SKETCHES IN LONDON.

BY JAMES GRANT,

AUTHOR OF

"RANDOM RECOLLECTIONS OF THE LORDS AND COMMONS,"
"THE GREAT METROPOLIS," &c. &c.

WITH

Twenty-Four Humorous Illustrations

BY "PHIZ," AND OTHERS.

"Many people wonder at the love of London. Why so? It is certainly the best *Summer* residence—none other is so cool.—The best abode in *Winter*—for none other is so warm.—The *rich* prefer it for containing every luxury; and for the *poor*, where can money be made to go so far?"—SIR F. B. HEAD.

THIRD EDITION.

LONDON:
WILLIAM TEGG, 85, QUEEN STREET, CHEAPSIDE.
MDCCCL.

PREFACE.

In presenting this volume to the public, the Author thinks it proper to mention that his object has been to exhibit life in London in some of the more striking aspects it assumes; and at the same time to lay before the reader such information respecting this modern Babylon, as may prove instructive as well as amusing. Everything the Author has described, has either come under his own observation, or been verbally communicated to him by friends who were cognizant of the facts stated, and in whose veracity he could place the utmost reliance; and he trusts that the work will be found to contain a great amount of information which is not only nowhere else to be found, but which is possessed of permanent interest.

With regard to the Illustrations by "Phiz," which embellish the volume, the Author can speak more unreservedly than he could do of the letter-press. They are among the happiest achievements of the genius of one who, though yet but young in years, is unquestionably, in this particular style of engraving, the first artist of the day.

London, September 1, 1838.

CONTENTS.

CHAPTER I.

BEGGING IMPOSTORS.

CHAPTER II.

DEBTORS' PRISONS—THE QUEEN'S BENCH.

CHAPTER III.

THE LUMBER TROOP.

CHAPTER IV.

THE VICTORIA PARLIAMEMT.

CHAPTER V.

PENNY THEATRES.

CHAPTER VI.

THE POLICE OFFICES.

CHAPTER VII.

WORKHOUSES.

CHAPTER VIII.

LUNATIC ASYLUMS.

CHAPTER IX.

BARTHOLOMEW AND GREENWICH FAIRS.

CHAPTER X.

COURTS OF REQUESTS.

CHAPTER XI.

GAMING-HOUSES AND GAMBLERS.

CHAPTER XII.

THE METROPOLITAN AND CITY POLICE.

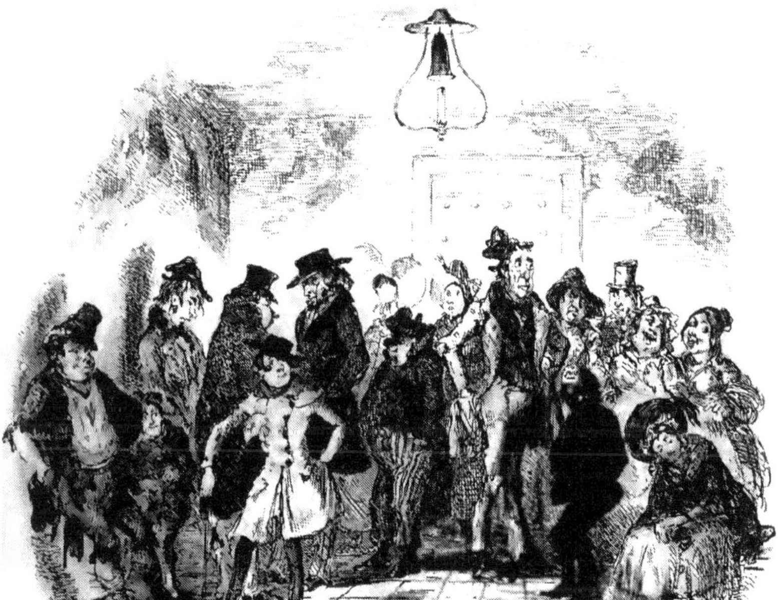

SKETCHES IN LONDON.

CHAPTER I.

BEGGING IMPOSTORS.

Begging-letter Impostors—Their supposed number—Probable amount of the money they receive—Probable number of letters they send, with the proportion of successful to unsuccessful applications—General materials of their letters—Occasional remarks on the result of their applications—Means by which they obtain available information regarding the parties to whom they apply—Modes of going to work—Illustrative anecdotes—Underwood and other begging-letter impostors—Specimens of their letters, &c.—Street-begging impostors—Their probable number, and the amount of their aggregate gains—Large sums which some of them have amassed—Expedients resorted to by them in the prosecution of their calling—Instances of feigned distress—Blind beggars—Speculations in the business of begging—Begging copartneries—Professional rehearsals—Meetings and carnivals of the fraternity—Crossings sweepers.

London is proverbial all the world over for the number and ingenuity of the tricks which are daily practised in it; but perhaps there is no department of metropolitan roguery in which a greater amount of ingenuity is displayed than in that of begging.

The London beggars are divided into a great variety of classes; but I shall confine myself to the begging impostors who ply their avocation by means of letters, and to those who by the assumption of distress which they do not actually feel, endeavour, in the open streets, to enlist the sympathies of the charitable and humane in their behalf.

Of the begging-letter class of impostors, it is exceedingly difficult to obtain statistical information so copious as could be desired. I have been at great pains to possess myself of as full and accurate particulars as are accessible. If I have not succeeded to the extent of my own wishes as regards the copiousness of my facts, I have great reason for reposing an implicit reliance on the accuracy of those I have ascertained.

I need hardly say, that it is impossible to ascertain what may be the average number of persons in the metropolis who make a trade of writing begging-letters. There can be no question that hundreds do so who are either never detected in the practice, or who if they are so by some of the individuals on whom they have sought to impose, are never publicly exposed; and consequently their names are unknown. A guess, however, may be made at the number of these men. The great majority of them confine their attempts at deception to the nobility and gentry. The reason is obvious enough; they know, in the first place, that the aristocracy are so much occupied with other matters, that they are less likely than the middle classes of society to put themselves to the trouble, in the event of any suspicion of attempted imposition, of detecting and prosecuting the offenders; in the second place, they know that, while the chances of detection are less with the nobility and the more affluent portion of the gentry, than with persons in an humbler sphere of life, they will necessarily, in the event of success, reap a much more abundant harvest from the former than from the latter. Half a crown, or five shillings, even were their tale of distress believed, would be all that they could, taking one case with another, expect to receive from persons in the middle classes of society; whereas, with the aristocracy they never dream of a successful effort being productive of less than a sovereign; while the average produce, from calculations I have made, and which they, as a matter of course have made long before me, is about fifty shillings.

Assuming, then, as before stated, that the vast majority of people who follow the avocation of writing and sending letters soliciting charity under got-up cases of distress, confine their business to the higher classes, I am enabled by means of data which are in my possession, to form something like a confident conjecture as to the average number of such impostors. Some time ago I saw a letter from a nobleman of a very humane and benevolent disposition, in which it was stated that, in the course of the year, he had received nearly three hundred and fifty begging letters, all of which were dated from London, and detailed trumped-up cases of the deepest distress. The noble lord, before remitting any amount of money in answer to either of the letters, took the precaution, which he had been led to do from having been so often imposed on before, of inquiring into the individual cases. And what does the reader suppose was the result? Why that forty-nine out of every fifty of the parties were gross impostors. And as these persons are, for the most part, men of great shrewdness, it is fair presumption that they would take care to find out who were the noblemen to whom they might apply with the greatest prospect of success, and, consequently, that the nobleman to whom I refer was not likely to be overlooked by many of them. In all the circumstances, I think it is a very moderate computation when I suppose the average number of those who live by begging-letter impositions to be about two hundred and fifty.

Another question will very naturally be asked—"What is the probable amount per annum which is averaged by the begging-letter impostors?" If I cannot answer the question with an absolute certainty, I have facts in my possession which enable me to speak with confidence as to what is near the sum. The highest which any one of the fraternity was in the habit of yearly deriving from his impositions, was very nearly 1000*l*. This may appear an incredible sum; it is nevertheless a true one. I shall have occasion to refer to the case more particularly in an after part of the chapter. The lowest sum earned by any of the supposed two hundred and fifty begging-letter impostors to whom I have alluded, cannot be under 100*l*. a year; but as a greater number are between this sum and that of 300*l*. than there are above the latter amount, I should suppose that if the average sum were estimated at the intermediate sum of 200*l*. we are pretty near the mark. This, then, would give no less than 50,000*l*., out of which the benevolent public of London, chiefly the nobility, are annually swindled by the begging-letter impostors.

I have been at some pains to ascertain the probable number of begging-letters which are, on an average, daily addressed to noblemen, gentlemen, and ladies in the metropolis. To speak with any thing like certainty on the subject were, of course, out of the question. From all the facts I have been able to learn, I should suppose that there must be at least, speaking in round numbers, 1000 such letters written every day by these impostors. Those who confine themselves to what they call the higher game, namely, the nobility and affluent gentry, do not deal to a great extent in epistles of this description, because the field is of necessity comparatively limited, and also because if they succeed in one case out of five they make a rich harvest, seldom receiving less than two sovereigns, in many instances five, in some ten, and occasionally, though very rarely, as high as twenty; but in my computation as to the probable number of begging-letters written daily in London, I include the class of impostors who chiefly, if not exclusively, confine their labours to epistolary applications to clergymen, dissenting ministers, and other persons of known benevolence, in the middle ranks of life. Instances consist with my own personal knowledge of an individual of this last class of impostors, writing no fewer than twenty of these letters in a day. Not long since sixteen letters of this description, all sealed and ready for delivery, were found in a basket at the house of one of these persons, in Blackfriars Road; and it was ascertained that all the sixteen had been intended to be forwarded to their respective destinations within a few hours after the discovery. If then some of these rogues are so indefatigable in their epistolary attempts on the pockets of the charitable and humane, as to pen twenty letters in one day, surely, considering their number, and after making every allowance for the comparatively contracted labours of the least industrious portion of the swindling community, there is nothing extravagant in the supposition that 1000 such letters are daily indited and forwarded to their several destinations in London.

As to the average proportion the successful bear to the unsuccessful applications in such cases, I have no data on which to ground even a confident conjecture. The comparative success in individual cases depends, as a matter of course, on the dexterity of the parties. To insure distinguished success as a begging-letter impostor, two things are indispensable; first, judgment in the selection of the persons on whose pockets the attempt is to be made; and secondly, skill or ingenuity in deciding on the form or mode of making it. These are just as necessary to success in this way, as the choice of a proper place and a skilful baiting of the hook, are to success in angling for any species of the finny tribe. The difference in the comparative success of the begging-letter impostors is very great. Some do not succeed in above one case out of twenty; others successfully practise their impositions every fifth time they make the attempt. I believe that this last amount of success is the most distinguished that any of them meet with.

It will appear on the first blush of the thing incredible, but the fact has in various cases been established beyond all question, that some of the more successful begging-letter writers keep their clerks, and sport their horses and gigs. This was the case with blind Williams, so well known in town some years ago. It was ascertained at the time, that his annual income, from his begging epistles, averaged from 600*l.* to 800*l.* He regularly employed two clerks, at a salary, if I remember rightly, of 80*l.* a-year, in the one case, and 50*l.* in the other. He also kept his horse and gig, and might often be seen "showing off" in the most fashionable parts of the town. He kept his mistress also, and on his death, his principal clerk, Joseph Underwood, of whom I shall have to speak hereafter, actually married her, regarding the printed documents and business materials* of her late "protector"—for so the term is in such cases perverted—as equivalent

* I shall afterwards have occasion to state of what this stock in trade consisted.

to a fortune. The other clerk of Williams also afterwards established a good business, on his own account, in the begging-letter way; but it was not nearly equal to that of his late employer.

A common practice in the begging-letter business is, for a number of impostors to enter into a sort of partnership together, it being found that the trade can generally be carried on most successfully that way. In such cases, however, they do not all "share-and-share alike." The company, if I may so speak, is formed on the banditti principle; in other words, they have always a head who acts in the capacity of a general, and all their movements or "operations," as they themselves phrase it, must be in strict conformity with his instructions. The late notorious Peter Hill, whose case was brought so prominently before the public ten or twelve years since, was the head of one of these companies or gangs. It was ascertained, beyond all question, at the period to which I refer, that the average amount of which the charitable public were daily plundered by the impositions of Peter and his gang, was upwards of 20*l*. His own share, after paying all the subordinates, or his "men," as he used to call them, and after deducting for expenses, in the shape of paper, postage, and other incidentals, was not much under 600*l*. a-year.

Of all the begging-letter impostors of whom I have heard, Peter was unequalled in the facility and success with which he could change his personal appearance. In the course of one day he could assume and sustain, with admirable effect, seven or eight different characters; so that those who saw him, and were conversing with him, at ten o'clock in the morning, might have been in his company at twelve, and never had the slightest suspicion of the fact. He had a pair of huge artificial whiskers, which he put on and off just as he pleased; and he had also a pair of moveable mustachios, which a Spanish Don would have looked on with envious eye. Of wigs, too, he had an abundant supply, embracing every variety of colour; while his wardrobe was so extensive, that you would have thought he had purchased the entire contents of some Jew clothesman's shop in Holywell-street. By these means, coupled with great natural cleverness, he was able to assume so many different characters, and to appear so very unlike himself, if there be not an Irishism in the expression, that, though the Mendicity Society had at one time no fewer than three hundred cases of begging letter impostures against him, and though its officers had repeatedly seen him in the police-offices, they passed him day after day in the public streets, without recognising him. I may mention one fact, out of hundreds, illustrative of the singular adroitness with which he managed to disguise himself, and to assume different characters; namely, that he applied personally one morning to the Earl of Harrowby, as an unbeneficed clergyman of the Church of England, in great distress, when he received a sovereign, and in the evening in the character of an unfortunate portrait-painter, when he again received a sovereign from the hands of the noble Earl, after having had a personal interview with his Lordship on both occasions.

The notorious Underwood, who was brought so prominently before the public three or four years ago, under innumerable aliases, was also the head or general of a gang of this description. He is the impostor to whom I have before alluded as having netted about 1000*l.* per annum as his own share of the plunder. He also kept his gig, and had a private clerk at a handsome salary. Underwood made one of the most successful single hits to be found, perhaps, in the annals of the letter-begging profession. Not many years since, he swindled the late Earl of Plymouth out of 50*l.* by one letter. I know several instances in which 20*l.*, 25*l.*, and even 30*l.*, have been got at once; but this is the only case which has come to my knowledge of 50*l.* being given at a time. When I come to describe some of the ingenious expedients resorted to by these impostors in the prosecution of their avocation, I shall refer to the way in which the above benevolent nobleman was swindled out of his 50*l.*, and shall, at the same time, make some observations on Underwood's qualifications for his profession.

The more experienced class of begging-letter writers conduct their operations on the most approved business principles. In addition to their constantly retaining clerks in their employ, whenever the success of their schemes will justify that expense, they keep their books in the most perfect order. There is not a merchant in the city who is more regular or correct in this way. They make a memorandum of each day's proceedings, which answers to the day-book of the merchant; while they have also a book corresponding with the ledger of the mercantile man.

All the begging-letter impostors who carry on an extensive business keep a regular diary of their proceedings. The following is copied from one of the morning papers of June last, as the journal of a notorious impostor named John Douglas, who was only liberated from the House of Correction, where he had been confined for his fraudulent practices, in September. I may just observe, that I some time since saw the original of the journal, but not having access to it at present, I am obliged to quote the extract from the morning paper referred to. It will be seen that, in most cases, the writer first mentions the name of the party applied to; then the assumed name in which the application is made; thirdly, the fictitious case of distress got up; and lastly, the result of the application where successful.

In some cases one or two terms are made use of, as "Derry" in the first entry, which are not so intelligible:—

Feb. 6.—Marquis of Bristol. Derry; Mary Cole; blind; seven children; three cripples.

Feb. 8.—Admiral Curzon. Ship Pallas; Sam Bowden, mate; seized for 4*l.* 4*s.* rent; paralytic stroke. Result, 2*l.*

Feb. 15.—Admiral Curzon. Ship Douglas; Powden, Mackey, and Bill Stroud, cripples, and two stone blind. Received 2*l.*

Feb. 26.—Sir Peter Durham. Lieutenant Spratt; leg off; hard up. Result, 20*l.*

March 12.—Countess of Mansfield. Widow; nine children; hooping cough; cholera morbus; measles.

March 14.—Lord Melbourne. Jane Simpson; father blind; mother dead; no money to bury her.

March 18.—Countess of Mansfield. Daughter supporting mother and grandmother by needle-work; lost use of both hands; furniture seized for 6*l.* 10*s.* Received 3*l.*

March 24.—Earl Fitzwilliam. Goods seized for 4*l.* 4*s.*; no bed; wife just lying-in. Result, 2*l.*

The above is, of course, but a mere skeleton or outline of the letters which are addressed. The writers dwell with an edifying circumstantiality, and expatiate with an amazing pathos, on the pretended cases of distress; and are great adepts at that sort of flattery of the persons addressed, which, to use their own expression, is most likely to "gammon" them. Of the admirable tactics of these epistolarian impostors I shall have occasion to speak at greater length by-and-bye, when I shall give some approved specimens of their correspondence.

Some of the begging-letter writers occasionally make droll remarks in their journals, as to the result of their applications. The following is a specimen:—

June 20.—Addressed the Duke of Richmond under the name of John Smith; case, leg amputated, out of work for six months, and wife and seven children starving. Result, 2*l.* Not amiss, but hope to be more successful next time.

June 25.—Letter to Bishop of London; name, William Anderson; case, licensed clergyman of the Church of England, but unemployed for four years, and wife dead three weeks ago, leaving five motherless children. Result, no go; too old a bird to be caught with chaff; but try it on again next week.

June 28.—Try Sir Peter Laurie; case, industrious Scotchman, but no employment; lived on bread and water for eight days, but no bread, nor anything to eat, for the last three days; name, John Laurie. Result, referred to the Mendicity Society, Sir Peter being too far north to be done; knowing rogues these Scotchmen; there is no gammoning them.

June 30.—Addressed Sir Peter Durham; case, lost a leg and arm in the service; was one of his men on board the ship Pallas; great destitution; not even as much as to get my timber leg repaired, being broken by accident; name, Jack Scraggs. Result 5*l.*; Sir Peter a regular trump; drink his health in a bottle of best Madeira; have at him again in a fortnight or so; plenty more cases to be got up; plenty more names to assume.

July 4.—Address Lord Wyndford; name, Samuel Downie; case, ruined by attachment to Toryism; have often detected treasonable conspiracies, and been a proscribed man by my former acquaintances in consequence; great hater of Reform, which means Revolution; ready to shed my blood in defence of Church and State. Result, long letter, enclosing half a sovereign; miserable work this: won't pay for consumption of time and paper; Wyndford a stingy customer; stingy old boy to deal with; cut the connexion at once.

July 6.—Letter to Lord Holland; name, Jonathan Manson; case, endured for a long series of years a species of living martyrdom for my zeal for Reform principles; was intimately acquainted with Muir, Palmer, and the other Scotch Reformers who suffered in 1794, for their principles; am now struck with palsy; wife dying, and six children without a bed to lie on, a rag to cover them, or a morsel of food of any kind to put into their mouths; most deplorable case altogether; dire necessity that induces to write; great outrage to feelings. Received 5*l.*, with a very compassionate letter; the compassion may go to the dogs, but the 5*l.* something substantial; jolly old cock yet; long may he live to lean on his crutches; will go it again; stick it into him at least once a fortnight.

July 3.—Wrote to Lord Brougham; directed to apply to the Mendicity Society; particularly obliged to his Lordship for his advice, but would have preferred a sovereign or two; have no wish to make the acquaintance of these Society gentry; wonder how his Lordship himself would like their bone-gruel, which they dignify with the name of soup, and to be kept to hard work at the mill to the bargain.

Unless some such journal or memoranda as this were regularly kept of the proceedings of these gentry, it would be impossible for them to do business at all. They would not only, by exposing their impostures, defeat their objects, but they would soon find themselves in Bow-street, or some other of the police-offices. The success of their schemes depends on the skill and dexterity with which they can vary their assumed names and pretended cases. If two letters were sent to any nobleman or gentleman soon after each other, with the same names or cases, their detection and consequent punishment would be a matter of almost moral certainty.

Those who are not in the secret, are at a loss to understand how the begging-letter writers manage to get acquainted with such circumstances, either in the cases of the persons whose names they assume, or in those of the parties they address, as could impose on the latter. The way in which the thing is managed is this:—They first of all ascertain who are the noblemen or gentlemen of the most benevolent disposition and ample means, and they then take care to learn what is the most probable way of procuring a favourable hearing to their got-up tale of distress. This done, their ingenuity is put to the rack, with the view of trumping-up the most plausible possible case. An instance or two will suffice to explain this more fully. Suppose I take the cases of Sir Peter Durham and Admiral Curzon, as gentlemen whose names have been already mentioned. The begging letter-writers, having in the first place ascertained that these gentlemen are distinguished for their benevolence of disposition, and for their strong attachment to the naval service, they then apply themselves to the procuring of some particulars respecting particular ships they commanded, and the men who served under them. They succeed in this by going down to Greenwich, and entering, as if it were by the merest accident, into conversation with some of the pensioners there, who, over a pot of porter or a tumbler of grog, are remarkably communicative on all matters pertaining to the naval service. They at once mention the day and date of particular engagements, and particular occurrences. They also learn who were special favourites with Sir Peter Durham, or Admiral Curzon, as the case may be; and then pretending to be one of those persons, they refer, with an edifying minuteness, to a particular occurrence. The imposition is thus in most cases effectual, and the gentlemen addressed believing the trumped-up tale of woe, and sympathising with an old sailor who served under them, naturally put their hands in their pockets, and send the applicant either one or two sovereigns to administer to his exigencies.

Where higher game is aimed at, that is to say, where the prize on which the impostor has his eye, is 10*l.*, 20*l.*, or 30*l.*, something more is done, with the view of practising the imposition successfully. They find out, from the sailors, who were the most favoured officers who served under the commanders, and what their pecuniary and other circumstances now are. They also contrive to possess themselves of the autographs of these officers, and then they set to work to draw out begging-letters, written in a hand as like theirs as possible. The letters thus written have the forged autographs of the officers in question attached to them; and so closely is the handwriting imitated, that in some instances even the parties themselves can scarcely detect the imposture, in so far as mere penmanship is concerned. I may mention, as an instance of the remarkable skill with which these impostors imitate the handwriting of other persons, and also as a proof of the infinite dexterity with which they draw up their letters, that in June last, when the impostor Douglas, already alluded to, was brought to Bow-street Office, Sir Peter Durham, from whom he had a few days before got 20*l.*, in answer to a begging-letter, written in the name of Lieutenant Pratt, an officer who formerly served under the gallant admiral,—the latter could not without great difficulty be made to believe that the application was not actually made by and in the handwriting of the lieutenant.

On ordinary occasions, they have four styles of penmanship. The first is a sort of handwriting which may suit "cases in general," as they are called; the second is that of an old man of education, say a clergyman or doctor, who has been reduced in circumstances; the third is that of a young lady; and the fourth, of an old lady. I have seen a great many of the original letters, written in each of these styles, which were manufactured by Underwood. They are remarkably characteristic in every point of view. The facility with which some of the impostors can, through long practice, imitate different handwritings, is of essential service to them. Indeed, the begging-letter profession could never be carried on with any measure of success without this capability of writing in a variety of hands; for being, as the rogues are, in the habit of sending a great many letters to the same parties in the course of the year, the mere assumption of different names would not, were the calligraphy the same, be a security to them against detection. I may mention, as one illustration of their skill in this way, that the impostor Douglas, already mentioned, got nearly 30*l.*, from Admiral Curzon, in the course of last year, in sums of 2*l.* and 1*l.* each, the letters having been all written in different names, with suitable variations in the penmanship. This consummate impostor was thus, in one sense, living as a pensioner on the bounty of the gallant and benevolent admiral, the latter supposing all the time that he had been administering to the necessities of as many different individuals as he had received different letters.

In the cases in which the begging-letter impostors give the names of men of education and respectability of character, the writers take particular precautions against detection, because the punishment, in the event of discovery, is usually much greater than it is in what are called general cases. The answers to their application are always directed to be made to some public-house, coffee-room, or hairdresser's or other shop, they having previously asked the persons in the house or shop to receive any letter which may come to their care with a particular address. This the parties, knowing nothing about the matter, and having the amount of postage left with them, readily engage to do. The impostors then make a point of watching for the postman outside, at the time they expect an answer, to see whether he calls at the place to which they requested their answers might be sent. Their object in watching for him is to see that no police or Mendicity Society officer accompanies him, for the purpose of pouncing on the letter-writer as an impostor. This they look for as a matter of course, in the event of their imposture being detected by the party on whom it was attempted to be practised.

Whenever the begging-letter writers are fortunate enough, which they frequently are, in getting, along with some sum of money from a nobleman or person of distinction, a letter expressive of sympathy with their supposed distress, such letter is looked on as quite a windfall. It is immediately enclosed, with a begging-letter from themselves, to the various affluent and charitable friends of the party, and usually insures some similar donation from them. The friends of the party take it for granted, that before such party would have written the sympathetic letter, he would have taken special care to satisfy himself that the case was one of a legitimate kind. One such letter has often been productive of an abundant harvest, without the impostors being put to any other ingenious shifts to make a plausible case. The late Earl of Plymouth once wrote a letter of this kind to a consummate impostor, at the same time enclosing a 20*l.* note, which enabled the rogue to levy contributions, without any trouble to himself, to an immense extent, on the aristocratic connections and acquaintances of that very benevolent nobleman.

But the most successful mode of letter-begging, when dexterously managed, yet remains to be mentioned. It is this:—The impostor, instead of applying to the party, on whose pockets he meditates an attempt, either by means of some trumped-up case of a general nature, or by passing himself off as some given individual, pretends to be himself a man of substance, and to have drawn out, from motives of the purest benevolence, a representation of the case of some unfortunate person, whose name and designation are always given with an edifying accuracy. The impostor, in such cases, always sends to the party applied to, a list of pretended subscriptions for the benefit of the alleged sufferer, along with the details of his afflicting case; and on this list, he himself figures as one of the most liberal of the benevolent subscribers. The letter always winds up with an assurance that any remittance which may be made to the writer on behalf of the unfortunate party, will be most strictly applied to his relief, and that in the way which will be least likely to wound his feelings. As clergymen in reduced circumstances are, of all other classes of men, those who excite the most deep and general sympathy, the name of some clergyman is usually preferred in such cases to that of any other individual. This mode of letter-begging is, as I said before, generally the most successful, where skilfully managed; but it requires very great ingenuity to do it well.

I alluded on a former occasion to the fact of 50*l.* being got on one occasion by the impostor Underwood from the late Earl of Plymouth. The mode of application which I have just described, was that which the impostor adopted. I may add that, so pleased was he with the success of his expedient, as well he might, and with the princely though mistaken liberality of the noble Earl, that immediately on receiving the 50*l.* note, he called on two of his brother impostors, and invited them to dinner in a fashionable hotel at the west end, by way of celebrating his good fortune. Repeated bumpers were dedicated to the health of his Lordship, and the most anxious wishes were expressed that he would soon, by another proof of his unsuspicious disposition and princely liberality, give occasion for the dedication of a few more bumpers to him. Upwards of 5*l.* out of the 50*l.* were spent before the trio of rogues rose from their seats.

A few years since, one of the impositions of the kind described above was detected under very curious circumstances. The impostor—whose name I forget, though it was mentioned to me by a gentleman who was personally privy to the circumstances connected with the detection of the imposition—having trumped-up a most affecting case of distress, in which a clergyman of the Church of England, whose name I forbear to give, because he is still alive, was represented as the suffering party, applied to Lord J——— for any donation he might think proper to give on behalf of the afflicted divine. Along with this application there was a pretended list of subscriptions given towards the same benevolent object; and the impostor, who on this occasion assumed the name of John Hughes, took care to call his Lordship's attention to the fact of his own name, though in comparatively limited circumstances, being on the subscription list. Knowing that there was a clergyman of the name of Mr. G———, whose living was anything but large, and seeing so many names heading a subscription list on his behalf, he generously sent "John Hughes, Esq.," a 5*l.* note, to aid in administering to the necessities of the unfortunate clergyman; adding in the note which accompanied the donation that if, afterwards, it should be necessary, he would have great pleasure in remitting another 5*l.* to alleviate the distresses of a worthy man. In precisely ten days afterwards, another letter was received by Lord J———, to which was appended the signature of "John Hughes." The letter, as the reader will anticipate, was highly eulogistic of his Lordship's humanity, benevolence, and so on; and stated that the writer, "Mr. John Hughes," was so affected with the continued distress of the clergyman, that he had given him, though he could ill spare it, an additional 2*l.* The conclusion of the epistle of course was, that a more charitable action could not be performed by the noble Lord than that of bestowing the second 5*l.* on Mr. G———, which he had before so generously intimated his intention to give. It is unnecessary to observe that Mr. John Hughes again expressed his readiness, from motives of the purest disinterestedness, to take the trouble of conveying the additional 5*l.* to the distressed clergyman. When Lord J——— received the begging letter, he was in the act of putting on his hat to go to a public dinner in aid of the funds of a charitable institution. But for that circumstance the second 5*l.* note would have been immediately entrusted to the care of Mr. John Hughes. The noblemen and gentlemen who sat down to dinner were about two hundred in number; so that it was impossible for any one to see all who were present. After the cloth had been removed, oratory became the order of the evening, and at length the Rev. Mr. G——— was announced as about to address the company. Lord J——— was thunderstruck at the announcement: he was still more confounded when the veritable reverend gentleman stood up, with his face redolent of health, though Mr. John Hughes's letter of that morning represented him as not only bed-ridden, but unable to move either arm or leg. His Lordship waited patiently until the reverend gentleman concluded his speech; and then, determined if possible, to have the mystery cleared up, he advanced to him and congratulated him on his "sudden recovery."

"Sudden recovery!" said the clergyman, in a tone of surprise.

"Yes; from your illness."

"My Lord, you must have been misinformed: there has been nothing the matter with me."

Here again his Lordship looked unutterably confounded.

"Were you not ill ten days ago?" he inquired, after a moment's hesitation.

"Not in the slightest degree," was the answer of the reverend gentleman.

"Nor this morning, either—not confined to bed this morning?"

"Certainly not, my Lord. I have reason to be thankful, I never enjoyed better health in my life than I have done for the last few weeks."

"Well, this *is* certainly strange," said Lord J———, emphatically.

"May I ask, my Lord, what made you think I was ill?" said the reverend gentleman.

"Why, your friend, Mr. Hughes, assured me you were so."

"Mr. Hughes!" exclaimed the clergyman in accents of astonishment. "Mr. Hughes!" he added, putting his two fore fingers to his lips, and looking on the floor, as if trying to recollect which of his friends rejoiced in the name of Mr. Hughes. "My Lord," he observed, after a pause of a few seconds, "I am not personally acquainted with any gentleman of that name."

"Well," said his Lordship, "you certainly do astonish me."

"Did this Mr. Hughes communicate the fact of my alleged illness to your Lordship verbally?"

"No, it was by letter."

"Has your Lordship got the letter with you? Possibly I might know something of the handwriting."

His Lordship, fearing the nature of the contents might wound the feelings of the reverend gentleman, hesitated for a few moments to return any direct answer to the question; but the idea then flashed across his mind that the whole affair had been got up by some swindling impostor; and putting his hand into his pocket, he drew out the second letter, the one he had received that morning.

The feelings of the reverend gentleman will be better imagined than I could describe them, when he saw himself represented as if at the very gates of death, in a state of absolute destitution, and the subject of a subscription list, on which his Lordship's name, and that of "Mr. John Hughes" were the most prominent. Some other parties were consulted as to what ought to be done, and it was agreed that his Lordship should, with the view of detecting and punishing the fellow, enclose another cheque for *5l.* on his bankers, to Mr. John Hughes, for the benefit of his friend, the Rev. Mr. G———, only taking care that a police-officer should be previously instructed to be in readiness at the banking establishment, which is in Fleet-street, to take him into custody the moment he presented the cheque and received the money. The remainder of "Mr. Hughes's" history is soon told: he figured shortly after at the Old Bailey, and then quitted this country for the antipodes, the expenses of his voyage being defrayed out of the public purse.

Other and very ingenious expedients adopted by the more enterprising of the begging-letter fraternity, in the prosecution of their deceptive purposes, yet remain to be mentioned. One of these expedients is, to have a very large quantity of warrants of distraint, for house-rent or taxes, always on hand, regularly printed, and filled up in the usual form. These they enclose in letters to persons of known charitable disposition, detailing most affecting cases of domestic misery, and supplicating assistance. At the same time they enclose a certificate as to character, and a testimony to the facts stated, either from the pretended churchwardens of the parish whence the letter is written, or from some surgeon or other professional man residing in the neighbourhood. This mode of imposture, when skilfully executed, is usually a most profitable one. Another, somewhat similar, is that of having pawnbrokers' duplicates printed in the usual form, and the blanks duly filled up with dates, names, and so forth, in writing. These are sent, at any time, to charitable persons, the impostors pretending that the articles of furniture, clothing, &c., mentioned in the duplicates, have been deposited with the pawnbrokers under the most distressing circumstances, and from dire necessity, and imploring something to enable them to redeem the articles, and thus save their families from dying of cold or destitution. But though such fictitious pawnbrokers' duplicates are forwarded at any time to persons of a charitable disposition, with the view of swindling them out of their money, and are successful to a very great extent, they are found particularly serviceable when a pawnbroker's shop has been destroyed by fire. In such cases, availing themselves of the information given by newspapers regarding the calamity, they forge the name of the party, and send the fictitious duplicates as those of valuable property they had pledged, and which, being all destroyed, leaves them in utter destitution. The accompanying letter fervently supplicates, as a matter of course, some assistance, to enable the parties, viz. the impostors, to rescue their family from absolute starvation. This expedient is, in most cases, a peculiarly successful one. It is in many instances most abundantly productive to the impostors. Underwood used to regard the destruction of a pawnbroker's shop by fire as a great windfall. His duplicates, on such an occurrence, were diffused through all parts of town in a day or two after the accident; and rich was the harvest he reaped from his tact and ingenuity.

And this reminds me of the promise I made in an early part of the chapter, to explain what was meant by the printed materials and other stock in trade which Underwood got by way of fortune, when he married the mistress of his former employer.

Old Blind Williams, as he was always called. These materials and stock consisted chiefly of an immensely large quantity of printed warrants of distraint for rent or taxes, pawnbrokers' duplicates, the names and residences of persons most easily imposed on, with the journal of all the letter-begging transactions of his deceased master.

And here I may remark, that, taken all in all, this Underwood was one of the most ingenious impostors ever known on town. He was the natural son of one of our London aldermen, and possessed all the advantages which a classical education could give him. But mere education could never of itself have made him the man he was. He was a person of great natural talents, which had been improved by constant exercise. I have known other begging-letter impostors, who displayed very considerable resources in the practice of their profession, but they all fell far short of him. Their expedients were limited in number, his were boundless. And they were as ready as they were inexhaustible. I have referred to the four classes of penmanship used by the impostors; each of these he could vary to an incredible extent. Other contemporary impostors were generally obliged to call in the assistance of other persons to insure variety, and consequently escape detection, in their handwriting. Those of them who carried on business to any extent, were obliged to have, at any rate, some female to imitate the penmanship of a lady: Underwood needed no such assistance. He was everything himself: he was, to use another expression which a mathematical friend of mine is particularly partial to, "a self-contained personage." And not only could he write every variety of calligraphy, but his intellectual resources were ample even to excess. He could write on any subject; he had not only the ingenuity to assume every conceivable character, but he could immediately, on assuming such character, sit down and write in that strain which was most consonant to it. I have looked over a large collection of his letters, and have been at a loss to know whether I ought most to admire the mechanical dexterity which enabled him to write so great a variety of hands, or the intellectual resources, which the appropriateness of his sentiments and style to the various characters he assumed, proved him to be possessed of. His inventive powers were of the first order. If the faculty of creation be one of the principal attributes of genius, Underwood was a genius of the first magnitude. The force and felicity of his imaginative facts were remarkable. Had he turned his attention to novel-writing, instead of to the profession of a begging-letter impostor, there is no saying how high his name might at this moment have stood in the current literature of the country. United as were his inventive powers to great facility and force of composition, he must certainly, had he applied himself to the production of works of fiction, have attained to no ordinary reputation. It can hardly be necessary to say, that a man of so much ingenuity was successful in his profession. I am assured by a gentleman whose means of ascertaining the fact must have been equal to those of any second party not one of his coadjutors in crime, that his annual income from his begging-letter practices must, as already stated, have been close on 1000*l.* He was repeatedly detected and imprisoned. He died in Cold-bath-fields' Prison, in the spring of the present year.

Before I proceed farther in my observations on the begging-letter class of impostors, it may be right, in order to show with what ingenuity they go to work, to give a few specimens of their epistolary talents. The following letters were written by the notorious Underwood, of whom I have just spoken; and as I have seen the originals, it may be right to state, that they are given without the alteration of a single word. The first is addressed to Lord Skelmersdale, and is signed "Mary Burn." It will be seen, that in this instance Mr. Underwood assumes the character of a widow.

"My Lord,—It is with most agonised mind and heart I presume to address these few lines to your lordship's notice, whom I have had the honour of knowing by sight for a great many years, and also your lordship's seat (Latham House), at some small distance from which I lived with some late relations, in the years 1797 and 1798. I am, however, a native of Preston, where I am descended from a respectable family, named Grimshaw. My parents have been dead many years, and I am the widow of a late respectable schoolmaster, who was proprietor of a boarding-school at Guildford, in this county, for a number of years, but who unhappily died of fever some five years ago, when I was left with four children, under eleven years of age, and obliged to dispose of my premises for the purpose of settling my husband's few debts, defraying funeral expenses, &c. Since then, my lord, I have kept a day-school, in the parish of St. George, Southwark, and held the situation of governess at a Sunday-school, although the emolument arising from the situation is scarcely worth my acceptance; but through its having pleased the Almighty to deprive me of the use of my lower extremities by rheumatic gout, during the last seventeen months, during which period I have been wholly prevented from attending to the duties of my avocation, in conjunction with the great expense attending the support of my family, have been the means of reducing me, from a comfortable station in life, to that of extreme and heart-rending distress; inasmuch as, being unable to pay my rent, my furniture has been distrained, and is now under the hands of my late landlord, or his broker; and I have been obliged to quit my late residence to save myself from an arrest and incarceration for a small debt incurred for the necessaries of life. I am become a great cripple, a melancholy spectacle; and but for the kindness of a friend, I and my fatherless children would have been driven into the workhouse, or have become poor houseless wanderers. However, through God's blessing, and the aid of humanity, I have been enabled to pay one moiety of the rent, for which my goods and chattels were seized, and I am allowed until the 24th instant to pay the rest; but am unable to do so, except through the aid of charitable assistance. In addition to which, my lord, I am sadly fearful, and under the apprehension that my present place of abode will be discovered, and that I shall be arrested, torn away from my dear children, and incarcerated for the small debt above alluded to, which is only 1*l.* 17*s.* 6*d.*, and which accumulated for bread only. I know not what to do, my lord; I am almost distracted, while my dear children, who are as innocent as lambs, during the last six weeks, appear to me to be quite happy with bread, potatoes, or whatever I can give them, which is a great consolation to me. In reflecting, this morning, on my unhappy situation, considering to whom I should apply, it suggested to my mind, from some little knowledge of your lordship's disposition, that your lordship would, in all probability, be pleased to afford me some small pecuniary assistance towards helping me to surmount my difficulties, and for which I humbly appeal to your lordship's goodness and generosity. I assure your lordship, that whatever assistance you may be pleased to render, I shall remember it with gratitude to the end of my life. I beg to subscribe myself, my lord, your lordship's most humble servant,

"2, Cross Street, Newington Butts. "MARY BURN."

This letter was written in quite a lady-like hand, and was accompanied by a certificate from a pretended Mr. Mansfield, surgeon, London Road. Mr. Mansfield, *alias* Mr. Underwood, was, of course, very eloquent in his commendation of the excellent moral character of "Mary Burn," *alias* Joseph Underwood, and most earnestly recommended her distressing case to the favourable consideration of his lordship.

The following letter, from the same voluminous epistolarian, was addressed to the Earl of Stamford and Harrington, and is dated July 1st, 1833. The character assumed on this occasion is that of a young lady, who had been seduced from her "tender parent's" roof by a gentleman, under promise of marriage. But the young lady, *alias* Mr. Underwood, will speak much better for herself than I could: let her tale therefore, by all means, be heard.

"My Lord,—It is with shame, indescribable shame, I presume to address your Lordship with these lines; but from having a knowledge of your Lordship's person from my infancy, and through the report of your Lordship's sympathising and benevolent character, I am about entrusting a most unfortunate affair to your Lordship's honour and secrecy. I am really ashamed to detail my misfortunes, my Lord, but I must; I must acquaint your Lordship. I know of no other person so likely to render me some assistance in the hour of need, and to save me from perdition and a premature grave, as your Lordship, whose humanity does honour to the feelings of a susceptible heart. Allow me to acquaint your Lordship, that I am a native of Warrington, Lancashire, and the youngest daughter of a gentleman who, for a number of years, held the rank of lieutenant in the British army, and who died in the year 1815, when I was but a year old, leaving my mother, who has for some years resided at Bolton-le-Moor, with five children (all girls) to support on a small stipend; that at Christmas last, I was prevailed on, by a person calling himself a gentleman, under the most solemn promises and assurances of marrying me as soon as we arrived in London, to leave my dearly beloved mother at Bolton, without her consent or knowledge; that he has forfeited his promises and assurances; and since I have been here, through my having frequently reproached him for his ungentlemanly and dishonourable conduct, he has left me in a most destitute condition. A few days subsequently he sent me the *enclosed letter* as a sort of an excuse; but, through my having spared no pains in referring to the sheriff of this county, Surrey, Sussex, Middlesex, and the city of London, I have ascertained that no such person has been arrested or is in custody; for in fact, no writ has been issued against any person of his name, and that therefore his letter is nothing but a subterfuge for his absence.

"Oh, my Lord! I am *ruined* and *undone*. I am lost, totally lost—lost to my dear mother, who *knows no tidings of me* or my misfortunes—lost to my dear sisters—lost to all my young friends and acquaintances in Lancashire and Cheshire—lost to all respectable society—have lately been turned out of my lodgings for the arrears of my rent, in the sum of seven pounds, for which my *trunks* and *wearing-apparel* have been, and *still are, detained* and withheld from me—that *I am much* in *want* of a *change* of *linen* and *dress*—have no home or habitation to dwell in, with the exception of a miserable place I am allowed just to enter and sleep in at night *only*, at a poor widow's, who has a large family and several lodgers, and whose house I consider would be an unsafe and improper place for your Lordship's letter to be addressed to, which has induced me to take the precaution of begging your Lordship to address it as above. My sufferings are extremely great, my Lord. I have frequently walked from here to Dean Park, a distance of some miles, and there spent the whole of the day in solitude, without breaking my fast, or having the means to break it. Oh, my Lord! I am suffering, justly suffering, for my act of imprudence; but the art and deceptions which have been used to ensnare and ruin me are really beyond human imagination, as letters and other documents, which I have in my possession, will fully prove; yet nothing will erase the stain, the everlasting stain, from my character. This is what I feel, my Lord, above all. I hate myself, and despise the wretch, the invidious and despicable fellow, who has caused it, and all my sufferings. I am sadly fearful your Lordship will form a bad opinion of me; but, when I inform your Lordship that I am yet under nineteen years of age, and him who thus deceived me is thirty-three years' old, and, in my opinion, prone to deceive and ruin the young and virtuous of my sex, that you will be pleased to permit my inexperience to plead a little in extenuation of my offence, and I hope to mingle your pity with your censure. I am gradually wasting away through the want of food and nourishment, and, without the aid of humanity, must inevitably fall a victim to poverty and starvation. To acquaint my beloved parent with my unparalleled misfortunes and sufferings would, I am sure, be more than she could bear; it would certainly be the means of confining her to her bed, if not sending her to a premature grave. In this unfortunate situation, I humbly venture, in appealing to your Lordship's humanity, for a small pecuniary assistance, to help me to discharge my late landlord's demand, and to redeem my trunks and wearing-apparel; which done, I will immediately set out for Bolton, where I have no doubt of being able to prevail on a lady, a most intimate friend of mine and my family's, to call on my mother, and interpose in my behalf, and for my reconciliation with her. It is true, I acknowledge, with a sincere and contrite heart, I have erred in the respect above named, but *in no other* case, can the world, or any individual in it, say I have. I have honestly and candidly told your Lordship the *worst* of *myself;* and, as soon as I reach Bolton, I will take care your Lordship shall be furnished with a memorial of my abilities, qualifications, and *general* character, from a gentleman of unquestionable character, who at present knows nothing of my sufferings, yet has known me from my cradle, and my family a great many years, and who, I have no doubt, will exert himself, under this unfortunate affair, to obtain the situation of teacher or governess in some respectable family for me, which I trust I am competent for, and which I shall prefer, under my unhappy circumstances, to my staying at Bolton, and living with my mother and sisters, the latter of whom might in all probability, on some occasion, be induced to reproach me for my misconduct, the more particularly as I am the youngest. I consider, therefore, that I should be far happier in a situation, and am convinced I can be recommended by some few of the most respectable characters at Bolton, where, to say the truth, I shall be ashamed to be seen. Let me beseech you, my Lord, under these circumstances, to take the particulars of my misfortunes into your Lordship's most serious consideration, and to *pause* ere you put a negative: for on your Lordship's answer depends much—much more than I can possibly describe; my *fate even depends on it,* I in *truth declare;* and I trust, though your Lordship may in some measure blame me for my imprudence, yet, when you consider the art and deceptions that have been used against me by a most wicked man, that you will sympathise with me, and not suffer my supplications to be made in vain; assuring your Lordship that your assistance will be the means, or part of the means, of rescuing an orphan daughter of a British officer, under unparalleled distress, *from entire destruction,* and *a miserable death;* that although it perhaps may never be in *my power* to return it, or compensate your Lordship for it, I have no doubt but your Lordship will feel amply satisfied and gratified in being convinced that your aid had the desired effect. This I promise shall be done, my Lord, not by my own hand, but by one whose honour, word, and testimony, none can dispute. I now beg leave to leave my case in your Lordship's hands, anxiously waiting the favour of your Lordship's reply, with the return of the enclosed letter for Mr. Henry Mannings, which, with a number of other letters and documents I have of his, will be absolutely necessary to show to my mother, and also to produce in a court of law some day; for I am convinced, he has got property both in the county of Lancaster and Cheshire. My Lord, I have the honour to remain, with the greatest deference and respect, your Lordship's most humble servant,

"MARTHA TURNER."

This letter was written in a small neat lady-like style. Indeed, one would think it impossible that any other than a female could have written such a hand. The letter was accompanied by another, purporting to be from the pretended seducer, which was written in a gentleman's hand. The latter was as follows:—

"My dearest Martha—It is really most revolting to my feelings to be obliged to tell you, that, through some gambling transactions in which I have been unfortunately engaged, I have been arrested, and am now locked up in a sponging-house for a debt I am wholly unable to pay. I care but little for myself, my dear girl; but for you I feel most deeply, and I am wholly at a loss how to advise you for the best. I know well that I merit your anger for what is past, but the reproaches of my own conscience are, I assure you, sufficient punishment for the injury I have done you. If fortune should ever shine upon me, I will acquaint you with it, and fulfil all my pledges. Pray endeavour to console yourself, my dearest Martha, and lose no time in endeavouring to return home, in order that no greater evil may happen you. Please give the bearer my pocket-book, which contains some memorandums and a bill of exchange, which would be of no use to you. In my portmanteau you will find a new case of surgical instruments, which you can convert into your immediate use. I have the honour to remain, my dearest girl, with unalterable truth, your unfortunate

"WILLIAM HANDS.

"*George Street, Blackfriars Road.*

"P.S.—Don't ask the bearer any questions respecting me."

There was also, in addition to this last letter, the accompaniment of a certificate, purporting to be from a clergyman in Margate, testifying to the truth, from personal knowledge, of all the facts stated by the unfortunate pretended victim of seduction. The certificate was written in a different hand from the letter of Mr. Hands the seducer, and was an admirable specimen of the style of penmanship most characteristic of clergymen.

I am sure my readers will concur with me, that in point of ingenious invention, the above letters might put our modern novelists to the blush. The creative powers of these writers will not stand a moment's comparison with those of the author of the above productions.

Hitherto I have spoken only of male begging-letter impostors. These characters, however, are not confined to persons of the masculine gender. Even among the female sex there are occasionally some very dexterous begging-letter impostors to be found. By far the most noted and successful of the present day, is Harriet Reid, alias Harriet Minette. Not content with getting up cases of distress of every possible variety, and reciting them in a most pathetic manner, she introduces into all her letters, more or less liberally, a dash of the romantic. The last time I heard of her, was in June 1834, when she was brought before the magistrates of Marlborough street, on a charge of endeavouring to obtain money by a fraudulent letter from the Rev. Mr. Leigh, the rector of St. George's Bloomsbury. The letter extended to four folio sheets of paper, and was written as if from some gentleman who was a mutual friend of Mr. Leigh's and of Miss Harriet Reid, *alias* Mrs. Harriet Minette. The penmanship was bold and masculine, and no one could ever have dreamed that it emanated from a female hand. The following was written on the envelope:—

"The enclosed, dear Leigh, tedious as it is, for Heaven's sake, peruse most carefully; the cause of it must at once excuse it. It contains a melancholy occurrence, indeed, one which, while it engages your attention, must cut you to the heart. Poor Mrs. Minette will soon be lost, unless immediately seen after. O, Leigh! I am all anxiety about her—in agonies until you receive this—then all will be well. Heaven crown your efforts with success! Even now, should the memory of the past be granted us, you must look down on your bounty to her with rapture!"

From the long letter, all written in a similar strain, I give the following extract, which, as in the one just given, appears without the alteration of a single word:—

"Poor Mrs. Minette! I shall surprise you when I tell you of what family she is by the mother's side. She is related to yourself; but I must not explain who she is, or who I am, at present! Oh! may Heaven, in its infinite mercy, avert the blow that now seems impending over this poor unfortunate lady. Continue your bounty to her, and you will soon learn what she is. She is thoroughly amiable, Leigh, and to me somewhat dear! Her mother married a man of inferior birth, and her relations discharged her. She married Minette, a villain, who has thrown her, after riding in her carriage, on the wide world in helpless adversity. As I told you, Leigh, in my first letter, she is an amiable unsuspecting creature—artless—being truly warm in her friendship and love. Silly young creature as she is, we must, however, save her some pangs. Do something, dear Leigh, for her support—recommend her to your friends—set her up in a school, and get her some pupils; but don't let her teach Italian, as that would bring her sorrows to her mind. But now for the more immediate melancholy purport of my letter. She will be lost unless you save her; but I know you won't let her want. I am in an agony of mind about her. I shudder to name the subject, but I must. On Sunday, a friend of mine, on her way to church, saw Mrs. Minette walking to and fro, in an unfrequented path, by the side of the river. She accosted her, but the unfortunate lady seemed quite lost. It is too clear, Leigh, her wicked thoughts. Dear Leigh, watch her narrowly. Things, at all events, look black. Take her under your care—reason with her—give her books—let her have a doctor, and see her take her physic; but don't hint a word to her of what you do; it might wound her sensitive feelings. She respects you—calls you her benefactor. Adopt her, then, as your protégée. Let her read to you, and come to you at church. Providence must surely have thrown her in your way, and made you his agent in delivering her from the fangs of Satan. Give her a few pounds, and Heaven bless you!"

What a pity that Mrs. Harriet Minnette did not apply herself to novel writing! Why, the letter from which I have only given a short extract, in conjunction with what was written in its envelope, contains more of the romantic than will be found in many of the three volume works of fiction which ever and anon emanate from the establishments of the west end bibliopoles. There are dashes of the pathetic in the extract I have given, which even Goethe himself would have readily admitted into his "Sorrows of Werter."

Who could resist such an appeal to one's feelings? The Rev. gentleman to whom it was addressed could not. He proceeded forthwith to the residence* of the lady herself. She at once appeared in her proper person, and a dashing personage she was; but though the subject of his correspondent's letter was there to be seen as large as life, the worthy divine was as much perplexed as ever, as to who his very familiar correspondent, who had taken such an intense interest in the fate of "Mrs. Minette," could be. He had not been many moments in the lady's company when he began to have some shrewd suspicions that all was not right. He, therefore, cut his visit to Mrs. Harriet Minette short, and proceeding direct to the office of the Mendicity Society, deposited the lengthened and sentimental letter with which he had been honoured from her

* In High Street, Bloomsbury.

ladyship, in the hands of one of their officers. The result was that Mrs Minette had the honour of a public interview with the magistrates of Marlborough street office, who kindly undertook to guarantee to all parties interested, that society should not have, at least for three months to come, to suffer the calamity of losing poor Mrs. Minette by her throwing herself into the river when under the ascendancy of "wicked thoughts." In other words, she got a quarter of a year's free lodgings provided for her in a well-known public edifice in Cold-bath-fields.

The most extensive begging-letter impostors at present, are the person Douglas already named, and another individual of the name of Johnson. Both have already been often in prison for detected attempts at imposture. Indeed, all the impostors of this kind spend a very considerable portion of their life in prison. However, this circumstance does not surprise them; for they have beforehand taken it into account, as a contingency to be expected, in their estimate of the comparative pains and pleasures which are connected with the pursuit of their profession.

Of all the begging-letter impostors of whom it has been my fortune to hear, there is none for whose fate I ever felt the slightest compassion, with the exception of one of the name of David Jones. This poor fellow had a world of spirit and enterprise in the pursuit of his self-chosen avocation, but nature never intended him for it; for he possessed no variety of mental resources, nor could he in any case disguise his hand-writing. He always, too, prosecuted his profession under the most dangerous circumstances; that is, by forging the signatures of particular individuals. About ten years ago, he adhibited the name of a Mr. Alderson to a fraudulently got up case, and passed himself off as a Mr. James Smith. He was convicted at the Old Bailey, and sentenced to seven years' transportation. Will my readers believe it? On the very same day on which he returned from New South Wales, he wrote the very same letter, word for word, as that for which he had been transported, and adhibited the same name of James Smith to it! One would have thought that the lapse of seven years, especially in the capacity of a convict in New South Wales, which of course must have prevented any other than a very sparing use of his pen,—one would have thought that this would have made some considerable change in his hand-writing. But no; the penmanship of James Smith before he left England, and that of James Smith after his return, were so very similar that you would have thought both the letters, for I have seen them both, were written within an hour of each other, and with the same pen. The poor fellow was detected, and taken into custody on this his very first attempt after his return. He was sentenced to a long term of imprisonment, before the expiration of which he died. I may mention that begging-letter writing, by means of forged names, seems to have been, in his case, a family vice; for the poor fellow's father is now, if still alive, undergoing the sentence of transportation for life, for a fraud which he committed on the late Lord Dudley and Ward.

I come now to speak of the other class of begging impostors. I mean those who are to be seen openly following their profession in the streets. The number of beggars is astonishing. Ten years ago it was estimated at 7,500; I am sure the number has not diminished since then; my impression is, that it has, on the contrary, considerably increased. I think it may be safely enough assumed, that the present number of beggars of this class, to be seen in the streets of London, is not under 8,000. It will startle those whose attention has never been called to the subject, when they are informed, that of the beggars who in so great a variety of ways, audibly and silently, solicit alms in the public streets, there is only one out of every twenty who is a proper object of charity; the remaining number are impostors. In a case of this kind I would not, lest I should in any instance dry up the stream of charity where it ought to flow, trust to my own calculations: the result I have mentioned, is given as one of undoubted accuracy, in a pamphlet published about two years since, by the Hon. and Rev. Baptist Noel, one of the most amiable and humane men in the metropolis. But suppose we take the proportion of street-beggars who are real objects of charity to those who are not, at nearly one in sixteen, that will give, on the above computation, the immense number of 7,500 of this class of impostors who are constantly on town. I have made inquiries of a gentleman who has been officially occupied with the subject for the last few years, as to what may be the average amount which the street-beggars annually receive from a generous but too confiding public; and he says that very few of them average less than thirty shillings a week. In order, however, that we may be under rather than above the mark, let us take the average at twenty shillings per week, and this will give the immense sum of 7,500*l.* per week, or 350,000*l.* per year, which these persons levy on a charitable public.

But though I have taken the average of the weekly individual proceeds of these impostors at twenty shillings, and though the gentleman to whom I refer estimates these proceeds at above thirty shillings, they do in many cases amount to a great deal more. I know of a boy, not yet fourteen years of age, who averages from ten to twelve shillings per day, and thus by simply holding out a paper before him, while sitting on some door step, with the words written on it, "A poor orphan boy." This juvenile impostor has been actually more than fifty times in Bridewell or the House of Correction, for begging in this way in the streets. He has been frequently brought before the police magistrates by his father, who is a most respectable man, and in easy circumstances, in the hope of reclaiming him from his mendicant practices; but the little rogue has proved incorrigible, and has been given up by his parents as such. It may be asked how he spends so much money. A good deal of it is spent at the theatre, to which he goes with a regularity equal to the actors themselves, and in treating other youthful rogues with whom he is in the habit of associating. It is in order that he may get money to spend in this way that he persists in begging.

There are various instances on record, so clearly authenticated as to leave no room whatever for doubting them, of London street-beggars having amassed fortunes, varying from 1,500*l.* to 3,000*l.* In one or two very rare instances they have been still more fortunate. Some years ago a woman, who had stood with a broom in her hand for about a quarter of a century in the neighbourhood of Charing Cross, died worth nearly 3,000*l.* She got the name, among the fraternity, of the banker, because she was in the habit of lending small sums to others, at an enormous rate of interest. She sometimes also lent considerable sums to tradesmen, but never unless she received an exorbitant rate of interest. It was proved by a bill found in her possession, after her death, that she had lent one tradesman in Westminster 50*l.* for three months, but at the monstrous interest of fifty per cent. per annum. But the most extraordinary instance of good fortune in this way I ever heard of, was exhibited in the case of a man, a black, who for nearly thirty years swept another crossing at Charing Cross. He actually saved in that time, by his profession, 8,000*l.* The case of this sable personage is alluded to in "Blackwood's Magazine" for August last, where the writer calculates the yearly average proceeds of the man's broom at nearly 300*l.*,—the above named 8,000*l.* being found at his death, in the wretched hovel in which he vegetated; so that none of it could have been the proceeds of interest on stock. Another woman, who for many years swept a crossing in the Kent road, left at her death 1500*l.* to a clerk in the Bank of England, simply because he was in the habit of giving her a penny more frequently than any other passer by she knew. I have mentioned, in my First Series of "The Great Metropolis," the case of the black man with one eye and snow-white hair tied behind, who died some years ago, leaving many hundred pounds to one of the late Alderman Waithman's daughters, all of which money he had amassed by means of his broom at the crossing, on Bridge street side, from Ludgate street to Fleet street. The reason why this old black left his money to Miss Waithman, was that she not only gave him a penny or a halfpenny more frequently than any one else, but enhanced the value of the gift by condescending to accompany it with a gracious smile. The only other instance I shall mention of crossings sweepers having amassed large fortunes, is that of a black man, who some years ago returned to his native country, the West Indies; carrying with him, as the savings of a long professional life, from 1,500*l.* to 1,800*l.*

But though a great many of our street beggars might, in the course of twenty or thirty years, save as much in the prosecution of their avocation as would enable them to retire on a handsome independency, the great majority of them are extravagant and dissipated, and consequently live up to their income. Not many years ago, one of them, a man about forty years of age, actually paid to the landlord of a public-house, in the neighbourhood of Oxford street, fifty shillings per week, for a considerable time, merely for what he ate and drank there. Thirty shillings have been frequently the result of one day's skilful prosecution of street mendicancy. It is a fact, which has been proved to the satisfaction of several persons who had the curiosity to inquire into it, that a gentleman having some years ago, in 1830 I think, accidentally met with an old schoolfellow, begging in the streets,—offered to procure him a situation which he had then at his disposal, the remuneration for which was either 80*l.* or 60*l.* per annum, I forget which, and a free house; but the other at once refused it, saying he preferred his present mode of life. Begging, however, it is but right to state, is not now so profitable a business as it was thirty years ago. I am assured that two of the fraternity, a young man and an old one, having met one day accidentally in the streets, the young man inquired at the other, what success he had met with that day: "Ah," said the old man, fetching a deep sigh, "Ah! Tommy, very poor indeed, my boy; begging is not now what it was in my earlier days; it is 50*l.* a-year worse than when I began the trade."

The expedients resorted to by the street-begging fraternity of impostors, are of an infinitely varied kind. Some of them must appear incredible to my readers; they did so to myself when I first heard them, and until the testimony of individuals, whose statements I could no more question than I could my own existence, established their truth beyond all possibility of doubt. All sorts of physical ailments and infirmities are assumed; but to be blind and lame seem to be two of the most favourite artifices. I could relate numerous anecdotes respecting the pretended want of vision, want of legs, or at least the want of the use of them, of London beggars; but I am afraid of extending the chapter to too great a length. Another expedient very generally resorted to by the impostor portion of the London beggars, is that of pretending to be quite feeble, either from want or illness; and in that assumed character, either leaning against the wall of some house, or sitting on the steps of some door, or other place where there is a great thoroughfare. Not long since, a man, seemingly about fifty years of age, was sitting, with nothing but rags on his back, on the steps leading to St. Andrew's Church, Holborn, which, as most of my readers know, is one of the most crowded parts of London. The day was cold, and the person not only appeared to be suffering severely from the inclemency of the weather, but looked as if he had been in the last stage of consumption, and in a state of utter debility. To produce the latter impression, and to impart as much as possible of a pale complexion to his countenance, which he could any time cause to assume a most sickly expression, he had wrapped up his head in a white napkin, which having extended over his ears, he tied under his chin. A more spectre-like appearance, I am assured by a gentleman who witnessed the scene, could not have been exhibited by a human being. The ghosts which are personated in the theatres by those who act the part of the elder Hamlet, have not a tithe of the unearthly appearance which this personage had. The thing took amazingly. You not only saw the deepest sympathy in the countenances of the spectators, but every now and then you saw pence, in one or two instances silver, finding their way into his hat, which was of course lying beside him in the position most convenient for the ready reception of whatever portion of the circulating medium should come that way. "The poor man's dying," said one.

"See how he gasps for breath!" observed another.

"Poor creature, he won't live an hour!" remarked a third.

"Why don't some one——" A lady was in the act of making some sympathetic observation, when, before she had time to finish her sentence, he started in a twinkling to his feet, and rushing through the ring formed by the spectators, darted down Holborn with a rapidity which would have bid defiance, I will venture to say, to the racing capabilities of the most nimble of the assembled spectators. Had the man actually risen from the dead, and come up from under the stones on which he sat, they could scarcely have looked more surprised at each other. The mystery was soon explained. While the kind and compassionating people were thus lost in amazement at what they had witnessed, an officer of the Mendicity Society made his appearance. The impostor, as they say in Scotland, had caught a glimpse of him with the tail of his eye coming down Holborn Hill, when some yards distant; and not relishing a month or six weeks in Bridewell, he thought it the best way to take to his legs at once. About two years since another begging impostor was often to be seen in Holborn, in the neighbourhood of Gray's-inn lane, who appeared, from his way of walking, or rather of crawling, to be an impersonation of weakness itself. People were afraid to touch him in passing, lest they should upset him in the street. You would have fancied that a breath of wind would have laid him prostrate on the ground beyond all possibility of resistance. An officer of the Mendicity Society, who saw one evening in twilight with what success he was imposing his pretended infirmities on the public, took him into custody. He walked some forty or fifty yards without offering any resistance, and without giving expression to even a murmur; but having then come to a rather retired place, he suddenly wrested himself from the officer's grasp, and beat, or to use his own expression, "walloped" him so severely, that he was four months afterwards confined to his room. He is still alive, but has not entirely recovered, and never will recover, from the effects of the maltreatment he received at the hands and feet of a ruffian, who but ten minutes before one would have thought did not possess sufficient physical power to hurt even a fly. The poor fellow's injuries are so great that he has not the slightest chance of ever being able to do any thing towards his own support.

There are a great many blind beggars in the metropolis. Those who really are blind, and are, consequently, not in that sense impostors, are, in many instances, led by dogs in their various professional peregrinations through town. Some of these dogs are so skilfully trained up in the parts they have to perform, that they look almost as imploringly to the passers-by for alms as their masters could do, had they the use of their vision. The sagacity of some of these animals, too, also enables them, in many cases, to distinguish between those persons who are likely to give anything, and those who are not. Most of these dogs carry a small tin box, in their mouths, to receive the gifts of the charitably disposed. By far the most successful beggar, through the assistance of a dog, of whom I have ever heard was Charles Wood, a blind man, who lived upwards of twenty years ago. As that was long before I resided in the metropolis, I will give the account of this singularly dexterous and successful beggar in the words of an author already alluded to. This writer says, "Wood's dog, which was certainly a most extraordinary one, he declared to be 'the real learned French dog Bob,' and extolled his tricks by the following address:—'Ladies and gentlemen, this is the real learned French dog; please to encourage him: throw anything down to him, and see how nimbly he'll pick it up, and give it to his poor blind master. Look about, Bob; be sharp—see what you're about, Bob!' Money being thrown down, Bob picks it up, and puts it into his master's pocket. 'Thank ye, my good masters; should any more ladies and gentlemen wish to encourage the poor dog, he's now quite in the humour; he'll pick it up almost before you can throw it down!'" This ingenious mendicant is said to have realized a large sum with the aid of his "real learned French dog Bob;" but as I have not been able to ascertain the amount, I will not indulge in any conjectures on the subject.

There was one other blind beggar whose dog displayed such extraordinary sagacity, that I cannot forbear adding a word or two regarding the mendicant and his four-footed leader. The beggar was none other than George Dyball, who was so notorious in town a good many years since, and celebrated as the favourite pupil of the mendicant whom Flaxman, the eminent sculptor, chose as his model for his admirable statue of "The Jolly Beggar." He always dressed as a sailor, though he never put foot on board a ship in his life. His dog, which went by the appropriate name of Nelson, would lead him to any particular part of town which he named; and, incredible as it may appear, the fact has been established by personal observation, that the dog, by choosing the best road, and taking the nearest cuts, would, in many cases, conduct his master to the place in question in the same space of time that an ordinary-paced walker would have taken to go by the usual route. But Nelson could do much more than this. He was actually instructed, by his ingenious and roguish master, to make a sort of response to the latter's petition,—"Pray pity the poor blind!" This response the animal made by uttering a most impressive whine, accompanying his doleful language, if so it may be called, by raising his eyes, and giving a most significant and imploring turn to his head. But if he failed to attract the attention of the spectators passing by, he would sometimes rub the tin box he carried in his mouth against their knees, by way of an additional appeal to their charitable feelings. And when successful in his solicitations, Nelson would lay down the box in the street, take out the money deposited in it with his mouth, and. putting it into the hand of his master, wag his tail in token of his happiness at his good fortune.

There was another blind mendicant, who for many years levied contributions on the west-end people, in Bond-street and the neighbourhood, under the guidance of a little dog he called Blucher, after, I believe, the great Prussian General of that name. The only sentence this man was ever heard to utter, was a short apostrophe addressed to his dog, whenever he supposed, from the absence of the sound of people's feet, that no one was within hearing. And what does the reader suppose the apostrophe was? Why this—"Look after the money, Blucher!" the little dog carrying in his mouth a tin box for that purpose.

The most successful of the impostors assuming the character of a dumb person, that have ever been brought under my knowledge, was that of a stout ruffian-looking fellow, who used, in the prosecution of his mendicant avocation, to perambulate the streets in the neighbourhood of Holborn-hill. He was in the habit of going up to ladies, to whom he restricted his attempts at imposition, and uttering the most unearthly and unintelligible sounds, looking at the same time most piteously in their face. One day he thrust himself in before two young ladies, who were walking along the pavement in Ely-buildings, and looking wildly yet imploringly at them, muttered out, "Hum, hum, hum," in such frightful tones, that one of the young ladies could not divest her mind either of his personal appearance or of the unearthly sounds of his voice for some days afterwards, and was very ill in consequence. A policeman, who had seen the conduct of the fellow and the alarm of the ladies, took him to the station-house, and brought him up next day before the magistrates at Hatton-Garden. On being placed at the bar, the presiding magistrate asked the policeman the nature of the charge against the prisoner. The former having stated the circumstances under which the prisoner was taken into custody, the magistrate inquired whether he was really dumb?

"Not at all," was the answer.

"All pretended, is it?" said the magistrate.

"It is, your worship; he can speak as well as I can," replied the policeman.

"Well, Sir!" turning to the prisoner, "we'll hear what you have to say to this."

"Hum, hum, hum," growled the fellow.

"O, you can't speak yet, eh!" said the magistrate sternly.

"Hum, hum, hum," was the only answer.

"I'll give you three months in Clerkenwell prison; perhaps you may recover your organs of speech by the end of that time," observed the magistrate.

The prisoner looked fiercely at the magistrate, but uttered not a word, not even a "hum."

"Take him away, officer."

This injunction had a miraculous effect on the prisoner. "Please your vorship, I'm surely entitled to the eighteen shillings this 'ere policeman took from me, any how," said he, with a fullness and distinctness of enunciation which would have done credit to the most accomplished orator of modern times, and amidst convulsions of laughter from all present.

One of the most extraordinary assumptions of distress, and unquestionably one of the best sustained, which ever came under my own observation, occurred some years ago, in a street in the neighbourhood of Shoreditch. The impostor in this case affected to have been suddenly seized with a species of epileptic fits. I was not present at the commencement of the performance, but understood that he first pretended to fall with his back to the wall, and then threw himself down, without injuring himself, till he was in pretty nearly a horizontal position. He foamed at the mouth at a furious rate; his eye looked dim and glassy; and his whole body was dreadfully agitated. A number of persons were soon congregated around him, and one or two silver pieces, if I remember rightly, were put into his hat by ladies. I confess that I myself was for once completely deceived. I did believe the rogue laboured under some serious affliction. I could not suppose that any one would ever think of assuming that peculiar kind of distress, if they could; and I did not believe that they could assume it so effectually as to impose on the spectators, if they would. I was soon undeceived. A policeman chanced to pass that way, and coming in to see what the passengers were stopping to gaze at, he exclaimed, "Ah, Jim, my boy, is it you again?"* at the same time seizing him in the most unceremonious manner by the breast of the coat. "Come away, my lad; a good shake from me, you know, always cures you," giving him two or three sound shakes, not, I should suppose, very unlike those which the Newcastle apothecary gave to his patient. The impostor affected to look up in the face of the policeman, just as if he had recovered from a delirium, and observed, "O yes, I'm always better after a shake or two from you!"

In the winter season the most approved mode of practising deception among the street-begging impostors, is to appear in a state of almost nakedness. They calculate on their ragged appearance in inclement weather appealing more forcibly to the feelings of the passers by, than any ordinary artifice to which they could have recourse. In some cases their clothes, if such they must be called, are in so tattered a condition, that one cannot help wondering how they manage to get them to hold together. I am sure that many of my metropolitan readers

* This had reference to recent impositions of a similar kind.

must often have been struck with the tattered appearance of a slender skeleton-looking woman, with the fragment of a black straw-bonnet on her head, who is frequently to be seen in Fleet-street and the Strand, in inclement weather. Her wardrobe is literally a bundle of rags, and they seem somehow or other to fit so well, as to give her the appearance of being in stays all over. This destitute-looking creature is seldom to be seen except in cold or rainy weather. Her Bardolphian nose and blotched face afford presumptive evidence that she expends in the gin shop whatever she receives in charity. It is not that she cannot get better clothes wherewith in some measure to protect herself from the inclemency of the weather: it is that her tattered appearance works more powerfully than any ordinary expedient would, on the sympathies of those who see her. Suppose she were to receive half a dozen gowns in a day, from persons compassionating her situation, she would never put one of them on. Her begging speculation in that case would cease to answer; all of the gowns, in the supposed instance, would forthwith find their way to the pawnbrokers, and the proceeds to the palaces whence blue ruin is vended. It is a favourite practice with begging-impostor mothers, to compel their children to remain in some gateway, or other place fronting the public street, without shoes or stockings, in the coldest days of winter; because experience has taught them, that, in addition to money, gifts of shoes and stockings are often made to them. Some time ago, it was ascertained beyond all question, that one mother who compelled her two children, of the respective ages of ten and eight, to stand shivering in the cold in the winter season, in a gateway in Broad-street, Holborn,—actually averaged four shillings per day for the price of shoes given her children to wear, but every pair of which was nightly sold to a second-hand shoe dealer in Monmouth-street. One of the most skilful impostors in this way who ever came under my own observation, was a dark looking man about thirty years of age, who stood, a very considerable portion of last winter, without shoes or stockings, or anything to cover his head, in the gateway leading from Amen Corner, Paternoster Row, to Stationers' Hall Court. He was a stout healthy looking fellow, and my opinion is, that he had become so inured to the cold as to feel little inconvenience from it. He was all ears to catch the sound of any footstep coming from either side before the party made his appearance, and the moment he did hear any such footstep, he assumed, with a truth to nature I have seldom seen equalled, a fit of violent shivering. The stratagem answered well; he collected considerable sums. He was never to be seen in a mild day. In fact, all this class of impostors disappear in good weather. They are clothed in a comparatively comfortable manner in summer, because a ragged aspect would not tell at that season of the year.

But of all the expedients ever resorted to for the purpose of extracting money from the pockets of the charitable, by imposing on them through fictitious cases of distress, those adopted by a fellow, a few years since, were incomparably the most extraordinary. Will it be believed that this rogue, who was an excellent swimmer, was in the habit of pretending attempts at suicide, by throwing himself into the Thames, with a view to work upon the feelings of whoever chanced to see him after being taken out of the water? He always contrived to select a part of the river near which there were a number of bye-standers, while another person, who was a party to the affair, took care to give the alarm, and call aloud for some boat in the vicinity. Whenever the fellow pretending to have attempted suicide was brought out of the water, the other, affecting to have been passing accidentally at the time, addressed the spectators, and said that the unfortunate man had been induced to make the rash attempt through the greatest distress, and that this was the fourth or fifth time he had sought to put an end to his life, and that within a very short period. Every spectator who had a heart within him, believing, as all always did, the got-up tale, put his hand into his pocket, and gave something to "the poor unhappy man." The collections thus made often amounted to two or three pounds. This daring expedient, however, was only convenient in the summer season; winter was much too cold for doing the thing comfortably. It will be asked, in what way, then, did this consummate rogue manage to live in winter? Why, by affecting to commit suicide by hanging himself in some public place, in the evenings. He used to fasten a rope to some lamp-post or other projection at the corner of a partially frequented lane or street, and then encircling his neck with another part of the rope, he would scale the lamp-post-or other projection, as if about to throw himself down again and thereby hang himself; but always at this critical moment his partner in imposture made his appearance, and, cutting the rope, prevented the rogue from carrying his pretended purpose into effect. Of course an assemblage of people presently gathered around; the same story of distress was vamped up; the deepest sympathy was expressed for the "unhappy man;" and the shillings and sixpences were forthcoming from every pocket, accompanied with the warmest commendation of the humanity of the other rogue. But the leading performer in this drama of imposition on the benevolent public, was eventually constrained to relinquish his part. The catastrophe was one evening very nearly realised in all its horrors. In ascending a lamp-post, after the rope had been fairly round his neck, he slipped his foot and fell, and would actually have been hanged but for the opportune appearance of his friend, who cut him down. From that moment he ever afterwards had such a horror of a rope, that the very sight of one made him turn pale.

I may here mention, that in the summer of last year, I myself saw a woman conducted by two policemen to Bow-street, who having taken a boat at Waterloo Bridge under the pretext of wishing to cross the river, threw herself into the water when the boat had gone a few yards. She was brought out of the river, after being for several seconds fairly immersed in it. The policemen mentioned to me, that she had done the same thing, at the same place, in open day, several times before. Whether it ever was productive to her in a pecuniary point of view, I cannot tell; indeed, I do not know whether it was done with that view; but certainly when I saw her, which was a few minutes after she was taken out, she seemed to regard the circumstance as a mere matter of course.

Among the many expedients resorted to by the female begging impostors, to excite the sympathies of the humane and charitable, that of having two children, representing them as twins, is a very common one. The usual practice in such cases is to borrow from some acquaintance a child as like their own in age and size as possible. In some cases, where the impostor has no child of her own, she procures the loan of two children from acquaintances, making a compensation to the parties out of the proceeds of her imposition.

Those in the habit of observing what is passing in the streets, can hardly fail to have been struck with the circumstance of the apparent age and size of the alleged twins remaining the same for a long time. I know a lady, who was for a long time in the habit of giving, every Saturday night, a small sum to a woman she always saw on that evening sitting in Clare Market, with a couple of pretended twins. She at length began to feel surprised that the babies, as she called them, never appeared to grow bigger. This led to enquiries, and to the consequent detection of the imposition. But the most singular case of this kind of which I have ever heard, was one which was proved before a committee of the House of Commons some years ago. The case was that of a woman who had regularly, at the same hours, occupied the same spot for ten years, all the while exhibiting two children as pretended twins.

But by far the most ingenious expedient I ever heard of as being resorted to by any of the impostor sisterhood, in connection with children, was that employed about six months ago by a woman who usually restricted her efforts at imposition to the west end. This woman was, about the time I have mentioned, seen standing one cold winter's day, at the corner of Davies-street, Berkeley Square, shivering from the inclemency of the weather, and seemingly in a state of the greatest misery. She stated, in answer to enquiries made by some ladies, who in passing commiserated her condition, that her great concern was about her "dear baby," and not herself. "The dear infant," she said, giving something she held in her arms a gentle pressure to her breast, "the dear infant has not tasted any nourishment to-day, I having no milk to give it owing to the destitute condition in which I am placed."

The ladies looked at each other in a very sympathetic manner, and one of them put a trifle into the woman's hand, desiring her to go and get some food for herself, that she might be able to suckle her baby. Just at this moment a plainly dressed man advanced to the spot where the woman stood, who was now surrounded by a small crowd of persons. "What's the matter?" he enquired, as he elbowed his way past some of the spectators. "A woman and child starving," was the answer of one of the ladies in the crowd. On getting nearer the woman, he at once recognised her as a person he had seen in similar circumstances but a few days before. "Is the child ill? just let me see it if you please," he observed, at the same time putting out his hand, and pulling the woman's cloke forcibly aside. Down dropped something bulky on the pavement. "O the dear child's killed!" shrieked the female bystanders, as if with one voice; and a feeling of horror came over the minds of all the male persons present. On taking up the supposed child, what does the reader suppose it turned out to be? Why, a bundle of rags made up as the effigy of a child!

It will appear a startling statement to those who have never paid any attention to the subject, but it can be proved to be a fact by several of the police magistrates, that in street-mendi cancy, as in almost every thing else, there have been a great deal of speculation and several co-partneries of late years. Two or three persons take a house, and receive into their keeping a number of beggars; just as certain women do those poor females who call themselves unfortunate girls. They take them on the condition of receiving every day all they collect, they providing them with bed, lodging, food, &c., and allowing them in some cases, though not in all, a certain per centage on what they receive. One inducement to the working mendicants to accept these terms, is that they have a sort of home to remain in, at least for some time, if they are unable to ply their vocation, or if not successful in it. Another inducement is that they enjoy, in this way, the society of kindred spirits. It was proved by undeniable evidence—if I recollect rightly, or oath—about three years ago, in one of our police offices, that certain parties, residing in the neighbourhood of Saffron Hill, had no fewer than about thirty beggars, chiefly Italian boys, living in one house; and that in order to insure a profitable result from the speculation, the younger ones were threatened with exclusion from the house on their return at night, if they did not bring home a certain sum. It was established at the same time on the clearest evidence, that a trade had been carried on for some time by the same parties, in the importation of these boys, who pursued their avocation by means of a hand organ, a white mouse, or something else to afford an excuse for begging. It was stated, in April 1834, by an Italian gentleman named Lucioni, before Mr. White, one of the magistrates of Queen Square police office, that there were then no fewer than 4,000 of these boys in England, and that many of them were sent to beg through all parts of the country. The same gentleman also stated that the boys were most cruelly used by their masters. "The food of the poor lads," said he, "when they came home at night, and when the pence were taken from them by their masters, consisted of the very worst rice that could be procured, potatoes, and the rinds and scraps of bacon, bought at the cheesemongers', which are all boiled up together; they were then all huddled into a room to lay upon straw. Their masters," he added, "dress in the most fashionable style; wear gold chains, brooches, rings, &c., about their persons, and frequent the west end." I am assured, that in several instances, these speculators in youthful Italian mendicants, have made a fortune by the business and returned to their own country, where they have purchased small estates and are now living in independence. In a great many other cases parents make a trade by sending out their children to the streets, threatening to beat them if they return without a certain amount of money.

Two or three cases have come to my own knowledge, of begging companies being formed on the most approved principles, and street mendicancy being carried on, on a system of the most perfect organization. The most singular instance of this kind occurred about fifteen years ago, when several rogues, all of whose names were given me, entered, with the view of plundering the lieges, into a brotherhood, so close and cordial that that of freemasons, were compared with it, unworthy of the name. They divided the metropolis into districts, each having his own "beat" duly assigned him; and availing themselves of a London Directory, they easily found out the names and occupations of such individuals as they thought the most likely subjects for being imposed on. Each of the number of the fraternity averaged from twelve to fifteen shillings per diem, allowing only six working hours to the day. Their head-quarters were in the Commercial Road, where they had their jollification every night. The brotherhood lasted for some years. What the causes were of its eventually breaking up, I have not been able to learn.

Most of the begging companies or co-partneries which exist in different parts of London, hold stated meetings at the place patronized by the leading commanders of the band. Such place is always considered head-quarters. When new troops or partners are admitted, or rather when they are candidates for admission to the honour and advantages of membership, it is customary to examine, with great care, their pretensions. If they are not deemed fit for the profession; if, in other words, it is supposed they are not likely to prove profitable to the general concern, but rather, from their ignorance of their business, to be a burden upon the existing members, they are rejected at once. If a favourable opinion be entertained of their mendicant qualifications; if, in other terms, they are looked on as skilful impostors, they are received into the brotherhood with open arms

But the most amusing part of the proceedings of a begging association usually takes place at the formation of the company. A sort of rehearsal, such as takes place in a theatre when a new piece is about to be produced, is then duly gone through, in which the pretensions of each member of the fraternity to the part he assumes are put to the test by the leaders of the gang, assisted by the opinions of some of "the friends." About two years since, a young man, now, I fear, dead—for he was then in a very delicate state of health, and I have heard nothing of him since—about two years ago this young man* was seized with so unconquerable a desire to make himself personally acquainted with the habits, conversation, &c., of the leading mendicants in town, that he actually put on a suit of ragged clothes, and spent a whole night with fifteen or twenty of them in a house in St. Giles's. From his account of what he saw that night, I hope to be able to convey to the mind of the reader some idea of what takes place at one of the rehearsals to which I have referred. The best way to do this will be to refer to a particular case. In the formation of a company it was lately proposed to establish, in consequence of a dissolution, caused partly by deaths and partly by differences, in an old one, there were three persons who took the lead in the matter. What was rather unusual, these three persons belonged to the different sections of the United Kingdom. The first was

---

* Leigh Hunt referred to this young man in one of the numbers of his "London Journal."

an Englishman, the second a Scotchman, and the third an Irishman. At all rehearsals it is an invariable practice to have an ample supply of gin, and, if the funds will permit, something in the shape of boiled ham, bacon, or other butcher's meat. On the occasion to which I allude there was no lack either of "summut" to drink or "summut" to eat.

"Now, then, Mick Ryan, my honey!" said the Irishman, whose name was Murtach O'Flannagan, to a countryman of his own, who wished to become a member: "now, then, what character would your jewel of a self be after a-takin' up."

"Och, it's meself would like to go upon a pair of sticks," answered Mick.

"A pair of sticks!" said Tom Smith, the Englishman, evidently at a loss to know Mick's meaning.

"O, he means twa stalves," observed Charlie Mackay, the Scotchman.

"Stalves!" exclaimed Tom, evidently as much in the dark as before; "stalves! what's that?"

"Sure an' it's what you English call crutches that he manes," interposed Murtach.

"O, crutches is it?" said Tom, surprised at his own stupidity.

"And do you think, man, that ye can gae like a cripple?" inquired the Scotchman. "Lat's see fat ye can do that way," taking two crutches from a nook of the apartment and putting them into Mick's hand.

"Aye, come let's see how you can walk on crutches," said Tom Smith.

"Do, come, Mick, my darlint, and be after showin' us what it's yourself can do in that same way," echoed O'Flannagan.

"Joe Higgs, don't you be a swallowin' that ere bakun faster nor you're a roastin' on it," said Smith, by way of parenthesis, to a hungry-looking fellow who was turning a piece of bacon with his fingers on a gridiron, which had evidently seen much service in that way.

"I vas only a lickin' o' my fingers, because as how they were burnt by this ere fat," said the personage who was presiding at the gridiron, without deigning to lift up his eye from it.

"Well, don't do it no more," observed Smith, turning towards Mick, who by this time had put the crutches in a proper position for a start.

"Noo," said Charlie Mackay, "noo, man, gae awa till we see fu' the stalves becomes you. I wish I had a drap o' Highland whiskey, the real Glenlivat. I dinna like that stuff o' gin," he added, addressing himself to Tom Smith, who at this moment was in the act of tendering him a bumper of blue ruin.

Mick made two or three tottering steps through the room, leaning on his crutches.

"Och, thunder and lightnin'!" exclaimed O'Flannagan, "that will never do. Ned Stubbs," he continued, addressing himself to a little ragged fellow, who held in his hand a pewter pot full of gin, "Ned Stubbs, my boy, just give me a mouthful of the cratur to comfort my poor sowl wid."

"You walk too stately like," said Tom Smith to the candidate for membership.

"Aye, you must put yoursel' a little mair twa-fall*, man, before you can do ony good!" observed Charlie.

Mick, obeying the instructions given him, put himself into a diagonal position, and crawled away three or four yards farther.

"By the powers!" exclaimed Mick's countryman, a gleam of joy irradiating his countenance as he gazed on Mick, "By the powers! that same's just the thing. Isn't it, my jewel?" turning to Tom Smith.

"It is to a hair; nothing could be better," answered the latter. "I say, O'Flannagan," added Tom, winking knowingly at the Scotchman, "He'll do capital well—eh?"

"Naething could be better: it's true to nature," replied Charlie Mackay.

"You'll make a trump of a 'un; take a glass of gin," said Smith, addressing himself to Mick, and handing him a glass of Fearon's best, which Mick drank off with due expedition, licking his lips after it, as much as to say, "I would have no objection to another of that same."

"Fred. Jones, vot character would you like to appear in?" inquired Smith, turning himself to a skin-and-bone-looking little Welshman, with a most demure expression of countenance, —just as if he had been made for frightening away the crows from the corn; "vot character would you prefer?"

"Voy, I don't know as how I knows myself," was the luminous and satisfactory answer.

"My opinion is," said Charlie; "my opinion is, that"——He was about to deliver his opinion, but was interrupted by Murtach exclaiming in a voice of Stentorian power—

"Och, bad luck to that spalpeen in the corner there! By my sowl he's drinkin' the last dhrop of the gin." Here Murtach pointed to a stout athletic fellow, with a face as black as the remains of the hat he had on his head, who was standing with his back to the others, with the pewter jug of gin at his mouth, and emptying it as fast as the liquid could find a passage down his throat.

* Twofold.

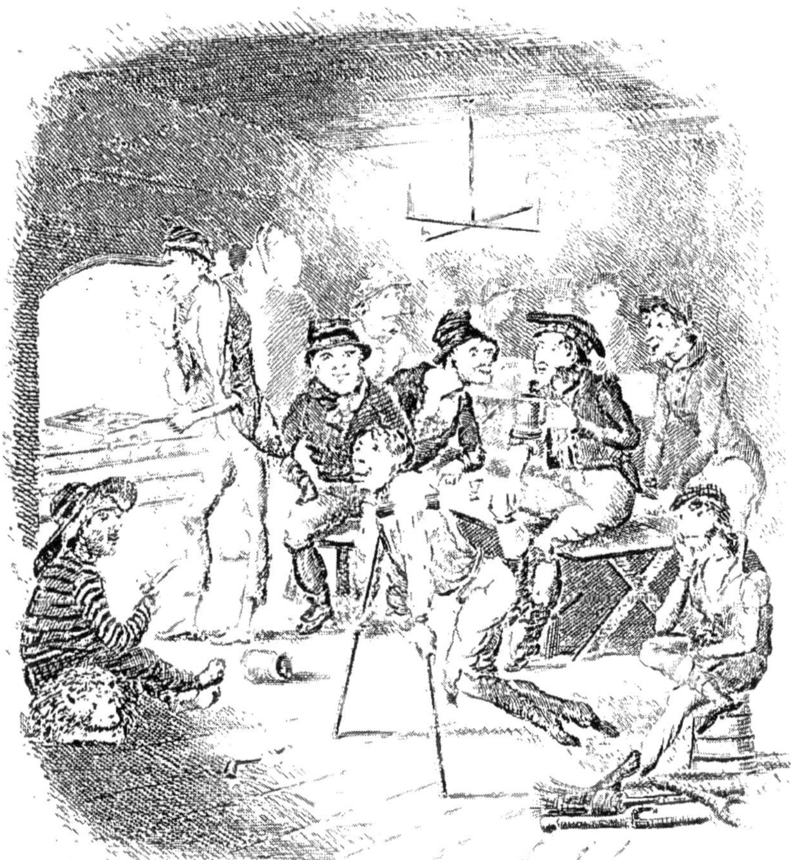

"Vy that's too bad, Harley; you ought to be ashamed of yourself," said Mr. Smith.

Why or wherefore this personage was called Harley, or whether that was really any part of his name, I have not been able to ascertain; but he turned about, and putting a bold face on the matter, insisted that he was not drinking the gin, but had only put it to his lips without being aware of the circumstance.

"Mackay," said Smith, apostrophising the Scotchman, "you were a-going to say something about Fred."

"I was just going to say that I dinna think he'll need any ither character than he has by nature. I think his very awfu' looking face will be enough to get him plenty o' bawbees."

After some further discussion it was agreed that Fred. Jones should, in the first instance, take the streets in his real character, and that if that was not found to answer, it should afterwards be taken into consideration what other one it would be most advisable to assume.

"Timothy Soaper, I think you said you would prefer wooden leg and an arm crutch—did you not?"

This was addressed by Smith to a young, healthy-looking fellow, with a straw broad-brimmed hat, who was sitting cross-legged on the floor, in the neighbourhood of the hearth-stone, munching the remains of a quartern loaf, and a piece of bacon half raw.

"Yes," he answered in a gruff tone, assuming a perpendicular position; "yes, I thinks as how I'll try that ere."

"Come away, then, my darlint, and try on the wooden leg," said O'Flannagan.

"Ned, my boy, jost gie us a wooden leg out of that ere nook," said Charlie, pointing to a corner of the room in which there was a very large assortment of wooden legs, crutches, brooms, tattered garments, and everything necessary to equip one in any particular character which either of the mendicants might think proper to assume.

A wooden leg having been produced, Soaper advanced to have it put on. Mackay undertook the task of strapping it. The knee having been fairly inserted, he proceeded to fasten it, when pulling the strap too hard, Soaper roared out as lustily as if he had been undergoing the operation of tooth-drawing.

"Be aisy, be aisy!" said O'Flannagan to Charlie, "and don't be after killin' him quite."

The knee of Soaper was fairly fastened, and he made several steps through the place, but he did the thing so very clumsily, and the foot which protruded behind him, notwithstanding its being wrapped in rags, looked so very unlike a lame one, that the three leading personages in the company came to an unanimous conclusion that he would never do in that character.

"Then," said he, on hearing their decision, "I'll take up again the one vot I use to be in;" clapping his fingers on his eyes to denote that he meant the character of a blind man.

This did not altogether meet the view of Smith, Mackay, and O'Flannagan; because the candidate had not done great things in that character before. It was, however, agreed that he should appear in it for some time, until they saw whether any better one which he could sustain with effect, should suggest itself.

There was another candidate, a fat shrivelled-faced middle-aged man, deeply pitted with the small-pox, who also aspired at sustaining the character of a blind beggar. He had before "tried it on" by appearing to shiver with cold at the corners of streets, but as he had not found the thing so profitable as he expected, even in the winter season, he saw clearly, now that summer was at hand, that it would not answer at all! He had therefore thought of trying what could be done by personating the character of a blind man, and had, with the view of ensuring success in his new line, been for nine weeks trying how mournfully he could repeat the words "Pity the poor blind!" "Let us hear you," said Smith.

"Yes, sure," said O'Flannagan, "be after repating it to us."

The other did so, and drawled out the words in so touching a tone, that one would have thought it impossible for any human being to resist his appeals for a few pence.

"Charlie, my boy," whispered Smith, into the Scotchman's ear, the moment he heard the peculiar twang of the candidate; "Charlie, my boy, this fellow vill do; blow me tight if he don't."

"Jim Burgess, vat vould you like to be?" said Smith, to a black curly-headed copper-faced, thick-lipped personage, sitting on a broken chair, who all this time had never opened his mouth.

"I vould likes to be a negro character," answered Jim.

"Och! by the mother that bore me, but that's just the thing for him—isn't it, Jim?" said O'Flannagan, turning to Smith.

"I thinks so too," said the latter. "With a little wet soot on his ugly face he'll look the character to a hair. Bring the wet soot here, Mac."

The Scotchman brought the commodity with all expedition, and Jim lost no time in thoroughly besmearing his frontispiece with it. "Och, by the powers!" exclaimed O'Flannagan, as he gazed on the sooty visage of Jim; "Och! by the powers! but he'll make the fortune of us all."

Two other candidates were admitted, who were each confident that a legible written label, with suitable words, would, with the

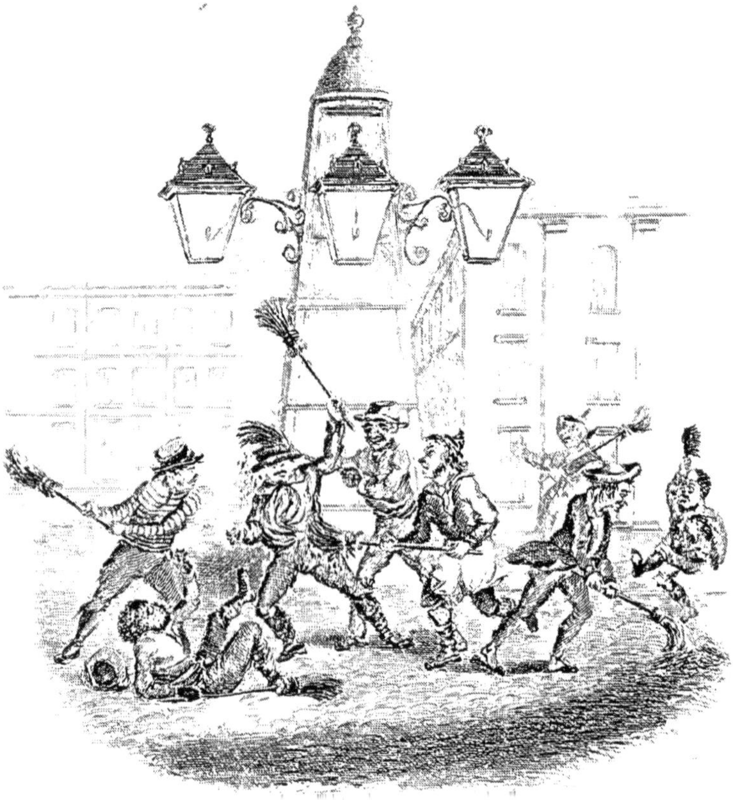

advantage they possessed of a most distressed personal appearance, insure a very fair measure of success without resorting to any other expedient. The one was to hold out his label in his hands, and the other was to have it affixed to his hat. The label of the first was agreed to be "Out of Employ;" that of the other "Great Distress." The last was to be the one which was to be affixed to the hat. Both were certainly very short and very simple.

But I must not go into further details respecting this rehearsal of the beggars. Some there were who claimed to be admitted into the society on the ground of their powers of enduring cold, and consequently being able to appear half naked in the streets; while others thought they might, without any thing of an adventitious kind, confidently trust to the power they possessed over their features, by which they could assume the most frightful conceivable expression of countenance. The scene was altogether one of ineffable richness, to which no justice can be done by mere description. The rehearsal having been completed and the arrangements for commencing operations next day been concluded, the party ordered a fresh supply of chops, ham, bacon, gin, porter, and spent one of the most jovial evenings ever witnessed even in St. Giles's,—which is by far the most jovial locality in London. Who could have believed, that next day the rogues would be seen crawling about the streets the very personification of apparent wretchedness and destitution?

I have often thought that of all modes of street begging, that of sweeping the crossings is the least troublesome and the most profitable. The latter opinion will, I am sure, be concurred in by all who have read the statements formerly given of individual instances of fortunes having been made in this branch of the mendicant professsion. Of course, then, it is an object to get possession of a good stand; for if once fairly in the possession of one of the fraternity, the tenure will remain undisputed for the party's life. The crossings-sweepers are great sticklers for prescriptive rights. If any new comer were to attempt, either by physical force or otherwise, to dispossess one of the brotherhood from that small portion of the metropolitan territory which he has professionally occupied before, all the brooms in London would be uplifted against him before he knew what he was about, and he would have cause to bless his stars if he escaped being scrubbed or "broomed" to death. The crossings-sweepers never fight with any other weapons than their brooms. A scuffle between two or more of them is a rich scene; it is one of the richest which a person will see in a life-time. Whenever a crossing-sweeper dies, it is a great matter to be the first to take possession of the vacant spot. This priority of possession is to insure it to the party for life. Hence if the circumstance should chance to transpire that one of the brotherhood is dangerously ill, the greatest anxiety is evinced to be the first, if possible, to take possession of his vacant post, after he has breathed his last. The number of aspirants after such a productive stand, that is, one in a good part of the town, when the existing occupier is understood to be dangerously ill, is incredibly great.

In some cases, as in that, for instance, of the black formerly referred to, who retired with a fortune of fifteen hundred pounds, and returned to his native country, the West Indies; in some cases, the possessors of a good stand dispose of it just as men do other trades. It was proved, a few years since, before a select committee of the House of Commons, that begging businesses had actually been sold for considerable sums.

I have often been struck, as I am sure every one who has passed through the streets of London must have been, with the great number of black men who possess lucrative stands. How it happens that so many of these ebony personages have been so fortunate, compared with the white population of London, is one of those things which are beyond the reach of my philosophy.

I have already remarked that, with very few exceptions, all the London beggars live up to their means; and that what they earn, or rather swindle out of a benevolent and confiding public, is spent in eating and drinking. The luxuries in this way, which some of our street mendicants can often boast of, would appear incredible to those who are unacquainted with the subject. But gin is the great thing with most of them. I knew one, and only one, who spent a considerable portion of his professional proceeds in the article of dress. This man, who used to be seen daily in the neighbourhood of Holborn, decrepit in appearance, and with the most ragged wardrobe that was ever fastened about the human body, regularly gave up his avocation at six in the evening, and in about an hour afterwards, was to be seen in the parlour of a public-house in Gray's Inn Lane, where he remained till eleven at night, smoking his pipe and drinking his brandy and water, and dressed in a suit of clothes, with his legs encased in top boots, which no gentleman would be ashamed to wear. The gentleman to whom I am indebted for this interesting fact, tells me that he has missed this mendicant for some time, and has not been able to learn what has become of him. Very few of the fraternity, however, waste much of their gleanings in apparel; the belly is the great thing with the vast majority of them: they are great gourmands. Not more partial is an alderman to his turtle soup, than are these gentry to the good things of this life. There are several of them who "spit" their goose or duck at least three times a week. There are also numbers who hold regular convivial meetings, at which some remarkable gastronomic feats are performed. On some special occasions they regularly elect their chairman, and have their series of toasts, their speeches, and songs, as on other great public occasions. It is known to several persons, that George the Fourth, when Prince of Wales, went, on one occasion, with his friend Major Hanger, to witness the scenes which take place at these guzzlling exhibitions of the mendicants. Tutored as the young prince was by Sheridan and others of his boon companions in all sorts of frolics, he enjoyed the scene for some time. At last, however, a circumstance occurred which somewhat disconcerted him. The beggar who presided on the occasion as chairman, after a temporary pause in the merriment of the evening, rose, and pointing to the Prince said, "With the permission of the company, I calls on that ere gemman with the clean shirt on, for a song." A round of applause from the rest of the "jolly beggars" showed how eagerly they responded to the appeal thus made to his Royal Highness. He winked significantly at Major Hanger, and then stammered out the expression of a hope, that as he was no singer the company would excuse him.

"Not a bit of it," said the chairman.

"Ve'll have no denial, young man," said another of the jovial crew.

"Perhaps, gentlemen, you'll allow the gentleman to sing by proxy," interposed Major Hanger.

"Proxy!" said several voices at once, "vat's proxy?"

"O, another person singing for him," answered the major.

"O certainly, if he can find one," said the chairman, looking round for the concurrence of the company in his sentiment.

"O, there can be no objections to that," observed a dozen voices at once.

"Come then, H——, you must do it yourself," said the prince, addressing himself to the major. The latter promptly responded to the appeal, and sung amidst great applause a well-known ballad—well-known, I mean, among the fraternity themselves—called "The Beggar's Wedding."

"Gen'l'men," said the proprietor of a little unwashed and unshaved face, and a nose of remarkable flatness, who sat opposite the chairman, "Gen'l'men, let us drink the health and song of the gen'l'man vot's just sung."

"Gen'l'men," shouted the chairman, drawing his own glass towards himself; "gen'l'men, fill your glasses."

Every glass was full to the brim in a moment.

"The gen'l'man's health and song," said the chairman in Stentorian accents.

"The gen'l'man's health and song," shouted a host of voices, and in an instant every glass was emptied of its contents, except that of the Prince.

"I say, young man, vy don't you drink to your friend?" said a round faced mendicant, who sat opposite his Royal Highness, his eyes rolling in a fine frenzy through the inspiring influence of the liquid he had so copiously quaffed.

"O, I beg your pardon, Sir," answered the Prince, who had been for the moment lost in surprise at the ecstasies of uproarious merriment he witnessed every where around him; "O, I beg your pardon, Sir, for the omission, it was quite accidental, I assure you." This was addressed to the personage who had challenged him for not drinking to the major.

"Vell, vy don't you do it now?" inquired the other, who was a very consequential personage in his own estimation.

The Prince filled up his glass, and having drunk off the contents to the health and song of Major Hanger, held it out in his hand in an inverted position.

"Bravo! you're a trump!" "Go it, clean shirt!" shouted a dozen voices.

"Three cheers for the gentleman who has favoured us with so excellent a song!" exclaimed the Prince, beginning to feel himself more at home. As he spoke he rose, and waved his hand with his empty glass in the air, as if to lead the plaudits of the others. All present were on their legs in an instant, and deafening and universal were the cheers with which the major was greeted. The scene was kept up with great spirit and eclat, until at least one half of the "jolly beggars" had drunk themselves asleep, and lay like so many masses of inert clay on the floor, in a horizontal position. The Prince often afterwards spoke of this adventure. He never mentioned it in the hearing of Sheridan, without the latter feeling the deepest regret that he was not an actor in so rich a scene of low life.

The beggars, at all their carnivals, adhere most scrupulously to the good old custom of having their toddy made in a large bowl, usually a pewter one. They hold that there is nothing like brotherly feeling in the modern practice of every one having his toddy made in a tumbler of his own. They are great Tories as regards all ancient usages; they have a perfect horror of innovation in such cases.

They are, for the most part, early risers, and will walk any distance in the morning, before setting out professionally, to visit those public-houses which are most largely patronized by the fraternity. There is one public-house in Oxford-street, which used to be,—and I have no doubt still is, though I cannot speak positively to the latter fact,—crowded with them by six o'clock in the morning. The landlord of this house has repeatedly mentioned that, on an average, about one hundred and fifty mendicants were in the habit of visiting his house in a day, and he has always added that he would never wish to have any better customers; for it was quite a common thing for the majority of the number to have individually their half pint of gin before nine in the morning.

In those lodging-houses which were formerly open to the begging fraternity promiscuously, and where business was carried on on a large scale, it was found, from experience, necessary to take certain precautions against the abstraction of any of the articles of furniture. Mother Cummings, who died a few years since, and who for a long period kept a lodging-house in a low street in Bloomsbury, always made a point of turning the key on her customers when they went to bed, and then unlocked the door with her own hand in the morning. By this means she prevented any of them making away with any articles of furniture in the course of the night; and as she witnessed every one of them quit their hovels in the morning, the idea of felony in the case of her property was out of the question. I may here mention, that Mother Cummings, while she was alive, kept by far the most extensive lodging-house for mendicants, of any of her contemporaries. She has been known to have had, on repeated occasions, upwards of eighty lodgers in one night. And, strange as it may seem, it was proved to be a fact, that she had one round bed in which, when there was an unusual demand for accommodation, eighteen or twenty persons have been huddled together for the night. Mother Cummings made always a distinction between the better and inferior class of mendicants. With this view she had two prices for accommodation for the night. The charge for a bed in ordinary circumstances was two-pence per night; but if any one chose to indulge in the luxury of clean straw, the charge was four-pence. The choice, therefore, of the different applicants for lodgings, in the matter of their bed, enabled her at once to range her customers into two classes; and both were treated by her with a measure of attention corresponding to the place they occupied in her estimation.*

It would seem as if some improvement had taken place of late in the morals of the mendicant gentry; for until about twelve

* Mother Cummings eventually retired from business, having amassed a considerable amount of money. She took a private house in Somerstown, where she died. The news of her death spread like wildfire among the fraternity, and her funeral was attended by an immense number of her former lodgers.

years since, not only was it necessary to lock these personages into their hovels at night, but it was found equally necessary that the knives and forks, the tongs and poker, and every other portable article in the places they used to frequent, should be fixed by iron chains to the table, or the walls of the house, as the only means of security against their being stolen. There was a sort of low eating-house in St. Giles's, that used to be largely frequented by the brotherhood, which furnished the last instance, so far as I am aware, of this precaution being taken against theft. That house was thrown down some years ago, preparatory to improvements in the neighbourhood; and I am not aware of either the locking-in or the chaining system having been resorted to in any subsequent case. It is gratifying to hear of an improvement in morals among any class of the community; there are few classes in which there is yet room for greater improvements than among the mendicant fraternity.

CHAPTER II.

DEBTORS' PRISONS—THE QUEEN'S BENCH.

Debtors' Prisons—The various debtors' prisons—The average number of prisoners in each—The Queen's Bench; extent and nature of the accommodation in it—The practice of chumming prisoners—Shops, business, &c.—Story of the Pie-man—The tap-room—Eccentric characters—Tom Snaggs—Circumstances under which persons are imprisoned—Partiality of some of the prisoners to the Queen's Bench—Striking instance of this—Efforts made by some of the prisoners to keep up their former dignity—Story of a dinner—Various classes of persons in the Queen's Bench—Changes in the external appearance of the better class of prisoners after they have been a short time in the place—Unexpected meetings of friends in the Bench—Illustrative anecdotes—General observations, and anecdotes.

The question of imprisonment for debt having been of late so often under the consideration of the legislature, the attention of the public has been drawn to it within the last few years much more generally than at any former period. Intimately connected with this subject is that of the Debtors' Prisons in London; and as very few, with the exception of those who have had the misfortune to be inmates, know any thing regarding these places, I shall devote this chapter to them. I have only one preliminary remark to make, which is, that all the facts and anecdotes which I shall give relative to the Queen's Bench Prison, have been verbally communicated to me by persons in the place, in the course of repeated visits which I lately paid to it, for the purpose of obtaining such information.

The Debtors' Prisons in London are five in number. They are, the Queen's Bench, the Fleet, the Marshalsea, White Cross-street, and Horsemonger-lane prisons.

As I shall afterwards have occasion to speak at considerable length of the first-named prison, I shall make a few observations on the others in this part of the chapter. The Fleet is a prison for the confinement of persons under process of debt issuing out of either the Court of Common Pleas, or the Court of Exchequer; or for the confinement of parties who have been guilty of contempt of either of these courts. The Fleet is also the place of imprisonment for persons who are held guilty of a contempt of the Court of Chancery, or of the Duchy Court of Lancaster. There is a certain space without the prison which is called "The Rules." Within this space the prisoners are permitted to reside at large, on furnishing satisfactory security against their escape.

This is done by a warrant of attorney to confess judgment, and on paying the warden of the prison a certain per centage upon the debt, the amount of which per centage varies according to the magnitude of the debt, and the circumstances of the debtor, but never exceeds five per cent. on the first 100*l.*, nor two and a half on the second. The space within the rules embraces a circumference of three miles, and includes the London Coffee House. Day rules may be had any day, during term, on which the Courts of Common Pleas and Exchequer respectively sit, on applying to the warden, and furnishing the same kind of security as in the case just mentioned. A day rule enables the prisoner to go at large during the particular day for which it is granted, from the opening of the prison gates in the morning till eleven o clock at night. The expenses of a day rule, exclusive, of course, of the amount of security required, are four shillings and sixpence. Of this sum the warden gets one shilling; the clerk of the papers one shilling and tenpence; and the officers of the court, who grant the rules, receive the remaining one shilling and eightpence. With regard to "chumming" and other internal arrangements of the prison, I shall not say any thing here, as they will be fully described when I come to speak of the Queen's Bench; the arrangements being essentially the same in both places. The verage number of persons confined in the Fleet is about 230.

The MARSHALSEA PRISON is situated in Southwark. The number of persons confined in this prison is always much smaller than in any of the other prisons in the metropolis. The reason of this is, that it is restricted to the reception of two classes of men; first, officers and privates of the Royal Navy under sentence of naval courts-martial for mutiny, desertion, &c.; and, secondly, persons committed for debt or contempt, by the Palace Court, whose jurisdiction extends to the distance of twelve miles round the Palace at Westminster. It has no rules like the Fleet: once consigned to it there is no getting out again, until you are liberated altogether. The prisoners in this place are obliged to find themselves in their own bedding, furniture, fuel, and every thing else. Their number does not average more than 130.

WHITE CROSS-STREET PRISON is a place appropriated exclusively to those who are debtors to society. It is divided into three departments; the first is set apart for those persons who are freemen of the city of London, and is called the Ludgate side of the prison; the second is set apart for persons within the jurisdiction of the city, and is called the London side; and the third is appropriated to the reception of those arrested in the county, and is called the Middlesex side. The number of persons committed to this prison is much greater than in the case of any other of the metropolitan prisons. This is to be accounted for from the fact, that the majority of those ordered for imprisonment by the

Courts of Requests, are sent to this place. And such is the facility of the debtor and creditor law in consigning human beings to prison, that a person has only to go and swear a debt of a shilling or sixpence against any other party, before the City Court of Requests, to have that party, if unable or unwilling to pay the debt, shut up in this prison for twenty days. The number of persons annually committed to White Cross-street prison is supposed to be very nearly 2000; and the average number of persons always confined in it exceeds 470. Its locality is in the City.

Horsemonger-lane Prison is very similar in its constitution to that of White Cross-street. It is situated on the other side of the water, at no great distance from the Queen's Bench prison. A large proportion of its inmates consists of persons committed on process issued by the Courts of Requests. The average annual commitments are about 1200, and the average number of individuals confined in it at a time is upwards of 100.

The Queen's Bench Prison, from its greater importance, is deserving of a more detailed notice than either of the others. It is situated in the Borough of Southwark, and embraces, with its open space, about four acres of ground. The principal building is 300 feet in length, and has a good deal of the appearance of a barracks. The whole is enclosed by a wall 35 feet in height; and which, to render the assurance of the safe keeping of the inmates doubly sure, is surmounted by large iron spikes. The exterior of the building is gloomy, owing partly to the dingy hue of the bricks, and partly to the smallness and plainness of the windows. The entire number of rooms within the walls of the Queen's Bench prison, is 225, of which eight are called "state rooms," and are set apart for the better class of prisoners. Half-a-crown a-week is paid as rent for one of these rooms. For the other rooms, with the exception of a few back ones which poor prisoners occupy rent free, the inmates pay one shilling weekly, and have to provide their own furniture. If, however, two persons are appointed to the same room, they are only charged sixpence each; if three, only fourpence each. In addition to the 225 rooms, there are a coffee-house and public kitchen, and a public-house. At one end of the prison there is a kind of market, consisting of several sheds, occupied by butchers, poulterers, green-grocers, &c., each tenant paying a weekly rent of one shilling. These shillings, with the amount received for the various rooms, go into the pockets of the marshal, and are one source whence he receives his remuneration. His other sources are fees on commitments and discharges, or for granting the rules, or the liberty of living within the walls of the prison. The last-named source is the most productive one, as may be inferred from what I have said when speaking of the rules of the Fleet Prison. Altogether, the marshal's emoluments are usually, or were lately, after deducting drawbacks, worth nearly 3000*l.* a-year.

Should the number of prisoners happen, which is very rarely the case, to be under the number of rooms in the place, then each prisoner is entitled to a room to himself on the payment of one shilling rental weekly. When the shilling cannot be paid, the marshal, as before stated, foregoes his claim, and allows the party to occupy his apartment rent free. The rooms are all very small; they must of necessity be so, from the number there is of them in so limited a space.

When there is more than one person to each room, which, as just observed, is almost always the case, the new-comers are, what is called "chummed" on the previous inmates. The system of "chumming" is difficult to be understood, to one who has not been an inhabitant of the place. It was some time before I could comprehend it: I shall explain it as well as I can. When a prisoner is first confined within the walls, he is entitled to what is termed a "chum ticket," which is a small piece of paper on which one of the officers of the prison, called the chum-master, writes the name of the party, and the number of the room in which he is to be "chummed." With this ticket he proceeds to the room in question, and showing it to the inmate, the latter must either share his apartment with him, or pay him five shillings, by way, as the phrase goes, of purchasing him out. If the new comer be offered the five shillings, he is compelled to take it, and then go and provide himself with the share of some other room, as he best can. The chum-master generally takes care to chum a poor prisoner, to whom the five shillings must be a great object, on one who is able to purchase him out. There are always a number of poor people in the place who will be glad to let any new prisoner have a part of their room for one shilling or eighteen-pence a week; so that the new prisoner gains four shillings or three-and-sixpence per week by the transaction. When the prison is full, the previous inmates are liable to have two persons chummed on them, so that, if they are desirous of possessing their rooms to themselves, they must pay ten shillings a week to the "chums," exclusive of their own shilling in the shape of rent to the marshal. Some years ago, instances occurred in which three persons were chummed on one individual who previously tenanted a room. Since then, however, an act of parliament has been passed, prohibiting the chumming of more than two individuals on a previous inmate. This, however, does not prevent a greater number than three individuals lodging and sleeping in one room. The anxiety of the poorer class of prisoners to save a few shillings per week, by congregating together in one room, has often led to six or eight persons vegetating together in a dark dirty apartment, measuring only sixteen by nineteen feet. In other cases, the same desire to save a trifle wherewith to administer to the necessities of the belly, leads numbers of the poorer order of prisoners to sleep on the benches in the tap-room, without any other covering than their clothes. It was stated in a report drawn up on the subject some years since, by a committee of the House of Commons, that as many as forty-eight persons have slept in this way in the tap-room at once. Why should we wonder, then, that the imprisonment of the poorer classes in the Queen's Bench proves, in many cases, the pathway to a premature grave; and that, in others, the constitution receives a shock from which it never afterwards recovers?

There is a class of tickets called "in-chum tickets." This means that the chum-master gives a new-comer, who wishes to have as comfortable a room as possible rather than the five shillings and the certainty of being obliged to live with other persons of the lowest class, a ticket on a previous prisoner who is known to be willing to receive into his room any person in the same rank of life as himself, in order that he may be spared the necessity of paying five shillings weekly to purchase any one out.

Formerly, the practice was to chum all new prisoners on the junior inmates, in the first instance, in order that those who had been longest in the place might have the chance of exemption, as a sort of privilege to which their long residence in the prison was supposed to entitle them. It accordingly often happened, that all the junior inmates had persons chummed on them, while those who had been there for a number of years escaped entirely, except in those cases when the prison was so crowded that there were chums for every person in it. A different course has been adopted for some time past. The practice, I believe, has been of late, to begin the process of chumming with the senior prisoners, regularly descending downwards to those who have most recently entered the place. This is a very improper arrangement; so, at least, I am assured by those who have been some years within the walls of the building. In order that I might glean as much original information about the place as possible, I spent the greater part of a day in it, in August last; and on that occasion, the hardship of saddling all the new-comers on the oldest inmates, in the first instance, was depicted to me by some of the latter in the strongest and most feeling terms. They say that the thing is most partial in its operation, inasmuch as that, while the senior prisoners have to submit almost all the year round to the calamity of having mere novices in the ways of the prison chummed on them, the "six-week" class of persons, that is to say, those who only come to the prison for a six weeks' probation there. prior to their transit through the

Insolvent Debtors' Court, often escape altogether. As far as I can comprehend the merits of the case, this ought not to be. "And if I were the marshal," as one of the prisoners of a long-standing date emphatically observed to me, "it should not be." But I am not the marshal, any more than the party making the observation, and therefore cannot redress the grievance.

Some of the prisoners, who manage to get their rooms decently done up and furnished, let them out to those new prisoners who can afford to pay for them. A guinea a week is often got in such cases for a room; while the party letting it goes, perhaps, and shares one, with some one in the same rank of life, at half-a-crown. There are generally one or more prisoners who let out articles of furniture to those who wish to speculate in furnished lodgings in the Queen's Bench.

There are always, in addition to the butchers, green-grocers, &c., formerly mentioned, a number of tradesmen, prisoners in the Queen's Bench, who pursue their respective callings there. When I last visited the place, which was two months ago, I found almost all the apartments on the ground-floor tenanted by what Robert Owen would call the sons of industry. One of these rooms is converted into a sort of bazaar in miniature, brimfull—that is to say, if one may judge from a passing glance at the window—of the most miscellaneous assortment of merchandise ever collected together; while no individual article could possibly have cost more than three-halfpence. Next door to this depot of small-wares, was a barber's shop. But the best of it was, that the man of soap and suds arrogated to himself the professionally aristocratic title of "hair-dresser and perfumer;" and, to complete his pretensions, he added, on his paper placard—which rejoiced in broken-backed and deformed letters, evidently the triumphs of his own pen—"From Regent-street." Then followed, in characters formed of more colours than I can enumerate, but in which the black, blue, and yellow predominated, the words "Shave for a Penny." Hear this, ye hair-dressers and perfumers of the aristocratic Regent-street! Here is one of your number—if his own story may be credited—who scrapes the lower extremities of the frontispieces of her Majesty's subjects in the Queen's Bench, "and all for the small charge of one penny!" If Tonsor's razors be no better than his orthography, I envy not the unfortunate wights who are doomed to encounter the operation of shaving at his hands: far rather would I, were I in their situations, turn Jew at once: I mean as regards the article of my beard. The aforesaid inscription or sign-board, appeared thus: "Mathew Maggs, Har Drsr and Parfoomr frome Regnt Street—Sheve for a Peny."

A few doors from this importation from Regent-street. is a

room in which tailorifics are practised by a knight of the thimble, whom some ill-natured creditor—so, at least, it is intimated on the sign-board—transferred to that locality from the "exquisite" regions of New Bond-street. I could not help compassionating poor Snip, as I thought of the mortification he must feel when he reflected on the contrast between "decorating" the very *élite* of aristocratic dandyism in New Bond-street, and patching the tattered corduroy unmentionables of the poor mechanics in the Bench. But I find—and, I doubt not, so does the industrious man of buckram now in the Bench, though late of New Bond-street—that there is no use in moralising on such things. We live in a changeable world; and I admire the philosophy of the man who can adapt himself to circumstances which he can no longer control. It were an endless task to enumerate the various descriptions of "callings" pursued in this part of the Queen's Bench. The range of rooms on the ground-floor is, in fact, almost exclusively occupied by an industrious colony of merchants and operatives. At the back part of the buildings, again, which is chiefly tenanted by the very poorest of the prisoners, there are shops of an humbler class. The first one which attracted my notice was set apart for the sale of sausages, and had a placard in the window with the words, after the name of the vender, "Sausage-maker to the Queen." This may appear a joke; I assure my readers it is nothing of the kind. The fact can be attested by every person who was in the place some few months ago. Whether this sausage-maker to her Majesty be still engaged in the useful occupation of vending these articles to her subjects, is a question which I cannot answer. The stock in hand, when I passed the window, consisted of half-a-dozen,—not one more nor less. As to the quality of the sausages, I am not competent to speak, not having tasted them. If, however, one may judge from appearances, I should doubt whether they were what they were warranted to be, namely, "prime 'uns." Let me not be understood by this as "insinuating," as the American was charged with doing when he one day went up to a sausage vender in New York, and asked him very significantly whether "them 'ere saussengers were good 'uns?"—let me not, I say, be charged with "insinuating" that the half-dozen sausages I saw in the window in question were not of the best quality. They *may*, to use the words of the Yankee just referred to, have been "werry good saussengers, for anything as I knows to the contrary; but this I knows, as how they did not *look* werry like good 'uns." I would say further, in favour of the sausage manufacturer alluded to, that though the assortment which greeted my vision as I passed the back part of the building were not particularly attractive in appearance, they may have been a bad lot owing to accidental circumstances, and by no means fair specimens of the quality of sausages manufactured and vended in the same quarter.

Next came "The Original Shop For Cleaning Knives, Spoons, And Boots." Why forks were omitted in the brief catalogue of articles cleaned, I have not, up to this moment, been able to divine; however, I have a strong impression that the tenant of the shop will suffer but little, if at all, from the omission. I saw no appearance of any business doing in the cleaning of either of the three other articles; and though forks had been included in the list, I am afraid the insertion would not have increased the custom. The fact I take to be, that those in the Queen's Bench who ever enjoy the luxury of clean knives, spoons, or boots, must perform the polishing operation themselves. I am sure I need not add, that, to a very large proportion of the unfortunate inmates, the luxury of knives, spoons, or boots, clean or otherwise, is one of which they never partake while within the walls.

But I must not take up more of my space with the shops in the Queen's Bench prison; nor shall I, having already alluded to the different kinds of stalls kept in the open air, advert again to them. It is right, however, I should here mention one species of merchandise carried on in the prison to which I have not before alluded. I refer to a portable stand, kept by an old man who never gets any other name than John, for the sale of penny pies, "all hot." This antiquated worthy is most eloquent and incessant in praise of his pies. All day long does he heap the most superlative commendation on them. An African says, "Strike me, but do not curse my mother:" John will a thousand times sooner submit not only to be abused, but even personally assaulted, rather than that a word should be said against the quality of his pies. His character as pie-man is dearer to him than life itself. If he had a purse, which he has not, he would say, in the words of Shakspeare, with an emphasis superior to any with which the phrase has ever been repeated before, "Who steals my purse, steals trash; but he who filches from me my good name,"—that is to say, as a pie-man,—"takes from me that which not enriches him, but makes me poor indeed." "Let me have one of your pies, John," said a hungry-looking cobbler, while I was one day present, as he gazed on the assortment before him, at the same time laying down a penny on the tin stand.

"Will you have an eel 'un, or a pork 'un, or a weal 'un?" inquired John.

"Whichever's best," was the answer.

"That's vich vay people's tastes goes," said John. "They are all of the werry best quality as can be made," he added.

"I thinks I'll take an eel 'un," observed the cobbler, eyeing the whole lot as eagerly and hungry-like as if he could have swallowed every one of them at once.

"An eel 'un?" said John, as he handed him the desired commodity.

"O, this is a cold 'un!" exclaimed the cobbler, laying it down again the moment it had been placed in his hand. "Vy don't you give me a hot 'un at once?"

"And vy didn't you ax for a 'ot 'un?" answered the pie-man, somewhat tartly. "How vas I to know as how you liked a hot 'un in pref'rence to a cold 'un?"

John rummaged through his entire stock of pies, in quest of an "'ot eel 'un," but the search was in vain. "Not got any 'ot eel 'uns," he intimated in accents which showed that he possessed that caloric, as the chemists say, in his temper which was lacking in his eel-pies.

"Then let me have a hot weal 'un," said the other, gruffly, being manifestly more powerfully impelled to the step by hunger than by choice.

"There's a weal 'un, all 'ot," exclaimed the pie-man, with an evident air of complacency, as he transferred the article to the mender of shoes. The latter conveyed it to the interior of his person, through the conduit of his throat, with amazing expedition.

"It tastes queerish, old chap," said the cobbler, looking rather droll, in a second or two after the pie had accomplished the passage of his mouth. "I say, I vishes to know vether that 'ere pie wich I ate *vas* a weal pie?" he added somewhat sharply.

"Yes, it vas," answered John, in still angrier accents.

"Vy, it doesn't *taste* like a weal pie, anyhow, that's certain," observed the other.

"None of your insinivations, you ragamuffin-looking feller: you says that bekase ye've got no money to get no more on 'em."

"Never mind that 'ere person there, John," interposed a ragged starved-looking youth, about sixteen, who was employed to supply the racket-players with balls.

"He's werry imperent, to make any reflekshuns o' the kind. He vishes to ruin my professional respectability of karackter," remarked the pie-man.

"He's not worth the mindin', John," said the young fellow, with a knowing wink at the cobbler. "Let me have one o' your pork 'uns," he immediately added.

"Have you got a penny?" inquired John, significantly looking the youth in the face, and not stretching out his hand to supply him with the desired commodity.

"I should think I have," answered the other drily. "It's time enough to give it though, ven I gets the pie."

"I von't do no sich thing, without the penny first."

The youth made a form of fumbling in his pocket in search of a penny, but none, of course, was to be found. "I finds I've lost the penny, John: vill you just give me the pie on tick, and I'll pay you to-morrow."

"I von't do nothin' o' the kind," answered John, energetically. "You owes me three hap'nies already."

"O, wot a thundering lie!" exclaimed the other. "I owes you nothing but one ha'penny."

The cobbler telegraphed the little rascal encouragingly.

"You're a little too fast, young man; but mind, I stands none o' that 'ere gammon—dash my vig, if I do!" said the pie-man, shifting one of his "weal 'uns" from one part of the tin case to another.

"I only owes you a ha'penny, old chap, and no mistake," reiterated the other. "I say, John, you gets more hobstinate as you gets older," he added, looking the "all 'ot"-man jeeringly in the face.

The latter took no notice of the remark for a few moments; but then, as if suddenly seized with a fit of boundless indignation, he shouted out, giving the words the accompaniment of a lusty application of his fist to the tin concern before him,—"If you says that 'ere agin, I'll smash every bone in your ugly carcase to pieces. I'm bless'd if I don't."

The cobbler again winked at the youthful tormentor of the pie-man, by way of encouraging him to proceed. The latter, taking the hint, observed, "I don't vonder that that 'ere gemman," pointing to the shoe-surgeon, "shouldn't like them 'ere pies; 'cos they're made of cats'-meat."

John's eyes flashed the "fire of infinite indignation" at the base and unfounded imputation; and, bristling up, he thundered out the threat of making cats'-meat of the body of the "imperent Old Bailey-looking youth," provided he could lay his hands on him.

"Vy, old 'un, you knows as how I got a bit of an 'oss's hoof in that 'ere consarn I got from you yesterday, and vich you called a weal pie."

"Blow me tight, young gallows, if I don't pound your ribs to powder!" shouted John, and with that he made a bound towards his juvenile tormentor; but his apron having got entangled somehow or other in the feet of his tin machine, the latter was upset, and the whole stock of pies hot and cold, whether made of pork, veal, or eel, or any other animal, was scattered in

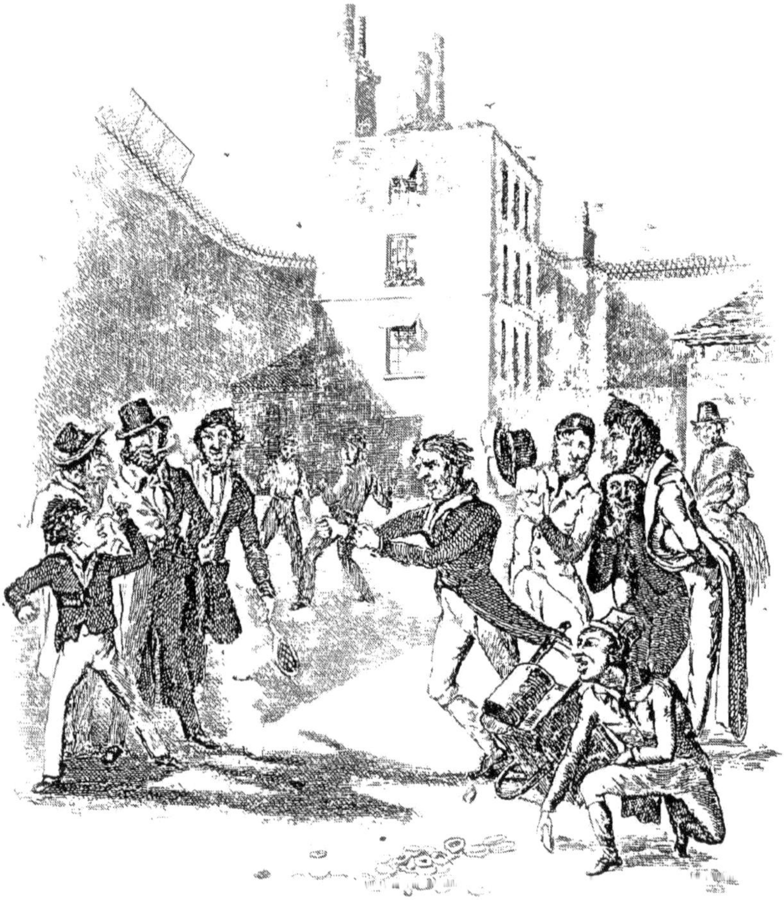

all directions. Possessing, as they all did, the circular form, some of them rolled themselves to an amazing distance. The little rascal, however, who was the cause of the disaster, took care to run much farther and faster.

A crowd of prisoners immediately gathered around the subverted stand of the pie-man, some condoling with him in his affliction, and others assisting in collecting the widely-circulated pies. John himself held up his hands, and looking aghast at what had happened, growled out curses loud and deep on the head of the "gallows-looking young feller" who had caused the disaster.

In less than a minute, the whole of the runaway pies were brought back, and replaced on the stand, which had been kindly restored to its proper position for their reception. Some of them were, as an American would say, "pretty considerably covered with mud;" others were so much broken and shattered, that the contents of the interior were exposed to the unhallowed gaze of every spectator.

John looked with a most rueful countenance at his stock of pies. And it was no wonder; for the muddy aspect of some, and the fragmentary appearance of others, were very materially aggravated by the collectors of them having huddled them up together in a heap, just as if they had been intended for pigs'-meat.

"I can never sell them 'ere pies to any respektable customer," said John, in doleful accents, as he gazed on the confused heap before him; "'cos, if I did, it would lose my karakter. O, wot shall I do?" he added with great emphasis, and wringing his hands.

At this moment, a humane gentleman, who had the day before been received into the prison, advanced to the spot to see what was the matter. He was informed of the disaster, and how it had happened. "How many were there of them?" said he, addressing himself to John.

"Just three dozen and a half, Sir," was the answer.

"Is there any one here who will eat any of them?" asked the gentleman, looking round among the poorest and most hungry-like parties in the little crowd.

"I vill!" "I vill!" shouted at least two dozen voices at once.

"Then let these people have them," said the gentleman, putting three-and-sixpence into John's hand.

The words were no sooner uttered, than there was a brisk scramble among the proprietors of fifteen or sixteen unwashed paws, to possess themselves of the pies. In an instant the whole vanished. Most of the parties, instead of waiting to carry them to their rooms, and eat them there, set to work, and despatched several of them at once. What is worthy of observation is, that one and all of those who tested the qualities of the pies declared, in the hearing of all present, that they were incomparably the best they ever tasted. This, coupled with the three-and-sixpence, was compensation of the most ample kind to John for the extreme misery caused by his youthful tormentor. His countenance brightened up, and he looked the very personification of self-complacency as he heard the praises of his pies thus publicly proclaimed; and he withdrew with his empty tin stand, observing that the young rascal could have got no greater punishment than to be denied the luxury of a " prime weal 'un."

The Queen's Bench has its general and twopenny post-offices. In both establishments a good deal of business is done, chiefly consisting of letters sent by the prisoners to their friends, supplicating pecuniary assistance.

There is one room in the place which is contradistinguished from all the other apartments. It is called the strong-room, and is appropriated to the reception of those who commit criminal acts in the prison. They are doomed to a fortnight's or month's solitary confinement, according to the magnitude of their offence, or the light in which the marshal happens to view it, he having the power in all such cases vested exclusively in his own hands.

The tap-room of the Queen's Bench is decidedly the most interesting locality in it. It is but very imperfectly lighted, and is vaulted at the top, while the walls, instead of being lathed and plastered, exhibit the bricks of which they are composed. When I last saw it the walls and vaulted ceiling seemed to have, some short time before, undergone the process of white-washing. I should suppose, judging from my recollection of its size, that it is about sixteen feet in length by twelve in breadth. There are four boxes, if so they must be called. The tables, which look as thick and strong as if they were cut out of a solid piece of wood, are all covered over with every variety of figures, to say nothing of their exhibiting all the letters of the alphabet in glorious confusion. They were, I suppose, originally meant, as successively carved out, to signify the initials of the names of the parties who engraved them there; but they are now so incorporated together, and with representations of horses, cows, dogs, cats, hens, &c., that the tables exhibit one mass of hieroglyphics. Some of the letters, and also of the pictorial abortions—for such they assuredly are—are two or three inches in length, and engraved full one quarter of an inch in depth in the tables. The appearance of the majority of the inmates of the tap-room is in perfect keeping with the place. There you see a variety of "waft" characters: judging from their beards, you would come to the conclusion, that there were not only no barber, but no razor in Christendom. As for washing their faces—I speak, of course, only of a portion of them—that is an idea that never enters their head. That would require soap, provided it were to be done effectually; they have got none. It would also require trouble, a thing they do not like to put themselves to. Their hats are almost, without exception, either crownless altogether, or they contain so many perforations as to answer all the purposes of first-rate ventilators. A whole brim is a perfect rarity; the last remains of the wool have vanished, so that it is sometimes a very nice question to settle the original colour of the article. Their coats have in many instances degenerated into jackets; while in others, one tail remains to indicate what the article of apparel originally was. As for the other portions of the generality of the wardrobes to be seen in the tap-room of the Queen's Bench, I will not attempt to describe them, because I know I should not succeed. The group of characters which are always to be seen in this classical spot, presents an edifying appearance, heightened as is the effect of that appearance by the various employments in which they are engaged, and the attitudes in which they are to be seen. That dark-looking man, with the reserved expression of countenance, cooped up in the corner of the nearest box as you enter, and reading the advertisements of a double-sheet "Times" with as great an apparent avidity as if he would eat them,—is one of the most respectable individuals in the room, which is the chief cause why he takes so little interest in the occupations of others. You see that thin-visaged personage, "whose tattered clothes his poverty bespeak," standing at the fire-place, turning over seriatim the three or four dozen herrings which are the property of a little bandy-legged man who visits the Bench four or five times every day, for the purpose of vending his finny commodities: you see this personage, do you not? He is a "rum customer," as the herring-merchant calls him, for he never purchases but one per diem, and before he commences his negotiation as to price, he examines and re-examines every bloater in the basket. Even when he has fixed on the herring he prefers, he usually spends a quarter of an hour before he concludes the bargain. In the box directly opposite the fire-place you see four or five favourable specimens of regular recklessness; they are just as comfortable inside as out, always provided they get plenty of beer. The one half of the day they sleep with their heads resting on the table, and the other they spend in swilling Barclay and Co.'s Entire. And what is worthy of observation is, that as if actuated by a sort of Siamese sympathy, they address themselves, as Don Quixote would say, to sleep, and awake from their slumbers much about the same time. Give them beer enough, and they will never seek to pop their heads, far less their feet, out of the walls of the place. Mahomet, were he still alive, might keep his paradise to himself for anything they care: they are in a perfect elysium as it is. In another box there are four or five strange-looking broken-down personages, enveloped in so dense an atmosphere of smoke, manufactured by themselves, that it is with difficulty you can recognise their features. The head of one of them is buried amidst a heap of empty pewter pots, and his face is immersed in a pool of heavy wet, which one of the others has made, without awakening him from his profound sleep. Six or seven other "gemmen," as they call one another, are knocking one another's hats down over each other's eyes, and displaying their ingenuity by inventing new tricks at each other's expense. Those three persons in the seat farthest off, with unwashed faces, and beards which would defy any razor in London, in earnest conversation together,—are just as busy and united as they can be in abusing Sir John Campbell and the Whig Ministry, for not passing the abolition of imprisonment for debt bill. If these same Whigs, as Dr. Wade would say, only heard what the triumvirate are saying, it would make their ears tingle again. Sterne himself, had he flourished in our time, and been present on the occasion, would have found some new hints which would have been well worth his consideration in framing his celebrated curse. The man in the opposite side of the box, with a most revolutionary head of hair, and a most republican-looking countenance, is quite occupied in signifying his assent to every word they say, by a hearty nod, and in withdrawing his pipe at intervals from his mouth, to enable him to mutter an audible concurrence. The middle-aged little "gemman," with the flannel jacket and one eye, who is leaning with his back against the box opposite the fire, owes the extraordinary elongation of his countenance to the fact of his having spent his last "bob," knowing as he does that no "tick" is to be had in "this here shop." See the envious glance he every now and then casts at those who have the luxury of a pot of beer before them, or of a "pipe o' baccy" in their mouths. Poor fellow, his misery is aggravated by contrast. Others again are quite uproarious. Nature has given them first-rate lungs, and they are constitutionally disposed to make the best possible use of them; in which disposition they are ably assisted by the oceans of "Entire" which they are everlastingly swigging. Every one has heard the observation, that some people are born with a silver fork in their mouths; you cannot help fancying, from the enthusiastic devotion of some of the inmates of the Queen's Bench tap-room to heavy wet, and from the circumstance of the lower part of their visages being constantly inserted in pewter pots, that they have been born for no other purpose than to chronicle the turbid liquid of the London brewers.

But the scene altogether is one to which no description can do justice. On a stone painted black, above the fire-place, I observed the words, written in chalk, "Tuesday, August the 29th, 1837." I inquired the meaning of this, and found that it was a regular practice to chalk up the day of the week and the day of the month, in the same way all the year round; as, otherwise, many of the poorer and more ignorant of the prisoners would have no idea of either. Connected with this diurnal chalking affair I may mention an anecdote of one of the prisoners, who was under thirty years of age, and evidently a tailor. He rejoiced in a tolerable wardrobe, certainly the best in the place; a circumstance, however, which might be satisfactorily accounted for from the fact, that he was the most recent importation to the prison. But though his exterior appearance was not amiss, he soon gave woeful proof that he was most miserably furnished within. In fact, he was as ignorant as his own goose. When I asked the reason why the aforesaid "Tuesday, August the 29th, 1837," was chalked on the black stone above the fire-place, he, addressing himself to the brother in adversity next to him in a geographical point of view, at once chimed in with me, and said, "Aye, and *vy* is that 'ere put up there?" Snip got, I need hardly observe, the same answer as myself. "Very good," retorted he, "but I think as how they might have spelt 'August' right, any how."

The word *was* correctly spelt.

"If you spelt that 'ere word any other way, you would spell it wrong," observed a middle-aged man, withdrawing his pipe from his mouth to let a small condensed cloud of smoke escape.

"It's all you knows about it," said Snip, "ven you says so."

"What way would you spell it, then, old dunderhead?" inquired another, opening his eyes, as if just awakened from sleep, and closing them again the moment he had put the question.

"August, august, a—ag—ags," said the man of buckram, making an ineffectual attempt to master the orthography of the word. "Vy, I don't know as how it should be spelt, but this I knows as how that 'ere vay is a rum 'un," he added.

Poor Snip looked as if particularly confounded.

"And how do you know that it's wrong, when you can't spell it?" inquired the first of his opponents.

"I *do* know it though," he replied, assuming a bold front.

"You're a downright dunce," interposed his half-slumbering, second opponent, again thrusting his face down in his breast when he had paid Snip the flattering compliment.

"I say you're a———"

"A what, Sir?" interrupted the other, starting up to his feet, and having the appearance of anything but a slumbering man.

"A ras———"

Snip was prevented completing his sentence by another of the prisoners first clapping his hand on his mouth, and then drawing him out of the place by the breast of his coat, he meanwhile darting a most furious glance at his opponent.

"You are a ———," repeated the tailor, twisting about his head as his friend was dragging him out of the room; but the renewed application of the aforesaid open fist to his mouth, again prevented the completion of the sentence.

"Only say that again, you blundering blockhead, you nineteenth part of a man," shouted his lately slumbering adversary, "an' I'll knock your ivory down your throat."

"I do say you're a ———." Snip again made an effort to apply some ugly epithet to his opponent, but the latter part of the sentence was lost, in consequence of the violence with which his friend shut the tap-room door as he got the "nineteenth part of a man" outside.

But for the timely interposition of the latter, a regular affray must have taken place; and the probability is that the consequence would have been a broken head to both parties. Hence the result would have been certain, namely, that both would have got a month's location in the strong-room. I thought with myself how narrowly Pope's lines escaped an exemplification,— "What dire effects from trivial causes spring!"

But decidedly the most eccentric character with whom I came in contact, in the course of my visits to the tap-room, was a personage who went by the sobriquet of Tom Snaggs. He was altogether an extraordinary personage. He was as different in appearance and manners from all the other human beings I have ever met with, as if he had belonged to some other species, or been projected from another planet, in consequence of some eruption; just as philosophers tell us of meteoric stones being thrust from the moon into our world, through some volcanic or other powerful agency. Tom belonged, as the phrase is, to the lower classes. He was a singularly odd-looking character. His face was thin, and as much shrivelled as if he had been dried in a kiln for the purposes of preservation in the collection of some naturalist. His complexion bore a strong resemblance to the colour of a radish; while his long lean neck, which was much exposed in consequence of the absence of a neckerchief, had precisely the appearance of a plucked turkey. In the expression of his countenance, there were actually blended all the peculiarities of physiognomy presented in the faces of Lord John Russell and

Mr. Goulburn. His eyes were especially remarkable; they seemed the most tractable pair I have ever seen in human head. At one time their mutual affection was so powerful, that you would have thought they would actually embrace each other. But for the obstruction presented by the bridge of Mr. Snaggs' nose, I am sure they would have done so. Never did two "peepers," as Tom himself called them, look so lovingly towards each other. If they had possessed the faculty of speaking, attributed by the fabulists of old to inanimate things as well as to beasts, birds, and fishes, I can well imagine with what cordiality they would have concurred in anathematizing the aforesaid section of Tom's nose, because it interposed to prevent a closer intimacy. At other times, both the luminaries of our hero darted off at a tangent, and looked in the most opposite directions, just as if some ground of deadly quarrel, unknown to any but themselves, had suddenly started up. This latter singular attribute in Tom's eyes may be best illustrated by the remark, that had he been sitting in the centre of a large room, with his face directly to the opposite wall, he would have seen, without moving his head in the slightest degree, two persons coming into the room at either end, with the same distinctness as if his gaze had been exclusively directed to one: Every one has heard a great deal about the "seeing capabilities" of Argus, with his century of eyes. Had Tom possessed two additional ones of the same power in the back of his head, he would, I doubt not, have been quite as well furnished, for all practical purposes, as the hundred-eyed personage of antiquity whose name I have just mentioned.

Tom's wardrobe was in tolerable keeping with his personal appearance. He was wrapped up—and this, be it remembered, in the warmest weather of last summer—in a dreadnought coat of most ample proportions. It was of a brown colour; and I beg to be understood as not exaggerating in the slightest degree when I say, that the wool or pile was about half an inch long. I would have given something to know the weight of the article; but had not an opportunity of gratifying my curiosity. If Tom, instead of vegetating in the tap-room of the Queen's Bench, where, in addition to the oppressive warmth of the weather, there is always a blazing fire kept for culinary purposes; had Tom, instead of this, been the inmate of some habitation in the polar regions, formed of snow, he would not, one would have supposed, have required any addition to his clothing. I have a strong impression that he must have a good deal of the salamander in his composition; for amidst all this excessive warmth of weather, and his constantly wearing this mountain of a great coat, he always took care to take the seat next to the fire. He evinced an unconquerable aversion to solid meat, at any rate, he ate nothing, so far as I saw, during the day I was there; and I did not learn from any one that he ever, under any circumstances, put his masticators into requisition. Let me not be understood as insinuating by this that Tom Snaggs lived on chameleon's fare; that would be doing him an injustice of which I would not, on any consideration, have the sin on my head. Everybody must be aware that there is an intermediate alternative, if I may so speak, between not eating any solid food and living on the thin and unfattening air. Tom lived on Barclay, Perkins, and Co.'s Entire; and I doubt if these gentlemen, amidst their myriads of customers, could ever boast of a better one than Tom. To thrust his head into a pot of their frothy liquid, was the very first act he performed in the morning; to do ditto was his last employment in the evening. To say that he was similarly engaged during the whole of the intervening day, would be an exaggeration; for drinking heavy wet, as well as eating solid food, requires that there should be at least temporary pauses, to allow one, were it for nothing else, to take his breath. But this I can say, that there was rarely an hour of the day in which Tom had not his jug of beer before him.

His manners and conversation were quite as singular as his appearance; and most largely did he contribute to the amusement of those who frequented the tap-room. He possessed much natural shrewdness, and was happy in turning the laugh against those who sought to raise it at his expense. I saw at once, on entering the place, that he was a character. He was in the act at the time of carrying on a political discussion with a shoemaker of the middle size and of a pug-looking dark-complexioned countenance.

"You don't know your own principles, Tom," was the first observation which greeted my ears, as I walked up towards the fire.

"Don't I?" said Tom emphatically.

"No you don't; I'm bless'd if you do."

"I 'spose you thinks, old leather-mender, as how you knows your'n," observed Tom, raising the jug of beer to his mouth.

"I'd be 'shamed of myself if I didn't," answered Crispin, taking out of his waistcoat pocket and unfolding a small dirty paper which contained the remains of his limited stock of tobacco.

"Then vat is your sentimens?" inquired Tom.

"Vy, I'm a Radical to be sure," replied the other, with emphasis.

"A Radical, eh! I'm blow'd if you an't like un."

"Yes, and vill be while the world lasts," added Crispin.

"You're quite sure of that 'ere, are you?" observed Mr. Snaggs.

"I am quite sure of it," answered the other, with great emphasis. "I'll stand by my principles while I has a button to my coat. May I be ——— if I don't," he added with increased energy, giving a violent blow with his fist on the table.

"If you don't stand by them any longer than that 'ere, I think that vont be very long," remarked Tom, significantly eyeing his opponent's coat, which had only two buttons remaining.

"None of your ignorant jeers, Tom. I'll be hanged if I stand them," said Crispin, pulling himself up and assuming a most valorous aspect.

"Vy this is liberty-hall," retorted Tom. "Every one has a right to speak vat he thinks in this 'ere place."

"I won't be insulted by no man as vas ever born," said the testy shoemaker.

"Vy you speak as if you were the prime minister, old shoe-doctor."

"I have a right to speak as I please, you stupid jackass."

"And so have I," observed Mr. Snaggs, winking at the bystanders. "Ve lives here in liberty-hall, don't ve, Harry?" he added, addressing himself to a sturdy son of Vulcan, who was lighting his pipe with a match.

"To be sure we do, Tom, my boy," answered the latter in encouraging accents.

"I don't vant to have anythink at all to say to an old fool like you," remarked Crispin, in a pettish tone.

"Vy, if so be as I be an old fool, we're well met, my chap."

"Vat's that, you old dotard, you were a-calling me?" inquired the shoemaker, looking fiercely at Tom.

"Should you like to hear it again, old boot-butcher?" answered Tom, with provoking coolness.

"You'll better take care of vat you say, that's all," was the only reply.

"You said take care, did you not, old Radical?" rejoined Tom, drawing the jug of beer towards him.

"I did," was the answer.

"You're a Melbourne chap, are you not?"

"Vat's that to you, I should like to know?" was the reply.

"Because as how all you Radical-looking fellows are Melbourne chaps."

"I vont stand this 'ere any longer. I'll be ——— if I do," shouted Crispin, as he suddenly started up to his feet, and assumed a menacing attitude.

"Vy you're a-standin' it now," said Tom, with provoking coolness; "you're on your legs, are you not, old leather-head?"

"I say you're a ———"

"And you're a Radical," interrupted Tom, before his opponent of the bodkin and the awl could complete his sentence.

"If you say that 'ere agin, I'll knock your rascally head into atoms with this here veapon," said Crispin, now worked up to an alarming pitch of anger, and brandishing in his right hand a last which he chanced to have with him at the time

"You're a Radical, and a Melbourne chap too," repeated Tom, with the most perfect composure, and knocking on the table with a jug, as an intimation to the waiter to bring him another pint of beer.

"Just say that agin, you vagabond-looking fellow, and as sure as I'm a livin' man I'll ———."

"Holloa! what's the matter?" interrupted one of the officers of the prison, who happened to enter at the moment.

"O nothin' at all," answered Crispin, softening down all at once into the calmest tone,—a fear of a month's confinement in the strong-room having suddenly flashed across his mind; "O nothin' at all, I was only a-showin' Tom Snaggs the vay in which I once heard two men a-quarrelling in the streets; vasn't that it, Tom?"

"Here's jolly good luck, my boy!" said Tom, by way of response, thrusting his mouth into the jug, and taking a hearty draught.

"Gemmen," said Tom, as soon as the officer withdrew, "Gemmen, I'll sing you a song, vich is better than disputing about politiks."

"Aye, do!" shouted every person present.

Mr. Snaggs chanted six verses of a song, which afforded internal evidence of its being one of his own composition. I was struck with one very appropriate idea which Tom introduced. It contained an admission that he had contracted debts which he was unable to pay.

"Sing the song over agin, Tom, if you please," said a short, squatting consequential personage, who had been a butler in a gentleman's house, addressing Mr. Snaggs in a tone of offensive authoritativeness.

"If you have a servant," answered Tom, "ask him to execute your orders; I don't quite like being spoken to in that 'ere way. I'm not hobligated to sing to please you, my little pot-bellied chap."

"True, Tom; quite right, Tom," cried a dozen voices.

"But I'll tell you vat," he resumed, addressing the ex-butler; "I'll tell you vat, I'll sing it over agin for a pint of beer."

"Done, Tom; you shall have it. Come, begin," said the admirer of Mr. Snaggs' vocal talents.

"Von't we better have the beer a'fore we begins? It clears and improves the windpipe, you knows," observed Tom.

"O, certainly, if you prefer it," was the answer.

"Vell, I *do* prefer it," said Tom, emphatically.

The beer was ordered, and was forthwith on the table. Tom took a liberal draught of the beverage, and keeping fast hold of the handle of the jug, treated his co-inmates to a repetition of the song.

"That's a true part of it, Tom, which says you have contracted debts you'll never be able to pay."

This was spoken by a tall demure-looking personage, who had been some time an apothecary in a small town in the neighbourhood of London.

"Is it?" said Tom, looking the apothecary sarcastically in the face.

"Never mind, Tom," said an attorney's clerk; "never mind, so as you gets out."

"I don't vant to get out," interposed Mr. Snaggs, hastily.

"You don't, eh?"

"No, I don't; and surely I knows best myself."

"Certainly you must, Tom," said I, now venturing for the first time to make a remark, with the view of eliciting more fully some of his more eccentric traits of character.

"Yes, I *does* knows best," repeated Mr. Snaggs, giving a knock on the table with the bottom of the pewter pot, which made the greater part of its contents leap out in the faces of those who were next to him.

"And are you so much attached to this place?" I inquired, in as encouraging a tone as I was master of.

"Quite delighted with it, Sir; it's a perfect paradise."

"Well, Tom, I can't fancy anything which could make the place so attractive."

"Lots of beer, Sir, and plenty of racket: call you that nothing, eh?"

Tom looked up in my face with an air of infinite self-complacency, and then decanted the remainder of the beer in the pot before him. I was about to answer his question when he resumed.

"But I've other reasons, and better 'uns too, for preferring to remain here: blow'd, if I haven't!"

"Can you mention them, Mr. Snaggs?"

"I can mention one on 'em."

"What may it be, Tom?"

"Vy, Sir, if so be as I must speak the truth, I likes this place, because I'm out of the reach of my vife; bad luck to the 'ooman!"

"Ah, Tom! you're married, then?"

"Aye, I believe you; married, indeed!" answered Mr. Snaggs, fetching a deep sigh, and accompanying it with a most significant shake of the head.

"So, then, you are no advocate for matrimony, Mr. Snaggs?"

"Vy, I says nothink against being spliced once; but, I'm bless'd, if I likes second 'uns."

"Second what, Tom?"

"Second vives, Sir."

"Oh! married a second time, then?"

"Vy, yes, I be's, as I knows in experience," replied Tom, with a very emphatic groan. "People," he added, "says second thoughts is best; I'm bless'd, if second vives be; they are all reg'lar bad 'uns."

"And you don't, then, approve of second matches?"

"Matches!" exclaimed Mr. Snaggs, starting up, and looking surprised at my using the word. "Matches! May I never swig another pint of beer, if so be as there be any match in it. I knows as I'm more than matched, anyhow."

"Yes, Tom," interposed a dark-looking, little-faced man, withdrawing his pipe from his mouth to enable him to articulate more distinctly. "Yes, Tom, you've been regularly done by your second wife."

"You may say that, Ben, my boy; she's a precious bad 'un But its all my own fault; blow'd, if it ain't."

"How so, Tom?"

"Vy, because I vas so big a fool as to take the 'ooman on character," replied he, looking at the beer-pot.

"On what, Mr. Snaggs?"

"On character, Sir."

I intimated to Tom that his meaning was beyond my comprehension.

"What I means, Sir, is this 'ere: I took the chap,"—an odd term to apply to one's wife,—"I took the chap on the faith of a good character I got of her from one of her former acquaintances, without knowing anything about her. Made short work of courtship, Sir,—knew her only for seven days,—married the eighth."

"That was certainly making short work of it, Tom."

"You're right, Sir; never take any vife on character agin; never be in such a hurry to get married agin. Made a deuced bad speculation of it."

"Possibly Mrs. Snaggs may improve, Tom."

"Improve!" he shouted. "Did you say improve?"

"I did, Tom; it is to be hoped she will."

"Vy, if she improves, all I can say is this,—it will be like the cow's tail,—in the wrong direction. She improve! You knows nothing about her, Sir, otherviso you vould never say so."

"Ay, Tom, you're a very unfortunate person," suggested one of his boon companions.

"That's a truth, Henry, my boy; however, I'm out of the

reach of the hussey here. Plenty of freedom in this 'ere place. Here's the liberty-hall of the right sort. May I be scragged (hanged) if I ever seeks to leave this place so long as they lets me remain in it." Mr. Snaggs again had recourse to a liberal potation.

"Does your wife never come to see you, Tom?"

"She come to see me!—not though I vas a dyin' by the yard. I've now been nine veeks in this 'ere paradise, and she's never come to see me once. No loss, as to the matter of that; never vish to be vhere she is; but I vish she had sent me a clean shirt. I've only had this one," pointing to a piece of linen in his breast, whose soiled appearance afforded presumptive proof of the truth of his statement; "I've only had this one for the last nine veeks."

"Too bad, Tom," said his friend Ben, who had on one or two former occasions interposed a word or two of modified commiseration. "Too bad, Tom; it is, indeed."

"Never mind," observed Mr. Snaggs, looking into the pot before him to see if there was any remnant of the turbid liquid in the bottom. "Never mind; one consolation, anyhow."

"What's that, Mr. Snaggs?" inquired a short, flabby-faced-looking personage, who all the while had been standing before the fire, but had never until now opened his mouth. "What's that, Mr. Snaggs?"

"Vy, I left her at home without a farthing; consequently she's on starvation allowance;" and his two eyes sparkled with delight as he made the observation.

"O, Tom, Tom!" observed Ben, "you're just as bad as she is. Come, that's werry wrong."

"You knows nothing about it, you booby; you have never had a second vife, or you vouldn't say so."

"Why, Mr. Snaggs, you might as well beat Mrs. Snaggs to death, as starve her to death," observed a rather respectable-looking man, of a reserved expression of countenance.

"O, Sir, she von't die; she'll neither be starved to death, nor beaten to death: second vives has as many lives in 'em as an eel."

"I say, Tom, you vouldn't speak in that 'ere way, if your vife vas in this 'ere place to hear you," remarked his friend Benjamin.

"O, vouldn't I, Ben, my boy? Aye, that I vould, and give her a good wallopping to the bargain."

"Come, come, Tom; you don't mean to say you would beat Mrs. Snaggs?" observed the aforesaid respectable reserved-looking man.

"Say it; aye, that I do; and vat's more, Sir, I vould do it too." As Tom spoke, he gave a violent knock with his fist to the crown of his hat, which forced the article down over his eyes. "I vish," he continued, with great energy, and raising up his hat again; "I vish I had my vife here just now. O, vouldn't I wallop her so, I'm ———!"

Here Tom, who had risen from his seat to show his auditors, by a forcible flourish of his right hand in the air, with what effect he would "wallop" Mrs. Snaggs, suddenly paused in the midst of a sentence, and, in an instant afterwards, uttered an exclamation of "Oh, Lor!" and turning as pale as death, fell back in the box.

"O, you rascal, you! I'll give it you!" shouted a strong masculine, virago-looking woman, who had that moment entered the tap-room. As she spoke, she rushed up to the place where Tom was sitting, shaking her hand at him all the way, while her eyes glared with ungovernable rage. The stranger woman, it was soon discovered, was no other than the redoubtable Mrs. Snaggs herself. What passed between the couple I will not mention, on the ground of the acknowledged impropriety of taking any notice of matrimonial quarrels.

It is interesting to reflect on the various circumstances under which the inmates of the Queen's Bench Prison have been brought there. The vast majority, as may be inferred from other parts of this chapter, have to attribute their deprivation of liberty to their own folly and utter want of principle. They are men who care nothing about the sufferings they entail on individuals and families, and the injury their bad example reflects on society, provided only their own humours can be indulged, and their propensities gratified.

There are others who are there because they either are, or fancy themselves to be, the victims of injustice. There is at the present time, or at least there was some few months since, a young gentleman, the representative of a family of wealth and antiquity in one of our English counties, who has spent the meridian of his life in prison, rather than relinquish, in compliance with the decision of a court of law, what he conceives to be his right, and what he thinks would be doing an unpardonable injustice to his family were he to give it up. To his determination not to part with property which he holds to be by every consideration of morality and justice the property of his family, and which, regarding himself as a trustee for them, he feels bound to protect,—he I have no doubt still adheres, though with the certain prospect before him, if he does not change his resolution, of perpetual imprisonment. In this there is much to admire; it is a specimen of heroism and self-denial in what the party conceives—whether right or wrong does not affect the question—a good cause,—worthy of the best days of ancient Greece or Rome;

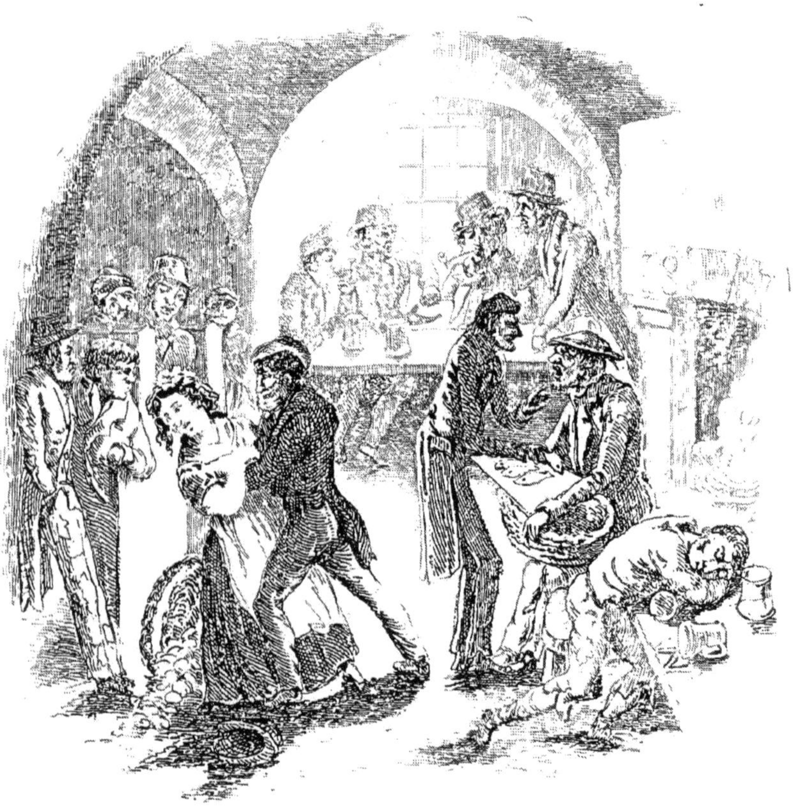

for his own pecuniary circumstances, altogether independent of this case, are so ample that they would enable him to move in what is called fashionable life.

A third class of persons are confined in the Queen's Bench Prison from adverse circumstances over which they had no control. These are the only persons who feel their incarceration to be a punishment, and yet they are the only inmates of the place who ought *not* to feel it a punishment; for they did everything which, human exertion made in an honest and honourable way, could do, to meet the demands of their creditors, and consequently escape imprisonment: they are the victims of adversity brought about by an agency not their own. One would think that this reflection would tranquillise their minds, and reconcile them to that which no exertions of theirs could have shielded them against. Such, however, is not the fact: they are degraded persons in their own estimation, and neither the dictates of reason nor the representations of friends can remove the erroneous impression. Their susceptibility on the subject is in some cases so excessive, that they are impelled to the frightful alternative of committing suicide. In other instances, though their sense of religion guards them against a step so revolting to society, and so opposed to revelation, their sense of self-degradation preys so forcibly on their minds, that they pine away, and eventually die under it. I could mention many instances of this; but it is unnecessary, as most of my metropolitan readers will be able to recal to their minds cases of the kind which consist with their own personal knowledge. There are at this moment three or four individuals in the Queen's Bench Prison, whose sense of self-degradation, in consequence of their incarceration, is so great, that they never venture out to the open area allowed the prisoners, nor on any account suffer themselves to be seen by their fellow-inmates. They shut themselves up in their narrow cells all day, brooding over their adversities, though these are not the consequence of any misconduct of their own; and never cross the threshold of their rooms until it has become quite dark. Even then they wrap themselves up in cloaks, lest any one should by accident get a glance of their features. I know instances of this kind, in which other parties, who have no feelings of shame, but who rather glory in their confinement though entirely the result of their own misconduct, have lived for upwards of twelve months in the next room to the individuals to whom I refer, and yet have never been able by any accident to get a glance of their features. What stronger argument than this could be urged against the principle of imprisonment for debt? That principle subjects the very parties to punishment who ought not to be punished, because their embarrassed circumstances have been brought about by causes which it was not in their power to control; while those unprincipled persons who really do deserve punishment, do not feel confinement within the walls of a civil prison to be any punishment at all. The honest man is thus punished, while the rogue virtually escapes. It is high time that in this Christian country and this enlightened age, so monstrous a state of things were put an end to.

There is a fourth class of persons who are confined within the walls of the Queen's Bench Prison from choice. This may appear a startling announcement; it is a true one nevertheless. I do not mean to say that such persons are numerous; they are, on the contrary, extremely few; but they do exist. It is only a few months since, that an extraordinary instance of this kind was pointed out to me, in the person of a man apparently about fifty-five years of age. This individual was first confined in this prison about eighteen years ago; and after being fifteen years an inmate, he was liberated. At first he fancied that his liberation would add to his happiness, and consequently rejoiced at the circumstance. He had not, however, been many days out, when he began to feel himself in the midst of a social desert, though living in the neighbourhood of Newport Market, which is in the very centre of London. All his former acquaintances were either dead or removed to other parts of the country, or, at all events, to places which rendered it impossible for him to obtain any traces of them, far less to hold intercourse with them. The desolateness of his new position was rendered still greater by contrast. The new acquaintances he had formed in the Queen's Bench Prison were all left behind him; so were the exercises and amusements in which he was wont daily and hourly to indulge when an inmate there. Even the very stones of the pavement, the walls of the building, and the place altogether, had become, through so lengthened and intimate an acquaintanceship, dear to him. These things all rushed on his mind; they haunted it by day, and he dreamed of them by night. The man, in other words, was miserable in his altered position. He felt as if he had been alone in the world—as if he had been, in one sense, the "last man," and he literally shed tears at the thought of his freedom. It was feared by some, who were acquainted with the circumstances, that he would either pine away, or, if he did not, that he would lay violent hands on himself. It was suggested to him that he should return to the Queen's Bench Prison. In that suggestion he at once and most cordially concurred; but he did not, at the moment, possess the requisite qualification: he was not then in debt. He soon, however, did acquire it, and was again confined in his old quarters, where

I saw him some months ago, one of the happiest of the three or four hundred inmates in the place.

I am sure that most of my readers will readily remember a story which is very similar to this: it is the only parallel one which my memory can bring to my mind at this moment. I allude to the well-known story of the man who had been forty years a prisoner in the Bastile of France. When the populace burst open the doors of that building, and liberated the prisoners, an old man, whose appearance had, by forty years' confinement in a dark dungeon, become almost unearthly, was found among the number. He was carried to the part of the town in which he had lived previous to his imprisonment. The whole aspect of the place was altered, and he could discover no trace of even one solitary former friend. The aged man felt himself, as it were, in a new and strange world. The very light of heaven proved a burden to him; he felt he could not long survive in the altered circumstances in which he was placed; and, with tears streaming down his cheeks, he implored those who had liberated him, in mercy and for Heaven's sake, to have the humanity of carrying him back again to his dark and gloomy dungeon in the Bastile. Habit is, indeed, a strange thing: there never was a more just observation, than that it is a second nature.

It is curious to witness the efforts which are made by some of the inmates in the Bench to keep up their former dignity,—in appearance, at least,—in despite of their altered circumstances. There are scores of persons there who fancy themselves as important (and are infinitely surprised and mortified to find others do not also think them so) as when they were living in the greatest splendour, residing in princely mansions, and keeping up magnificent establishments. Though practically on the same footing with the humblest of their co-inmates,—with this difference, that, having more money at their command, they can procure greater comforts in some respects,—they affect to look down on all others as if they were not of the same species. This is ridiculous enough out of prison,—in prison it is peculiarly so; for a place like the Queen's Bench is, to all intents and purposes, a republic. When the purse of such persons is empty, their attempts to keep up their fancied dignity not only often reach the *ultima thule* of ridiculousness; they are sometimes amusing in the highest degree. A lady formerly moving in the highest circles of society, who had for several years been one of the inmates, determined, within the last twelve months, or it may be a little more, to ask four others of her West-end friends to dinner one Sunday afternoon. The invitations were duly forwarded, and answers, accepting them, were received in due course. Unfortunately, the lady had not a sovereign in her possession, and what was the next worst thing, she had neither credit enough with any of her fellow-prisoners to get the loan of a few, nor with the individual who furnishes the dinners to get a dinner—to use the phraseology of the place—"on tick." She had, in other words, a heavy score in that quarter already. What was to be done? It would be a fearful wound to her pride, an awful outrage on her dignity, to ask friends to dinner and yet have nothing to set before them when they came. She saw there was no alternative but to endeavour to do something by some means or other, with the party who acted as "provider" on such occasions. After in vain using every argument and entreaty she could think of, to induce him to furnish the requisite repast, and add the bill to the previous account, she at last proposed that he should have a dinner, consisting of certain things which she mentioned, ready by six o'clock next Sunday afternoon; adding, that she would by that time receive some money, and pay him the amount before she would ask him to lay the things on the table. To this he agreed, at the rate of a guinea a-head, not doubting that when the guests were come, they would rather pay for it than see their friend and themselves made ridiculous. At all events, he determined that, if the amount of the bill was not forthcoming, not a morsel should be tasted, either by mine hostess or the guests. The day appointed arrived; so did the hour, and so did the friends. The lady was as unencumbered by the circulating medium then as before. She had not a shilling in her possession. To ask the loan of the requisite sum from the friends she had invited,—in other words, to ask them to pay for the dinner of which she had asked them to partake,—was an expedient to which she was most unwilling to resort. Telling her friends that dinner would be on the table presently, she begged to be excused for a minute or two; and so saying she hurried off to the party engaged to provide the feast. She renewed her entreaties for credit once more, and was most prodigal of her protestations that the amount of that particular bill, as well as the old score, would be honourably and cheerfully paid in a few days, by which time she was sure of a liberal remittance from her friends. But all would not do; the "provider" was inexorable. His motto, after the experience he had had already, was—"No money, no dinner." She left him, and returned to her friends, thinking that if his heart did not soften, the circumstance of the dinner being sure to be spoiled, if not speedily eaten, and his thus losing money by it, would in two or three minutes operate favourably on him. The lady told her friends on her return, that dinner was not quite ready, but would be in a minute or two. They, of course, assured her they were in no hurry. About three minutes afterwards a knock was heard at the door. Mine hostess immediately opened it. "Are you, ma'am, to have the dinner, or not!" inquired a voice on the landing.

"Hush! hush! don't speak so loud," answered the lady.

"Say at once, ma'am, whether I'm to bring it, or not."

"Yes, do; bring it presently; we're all waiting for it," said she, in an under tone.

"The money, then, if you please, ma'am."

"O, do bring it, and I'll pay you to-morrow; I will indeed."

"No, ma'am, not a morsel shall be brought without the money: if you do not pay first, before I quit this place, I shall go and dispose of it at a reduced price to the other prisoners. On that, ma'am, I'm resolved," said the "provider," laying a peculiar stress on the word resolved, and giving a forcible stroke with the palm of his right hand to one of his legs a little above his knee.

This announcement, coupled with the energetic manner in which it was made, alarmed the lady. She saw that if the dinner was not got by some means or other, without loss of time, it would not be got at all. The thought was horrifying; it was still more so, if possible, to think that it should be disposed of to, and be eaten by, the vulgar herd of prisoners; that their palates should be regaled by the dainties provided for herself and friends. "O! the very idea was enough to annihilate one!" She opened the door, and rushed half frantic into the room. "My dear friends, how awkward! O, I can scarcely utter a word! but the truth is, that I have been disappointed in a small remittance I expected yesterday, and which I am sure to receive to-morrow; and this brute of a man is so rude and unmannerly as not to give me credit even for a few hours. I'm quite ashamed; indeed, I am!"

The explanation of the cause of the non-appearance of the dinner was unnecessary; the party had overheard every word that had passed between the lady and the other party.

They were as much confounded as herself; each looked at the other; and what aggravated the unpleasantness of the circumstances in which they were placed, was the fact that they had not above a guinea amongst them all. In fact, not dreaming of so "untoward" an affair, they had not thought of taking any money with them. The confusion of the intended guests was only made so much worse by the countless apologies and unspeakable mortification of their friend, the lady prisoner. And if anything could have added yet more to the confusion of the lady's friends, and rendered her own mortification complete, it would have been the fact of hearing the party providing the dinner singing out, in tones sufficiently stentorian to make all the prisoners hear it, as he walked up and down the place—"A dinner provided for ———— *, to be disposed of in small portions, at reduced prices. The lady's friends were obliged to return home with empty stomachs, and she herself has not yet recovered the shock which her pride received on the occasion.

I am convinced that the deprivation to which I have referred of that respect and obeisance which are paid to the aristocracy outside the walls of the prison, embitters their situation within, much more than the mere confinement itself. In the course of my visits to the place I have been often struck with the crest-fallen appearance of the scions of the aristocracy, when I have seen them walking about on the pavement without any one deigning to take the slightest notice of them. Those only who have been accustomed to be treated with the greatest deference, and to have all manner of respect shown to them, just as if they were a sort of superior beings, can form an idea of the depth to which those persons fall in their own estimation, when they are reduced to a level with the humblest individuals in the land.

It is worthy of observation, that there are generally a fair sprinkling of the nobility in the Queen's Bench. Considering the proportion which the aristocracy bears to the other inhabitants of the country, their relative number in the Bench to the other prisoners is strikingly great. Take the aristocracy, strictly so called, of the country at 5000, and the population of the United Kingdom at 25,000,000, that would give only one aristocrat for 5000 of the people. Go to the Queen's Bench, and you will usually find the nobility to be, to the people, in proportion of one to one hundred and fifty; which conclusively shows that, considering their relative numbers, they much more generally incur debts they are unable or unwilling to pay, than those in the lower walks of life.

It were desirable for the sake of what Lord Grey would call "the order," that the number of the nobility, who from time to time grace the Queen's Bench, were not so great; but there is another class of persons whom every one must much more regret to see there. I mean the clergy of the church of England. The number of clergymen imprisoned in that place for debt is relatively great. Not long since there were no fewer than nine or ten at once. I know of nothing more prejudicial to the interests of that religion, whose ministers they profess to be, and whose principles they solemnly swore on the day of their ordination to have adopted from conviction, than that, through habits of extravagance, to use no harsher terms, they should render themselves amenable to the civil jurisprudence of their country. A clergyman in the Queen's Bench, through misconduct of his

* The name was pronounced in full.

own, is a most painful spectacle. Not only is his own usefulness ever afterwards impaired, but scandal is, through his means, brought on Christianity itself. It is due to the Dissenters to say, that while the Queen's Bench prison is scarcely ever—I doubt if it be ever—without several clerical inmates, the circumstance of one of their ministers being confined within its walls, is an occurrence which hardly ever takes place.

There are always a considerable number of attorneys and barristers in the Queen's Bench. I need scarcely say that in the great majority of cases the attorneys were without practice, and the barristers briefless, before their entrance. Some of the former, however, manage to raise a tolerable business within the walls of the prison. Strange as it may appear, it does sometimes happen that persons have to date their prosperity in life to their incarceration in the Queen's Bench. One remarkable instance consists with my personal knowledge. The party was a barrister, but had never in his life had a single brief in his bag. I am not sure, indeed, having no use for it, whether he had a bag at all. He was sent to vegetate for ten or twelve months in the Bench. While there he contracted an intimacy with one of the prisoners of some station in society, and of considerable wealth, though, through some illegal proceedings, temporarily deprived of it. The case was laid before the briefless barrister, and having abundant time on his hand he made himself completely master of it in all its bearings. On his liberation he undertook to bring it before the proper tribunal, making his remuneration entirely dependent on his success. He did succeed: the party was liberated, and he amply rewarded for his trouble. But the remuneration he received was but a very subordinate portion of the benefit he derived from the case. Possessed of very respectable natural talents, and knowing the case so thoroughly, he made so creditable a professional appearance in court, that briefs, from that time, poured in on him in copious abundance. This was the tide in his affairs of which Shakspeare speaks: he wisely took it at the fountain, and it led on to fame and fortune.

Of military men there is always a good number in the Queen's Bench Prison. They consist of all degrees of rank in the service, from the general down to the officer of the humblest grade. You can easily distinguish them from the rest of the prisoners by the stiffness of their gait.

But of all classes of men to be found in the Queen's Bench, that of authors, in proportion to their relative numbers to society generally, is by far the most numerous. On some occasions they are to be seen in crowds, in that locality. Napoleon called the English a nation of shopkeepers; and when George the Fourth visited Scotland, mistaking the holiday clothes in which the people were dressed to greet his arrival, for the apparel in which they daily appeared, he called the Scotch a nation of gentlemen. Were a foreigner, again, to make his first place of visit, on his arrival in this country, the Queen's Bench, he would, from the number of literary men he would find among the inmates, immediately come to the conclusion that we were a nation of authors. Formerly, when the privations and misfortunes of authors were adverted to, the garrets of Grub-street were mentioned as the place where literary men were chiefly to be found pining in want and wretchedness. The miseries of authorship are still more forcibly illustrated in the Bench. It is, beyond all comparison, the worst trade going. For one man that succeeds in it, thousands fail. No wonder that Sir Walter Scott always admonished young men of literary tastes, not to dream of earning their bread by their writings. Had he ever visited the Queen's Bench, he would have been still more earnest in his cautions to them not to lean, as he himself used to say, on so broken a reed. I have heard of literary men who had themselves largely experienced the wretchedness of making literature a profession, giving it as their most earnest advice to their sons, never to think of making authorship a trade; and they have enforced their counsels and cautions by a reference to particular cases of misery which have resulted from the attempts thus made to earn their bread by their literary labours. If such parents were to take their sons to the Queen's Bench, and by that means bring before them examples in wholesale, demonstrative of the pains and penalties of living, or rather endeavouring to live, by literature,—their counsels would have a much greater chance of making a permanent impression, and of producing the intended effects.

The number of female prisoners in the Queen's Bench bears but a small proportion to the male. I should think that, on an average, there is not one woman for seven or eight of the male sex.

It is curious, on a visit to the Queen's Bench, to contrast the external appearance of the higher classes of the prisoners, after they have been a short time in the place, with what it was before their admission. The metamorphosis they undergo in the course of a few months is almost incredible. It is sometimes so complete, that their own friends, one would think, would have some difficulty in identifying them. Were they to meet them accidentally in the street, I am sure they would pass them by without recognising them. It is quite a common thing to see noblemen and gentlemen, who but a few months before were dressed, or, as a tailor would say, "decorated," in the extreme of fashion;

persons, on whose apparel Stultz, and Willis, and Crellin, and our other first-rate tailors, had expended all their ingenuity and taste, in order to make an exquisite fit; it is, I say, quite a common thing to see such persons in the Bench nothing better than the mere wrecks of dandyism. In some instances, you see their wardrobe "all tattered and torn," just like that of the little hero in the nursery-book, price one halfpenny, "who kissed the maiden all forlorn." In many cases parties who on their introduction to the Queen's Bench were dandies of the first water, have not the means of "keeping up the steam of Beau Brummellism;" they have no cash, and what is worse for them, no credit. In other cases, they have no inducement to sustain their reputation as dandies: they see nobody, and are seen by nobody, as they themselves phrase it. Hence they get careless in the article of apparel; and that carelessness eventually degenerates into slovenliness. The brush comes in contact with their clothes: button after button drops off without being replaced, until they are pretty nearly buttonless. There is a hole here, and a rent there. "The shine" is taken out of their shoes, and is not put into them again. If Warren had no better customers than the inmates of the Queen's Bench, he would be obliged to advertise less. The columns of so many country papers would not be enriched by the poetical praises of his "unrivalled," nor would those journals be so often embellished by the picture of the cat fighting with her own shadow as reflected in the well-polished boot. Then there are the hats of these broken-down demi-dandies: they are, indeed, "shocking bad" ones, if they are worthy of the name. The pile is gone, the colour is faded; they are broken and bruised all over. As regards their beards, again, they find it the least troublesome course to let them have their own way of it; hence the chin, which on their entrance was scraped by some tonsor as bare as if no crop had ever grown on it, is embellished by a most abundant harvest of hair, which is dignified with the name of mustachios.

There are always some persons in the Bench who illustrate the old proverb of not learning wisdom from experience. A few months since, there was a lady there, who had, after having been for seven years an inmate before, procured her liberation. By a curious coincidence, within a few days of her discharge she had the further good fortune of coming into the possession of property which had been left her by a deceased relation, to the amount of 4000*l.* This might have kept her comfortable for life, as she had no one dependent on her for support. In a few weeks afterwards, she saw an advertisement in "The Times" newspaper, in which the advertiser intimated his desire to meet with a party, commanding a capital of 4000*l.*, to enter with him into a speculation which he pledged himself would, the very first year, yield a return of 50 per cent. on the money embarked in the affair. The lady answered the advertisement; it was too tempting a prospect to be slighted. A personal interview followed. The advertiser, who was an exceedingly plausible person, assured her that he had discovered a method of making candles of the first quality without tallow, and that, if he had the command of 4000*l.*, wherewith to erect the necessary machinery, and to fit up suitable premises, the party advancing the sum should be received as full partner into the concern, and that the fortunes of both would be made in a few years. The simple lady was exceedingly pleased with the scheme; she advanced the last farthing of her money; the ingenious rogue was, of course, no more heard of; and, in exactly twelve months afterwards, she was sent back to her old quarters in the Bench.

Very unexpected meetings sometimes take place between near relations or intimate friends, in the Queen's Bench. Not long since, a woman, moving in a respectable sphere of life, was committed, as the phrase is, to the custody of the Marshalsea. She had not been three hours in the place, when she was surprised to see her daughter, who had lived in lodgings of her own, make her appearance in the coffee-room. "Mercy on me, Matilda! how did you hear so soon of my being here?" she exclaimed, advancing to embrace her daughter. The latter uttered a shriek, and fainted away at the sight of her mother. She had not heard of her parent's incarceration. The coincidence of both being imprisoned in one day for their individual debts was curious enough. We often hear of agreeable surprises: this was a surprise of a very different kind: it was a most *dis*agreeable one for both parties.

But a meeting of two friends in the Queen's Bench, under still more singular circumstances, occurred a short time ago. Mr. Bagster, a literary man in a small way, was most devotedly attached to Miss Bridget Shrimps, who had been many years known as a dress-maker, in the neighbourhood of Leicester-square; and his ardent affection was reciprocated on her part. Never, indeed, did novelist lavish more high-wrought encomiums on the ardour of the attachment entertained towards each other, by any couple of imaginary lovers which his own fancy called into being, than were merited by Mr. Bagster and Miss Shrimps. Their love was on the eve, as it was right it should do, of attracting each other, by a sort of Siamese sympathy, towards the hymeneal altar. Just three days more, and Miss Shrimps would have been metamorphosed into Mrs. Bagster; but "the course of true love"—the reader can complete the sentence. Mr. Bagster was one evening on his way, through Coventry-street, to Miss Shrimps, to renew to her his protestations of ardent and unalterable attachment, and to make some necessary preparations for the approaching nuptials, when he received a rather smart tap on the right shoulder. He turned about, and encountered the physiognomy of a personage whose visage, even in the contemplation, had been associated for six months before with very unpleasant feelings. Mr. Bagster was landed in an hour or two afterwards in the Bench. That night did pass away; but it was an age to poor Mr. Bagster. The image of Miss Shrimps haunted his mind continually, not even allowing him one moment's repose. He thought next day what a wretched person he must be if he was kept many weeks from the embraces of Miss Shrimps. On the afternoon of the second day, he sat down to unburden his mind by pouring into her ear, through means of a letter, his woes, caused by his sudden and unexpected separation from her. The letter, so far as it had proceeded, was instinct with affection: it was full to overflowing of protestations of undying attachment. "O, Miss Shrimps! my ever adored and ever adorable Miss Shrimps! how shall I endure the pangs of separation from you! Last night was an age; this night will be an eternity, because of my not seeing you. Your presence here would convert this miserable place into a para—" Mr. Bagster was in the act of completing the sentence, by inditing the word "paradise," when interrupted by what he thought a gentle knock at the door. "Who's there? Any one there?" said he, leaving the word "paradise" in its incomplete state, and raising his head and looking towards the door. He resumed writing.

No answer was returned to his queries.

"Yes, my——"

He was again interrupted by what he conceived to be another gentle knock at the door.

"Any person there?" he again inquired, in a subdued tone of voice, directing his eye towards the door.

Still there was no answer to his question.

"It's all imagination with me," he observed to himself.

"Yes, my dearest!" resuming his epistolary employment; "yes, my dearest Bridget, your presence, which is but another name for happiness, would convert even this miserable place into a perfect paradise; but how——"

A loud knock, which there was no mistaking, interrupted Mr. Bagster a third time; and throwing down the pen, he started to his feet, and threw the door wide open in a moment. A female figure appeared before him. "Bridget!" he exclaimed, with an expression of countenance which showed that he could hardly credit the evidence of his eyes.

"O, Francis! O, my——" The remainder of the sentence was lost, in consequence of Miss Shrimps thrusting her face into Mr. Bagster's breast. Mr. Bagster opened his arms as wide as their length would admit of, to receive his Dulcinea, and then, pressing her to his bosom, exclaimed, with a most emphatic sigh, "O, Bridget! Bridget! O."

"Francis!" faintly ejaculated Bridget, looking up languishingly in her lover's face.

"Bridget, my dear!" responded the latter, with a sort of sob which defies specification.

Miss Shrimps looked up in Mr. Bagster's face, but uttered not a word.

Mr. Bagster looked down in Miss Shrimps's face, and was equally silent.

"This *is* a meeting," gasped Bridget after a minute's pause; "a meeting ——"

"It *is* a meeting, my dear!" answered Mr. Bagster. "But, come inside." As he spoke, he led Miss Shrimps into his room, seated her on a chair, and after both had begun to recover from the effects of so unexpected an interview, Mr. Bagster handed to Miss Shrimps the letter he had been writing.

She forthwith commenced reading it, and on coming to the tender passage which Mr. Bagster had been in the act of inditing when she knocked at the door, she threw down the letter, and thrusting her arms round his neck, cordially embraced him.

"O, Bridget! I'm so delighted you're come. But how shall I bear the pang of parting from you when the gates are about to be shut in the evening?"

"My dear Francis, I'll stay here; I won't leave you."

"But you must, my angel; all strangers must quit previous to the gates being shut."

"O! but they won't ask me to go."

"Indeed they will, my dear; they never allow any one but the unhappy inmates to remain."

"Francis! Francis! How shall I tell you ——"

Here Miss Shrimps gasped for breath, and seemed within a few degrees of a regular swoon.

"Tell what, my dear?" inquired Mr. Bagster eagerly.

"*How* shall I tell it?" repeated Miss Shrimps, with additional emphasis.

"*Do* tell it, my dearest Bridget."

"*I* am an *inmate*—a *prisoner*, Francis," answered Miss Shrimps, and she again buried her head most poetically in the breast of Mr. Bagster.

"You don't say so!" exclaimed the latter, starting back on the first intimation of the fact.

"I do, indeed," rejoined Miss Shrimps, clinging still closer to Mr. Bagster.

"Bridget! my adored Bridget! I'm happy to hear it," observed Mr. Bagster with great emphasis, after a moment's reflection; and as he spoke, he pressed Miss Shrimps with redoubled vigour to his bosom.

"O, I'm *so* happy to hear you say so!"

"I was afraid, Bridget, that I might forfeit your affections when you discovered that I was in embarrassed circumstances."

"And I laboured under a similar apprehension when you found out the state of my pecuniary matters," rejoined Miss Shrimps.

"We are now again on a footing of perfect equality," remarked Mr. Bagster.

"Quite so," answered Miss Shrimps; and the lovers again embraced each other.

They were both liberated in six weeks; and before the seventh week had passed away, Miss Shrimps was transformed into Mrs. Bagster.

And there was, after all, more philosophy in the mutual congratulations of the lovers, on finding themselves both in prison for debt, than might appear on the first blush of the thing. The one would not, in the bickerings which are incidental, as if by some sort of moral necessity, to the matrimonial state, be able to reproach the other with a stigma which attached equally to each. The same philosophy dictated the mutual confessions of Dr. Johnson and the lady to whom he was paying his addresses, immediately before their marriage. "I had a near relation who was hanged," said the lady, in order that the Doctor might not afterwards have any ground for accusing her of concealing the fact, or of reproaching her, with any justice, with the circumstance. "My dear," said the lexicographer, "there is no inequality in our circumstances in that respect; for though no near relation of mine has been hanged, I have at least twenty who deserve to be so."

I have alluded, in a former part of the chapter, to the length of time which some of the present prisoners have been inmates of the Queen's Bench; and also to the causes, in some cases, of their protracted imprisonment. There is one of these individuals who has been fifteen or sixteen years in the place, simply because he refuses to answer certain questions put to him by the commissioners of bankrupts. He has been several times before those gentlemen, and might, at any time since he was first committed, have procured his liberation by saying either "Aye," or "No" to their queries. But no consideration will induce him to use either of these monosyllables in connexion with their questions, though he has no particular objection to the words in other circumstances. On one occasion he was brought before Lord Brougham, then Lord Chancellor, with a view to the overcoming what the commissioners of bankrupts call his obstinacy; and his Lordship made every effort in his power to get either an affirmative or negative answer to the questions referred to; but without effect. "Why, my good man," said his Lordship, in the most winning tone of which he was master,—never, by the way, very winning at any time,—"why, my good man, would it not be a very simple thing to answer affirmatively or negatively the question put you?"

The prisoner was silent.

"Your conduct is most extraordinary," added his Lordship, giving a twitch or two to his nose.

Still the prisoner uttered not a syllable.

"You are not asked to answer the questions in any particular way, but only to give such answers as are in accordance with the truth."

Not a word proceeded from the prisoner.

"Can't you," resumed his Lordship, in his usual tart and hasty manner, and imparting a variety of very violent twitches to the aforesaid part of his face; "can't you say 'Yes or No?'"

Whether his Lordship was aware that, in putting the matter to the prisoner in this way, he was quoting the title of one of Lord Mulgrave's novels, I cannot say; but the prisoner continued as mute as before.

"Then, Sir, you won't say either 'Yes or No?'" repeated Lord Brougham, with additional warmth.

"No," said the prisoner, in an audible voice.

"O, then," observed his Lordship, in a subdued tone, and his countenance assuming a much milder expression; "O, then, you mean, at last, to answer the questions in the negative, do you?"

"Certainly not," answered the prisoner in a firm and steady voice. I meant by 'No,' that I did not intend to answer them either way."

"Officers," shouted Lord Brougham, addressing the parties in whose custody the prisoner was; "officers, remove this person back to prison." And he was re-transferred to the Bench accordingly, where he has remained ever since.

There are some prisoners, again, who, so far from going into the Bench with the determination of remaining there for a lengthened period, enter it with the full determination, and under the assured conviction, of not being in it above a few weeks at furthest. There was some months since, and I suppose is still, an individual in it, of the name of Such, who has been an inmate, without once crossing its threshold, for more than twenty years, who on his incarceration felt so assured of his being liberated next day, that he observed to Mr. Sams, a fellow-prisoner who had been a previous acquaintance, that he had come to a resolution not to take off his boots while he remained there. "Don't be too sure of regaining your liberty so promptly," observed the other.

"If I don't get out to-morrow, I'll jump down my own throat," rejoined the other.

This promise to jump down his own throat was a favourite

expression of his, when pledging his word to anything which he was confident would occur.

The hour for shutting the gates next evening arrived, without any appearance of Mr. Such being liberated. "Come, now," said Mr. Sams, on the bell being rung for the departure of strangers,—"Come, now, I suppose you'll have no objection to take off your boots?"

"Take them off! Certainly not; perfectly sure of getting out to-morrow. If I don't, I'll jump down my own throat; blame me, if I don't!"

"P'r'aps you would like your boots cleaned, Sir?" said a man of all-work, on seeing the unpolished aspect they presented next morning, as Mr. Such promenaded the pavement.

"O, not at all, my good man. I'll have them cleaned in the Tavistock Hotel in a few hours."

"Vould'nt you better have them done now?" inquired the other, having an eye to the penny which was his usual charge.

"Certainly not: I'm resolved they shall never come off my feet while here; far less, have them cleaned."

"Vell, Sir, but you knows as how, if you don't get out o' this here place so soon as you expects, you must take them off to get them cleaned, for decency's sake."

"O, I'm quite certain of getting out to-day: there can be no mistake about the matter. I'll jump down my own throat, if there be."

That day passed away like its two predecessors, and still Mr. Such's efforts to procure his liberation were unsuccessful. "Come, come," said his friend, "don't be so foolish; off with your boots, and go to bed at the usual time, and in the usual manner, like other people."

"Will I!—Not for worlds. I have pledged my word that I shall not take off my boots while I remain in this place. However, I know the causes why I have not already regained my liberty. All owing to accidental circumstances: but sure to be out to-day. Here goes, if I don't." As he uttered the last sentence, he pointed his finger to his open mouth.

Nearly a month elapsed, during every day of which Mr. Such was repeatedly urged by one or more of his fellow-prisoners to take off his boots; but to each of their entreaties he replied by a threatened descent of his own throat, if he did not get out before night. By the close of the fourth day of his incarceration, he was so uncomfortable and exhausted with sitting up all night, or only lying down for a few hours with his clothes on, that he was obliged to go to bed like other people, only that he neither doffed his boots nor trowsers. Just about the commencement of his fifth week, his toes began to peep out between the soles and uppers of his "understandings,"—as he sometimes facetiously called his boots. This was deemed by Mr. Sams a fortunate circumstance. He thought the boots of Mr. Such must come off now, whether he was willing or not. " Mr. Such," said he, " your boots want mending."

" Why, I know that," observed the latter, coolly.

" Take them off, and I'll send for a cobbler to have them mended."

" O, not at all, Mr. Sams; though equally obliged to you for your kind offer."

" Why, really, Mr. Such, you are carrying the joke a little too far. You look quite ridiculous with your toes staring people in the face that way," pointing to his feet.

" Can't help it; it will only be for this one day more. I'm sure to be out before nine this evening. If I be not, I'm down directly." The latter sentence was accompanied by the appropriate action of again pointing to his open mouth.

" Come, come, no more nonsense, Mr. Such. Let me bring you a cobbler at once."

" O, bring him by all means, if you please; only, if my boots are to be mended, they must be so on my feet."

" Well, Sir, have your own way of it. Keep them on till doomsday, if you wish it," observed Mr. Sams in an angry tone, as he quitted Mr. Such's room. Mr. Sams determined with himself that he would never again utter a syllable to him on the subject.

In about a fortnight afterwards, one of the prisoners, in passing Mr. Such, chanced to accost him with " Not out yet, Mr. Such?" He was surprised at not receiving the usual reply of " I will be out to-night, though. If I don't, down my own throat I go."

" You should be advised, and take off your boots, Mr. Such."

" *I* won't take them off," replied Mr. Such, in a subdued tone, looking significantly at his feet.

" Will you allow *me* to take them off?"

" O, if you wish it, I have no objections; only, I don't do it myself: I won't break my word."

The other endeavoured to release him from the state of living martyrdom in which he had been for seven weeks, but found his legs were so swollen, that the boots could not be got off in the usual way. They were obliged to be cut off in pieces. When the process had been completed, and Mr. Such saw the fragments lying before him, he observed, with something between a sigh and a groan, " O, there they are! I have now no longer any wish to regain my freedom. Here I am willing to live and die." From that time, nearly a quarter of a century ago, the eccentric gentleman has never been heard to express a desire to get out of the Bench; while his favourite threat of jumping down his own throat has never since escaped his lips.

CHAPTER III.

THE LUMBER TROOP.

Origin of the Troop—Distinguished members—Coat of Arms—Troop Hall—Admission of distinguished members—Remarks on the Charge delivered on the admission of Troopers of distinction—System of punishments adopted by the Troop—Scenes which sometimes occur on the proposed exaction of fines—An instance given—Visit of the City Members to Troop Hall—Their speeches on the occasion—The uproarious scenes which sometimes occur—Specimen of one—Miscellaneous Observations.

The period at which this body was first formed, cannot now be ascertained. Ask a member of the "Ancient and Honourable Lumber Troop," the time when it was first instituted, and his answer will be—"Its origin is lost in the mist of ages." This, at any rate, is the answer I have always got from the Troopers when I have questioned them as to the origin of the Troop. Some intelligent persons are of opinion that it was originally instituted to commemorate the destruction of the Spanish Armada, in Queen Elizabeth's time. I do not see any probability in this hypothesis; for so far as I am acquainted with the annals of the Lumber Troop, I can discover no connexion which it could ever have had with that event. Others are of opinion that it was founded in the reign of Queen Anne. This theory also appears to me to be untenable; for some of the writers in the commencement of that reign, allude to it as a body of some standing. Besides there is a portrait of some noted Trooper of a former period, in the Hall, which, from the style of painting, coupled with the costume of the Trooper, could not have been taken posterior to the time of the second Charles.

But though the precise time of the institution of the "Ancient and Honourable Lumber Troop" is thus involved in uncertainty, there seems to be a pretty general concurrence of opinion as to the circumstances under which it originated. The general impression among the members themselves is, that it originated in the circumstance of a few boon and frolicsome acquaintances being in the habit of meeting together to spend their evenings in the same public-house, and that one of the number having, in joke, proposed that they should call themselves a Troop, for the purpose of burlesquing the then trained-band of London, immortalized by Cowper in his John Gilpin,—they agreed to the proposal; and that afterwards, by way of ridiculing themselves, or rather of having their joke at each other's expense, they called themselves the "Lumber" Troop; meaning that, instead of being available soldiers, they were no better than so much mere lumber. If this hypothesis be correct, we can have no difficulty in coming to the conclusion that the very imposing adjectives of "Ancient and Honourable" were prefixed in the same spirit of burlesque.

From first to last, there have been many members of distinction in the Lumber Troop. Such persons, however, have joined it, in most cases, from a pure love of fun. Prince George of Denmark, the consort of Queen Anne, was a Lumber Trooper; and so was Hogarth, the prince of humorous painters. In fact, Hogarth joined the Troop with the view of forwarding his professional business. Some of his best subjects were selected from Troop Hall. John Harrison, of Bell-yard, Temple-bar, an eccentric personage, who kept a tobacco-shop, and went to all the meetings of the Troop with his pockets stuffed with tobacco, which he sold in retail to the Troopers, is supposed to be the character whom Hogarth represents in his "Modern Midnight Conversation," as leaning over the parson when challenged to drink to a particular toast. The allusion will be better understood by the following lines:—

"Warm'd and wound up to proper height,
He vows to still maintain the fight;
The brave surviving priest assails,
And fairly ——s the first that fails;
Fills up a bumper to the best
In Christendom, for that's the taste:
The parson simpers at the feast,
And puts it forward to the rest."

One thing is clear, from this morsel of poetry,—if the latter word be not a misnomer,—namely, that the Troopers of a century since were equally renowned with some of their descendants of the present day for their love of jollity. Hogarth, in return for the professional advantage which he derived from the Troop, through the oddities of some of its members, made it a present of a design by himself for a coat of arms. As most people will be curious to see what so great a genius designed for so droll a body of persons as the Ancient and Honourable Lumber Troop, I here give a correct engraving of it, only premising that a similar engraving is given on the ticket of every member on his admission.

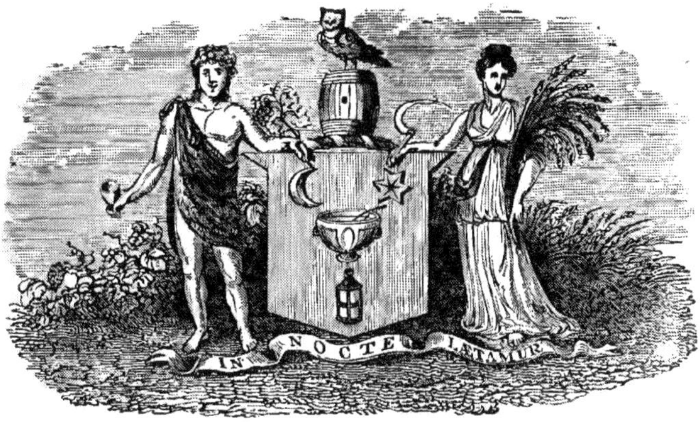

There is a common impression among the members of the Troop, that Prince Blucher, the celebrated general, was a Trooper. Past-Colonel Birch assures me that such was not the fact; but adds, that the mistake is a very natural one, as one of his most intimate friends, who was almost always in his company when in this country, joined the Troop, and received from it, on the occasion, the very appropriate present of a brace of pistols. The late Alderman Waithman evinced a lively solicitude in the fortunes of the Troop: so did Sir John Key, for a time. The latter gentleman, indeed, when lord mayor, gave a considerable number of the Troopers, and their wives, a grand ball and supper at the Mansion-house. Sir John Hobhouse was also a Trooper, when member for Westminster: but all these gentlemen had political objects to serve by joining the Troop, the members being, almost to a man, of liberal opinions in politics. I shall afterwards have occasion to refer to the fact of the present members for the city of London being Lumber Troopers for the same reason.

Troop Hall, the "head-quarters" of the Troop, is in Bolt-court, Fleet-street, in the very house where Dr. Johnson so long lived, and where many of his greatest works were written. This place is called the Doctor Johnson Tavern, and is kept by Mr. Beck, the Suttler of the Troop. Troop Hall is open to the public on the payment of twopence by each individual who enters. As he presents himself at the door, he is asked whether he be a Trooper or visitor, and on answering that he is the latter, his name is inserted in a book as such. If he do not wish to give his right name, he can assume one for the occasion. When he takes his seat in the Hall, he is politely waited on by one of Mr. Beck's servants, who coaxingly looks in his face, and says "What will you take, Sir?" The visitor may order a pint of ale, or some brandy-and-water, or anything else in the subterranean regions of the suttler; only if it be heavy-wet, the favourite beverage, according to the Tory journals, of Dr. Wade, he will not be allowed to drink it out of "the pewter," that being contrary to a formal resolution of the Troop; but out of a glass. The Troopers also order what they please, provided they pay for it; but until about thirty years ago, the immemorial practice was to pay sevenpence on their entrance; they being allowed to drink, without any further charge, as much porter as they pleased, and to call for as much tobacco, technically termed "Troop-sand," as they could consume at the sitting. This regulation was found to answer extremely well for the suttler, for a time; but some blacksmiths, whose throats were full of smoke, thought that to join the Troop was an excellent way of giving them, at a cheap rate, a thorough "clearing out," as they themselves used to say; but the suttler made the discovery that the quantity of "Entire," requisite for the purifying operation, cost himself at least twice the sum of sevenpence. Hence the change to the charge of twopence on entering, and paying for whatever should be ordered.

Troop Hall is a spacious room, beautifully fitted up with a variety of military trappings. On the walls are hung a number of well-executed portraits of distinguished Troopers, while on the table or bench, where the Colonel presides, there are two mortars; and projecting from the wall, at the Colonel's back, are twenty-one guns, and a sword seven or eight feet long.

The Lumber Troopers have certain great occasions, on which new members of importance or celebrity are admitted into the fraternity, amidst much show of pomp and circumstance. It is impossible to describe the interest which the Troopers generally manifest on such occasions. There is a peculiar animation in their eyes, and their countenances glow with an unusual brightness. Not more important is the coronation of a sovereign to other people, than is the admission of a member, amidst "the proper forms," to the Troopers. They magnify it into an importance of which the uninitiated can form no conception. The ceremony has nothing very complicated about it. After being declared duly elected, the affair begins. The first thing to be done, is to present the newly-made Trooper to the Colonel, whose self-importance on such occasions is so great, that it is matter of wonder that there is not a realization of the fate of the frog in the fable, which would not rest satisfied with the proportions which nature had assigned it, but must needs distend its little body in the hope of forcing itself out to the dimensions of the ox. Every one knows what was the result. Every Colonel of the Lumber Troop is, in like manner, so self-consequential on the great occasions to which I refer, and struts about with an air of such importance, that it is really surprising no explosive accident occurs to him. When the new-made Trooper is presented in due form to the Colonel, which is always done by the Serjeant, the robe-master standing by his right hand, thus addresses him: "Sir, allow me to invest you with the star and ribbon worn by William the Fourth's grandfather, when Prince of Wales." The robe-master always assumes a very dignified aspect when performing his part of the ceremony. He moves as stiffly as if he were a piece of wood, instead of a human being, only that when he comes to extend his hand to bestow the ribbon and star on the newly-created Trooper, he does contrive to make a bow, and thereby shows that there are joints in his body. The robe-master then decks out the person of the newly-enlisted Trooper with the insignia of the corps, by attaching the ribbon to his left shoulder, and affixing the star to his left breast. This done, you see the countenances of all the Troopers beaming with ineffable joy at the circumstance of receiving a new comrade; and that joy is so great that, but for their rising to their feet, and giving vent to it in roars of applause which would almost drown the thunder of their own artillery, there is no saying what might be the consequences. Some of them, indeed, might die from the very excess of their joy and happiness. Of the feelings of the party himself, when he sees the ribbon floating from his shoulder, and beholds the star decorating his breast, I will say nothing: no description could do them justice. Grattan, the Irish orator, in one of those beautiful figures of speech of which he was so distinguished a master, speaks of a man walking forth in all the majesty of freedom. I wish Grattan had seen a newly-made Lumber Trooper strutting about in all the majesty of a "comrade." I am convinced, if he nad, he would have blushed at the thought of having used the metaphorical expression to which I have referred, as applied to one's emancipation from slavery. He would have seen how vastly superior—at least, in the party's own estimation—was the majesty of the Trooper to that of the freeman.

The next part of the initiatory ceremony is for the Colonel to fill his cup with ale, and drink to the new-made comrade. The Colonel having quaffed the contents, which most of the colonels are remarkably expert at doing, he is to transfer the empty cup to the robe-master, who takes it, and, filling it to the brim, hands it to the new-made comrade, saying, "Take this in your right hand, and repeat after me—'To the Colonel, the rest of the officers and comrades, and prosperity to the Ancient and Honourable Lumber Troop:' drink this toast: it is the only thing we have to require of you." The new Trooper repeats the words audibly, swills the ale, and is then pronounced a comrade. He is next addressed by the Colonel in the following lines, which are called "The Charge:"

Let the Freemasons boast of what they please,
Or Gormagons (of origin Chinese),
The Troopers are as ancient as these.
To this illustrious Troop you have now a right:
We are merry, drink, and sing, but seldom fight.
We had rather meet within this house to dine,
Than beat a march t'other side the Rhine.
But should our country's foes our rights invade,
And our great noble king * require our aid,
No Troop more ready then to take the field,
The first to battle, and the last to yield.
To show that we are free from war's alarms,
Bacchus and Ceres both support our arms:
A bowl of punch does in the centre flow;
The moon and stars above, lantern below.
For crest there stands a butt of Domine,
Perch'd on the top of which an owl you see;
Apparently, this emblem well implies,
That Troopers, though they're merry, still are wise.
Our motto (——–) means, if you construct it right,

In nocte lactamur.

The merry Troopers revel in the night.

Now for your profits;

You've twenty pounds a-year as private man;
To get which sum, you must do the best you can;
Lend to the Troop a buck oft as you please,
Breeches made of its skin shall be your fees.
If, on a march, you're pennyless and dry,
And ————, † our suttler's house, is nigh,

* Of course the phrase "great noble queen" ought now to be substituted.

† A blank is left here to be filled up with the name of the suttler for the time being. Mr. Beck, of the "Doctor Johnson," being the present suttler, the reader can write his name in the blank.

Boldly advance, and claim a Trooper's due—
Some bread and cheese, a pint of ale (not two).
Don't impose on us—pray have a care;
For if your pockets are search'd, and money there,
'Tis not only paying for your bread and cheese,
But expulsion you've to fear, should the Colonel please.
If you at midnight chimes, when Troopers roam,
With strength renew'd should seek your happy home,
And being too much prim'd,—unlucky wight!—
Should chance to offend the guardians of the night,
And are by constables, who'll hear no reason,
Under strong guard sent to the nearest prison;
Next morn, before the justice takes his chair,
Send for the Colonel or the Treasurer:
You'll quickly be discharged, if they appear.
But if they come not to afford you aid,
And your discharge thereby should be delay'd,
Why then submit to law, and pay your fees,
And the Troop will contribute *what* they please.

The following song used to be always sung by the assembled company immediately after the delivery of the Charge; but it has been omitted on some late occasions:

SONG.

We are full ten thousand brave boys,
  Content with a competent wealth;
And we make an agreeable noise
  When we drink to our Colonel's good health.

We scorn to accept any pay,
  Each man keeps himself and his steed:
We frequently moisten our clay,
  And fight for the King * when there's need.

Our Troop is of excellent blood,
  Each man has a generous soul;
I'm sure it will do your heart good
  To go and join the jolly Troop bowl.

There is another verse, but it is not altogether fit for the public eye, and therefore I omit it.

The newly-made Trooper then descends from the elevated place which had been the theatre of all his glory, into the midst of his comrades, by whom he is received with an enthusiasm equal to any thing of the kind with which the most dis-

* Read the Queen now.

tinguished conquering hero of ancient Greece or Rome, was ever received by his grateful and admiring countrymen.

The task of commentator is one which I do not often take upon myself, but here the temptation is too great to be resisted. By whom the above piece of poetry, if so it must be called, was written, is as great a mystery as is the authorship of Junius. My researches on the subject have only conducted me to two certain conclusions; which conclusions are, that it was written in Pope's time, but not by Pope himself. There is internal evidence of the clearest kind, that the versifier who *did* the affair, must either have been by nature as destitute of brains as the artillery of the Troop, or that, if he ever had any, they must have been "stole away" by the ale or brandy of the suttler. But let the poetry of the "Charge" and its authorship pass; and now for a word or two on the Charge itself.

The first line which deserves notice is the fourth:

"We are merry, drink, and sing, but seldom fight."

This is partly true and partly not. The first clause is perfectly correct in point of fact: the latter clause is to be received with certain qualifications. A "merrier" race than the Lumber Troopers are not to be found. They are the most hearty and jolly assemblage of beings with whom I have had the fortune to meet. The merriment of some of the comrades occasionally verges on "Merry Andrewism" itself. If any one wishes to see a specimen of Lumber Troop merriment, let him visit the "head-quarters" on any of the evenings on which there is a particular muster of the Troop. There his eyes and ears will afford him ample proof of the attainments of the Troopers, both in the art of drinking and singing. See how constantly and actively the waiters of the suttler are engaged in meeting the demands of the comrades, officers and all, for ale, stout, gin, brandy, and so forth; and see how suddenly the new supplies vanish. "Bring me another go, William," is a command enjoined on the poor fellow before he has had time to give the change for the one he has just brought. And while one set of Troopers are thus displaying such dexterity at absorbing anything and everything in the shape of liquids which comes before them, another set are putting their vocal capabilities to the test. Some are singing, others are roaring: between the two classes of performers, there is no lack of sound.

But the Troopers, it seems, if the statements of the "Charge" may be credited,

"Seldom fight."

It is quite true that they are as innocent, as the most peaceably disposed people in Christendom could desire, of ever fighting with deadly weapons, or with any of their country's enemies: nevertheless they do have their occasional skirmishes among themselves. Their weapons in such cases, are usually their tongues; but these last are sometimes followed by their fists. Pugilistic encounters, however, are, it is but justice to the Ancient and Honourable Lumber Troop, to say, of very rare occurrence. They are not only, taken as a body, the most pacifically disposed set of soldiers, in reference to other people, I have ever seen, but they usually breathe a most peaceable spirit as regards each other. It is not to be denied, that a little martially-inclined personage, who is remarkable for the quantity of Edinburgh ale he drinks, without at all exhibiting the slightest symptoms of a tendency to inebriety, but who having, on a late occasion, so far forgot himself as to intermingle four "goes" of brandy-and-water with half-a-dozen glasses of his favourite beverage; it is, I say, quite true, that he, on a recent occasion, sallied out to the streets, and meeting with no fellow-mortal who would accept of his challenge to fight, "pitched in," to use his own elegant phraseology, to a lamp-post. It is unnecessary to say that in this conflict he came off second best. He not only knocked his hands, but his head, against his metallic antagonist, of which conclusive proofs were afforded by his person for several weeks afterwards. There are various other instances in which the heroes of the Lumber Troop have, on leaving head-quarters, quarrelled with policemen, and after a regular fight been safely transferred to the watch-house, which a Trooper always calls the Black Hole. And there is one recent instance of a Trooper going home, and, in the ardour of his military zeal, giving his wife a sound beating, under the idea that she was one of some imaginary "enemies" that were running in his mind. But these are only exceptions to the rule; and they occur so seldom, that it is hardly fair to allude to them. As a body of martial men, the Troopers are the most harmless and peaceable personages in Christendom. Their artillery has not only never destroyed the life of a single human being, but it has never discharged a single ball.

Let me not be understood as at all reflecting on the bravery of the Troopers, when adverting to the fact that they have never been engaged in any great martial enterprise. They don't undertake to peril their lives in war, except their country were unhappily invaded by some foreign foe. In such a case, if their own word may be taken, they would distinguish themselves in the battle-field by deeds of surpassing prowess. Hear what they say:

> "But should our country's foes our rights invade,
> And our great noble King (Queen) require our aid,

> No Troop more ready then to take the field ;
> The first to battle, and the last to yield."

Brave boys! Captain Bobadil himself was not a bit more valorous at his own fireside, than are the Ancient and Honourable Lumber Troop in Troop Hall. They would put to the blush the forty-second regiment of Scottish Highlanders, who won for themselves so brilliant and enduring a reputation on the field of Waterloo. Even the valour of the heroes of Thermopylæ would shrink from a comparison with the martial exploits of the Troopers, did circumstances call the latter to the field of battle.

Passing over various points in the "Charge" which invite comment, I come to the line—

> "If you at midnight chimes, when Troopers roam," &c.

This roaming at midnight is one of the worst things connected with the Troop. It is the grand objection which many wives have to their husbands enlisting under its banners. Why don't the more domestic class of the Troopers endeavour to procure a law for the expulsion from the body of those who, on quitting Troop Hall, do not go direct home?

The natural consequence of "roaming at midnight chimes" is clearly predicted:

> "And are by constables, who'll hear no reason,
> Under strong guard sent to the nearest prison," &c.

The number of "unlucky wights" belonging to the Troop, "too much prim'd," as the "Charge" has it, who are nightly sent to prison, is greater than is usually supposed, owing to the circumstance that, from regard to the character of the corps, they seldom represent themselves as members of the Ancient and Honourable Lumber Troop. The phrase "constables who'll hear no reason," is exceedingly just and happy. Policemen are the most unreasonable class of men who are to be met with, when they chance to encounter an "unlucky wight" of a Trooper, "too much prim'd," roaming about "at midnight chimes."

A word or two now on the "Song." The first line announces an important fact:

> "We are full ten thousand brave boys."

The number of Troopers necessarily varies: at present the number is estimated at from 8000 to 9000. They are scattered abroad, not only through the British empire, but over all the world. There is not a part of the civilized globe where Lumber Troopers are not to be met with; and when two comrades do happen to meet in some distant part of the earth, the friendship they evince for each other, and their mutual joy at the meeting, baffle all description. But though the number of Lumber Troopers be what I have mentioned, they seldom muster above 1000 strong at a time. The great gatherings with them are at the annual meetings for the election of the Colonel and officers.

> "And we make an agreeable noise
> When we drink our Colonel's good health."

That the Troopers do make a *noise*, when in their more uproarious moods, nobody who has ever been in their head-quarters can deny. But that this noise is *agreeable*, is a point on which a difference of opinion obtains. Ask the good people of Bolt-court, that being the place nearest to Troop-hall, whether they think the noise caused by the "comrades" *agreeable?* They will, on the contrary, one and all, pronounce it to be of a most *disagreeable* kind. Those of them, indeed, who are conversant with Æsop, will quote for you the fable of the Boys and the Frogs, observing that the "noise" may be amusement to the Troopers, but that it is death, or a species of living martyrdom, which is the next greatest earthly evil, to everybody else.

> "Our Troop is of excellent blood:"

This remains to be proved; and until it has been so, there will be a difference of opinion on the subject. Why do not the Troopers achieve some glorious exploits, to set the question as to the quality of their blood, at rest?

> "Each man has a generous soul."

Far be it from me to deny this; only it were as well that the Troopers gave some proof of the thing by performing some glorious *deeds:* others would then be forward to admit the fact. Coming from the Troopers themselves, it smacks of egotism, to say the least of it.

> "I'm sure it will do your heart good
> To go and join the jolly Troop-bowl."

This is all true. The Troopers, as before mentioned, are the most "jolly" set of mortals in Europe: only see them over their "Troop-bowl," and then doubt it who can. But I will not expatiate on this topic further; abundant proofs of the jolly disposition, and jolly conduct of the Troopers, will be found in this chapter.

The system of punishments which obtains in Lumber Troop Hall, is as lenient as the most strenuous advocates for a gentle code of penalties, could desire. The soldier who is found asleep at his post in her Majesty's army, subjects himself to the penalty of death: in the Lumber Troop, the punishment to the officer who takes a nap is one shilling; and for the same offence, when committed by a private, sixpence. The soldier who gets drunk in her Majesty's service, when on duty, incurs the penalty of as many lashes as the surgeon of the regiment conceives may be inflicted without actually flogging the soul out of the body: an officer in the Lumber Troop who gets drunk, escapes on payment of a shilling; and a private, on paying the penalty of sixpence. There are various other still more lenient punishments for minor offences; but it is unnecessary to refer to them.

The proposed or actual exaction of the fines often leads to amusing scenes in Troop Hall. Some time ago, on a rather important occasion, the gallant Colonel himself * either had so forgotten himself as to have degenerated into a temporary doze, or was supposed to have committed that outrage on the dignity of his office. "I'm blow'd if that 'ere comrade there," pointing to the Colonel, "bean't a-sleepin'!" shouted a Mr. Jambo, a green-grocer of homely manners, and of a still more homely personal appearance, who had been made a Trooper the week before, and who having the rule against sleeping on duty fresh on his mind, deemed it proper, in the plenitude of his zeal as a new recruit, to give intimation of the circumstance.

"Do you hear that, Colonel?" said another officer who was sitting next to him, giving him a gentle shake by the arm, his head being at the time drooping in his breast.

"What is it?" said the gallant gentleman, in a gruff and drowsy voice, not deigning to raise his head to its usual position.

"Why, you're charged with being asleep."

"Who charges me with it?" inquired the Colonel, in a smart and determined tone, and looking up with neck erect, as if strongly resenting the dishonourable imputation.

"Why, comrade——What's the Trooper's name who preferred the charge?" As the officer, whose name I did not learn, spoke, he looked in the direction of the Trooper making the charge with great eagerness, not doubting that as he had forgotten his name, he would come boldly forward at once, and avow himself.

"My name is Jambo," said the valiant green-grocer, with much energy.

"Oh, aye; comrade Jambo," observed the officer, nodding to the vender of vegetables.

"Comrade Jambo!" echoed a hundred voices at once.

"You said, did you not, comrade Jambo, that the Colonel was asleep?" inquired the officer in question, encouragingly.

* Not the present Colonel.

"I did, and I *does*," shouted Mr. Jambo, with an air of immense importance.

"I say it's a ———" Here the Colonel was about to say something in a loud and energetic tone; but having checked himself, as if conscious he had been on the eve of uttering some great verbal impropriety, he continued in a lower voice. "I say it's a downright untruth."

"Order! order!" shouted a score or two of very excellent voices.

"I say, with comrade Jambo," remarked a little pot-bellied proprietor of a neighbouring public-house; "I say, with him, that the Colonel *vas* asleep."

"And so do I," said another Trooper.

"And me too," added a third.

"And a lot on us saw him," cried a fourth. Who the latter Trooper represented, it was not so easy to ascertain; unless, indeed, they were the proprietors of eighteen or twenty voices which severally exclaimed "I saw him a-sleepin'."

"Brother officers and comrades," said the gallant Colonel, rising up, and addressing the Troopers with as important and dignified an air as if he had been some general of celebrity addressing his soldiers on the eve of some great battle. "Brother officers and comrades, I deny the charge; there is no truth in it. I was not asleep. Comrade Potter, did you see me asleep?"

"No, I didn't," answered the latter, with an edifying promptitude, as he rose up in the body of the room.

"I thought so," observed the gallant Colonel, in a tone of self-gratulation. "Comrade Dunderhead, did you see me a-sleepin'?"

"Certainly not, Colonel," answered a very bustling consequential-looking personage, with a face as red and glowing as a full moon, at the farthest end of the room, the appeal having been made to him.

"Or did you see it, comrade Short?"

"See what?" answered a little man, with infinite good-nature in his physiognomy, who was just entering Troop Hall.

"See me asleep?" repeated the Colonel.

"I object to the question being put to him," interposed comrade Cotton, with great warmth. "He can't know nothin' about it; for he was not in the Hall at the time."

"Raally, gintlemen," said an unadulterated Irishman, mounting one of the chairs, while his face displayed the most intense anxiety mingled with benevolence; "raally, gintlemen, that person," pointing to the Colonel, "ought not to be condemned without the clearest proof. Remember, gintlemen, that if he be found guilty of slaping at his post, he'll be shot dead for it. And, gintlemen, it's——"

While poor simple Pat was thus interposing, from pure humanity in favour of the gallant Colonel, he was interrupted by comrade Joss inquiring whether he was a Trooper.

"I don't know what you mane, Sir."

"Do you belong to the Ancient and Honourable Lumber Troop?"

"Is it, am I a soldier, your honour manes?"

The Troopers looked each other in the face.

"Have you joined this body?" inquired another, thinking the question might be more level to the capacity of the Irishman when put in that form.

"Och! sure and it's myself did join, when I came into this same place a few minits ago. And it's myself could not bear to think of that gintlemin being shot for slapin', if he didn't slape at all at all."

It was now clear to all that poor Pat was no Trooper; but that having been recently imported from the Emerald Isle, he had gone into Troop Hall simply because he saw the door open, and others entering; and that confounding the Troopers, from the strictness of the military phraseology he heard spoken in the Hall, with a regular military force, and knowing that to sleep on duty was death to the soldier,—he became alarmed for the fate of the gallant Colonel.

"Fellow officers, and comrades all," said the Colonel, in a stentorian voice, and giving a smart knock on the table to command attention; "fellow officers, and comrades all, I pledge my honour, as the Colonel of the Ancient and Honourable Lumber Troop, that I was not asleep."

Loud cheers from the gallant Colonel's special friends followed the emphatic declaration.

"I say you was," shouted comrade Jambo, in an equally loud and energetic voice.

"And so do I," said comrade Collins.

"And I too," observed comrade Wink.

"And I also," bawled out some dozen comrades all at once.

"I rise to order," said comrade Slow, assuming a perpendicular position, and looking immensely dignified and indignant. "Really, if such a scene as this is to be any longer exhibited, it will cover the Troop with deep and indelible disgrace. Possibly there is a little mistake on both sides." (Cries of "No mistake," from both parties, with tremendous uproar.) "Really, comrades," continued comrade Slow, "if this sort of work is to go on much longer, there is no saying——"

"I beg pardon for interrupting you, comrade Slow," interposed some other comrade, whose name I could not learn, addressing himself to the Trooper who was playing the orator; "I beg pardon for interrupting you; but possibly the suggestion I have to throw out may set this matter to rest. It——"

Here the speaker was himself interrupted by some of the other comrades singing out, "Out with the suggestion at once, then." (Cries of "Order! order!")

The other resumed, on order being restored. "If comrade ———, what do you call him?—I do not know the gentleman's name,—would only be kind enough to hold his tongue till I finish my sentence, he would then be at liberty to speak as much and as long as he pleases. What I was going to say, officers and comrades, was, that possibly the Colonel had only been dozing."

"I deny the fact," said the Colonel, indignantly.

"What is the difference between dozing and sleeping?" inquired comrade Smallshins in an under tone, addressing himself to comrade Trench, who sat opposite to him.

"Bless'd, if I knows," answered Trench, who was a journeyman blacksmith.

"*I* knows the differens," observed a diminutive, thin-faced, unshaved Trooper, on the left hand of comrade Smallshins.

"Then, what is it?" inquired comrade Trench.

"O, I knows,' replied the other, with a significant shake of the head, which was promptly followed by a copious draught of the suttler's best ale.

"And why don't you tell us?" inquired Smallshins, slightly offended at the reserve of the little thin-faced personage.

"Vell, then, the differens is this," answered the latter, looking as wise as if he had been a second Solomon; "ven a man sleeps, he *is* asleep; but vhen he's a-dozin', he is neither asleep nor avake."

"O, that's it, is it?" said Trench, with marked emphasis, as if he had clearly comprehended the luminous distinction.

"That's it!" nodded the other, with quite an oracular aspect, withdrawing the pipe from his mouth for the double purpose of uttering the couple of words, and ridding the interior of his speaking-box of an immense quantity of smoke which had accumulated in it.

This conversation between the two Troopers was carried on in an under tone, and was confined to themselves. It consequently offered no interruption to the discussion which was then proceeding among the Troopers, as a body, respecting the alleged fact of the Colonel having resigned himself for a moment to the embraces of Morpheus.

"Comrades!" shouted comrade Slow, "our Colonel denies that he was even dozing. I——"

"I do!" interrupted the Colonel, with prodigious emphasis; "and I will rather re——"

Here the gallant gentleman was interrupted in his turn by comrade Slow, who protested against being interrupted by the Colonel. "Comrades!" continued Mr. Slow, knocking his fist on the table with great warmth; "comrades, you all know it is the duty of the Colonel to preserve order, and to procure a patient hearing for any Trooper who chooses to address the Troop; but instead of this, he himself——"

"I deny it, Sir." (Loud cries of "Order! order!")

"Will you allow me to make the charge, Sir, before you deny it?" (Tumultuous applause.)

When the cheers had subsided, comrade Slow resumed. "I was about to state, my brave comrades," laying great stress on the word "brave;" "I was about to state, when interrupted by the Colonel,—by the *Colonel*, comrades,—that instead of keeping order, as from the nature of the important office he fills he is bound to do, he is the first to set the example of *dis*order." (Loud cheers, mingled with equally loud hisses, and deafening cries of "Order! order!")

Here the Colonel rose, and looking a perfect tempest of indignation at the indignity cast upon him, or, as he himself termed it, the outrage offered to the office he filled, was about to address the Troop, when an officer of an inferior grade interposed, by stepping in before him, and thus intercepting his view of the Troopers. "Really," said the interposing party, "if this unseemly squabble be not put an end to, the Ancient and Honourable Lumber Troop will be disgraced in the eyes of the civilized world." (Loud cries of "Hear, hear!")

"You're right," exclaimed some unknown comrade in the body of the Hall; "and, therefore, the best way to put an end to this unsoldierly squabble, will be to take the sense of the Troop on the question."

"On what question?" inquired a short thick-set cheesemonger, rejoicing in the appropriate appellation of comrade Stilton.

"Why, the question of whether the Colonel was or was not asleep?" replied the other.

"Oh, that's it, is it!" observed Stilton, seemingly quite enlightened by the reply.

"But I cannot put the question myself," said the Colonel, in a subdued tone, doubtless from a conviction that his acquittal from the serious charge would be carried by a large majority.

"Oh, I'll put it," said the officer before alluded to. "As many of the Troop as are of opinion that the Colonel was asleep, will please to signify the same by holding up their hands." Twenty-six hands responded to the call.

"You that are of opinion that the Colonel was awake, will hold up yours." The identical number of twenty-six, including the fist of the officer putting the question, was again held up, amidst loud laughter, and cheers from those who espoused the Morpheus side of the question.

"The numbers, fellow officers and comrades," said the officer, "are equal; but I see a great many Troopers who have not voted at all."

The reason why many did not vote, was that they had not been paying any attention to the Colonel before the charge was made, while a considerable number declared that they could only conscientiously vote for the dozing view of the matter. "Then I say now, as I said before," observed the Colonel, thrusting up his right hand in a perpendicular position, "that I was *not* asleep."

"Carried, by a majority of one, that the Colonel was *not* asleep," said the officer.

The announcement was received with deafening plaudits by the friends of the gallant gentleman, and with much dissatisfaction by the hostile party.

I have before stated, that among the distinguished members of the Troop may be mentioned the four representatives of the city of London; namely, Mr. Alderman Wood, Messrs. Grote, Crawford, and Pattison. These gentlemen, however, are not Troopers on whom much dependence is to be placed. I am pretty confident I may say, without any breach of charity, that the honourable gentlemen whose names I have just mentioned, only join the Troop for electioneering purposes, and that they never bestow a thought either on it or its affairs from one general election time to another. Of this I am certain, for I heard some of themselves state the fact at the last general election, that they never attend any of its meetings, except one or two immediately previous to the polling-day. When an election is about to take place in the city of London, a special meeting of the Troop is invariably called, to receive, in true military style, comrades Wood, Grote, Crawford, and Pattison, each of whose names being at the particular period minus the magical M.P., and the parties being anxious to have the appendage restored, submit with an exemplary patience to all the nonsensical ceremonies observed on such occasions. I was present at the last visit of Messrs. Wood, Grote, Crawford, and Pattison, to the head-quarters of the Troop, where their "comrades" were all met to receive them. There sat the Colonel, whose name I forget just now—which, however, is no great matter, and will, I dare say, be no great privation to the reader—there sat the Colonel on a sort of elevation at the farthest end of the room, regularly equipped in what I suppose was the military uniform of the Troop. Instead of a sword, or any other warlike weapon, he held in his hand a brass hammer; so, at least, it appeared to me; and anything more necessary or appropriate he could not have grasped. The "use," as Shakspeare would have said, to which this hammer was to be applied, was that of giving the noisy a hint to be silent, by a rather smart knock on a sort of desk which lay before the Colonel; and which desk, let me observe in justice to it, possessed the most wonderful acoustical properties I have ever witnessed in any thing of the kind. I have often admired the sounding capabilities of a little red-looking box on the table of the House of Commons, especially when thumped by Sir Robert Peel; but the sounds evoked by the hammer of the gallant Colonel of the Lumber Troop from the small desk, which on this occasion lay on the table before him, would, I am convinced, have made the box on the table of the House of Commons quite ashamed of itself. And it was of no ordinary importance to the proceedings of the Lumber Troop on the evening in question—as it is, I doubt not, to its proceedings on every occasion on which it meets—that this desk should be able to perform the function of emitting sounds of first-rate power; for really the noise of the Troop was so great that it would have drowned any ordinary sounds which the Colonel, by means of his hammer, might have made, and consequently his commands could not have been heard. Need I add that, according to all the admitted rules of sound reasoning, if they had not been heard, they could not have been obeyed? To speak a truth, "the men" were not over prompt in their obedience to the commands of their gallant Colonel as it was; but this, though bad enough in itself, was not quite so bad as it would have been had they not been obeyed at all.

Comrades Wood, Grote, Crawford, and Pattison, were received, on entering the "head-quarters" of the Troop, with all due honours. Their fellow-soldiers, though bearing no musketry with which to greet them on their appearance by firing a salute, could nevertheless boast of weapons of another kind, which were duly charged. Each had his "go" of brandy-and-water, or some other "ardent spirit" and water, before him. The four gentlemen visiting the Troop must have been highly gratified with the display of "ardent spirits," in a double sense, before them; for it is only doing the Troop justice to take for granted, that all "the men" composing it are, as all soldiers ought to be, "ardent spirits." Comrades Wood, Grote, Crawford, and Pattison, having been greeted with thunders of applause on their entrance,—I do not mean the thunder caused by artillery, but the thunder caused by the throats of the troops,—marched up in regular military style to an open space set apart for them on the right hand of the gallant Colonel who presided on the occasion. On reaching their destined station in the "head-quarters" of the Troop, their comrades set up another loud shout of applause. And no wonder though they did; for what soldier would not rejoice once more to meet with an old fellow "trooper" after an absence of several years? Every face beamed with delight at seeing Comrades Wood, Grote, Crawford, and Pattison, once more in Troop Hall. The latter, I doubt not, were much gratified with their reception; for many of their fellow-soldiers had votes to bestow at the approaching elections, and those who had not could influence persons who had. The thing, therefore, was all perfectly intelligible on both sides.

A great many little matters, which, not being a military man, I cannot well describe, having been disposed of, Comrade Wood, as being, I suppose, the senior of the other three as a member of Parliament, if not of the Ancient and Honourable Lumber Troop,—first rose to address his fellow-soldiers: and really I had no previous conception, that one of whom I had never heard a word, except in his capacity of politician or citizen, could be so intimately conversant with military phraseology, as the worthy Alderman—I must still occasionally call him by his civic title—proved himself to be. After adjusting his collar, and standing up *à la militaire*, he commenced thus:—"Colonel, officers, and comrades!" and then proceeded to express the supreme satisfaction with which he again met his gallant companions in arms, after an absence of three years. He assured them, however, that though not with them, he had not been an idle soldier, but had been fighting for them and for his country. It was true, he continued, that the battles in which he had been engaged, since he last appeared among his fellow-soldiers of the Ancient and Honourable Lumber Troop, were bloodless battles; but they were not less important battles on that account. He referred, he added, to the battles in which he had been engaged in the House of Commons with the common enemy of the country and the human race. Need he say to whom he alluded? (Cries of "The Tories, of course.") Yes, said comrade Wood, the Tories; and he was ready to go and battle with them again; and he hoped his gallant comrades would, in the true spirit of soldiership, assist him in his ambition again to measure swords with the enemy on the field of conflict in the House of Commons. Comrade Wood, still standing in that stiff and upright position peculiar to military men, went on at some length in the same strain, amidst the loud applause of his fellow-troopers. And not content with his soldier-like aspect and warlike phraseology, he actually endeavoured, and with tolerable success, to mimic the mode of pronunciation, in addressing his fellow-soldiers, which dandy officers sometimes adopt. The word "here," the gallant gentleman pronounced "eeor;" and the word "years,' "ye-o-ars;" and so on with most of the other terms he used in the course of his military harangue.

Comrade Grote's turn came next. The gallant gentleman deserves all praise for the attitude he assumed while delivering his oration. He pulled himself up immediately on starting to his feet, and looked as stiff and erect all the while he retained his perpendicular position, as if he had been for a long series of years in the army; but the matter of his address to his fellow-soldiers, was not at all in keeping with the military character. In imitation of the gallant gentleman (Comrade Wood) who preceded him, he certainly did manage to begin with "Colonel, officers, and comrades!" but scarcely had these soldierly terms crossed his lips, than he flew off at a tangent to the subject of the ballot; and, to make the matter worse, he never found his way back to military topics or military phraseology during the whole course of his somewhat lengthened address. It is but right, however, to say that, though his speech was so unmilitary, if I may invent a word, it was vociferously applauded by the Troopers. If I may hazard a hypothesis, I should say that the secret of this was, that the time chosen by Comrades Wood, Grote, Crawford, and Pattison, for this visit to the head-quarters of the Troop, being, as before stated, on the eve of a general election, the soldiers assembled on the occasion merged their character as military men, for the moment, in that of politicians.

Next came Comrade Crawford. This gallant gentleman appeared to me the most unsoldier-like personage I have ever seen. He had not a particle of the manner of a martial man about him, and could not manage to string a couple of military phrases together. Instead of standing, like his two comrades, Wood and Grote, in the erect and dignified attitude of a soldier, he, in the fervour of the fit of speechification with which he was seized, repeatedly put his person into a diagonal position, and to scores of other positions which I will not name, because I cannot; into every position, in a word, except that which became a hero of the Ancient and Honourable Lumber Troop to assume. His attitude sometimes resembled that of a disciple of Tom Spring or Dutch Sam. Had I been the Colonel, I would have ordered him off at once to the awkward squad department of the service, and given peremptory instructions to the officers to see that he was properly drilled into his military movements before he again undertook to exhibit before his fellow-soldiers. The applause with which his performances were received was very faint and feeble indeed, compared with that with which the addresses of the two gallant gentlemen who preceded him were greeted. Whether it was owing to the ignorance of military phraseology and military attitudes which Comrade Crawford displayed, I cannot say; but the fact was that the Troopers, generally, before he had finished his address, began to exhibit manifestations of insubordination; and it was with no inconsiderable difficulty, aided as he was by the hammer before referred to, that the gallant Colonel could maintain order. Not content with telegraphing Suttler Beck, the proprietor of the head-quarters of the Troop, and his waiters, by winking with one eye and making significant motions to "charge" their glasses again with brandy-and-water, and to bring them a fresh supply of "'baccy;" not content with this, some of the more undisciplined of the band uttered a variety of ludicrous expressions, and conducted themselves altogether in a most unmilitary manner during the time their gallant comrade was addressing them.

Knowing that Comrade Pattison's turn would come next, and feeling so disappointed by the unsoldier-like address and deportment of Comrade Crawford, I had withdrawn my eye and attention from the latter military gentleman for some time before he resumed his seat, and fixed both on Comrade Pattison. I felt for him; and, what is worthy of mention, though I saw others who were suffering from the closeness of the room and the atmosphere of cigar and tobacco smoke within which they were enveloped,—I somehow or other felt for nobody but himself. I never saw a human being look more uncomfortable in my life. The infinite "jolliness" of countenance which I had always before seen characterize him, and which I had persuaded myself could only disappear with life itself, had completely vanished before his turn came to harangue his fellow-soldiers. Poor Comrade Pattison! I can fancy I see him at this moment. Not more out of its element would a fish be on dry land, than was the gallant gentleman on that occasion in the head-quarters of the Lumber Troop. And no wonder, truly; for, in addition to the unmeaning military jargon he was, the whole of the evening, doomed to hear—the soldierly attitudes he saw everybody around him attempting to assume—and a closeness and unpleasantness of atmosphere which could only have been surpassed by that of the memorable Black Hole of Calcutta, which proved so awfully destructive of life to those who were doomed to breathe it; in addition to all this, some of the Troopers who sat opposite to him kept up—whether intentionally or not it is not for me to say—a constant battery of smoke at his face. They emitted it *at* him in such continued streams, that it appeared to him for some time quite a matter of choice, whether he should suffer martyrdom from the suffocating volumes of tobacco smoke which came from across the table; or whether he should come by it by hermetically sealing his mouth with the view of shutting out the tobacco exhalations. It required no great stretch of imagination to arrive at the conclusion, that he was all this while contrasting, in his own mind, the blessings of the Bank parlour with the miseries he was then enduring. At length his turn came, and with wonderful alacrity did he take to his pedestals. For some moments before, he was all but invisible through the dense clouds of smoke which filled the place: not more smoky, indeed, could it have appeared though all the artillery of the Troop had been for some time before engaged in discharging a succession of rounds. I had my fears that when he rose, I might not get a sight of him; but from some cause or other, which it is beyond the reach of my philosophy to explain, the smoke, contemporaneously with his rising to address his comrades, did partially disappear in the immediate locality of the spot where he had taken up his position, and I got a tolerably fair view of him. The remaining smoke, however, had the effect of operating, in so far as my optics were concerned, as a magnifying medium; for great as are the geometrical dimensions or physical proportions of Comrade Pattison at any time, they now appeared to me of a vastly increased magnitude. But let that pass. Comrade Pattison made short work of it: his speech had the merit of brevity. It was pre-eminently short; and because short, it was sweet. He proved that he was no wordy warrior: this appeared to me to augur well for him as a Trooper. I always find that those persons do the most who say the least. He resumed his seat with all due expedition, and in a few seconds after was to be seen in Fleet-street. I am strongly of opinion that Comrade Pattison would rather lose his election next time for the city of London, than spend such another hour or so with his fellow-soldiers at their head-quarters at Mr. Beck's, Bolt-court.

I have already referred to the artillery or musketry of the Lumber Troop. Which is the proper term, is more than I can determine; for their fire-pieces are in the form of cannons, though not larger than guns. Some of the London journals gave great offence to the Troop, by calling their fire-pieces *pop-guns*, a few weeks ago. They have also two mortars of decent dimensions. The Troop only discharge their artillery on great occasions: the last time, I believe, was when the ever-memorable Mary-le-bone Festival of 1836, took place at St. John's Wood. The moment that Mr. Wakley, the member for Finsbury, arrived at the scene of that great festival, there were nearly five thousand persons, including the ladies, present. Several rounds were

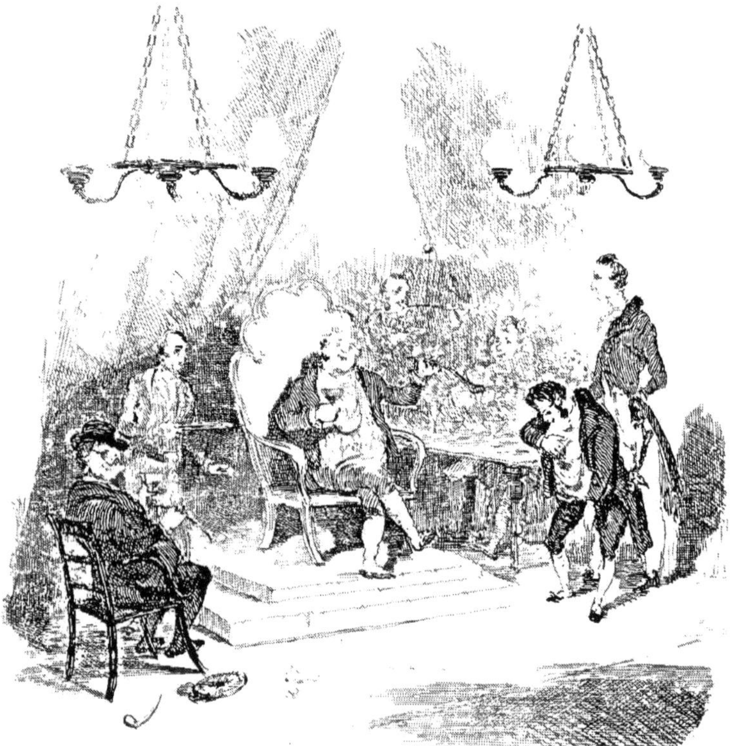

fired, to testify the respect of the Troop for Comrade Wakley. It was proposed, and also eventually agreed to, to fire the guns on the occasion of the late visit of her Majesty to the city of London. One of the Troopers, a past suttler, however, through his individual interference, prevented the intentions of the Troop being carried into effect. He communicated to the Lord Mayor the resolution of the Troop, and the circumstance being brought before a Court of Aldermen, they interdicted all firing in the City on that day. As might be expected, the conduct of this comrade became the subject of discussion on the next meeting of the Troop, which took place on Wednesday evening, the 1st of November. Of all the scenes which it has ever been my lot to witness, that which was exhibited on the evening in question was, out of sight, the most extraordinary. I will venture to say that it was unparalleled even in the annals of the Troop itself. At all events, all the Troopers with whom I have conversed on the subject, say they never saw anything like it. In attempting to give some idea of it, I seriously assure my readers—and scores of individuals who were present will bear testimony to the truth of what I say—that so far from exaggerating the exhibitions of that evening, no description can come up to the reality.

The motion before the Ancient and Honourable Lumber Troop, when the scene began, related to the rescinding or suspension of a resolution which had been come to at the previous meeting, expressive of the intention of the Troop to salute her Majesty, by a volley from Troop Hall, when she entered the City at Temple-bar. Four or five Troopers were reproaching comrade Stout for having communicated the intention of the Troop to the City authorities, and thus frustrated their wishes, when he observed that he had been deputed by some other Troopers to do what he had done.

Seven or eight comrades—"Who deputed you to do it? Name, name." (Loud cheers, and cries of "Hear, hear!")

Comrade Stout raised his glass of brandy-and-water to his mouth with infinite coolness, but uttered not a word.

Comrade Blood—There's a pretty go of it, to undertake to do anything of the kind, and then shelter himself under the authority of some other Troopers. (Hear, hear, hear, he-ar! and laughter at the drawling way in which the last "hear" was pronounced.)

Comrade Stout—I say that I did not shelter myself under the authority of any one. (Cries of "Oh, oh!" "Attention!" and great uproar.)

Comrade Blank—Colonel, officers, and comrades, I rise to order. I protest against this proceeding. We have nothing before us. If we are to have a debate, let us have something to debate about. (Cries of "So we have," drowned by cries of "We have not.")

Comrade Blank, with prodigious emphasis—I say we have *not:* the resolution has not yet been read.

A perfect hurricane of cries of "Read the resolution," "Read the revolution," succeeded the last observation.

Major Stumps—The resolution is on the books, and therefore there is no necessity for reading it.

Deafening cries of "There is, there is," "Read it, read it," followed this remark. In the midst of this uproar, eight or ten Troopers rose all at once in different parts of the Hall, each protesting, in the loudest tones, and with the most violent gesticulation,—"I'll be heard; I'm determined I'll be heard." The Colonel in the meantime kept knocking as regularly with his brass hammer on the table as if he had been a blacksmith at the anvil, accompanying every knock with a loud call for "Attention." Past-Colonel Birch, on the other hand, who acted as vice-chairman at the other end of the room, took the whole thing with the most perfect coolness, smoking his pipe as if he had been sitting at his own fireside, and never uttering a word, or making any attempt to restore subordination among the disorderly Troops, beyond an occasional gentle application of his hammer to the table. Amidst the Niagarian roar of Lumber Troop voices, which threatened to "split the house," as one of the visitors observed, that of Comrade Blood occasionally rose above all the rest. He was heard repeatedly to say, though no one paid the least attention to him — I rise to a pint — (Cries of "A pint of half-and-half," and laughter,) — of order; and I von't be called down by any one. Not by any comrade, he continued, after an expressive pause, and flourishing his right hand above his head in the air. I'm an old officer of this 'ere anshent and honourable Lumber Troop.—(Loud cries of "No, no.") Who's that a-saying "No, no," I should like to know? Several voices here said—"I say it," followed by roars of laughter, and an extraordinary scene of confusion, in the midst of which, Comrade Trope was repeatedly heard roundly rating the waiter for not bringing him a fresh supply of troop-sand.

At this moment, another Trooper named Tickler, rejoicing in the rank of lieutenant-colonel, who had been on his legs for the previous five minutes, but without uttering, or even attempting to utter a word, now laid down the glass of ale he held in his hand, and said, in a voice of stentorian power, "I'll stay here till the Troop break up, rather than be defeated in my attempts to obtain a hearing." (Cries of "I wish you may get it," drowned amidst exclamations of "Hear him, hear him.")

Lieutenant-colonel Tickler here looked at his watch: it wanted precisely two hours to the usual time of breaking up the meeting. At this moment, some one behind the gallant officer, as a proof of his respect for the Troop, and his own acquisitions in military discipline, put an open handkerchief with a yellow ground, and liberally embellished with large black spots, around his head, which made the upper story of the Trooper look wonderfully like a leopard's hide. The walls of Troop Hall literally resounded with the peals of laughter which followed. Not even the gallant Colonel himself who presided, could in this instance refrain from joining in the universal laugh, however indignant he must have been at the deplorable want of military respect which the party had exhibited.

When the roars of laughter had subsided, which they eventually did from the mere exhaustion of the Troopers, the cry of "Read the resolution" was again raised with redoubled vigour.

Lieutenant-colonel Tickler — Troopers may assail and attempt to annoy me in any way they please, but here I'll stand till I'm heard. I've got plenty of time. My time is of no importance. (Laughter, mingled with groans and hisses; in the midst of which, the gallant officer took out his box, and assisted himself to a pinch of snuff with the most perfect composure; after which he called for another go of brandy and water—the water to be quite hot.)

The Colonel here interposed with success, for the first time, and said, addressing himself to Lieutenant-colonel Tickler—If you wait till the resolution is read, I'll hear you for an hour, if you like. (Loud cheers, in which the Lieutenant-colonel cordially joined.)

At this moment, another officer, whose name I could not learn, rose, and was proceeding to address the Troop, but had not uttered many words, when his voice was drowned amidst the universal uproar which followed.

The resolution was at length permitted to be read; on which Comrade Blank rose, and moved—"That the standing order of the body be rescinded."

Lieutenant-colonel Tickler—Not "body;" "Troop," Sir, if you please."

Comrade Blank—Then "Troop," if you wish it, Mr. Critic; but I contend that the Troop is a body. (Loud cries of "No, no," and "Yes, yes," amidst stentorian instructions to the waiters to bring more troop-sand, and to fill up certain glasses again.)

A Trooper—The effect of the motion will be, if carried, to prewent the firing of the artillery on the Queen's wisit to the City. I vish to know vy ve should not persist in our original intention?

A host of voices—Because we've got a letter from the City authorities a-forbiddin' it. (Loud cries of "Read the letter.")

Comrade Jones—I advise the Troop to be cautious; for the public press is ready to hold us up to ridicule. (Tremendous cries of "No! no!" with equally loud exclamations of "Yes! yes!")

Comrade Jones, with an emphatic application of his fist to the table—I say *yes*, though. They ridicule us as smokers, revellers, and *uproarious* persons. (*Roars* of laughter.)

Comrade Blank—I rise, Colonel, officers, and comrades, to order. ("Hear! hear! hear! hear! hear.") Comrade Jones is quite out of order. He is not speaking to the question.

Comrade Jones (to Comrade Blank)—If you don't like my speech, I'm blow'd if you don't have a precious dose of it. (Deafening peals of laughter, mingled with cries of "Oh, oh!")

After a moment's pause, Comrade Jones gave a significant shake of his head, and said energetically—I say he *shall*, though; aye, and so shall the *Troop* too.—(Renewed bursts of laughter, with loud expressions of disapprobation.) I repeat——(Loud cries of "Question! question!") I'm astonished—(Here comrade Jones scornfully tossed his head, and curled his lip)—I'm astonished at those who cry 'Question.'—(Renewed cries of "Question! question!") Yes, I do say I'm asto——(Renewed cries of "Question! question!" from a score of voices.) Will any person tell me that I am not speaking to the question?

The ludicrous gravity with which this last sentence was spoken was so great, that another universal shout of laughter resounded through the room, as if all the Troopers had been subjected in a moment to the effect of a mental electrical agency,—if there be not an impropriety in the expression.

Comrade Jones—I repeat the question: will any man tell me that I am not speaking to the question?

Comrade Blank (winking at a friend)—I do.

As Comrade Blank uttered the last two words, he took a liberal draught of cold water.

Comrade Jones (assuming an aspect of great seriousness):—Will you tell me your name, Sir?—(Loud cries of "Order! order!")

Comrade Blank (quite coolly)—There is no occasion. (Laughter and cheers.)

Comrade Jones—I must know what comrade I am addressing. (Loud cries of "Order! order!" "Chair! chair!")

Comrade Blank—My name is Fergusson. (Loud laughter.)

A Trooper (with great energy)—I say that person's name is *not* Fergusson. (Tremendous uproar, during which the gallant Colonel in the chair, seeing the utter impossibility of preserving order, wisely determined, to use the phraseology of a Trooper, to let the unruly and awkward squad have their full swing.) The Trooper resumed, addressing himself to Comrade Blank—You, Sir, are humbugging the Troop. Yes, Sir; you are, Sir. (Cries of " Shame ! shame !")

Comrade Jones (looking Comrade Blank fiercely in the face) — You, Sir, have some *aliases*, perhaps. (Renewed cries of " Order ! order !" and a frightful storm of uproar.)

The gallant Colonel, seeing the altercation and uproar were likely to be protracted to midnight, if not put a stop to, here interposed, and said that both comrades were out of order: Comrade Blood, in not asking the gentleman's name through the Chair; and he in giving a wrong name.

Comrade Blank—Very good, Colonel: my name is not Fergusson. I'll tell you what my real name is, if Comrade Jones sits down.

Comrade Jones—No, I won't. (Loud laughter.) Yes, I will. (Renewed peals of laughter.) William, fill up this glass again.

Comrade Blank—Now, then. I'll first tell you why I called myself Fergusson; and then (looking towards Comrade Jones) I'll give you my real name. It is—

Comrade Jones—I won't have it. (Loud laughter, and cries of " Oh ! oh !")

Comrade Blank—I won't answer any question unless I'm heard. My name is Blank; and if comrade Jones wishes my address, it is— (Here a tremendous burst of applause greeted Comrade Blank for the manly and courageous course which he adopted.) The reason why I gave a wrong name was, that I wished to have a little bit of pleasantry at Comrade Jones's expense. (Deafening cries of " Order ! order !" " Chair ! chair !" " Waiter, bring me another go of gin-and-water ;" " More troopsand here," &c.)

Comrade Jones—I'm quite delighted to hear it. (Loud laughter.) I assure— (A cry of " Order !" here proceeded from some one in the body of the Hall.) Who calls 'Order,' I should like to know? Will anybody call 'Order' again? I assure friend Blank that—

Comrade Blank—I rise to order, Colonel. I insist on my right to be called comrade. (Great applause.)

Comrade Jones (sneeringly)—Well, then, *Comrade* Blank gives me his address as if I wished to call him out. I never fights with any other weapon than this 'ere, (pointing to his tongue, amidst great laughter and loud cheers.) I wish, (continued Comrade Jones, looking to the Colonel;) I wish the Colonel would keep his brother officers in summut better order.—

(Loud cheers and laughter, mingled with a cry from the middle of the Hall, "William, bring me some more 'baccy.")

The Colonel—O, but I can't. (Shouts of laughter.)

Comrade Strap—I rise, Colonel, to move—

Comrade Pewter—I rise to order. I say—

Comrade Strap—*I* say, Sir, you hold your chat. (Laughter, and cries of "Order! order!') I'm in possession of the chair and the Troop, Sir. I move, as an amendment to the motion for rescinding the resolution, that it be allowed to stand; my object being, that the guns should be fired on her Majesty's visit to the City.

Comrade Blank—I rise to object to the amendment. I maintain—

Comrade Jones (interrupting Comrade Blank*)—You assume too much, young man.—(Loud laughter.) You cannot object to it till it is seconded.—(Renewed laughter.)

Past-Colonel Hodson—I've seen many scenes in this place, but I've never seen any one equal to this. ("Hear! hear!") We are betrayed by Troopers. (Cries of "We are, we are.")

A Trooper (in a small penny-trumpet sort of voice):—Yes, ve is. I says it, too, past-colonel. Dash my buttons if we ain't a-being burlesqued! (Cries of "Hem! hem!")

Comrade Franks—All this has come from the doings of a disappointed past-suttler. (Immense applause.) Yes; von vot now vishes to disgrace this 'ere Troop. (Renewed plaudits.)

Here Comrade Blank handed up to the Colonel the motion he had made, as altered, and moved that it be read.

The Colonel commenced reading the resolution; but when he got to the third line, he made a dead pause.

Cries of "Read, read!" and "Go on!" resounded from all parts of Troop Hall.

A Trooper—It's very easy to bawl out—anybody could do that—'Read, read!' and 'Go on;' but *can* the Colonel read the writing?—Some more 'baccy, vaiter."(Loud laughter.)

The Colonel—No; I can't; and I don't think anybody could. (Laughter and cheers.)

Comrade Blank—Give it to me, and I'll read it. (Cries of "No, no; it must be read by the Colonel.")

Comrade Blank—Then I insist that the Colonel read the alterations made with the pencil.—Waiter, bring me some cold water. (Loud laughter.)

The Colonel again closely scrutinized the pencilship, but was still unable to proceed.

Comrade Blank—Oh! you can't read it.

---

* Comrade Blank is a young man.

Comrade Sprat—I rise to order. There's another insult to the Colonel. I'll take (to the waiter) another go of brandy-and-water, William.

The Colonel (his face brightening up at the circumstance of being at last able to decipher the MS.)—Comrade Blank requests me to read the pencil writing *exactly* as it is. It is this, then, officers and comrades: "That the s*l*anding orders—" (Loud laughter, and yells of "Oh! oh! oh!")

The Colonel—I don't doubt that it means s*t*anding orders; but I have read it as desired, exactly in the way in which it is written.

A Trooper (addressing himself very indignantly to Comrade Blank)—Yes, Sir, you never scores the tops of your t's.

"No, you don't, Sir," echoed a dozen voices, their proprietors severally standing up as they delivered themselves.

A Trooper—You *ought* to score your t's, Comrade Blank.

Another Trooper (with great emphasis)—And *vy* don't you do it, Comrade Blank?

Comrade Scraggs—Really, if we go on at this rate, we'll never get through the business before the Troop (Loud cries of "Hear! hear!" and of "Question! question!")

Comrade Tugworth—I move that the amendment be put to the vote.

A Trooper—Vat *is* the amendment? May I be pounded in a druggist's mortar, if I knows.—Vaiter, just bring me a little more troop-sand. (Peals of laughter.)

Comrade Duckster—We can't put the amendment, because it's not formal. ("Hear! hear!")

Comrade Blank—O, never mind formalities: don't stand on them.—(Loud cries of "Order! order!" "Chair! chair!" and a scene of uproar, which defies description, followed this proposal to depart from the rules of the Troop.) The scene continued for some time; and during the greater part of it, a forest of hands were seen cleaving the air, and at least one half of the Troopers present were either on chairs, or on their legs on the floor; while the noise occasioned by the almost universal exclamations or apostrophes to the gallant Colonel, was not only discordant in the highest degree, but absolutely deafening. The Colonel wisely leaned back in his chair until the Troopers had in some degree exhausted themselves; while the past-colonel, who presided at the opposite end, renewed his old practice, on such occasions, of applying his hammer, with a slow but steady hand, to the table, at the rate, on an average, of ten times a minute by the Lumber Troop clock.

"I never saw such an unruly Troop," said the Colonel, with marked emphasis, and much vehemence of gesture, after order had been in some degree restored. "I never saw such an unruly Troop: I'll leave the chair directly."—(Loud cries of "No! no! Colonel; *don't* do that;" amidst a renewed scene of disorder and uproar.)

Comrade Tapster—The Colonel must put the original motion.

(Loud cries of "No! no!" "The amendment first,") followed the proposition, and the noise and confusion became still greater than before. Eight or ten Troopers were seen—for they could not be *heard*—addressing the Colonel at once; while others, in different parts of the Hall, were disputing with and abusing one another at the full stretch of their voice. Almost every one present was on his legs; while growls of "Bow, vow, vow!" groans of every kind, and zoological sounds in all their varieties—many of them I am certain never heard before in any menagerie—issued from every part of the room. And to complete the ludicrousness of the scene, voices were now and then heard calling on the waiter to bring a fresh supply of troop-sand, gin with cold water, brandy "vith varm vater," &c. Order being again in some degree restored,

Comrade Manson said—Though I seconded the amendment, I never *meant* to second it."—(Roars of laughter.)

The amendment was then withdrawn, and the original motion declared to be carried.

Comrade Blank then rose, and said—I am now about to make a motion for a vote of censure on the officer who wrote to the Lord Mayor about the intention of the Troop to fire their guns on her Majesty's visit to the City; and in doing this, I beg to assure the Troop that I am not to be put down by opposition bullies. (Deafening cries of "Order! order!" "Chair! chair!" and cries of "Apologize," from comrade Tapster.) I *will* apologize; and (looking Comrade Tapster in the face) I will pay you in gold instead of copper. (Loud laughter.) I am prepared to— (Here Comrade Blank was interrupted by a growl, exceedingly like that emitted by a surly Newfoundland dog, from the left-hand corner of the Hall.) If you, Colonel, don't put a stop to this under-growling work, I'll sit down at once. Unless I be supported— (Here the interruption was renewed from the same quarter, only that the sound was different.) Can you not, Colonel, put a stop to the braying of this animal? (Loud laughter.) The press has been aspersed this night; and before I make my motion, allow me to vindicate the press of London from the aspersions thrown on it. (Cries of "No! no! that has nothing to do with the question.") Well, then, since I am denied the liberty of vindicating the character of the London press, I'll confine myself to the motion.

Comrade Blank then proceeded to denounce, in the most uncompromising terms, the conduct of their officer, in writing to the Lord Mayor; and several other speakers gave expression to their sentiments in the same strain, amidst peals of applause which made the walls of Troop Hall resound again: and yet, notwithstanding all this, and the groans and clamour also, which were directed towards him from all parts of the room, the criminated party smoked away at his pipe, supplied as it was with additional troop-sand, and swilled suttler Beck's sparkling ale, as if nothing had been the matter. When his turn came to address the Troop in vindication of himself, he coolly rose, and after looking about him for some time, began in the usual military phraseology of "Colonel, officers, and comrades;" but before he proceeded farther, he was assailed by such a volley of yells, hisses, groans, and all sorts of menagerie sounds, that a discharge of the Troop's twenty-one guns, with their two mortars to boot, would have been comparative silence itself. The scene of uproar which had thus again commenced, lasted for nearly an hour, during which the accused Trooper took up his hat two or three times, and said he would "march" himself home for the night; but that he would be *happy* to hear his conduct discussed any other evening the Troop chose to appoint. On one of these occasions, he "marched" to the door of Troop Hall, but was induced to return again, on some Trooper promising he would be heard. The second presentation of himself, however, only served, if possible, to add to the uproar. Eventually he desisted from the attempt to address his comrades; but by this time almost every couple of Troopers in the Hall had involved themselves in a nice, snug, private quarrel of their own. The most noisy and the most distinguished of the number was a "man with a Macintosh;" but whether he was a Trooper, or only a visitor, nobody seemed to know. He conducted, with very great spirit, indeed, a smart quarrel with sundry Troopers at once. But his most formidable opponent was a knight of the thimble. "You're a tailor, Sir," said "the man with the Macintosh" to his valorous adversary, who was a tall lean personage.

"And you're a wagabond," retorted Snip, giving a smart knock on the table.

"Sir, I repeat, you're a *tailor*," said the other, sneeringly.

"And I say you're *vorse* nor a wagabond."

"Hold your tongue, old thread-the-needle."

"Sir, if you say that 'ere agin," said Snip, now wrought up to the highest pitch of passion,—"I'll knock your——; I will, as sure as I stands in this 'ere place."

"You'll do what, Sir?" observed the "man with the Macintosh," eyeing the knight of the thimble steadily.

"Just call me a tailor, agin, Sir."

"You are a tailor."

"I von't stand this insult any longer, may I——!"

Here the hand of the tailor was raised, with the view of suiting the action to the implied threat; but it was arrested in its descent towards the person of his antagonist by a friend who chanced at the moment to have elbowed his way towards the particular part of Troop Hall in which the embryo pugilists were stationed.

"What's all this about?" inquired Comrade Spunk, addressing his friend the tailor.

"It's that 'ere person has been a insultin' of me and my trade," replied the latter, pointing to the "man with the Macintosh."

"In what way?"

"Vy, he has called me a tailor, vich is no fault of mine. I couldn't help it, if my father put me to learn that 'ere bisness."

"Pooh, pooh!" said the other; "if that's all, it is not worth fighting about."

"Ay, but——"

The insulted tailor was about to say something, when the Colonel suddenly rose from his seat, and said that, as no attention was paid to him, there was no use in his sitting there.

"Good night, then, Colonel—I'm off," observed the "man with the Macintosh."

"And I'll be marching too," said another, taking up his hat, and walking himself out of Troop Hall.

"And we'd better all be gone," shouted a third.

The suggestion was received with acclamation; the Colonel observing that he had sate there for five hours without relief. The Troopers then quitted the Hall in a most irregular and unsoldierlike manner, without having either adjourned the discussion, or come to any decision on the motion before it.

I have always observed that the uproarious scenes which are so common in Troop Hall, occur when there is the greatest muster of the Troopers. When the attendance is but limited, nothing could pass off more smoothly or quietly. All are on the most friendly terms,—as comrades ought to be. They smoke their pipe, quaff their go of brandy-and-water, and enjoy their song in the most perfect harmony. The Colonel, Past-Colonel Birch, the Secretary, and a great many others whom it is unnecessary to particularize, are as pleasant and intelligent men as any one could wish to spend a social hour with.

One of the principal amusements of the Troopers, when there is no important business to transact, is to hear one another sing. And I have much pleasure in mentioning, that there are some very excellent vocalists among the body. I have repeatedly heard singing in Troop Hall which would do no discredit to persons who live, as Shakspeare would say, by "discoursing the sweet music" of their voices. And what has always been to me the source of supreme gratification, is the promptitude with which every Trooper responds to the call of the Colonel, when he appeals to some particular comrade for a song. I am far from meaning to say that there are no unmusical or inharmonious personages in the head-quarters: that could not be expected when there usually is so strong a muster; but this I will say, that I never heard a Trooper refuse to comply with the request of the gallant Colonel, when demanding a song, on the ground that he could not sing. Every visitor to Troop Hall must have contrasted this readiness to "favour the Troop with a song" with the hesitation and excuses, and affected inability to sing, which are so common in private society. To be sure, there are several Troopers who exhibit no variety, either in the matter or style of their singing. They have but one song, and but one way of singing it: still they show their subordination by so readily complying with the call of their Colonel for a song. They do their best, and more cannot be expected from any one. There is one Trooper who has for years treated his comrades to the same song almost every night he has been present; and yet, notwithstanding the frequency with which he has repeated his vocal performance, he still sings the song with as much zest as he did the first time. It is due to the Troop to say, that, judging from the plaudits with which they receive it, and the fervour and unanimity with which they join in the chorus, they are no less pleased than the gentleman himself. I am sorry that I do not now recollect some of the verses of this song; for, if I did, I would give a specimen or two, because I think there are some clever things in it. The chorus, as well as I can remember, is something like this:

"Now listen to me, if you please,
And I'll soon prove my words,
That the world is but a nest,
And we're all birds, birds."

It is impossible to convey any idea of the effect which is produced by a large body of the Troopers, causing the walls of Troop Hall to resound again by the fervour with which they sing this chorus.

Another Trooper is so devotedly wedded to a particular song, beginning with

"Mary's my lily, and Flora's my rose,"

that no consideration would induce him to sing any other. This Trooper is, I am told,—for I am not personally cognizant of the fact,—an undertaker by trade. He thinks he has a sort of prescriptive right to monopolize the singing of this song in Troop Hall. Not long since, a comrade treated the Troop to the same song. It was clear that the undertaker was mortified beyond measure at the circumstance,—the more especially as the vocal performance of his rival was greeted with loud applause. Every manifestation of approbation was like plunging a dagger into the bosom of the poor undertaker. Some of his friends observing this, expressed their opinion that he sang the song much better than his rival. Some admirers of the vocal capabilities of the latter, intimated their dissent from this. A fierce discussion in the first instance, and afterwards a rather violent altercation, as to the comparative merits of the vocal rivals, followed. It was eventually proposed that they should both sing again, and that the sense of the Troop should be taken as to whose vocal performance was most meritorious. The undertaker declined the competition that evening, on the alleged ground that he did not then feel himself in good condition for singing; but signified his readiness to enter the lists with his rival on the next meeting of the Troop. The proposal was agreed to. In the interim,—the interim, namely, of a week,—there was a constant clearing of throats, and an assiduous preparation on the part of the rivals for the grand vocal competition. Troop Hall was crowded on the next Wednesday evening, to enjoy the affair. Comrade Swan, the opponent of the undertaker, was called on by the Colonel for a song, and the other promptly responded to the call, by singing, in his best style,

"Mary's my lily, and Flora's my rose."

The applause was pretty cordial, and general; but the Troopers were surprised to find that nine or ten persons, sitting beside each other, and rejoicing in what Mr. O'Connell would call "churchyard-looking" visages, were wonderfully active, fervid, and unanimous, in their expressions of disapprobation of Comrade Swan's vocal exhibition. It was now the undertaker's turn to sing. After taking out of his pocket a handkerchief of a greater number of colours than Sir Isaac Newton ever dreamed of, and applying it to his forehead for the purpose of drying up a perfect pool of perspiration which had gathered there, in consequence of the agony of fear as to the result under which he laboured,—he gave two or three forced coughs, with the addition of a couple of hems, and then commenced. Before he had finished the first note, the assemblage of demure-looking personages, already referred to, burst forth, as if moved by some unaccountable sympathy with each other, into a literal roar of applause. Of course

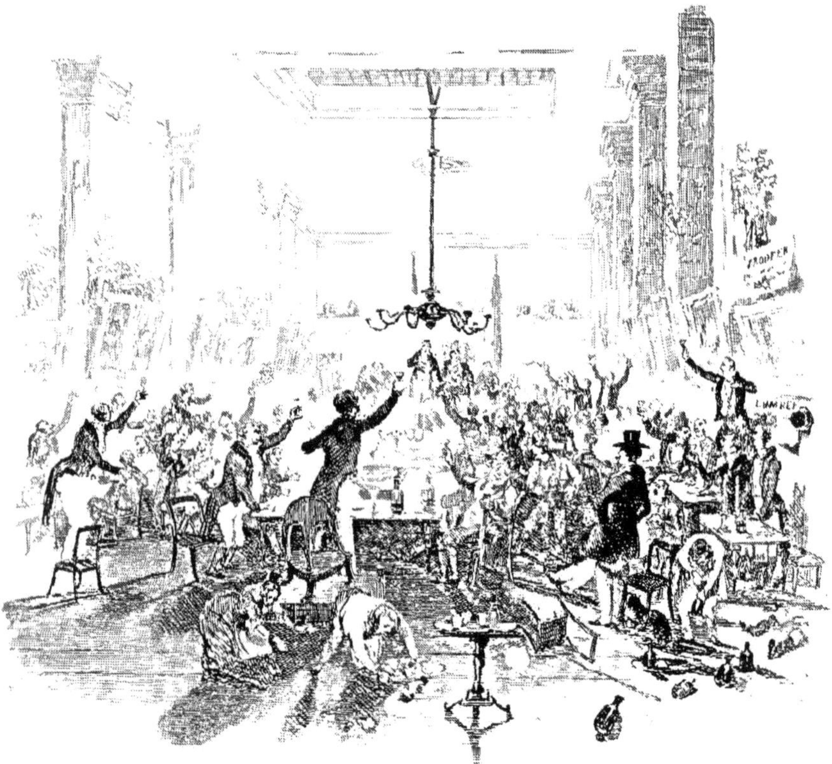

the undertaker's voice was drowned; while that of the Colonel, in calling "Attention!" "Silence!" and so forth, was scarcely in the first instance heard. Their cheers at last died away; but were renewed with undiminished energy when the undertaker had reached the end of verse the first. A regular round of applause from the same vociferous party followed the last word of each succeeding verse,—in which plaudits, several of the most disciplined of the Troopers, carried unconsciously away by their enthusiasm, could not refrain from joining. It was clear to all that the undertaker was greatly encouraged by these demonstrations of applause; for he waxed more and more confident, till he reached the end of the song, when he concluded by a vocal flourish, appropriately accompanied by a flourish of his right hand in the air, which afforded demonstrative proof that he already regarded himself as the victor. The melancholy-looking gentry, who had been so active in cheering the songster as he proceeded, rose to their feet as he resumed his seat, and waving their hats above their heads, rent the air of Troop Hall with their plaudits. A general, though more moderate manifestation of applause from the Troopers, confirmed the undertaker's anticipations of a triumph over his rival. The Colonel was about to put the question to the vote, as to who had sung "Mary's my lily, and Flora's my rose," best, when one of the proprietors of the demure physiognomies unguardedly shouted aloud, "Vy, master's von the day, to be sure: he be the best; blow me, if he ben't."

The Troopers first looked at each other with amazement, and then at the stranger who had made the unintelligible remark.

"Who are you, Sir?" said the Colonel, authoritatively.

"Who am I?" answered the other, coolly.

"Aye; *who* are you?" interrogated the Colonel, with increased emphasis.

"Vy, I be's in the sarvice of that 'ere gemman," pointing to the undertaker, "vot's jost a-been a-singin'; and ve came to this 'ere place to——"

Here another of the sombre-looking party suddenly started up, and clapping his hand on the mouth of the speaker, caused him to break off in the middle of the sentence.

"Come, do tell us what you came here for," said the Colonel, beginning to suspect that something was wrong. The undertaker's countenance exhibited double its usual longitude, as the gallant gentleman put the question.

"*Must* I tell?" inquired the other, with great simplicity.

"Certainly you must," exclaimed a host of Troopers at once.

"No, don't," whispered one of the demure-looking gentry.

"Order, Sir!" said the Colonel, with some sternness, looking the latter hard in the face. The undertaker now appeared as crest-fallen as if he had been about to be expelled from the Troop.

"Come, Sir," repeated the Colonel, "tell us what you came here for."

"Vy, then, if so be as I must speak the truth, master engaged nine on us to come here to-night, and to cheer his song, and to hinterrupt the gemman vot's sung before him. Ve are all in master's sarvice: ve assists him in performing funerals."

It is impossible to describe the effect produced on the Troopers by this unexpected disclosure of one of the undertaker's mutes. The conduct of the party, so unaccountable before, was perfectly intelligible now. The undertaker saved himself from a vote of censure in his own presence, for the deception he had practised, by snatching up his hat, and quitting Troop Hall with an edifying expedition. He has never since crossed its threshold.

I have often admired the polite way in which the Lumber Troop rid themselves of the presence of any comrade who has so far forgotten himself, and the respect due to the ancient and honourable body with whom he is associated, as to get drunk. The Colonel authoritatively desires the suttler, for the time being, to "see that gentleman safely conducted out of the Hall." A more genteel way of ejecting a troublesome customer, I hold it were impossible to imagine. The suttler, thus instructed by the Colonel, gently, in the first instance, takes hold of the inebriated comrade by the breast of the coat. If the latter offers no resistance, but resigns himself to the safe guidance of the suttler, good; all passes off quietly enough. But if he takes it into his head to refuse quitting Troop Hall, as intoxicated comrades often do, then he must expect to be handled a little more roughly. The suttler brings all the physical energy of which he is proprietor, to bear on the forcible ejectment of the refractory Trooper; and if he be not competent for the task himself, there are always plenty of comrades present, willing and ready on a moment's notice, to lend a helping hand in a work which so nearly concerns the honour and respectability of the Troop. My only surprise is, that the Troop content themselves with the mere ejection of such persons, and the exaction of a fine of a shilling or sixpence, according as the offender is an officer or a private. If I were a Trooper, one of the first motions I would make, would be, that such members of the body as could disgrace both themselves and the Troop in this way, should be expelled at once. It strikes me, that this would be the proper course to adopt, if the Troop are desirous of insuring well-conducted soldiers, and due decorum in the proceedings at head-quarters. I am sure I need not repeat that, under the existing system of discipline, singularly lenient as that system is, the breaches of military subordination are of rare occurrence, when the number of Troopers is considered. But the adoption of a more rigid code would have the effect of purging the Troop of all disreputable persons. And here let me observe, that I would be for bringing under the operation of the code I am recommending, all those comrades, whether drunk or sober, who persist in creating a disturbance in Troop Hall, by unnecessarily interrupting the due course of the proceedings. There are many individuals, as may be inferred from what I have said in a former part of the chapter, who join the Troop for no other purpose in the world than that of getting up what they call "scenes." There ought to be a law for the summary expulsion of such individuals. It was clear, that there were many of these individuals in Troop Hall on the evening of the first of last month, when the scene, of which I have attempted to give some idea in a previous part of the chapter, occurred. And had the strict system of discipline I am recommending obtained at that time, and been duly enforced, all the disturbance and uproar, which threw so much discredit on the proceedings that evening, would have been prevented. My plan would be very simple: I would hold it competent for any Trooper to move that any comrade, whom he supposed to be seeking to create a disturbance, or to burlesque the Troop, ought to be expelled Troop Hall at once. Let the question then be put to the vote, and there would at once be an end to the matter.

As it is, as before mentioned, any person wishing to enjoy two or three hours' peaceable and pleasant conversation at a cheap rate, may have it at the small charge of twopence, by going to Troop Hall in the capacity of a visitor, on the Wednesday evenings, when what is called the usual meetings of the Troop are held. The lovers of uproar and confusion—for singular as the taste is, there are some persons who only feel themselves in their element when in the midst of such scenes—may have their tastes gratified to their heart's content, by visiting Troop Hall on those evenings appropriated for the election of officers, or for the transaction of other important Lumber Troop business. The annual election of officers takes place about the middle of next month, when, as a matter of course, the usual amount of disorder, noise, and uproar, will be exhibited.

If any one is ambitious of being a member of the Troop, in order that he may have a right to take part in their discussions, and to vote on all questions submitted for discussion, surely the annual payment of five shillings is not too great a price for so important a privilege. Let no man be deterred from allowing himself to be put in nomination for membership, from an apprehension that his pretensions to the honour will be too severely scrutinized. There could not be a more unfounded apprehension. To speak the truth, there is not—unless under some very peculiar circumstances—any scrutiny at all. A Trooper proposes that Mr. So-and-so "be admitted a member of the Ancient and Honourable Lumber Troop;" another Trooper seconds the motion; and the Colonel, addressing himself to the party nominated, who receives a hint to assume a perpendicular position on the occasion, says—"Is it, Mr. So-and-so, with your own free-will and consent, that you are proposed for admission into this Ancient and Honourable Lumber Troop?" The party either answers "Yes," or gives an affirmative nod; and is that instant pronounced by the Colonel to be a Trooper.

It is really amusing to hear the Troopers talking in regular military style. Many of them can do it with the strictest propriety. I doubt if Wellington himself be more conversant with military phraseology than are some of the Lumber Troopers of the greatest standing. I am almost convinced that the officers do, on particular occasions, forget that they are plain citizens, and that they actually, for the time being, fancy themselves to be officers of regular regiments of soldiers. Even their written addresses are penned in the genuine military style. Let any one who doubts this, visit Troop Hall at his convenience, and he will see the walls placarded with the following:

TROOPERS!

SUPPORT YOUR BENEVOLENT FUND!

And here let me give expression to the hope, that the appeal thus made to the Troopers will be promptly responded to, and that a liberal support will be extended to the Benevolent Fund; for the object of that fund is truly benevolent, being nothing else than to assist Troopers who, by ill health, old age, or adverse circumstances, are fit subjects of relief by those who are more fortunate in the world.

There are two of the rules of the Lumber Troop which appear to me to be exceedingly injudicious, in so far as respects the enlistment of new soldiers. I refer to the rule which prohibits the drinking of ale or porter out of any pewter vessel; and to that which denies the members permission to eat anything in the character of Troopers.

With regard to the first prohibition, everybody knows that there are many persons who would rather not drink ale or porter at all, than drink either out of a glass. Their affection for pewter pots is so great, that one cannot help thinking there is something in the peculiar metal itself as palatable to their taste, though only put to their mouths, as is the liquid which it contains. One of the late Irish M.P.'s was so devotedly attached to drinking porter out of a pewter pot, that he rather preferred running the risk, when he went into any tavern, of being voted, as he used to say, "ungenteel," than submit to the privation of not having the liquid in a pewter pot. His plan for concealing his metallic partialities from the other persons in the room, was to instruct the waiter, when he brought in the porter, to place it under the table. This done, the ex-honourable gentleman bowed down his head, and took draught after draught of Whitbread and Co.'s "Entire," as occasion required, replacing the pewter pot with its contents, each time, in its locality beneath the table. Supposing, now, that the quondam M.P. for D——, had intended to join the Lumber Troop, the circumstance of pewter vessels being prohibited in Troop Hall would, with him, have been an unconquerable objection to his becoming a comrade. And I have no doubt whatever, that many others who would have shed a lustre on the Troop, have been deterred from enlisting themselves under its banners for the same reason.

As regards the prohibition of eating anything in the head-quarters, I am no less convinced that it has largely contributed to keep down the numbers of the Troop. Many people have no notion of sitting for hours in a public-house, swilling ale or porter, or quaffing go after go of brandy-and-water, without partaking of something of a solid kind. It is only a short time since the Troopers had a practical illustration furnished them of the strong disapprobation with which some persons regard the rule which prohibits eating, as well as drinking out of the pewter. A stout country-looking man, whose dialect clearly proved that he was a recent importation from Yorkshire, chanced to drop one evening into Troop Hall, without knowing anything of the Troop. William, as usual, before the visitor had well seated himself, seductively inquired, looking up in his face, what he would take. "A pint of half-and-half," was the answer.

"Yes, Sir," said the waiter, and away he flew to meet the wishes of his customer. In an incredibly short time he returned with the liquid in a glass vessel, and was in the act of depositing it on the table before the Yorkshireman, when the latter said, "Be kind enough to bring it me in the pewter."

"No pewter jugs allowed, Sir, to-night."

"Why not?"

"Oh, Sir, because it's a rule of the place."

"Coom, coom, none of your nonsense," said the other, as if looking on the thing as a joke.

"Quite true, Sir, I assure you," repeated William, with much politeness.

"Are you serious?"

"Perfectly so."

"Oh; then there is no help for it, I suppose. Just bring me a crust of bread and cheese."

"Can't, Sir," said the waiter.

"Can't bring a customer some bread and cheese!" said the Yorkshireman, looking as much amazed as if he were at a loss to know whether or not he ought to credit the evidence of his ears. "Why, good man, I don't want it for nothing: I mean to pay for it."

"Don't doubt that, Sir; but can't bring it. It's contrary to the rules."

"What rules?" inquired the other, with considerable emphasis.

"The rules of the Troop, Sir."

"The Troop! What Troop?"

"The Ancient and Honourable Lumber Troop, Sir."

The countryman was as much in the dark as before; but some one sitting beside him entered into such details as eventually enabled him to form some idea of the nature of the institution.

"But still," he observed, after the other had concluded his explanations; "but still, I don't see why a man should coom into a public-house to be refused bread and cheese, when he is willing to pay for it.—Waiter, you bring me some."

"Can't do it, Sir," answered William, pathetically.

"But I insist that you shall. I have a right to demand it," said the other, with considerable warmth; his Yorkshire blood rising some degrees at the reiterated refusal to meet his wishes.

A regular squabble ensued between the countryman and several of the Troopers around him, in consequence of their asserting the propriety of the prohibition.

"Who is that gentleman?" inquired the Colonel, while the altercation was at its height. "Is he a Trooper?"

"He is only a visitor," answered two or three voices at once.

"Then, Mr. Beck, you see that gentleman conducted safely along the passage," said the Colonel.

Mr. Beck advanced for this purpose, when the Yorkshireman dared any man to lay a hand upon him, but signified his intention of quitting Troop Hall of his own accord. He accordingly proceeded along the passage, and on reaching the door, took the knob in his hand, and, turning about, shouted as loud as he was able, "What a precious starved squad you must be, when you never goes to mess!" and so saying, he violently slammed the door, and *bolted* out of Bolt-court.

CHAPTER IV.

THE VICTORIA PARLIAMENT.

Meeting of Parliament—Taking the oaths—Introduction of a new Peer into the House of Lords—Further observations on taking the oaths—Mr. O'Connell's manner in taking the oaths—Opening of the Parliament by her Majesty in person—Appearance of the House of Lords on the occasion—Conduct of the members of the House of Commons on being summoned into the presence of the Queen—The Queen's delivery of her speech—Her Majesty's personal appearance—Moving the Address in the Lords, in answer to the Queen's speech—The Duke of Sussex—Lord Portman—Lord Brougham—The Address in the Commons—Lord Leveson—Mr. Gibson Craig—Scenes in the House of Commons—A missing amendment which had been moved by Mr. Daniel Whittle Harvey—Parliamentary débuts in the present session—Mr. Blewitt—Mr. D'Israeli—Remarks on the reception of the latter gentleman by the House—New members—Miscellaneous observations.

The day appointed for the meeting of the present parliament was Wednesday, the 15th of November. On that day the Commons limited their proceedings to the re-election of Mr. Abercromby as speaker. In the Lords, they were confined to the usual formality of reading her Majesty's writ,—the Commons being assembled at their Lordships' bar,—authorising the meeting of the new parliament. Thursday, Friday, Saturday, and the early part of Monday, were occupied with swearing in the members of both Houses. The oaths taken on these occasions are two: the oath of allegiance, and that which disclaims all faith in the Roman Catholic religion. No member in either House can take his seat, or vote on any question, until he has taken the first oath. The second, as a matter of course, is only taken by Protestants. For the Roman Catholic Peers, and the Roman Catholic Commons, a different oath is provided: they are made to swear that they will do nothing in their capacity of members of the legislature to deprive the Church of England of any part of its property, nor seek to injure it in any way. It was curious to witness the exposition lately given in both Houses, of the peculiar notions of particular individuals on the subject of the Roman Catholic religion. Lord Melbourne, Earl Mulgrave, and others of the more liberal Whigs, seemed, judging from the careless and indistinct manner in which they muttered over the words of the oath, to look upon it as a piece of mere mummery; while Lords Kenyon, Roden, Winchilsea, and others of the ultra Tory party, repeated the words with a seriousness of countenance, and an emphasis of manner, which showed that they felt what they uttered. The oath in question disclaims all belief in the doctrine of transubstantiation, or in the propriety of praying to the Virgin Mary, or other saints. The praying to saints, and the sacrifice of the mass, the parties taking the oath declare to be idolatrous. All acknowledgment of the authority of the Pope is also disclaimed. In the House of Lords, the Lord Chancellor sat as motionless and mute on the woolsack, while the two clerks were administering the oaths to the Peers, as if he had been a statue. I have often pitied the noble and learned Lord before, while doomed to witness the nonsense which such men as Lord Londonderry and the Duke of Newcastle were inflicting on the House; because, while other Peers can escape the visitation by quitting the House, he must remain on the woolsack to hear every word they utter; and what is more, must, as a matter of courtesy, appear to listen with respectful attention to everything they say. Great, however, as has been my compassion for the Lord Chancellor on the occasions to which I refer, it never was half so great as when witnessing him on the woolsack during the four days he was compelled to sit there while the oaths were being administered to the Peers. His Lordship's face is grave at any time: on the occasions to which I allude, it was peculiarly so. And no wonder; for what could be more tiresome than to have his ears dinned by hearing the same everlasting oaths so often repeated? Nonsensical speeches, if they have no other recommendation, have at least this one—that there is variety in them. Here all was an unbroken monotony; and what is more, a monotony of a very unpleasant kind. To be sure, a Peer, either on his entrance, or after he had taken the oaths and his seat, now and then advanced to the woolsack, and shook hands with the noble and learned Lord; but this was scarcely worthy of the name of variety. The most interesting little episode which occurred while I was present, in the four days' *sederunt* of his Lordship, took place when the new Bishop of Hereford was being admitted to the House as a spiritual peer. One of the leading officers of the House, whose duty it is to see that none but Peers be permitted to pass the bar, having observed the right reverend prelate standing outside the bar, with some other bishops behind him, while the Bishop of Durham, who had undertaken to introduce him, was motioning him to follow,—sprang to the bar from the centre of the House, where he chanced to be standing at the time, and inquired audibly of the reverend prelate, whether he had brought his writ with him?

"I have," answered the right reverend prelate; and as he spoke, he produced the important piece of paper.

"Then you may walk in," said the officer, opening the little iron door, and admitting his reverence.

The latter, preceded by the portly Bishop of Durham, and followed by another ecclesiastical dignitary, then advanced to the table of the House, where the clerks were in readiness to swear in the new member. One clerk stood on the ministerial side of the table, and the other on the Tory side. Whether this was indicative of the respective political views of the parties, or was the result of pure accident, or agreeably to some usual arrangement, are points on which I can give no opinion; nor is the matter of much importance either way. I allude to the circumstance of the two clerks being thus, as regarded local position, pitted against each other, for the purpose of mentioning, that the clerk on the ministerial side handed over to the one on the Tory side, a small slip of paper, carefully folded up. The latter opened the piece of paper, and began reading thus:—"To our trusty and well-beloved, James, Earl of—" Here he suddenly paused, and looked confounded. The fact flashed on him that he had been reading the wrong writ, and tossing it over to the clerk, on the opposite side, from whom he had received it, indicated by his looks that he thought his colleague had committed a very stupid blunder. The error, however, was forthwith rectified, by the proper piece of paper being handed over to him whose duty on the occasion it was to read aloud the authority on which the new bishop was about to be recognised as a member. Instead of "the Earl of," the words "right reverend father in God" greeted the ears of every one present. The reverend prelate then proceeded to take the oaths; which having done, he laid down the paper and the New Testament on the table, and looked about him with a strangeness of manner which denoted that he was in a place which was new to him. A few seconds passed before the Bishop of Durham, who acted on the occasion as his "guide, philosopher, and friend," gave any indication of an inclination to budge from the spot on which he stood; during which time the new spiritual peer looked as if he had been saying in his own mind, "Well, I wonder what comes next!" The thing that came next was, that the Bishop of Durham, instead of going the nearest way to the bench of bishops, in order that the new-made spiritual legislator might comply with the form of "taking his seat," took the most circuitous way to the ecclesiastical locality which he possibly could,—the Bishop of Hereford and the other unknown bishop following his reverence with a most exemplary docility. The form of taking the seat having been gone through, the Bishop of Durham introduced the Bishop of Hereford to the Lord Chancellor, sitting, as before mentioned, as if "the sole inhabitant of some desert isle," on the woolsack. His Lordship seized the extended hand of the newly-admitted spiritual peer with so much energy,—arising doubtless from the cordiality with which he congratulated him on being added to the members of the House,—that he almost pulled him down on his own knee. After about half a minute's conversation with the noble and learned Lord, the Bishop of Hereford left the House, in the company of his right reverend friends.

In the swearing-in of the members of the Lower House, there were also many amusing circumstances to be seen. It was not only amusing, but sometimes laughable, to see those gentlemen returned for the first time, when about to take the oaths. The members, including old and new, advanced to the table on several occasions in droves of from a dozen to a dozen-and-a-half; and anything more awkward than the movements of the newly-fledged legislators it were impossible to imagine. But decidedly the best scene of all was exhibited on Friday, when upwards of one hundred members were sworn in at once. Some of the new M.P.'s stared at the huge proportions of the Speaker's wig, as if they had been afraid of the article; but what chiefly embarrassed them was, to ascertain the position which they ought respectively to occupy at the table. They dashed against each other, displaced each other, and trod on each other's toes, just as if engaged in a regular jostling match. An Irishman would have thought the thing an imitation of a row. At one time, two or three were seen snatching at the same copy of the New Testament; and immediately after, the same two or three legislators were seen holding the book at once with an air of great gravity. The limited supply of the sacred volume—limited, I mean, as compared with the number of gentlemen being sworn in at one time—rendered this necessary. The various moods of mind in which the oaths were evidently taken, afforded matter for curious reflection. Those of liberal politics, and of latitudinarian notions respecting denominational differences in religion, clearly regarded, like the Whig Peers, those portions of the oath which relate to the Roman Catholic faith as a species of mummery; for they hummed over the words in that careless and impatient manner in which a school-boy repeats an ungrateful task. They often looked, on the sly, off the printed slip whence they read, just as boys of a trifling disposition do at school when they fancy the eye of the pedagogue is not on them. The Tories, on the other hand, and all who entertained a conscientious horror of the Roman Catholic religion, were remarkably serious and emphatic when repeating the portions of the oath which apply to it. I think it would have been no difficult matter, without any particular pretensions to a practical knowledge of the

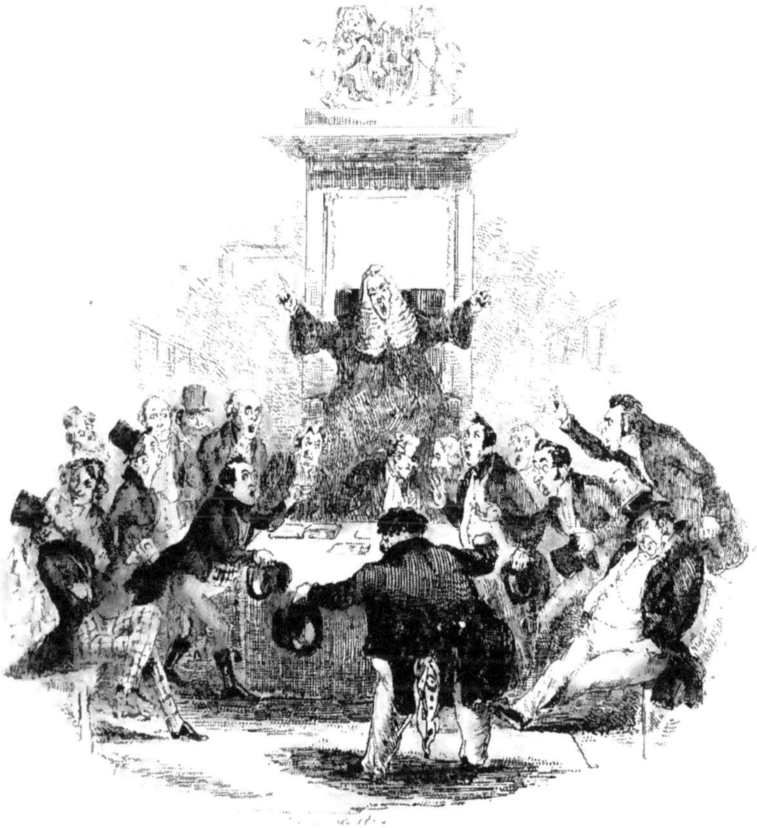

system of Lavater, to have distinguished between the more devout of the Tories and the more latitudinarian of the Liberals, from a simple glance at their several countenances while reading the denunciations against certain points in the Roman Catholic faith. The grave visages of the former exhibited a marked contrast to the careless physiognomies of the latter.

The circumstance of so many persons audibly repeating the same words at once, had a singular effect on the auricular organs. Only fancy that you hear upwards of one hundred individuals, all repeating in loud tones the same words after the clerk of the House of Commons,—words, too, which many of them had never pronounced before,—and you will easily conceive what must have been the variety of voices, and the deviation from the proper time in the delivery, which must have been exhibited on the occasion. Anything more inharmonious, it has happily been but seldom my lot to listen to. It needed not aught of the prophetic spirit, after hearing the voices and elocution of many of the honourable gentlemen, to predict that they were not destined to achieve any remarkable oratorical triumphs on the floor of the House of Commons.

While the large assemblage of members, of whom I have been speaking, were undergoing the initiatory process of taking the oaths, a rather awkward circumstance occurred. I refer to the fact, that at the same time another of the clerks was engaged in administering a different oath to six or seven Roman Catholic members standing at the same table; so that the latter were obliged to submit, without even a word of murmur, far less of remonstrance, to hear themselves denounced by the Protestant members as idolaters, for whom a certain doom, which I shall not here mention, is in sure reserve. This might have been avoided by administering the oath to the Catholics at an after period

Mr. O'Connell came into the House by himself. His ever smiling and ample countenance, redolent of health and of a cheerful disposition, delighted all present as his athletic person was recognised passing the bar, and swaggering up towards the table. It is a positive luxury, in an assemblage where there are so many artificial dandies and sprigs of fashion, to witness the plain, farmer-like appearance, and unsophisticated manners of Mr. O'Connell. Advancing to the corner of the table, on the ministerial side of the House, next the Speaker's chair, the honourable member intimated to one of the clerks that he was ready to take the oaths. The clerk, having placed the oath of allegiance in his hand, forthwith commenced reading it. Mr. O'Connell not being able to read without the aid of an eye-glass, and not having taken out of his pocket that necessary auxiliary to his vision in time to enable him to start with the clerk, was obliged to repeat the words, for some time, after the clerk, without knowing whether the latter was reading correctly or not. All this while, the honourable gentleman was making a most active search for his glass, first in one pocket, then in another; when eventually alighting on it, he promptly raised it to his eyes, and carefully read the remainder of the oath,—as he also did the one administered only to Roman Catholics,—from the printed copy before him. It was amusing to observe the slow and cautious way in which he repeated the words after the clerk before he was in a condition to read the oath, contrasted with the rapidity of his utterance when reading it himself off the printed copy. In fact, he had hardly commenced reading the document, when it must have struck all present that, instead of following the clerk, he was rather in advance of him. It looked, indeed, as if there had been a regular match between the two as to who should read the oath most rapidly; while it was beyond all question that Mr. O'Connell was the winner. While this exhibition of rapid-reading rivalry was going on, Mr. O'Connell, instead of taking the document in his hands, as the members usually do when going through the ceremony of being sworn in, laid it on the table, and applying his glass to his eyes with his left hand, thrust the fingers of his right one between his black neckerchief and his neck, at intervals of a few seconds, until he had got to the end of the oaths. Mr. O'Connell read the whole of the oaths in a distinct and audible, though rapid, manner; but was repeatedly observed to lay peculiar emphasis on particular expressions. He laid remarkable stress on that part of the oath of allegiance which refers to the Queen in particular. If any one had doubted the honourable member's loyalty before,—which no one, so far as I am aware, ever did,—they could no longer resist the conviction that he was not only a loyal subject, but that he was one of the most loyal subjects in her Majesty's dominions. Having got through the ceremony of swearing in, Mr. O'Connell took up the Roman Catholic oath, and then contemptuously tossed it down again on the table, as if he had either had some private quarrel with it, or deemed it an altogether unnecessary affair. This done, he glanced some half-dozen of his own peculiar smiles at some of the honourable members beside him, and then went over to the Speaker, with whom he cordially shook hands, and held a brief confabulation: after which, he took his seat for a few seconds, and then waddled out of the House again.

Nearly all the members of both Houses had taken the oaths by four o'clock on the Saturday. Those who had not done so, took them early on Monday, that being the day appointed for the Queen's opening the parliament in person, and no member

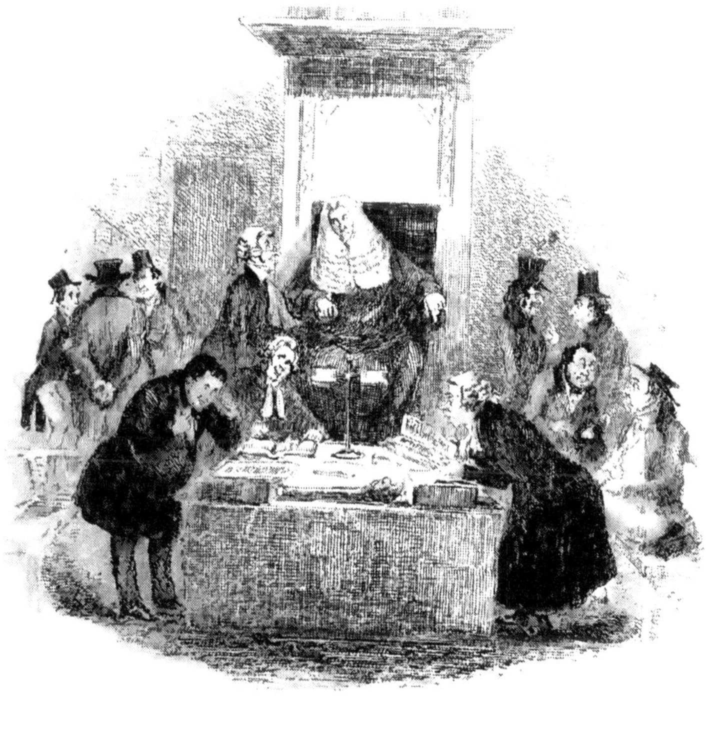

of either House being qualified to vote on any division that might take place on the Address, until the oaths had been taken.

The opening of a new parliament by the sovereign in person, is, at any time, a most interesting circumstance, and never fails to attract a large concourse of persons, not only to the vicinity of the parliament-house, but to every part of the line of procession. The interest of such an occurrence was, on this occasion, greatly heightened by the circumstance of this being not only the first parliament of the sovereign, but of that sovereign being an amiable female of the tender age of eighteen. Loyalty and gallantry, therefore, both combined to draw out the population of London on the occasion of Victoria's opening her first parliament in person. And as has hitherto been the case, on all the occasions in which our young Queen has appeared in public, the weather, on the day in question, was propitious in the highest degree. Under all these circumstances, it is not to be wondered at if the assemblage of persons who greeted Victoria with their plaudits on her way to and from her parliament, was far greater —as I am convinced it was—than were ever congregated together under similar circumstances. I have witnessed the openings of several parliaments by the sovereign in person; but the concourse of people on such occasions was nothing to what it was on the present. From Buckingham Palace to the Horse Guards there were two unbroken lines of persons as closely wedged together, ten or twelve deep, as it was possible for them to be; while from Charing-cross, down to Arlington-street, a distance I should suppose of about half-a-mile, the broad pavement on either side exhibited one dense mass of human beings. It is hardly necessary to say that the windows and tops of the houses, and every spot which could command a glimpse of the procession, were most thickly tenanted. In the fronts of most of the houses in Parliament-street, scaffoldings were erected, many of which were let out, while others were confined to the accommodation of friends. Palace-yard, again, exhibited one dense mass of cabs, coaches, carts, waggons, and vehicles of every kind, which were also let out for the occasion; and many a Jehu made a much more profitable couple of hours' work by letting out his vehicle in this way, than he could have done by driving about in the streets from morning to night with ordinary "fare." To compute, with anything like confidence of being near the mark, the number of persons who, on the 20th of November, were assembled together to get a glance of their young Sovereign, is what no man would undertake to do. Forming a rough conjecture on the subject, I should say it could not have been much under 200,000.

So early as twelve o'clock, the interior of the House of Lords was nearly filled by peeresses and their daughters; by one, it was quite full; and so great was the anxiety to obtain a view of the Queen while opening parliament, that even the gallery of the House of Lords was filled with the female branches of aristocratic families by twelve o'clock; all, as in the body of the House, in full dress. Lady Mary Montague gives a graphic description of the siege which a troop of duchesses, countesses, and other titled ladies, laid to the door of the gallery of the House of Lords when, in her time, some interesting debate was expected; and how, when they found, after a ten hours' assault, the gallery was not to be taken by storm, they succeeded in effecting an entrance by stratagem. The ladies, in the present case, were not under the necessity of attempting an entrance into the gallery by sheer physical force; for they had, in most cases, procured a lord-chamberlain's order of admission; but several of them effected an entrance by the persuasive eloquence of their pretty and fascinating faces, accompanied by a few honied words, which the officers could not resist; and which no man, possessed of an atom of susceptibility, to say nothing of gallantry, could, had he been in the officers' places, have withstood. But this was not all: not only did a number of ladies who had no order of admission from the Lord Chamberlain, meet with this wonderful facility of entrance; but some of them carried the joke still further, and actually took forcible possession of the front seat in the gallery, which is always specially and exclusively appropriated for the gentlemen of the press. This seat is capable, on an emergency, of containing, including a back form, about thirty persons, and yet only three reporters were fortunate enough to obtain admission; and even they, but for the accidental circumstance of having taken possession of their places the moment the door was thrown open, would also have been among the excluded. And what does the reader suppose would have been the consequence? Why, none other than this: that not one word of the important proceedings in the House of Lords, on the opening of the parliament by the Queen,—beyond a copy of the speech, which is always sent from the government offices to the newspapers,—could have appeared in next day's papers. Let the public imagine what an "untoward affair" this would have been, and be thankful that three gentlemen of the press were fortunate enough to secure their places in the gallery. The alacrity which the ladies displayed in possessing themselves of the seats set apart for the reporters, was truly astonishing. Philosophers tell us that nature abhors a vacuum, and that whenever one is created, she rushes in to fill it up. I am not myself philosopher enough to know with what expedition nature fills up such vacuums; but this I know, that she could not be much more prompt in her movements, than were the ladies in filling up the vacant seats intended for the gentlemen of the press, on this occasion. The three reporters already referred to, when they saw the rush of the ladies to take possession of the unoccupied seats, felt, in the first instance, inexpressible surprise; but on recovering themselves, the predominant feeling in their minds was one of gratitude to their stars that they had been fortunate enough to possess themselves of their places. There they sat for two long hours, amidst a large assemblage of the fairest of the fair, literally hid from the sight of those who were lucky enough to get a peep into the House from the door, by a forest of waving plumes of feathers of the richest kind. By one o'clock, the House had an appearance which, I am convinced may be said with truth, it has seldom, if ever, presented before. The whole of the benches on the floor and the two side galleries, were occupied by the female portion of the families of the Peers, all attired in their costliest and most magnificent dresses. I will not attempt to describe the effect produced on the mind of the spectator by the dazzling splendour of the jewellery they wore. Altogether, the spectacle was perhaps one of the most interesting of the kind ever witnessed in this or any other country. I have been in the House of Lords at the opening and proroguing of several previous parliaments by the sovereign in person; but on no former occasion was there any comparison with the scene in question, either as regarded the number of ladies present, or the imposing and brilliant aspect the place presented.

I could have wished that the opponents of Mr. Grantley Berkeley's motion for the admission of ladies into the gallery of the House of Commons, had been all present on this occasion: that is to say, provided there had been accommodation for them. There can be little doubt that, as respects a considerable number of these ungallant "honourable gentlemen," the real cause, though they have not the courage to own it, of their opposition to the admission of ladies into the gallery is, that they labour under the impression that ladies could not refrain from speaking to one another, and thus betray a want of proper respect for the House and its proceedings. As to the amount of respect which is due to the House and its proceedings, I beg to be excused from expressing an opinion; but this I feel bound to say, in justice to the sex, that the supposition that women could not, under any circumstances, refrain from speaking, is altogether groundless. It was proved to have been so on the occasion in question; and this under circumstances of a very trying nature; for all the ladies had to sit about two hours before the arrival of the Queen, and while there were no proceedings in the House; and yet everything was as quiet as the most devoted admirer of the "silent system" could have wished. I do not mean to say that the ladies remained all this time as mute as if they had been so many statues; but this I will say, without the fear of contradiction, that when one exchanged a word with another, it was done in a perfect whisper, so as to be audible, with few exceptions, to no one but her to whom it was addressed. If, then, an unbroken silence was observed by the ladies present, during the two tedious hours they were in the House without anything in the shape of proceedings to occupy their attention, what a groundless and ungallant imputation for the members of the House of Commons to say—and I myself have heard members say it in private,—that if ladies were admitted into their gallery, they could not refrain from speaking!

A little before two o'clock, a discharge of artillery announced that her Majesty was on her way to parliament. The first round startled many a "lady fair," as might be seen by the sudden and somewhat ungraceful nodding of so many plumes of feathers; but the momentary surprise over, every countenance beamed with joy at the thought that a sovereign of their own sex would in a very little time be seated on the splendid throne before them. A short time passed away, and the striking-up of a band of music on the outside, announced the near approach of her Majesty. A few moments more elapsed, and the thrilling tones of the trumpet intimated that Queen Victoria, though as yet unseen, was proceeding along the passage to her robing-room, and would be in the midst of them presently. That was a moment of intense interest, and it was visibly depicted in every countenance. Every eye momentarily expected to gaze on the youthful Queen, attired in her robes of state. In a few seconds more, Victoria entered the House. The Peeresses and all present simultaneously rose, while every breast throbbed with exultation at the sight of their sovereign. It was a sight to be seen, not to be described. The most lively imagination would fall far short of the reality: how fruitless, then, were any effort to attempt to convey any idea of it by mere description! There stood, in the presence of their young and interesting sovereign,—all emulating each other in doing homage to her in their hearts as well as outwardly,—the Peers and Peeresses of the land! It was a touching sight: it was a sublime spectacle: it was one which will never be forgotten by those whose happiness it was to witness it.

Her Majesty having taken her seat on the throne, desired the Peers to be seated. The intimation was known to be equally meant for the ladies. The Commons were then summoned into the royal presence. The summons was forthwith followed by a scene which strongly contrasted with that to which I have been alluding. There is a proverb, which is current in certain districts of the country, that some people are to be heard when they are not to be seen. The adage received a remarkable illustration in the case of the representatives of the people, on this occasion. No sooner had the door been opened, in obedience to the mandate of the Queen, which leads into the passage through which they had to pass, on their way to the bar of the House of Lords, than you heard a patting of feet as if it had been of the hoofs of some two or three score quadrupeds. This, however, was only one of the classes of sounds which broke on the ears of all in the House of Lords, and even of those who were standing in the passages leading to it. There were loud exclamations of "Ah! ah!" and a stentorian utterance of other sounds, which denoted that the parties from whom they proceeded had been suddenly subjected to some painful visitation. All eyes—not even excepting the eyes of her Majesty—were instantly turned towards the door of the passage whence the sounds proceeded. Out rushed, towards the bar of the House of Lords, a torrent of members of the lower House, just as if the place which they had quitted had been on fire, and they had been escaping for their lives. The cause of the strange, if not alarming sounds, which had been heard a moment or two before, was now sufficiently intelligible to all. They arose from what Mr. O'Connell would call the mighty struggle among the members, as to who should reach the House of Lords first, and by that means get nearest to the bar, and thereby obtain the best place for seeing and hearing. In this mortal competition for a good place, the honourable gentlemen exhibited as little regard for each other's persons as if they had been the principal performers in some exhibition of physical energy in Donnybrook Fair. They squeezed each other, jammed each other, trod on each other's gouty toes, and "punished" each other, as the professors of the pugilistic art phrase it, in every variety of form, without the slightest compunctious visiting. Hence the exclamations—in some cases absolute roars—to which I have alluded. The most serious sufferer, so far as I have been able to learn, was one of the honourable members for Sheffield, who had his shoulder dislocated in the violent competition to be first at the bar. Even after the M.P.'s were fairly in the presence of their Sovereign, there was a great deal of jostling and jamming of each other, which extorted sundry exclamations indicative of pain, though such exclamations were less loud than those before alluded to. The Irish members played the most prominent part in this unseemly exhibition; and next to them, the English ultra Radicals: the Tories cut but a sorry figure in the jostling match. The Liberals were, as the common saying is, "too many for them." I thought with myself at the time, what must the foreign ambassadors and their ladies who were present, think of English manners, should they unhappily form their notions on the subject, from the conduct on this occasion of the legislators in the lower House? It was a rather awkward exhibition for a body of men arrogating to themselves the character of being "the first assembly of gentlemen in Europe."

Her Majesty having taken the oath against Popery, which she did in a slow and serious, yet audible manner, proceeded to read the royal speech; and a specimen of more tasteful and effective elocution it has never been my fortune to hear. Her voice is clear, and her enunciation distinct in no ordinary degree. Her utterance is timed with admirable judgment to the ear: it is the happy medium between too slow and too rapid. Nothing could be more accurate than her pronunciation; while the musical intonations of her voice imparted a peculiar charm to all the other attributes of her elocution. The most perfect stillness reigned through the place while her Majesty was reading her speech. Not a breath was to be heard: had a person, unblessed with the powers of vision, been suddenly taken within hearing of her Majesty, while she was reading her speech, he might have remained some time under the impression that there was no one present but herself. Her self-possession was the theme of universal admiration. Nothing could have been more complete. The most practised speaker in either house of parliament never rose to deliver his sentiments with more entire composure. Nor must I omit to mention, that the manner of her Majesty was natural and easy in the highest degree: the utter absence of art or affectation must have struck the mind of every one present.

The speech being ended, Victoria descended from the throne, and with slow and graceful steps retired from the House to her robing-room, a few yards distant; nodding as she did on her entrance, to most of the peeresses whom she passed. In person she is considerably below the average height. Her figure is good; rather inclined, as far as one could judge from seeing her in her robes of state, to the slender form. Every one who has seen her must be struck with her singularly fine bust. Her complexion is clear, and has all the indications of excellent health about it. Her features are small, and partake a good deal of the Grecian cast. Her face, without being strikingly handsome, is remarkably pleasant, and is indicative of a mild and amiable disposition. She has an intelligent expression of countenance; and on all the occasions—three in number—on which I have seen her, has looked quite cheerful and happy.

On the conclusion of the Queen's speech, both Houses adjourned, as is usual on such occasions, till five o clock, when they again met to discuss the royal oration, and to consider the propriety of voting an address to her Majesty, expressive of the gratitude of the legislature for her most gracious speech.

In both Houses there was a large attendance of members, while the galleries were crowded with strangers. In proceeding along the passage which leads to the reporters' gallery in either House, immediately previous to the commencement of the debate, it was an interesting sight to witness the reporters of the evening newspapers, with a number of boys all ready to be despatched to their several offices with the copy in piecemeal so soon as prepared, sitting at a table, with the necessary apparatus of pen, ink, and paper before them, and each more eager than the other to give a practical proof of the accuracy and expedition * with which they could commit to paper, and then extend their notes for publication, the orations with which the minds of the various intended speakers were surcharged.

In the Lords, the address to the Queen was moved by the Duke of SUSSEX. To witness his Royal Highness on this occasion, was an interesting sight. Not only did the circumstance of his being for so many years a veteran in the cause of reform,—and that, too, in the worst of times,—necessarily give rise to a variety of associations, of the most hallowed kind, in the minds of all who wish well to the cause of human improvement; but there was something so exceedingly venerable in his personal appearance as could not fail to impart an unusual interest to everything which proceeded from his lips. There stood his tall and exceedingly stout person, immediately before the ministerial bench, not bowed down or decrepit by the load of sixty-four years, yet evidently feeble, in a physical sense, through the combined effects of advanced age and recent illness. His countenance wore a remarkably cheerful expression: it glowed with benevolence, and so far was an accurate index of his disposition. The tones of his voice, and the occasional energy of his manner, clearly showed that it was not from mere courtesy towards the ministers, that he had undertaken the task of moving the ad-

* The accuracy and despatch with which "The Sun" publishes its reports of the parliamentary proceedings, and of the speeches at public meetings, are really extraordinary; and can only be accounted for from the circumstance of Mr. Young being so fortunate as to have a *corps* of reporters, who unite the greatest zeal towards the establishment, with first-rate professional abilities. Mr. Young's achievements in parliamentary reporting are unparalleled in the annals of the press. One very extraordinary recent one may be mentioned in proof. On the motion of Lord Roden, in the end of November, on the subject of the present state of Ireland,—"The Sun" gave a verbatim report of the speeches down to eight o'clock, making upwards of seven columns in all, and had the whole published, in a *third* edition by *nine* o'clock, at which hour expresses were despatched to all parts of the country.

dress; but that it was to him a labour of love. He spoke with much distinctness, and with great seeming ease in so far as concerned the intellectual part of the exercise. He was audible in all parts of the House. His speech occupied nearly half-an-hour in the delivery, and was listened to with the deepest attention by both sides of the House. Considered as a mental effort, it would have been regarded as worthy of all praise from any noble Lord in the prime of life, and was such as but few of their lordships could equal: considered as the speech of one who has attained the age of sixty-four, and who has of late years been a severe physical sufferer, it must have been looked on as a great intellectual achievement.

Lord PORTMAN seconded the motion for the address. His Lordship having been but recently raised to the peerage, and not having made any speech before,—unless, indeed, a few desultory observations, arising out of some casual circumstances, be deserving the name,—his appearance on this occasion was regarded as his *début* in the character of a speaker in the House of Peers. Hence all eyes were upon him, to see how he would acquit himself. He spoke for more than half an hour, and acquitted himself in a highly respectable manner. The matter of his speech, without being brilliant, displayed considerable talent. It was occasionally argumentative, sometimes declamatory, always clear. His style was unassuming and plain: he never seemed to aim at being rhetorical. His manner was pleasant rather than impressive. One of his favourite attitudes was to rest both hands on the table for a short time, and then suddenly withdraw them to enable him to resume a perpendicular position. He usually kept his eye fixed on the two or three noble lords immediately opposite him. He spoke with some fluency, and without any seeming difficulty. His voice is of the treble kind. He did not speak in loud tones, but was sufficiently audible in all parts of the House. He had nothing worthy the name of gesticulation, beyond his resting himself by means of his two hands on the table, in the way I have described, and a slight occasional movement of the head. He is dark-looking, and has dark hair. His features are regular, and his countenance wears an intelligent aspect. He is rather tall, and of a stout frame. He is understood to be somewhat reserved in his habits, and is said to have a good deal of the quality which the French call *hauteur*. The noble lord is in the thirty-eighth year of his age.

There have been already a good many discussions in the House of Lords. Seven or eight of the debates have been of considerable importance; a very unusual circumstance so soon after the beginning of a session. I believe there were as many interesting discussions during the five weeks the House sat, before the Christmas holidays, as there were in as many months from the beginning of either of the last three sessions. To the circumstance of Lord Brougham being again present, and perfectly recovered in health, we are, in a great measure, to ascribe this. The noble Lord seems determined to make up by his activity this session, for his absence in the session of 1836, and his inactivity in the last session, caused by the indisposition under which it is now well known, though he himself tried to conceal it, he then laboured. I know from private sources of information, that he is resolved to make what is called a sensation this session. I have met with gentlemen who have had lengthened interviews with him, within the last few weeks, and they say that he is all eagerness for rushing fairly into the political arena in the House of Lords. He is in excellent spirits: he never was in better in his life. This, indeed, has been visible in his appearance and manner during that part of the session which is already past. He has all the appearance of excellent health about him. He looks as well, in point of physical vigour, as he did twenty years since, when, as plain Henry Brougham, he was day after day achieving such splendid victories both at the bar and in the senate. He is himself animated with the highest hopes of seeing, ere long, the complete triumph of those principles, both in politics and education, with which he has within the last few weeks identified himself in so remarkable a manner. His speech on introducing his measure for a system of national education, occupied upwards of two hours in the delivery, and was one of the most masterly speeches I ever heard. It was equal to anything the noble Lord ever himself achieved; and yet it was delivered under the most unfavourable circumstances. There were not above fourteen or fifteen peers present during the delivery of this address. Now, every person, who knows anything of public speaking, must be aware how dispiriting it is to the speaker to have to encounter the slight offered to the subject, if not to himself personally, by the absence of most of those whose duty it is to be present. Lord Brougham, however, did not seem in the least disheartened by the thinness of the House, but displayed great liveliness of manner as well as excellence in his matter. I am satisfied, indeed, that he would have delivered his two hours' speech with the same animation and spirit, had no other Peer than the Lord Chancellor been present. He is not a man to be dispirited by marked neglect, any more than by strenuous opposition. In regard to regularity of attendance this session, Lord Brougham has exceeded every other Peer in the House; always, of course, excepting the Lord Chancellor. I do not recollect missing him for a single evening while the House was sitting. The only Peer who would probably have been Lord Brougham's rival in the matter of regular attendance, is now out of the country: I allude to the Duke of Cumberland, *alias* the King of Hanover. His Hanoverian Majesty, as I mentioned nearly two years ago in my "Random Recollections of the House of Lords," was, for some years prior to his quitting the country, more regular in his attendance in the upper House than any other Peer of the realm. He was always the first to enter and the last to leave it.

The address in the Commons, in answer to the Queen's Speech, was moved by Lord Leveson, son of the Earl of Granville, and member for Morpeth. As this was the noble Lord's maiden speech,* all eyes were naturally fixed on him. What added to the interest of his moving the address, was the circumstance of his speech being the first after the regular meeting, not only of a new parliament, but of a new parliament under a new sovereign, and that sovereign a female of only eighteen. The proceedings on the election of speaker are only considered a sort of preliminary matter which has no proper connexion with the actual business of the session. The interest which the circumstances to which I have alluded gave to the speech of Lord Leveson, was greatly heightened by his exceedingly youthful, not to say boyish appearance. The noble Lord is very young to be entrusted with the representation of an important constituency, for he is only in his twenty-second year; but young as he is, he even looks still younger. He commenced with wonderful self-possession, under all the circumstances of the case, and spoke for about fifteen minutes with much seeming ease. His utterance was rapid rather than otherwise, and the words proceeded in regular order from his mouth. His voice does not appear to be powerful, but it is clear and pleasant. His articulation was sufficiently distinct, and in his pronunciation there was an absence of that dandified "fine-young-gentleman" manner of speaking, which is somewhat common among the sons of the aristocracy. His action was quiet and unpretending; in fact, beyond a slight movement of his right arm, and an occasional gentle turning of his head from one side to the other, there was nothing in his manner to deserve the name of gesticulation at all. In the matter of his speech there was little either to praise or blame. It was rather above mediocrity, which is all that can be said about it. But, in justice to the young nobleman, let me guard the reader against prejudging him on the score of talent, in consequence of my speaking of his maiden oration in the House as not rising much

* The noble Lord was first elected for Morpeth towards the close of last session; but never made any regular speech in the House before.

higher than mediocrity. Supposing he were a man of commanding abilities, he could not, in the circumstances in which he was placed, have made any striking display of his talents. The movers and seconders of addresses in answer to royal speeches, are necessarily tied down to certain topics; the topics, namely, embraced in the speech: and even in speaking on these topics, the mover and seconder are expected to be exceedingly guarded in what they say. They have no latitude either of thought or of expression allowed them. It is for this, perhaps, more than for any other reason that could be named, that no men of distinction as speakers are ever selected to move or second the address in either House; for Ministers would be apprehensive, were such men to be entrusted with the moving or seconding of such address, that they would, in some ill-starred moment, follow the impulses of their genius, and overleap the limits of discretion.

Lord Leveson's personal appearance is very prepossessing. His manner is modest: there is no assumption in it. He is under the middle height, and slenderly formed. His features are small; his complexion is fair; and his hair has something of a flaxen hue. He has a bright eye, and a rather intelligent expression of countenance. His face is exceedingly pleasing, and is not without a feminine expression. I am anxious to see how so young a legislator will acquit himself when he takes part in any important debate.

Mr. Gibson Craig, the new member for the county of Edinburgh, seconded the address which had been moved by Lord Leveson. Mr. Craig having been long known as an advocate of considerable distinction at the Scottish bar, great things were expected of him: great things, I mean, as to the manner of his speech. The delusion was dispelled before he had uttered half a dozen sentences. He completely broke down in the very outset, and never afterwards recovered himself. He commenced thus: "Mr. Speaker,—I rise, Sir, for the purpose of seconding the motion which has just been made by the noble Lord; and I—" Here he suddenly paused, and appeared to be labouring under great tremor. Not resuming his speech for some seconds, both sides of the House cheered him, with the view of enabling him to recover his self-possession, and of encouraging him to proceed. I am convinced that these cheers only aggravated the evil they were kindly meant to remedy; for though it is the custom, at all public meetings in England, to endeavour to encourage a tremulous speaker in this way, I do not recollect ever having seen the expedient resorted to in Scotland; and therefore it must have sounded strange in the ears of Mr. Craig,—if, indeed, he did not understand it in a light the very opposite of what was intended. I have seen it stated in several journals, that after he had uttered the first sentence, he actually sat down, and did not rise again. This is not correct. He remained on his legs at least five minutes; and during all that time did continue saying something or other, though that something was, to use one of his own favourite terms in the law courts of Edinburgh, often as "irrelevant" to the subjects, to which he should have confined himself, as it was possible to be. Nor is this all. Not only did Mr. Craig wander from the topics introduced into the royal speech, but he wandered from every other topic. His language, in other words, had often no meaning at all. One of the most experienced and accurate shorthand-writers, in the gallery, mentioned to me, a few days afterwards, that he could not, by any exertion of his intellect and judgment, extract anything like meaning or coherency from his notes of the learned gentleman's speech. Mr. Craig, on finding himself break down in the commencement, referred to the notes, which he held in his hand, of what he meant to say; but they afforded him no assistance worthy of the name. It is true, they did help him to an idea or two, when there seemed to be an utter absence of any in his mind; but the evil of it was, that he could not clothe those ideas in the proper phraseology, so as to make himself intelligible to his audience. He stuttered and hesitated, corrected and re-corrected his expressions, and then, after all, left his sentences worse at the last than they were at the first. His self-possession all but completely forsook him; and his nervousness was so excessive, that in many cases he could not pronounce the word even when it suggested itself to his mind. Hence, during a good part of his speech (if so it may be called), not a word was heard by those a few yards distant from him, though his lips continued to move. The most pleasant part of the matter, to all who were present, was to see him again resume his seat, which he did very abruptly.

Great surprise has been generally expressed, that a lawyer, so much accustomed to public speaking as Mr. Craig has been for many years past, should thus have completely broken down in the House of Commons. To my mind, there is nothing surprising in the circumstance. The causes of his failure appear to me as plain as can be. They were the peculiar circumstances in which he was then placed. These were different from any in which he had ever found himself before. It was the first day of the meeting of parliament, and the first time in which he had been on the floor of the House, except during the election of a Speaker, and while taking the oaths. Everything, therefore, was new to him. He found himself, too, overwhelmed with that undefinable sort of awe which almost every man, who ever addressed the House immediately on his introduction to it, has afterwards confessed that he felt. It will doubtless be urged, in opposition to this hypothesis respecting the causes of Mr. Craig's breaking down, that, on the same grounds, Lord Leveson ought also to have failed, as he may be said to have been also a new member. To this, I answer, that there was this difference between them,—a difference, it will at once be seen to be decisive in favour of my theory,—that Lord Leveson, not being a practised speaker, took the wise precaution of previously writing out and committing his speech to heart; so that he had only to repeat it, just as he did when giving one of his short recitations at school a few years since; while Mr. Craig, trusting to his extemporaneous powers of utterance, had not prepared his speech, but trusted to his consulting, if there should be a necessity, a few confused notes which he had jotted down on paper.

It was a most ill-advised thing on the part of Ministers to ask Mr. Craig to second the motion for the address, knowing as they did that he had never been in the House before. It was still more injudicious on his part to have undertaken the task. I do not at this moment recollect any previous instance of the kind; but I know several instances in which the most distinguished men have either broken down altogether, or comparatively so, when they ventured to address the House on the first day of their introduction to parliament. I have mentioned in my "Random Recollections of the House of Commons," that Cobbett once stated to me, that, bold and confident in his own resources as he was, he felt a degree of tremor come over him when he rose to address the House on the day of his first entering it, which almost unnerved him for the task; but that knowing every word he uttered would be severely criticised, he took the precaution of preparing his speech beforehand, and consequently managed to get through it in a passable manner.

The instances are innumerable in which men of first-rate talent have broken down in the House, when making their maiden speech, even after they have been some time in it, and consequently might be expected to have felt more at ease. The case of Addison, who rose up and said, "I conceive," three successive times, resuming his seat each time, because he was unable to proceed, and who did not eventually succeed in uttering another word, is known to everybody. Sheridan, also, in his first effort, completely failed; so did Erskine, and so also did the late David Ricardo. The truth is, it will generally be found that parliamentary failures most frequently occur in the case of great men. The reason is obvious: they are usually the most diffident: they want that assurance which is so common among persons who are below mediocrity. Such tenth-rate personages as Mr. Peter Borthwick never break down. Their stock of an overweening conceit of their own abilities is at all times, and under all circumstances, abundant; and they have consequently an ample supply of mere words for all occasions.

The nervousness of Mr. Craig, under the peculiar circumstances in which he was placed, I should have regarded as presumptive proof of his being a man of superior intellect, had I known nothing of him previously. Cicero mentions, that not only did his knees tremble, and his whole frame shake, when he first ventured to address an assemblage of his countrymen; but that he never, even after he had enjoyed for years the reputation of being the first orator in Rome, rose to speak on any important occasion without feeling himself oppressed in the outset by an excessive nervousness. Mr. Craig has the matter in him; and, as Sheridan said of himself in similar circumstances, "out it will yet come." I am much mistaken, indeed, if Mr. Craig does not, by the success of his future efforts, more than atone for the failure of his first attempt.

The Victoria Parliament has not, as yet, been productive of many of those uproarious scenes which are of such frequent occurrence in the House of Commons. Abundance of such scenes, however, are, I have no doubt, in store for those who are partial to seeing the "first assembly of gentlemen in Europe" making themselves ridiculous. All the scenes worthy of the name which have occurred hitherto, took place on one night; the night, namely, on which the conduct of the "Spottiswoode gang," as it has been called, was first brought under the consideration of the House. The House sat on that evening till a quarter past ten: and from five o'clock till that hour there was nothing but a continued succession of scenes. The usual discussions, indeed, constituted the exception, and the scenes the rule on that memorable night. Sir Edward Knatchbull had the honour of commencing, quite unintentionally there can be no doubt, the uproar and disorder which so largely characterized the after proceedings. He called Mr. O'Brien to order, in a few moments after the latter honourable gentleman had risen to animadvert on the "Spottiswoode conspiracy." Sir Edward Sugden soon after followed the example of Sir Edward Knatchbull, and lustily called out "Order!" Both baronets interrupted Mr. O'Brien, on the ground that he was irregular in making observations when presenting a petition. Several other members soon mixed themselves up with the question of "order," and a regular scene followed. Four or five rose repeatedly at once, amidst deafening cries of "Order!" "Chair! chair!" and so forth. Among those who seemed most eager to rush into an altercation on the point of order, were Mr. O'Connell, Mr. Wakley, Mr. Lambton, and last, though not least, Mr. Henry Grattan. The latter honourable gentleman is most liberal of his gestures on all occasions on which he speaks: when exhibiting in a "scene," he is particularly so. The interposition of the Speaker restored order for a time, but only for a time. Sir Francis Burdett made a speech, which called up Mr. O'Connell, but the latter honourable gentleman had no sooner presented himself, than he was assailed by a perfect tempest of clamour from the Tory benches. In the midst of all the noise and commotion which prevailed among the Opposition, and amidst all the din of voices at the bar, and the moving of feet on the floor of the House,—loud cries of "Spoke! spoke!"—meaning that Mr. O'Connell had no right to rise a second time,—were distinctly heard. The honourable gentleman stood with his arms folded across his breast, in an attitude of perfect calmness, and looked at the Tories opposite as if he had been bidding them defiance. At last, seeing the uproar continue, he threatened to move the adjournment of the House if the interruption was persevered in. He was then allowed to proceed for a few seconds, but was again assailed by cries of "Spoke! spoke!" "Order! order!" Mr. Hume now rose with the view of seeing what he could do for the purpose of allaying the storm of uproar which was raging in the House; but poor good-natured Mr. Hume was himself received with increased shouts of disapprobation from the Tory benches; and what aggravated the thing was, that a universal yell of "Chair! chair!" was set up before he had uttered a single word. Good-tempered as the member for Kilkenny proverbially is, this was really more than human nature could endure, and he exclaimed, with considerable sharpness and energy, looking "the enemy" fairly in the face, "Why 'chair,' when I have not—" The remainder of the sentence was lost amidst a most vociferous renewal of the general cry of "Order! order!" Amidst some half dozen who now rose to speak from the Tory side of the House,—some of them exhibiting an alarming superabundance of gesticulation,—Sir Robert Inglis was heard to say that he called Mr. Hume to order because the Speaker wished to make some observations. "But," shouted Mr. Hume again, starting to his legs, before Sir Robert had time to resume his seat; "but how am I out of order? and why call out 'chair,' when I have not yet spoken at all?" Loud laughter, accompanied by additional uproarious demonstrations, followed the observation. Eventually the Speaker's voice prevailed over that of the performers in the scene; and the scene itself was soon afterwards put an end to. In about twenty minutes, however, it was succeeded by another, though of a different kind. It was one to be seen: not to be described. Sir Francis Burdett having been keenly attacked by Mr. Maurice O'Connell, and having been asked by Mr. Handley whether, after subscribing to the Spottiswoode Fund, he would not feel it binding on him, as a man of honour, to abstain from voting on all matters connected with Irish elections,—all eyes were turned to him; but, instead of repelling the attack of Mr. Maurice O'Connell, or answering the question of Mr. Handley, he rose from his seat, and without uttering a word, made a low bow to the Speaker, and, with a steady pace, but a most ludicrous carriage, walked out of the House, as if he had been performing what soldiers call the dead march. The cheers of the Tories were deafening, while the laughter of the Reformers was so immoderate as to threaten serious injury to their sides.

Soon afterwards came the "last scene of all,"—the last, I mean, to which I shall advert,—in "the strange eventful" proceedings of this memorable evening. Mr. Blewitt, the new member for Monmouth, having concluded a speech of an hour's duration, by moving a string of resolutions nearly as long as the speech itself, condemnatory of the Irish Election Petition Fund, seemed perfectly at a loss as to whether or not he should press them to a division. The honourable gentleman, who is a little bustling man, leaped about from one part of the House to another, asking the opinion of different members as to what he should do; and then, when he had got a most abundant supply of advice, all to the effect that he should withdraw his resolutions, he seemed to be, as they say in Scotland, "in a peck of troubles" as to whether he should take it or not. It is impossible to describe the scene of confusion which the House presented at this time. The bar was so crowded with honourable gentlemen laughing and talking, and otherwise amusing themselves, that there was no getting out or in; while the floor of the House was promenaded by other honourable members, just as if they had been on the pavement in Regent-street. Mr. Blewitt at last said something about withdrawing four resolutions, and pressing the fifth; but the noise and confusion were so great, that nobody but himself and the Speaker seemed to know anything of the matter. Eventually, amidst the same scene of disorder, Mr. Blewitt withdrew the remaining resolution; but nobody being aware of the circumstance, Mr. Peter Borthwick, Sir Edward Knatchbull, Mr. Goulburn, Colonel Sibthorp, Sir Edward Sugden, and a number of others, all rose at the same time, some to speak on the resolutions, and others to ask whether or not they were still before the House. The scene which ensued defies description. Mr. Blewitt and some of his friends rose in threes and fours at a time, to assure the House that *all* the resolutions were withdrawn; while the Tory members not only started up in dozens to deny the fact, but were prepared, with great vehemence of gesture, to argue the point. Their friends, on either hand and at their backs, came forward with an edifying promptitude and unanimity to support their hypothesis, as to the non-withdrawal of the resolutions, by loud cries of "They are not withdrawn," "No, no," &c. Groans, yells, and other zoological sounds proceeded from several parts of the ministerial side, by way of answer to the exclamations and affirmation of the Tories. In the midst of this uproarious exhibition, the Speaker several times assured the House that the resolutions had all been formally withdrawn, and that there was no business before the House; but for some time they persisted in maintaining that he was mistaken. At last he satisfied the Tories, or at least seemingly so, that the resolutions were withdrawn, and order was once more restored. But so keenly did the right honourable gentleman feel the disrespect offered to him in the implied doubt of his word, that he next evening mentioned, that if such conduct were again repeated he would resign his office as speaker.

The most amusing circumstance, not coming under the category of "scenes," which has yet taken place in the House of Commons, happened in the second week of parliament. The occasion was that of the Chancellor of the Exchequer bringing the question of the Civil List under the consideration of the House. It will be remembered, that Mr. Daniel Whittle Harvey gave previous notice of his intention to propose an amendment to the motion of the right honourable gentleman. As is usual on such occasions, as a matter of courtesy, Mr. Harvey, before commencing his speech, handed to Mr. Spring Rice the amendment he meant to propose; but instead of handing the right honourable gentleman a copy of the amendment in question, Mr. Harvey handed him the original itself, and this, too, without providing himself with a copy. There can be no doubt Mr. Harvey's intention was to have asked his amendment back from Mr. Spring Rice before beginning his own speech; but having forgotten to do this, and also forgetting for the moment that the Chancellor of the Exchequer had his amendment in his possession, Mr. Harvey concluded an able and luminous speech by observing, with his usual volubility, that he now begged "leave to propose the following amendment." Mr. Harvey immediately leaned down to "pick up" his "following amendment" from among a quantity of papers which were lying on his seat; but no "following amendment" was to be found. It was then that the fact flashed across his mind that he had handed it to the Chancellor of the Exchequer, and that the latter gentleman had not had the politeness to return it. "My amendment," exclaimed Mr. Harvey, with some tartness of manner, "is in the custody of the Chancellor of the Exchequer. Be pleased to hand it me over." As the honourable gentleman uttered the last sentence, he looked anxiously towards Mr. Spring Rice, who was five or six yards from him, at the same time stretching out his hand to receive the document when it should be returned to him through the means of some of the intervening honourable gentlemen. Mr. Spring Rice looked amazed and confounded when the honourable member for Southwark so pointedly apostrophized him as being the custodier of his amendment. To be sure, he said nothing in the first instance; but it was very easy to see that he was inwardly ejaculating "Me, your amendment!" The fact was, that he also had become oblivious of the circumstance of the document being in his possession. However, in a few moments, the conviction was brought home to his mind that he was a defaulter in this respect; and forthwith he commenced a most vigorous search for the amendment, Mr. Harvey all the while standing in his place, with his eye as steadily fixed on the honourable Chancellor of the Exchequer as if he had been about to play the cannibal with him. Mr. Spring Rice searched his pockets: the missing amendment was not there. He eagerly and hastily turned over a miniature mountain of documents erected by his side on the seat on which he sat: still there was no appearance of the lost amendment. He then rose up, and advancing to the table, rummaged for some time among a heap of papers there: the search was still in vain. He resumed his seat, and inquired of Lord Morpeth, who was sitting beside him, whether he knew anything of the mysterious disappearance of Mr. Harvey's amendment. Lord Morpeth significantly shook his head, being just as ignorant on the matter as the Chancellor of the Exchequer himself. Lord Morpeth, however, kindly consented to assist in the search for the missing amendment; and great was the activity he displayed in turning and re-turning over, after Mr. Spring Rice, the various documents that lay on the seat and on the table. Long before this time, Mr. Harvey, tired of holding out his hand to receive that which was not likely to be forthcoming in "a hurry," had drawn it in, and, as if determined to take the thing as coolly as possible, folded his arms on his breast, and stood in that attitude with all the seeming resignation of a philosopher who patiently submits to a calamity over which he has no control. In the meantime, however, though thus motionless in one sense, he was not so in another. His tongue was occasionally set a-going. He remarked, on one occasion, with that bitter sarcasm of manner which is peculiar to himself, that this was the first document of his which ever had been taken so much care of by a cabinet minister. Roars of laughter, to the manifest mortification of Mr. Spring Rice, followed from both sides of the House. On another occasion, he observed that he was quite delighted to see that his amendment was so safe in the keeping of the Chancellor of the Exchequer, as that no one would have any chance of abstracting it. All this time, Mr. Spring Rice and Lord Morpeth were most exemplary as regarded the eagerness with which they prosecuted their search for the lost document. It is worthy of remark, that no one joined with them; but all, even the Liberal members, seemed to enjoy the sport. To the Conservatives, the affair was a rare piece of amusement. I observed some of them laughing heartily, who were never seen to laugh within the walls of the House before; and in whose existence, even out of doors, a hearty laugh might be said to be quite an era. Mr. Spring Rice, after "turning about and wheeling about," in search of the amendment, with an agility worthy of his namesake of Jim Crow notoriety, at length bethought himself of unlocking a small tin box, in which he keeps the more valuable of his papers, when, to his infinite joy, after rummaging for a few seconds among its contents, he discovered the missing amendment. He pounced upon it just as a Bow-street officer would on some offender, for whom he had been on a vexatious search, when alighting on him; and dragging the innocent amendment out of its place of concealment, held it up in his hand to the gaze of the House, exclaiming, as loud as his lungs would permit, and with an air of triumph, "Here it is! here it is!" "I'm happy to see that the right honourable gentleman prizes it so highly," said Mr. Harvey, in the sarcastic way to which I have alluded, "as to place it among his most valuable papers, and to lock it up in his box." Peals of laughter followed; and during their continuance, the amendment was handed over, through the assistance of two or three intermediate members, to the honourable gentleman whose property it was, who, as soon as it reached him, read it, amidst renewed peals of laughter. The bursts of laughter, which were thus resounding through the House, were much increased by the circumstance of Colonel Sibthorp, who was directly opposite Mr. Spring Rice, rising, with his own imperturbable gravity, and with his huge mustachios looking unusually large, to second the amendment. It certainly was a novelty in the proceedings of the House of Commons, to witness the most ultra Tory, perhaps, in the House, rising to second an amendment on a vital question, moved by one of the greatest Radicals. The shouts of laughter which followed the circumstance, had their origin in the impression that the gallant mustachioed Colonel had seconded the amendment in a mistake; but when it was understood that there was no mistake in the matter, and that the gallant gentleman was perfectly aware of what he was about, the Liberal members looked unutterable things at one another. It was at last understood that the Tories were, from factious motives, about to join the extreme section of the Reformers on that particular occasion, not doubting that, in the event of a division, ministers would be in a minority, and consequently be compelled to resign office. The circumstance, however, of the Chancellor of the Exchequer giving Mr. Harvey certain specific pledges, in reference to the treatment of the Pension List, induced the latter gentleman to withdraw his amendment, which of course prevented any division taking place.

The *débuts* made by new members have not been numerous. Those of Mr. Blewitt and Mr. D'Israeli have attracted most attention. Mr. Blewitt made his *début* by bringing forward certain resolutions connected with the Spottiswoode Subscription. He commenced by apologizing for venturing, so soon after his introduction to the House, to occupy its attention by undertaking to bring under its notice so important a subject as that embraced by the resolutions which he had given notice of his intention to move. There being a self-possession and confidence in his manner, which seemed at variance with his imploring the indulgence of the House, the Tories at once set up a loud and general laugh, mingled with other interruptions which it is not so easy to characterise. This appeared to embarrass the honourable gentleman in some small measure; but several cheers from the ministerial benches having immediately succeeded the interruptions from the other side, he speedily recovered his composure of mind, and proceeded to address the House in a distinct and steady voice. He kept his eye for some time as constantly fixed on the wig of the Speaker, as if it had been a crime of the first magnitude to withdraw his gaze from it for a moment. By the time he had been on his legs for about fifteen minutes, he waxed wondrously magniloquent. He evinced a singular partiality for expletives. He talked of the "purity and honesty of his motives," and so forth. He made repeated efforts to be impressive; but his intended pathos only ended in bathos. He regretted that he could not introduce honourable gentlemen opposite, to the recesses of the bottom of his heart. Of course he could not do this, as the "recesses of his heart," however capacious, could scarcely be expected to accommodate three hundred Tory gentlemen. Such rhetorical flourishes as this—and they were not few in number—caused, as might have been expected, loud shouts of laughter from the Tories; and even the honourable gentlemen who graced the ministerial benches could not, in several cases, refrain from joining in the merriment of those on the opposite side. For some time the interruptions from the Tories were renewed, chiefly however in the shape of laughter. At last the honourable gentleman degenerated into a more tame and monotonous manner

-t speaking; and the consequence was, that the Tories, instead of keeping up their merriment, entered, in most cases, into conversation with each other; while a few of them addressed themselves to sleep. The greatest inattention to Mr. Blewitt's speech, also prevailed on the ministerial side. During the hour he spoke, he only got two cheers, and these very faint and very partial ones. Mr. Hume, who sat immediately at the back of the honourable gentleman, repeatedly yawned and spoke to Mr. Bulwer, the celebrated novelist. Mr. Bulwer did not evince any greater disposition to engage in conversation with Mr. Hume than he did to listen to Mr. Blewitt, being, very probably, engaged in his own mind in inventing the plot of some new work of fiction. Mr. O'Connell sat on the other side of Mr. Hume; and I speak with all seriousness, when I say that the honourable and learned member for Dublin looked the very incarnation of melancholy. I never in my life saw his countenance wear an aspect of so much gravity. Towards the conclusion of his speech, Mr. Blewitt repeatedly paused; and there seemed, on one or two occasions, to be a general impression that he would not be able to resume, in consequence of his memory having proved unfaithful. He contrived, however, to recommence again, until, having unconsciously made some very ludicrous observation, a general and loud laugh from the Tory side of the House fairly drove the remainder of his speech out of his head; and not being able to resume the thread of his argument, though not losing his self-possession, he, after a short pause, observed in a very characteristic manner, that if the gentlemen opposite would not listen to his speech that was their fault, not his. This elicited another burst of laughter; when, after a temporary pause, he remarked, with much emphasis, that they (the Tories) had fairly laughed him out of a great part of his speech, and that, therefore, he must abruptly conclude by moving the resolutions. Mr. Blewitt then sat down amidst loud laughter.

Among the new members who have already made their *débuts*, Mr. D'Israeli, the member for Maidstone, is the best known. His own private friends looked forward to his introduction into the House of Commons as a circumstance which would be immediately followed by his obtaining for himself an oratorical reputation equal to that enjoyed by the most popular speakers in that assembly. They thought he would produce an extraordinary sensation, both in the House and in the country, by the power and splendour of his eloquence. How different the event from the anticipation! It was known for some days previously that he was to make his maiden speech in the course of the discussion respecting the Spottiswoode combination: he himself made no secret of the fact among his party, that he was labouring with an oration which he expected would produce a great impression; and this circumstance, taken in conjunction with the sanguine notions already referred to of his friends, as to his capability of achieving mighty oratorical triumphs, made the House all anxiety to hear him. When he rose, which he did immediately after Mr. O'Connell had concluded his speech, all eyes were fixed on him, and all ears were open to listen to his eloquence. Before he had proceeded far, he furnished a striking illustration of the old story about the mountain in labour bringing forth a mouse. For the first five minutes he was on his legs, the Tories met every burst of laughter, or other manifestation of ridicule which proceeded from the ministerial benches, with loud cheers. And it is particularly deserving of mention, that even Sir Robert Peel, who very rarely cheers any honourable gentleman, not even the most able and accomplished speakers of his own party, greeted Mr. D'Israeli's speech with a prodigality of applause which must have been severely trying to the worthy baronet's lungs. The latter honourable gentleman spoke from the second row of benches immediately opposite the Speaker's chair: Sir Robert, as usual, sat on the first row of benches, a little to the left of Mr. D'Israeli; and so exceedingly anxious was the right honourable baronet to encourage the *débutant* to proceed, that he repeatedly turned round his head, and looking the youthful orator in the face, cheered him in most stentorian tones. All, however, would not do. Mr. D'Israeli increased in the absurdity of his matter, and the ludicrousness of his manner, with every succeeding sentence he uttered. This, of course, called forth fresh bursts of laughter from the ministerial benches. At last, his own most devoted friends were obliged to abstain from all farther manifestations of applause. For a time he endeavoured to brave out the laughter and jeers of the gentlemen opposite; but it was visible to all, that when his own party ceased to cheer him on, he began to lose courage. There was not only less confidence in his manner; but, on one occasion, he intimated his willingness to resume his seat, if the House wished him to do so. He proceeded, however, with his speech; at one time talking a sort of sickly sentimentality which would have been scarcely endurable even in one of his own novels, but to utter which in the House of Commons indicated a most miserable taste; at another time, speaking downright nonsense. What for instance, could be more nonsensical than this passage? "When we remember that, in spite of the support of the honourable and learned gentleman, the member for Dublin, and his well-disciplined phalanx of patriots; and in spite of all this, we remember the amatory eclogue, (roars of laughter,) the old loves and the new loves that took place between the noble Lord, the Tityrus of the treasury bench, and the learned Daphne of Liskeard, (loud laughter, and cries of 'Question!') when we remember, at the same time, that with emancipated Ireland and enslaved England; on the one hand a triumphant nation, on the other a groaning people; and notwithstanding the noble Lord, secure on the pedestal of power, may wield in one hand the keys of St. Peter, and in the other—" The remainder of the sentence was lost amidst peals of laughter: but it is not probable that any after combination of words could have made sense of the passage. On another occasion he spoke of himself, amidst roars of laughter the loudest and most general I ever remember to have heard in the House, as being the *representative* of all the new members of Parliament. By the time he had got half through his speech, he was assailed by groans and under-growls in all their varieties, as well as with continued bursts of laughter. The uproar, indeed, often became so great as completely to drown his voice. Some of the peals of laughter lasted for a considerable time; and when it was thought that honourable members were literally exhausted, the recollection of the ludicrousness of the matter and manner of Mr. D'Israeli threw them into renewed convulsions of laughter before he could commence another sentence. At last, losing all temper, which until then he had preserved in a wonderful manner, he paused in the midst of a sentence, and looking the Liberals indignantly in the face, raised his hands, and opening his mouth as wide as its dimensions would permit, said, in remarkably loud and almost terrific tones,—"Though I sit down now, *the time will come when you will hear me.*" Mr. D'Israeli then sat down amidst renewed roars of laughter, which lasted for some time.

A more extraordinary exhibition altogether I have never seen in the House. Mr. D'Israeli's appearance and manner were very singular. His dress also was peculiar: it had much of a theatrical aspect. His black hair was long and flowing; and he had a most ample crop of it. His gesture was abundant: he often appeared as if trying with what celerity he could move his body from one side to another, and throw his hands out and draw them in again. At other times he flourished one hand before his face, and then another. His voice, too, is of a very unusual kind: it is powerful, and had every justice done to it in the way of exercise; but there is something peculiar in it which I am at a loss to characterise. His utterance was rapid, and he never seemed at a loss for words. Notwithstanding all the nonsense he spoke, I am convinced he is a man of talent, and possesses many of the requisites of a good debater. I doubt, however, if he will ever acquire any status in the House. His manner and matter created so strong a prejudice against him, that it will be exceedingly difficult, if not impossible, for him ever again to obtain a fair hearing. He seemed himself to feel deeply mortified at the result of his maiden effort. He sat the whole evening afterwards, namely, from ten till two o'clock in the morning, the very picture of a disappointed man. He scarcely exchanged a word with any other honourable gentleman. He did not cheer when his party cheered, Lord Stanley and Sir Robert Peel; neither did he laugh when they laughed. He folded his arms on his breast for a considerable part of the evening, and seemed to be wrapped up in his own unpleasant reflections.

Let me, before concluding my notice of Mr. D'Israeli's parliamentary *début*, mention, in justice to him, that however foolish his speech may have been, and however much calculated some parts of it were to elicit laughter from the House, yet, that the way in which he was assailed by the ministerial supporters, was most unbecoming, if not actually indecent. There was an evident predisposition on the part of many honourable gentlemen to put him down, if at all possible, without reference to the merits of his speech; and I have always observed, that when the Liberal members have come to a resolution of this kind, they never scruple as to the means they employ to accomplish their purpose. The Tories cannot stand a moment's comparison with them, in the matter of putting down a member. Not only are they, generally speaking, blessed with lungs of prodigious powers, but, on such occasions, they always give them full play. Their "Oh!'s" and groans, and yells, to say nothing of their laughing, or rather *roaring* capabilities, far exceeding anything I have ever heard elsewhere, not even excepting the ultra Radical assemblages which meet at White Conduit House, or at the Crown-and-Anchor. I am convinced that, on this occasion, Mr. D'Israeli was made to utter a great many foolish things which otherwise would not have escaped his lips; for I observed that he usually made some observations in reference to the interruptions offered to him; and that it was when doing so, or immediately afterwards, that he gave expression to the greatest absurdities. In the middle of his speech, when respectfully soliciting the indulgence of the House, especially as it was his first appearance,—a plea which one would have thought could not have been ineffectually urged in an assembly, "not only of the first gentlemen in Europe," but of men sitting there for the specific purpose of doing justice,—Mr. D'Israeli very emphatically said, that he himself would not, on any account, be a party to treating any other honourable gentleman in the way in which he himself was assailed. I did think that this appeal to the sense of justice and gentlemanly feeling on the ministerial side of the House, could not be made in vain. The event showed that I was mistaken. It had scarcely escaped the honourable gentleman's lips, before he was assailed as furiously and as indecently as ever. Mr. D'Israeli is a man of the middling height, rather slenderly made, and apparently about thirty-five years of age. His complexion is sallow, and his countenance has so much of the Jewish cast in it that no one could see it without at once coming to the conclusion, that he is of Hebrew extraction; which, I need not say, he is.

The number of new members in the Victoria Parliament is unusually great: it is no less than 158, being nearly a fourth part of the whole. The appearance of so many strange faces in the House had a curious effect on the old members during the first few days of the session. It awakened in the minds of those of them accustomed to reflection, a train of interesting reflections. They thought of the varied circumstances by which their absence from the new House was to be accounted for. Some were excluded from ruined fortunes; some because they had quitted the country; some because of their apostacy from the principles they had formerly professed, and in the faith of which they had been returned; others, from the fickleness of popular favour; and a fifth class, because they are now in their graves. The contemplative mind had only to follow out this train of reflection, by recollecting particular individuals who belonged to each of these five classes. On some occasions, old members seemed as if in a strange place; for on particular nights the new members, impelled by the novelty of the situation in which they were placed to be marvellously punctual in their attendance, whether the business to be transacted was important or not, far outnumbered the old stagers. The side galleries were, for the first three weeks of the session, nightly crowded by the newly-imported M.P.'s. And here I may remark, that new members have a particular partiality to the side galleries. By taking up their position in them, they are enabled to look down on the more experienced M.P.'s, and by carefully observing their movements, become acquainted with the forms and proceedings of the House. The awkwardness of new members, for the first few weeks of the session, can only be conceived by those who have witnessed it. Not only are they, with the few exceptions furnished in the case of some two or three self-confident or adventurous spirits, afraid to utter even one brief sentence on any subject which is under discussion, but they do not even know how to deport themselves as regards their moving from one place to another. The knowledge necessary for this, however, they soon acquire, by lounging about in the side galleries. Hence, in addition to the motive to frequent these galleries afforded by their anxiety to learn the forms and proceedings of the House, as regards speaking, they have a desire to avoid laughter at their own expense because of any awkward physical movement.

I do not recollect ever to have seen so many young members in the House of Commons as there are at present. Some of them have all the appearance of mere youths, whom one would suppose ought to be still under the strict guardianship of their tutors. How they came to be chosen as the representatives of constituencies does, indeed, seem passing strange. The idea of such youths having the destinies of a great country, in one sense, committed to their care, is something more than odd. There may be men of mature judgment among them; but their appearance is not calculated to inspire confidence in the wisdom of their deliberations.

Among the new members returned to the Victoria Parliament, there are a great many whose manner, both in the House and out of the House, is the most undeliberative-like that the human mind could fancy. In the House, you see them either talking to or laughing with each other—very often both together; or if not, they are to be seen standing in dozens about the bar, completely blocking up the passage, so as to deny other honourable gentlemen all egress and ingress. To sit quite quietly, and to listen with attention to what is going on, is a habit which, in most cases, they have yet to acquire. Then, again, to see them leaving the House smoking their cigars, and making a regular noise as they proceed up Parliament-street, you would suppose them to be so many sparks bent on what, in homely language, is called a spree. I could not help contrasting, in my own mind, the levity of demeanour exhibited by several of the young members on their way up Parliament-street, on one of the nights of the debate on the Spottiswoode combination, with the staid manner in which Mr. Hume, Mr. Warburton, Mr. Wallace, and others of the older members, walked themselves home. But this is a delicate topic, and therefore I will say no more on it.

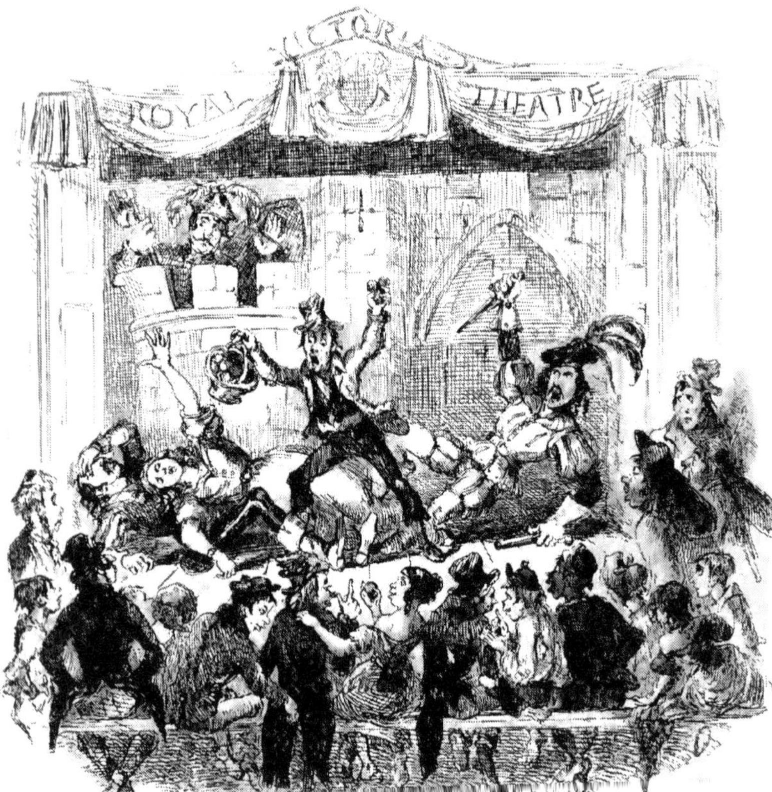
ROYAL
THEATRE

CHAPTER V.

PENNY THEATRES.

Their supposed number—Computed attendance in them—Their moral tendency—The manner in which they are fitted up—Destitute condition of the performers—Squabbles between proprietors and actors about pay—Differences among the performers—Abridging pieces—Character of the productions written by the actors—The intimacy which subsists between the actors and the audience—Dramatic taste of the audiences—Specimens of the pieces—The play bills—Mr. Guff and his bear—Mr. Abel Smith's two dogs—Quality of the acting—The suppression of the Penny Theatres recommended.

PENNY Theatres, or "Gaffs," as they are usually called by their frequenters, are places of juvenile resort in the metropolis which are known only by name to the great mass of the population. I myself knew nothing of these places in any other way, until I lately visited a number of them with the view of making them the subject of one of my sketches. With regard to their statistics, I must still confess myself to be, to a certain extent, ignorant. There exist no means for ascertaining satisfactorily either their number, or the number of the young persons in the habit of attending them. Other facts, however, I have succeeded in learning, though not without personal inquiry, respecting these cheap places of juvenile amusement. They exist only, as would have been inferred from what I shall afterwards have occasion to state, though I had not mentioned the thing, in poor and populous neighbourhoods. There is not a single one of them to be met with in any respectable part of the town. It needs but little if any philosophy to account for this. Respectable parents would never allow their children to visit such places. Their great patrons are the children not only of poor parents, but of parents who pay no attention to the morals of their offspring.

Though the number of Penny Theatres in London cannot be ascertained with certainty, it is beyond all question that they are very numerous. They are to be found in all the poor and populous districts. At the east end of the town, they literally swarm as to numbers. Ratcliffe-highway, the Commercial-road, Mile-end-road, and other places in that direction, are thickly studded with Penny Theatres. St. George's-in-the-Fields can boast of a fair sprinkling of them. In the New Cut alone I know of three. In the neighbourhood of the King's-cross there are several; while in the west end of Marylebone, they are not only numerous, but some of them are of a very large size. One of them, I understand, in Paddington, is capable of containing two thousand persons; and what is more, is usually filled in every part, or, as the proprietors say, is honoured with "brilliant and overflowing audiences." Incredible as it may appear, I am assured that, by some means or other, the proprietors of one of these penny establishments in the western part of the metropolis, have actually procured a license. In Marylebone, I know, some of them, conducted on a very extensive scale, have lately, in consequence of memorials to that effect being presented to the vestry by the more respectable portion of the neighbouring inhabitants, been put down as regular nuisances. It can scarcely be necessary to say, that all the other Penny Theatres are unlicensed. I should suppose, from all the inquiries I have made, that the entire number of these places, in London, is from 80 to 100. Assuming, as wishing to be under rather than above the mark, the lowest number to be correct, there will be little difficulty in making a conjecture which may approximate to the truth, as to the average number of youths in the habit of nightly attending these places. The average attendance at these penny establishments which have come under my own observation, I should estimate at 150; but then a large proportion of these places have, in the winter season, from two to nine distinct audiences; or, to keep by the phraseology of the proprietors, "houses," each night. About three-quarters of an hour's worth of tragedy, or comedy, or farce, or very likely all three hashed up together, is all that is allowed for a penny; and a very good pennyworth the actors think it is, too, though the little urchins who principally form the audience, often think very differently. At the end of the "first house," there is a clearing out of the audience, which is followed by the ingress of another set of "little fellows." If any one choose to treat himself to the second "entertainment for the evening," it is all well; only he must pay for his pleasure by the prompt production of penny the second; and so on, at each successive "house," till the last scene of all is enacted. In many cases, each "house" has its two pieces and a song, thus allowing about twenty minutes to each piece, and five minutes to the doggrel dignified with the name of song. Supposing, which certainly is a moderate computation, that forty out of the assumed eighty Penny Theatres have severally their plurality of "houses" every night, and average 450 patrons, that would give an entire aggregate nightly attendance of 18,000; to which, if we add, for the other forty penny establishments which are supposed to have only one "house" per night, 6000, we should have an entire average attendance on the Penny Theatres of the metropolis, of 24,000.

The audiences at these places, as has been already intimated, almost exclusively consist of the youthful part of the community. Now and then, it is true, you will see an audience diversified by some coal-heaver rejoicing in a dove-tailed hat, which completely overspreads his neck and shoulders; or it may be an adult chimney-sweep, whose sooty visage, with his head graced by a night-cap, is sure to attract the eye of the visitor; but grown-up personages are rarely to be seen in such places: youths, from eight to sixteen years of age, are the great patrons of such places. There is always a tolerable sprinkling of girls at the Penny Theatres; but, usually, the boys considerably preponderate.

No one who has not visited these establishments,—if, indeed, it be not a misnomer to use the word,—could have the faintest conception of the intense interest with which boys in the poorer neighbourhoods of London regard them. With thousands, the desire to witness the representations at the Penny Theatres amounts to an absolute passion. They are present every night, and would at any time infinitely sooner go without a meal than be deprived of that gratification. There can be no question that these places are no better than so many nurseries for juvenile thieves. The little rascals, when they have no other way of getting pence to pay for their admission, commence by stealing articles out of their parents' houses, which are forthwith put in pledge for whatever can be got for them; and the transition from theft committed on their parents to stealing from others, is natural and easy. Nor is this all: at these Penny Theatres the associations which boys form with one another are most destructive of all moral principle. The one cheers on the other in crime. Plans for thieving, and robbing houses and shops, and other places, by way of joint-stock concerns, are there formed and promptly executed, unless the little rogues be detected in the act. Then there are the pieces which are performed at these places, which are of the most injurious kind, as I shall afterwards have occasion to state at greater length. The dexterous thief or villain of any kind is always the greatest hero, and the most popular personage, with these youths; and such are the personages, as a matter of course, who are most liberally brought on the stage, if so it must be called, for their gratification. I have not a doubt that a very large majority of those who afterwards find their way to the bar of the Old Bailey, may trace the commencement of their career in crime to their attendance in Penny Theatres. The "gods," as Garrick used to call those who tenant the shilling galleries of our larger theatres, first formed for the most part, their dramatic predilections in the Penny ones.

The interior of the larger theatrical establishments is often the subject of laboured panegyric by the press, as well as of admiration by the public. There is what an American would call a pretty considerable contrast in this respect between the leviathan houses and the penny establishments. The latter are all a sort of out-door houses: most of them, before being set apart for histrionic purposes, were small stables, sheds, warehouses, &c. They are, with scarcely an exception, miserable-looking places. Judging from their appearance when lighted up, I suppose they must have a frightful aspect through the day. The naked bricks encounter the eye wherever the walls are seen; while, in an upward direction, you see the joist-work in the same naked state in which it proceeded from the hands of the carpenter. These establishments, in fact, have all the appearance of prisons: and would answer the purposes of punishment admirably, were they sufficiently secure against the escape of the inmates. The distinctions of boxes, pit, and gallery, are, with a very few exceptions, unknown. It is all gallery together. And such galleries! The seats consist of rough and unsightly forms. There is nothing below the feet of the audience; so that any jostling or incautious movement may precipitate them to the bottom. The ascent to the galleries is usually by a clumsy sort of ladder, of so very dangerous a construction, that he who mounts it and descends it without breaking his neck has abundant cause for gratitude. In many of these establishments, the only light is that emitted by some half-dozen candles, price one penny each. The stage and the lower seats of the gallery communicate with each other, so that should the actors or actresses chance to quarrel with the occupiers of the first row, in consequence of anything said or done by the latter—and such things do sometimes happen—they can adjust their differences by a fistical decision,—which, being translated into plain English, means, that they may settle their differences by having recourse to a pugilistic rencontre. The stages in all the Penny Theatres are of very limited dimensions, it being desirable, in the estimation of the proprietors, that as much space as possible should be set apart for the accommodation of the audience,—meaning, by the word "accommodation," that room should be provided for the greatest possible number of persons who are willing to pay their pence. In some places, the stage is so small that the actors must be chary of their gesture, lest they break one another's heads. On the article of scenery, the expenditure of the proprietors of Penny Theatres is not extravagant. They have usually some three or four pieces of cloth, which are severally daubed over with certain clumsy figures or representations; and these are made to answer all purposes. I am sure I need not add, that the wardrobe of these gentry is, for the most part, equally limited in quantity, and moderate in expense. The same dresses, in many of the establishments, serve for all pieces, no matter what their diversity of character. The costume that suits the broadest farce is found to answer equally well in the deepest tragedy. The "lovely bride," about to be led to the hymeneal altar, appears in the same apparel as the widow overwhelmed with grief at the death of her husband. The Ghost of Hamlet is to be seen in the same suit as Paul Pry.

Most of the Penny Theatres have their orchestra, if the term can be applied to a couple of fiddlers. In fine weather, the musicians usually stand at the door, because in such cases their "divine strains" are found to answer a double purpose: they attract the attention of the passers-by to what is going on inside, and they at the same time administer to the love of sweet sounds which may be cherished by any of the audience. In cold or rainy weather, the fiddlers take their station nearer the gallery, though even then they do not venture farther than the top of the ladder. In many cases, the proprietors dispense with music altogether, by which means the sixpence usually paid to the fiddler is saved; and that is, in most of these establishments, a very important consideration.

Shakspeare has given a touching picture of the wretchedness of a strolling player's life. He describes his wardrobe as a mass of rags, and his appearance that of starvation personified. The same description applies with equal truth to the histrionic personages who grace the boards of our Penny Theatres. Their costume is literally a thing of shreds and patches: in many cases the repairs made on the original garment have been so numerous, that not a vestige of it remains. As for their physiognomies, again, they must be guilty of bearing false witness, if a substantial meal be not an era in the history of the parties. The fact of Penny Theatre performers living, in a great measure, on chameleon's fare, satisfactorily accounts for the violent squabbles which often occur among them when the piece represented requires there should be something in the shape of an eating exhibition,—as to who has the best right to the slice of bread provided on such occasions. In November last, a very ludicrous scene, arising out of a squabble between two of the actresses as to who had the best right to a piece of bread which required to be munched, occurred at one of those establishments in the immediate neighbourhood of the Victoria Theatre. I do not recollect the name of the piece represented, but the leading characters in the plot were a Queen and a Duchess. These characters were sustained by two females, tall and bony, and with a most hungry expression of countenance. Everything went on smoothly enough for a time: never seemingly were there two more attached friends in the world, than her majesty and her grace. At length, her majesty ordered dinner to be provided for herself and the duchess. The servant in waiting promptly put a piece of board across two chairs, which was made to answer the purposes of a table admirably well. A piece of cloth, which had all the appearance of being the half of a potato-sack, was spread on the board as the only substitute for a table-cloth which the palace could furnish at the time. A slice of bread, about half an inch in thickness, was then brought in on the fragment of a plate, by one of the queen's servants, and laid on the table. Every one who saw it must have grieved to think that the sovereign, who but a few minutes before had been heard talking in pompous strains, as with an air of royal dignity she strutted across the stage, of her extensive empire and inexhaustible riches,—should not have had a better meal provided for her; but so it was. Her most gracious majesty and her grace the duchess had nothing for dinner between them but the one slice of bread: they had not even a morsel of butter, or a modicum of cheese. While dinner was being laid, they had, as became the dignity of their station, retired to the robing-room, which robing-room is made out of a corner of the stage, cut off by a small wooden partition, with a door to admit of egress and ingress. As this Lilliputian box adjoined the first row of seats, everything that passed in it was distinctly heard by a large portion of the audience, except when the noise, caused by the performances on the stage, was sufficiently great to drown the voices of the inmates. At this time, there being not only no noise, but nobody on the stage, every word that was spoken by either of the exalted personages in the little room, was audible to all in that end of the house who did not choose to put their fingers in their ears to exclude the sounds. In the first instance, a sort of whisper was heard in the inside; and for a time, as neither of the inmates was likely to make her appearance, it looked as if the dinner were to remain untouched. One could not help thinking, homely as the meal was, that this was a pity; for it was clear, from the eagerness with which some of the audience, especially a chimney-sweeper's apprentice, gazed on the slice of bread, that there were no want of mouths in the house that would have despatched the humble meal ordered by the queen, with an edifying expedition. The whisper, which was at first so faint as to be scarcely cognizable by the ear, soon broke out into sounds so loud as to be almost terrific. "I won't—

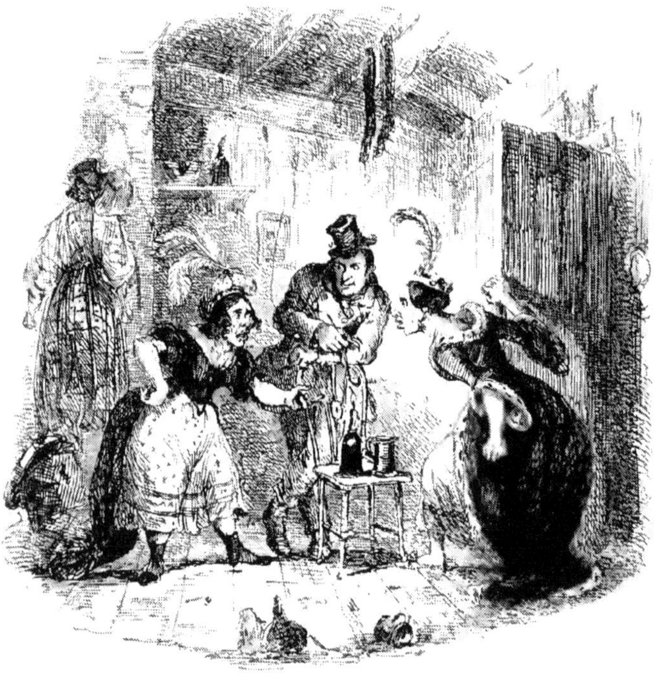

I shan't—I will not let her have it to-night again," said her majesty, advancing to the door of the little room, and looking quite savage as well as hungry.

"Let her have it to-night," said a voice, evidently that of a man, soothingly, "and it will be your turn to-morrow night."

"Oh, but I won't, though!" shouted the queen, with great energy. As she spoke, she came out of the robing-room, and walked, with all the appearance of offended majesty, a few steps along the stage. "I don't see why she should have it oftener than me," she added, wheeling about on her heels, and again approaching the Lilliputian apartment.

"You have had it twice for my once for a week past," said the duchess, apostrophizing her sovereign in very indignant accents.

The audience were all this time lost in utter ignorance of the cause of the scene; and it seemed for some time to be quite a question with many of them whether the parties to it were actually quarrelling with each other, or only acting. To any one of ordinary penetration, it must at once have appeared that there was too great a fidelity to nature for the scene to be acted; and that, therefore, there existed some real ground of quarrel between her most gracious majesty and her grace the duchess. The sudden appearance of the two amazons—for that was now the character in which they appeared—on the stage, where the quarrel rose to an alarming height, coupled with the frequent reference made to the slice of bread, soon satisfied the audience that it was the innocent cause of the deadly quarrel. The duchess, not only forgetting all personal respect herself for her sovereign, but regardless of the tendency of her disloyal conduct to lower royalty in the estimation of the audience, was unmeasured in her vituperation of her majesty. Her grace stoutly asserted that the queen had a stomach for everything; that she was never contented with her own share of victuals, but wished to have that of everybody else; and that were she to have her own way, she would waste all the proceeds of the establishment in administering to the cravings of her insatiable appetite.

"Miss," said her majesty, with much affected dignity, "you know you don't speak the truth."

"Marm," shouted the duchess, "I *do* speak the truth, and you know it too. You know you've got an appetite as there is no satisfying; you have, indeed, you starvation-looking 'ooman." As her grace spoke, she looked quite furiously at the queen, and strutted a few paces across the stage. The audience, as might be expected, were quite shocked at the insult thus offered to her majesty.

"You are a good-for-nothing individwal—indeed you are, Miss," retorted the queen, with great warmth, and violently stamping her foot on the floor.

It was now, for the first time, that those of the audience not previously acquainted with the actresses learnt that her majesty was married, and that her grace was single.

"Vy don't you divide it between you?" said a voice in the gallery.

"Yes," responded another of the penny spectators; "and that would set all to rights."

"Ay, do," said the actor already referred to, who all this time had been looking very much concerned at the quarrel that was going on between the queen and the duchess, but seemed afraid to interfere. "Ay, do, there 's good creatures; and that will end all disputes."

"Well, I don't mind though I do it this once," said her majesty, assuming an aspect of great condescension. The duchess also assented to the compromise without a word of murmur; and both sat down to the frugal repast the best friends in the world. The division of the slice, which was made by her majesty, appeared, as far as the audience could judge, to be of the most equitable kind. The exalted personages, however, were not allowed to eat their meal in peace. Before they had munched the piece of bread, a noise, like that of an infant screaming, was heard to proceed from behind the curtain, and, in a moment afterwards, a shrill tremulous voice from the same locality, evidently addressed to her majesty, was heard to say, "Make haste, Mrs. Junks—do pray make haste, for Lubella is crying for the breast." The matter was clear in an instant; the screaming proceeded from a young princess. Her majesty, to her credit be it spoken, did not allow the dignity of her situation to interfere with her maternal duties; but hastily snatching up the remainder of her share of the slice of bread, and poking it into her mouth, quitted the stage to administer to the wants of her infant princess, leaving the duchess to enjoy her dinner at leisure.

It is curious to contrast the actual condition of the histrionic personages who figure at the Penny Theatres with the circumstances in which they are often professionally placed. Their assumed character, I have frequently thought, must very materially aggravate the evils of their real condition. On the stage, they often appear as emperors, kings, dukes, empresses, queens, duchesses, &c., and as such talk, in pompous and boasting strains, of their inexhaustible wealth, their immense resources, and their vast power; when the real truth is, that they cannot command a single sixpence wherewith to procure themselves a homely meal; nor does their power extend so far as to induce any one to bestow on them a morsel of bread. How great the contrast between the poor creatures strutting about on the stage with the assumed dignity of monarchs, while they are at the very moment enduring the pains of hunger, and know not an individual in the world who would move a step to rescue them from the horrors of actual starvation.

The severity of the privations which these parties are often doomed to undergo, will at once be inferred when I state what are the usual salaries they receive. Fourteen pence per night, and this, be it observed, for performing, it may be, in six or seven pieces, is thought a high rate of remuneration for the histrionic services of a poor wight acting at a Penny Theatre. Tenpence, or five shillings per week, is the more common rate of salary. How the poor creatures manage to subsist at all on this, I am at a loss to know; for between rehearsals through the day, and committing new pieces to memory, they have not time, even if they had the opportunity, to endeavour to eke out a miserable existence in any other way. But even this is not all. I know many instances in which penny theatre performers have a wife and three or four children dependent on them for support. Mr. Hector Simpson, the proprietor of the Tooley-street penny establishment, and also of a theatre in the neighbourhood of Queen-square, Westminster, lately detailed several affecting cases of this kind to me. When I spoke of one in particular, in which each member of the family had not above three halfpennyworth of food per diem, I asked him how they managed in such a case to preserve existence

"That's quite a mystery, Sir," replied Mr. Hector Simpson.

"It is, indeed, a mystery. I cannot think how it can be done at all."

"They do it, though," observed Mr. Simpson, significantly shaking his head.

"But how?" I again inquired.

"Ay, that's the rub," observed Mr. Hector Simpson, quoting Shakspeare quite seriously, and still declining to enlighten me on the subject.

"But it appears to me," I added, "that the thing is physically impossible."

"Oh, you've come to physical impossibilities, have you? These are things we know nothing about, Sir; there are no physical impossibilities with us. Mr. Hector Simpson drew his hand across his beard as he spoke.

"I'm happy to hear it, Mr. Simpson; it's very fortunate for you."

"It's the case, Sir," said the latter, with an air of some importance; "it is, indeed, Sir."

In many cases the proprietors of Penny Theatres are as poor as the players. In other words, the speculation does not pay, and they are sometimes obliged to withhold the supplies, scanty as they are at best, from the poor performers. This, as might be expected, often leads to disputes between the lessees and the actors; and it does sometimes happen that, in imitation of the conduct which has of late been once or twice pursued at some of the larger theatrical establishments, the actors unanimously refuse to play until their arrears, or at least an instalment of them, are paid up. This usually has the effect of either prompting the proprietor to make some extraordinary exertions to raise what they call the "wherewith," or of breaking up the concern altogether. In those cases in which the latter alternative occurs, it does occasionally happen that, in imitation of the example set them some short time since, by the company at the English Opera House, the corps dramatique enter into the speculation on their own account, thankful if they are able, at the close of the establishment each evening, to divide among themselves as much profit as will make the remuneration of the services of each, tenpence or one shilling.

It sometimes happens that the proprietor of a Penny Theatre takes advantage of the good nature of some particular performer by allowing his salary to "run up," while he is pretty prompt in the payment of the salaries of others. Such proprietors, however, are sure to find in the end, that even the best-natured of mortals cannot be always trifled with, or unjustly treated, with impunity. "A hungry man is an angry man,"—so says the proverb; and never was there a truer adage. I need not repeat Lord Bacon's just observation, "that of all rebellions the rebellion of the belly is the worst." Hence when a good-natured actor is goaded on by hunger to quarrel with his employer in consequence of the non-payment of his salary, he usually assumes a very determined aspect, and acts with a decision and spirit which no one would otherwise have expected of him. At one of the Penny Theatres over the water, an amusing scene of this kind lately occurred. The fall of the curtain intimated that the first piece was over. A considerable space of time having elapsed without any appearance of the second piece being about to be commenced, the audience became impatient, and set up the shouts and exclamations usual in such circumstances. Eventually the curtain was raised; but, behold, the stage was unoccupied! After the lapse of about half a minute, cries of "Why don't you begin?" proceeded from all quarters; but for a time no one appeared on the boards to answer the question. The conduct of the audience eventually became alarmingly uproarious. Apprehensive of an actual riot, the lessee at last came forward, and begged the indulgence of the "ladies and gentlemen," on the ground that a temporary accident had occurred to the actor who was the leading character in the piece.

"Vat accident is it?" inquired an unwashed ragged youth in the midst of the audience.

"Vy, it was—hem; it was ——." Here the lessee hesitated, as if unable, on the moment, to invent some plausible answer.

"I say, old 'un, you seem at a loss," shouted a tailor's apprentice.

"Voy, I'm blessed if he knows vat to say," said another patron of the penny drama.

"Come, old chap, can't you tell us vat 's the matter," said a third.

"Vy, ladies and gemmen, he 's ashamed on himself," observed one of the actors, rushing on the stage. "The cause, ladies and gemmen, of this delay is, that I von't hact, because this 'ere person von't pay me my salary."

Cries of "Shame! shame!" proceeded from every throat in the house.

"*Vill* you allow me to explain?" inquired the lessee of the establishment, with great earnestness, looking imploringly towards his patrons, dignified with the name of an audience.

"No, don't you!" said the actor, casting a most piteous glance in the same direction,—"no, don't; he owes me a fortnight's salary, and I can't get a stiver from him."

The cries of "Shame! shame!" were here renewed with redoubled energy.

"I do assure you ————" The unfortunate lessee again struggled hard to obtain a hearing, but without effect. His voice was drowned amidst a volley of exclamations denunciatory of his conduct in withholding the poor actor's miserable salary from him.

"I will pay him to-morrow," said the lessee.

"Don't believe a word he says," observed the actor.

"I pledge myself to pay him to ——"

"Vy don't you do it now?" interrupted a gruff voice in the gallery, the proprietor of which was afterwards ascertained to be an errand-boy in the employ of a neighbouring cheesemonger.

"Ay, vy don't you do it now?" echoed the poor actor, whose lank cheeks bespoke his distressed condition; "you knows that no one can hact well without vittals, and I have not had a mouthful since yesterday."

The lessee renewed his promises to settle matters on the morrow.

"Oh, it von't do," said the actor, drawing back his head, and giving it a significant shake; I 've had a precious deal too many of your promises already, not to know that they are not worth a straw.

This short speech of the unfortunate actor was greeted with loud cheers and cries of "Bravo! bravo!"—"Go it! old boy."

"Vill you just allow me one word? Upon my honour——"

"We didn't know you ever had any," interrupted a small shrill voice.

"If he has, I never saw any of it," observed the refractory actor, with some sharpness.

"I *vill* pay you to-morrow," said the lessee, in soothing strains, addressing himself to the histrionic personage whose refusal to act had caused the unpleasant scene which was being exhibited.

"I will not move a step nor utter a word until I'm paid," said the latter, in a firm and audible voice.

"I really cannot pay it you just now; I have not got as much money at my own disposal.

"I'll take a part, then, just now, and the rest to-morrow," said the poor half-famished performer.

Loud cheers, mingled with cries of "Surely, the old chap can't refuse that," greeted the intimation.

"Here 's five shillings, just now," said the lessee, after fumbling some time in his pocket.

"And you 'll pay me the other five shillings to-morrow," said the actor, as he held out his hand to receive the crown.

"I vill."

"Then let the play commence," shouted the histrionic personage, advancing some paces on the stage with an aspect of great dignity, but still keeping the five shillings close in his hand, which by this time had been thrust into his pocket. The piece was accordingly begun, amidst the cordial applause of the audience, and it was a positive luxury to witness the spirit and effect with which the poor fellow now went through his part, compared with the feeble, spiritless, and inefficient way in which he performed his character in the first piece. And it is no wonder; for not only did he now see the prospect of "summut to eat to supper," but it was an epoch in his history to have five shillings in his possession at once.

But though many of the Penny Theatres are such losing concerns to the proprietors and all concerned, that it is with difficulty that either can obtain as much from them as will support life, there are some of them that prove profitable speculations. Mr. Hector Simpson has the supreme satisfaction of thinking, that if he loses money by his theatre at Westminster, he gains more than he loses by the penny establishment in the classic regions of Tooley-street.

The rentals of the Penny Theatres vary, as a matter of course, according to the size and condition of the house. Perhaps the average rental is fifteen shillings per week. In some cases, when a place is to be fitted up for the first time as a theatre, the proprietors of the house enter into an arrangement with the lessee, that when the latter thinks fit to leave the place, or is ejected from it by the proprietor, the latter shall take every thing in the shape of fixtures off the lessee's hand, paying him whatever money he expended in the article of fitting up. When such arrangements have been entered into between the parties, the lessee is expected to produce a separate bill for every thing he had, even in matters of the most trifling nature, for his fitting up. One of these lessees lately mentioned to me a variety of articles, for which he had separate bills to produce whenever he and the proprietor should tire of each other. Some of them are rather funny. Among the number, one for a pennyworth of nails, made out as all of them were, in due form, ran thus:—

Mr. Tobias Trunk,
Bought of SAUNDERS and RAFF,
One pennyworth of nails for his establishment in the New Cut £0 0 1
1837. Received payment,
Nov. 20. SAUNDERS and RAFF.

Let the reader only fancy three or four score accounts, all for articles whose individual price was under threepence, made out in the same way, and he will be able to form some idea of the regularity which the lessees of Penny Theatres are obliged to observe in their financial dealings with the proprietors. Mr. Tobias Trunk, observing that I felt considerably surprised at the circumstance of his asking a bill duly receipted for so trifling a purchase as a pennyworth of nails, said, with a significant shake of the head, and a slight twitch of his nose, "I have no doubt, Sir, you think this very strange; but still it is necessary it should be done. We never take one another's word in such matters; we must have black and white for every thing we do; we must indeed, Sir."

"But, Mr. Trunk," said I, "what did the merchants whom you patronized when making your penny and twopenny purchases think, when you asked them for a bill and receipt?"

"Bless my soul, Sir," answered Mr. Tobias Trunk, "they thought, as I suppose you do, that I was a little cracked."

"Oh, Mr. Trunk! that's too bad; I neither have said nor done anything that could justify you in concluding that I had formed that opinion of you."

"*You* have not; but I could easily see that they thought there was a screw loose in the upper part of my machinery; for they first looked as amazed at me as if I had asked them to make me a present of their property, and then observed that they were not in the habit of making out accounts for such small purchases."

"But still you managed to get them to do it at last, Mr. Trunk."

"I did, Sir, I persewered; and persewerance, as the world now wags, you know is everything."

"It certainly performs wonderful feats, Mr. Trunk."

"Wery vonderful feats, Sir."

Among the most amusing circumstances to be met with in the annals of penny theatrical establishments, are the squabbles which take place betwixt the performers in the private room, when contrasted with the ardent friendship and boundless affection they show towards each other on the stage. At one of these theatres in the New Cut, a very laughable instance of this kind occurred about six weeks since. Mr. Trotter appeared in the character of a gay Lothario, paying his addresses to an old and masculine-looking female, rejoicing in the appellation of Miss Honoria Chessmore. I will answer for it that two more devoted lovers than this interesting couple, never existed in a poet's imagination, far less in the regions of actual life, seen only as they trod the classic boards of the theatre in question; and yet, the moment they made their exit, in order that other of the dramatis personæ might appear on the stage, they renewed with a vigour and point seldom equalled, (surpassed were out of the question,) an old quarrel, which I afterwards learnt was of very considerable standing, respecting the share which each had in the emptying of a pot of beer which the lessee had left in the green-room, while none but themselves were present. After being engaged for about a minute, in an altercation on the subject, of so violent a nature that the whole of the audience who heard it, must have momentarily expected it would end in a throttling match, it became their turn again to appear on the stage. They did so with the strictest histrionic punctuality, and again embraced each other with a fervour of affection which it was a positive luxury to witness; while the words in which they conversed together, were of the most honied description that ever escaped human lips. By-and-bye it again became their duty to retire, to allow other characters to unfold the part of the plot with the developement of which they were entrusted, when the mortal quarrel about the pot of beer was recommenced with the same energy as before. These transitions from being the most deadly enemies, which they were in reality in the green-room, to the most devoted of lovers on the stage, were continued for about ten minutes, and afforded a view of human nature in its connection with the realities and assumed circumstances of life, which the philosopher might have contemplated with an interest of no ordinary kind.

In connection with the observations I have just made, I may mention that it often happens, that a husband and wife, not in the habit of living on the most affectionate terms at home, have to personate a married couple whom the author has described as living in a state of the purest love and of uninterrupted concord. The contrast between their appearance on the stage and at home, must, in such cases, forcibly strike the minds of all such parties, if not lost to all reflection. Not long since, a poor wight of a husband at one of these penny establishments, was so affected with the acting of his spouse in the character of a devoted wife, though a perfect Xantippe at home, that he could not help whispering in her ear in the midst of the performance—"Ah, my dear, I would give the whole world to see you as kind and affectionate at home as you appear just now." On the following night a new piece was produced at the same establishment, in which the poor hen-pecked fellow had again to sustain the character of husband, and in which his better half appeared in the character of his wife. In the case of the latter, however, there was this very important difference, as compared with her appearance the previous evening—that it now devolved on her to act the part of a wife who played both the tyrant and virago at home. Here her acting far surpassed that of the former evening, though it was wonderfully fair; because she now appeared in her natural character. She had now simply to exhibit on the stage what she had for years nightly practised without an effort at home. And so great was the resemblance of her manner on the stage, to what it was in her capacity of wife in the domestic relations of life, that the poor fellow could not help bursting out, looking significantly and with uplifted hands, towards the audience—"It's so like—jist the thing—that's the very way she goes on at home."

The histrionic gentlemen and ladies who grace the boards of Penny Theatres, are remarkably dexterous hands at mangling, or, as they call it, abridging pieces. Hamlet is often performed in twenty minutes; and Macbeth, and Richard the Third, and the other tragedies of Shakspeare, are generally "done" in much about the same time. Of all Shakspeare's plays, Othello is the greatest favourite of these establishments; very possibly because it is easier to assume the appearance of the Moor, than of any other of Shakspeare's heroes. A little soot smeared over the phiz of the actor undertaking the part, is deemed a sufficient external qualification for the part; whereas in many other cases, something in the shape of dresses is supposed to be necessary.

In the abridging of pieces the performers at the Penny Theatres are guided by no fixed rules. Time is the only counsellor to whose directions they will condescend to lend an ear. They will sometimes unwittingly devote perhaps ten minutes to the representation of some of the more interesting scenes in the first act, and then on being apprised that they have only ten minutes more to finish the whole, they overleap the second, third, and fourth acts, and very possibly land about the middle of the fifth. Should they even then be getting on more slowly than the lessee deems it right, and he wishes to have the piece "done out of hand," he desires them to come at once to the "last scene of all," which they do, and then enact that scene with an expedition with which it were in vain for any steam power to attempt to compete. I was lately very much amused on learning that at most of these places the lessee is in the habit of standing on one side of the stage watching the time, and that when it is within a minute or two of that which he has in his own mind allotted for that particular piece, he exclaims, "Time up!—finish the piece!—down with the curtain!" and it is all done as he desires. Scarcely have the words passed his lips, when the whole affair is over, and down falls the curtain. In those cases in which he knows how the thing ought to end, he is more precise in his directions. In the case of Othello, for example, when the time has expired, even though the performers should not have got beyond the first act, he says, "The time is up—commit the murder, and down with the curtain." Desdemona is then strangled in a moment, down goes the curtain, and out go the audience.

In several of these establishments, as many as from ten to twelve new pieces are sometimes produced in one week. In the theatre in Queen-square, Westminster, a round dozen new pieces were actually brought out in one week in the middle of last December. Of course, in such cases, but little pains are bestowed on the composition. Even suppose the writer, and there are seldom more than one or two writers for one establishment, had the talents requisite to the production of a tolerable piece, he can neither have the time nor the scope to display those talents to any advantage. With regard again to the performers committing pieces to memory, that were altogether out of the question. They are told a few of the leading incidents, and are either allowed to look at the manu script of the piece, and by that means endeavour to remember some of the phrases, or to express themselves in any words which occur to themselves. They are, in fact, obliged to do from necessity, what John Reeve used to be in the habit of doing from sheer indolence, namely, express themselves in the best way they can. And horrible work, as might be expected, from the very imperfect education of many of their number, do they usually make of it. They murder the Queen's English much more remorselessly than they do their own heroes; for, in the latter case, you sometimes see in their countenances, or demeanour, the operation of some qualm of conscience; but in the former there is nothing of the kind. To speak the truth, they remain ignorant, and will do so to the last, of the butchery of the English language of which they have been guilty.

But there is something still more ludicrous in the Penny Theatre productions. Their authors, who are always performers in the establishment, often begin not only to write them without having made up their minds as to how they will end, but even cause the acting of the first part to commence before the latter part is finished. When the author sees the length of time which the manuscript he has given out takes to act, he is then able to decide on the length to which he ought to extend the remainder of the piece. The performers, in such cases, after being made acquainted with the incidents, must do the best they can with them. An instance of this kind occurred about six weeks since, under my own observation. I asked the lessee what was the nature of the new piece which was then beginning to be acted. "Upon my word, Sir, I cannot tell you," was the answer. "I usually leave these things to the actor who gets them up," he added. After a moment's pause, he asked, for my information, the author-actor who chanced to pass us at the time, how the piece would end. "Vy," said the latter, whose name was Hardhead, "I'm not exactly sure yet; but I think I'll end it either with a murder or a suicide."

"Why not with both?" suggested the lessee.

"That certainly would give the piece a more tragic termination," I observed.

"Werry vell, then, I shall have both on 'em," said Mr. Hardhead, with the utmost indifference, as if it were quite immaterial in what way the piece should end; and with what the penny-a-liners call a "shocking case of suicide," and a "dreadful murder," it did accordingly end.

The dramatis personæ of the Penny Theatres keep up, in most cases, a very close intimacy with the audience. In many instances they carry on a sort of conversation with them during the representations of the different pieces. It is no uncommon thing to see an actor stop in the middle of some very interesting scene, to answer some question asked by one of the audience, or to parry any attempted witticism at his expense. This done, the actor resumes his part of the performance as if nothing had happened; but possibly before he has delivered half a dozen sentences more, some other question is asked, or some other sarcastic observation made by one of the auditory, in which case the performer again stops to answer or retort, as if by way of parenthesis. A cross fire is thus sometimes kept up between the audience and the actors for several minutes at a time, and, to my taste, such "keen encounters of the wits" of the parties are much more amusing than the histrionic performances themselves. Decidedly the best thing of the kind which I ever witnessed while collecting, by personal observation, materials for this chapter, occurred about four months since, in an establishment some forty or fifty yards off High Holborn. A poor fellow, short in stature, and half-starved in appearance, with a ragged coat, which, but for its tails, would, from its shortness, have been mistaken for a jacket, came forward in the midst of the piece to treat the audience to one of his best vocal efforts. I do not now recollect the name of the song, but it was one of course of a prodigiously comical kind; for all the songs at these establishments are remarkable for their excess of the comical. I could not help thinking with myself, what a difference there must have been between the poor fellow's actual mood of mind, and that in which the song made him appear. The audience, however, did not seem to be encumbered by anything in the shape of moralization, but were clearly resolved to have as much amusement as possible for their pence. Most heartily did they laugh at the most laughable things in the song. So far all was well; for they had an undoubted right, having paid for it, to exercise their risible faculties as much as they pleased; but in the middle of the song, a little urchin threw a potato at the vocalist, and hit him right on the forehead. As might be expected, he suddenly paused: and made a remarkably rapid transition from the comical to the tragic. He put his hand to his forehead, and looked for a few seconds terrifically at the part of the house whence the potato was projected. At last he stammered out, in half indignant half pathetic tones, "Who did that?"

"It was not me?" answered one.

"Nor me," said another.

"I didn't do it, any how," observed a third.

"Nor I either," shouted a chorus of voices.

"Perhaps *nobody* did it," said the poor fellow, with an aspect of great simplicity.

"Per'aps not," answered a little rogue, amidst peals of laughter.

"Whoever did it," said the songster, becoming better humoured as the pain abated; "whoever did it, might, at any rate, have boiled the potato first."

"Vat for?" inquired another of the patrons of the penny drama.

"I'll tell you what for ——"

Here the vocalist was interrupted by a voice—"O I knows vat for!"

"No you don't," said the actor.

"I do though."

"Vell, vat is it for?" inquired a little sickly-looking boy who sat beside him.

"Vy, bekase as how if it had been a boiled 'un, it would have been so soft as not to have 'urt him."

"No, that's not it," said the poor fellow.

"Vell, vat is it then?" shouted a dozen voices.

"I'm blessed if *I* don't know," said a tin-trumpet sort of voice, from the centre of the audience.

"Let's have it then," said the vocalist.

"Voy, bekase if as how it 'ad been a boilt, you could have eaten it."

A shout of laughter followed the clever observation of the urchin, in which the vocalist could not refrain from joining. He then endeavoured to resume the song at the place at which he was interrupted; but not being able to remember it, observed, with infinite good nature, "O, we must begin again;" and he did begin again, and end too, in excellent style.

I will just mention one other amusing proof of the familiarity which so generally subsists between the corps dramatique at Penny Theatres and the audience. It occurred about eight weeks since, at Cooke's establishment in the New Cut. The piece which had been performing was one of so awfully a tragic kind, especially towards the conclusion, that even two policemen, a class of men not said to be remarkable for their susceptibilities on such occasions, who had stationed themselves in a dark corner of the house, for the purpose of pouncing on two young thieves whom they expected to make their appearance that evening, could not refrain from affording some indications that they, any more than the rest of the audience, were not insensible to the touching scenes which were passing before them. The *dénouement* was at length at hand. The piece was a love one; and the lover, goaded on by the violence of the green-eyed monster's operations in his bosom, determined to be revenged both on his rival, and on the mistress of his heart, for countenancing the tender advances of any one but himself. No sooner had he formed his determination than he prepares to carry it into immediate effect. He procures a pair of pistols and a dagger. He loads the former, and concealing them, with the dagger, under his cloak, seeks a meeting with the intended victims.

That meeting he soon gets: he discovers them both together in very earnest and affectionate conversation. He discharges one pistol at his rival, and the other at his sweetheart, and then plunges the dagger into his own bosom. The whole three fall almost instantaneously; but as they fell, and while the audience were all wrapt in horror at the frightful tragedy, out came from behind the scenes a ragged boy, with a corduroy jacket, and a basket in his extended hand, and stepping over the bodies of the dying trio, as careless-like as if he had been walking on Waterloo-road, sang out, "Apples!—six a penny!" A little dog, at the same instant, as if the thing had been the result of concert, sprung also from behind the scenes, and set up a loud barking. The affair was infinitely ludicrous, and converted, as if by some magical influence, the horror and sorrow with which the audience were overwhelmed but a moment before, in consequence of the dreadful tragedy they had witnessed, into a loud and universal roar of laughter, which was only put an end to by the fall of the curtain.

The audiences at the Penny Theatres are peculiar in their dramatic taste. They are not only fond of extremes, but will tolerate nothing else. Comedy is completely proscribed by them; they must either have the deepest tragedy or the broadest farce. In the tragic way, they evince a remarkably strong predilection for "horrible murders;" and the moment that accounts of any such occurrence appear in the newspapers, a piece embodying the most shocking incidents in that occurrence is got up for representation at these establishments. The recent atrocity known by the name of the Edgeware murder, was quite a windfall to many of the Penny Theatres. Pieces founded on the most frightful of the circumstances connected with it were forthwith got up, and acted to crowded houses, amidst great applause. It will hardly be believed, yet such is the fact, that so late as November last—that is, full ten months after the occurrence took place—it was represented in these establishments to numerous audiences. The following is a verbatim copy of one of the placards, announcing it for a particular night, as the leading piece for the benefit of one of the performers:—

FOR THE BENEFIT OF MR. TWIG.

On Tuesday next will be performed the Grand National Dramar

OF

GREENACRE,

OR

THE MURDER *OF* CARPENTER'S BUILDINGS.

The farces, as I have just stated, are of the broadest kind: the broader and more absurd, the better do they take. At a penny establishment on the Lambeth side of the water, which my curiosity, and the desire of procuring accurate information, induced me to visit seven or eight weeks since, one of the most successful pieces consisted of such matter as the following:—

Enter Tom Snooks, Harry Finch, and Ned Tims.

Tom Snooks.—I say, Harry, will you lend me a tanner (a sixpence) till to-morrow?

Harry Finch.—I vould if I could, but blow me tight if so be as I've got one.

Tom Snooks.—I say, Ned, old 'un, can you do anything?

Ned Tims.—Voy, Tom, may I never smoke another pipe o' baccy, if I've got a stiver in the world.

Tom Snooks.—I say, chaps, as we are all poor alike, vat do you say to a goin' a robbin' o' some old rich fellers?

Harry Finch.—Capital, Tom, nothing could be better; don't you think so, Ned?

Ned Tims.—Voy, yes, if it were not for wot follows.

Tom Snooks.—Vat do you mean?

Ned Tims.—Vat I means is this 'ere, that I'm afear'd we might all three get scragged (hanged).

Tom Snooks.—Pooh, pooh! all nonsense.

Harry Finch.—Vell, Ned, I'm bless'd if I ever thought you were such a coward.

Ned Tims.—Vell, dash my vig if I cares vat be the consekence—I'll go. I say, chaps, hush—I'm blowed if there be not an old feller on the road there: let's begin with him.

Tom Snooks.—Done, Ned, done.

Harry Finch.—Come, Ned (patting him on the shoulder, and looking him coaxingly in the face), may I never have a button to my coat if you ben't a regular trump.

Enter an eccentric-looking Stranger.

Stranger.—Can you tell me, friends, how far I am from the next inn?

Ned Tims (seizing the stranger by the throat).—Your money or your life, Sir.

Tom Snooks.—Yes, my old bowl, your money or your life.

Harry Finch.—And this moment too.

Stranger.—Oh, ho! that's it, is it? But how do you know I've got any?

Ned Tims.—Then out goes your brains (putting his hand beneath a sort of cloak, as if grasping a pistol in his hand).

Stranger.—Why, my good friends, if the truth must be told, I'm quite as destitute of brains as of money: I've got none of neither.

Ned Tims (to the stranger).—Come, old feller, no gammon with us. If you don't fork out the yellow boys (sovereigns) presently, I'll send a ball through your carcass, which will make a passage broad enough to let a coach and six be driven through with ease.

Stranger.—You don't mean that?

Ned Tims.—We do, indeed. Don't we, young men.

Harry Finch.—Ay, that we do.

Tom Snooks.—Yes; and no mistake.

Here the appearance of some person puts an end to the dialogue, the trio of scamps taking to their heels without loss of time. In a short time afterwards, they again appear on the stage, when they are found in a very jocular mood, and conversing on a variety of subjects.

Tom Snooks.—They say the cholera is coming to wisit this town.

Harry Finch.—Vell, and vat about it?

Tom Snooks.—Voy, it's wery alarming.

Ned Tims.—But voy should they let it come into the town?

Tom Snooks.—But how can they keep it out?

Ned Tims.—Voy, by giving the toll-keeper strict orders not to let it pass the turnpike-gate on any account.

I shall only give one more short specimen of the sort of dramatic literature which is most popular at the Penny Theatres.

Harry Finch.—I say, Ned, old feller, do you know I've become a father this morning?

Tom Snooks.—Vat! a papa, Harry?

Mr. Finch nodded in token of assent.

Ned Tims (seizing his hand).—Ah, Harry, my boy, I wish you much joy. Pray, vot have you got?

Harry Finch.—Guess.

Ned Tims.—A boy?

Harry Finch.—No; guess again.

Ned Tims.—Per'aps a girl, eh?

Harry Finch (apparently with great surprise).—Bless my soul, Ned, I'm blow'd if you ain't a guessed it.

This has but little effect in the mere telling; but when spoken with a certain archness of manner, it sets the whole audience in a roar of laughter.

The play-bills of the Penny Theatres are never printed. The expense of printing is too great for the state of the treasury to admit of that. They are all written, and are seldom to be seen anywhere but on a board in the immediate neighbourhood of the various places. The titles of the pieces are always of a clap-trap kind. The following is a specimen :—

On Thursday next will be performed at Smith's Grand Theatre,

THE RED-NOSED MONSTER,

OR

THE TYRANT OF THE MOUNTAINS.

Red-nosed Monster - - -	Mr. SAVAGE.
The Assassin - - - -	Mr. TONGS.
The Ruffian of the Hut - -	Mr. DARTMAN.
The Villain of the Valley - -	Mr. PRICE SHORT.
Wife of the Red-nosed Monster -	Mrs. TAPSTER.
Daughter of the Assassin - -	Miss BLACK.

To conclude with the

BLOOD-STAINED HANDKERCHIEF,

OR

THE MURDER IN THE COTTAGE.

The Characters by the Company.

The Christmas holidays are the most productive seasons at the Penny Theatres. The Pantomimes "draw" houses "crowded to excess." The playbills, on such occasions, are written in unusually large and striking letters. The following specimen is copied, without the alteration of a word, or the slightest departure from the punctuation, from a placard which was exhibited at one of these establishments in St. George's Fields, on the 28th of December last:—

To. Day.
Will, be produced. A, splendid
(New) PANTOMIME
With, New. Scenery Dresses.
Tricks (and) Decorations, Written and
Got, up. under (the) Direction. of
Mr. CLARKE entitled

DR. BOLUS OR HARLEQUIN—THE FAIRY
Of. The
TEMPLE DIANA.

Albert, afterwards Harlequin - -	Mr. GUTHRIE.
Gobble, afterwards the Clown -	Mr. BUCKSKIN.
Dr. Bolus, afterwards Pantaloon -	Mr. DRINKWATER.
Runabout - - - - -	Mr. SMITH.
Dozey - - - - -	Mr. JONES.
Rosa, afterwards Columbine - -	Miss SHUTTLE.
Sunbeam, a Fairy - - -	Miss SHORT.
Fishwoman - - - - -	Mrs. SPRATT.

In imitation of the conduct of the managers of the larger establishments,—places which are professedly set apart, in a special manner, for the protection and encouragement of the legitimate drama,—the Penny Theatre lessees occasionally treat their audiences to the performances of the brute creation. I need hardly say that their boards are not sufficiently large to admit of the performances of elephants or of horses. The largest animal I have ever heard of as performing on the stage of a Penny Theatre, was a bear. Bruin was amongst the largest of his species, and was remarkably ferocious in his appearance, to boot. He was the property of a little, lank-cheeked, sharp-eyed man, named Monsey Guff. To his master, Bruin was very strongly attached, though a perfect brute to everybody else; and it is but justice to Mr. Guff to say that there was no love lost between them, for Mr. Guff was exceedingly partial to his bear. The affection of the parties for each other was far stronger than anything of the kind which goes by the name of Platonic. A very interesting practical display of their mutual attachment was afforded, under very trying circumstances, some years ago. It was arranged between the two that they should make the tour of Scotland together, to see what luck they should have in the way of an exhibition; for Bruin, under the able instructions of his master, had made considerable progress in the art of dancing. It is doubtful, indeed, whether he would have made greater proficiency had he been under the tuition of the most distinguished French master extant; for Mr. Guff thoroughly understood the genius of his pupil, which a stranger could not be expected to do. With the bear's acquirements in the art of tripping on the light fantastic toe, Mr. Guff confidently calculated on realizing a rich harvest from the tour in Scotland. He fancied that Bruin would be just the thing to "draw" the Scotch. Alas! how different the event from the expectation! Mr. Guff says, that he soon found, to his sad experience, that the Caledonians either had no "siller" to spare, or that they would not part with it. In the lower districts of the country, he, and his friend the bear, just managed to get a subsistence; but when they came to the Highlands, nothing but starvation stared them in the face. Before setting out on their journey, the parties came to a distinct understanding that they should live or die together; and for some days they bore their privations with a fortitude that would have done credit to philosophers of the first order. Mr. Guff says that not a single murmur escaped his lips,—unless, indeed, the occasional utterance of a wish to be back to England deserved the name; while poor Bruin, as far as his friend and master could understand what was passing within his mind—if a bear can be said to have a mind—

contented himself with wishing that he were once more in the polar regions. At length, however, matters reached a crisis: the hunger of Mr. Guff and Bruin became so great, that, as in the case of a shipwrecked crew who have been several days without food, no other alternative presented itself to them but that of the one eating the other to preserve life. The question, therefore, was, whether Mr. Guff should eat the bear, or whether the bear should eat Mr. Guff. It was true, that the animal could take no audible part in discussing the matter; but Mr. Guff, who says he clearly understood, on this occasion, Bruin's thoughts, from his physiognomy and manner, unhesitatingly affirms that the bear was perfectly willing to be sacrificed for the preservation of his master and friend; but that he (Mr. Guff) could not reconcile it to his notions of justice, or to his attachment to the bear, to entertain for a moment the idea of eating him up, without first drawing lots, and by that means giving him the same chance as himself for life. Mr. Guff was accordingly about to draw lots as to whether he or the bear should be the victim, when he happened, after having travelled through a bleak and barren part of the country, fifteen miles in length, without seeing a single house,—to discover smoke issuing from a small turf hut about forty or fifty yards before them. To the hut they both proceeded, and so far from the inmates, two aged brothers, being frightened at the sight of Bruin, as they had invariably found the peasantry to be before,—they were delighted to see him, observing that he recalled to their minds the repeated voyages they had made years before, when sailors, to the polar regions. Both Mr. Guff and the bear were treated to a homely but abundant repast, and from that day to this, Mr. Guff says that neither he nor the bear has ever known what hunger is.

But, of all quadrupeds, those teachable animals called dogs are most frequently introduced to the juvenile personages who grace with their presence the Penny Theatres. Some years ago, a Mr. Abel Smith had acquired a tolerable reputation for the exploits which he had taught a couple of Newfoundland dogs to perform. He used to tell a curious story about one of his engagements with the proprietor of a Penny Theatre. For some time he and his dogs confined their exhibitions to Sadler's Wells, which has been for more than a century, as many of my readers are aware, the leading establishment in town for appreciating merit in the brute creation, or anything in the shape of "astonishing" gymnastic performances in the two-legged class of animals. Mr. Abel Smith's dogs, like actors of another kind, eventually ceased to "draw" at the Wells;" and accordingly their engagement soon came to a termination. The proprietor of one of the penny establishments having been apprised of this, thought it would prove a profitable speculation if he could get a fortnight of Mr. Abel Smith's dogs on reasonable terms. He said the thing would be a novelty, at any rate, and could not fail to please, whether it paid or not. Mr. Cross, the Penny Theatre proprietor, consequently waited on Mr. Abel Smith. "Mr. Smith," said the other, "I have come to have a word or two about your dogs."

"Very good, Sir: very wonderful animals, Sir."

"They are said to be very clever, Mr. Smith."

"They *are* very clever, Sir."

"What terms would you propose for the use of them in my theatre, in Shoreditch, for a fortnight?"

"For a fortnight of successive nights?" said Mr. Abel Smith.

"Just so," answered Mr. Cross.

"Oh, we had ten shillings each per night at 'Sadler's Wells.'"

"Ah; but, Mr. Smith, you must remember, that while the price of admission to the boxes at Sadler's Wells is half-a-crown, the pit eighteenpence, and the gallery one shilling, I have got neither boxes nor pit in my establishment; and the price of admission is only one penny."

"Bless my heart!" said Mr. Abel Smith, looking surprised, "I'm not sure, Mr. Cross, if it would be respectable for us to appear on the boards of such an establishment."

"Well, certainly, Mr. Smith," said Mr. Cross, pulling himself up, "you do astonish me. This is the first time I have heard anything about the respectability of dogs."

"Do you mean to say we're not respectable, Sir?" remarked Mr. Abel Smith, with great emphasis, entwining his arms on his breast.

"Not at all, Mr. Smith. I assure you, nothing could be farther from my intention as regards yourself personally: I only meant your dogs."

"My dogs, Sir!" exclaimed Mr. Smith, with great energy, and looking Mr. Cross fiercely in the face.

"Yes, Mr. Smith, *only* your dogs."

"*Only* my dogs! I tell you what, Mr. Cross, those dogs are very respectable animals. I wish all animals with *two* legs conducted themselves with as much propriety." Mr. Abel Smith made two or three hasty paces through the room as he spoke.

"Do you mean any reflection on me, Sir?" said Mr. Cross, with much sharpness. "Do you mean to say that your dogs are more respectable than me?"

"I mean to say this," answered Mr. Abel Smith, with a firm and steady voice, but evading the question put to him; "I mean to say this, that I shall never stand silent by while the respectability of my dogs is called in question. I will not, Mr. Cross. They are noble animals; they *are*, Mr. Cross."

"Mr. Smith, you seem to labour under a strange misconception," observed Mr. Cross, in a more conciliatory tone. "I never impugned, nor meant to impugn, the respectability of your dogs."

"Then you admit that they are respectable?"

"I have no doubt they are, in their own way, Mr. Smith."

"Very good," said the latter, in a tone that showed he was quite satisfied. "Very good: if you wish to engage us, our terms are seven shillings a-piece."

"Seven shillings a-night; that is fourteen shillings altogether," observed Mr. Cross, in a slow and subdued tone, and fixing his eye on the hob, as if lost in a calculation as to what the entire sum would be which he would have to pay Mr. Abel Smith for the fortnight's performances of his dogs.

"Fourteen shillings!" said Mr. Abel Smith, with much surprise; "you're mistaken, Sir; it's a guinea."

"A guinea! How do you make that out? There's only two dogs."

"Very true, Sir; but there's *me*."

"Oh, but it is not necessary to have *you*, Mr. Smith. You don't act; you only say two or three words to the animals. which we can say ourselves."

"Sir," said Mr. Abel Smith, adjusting his collar, "if we don't go together, we don't go at all."

"Really, Mr. Smith, I think that is unreasonable."

"It shall be the case, Sir. My dogs and myself, or no dogs at all. Besides, Sir, the animals won't perform their wonderful feats with any one but myself."

"I don't see why they shouldn't."

"But I tell you they won't, Sir," said Mr. Abel Smith, in a gruff voice.

"Have you any objections to let me try them?"

"Oh, none in the least."

"Well, then, Mr. Smith, perhaps you would call in the first one, and see whether, on my running across the room and repeating the words you use, the animal does not seize me by the neck of the coat without doing me any infury."

"Oh, certainly, Sir. Stampheels! here, here, here."

A large lively-looking dog immediately responded to his master's call, and quitting a back yard, presented himself before Mr. Abel Smith and Mr. Cross.

The latter made a sort of run through the room, and uttered the words which Mr. Smith invariably used in Sadler's Wells when he wished the animal to perform the exploit of seizing him by the neck of the coat without hurting him; but the dog remained motionless at his master's feet.

"Well, Sir," said Mr. Abel Smith, triumphantly, "you are convinced now, I suppose, that the animals won't perform without me?"

"It strikes me," answered Mr. Cross, "that if you were to say, 'Go, Sir,' in a harsh tone, when I repeat the words, that he would go at once, and perform the feat."

"Very well, Sir; we shall try the experiment, if you wish it."

"Do, Mr. Smith."

Mr. Cross again made a bound across the room, repeating the particular words; on which, Mr. Abel Smith, addressing himself in an assumed angry tone to Stampheels, said, "Go, Sir!" The animal that moment started to his feet, and springing on Mr. Cross, seized him ferociously by the neck of his coat. He then threw him on his back on the floor, and gave two or three tremendous growls, as if he had been about to tear him to pieces. Here Mr. Abel Smith interfered, and by rescuing Mr. Cross from the paws and mouth of the animal, prevented the occurrence of any such catastrophe. Mr. Cross, as might be expected, was petrified with fright at the horrible situation in which he had been placed.

"Satisfied now, Sir, I presume, that the dogs won't do without me?" said Mr. Abel Smith, with an air of much self-complacency, addressing himself to Mr. Cross, on the partial recovery of the latter from his fright.

"Oh! quite satisfied, Mr. Smith," said the latter. "You shall come with the dogs, and you'll have your own terms."

Mr. Abel Smith has told this story about "me and my dogs" with infinite zest, a thousand times over, and he tells it still with a glee and earnestness of which no description could furnish an idea.

It is amusing to contrast the respect which the speculators in Penny Theatres pay to their audiences when going in, with the rudeness they often show to them when coming out. When a person is going into one of these establishments, he meets with every politeness from the proprietor, or the person whom he may have stationed at the door to take up the money. When coming out again, the audience are ordered to clear the way, just as if they were so many serfs at the beck of the proprietor or his servants. At some of these establishments, the audience are told on going out, in most authoritative tones, by the proprietor, to "make haste out of the way, to let in my fresh audience." The "fresh audience" are treated with all deference on their entrance, because they then pay their money; but they in due course become what I suppose the proprietors would call their *stale* audience, and meet with the same disrespectful treatment on their quitting the place which they saw those receive whom they encountered in the passage coming out, while they themselves were going in. And yet this is but a modification of a principle which is every day seen and felt in its operations in the ordinary affairs of life. So long as we are of service to our fellow men, they treat us with at least the outward manifestations of respect; but the moment we cease to be so, we meet with a very different treatment. The fable of the man who overlooked the ninety-nine times in which the greyhound had caught the hare, when the animal failed in the hundredth attempt, is hourly illustrated in every walk of life. Of course, there are exceptions, but they are comparatively few in number.

I must in justice say there are some such exceptions—for I know of two—in the case of the proprietors of Penny Theatres. Mr. Hector Simpson, to whom I have made such frequent reference already, is one. So respectfully does Mr. Hector Simpson treat his audiences, that he often goes into the pit unobserved by his company of actors, to see that they do full justice to the audience by fairly acting the piece; and if he sees that any part of the piece has been slovenly represented, or rather *mis*represented, or, worse still, not represented at all, he immediately starts up with the suddenness of an apparition, and sternly commands his actors to play the part over again, or to perform that which they omitted, adding, in indignant and stentorian accents, "I 'm determined that no persons in my employment shall insult my audience with impunity." Mr. Hector Simpson is most assiduous in enjoining on his performers, that they pay the utmost respect, on all occasions, to his audience. It is not improbable that this is one of the principal causes of the great success of his establishment in Tooley-street, while he sees so many other Penny Theatres around him in so deplorable a condition. There is one thing which, in this respect, is in Mr. Hector Simpson's favour: he never suffers the salaries of his actors or actresses to fall into arrear, which very naturally insures obedience to orders that otherwise might be slighted.

Hitherto I have said little of the quality of the acting at the Penny Theatres. In those cases in which the arrangements are such that pieces must be got through in a certain time, without regard to effect, there can, of course, be no good acting, even where there is the requisite talent on the part of the performers. In some of the establishments, however, where there are only two or three, instead of six or seven, "houses" in one night, and where the proprietor trusts to a superior order of acting drawing numerous audiences, and by that means making up for a reduced number of "houses," the acting is, in many cases, really good.

I have seen some pieces, both in tragedy and farce, represented at these establishments, with wonderful effect. Indeed, I am convinced that the acting, as a whole, in the cases to which I refer, would have been applauded at some of our more respectable larger theatres. This will appear the less surprising, when I mention, that many of those who are now subsisting on the miserable pittance they receive for their performances at Penny Theatres, were once great favourites at the larger establishments. One of these unfortunate persons was lately pointed out to me as not only the bosom friend of the late Mr. Munden, one of the most distinguished comedians of his day, but as having many years acted with him in important characters at Drury-lane, and most efficiently supported him in his most arduous parts. And now the poor fellow has only tenpence a night. I forbear mentioning his name, as that would only add to the unhappiness of his condition. It is really painful to think that one who had for so many years been a popular actor, should now, in his old age, partly from the infirmities of his advanced years, and partly from the fickleness of the public taste, be unable to obtain an engagement in any of the larger houses, and consequently be driven as a last resource against the workhouse, to toil night after night at one of these miserable places.* Yet so it is; and not in his case only, but also in that of many others. These unfortunate men, as will easily be understood, having been in the habit of acting well, now act well without an effort; it has become a sort of second nature to them. There are others, again, who have a natural talent for the stage, but who, having never been fortunate enough to get an engagement in any larger house, are obliged to

* It is generally admitted that there is no class of men more improvident than the members of the theatrical profession, taken as a body. In many cases, they have what, in speaking of the pieces in which they perform, they would call such "a run" of good luck, that in a few years they might, with proper economy, save as much as would place them beyond the reach of want; yet it so happens that very few of them have the prudence to lay aside a part of their earnings. They usually live up to their means; very often above their means, even when those means are abundant. They never contemplate for a moment the possible, not to say probable contingency of their popularity declining, and eventually dying away altogether; or of any of the accidents of life occurring to prevent their successful prosecution of their professional pursuits. They take for granted that they are to continue to run an equally prosperous career, and think it enough if they make the day and the journey alike; consequently, when a reverse of circumstances occurs, they have nothing to fall back upon, but are obliged to accept of any engagement, no matter how disrespectable, or how painful to their feelings, which is offered to them. But while I thus refer with regret to the improvidence which is so general among the members of the histrionic profession, it must be admitted, that from the extreme precariousness of that profession, the most provident are often unable to make any provision against a future period. I believe that between improvident habits and the precarious nature of their pursuits, there is more suffering among actors and actresses, than among the members of any other body that could be named.

vegetate in obscurity in these Penny Theatres; so that between these two classes of actors, good acting, where sufficient time is allowed by the proprietors, may often be witnessed at them. In the generality, however, of these establishments, there is no such thing as acting at all. The performers say what they like and do as they like. Stabbing and thrusting in the tragic pieces, and slapping one another's faces, and pulling one another's caps over each other's eyes in the farces, are the principal kinds of acting which are to be seen. The pleasure which would otherwise be enjoyed by those who can appreciate the good acting, must necessarily be much diminished by the consciousness that the actors are so miserably remunerated for their services. I have often wondered how they are able to keep up their spirits sufficiently to enable them to play their parts so well.

I may here observe, not having done it when speaking of the number of Penny Theatres, that they are rapidly on the increase. The oldest of them is of comparatively modern growth, and if they continue for a few years to increase as rapidly as they have done for the last five or six years, they cannot fail to attract the attention of the magistrates, if not the legislature itself. I am quite satisfied, from what I have myself witnessed at these establishments, to say nothing of what has been communicated to me by persons whose word or opportunities of acquiring correct information I had no reason to question, that they do incalculable mischief to the morals of the youths who frequent them.* Whenever the police have reason to believe that some particular boy has been guilty of any act of theft, or other crime cognizable by the civil authorities, they proceed as a matter of course to some spot in the neighbourhood of some of these establishments, not doubting they will meet with the youth of whom they are in quest, either when going in or coming out. But to expatiate here on the mischievous tendency of these places on the morals of the youths who frequent them, would only be to repeat what has been said on the subject in the opening of the chapter. My purpose in again adverting to the matter, is to impress, if possible, on the minds of the civil authorities, the propriety of shutting up the Penny Theatres. The process by which this may be done, is sufficiently simple and easy. The magistrates have only to indict them as nuisances, which they undoubtedly are, to the neighbourhoods in which

* I could indeed refer to particular cases in confirmation of the injurious consequences to the morals of both sexes from attendance on Penny Theatres, but that is unnecessary. One has only to spend a single half hour in one of these places to see and hear what is passing, to be convinced of their highly immoral tendency. A few visits to Penny Theatres by the moralist or philanthropist, could not fail to afford information which might be made conducive to the interests of society.

they are severally placed. This has already been done by the proper authorities in several districts in town. A year or two ago, two or three of them were put down in the east end. leading, if I remember rightly, out of Ratcliffe Highway; and within the last ten or twelve months, several of them, as before stated, have been shut up in the West End. The evil has already reached a sufficient height to justify the interference of the magistrate. Were it likely to abate of itself, that might afford some excuse for looking passively on these places; but when, as already stated, the evil is rapidly on the increase, instead of being on the decline, and when, as I have lately been assured by the proprietors of two of these establishments, they are likely to go on increasing to an extent of which no one has at present any conception, it is surely high time that the proper authorities interfered. As before observed, they must sooner or later be put down by the arm of the law; and consequently it were better they were put down now. Enough of evil has already been done by these places in the way of corrupting the morals of the youths in their respective neighbourhoods; let not the amount of that evil be increased, by not only suffering those already in existence to continue their nightly performances, and by that means extend the mischief, but by allowing new ones to be called into being in different parts of the town.

CHAPTER VI.

THE POLICE OFFICES.

Their Number and Names—Remarks on Bow Street Office—The Thames Police Office—The Magistrates—Number of cases daily brought before them—Yearly Expenses of the Police Offices—Their Expenses Forty Years ago—The Station Houses—Anecdote of a Prisoner—Scenes to be witnessed in the Station Houses—Exhibitions of Human Nature to be witnessed in the Police Offices—Specimens given—North Country Simplicity—The Poetical Cobbler—A Drunken Frolic—Case of alleged Horse-stealing.

In a work devoted to the metropolis, it were an unpardonable omission to pass over in silence the Police Offices. I will, therefore, make them the subject of the present chapter, and shall endeavour to enliven the statistical details which it will be necessary to give by the introduction of matter of a lighter kind.

The Police Offices of London are nine in number. They are thus enumerated in the Report of the Parliamentary Committee appointed in 1833 to inquire into matters connected with the police of the metropolis:—Bow Street, including the horse-patrol—Marlborough Street—Hatton Garden—Worship Street—Lambeth Street—High Street, Marylebone—Queen Square—Union Hall—Thames Police—City of London Police. In this list of the Police Offices, it will be observed that no mention is made of the Mansion House, Guildhall, or the Town Hall in Southwark. The reason of this is, that these three places are differently constituted from the other police establishments. The Mansion House, as every one knows, is presided in by the Lord Mayor for the time being, while justice is gratuitously administered in Guildhall, and the Town Hall, by one or more Aldermen. These last three offices are under the jurisdiction of the City authorities, who have a large police establishment of their own.

The oldest of the existing offices is that in Bow Street. It is at least a century since it was originally established for the purpose of administering justice. Until 1792, however, it was on a very different footing from what it has been since. Previous to that time, it was not established by act of parliament, but was simply an office used by the county magistrates, who gave their services gratuitously. Mr. Henry Fielding, the author of "Tom Jones," and other celebrated novels, was the first magistrate who received any remuneration for his services in administering justice in Bow Street. The precise time when he first received a salary is not known. To the circumstance of Fielding having been a London police magistrate, we are, in a great measure, indebted for some of his choicest works of fiction. The many-coloured scenes of life which he witnessed while discharging the functions of a magistrate there, furnished him with that intimate knowledge of human life which he displays so strikingly, and at the same time afforded him some of the happiest incidents which are to be found in his works.

In 1792, seven police offices were established by act of parliament in different parts of the metropolis. To each of these offices three magistrates were appointed, at a salary, respectively, of 400*l.* per annum. The other two offices were subsequently established, a growing metropolitan population having so much increased the amount of police business, as to render them necessary.

Bow Street Office has the most extensive jurisdiction among the police offices of London. It can take cognizance of any case which may occur in any part of the county, though its positive limits are the line of the city, which is at Temple Bar eastward, Holborn and High Street on the north, St. Martin's Lane on the west, and the river Thames on the south.

The only other establishment whose limits I shall mention, is, the Thames Police Office. My reason for specifying the extent of its jurisdiction is, that it is much greater than any of the remaining seven offices. The limits of this office upon the Thames are as far as the river runs between the counties of Middlesex and Surrey, Essex and Kent. The more common supervision, however, is confined to the busier and more active parts of the river,—namely, from Greenwich to a little above Westminster Bridge. The land district is restricted to the populous parishes of Wapping, Aldgate, St. Katharine's, Shadwell, and Ratcliffe.

All the police magistrates are either barristers-at-law or serjeants-at-law. This was not the case formerly: it is the effect of a recent resolution on the part of government, made under a conviction that it would prove highly essential to the ends of justice, and conducive to the respectability of the magisterial character, that the magistrates should be men, not only of general intelligence, but that they should be well acquainted with the law which they are called to administer.

The appointment of the magistrates is vested in the Home Secretary; and their continuance in office is dependent on the good pleasure of every successive individual who may hold that important appointment under his sovereign. The magistrates are liable to be set aside, without being entitled to any pension, at any time, should it suit the whim or caprice of the Home Secretary to come to such a determination. In this respect they are very disadvantageously circumstanced as compared with the judges; the latter being, from the very moment of their appointment, ever afterwards entirely independent of the crown. It is but right, however, to say that police magistrates are seldom dismissed from their situations, and never without some reason. The only recent instance was that of Mr. Laing, of Hatton Garden, who was set aside seven or eight weeks ago.

The salaries of the police magistrates were doubled some years since. They are now 800*l.** per annum. After they have served for a certain time, they may retire, if they wish it, on a pension of 500*l.* per annum. Mr. Halls, of Bow Street Office, retired on that pension about twelve months since. The police magistrates are prohibited from pursuing their professional pursuits as barristers, or engaging in any trade or business: it is expected that they shall apply themselves exclusively to the duties of their office. They have to sit every day during the week, Sunday excepted. They commence their sittings at eleven o'clock, and continue, in most cases, till five; and again sit an hour or two after seven o'clock. One out of the three magistrates always presides at each office. Hence the expression, the "sitting magistrate." One of the other two is always present, but takes no part, except in extreme cases, in the proceedings. Two magistrates must be in the office when hearing cases. They always sit by rotation; so that each magistrate is the sitting or presiding magistrate two days in every week.

The magistrates at the Police Offices have no control over the police constables. They have all a greater or less number of officers of their own, according to the amount of business done at each establishment. In Bow Street Office, the number of constables or officers at the disposal, and under the sole control of the magistrates, is ten. Their salaries are in most cases twenty-five shillings per week; but when they are sent to the country in pursuit of any party, the individual so employing them must allow them ten shillings each per day for his pay, twelve shillings for living, and pay all coach hire and other expenses besides. These constables are all appointed by the Home Secretary, the magistrates seldom interfering even so far as to recommend any

* The chief magistrate in Bow Street has a salaray of 1200*l.* a year. There is no chief magistrate at any of the other offices.

particular person for the situation. They are always dressed in plain clothes, and have no connexion, and but very little intercourse, with the other policemen. The magistrates employ them in all those cases in which they have themselves received private information either of an actual or intended violation of the law. If, for example, information were communicated of a contemplated duel, the magistrate to whom such information is given, immediately despatches two of his own officers to arrest the parties. The magistrates never employ the ordinary police. In the other offices, except the Thames Street Office, the number of constables retained by the establishment is seven, eight, or nine, according to circumstances. In the Thames Police Office, there are nearly as many constables as in all the other offices put together: the number is seventy, exclusive of thirty-one surveyors. The reason why so great a number of officers is required at this establishment, is the circumstance of all the business connected with the river being under its jurisdiction. The parties in the employ of this office have to look after all illegal transactions on the Thames. The whole number of persons employed as constables in the Police Offices is about one hundred and forty.

The number of cases daily tried before the Police Offices of London considerably varies. Some days it is as high as ninety, other days it is as low as sixty. The Edinburgh Review, in its last number, estimates the average number at seventy. The writer grounds his opinion on an examination of the police sheet for a given day. Probably seventy is about the average number. Of course it will be understood, that I am here speaking only of the number of cases for larceny, and those other crimes which, if proved, would render the party liable to be tried at the central criminal court. I exclude altogether what are called night charges: that is, quarrelling with the policemen, getting up a row, or being drunk. If those cases were to be included, the number would be nearer three hundred; for instances have occurred in which upwards of ninety persons have been shut up in Bow Street Station-house alone, in one night.

The police sheet, which passes between all the offices every day, and to which the Edinburgh Review refers as its authority for the supposition that the average daily number of cases of the class of offences to which I allude, is seventy, divides that seventy into three descriptions of cases. It gives the summary convictions or commitments for trial at the Old Bailey Sessions at sixteen; the remands twenty-seven; and the discharges as twenty-seven.

The yearly expense of the nine Police Offices is upwards of 50,000*l.*, making that of each to be on an average somewhat about

5500*l*. One considerable item of expense at each of these establishments is the salaries of clerks. There are three or four clerks at each of the eight offices, and double the number at Thames Street Office. Their salaries vary from 400*l*. to 120*l*. per annum.

Connected with the Police Offices there is a Receiver, at a salary of 500*l*. per annum. The following tabular view will show at one glance the various kinds of officers at the different police establishments, with the salaries they severally receive for their services. It is taken from the parliamentary returns of 1835:

PAY OF EACH CLASS OF OFFICERS.

Chief Magistrate of Bow Street, 1200*l*. per annum.

Police Magistrates, 800*l*. per annum each.

Receiver of the nine Police Offices, 500*l*. per annum.

Chief Clerk of Bow Street, salary 250*l*., increasing 10*l*. per annum to 450*l*.

Second Clerk, salary 180*l*., increasing 8*l*. per annum to 300*l*.

Third Clerk, salary 120*l*., increasing 5*l*. per annum to 250*l*.

Constables and Police Officers, 25*s*. per week.

Thames Police Principal Surveyor, 160*l*. per annum.

Inspecting Surveyor, 100*l*. per annum. Twenty Surveyors, from 75*l*. per annum to 90*l*. per annum each.

Thames Police River Constables—thirty at 23*s*. per week each; forty at 21*s*. each.

The following were the expenses of each of the offices in 1835, including contingencies:—

CONTINGENCIES. £.	s.	d.	OFFICES.	TOTAL EXPENSES. £.	s.	d.
1263	11	4	Bow Street	9768	14	2
432	1	0	Queen Square	4574	7	2
351	1	10	Marlborough Street	4402	10	0
246	0	0	Marylebone	3978	17	5
280	4	11	Hatton Garden	4250	18	3
365	4	4	Worship Street	6106	9	4
205	10	5	Whitechapel	3775	6	4
329	19	0	Union Hall	4152	4	10
763	19	11	Thames Police, including the River Force	10,712	17	11

Making the aggregate expenses of the nine Police Offices, in 1835,—51,724*l*. 5*s*. 5*d*.

Connected with Bow Street Office, as before stated, is the Horse Patrol, the expenses of which, in the same year, were 10,169*l*.; making, if the cost of both departments be put together, the expenses of that office, in 1835, about 20,000*l*.

Forty years ago, the expenses of Bow Street were not above one-third of what they now are, as will be seen from the following table:—

	£.	s.	d.
Three Magistrates, at 400*l.* per annum each	1200	0	0
One Clerk at - - - - - - -	160	0	0
One Clerk at - - - - - - -	130	0	0
One Clerk at - - - - - - -	100	0	0
One Extra Clerk - - - - - -	80	0	0
Six Officers, at 11*s.* 8*d.* per week - -	182	0	0
An Officekeeper - - - - - -	35	0	0
A Housekeeper - - - - - -	35	0	0
A Messenger - - - - - - -	35	0	0
An Assistant Gaoler - - - - -	17	10	0
Attached to the office there is a patrol, consisting of sixty-eight persons, divided into thirteen parties, each having a captain at 5*s.* per night, the men having 2*s.* 6*d.* per night, amounting in the whole, annually, to about - -	3695	12	6
There is also paid to the clerks, on account of the patrol - - - - - - -	71	0	0
And in remuneration to the magistrates, in lieu of fees and perquisites, and for special services	900	0	0
	£6641	2	6

The amount of gratuities, and penalties levied at each of the nine offices in the same year, is thus given in the parliamentary paper whence I have copied the above statistics:—

	£.	s.	d.
Bow Street - - - - -	1528	16	4
Marlborough Street - -	1040	3	0
Queen Square - - -	1007	12	11
Hatton Garden - - -	1112	3	9
Worship Street - - -	804	6	11
Whitechapel - - -	799	4	0
Marylebone - - - -	1025	7	1
Union Hall - - - -	1312	17	2
Thames Police - - -	753	6	10
Making a total of - - -	£9383	18	6

Of this sum upwards of 1000*l.* consisted of fines exacted from parties who had committed assaults on the police. The money thus collected is applied to the expenses of the several offices.

Of the expenses of the three City Police Offices, I have said nothing. As the magistrates there receive no salary, the expenses are confined to the pay of a few officers, and do not much exceed 500*l.* per annum.

The Police Offices are for the most part ill ventilated, confined, sombre-looking places. They are not at all worthy of a great city like London, and the important space they fill in the public eye. There is a great want of room in them, considering the amount of the business which has to be transacted. They are often crowded to suffocation, to the great annoyance of every one who has occasion to be present. They are also, with two or three exceptions, in badly chosen situations.

The cells in the station-houses belonging to them, in which prisoners are locked up over the night, are in striking keeping with the offices. These cells are most uncomfortable places: they are so, apart from the unpleasantness of feeling which arises from the disgrace of the thing, in all those cases, where the party is not so intoxicated as to be deprived, for the time, of his reflecting powers. They are narrow, damp, dark, and cold. In some of the station-houses they are on a level with the streets; in others, they are under ground. In either case they are the most miserable receptacles into which a human being could be put, short of burying him alive. When the number. of prisoners is few, each one has often a cell for himself. When an "apartment" cannot be spared to each, owing to the number of candidates for admission, two, in some cases it may happen three, four, or five, are shut up together in one little cell. It is often curious to reflect on the strange errors as to where a party is, and with whom he is, into which he falls on recovering from that state of extreme intoxication called "dead drunk." A few months ago I was amused with the account given me by one who was in the same cell, of the conduct of a young man, whose name I afterwards ascertained to be Snitch, and who had been deposited in the station-house about twelve o'clock the previous evening, in a state of such entire intoxication, that but for the circumstance of his breathing, you would have concluded he was dead. Until five o'clock in the morning—it was in the summer season—he slept as soundly and lay on the stones as quietly as if he had been in his grave; but he then all at once opened his eyes, and sitting up, looked for a moment wildly around him. His eye at last lighted on his fellow prisoner; and after a temporary gaze on him, he uttered in accents of a most unearthly kind, "Where am I? Who is that? Sophemia! who is that?" Who Sophemia was, whether sister, sweetheart, or wife, was at the time a mystery; but it was clear the unlucky wight fancied he was in his own home, and that he had metamorphosed his companion in trouble into an apparition. His horror and bewilderment seemed for a few seconds only, to increase when the other spoke to him. He had not the most remote idea of where he was; nor, when acquainted with his temporary "local habitation," could he recal to his mind a single circumstance connected with his capture by the police, or his conveyance thither. His latest reminiscences did not come within two hours of the time at which the police took charge of him. He was then, he stated, admiring "a show of beauties" in the saloon of Drury Lane Theatre. The period which elapsed from that hour, which he stated to have been ten o'clock at night, down to the time of his waking in the station-house next morning, which, as before stated, was five o'clock, was a perfect blank in his existence. Had he been literally dead, he could not have been more oblivious of what had occurred in his personal history in the interim. But the most interesting circumstance in the affair, was his ignorance of the offence for which he was locked up, coupled with the intense anxiety he manifested to ascertain it. What could it be? Was it murder or manslaughter? Was it committing some serious assault? Was he a prisoner for felony? Could he have smashed people's windows? What in the name of wonder could he have done to justify the police in confining him in the dungeon—he was in a cell below ground—in which he then found himself? These and a dozen other questions suggested themselves to his mind, and filled him with the most horrible fears. His awful apprehensions were not lessened by observing that his hat was shattered to pieces, and that one of the tails of his coat had been entirely torn away. At last, no longer able to endure the frightful forebodings of what might be the disclosures when brought before the magistrate, he turned to his brother in adversity, having been by this time satisfied that he was a fellow mortal, and with a most dolorous expression of countenance, and in truly touching accents, said, "Pray, Sir, can you inform me for what crime I was brought here?"

"I know *one* violation of the law with which you are charged," answered the other, quite coolly.

"Violation of the law, Sir?" said the terrified party, with great earnestness.

"Of course; otherwise you would not have been here."

"Pray, Sir, *do* inform me of its nature! Was it a *serious* breach of the law?"

"*Very* serious," answered the other, with some emphasis.

"No life lost, I hope?" gasped Mr. Snitch.

"Why, the policemen who brought you here did say something about being uncertain whether some person of whom they were talking, were living or dead."

"I'm a lost man!" groaned the poor fellow, violently striking his forehead. A public trial, a verdict of guilty, transportation for life—if not suspension by the neck—with all their concomitant horrors, were ideas which in a moment crowded on his mind. "Oh, Sophemia! that ever it should have come to this! Little did I think——"

"Don't be so much alarmed," interrupted his companion; "possibly your fears are worse than the reality. It may have been yourself the policemen alluded to, when they spoke of its being uncertain whether the party was dead or alive."

"My dear friend," said the poor frightened youth, seizing his fellow-prisoner with a cordial grasp by the hand, "do you really think that is the fact?"

"I hope it may be so," replied the other.

"My dear Sir, you delight me. I feel as if——"

At this moment a friend, to whom the other had written to come and bail him out, arrived, and he was liberated,—leaving the unhappy youth to himself to be tormented between his doubts and fears until he appeared before the magistrate, as to what crimes he had committed while drunk.

I was present at the police-office when the charges for the night were brought before the magistrate. After several others had been disposed of, the magistrate said, in his usual sharp and hasty manner,—"The next charge on the list."

"Sophemia Burgess!" bawled out one of the officers, at the full stretch of a powerful voice, opening, as he spoke, a door which communicated with a passage leading to another room, where the undisposed "charges" were congregated together.

In a few seconds, Mr. Snitch was conducted to the bar. His pale countenance, with the marked expression of horror which was depicted on it, told in silent but impressive terms of the agony of mind under which he laboured. His unshaved beard, his dirty face, the crumpled breast and collar of his shirt, and sundry patches of mud which still adhered to his apparel, were in strict keeping with his one-tailed coat. Taken altogether, the appearance of Mr. Snitch was so much in character with the usual effects of a drunken debauch, that it needed not the testimony of any living witness as to the way in which the unfortunate wight had spent the previous night.

"Why, officer," said the worthy magistrate, with some tartness, "you have made a mistake. You have brought me a man instead of a woman."

"It's quite right, your worship."

"It's what?"

"Quite right, your worship."

"Why, the name on my list, of the next charge, is Sophemia Burgess."

"This *is* Sophemia Burgess," said the officer, with a steady voice.

The magistrate looked at the officer with an air of infinite surprise; and Mr. Snitch's pale face coloured deeply, as well as indicated the utmost amazement, when the name was mentioned. The latter rapidly glanced his eye round the office, as if looking to see whether some person of that name, with whom he was on terms of intimacy, was in the place. It was afterwards ascertained, that Sophemia Burgess was a young lady to whom he was paying his addresses; and as she still absorbed his thoughts so long as he was able to think, he had stammered out her name when asked his own.

"Why," said the worthy magistrate, addressing himself, with increased sharpness, to the policeman,—"why, Sophemia is a woman's name, not a man's."

"That *is* his right name," insisted the knight of the bludgeon.

"Is that your name, Sir?" said the magistrate, addressing himself to Mr. Snitch.

"It is not, Sir," answered Mr. Snitch.

The magistrate now looked quite ferocious at the policeman, as if he had meant to say, "What have you now to say for yourself, you blundering blockhead?"

"That *is* the prisoner's name, your worship," repeated constable H, of the G division, without the slightest disconcertion of manner.

"Is that the name he gave you, when you took him into custody?" inquired the magistrate.

"No, your worship; he was not able to give any name at all."

"What! was he so drunk as that?"

"He was, your worship, dead drunk: he could neither move hand nor foot, let alone speaking."

Mr. Snitch hung his head still lower, and audibly groaned.

"And how did you come to know his name, then?" continued the magistrate.

"Vy, your worship, a person who had seen him before he was quite so bad, told me he had inquired his name, and that, with an effort, he managed to answer, 'Sophemia Burgess;' but, besides that, we found in his pocket a card with her name on it."

"And you mean to say, Sir, do you," said the magistrate, addressing himself to the prisoner, "that Sophemia Burgess is *not* your name?"

"That is not my name, Sir."

"Well, then, will you tell the bench what *is* your name?"

"It is Tugworth Snitch, Sir."

Mr. Snitch had no sooner mentioned his right name, than he reproached himself for his stupidity in not giving an assumed one; but the rapidity with which the magistrate proceeded to dispose of the charge, left but little time for reflection on the subject.

"Well, Sir, you hear the charge: what have you to say in your defence?"

Mr. Snitch whispered in tremulous accents, that he was not aware of what specific offence he was charged with.

"Why, with being in a state of beastly intoxication," said the magistrate, with some acrimony.

Mr. Snitch's countenance brightened up, as if a poet's paradise had all at once opened on his view, on thus hearing that the charge against him was confined to being drunk.

"I am sorry for it, Sir," answered Mr. Snitch, in a tone of mingled penitence and joy. "I never was in the same situation before, and hope I never will be again."

"I hope it will be a warning to you, Mr. Tugworth Snitch: you have great reason to be thankful that you were not run over, and killed by some vehicle, when the policeman found you rolling in the mud."

Mr. Snitch was silent, and looked as if he assented to the proposition.

"You are fined five shillings, for being drunk," said the magistrate. "Officer, the next charge," he added, in the same breath.

Mr. Snitch paid the fine, and retired from the bar, rejoicing that matters were not much worse.

Some extraordinary scenes are to be witnessed in the station houses, when all the "charges," as the prisoners are called, are brought forward from their different cells, to one place, immediately prior to their being transferred to the police-offices. Not long since, I saw an odd exhibition of this kind in the Vine-street station-house. The number of persons who had been shut up during the greater part of the night, was fifteen. It will at once be concluded, that they consisted of both sexes; but it will not be so readily inferred, though such was the fact, that a majority of the company belonged to the female sex. There may be, in the estimation of some persons, but little gallantry in making this statement; but gallantry, in such cases, must give way to the truth. A more motley assemblage than that to which I refer, it has never been my fortune to behold, either at a station-house or elsewhere. It embraced all ranks as well as both sexes. There were parties moving in the higher walks of life, and there were the very humblest of mankind. There were persons of every shade of character; from those of correct morals, who had been consigned to a gloomy cell simply because they had refused, in going home, to submit obsequiously to the behests of a capricious policeman, down to the most worthless and depraved creatures to be met with in this vast metropolis. And their external aspect exhibited as great a variety as did their moral character. There was the tastefully-dressed man of fashion, and the poor mendicant, wrapped up in a mass of dirty rags. There were some, both men and women, whose apparel, at the best, had only been of an humble description. There were others who were what is called "elegantly attired" the previous night, whose clothes were either torn to tatters, or covered over with mud. Hats without crowns, and minus the greater part of their brims to boot; coats converted, by the tails being torn off, into jackets; straw and silk bonnets transformed into shapes which the milliners who made them never intended; shawls and gowns either torn into fragments, or affording abundant evidence that their wearers had recently been paying their respects to the pavement, were among the things which gave variety to the scene. Then there were the langour and heaviness of manner caused by the dissipation of the preceding night, which were so visibly impressed on the countenances of many: to say nothing of the unwashed faces, unshaved beards, and unbrushed clothes of others. The odd effect which all this was so well calculated to produce on the mind of him who had slept comfortably in his bed at home, and was but an accidental spectator of the scene, was very materially heightened by the hanging down of the heads of those who were particularly ashamed of the situation in which they were placed, and the significant looks which others exchanged with each other, as if they had meant to say, "We are brethren and sisters in adversity." Altogether, it would have been difficult to have fancied a group in which there could be a greater diversity of external appearance, or in moral or social character. For a time they were doomed to be separated: instead of being all conveyed together to the police-office, they were transferred thither in separate detachments of ones, twos, or threes. Those of them who could afford to pay for a hackney-coach, and preferred incurring the expense to being walked to the police office in Great Marlborough-street, in the company of a policeman, had it in their power to avail themselves of the services of Jehu; while those who were less favourably circumstanced, or grudged the coach fare, were obliged to submit to encounter the rude and unhallowed gaze of every unmannerly person they met on the way. The separation of those who had parted at Vine-street station-house was but of a temporary kind. At the police-office they were all destined to meet again, previous to being severally called before the magistrate. Here they were all huddled together, and pent up in a small space, as if they had been so many black cattle for sale in Smithfield-market. They were introduced to another lot in the same predicament as themselves, who had been deposited in the course of the night in some other station-house. Here, again, the scene was worth seeing. It was on a still more extensive scale. What struck me particularly was, the genuine republican character of the assemblage. The most strenuous advocate for the extinction of all conventional differences in society, and for the substitution of the most thorough equality, would have been gratified with the spectacle to his heart's content. The highest and the lowest—the most elegantly attired and the most ragged in their apparel—stood there on precisely the same footing, and treated each other in the genuine republican style. It was altogether a truly curious spectacle to witness, and one which could not fail to lead to an interesting train of reflection in a meditative mind.

Perhaps there are no places in the world, in which a more complete insight into human nature, in all its simplicity, extravagances, eccentricities, follies, and viciousness, may be had, than in the police-offices of London. The cases which daily come before the magistrates, develope at one moment deep-laid schemes of unredeemed villany; in the next, instances of such perfect simplicity or "greenness," as no one could have previously deemed of possible existence. I will give a few of the more interesting cases which have lately occurred in several of the offices, which will go far to confirm what I have just said about the complete exhibition of human nature, in all its aspects, which is to be seen at these establishments. For the sake of classification, it may be as well to give the cases such headings as it is very likely they would have received, had they been written for the daily newspapers. It may perhaps be right to mention, that none of the cases have before appeared in print. The first is a case of

NORTH-COUNTRY SIMPLICITY.

Thomas Watson, whose broad manner of speaking would of itself have been sufficient to satisfy any reasonable person, that he was a recent importation from the land o'cakes, came forward to prefer a complaint against a young gaudily-dressed damsel, well known in the neighbourhood of Covent-garden. Mr. Watson was seemingly about twenty years of age, of a copper-coloured physiognomy, thick lips, broad flat nose, and of a most good-natured, unsuspecting expression of countenance. He was clad in his holiday clothes, and had what is called a decent, though sheepish, appearance. "Well, Sir, what is your complaint?" said the magistrate, in a tone of kindness, being struck with the manifest simplicity of the young man.

"It's aboot the loss of my siller, Sir; may I speek a word or twa?" said the Scotchman.

"Certainly," answered the magistrate. "That's the very thing I was requesting you to do. State your case."

"Weel, Sir——"

"But, pray, what are you?" interrupted the magistrate.

"Do you mean, Sir, what country I belong to?"

"Oh, no; I don't want to know that: that is sufficiently clear without your telling us."

"Do you mean, Sir, what line of life I follow?"

"Precisely so."

"Aw, then, Sir, I'm a mekanic."

"But what is your trade?"

"I'm a heckler, Sir."

"A heckler!" exclaimed his worship, evidently at a loss to know what the simple Caledonian meant.

"Yes, Sir, a heckler," repeated the latter, with great innocence.

"It means, your worship, a flax-dresser," interposed a sergeant of the police, who was himself a transplantation from the north of the Tweed.

"Oh, very good; I see," said the magistrate. "Pray go on with your story," he continued, addressing himself to Mr Watson.

"Weel, Sir, as I was a-going to tell you, I came up to Lunnun, to an uncle wha's in a good way, thinkin' he might do something for me, as I dinna like my bisness very weel: but on comin' up here, I found that he had left his former house, and the folks that live in it couldna tell me whar he had gane to."

Here the young man stopped, as if he had finished his story.

"Well, go on," said the magistrate; "you have not yet told the Bench why this female is brought here."

"I'll tell you that the noo," resumed the other. "It was near ten o'clock at night," he continued, "when I reached the place which is called the Strand, whar my uncle formerly lived; and findin' that he was not there, I made up my mind to go into the first public-house I could see, to ask for lodgings for the night. Jost whan I cam' to this resolution, I met this young leddy, wha,' as I thought at the time, cam' in o'er to me with great kindness, and spoke to me."

"What did she say?" inquired the magistrate.

The poor Caledonian coloured, and hung down his head.

"Come, don't be so modest. Tell us what she said. Something tender, I suppose?"

"*Very!*" answered the young man, in a tone something between a groan and a sigh.

"Why," said the magistrate, observing the blushes and hesitation of Sawney, "she seems to have made an impression on you!"

The Scotchman only coloured the more.

"Come," resumed the magistrate, with some sharpness, "you must lay aside your modesty, and tell us what she said."

"Weel, I will," answered Mr. Watson. "She said ——"

Here he again faltered, and looked as if he could have sunk into the earth.

"Come, out with it," said the magistrate.

"She said, 'Ah, my dear! how do you do?'" (Loud laughter.)

"And you thought, I dare say, that there was something very kind in her saying that?"

"I did, indeed, Sir: I thought she must be a tender-hearted creatur to speak to a perfect stranger like me in that way." (Renewed laughter, in which the magistrate joined.)

"And what more passed between you?"

"I thaunk'd her kindly for her condescension, and hoped she was weel hersel'."

"Ladies are not in the habit in your country, I suppose, of speaking in this way to strangers?" observed the magistrate.

"No, Sir, they are not: besides, what made me think mair of this leddy's kindness was, that she was so brawly dressed. She had on a veil, Sir."

"Well, but you have not told us what passed between you."

"When I thaunked her for her kindness, she asked me whether I was not newly come to toon; and I told her that I was, and that I had been inquiring about an uncle, but could not find out his hoose. She then asked my uncle's name; I said it was John Watson. 'Oh!' says she, 'I know him quite well: but it's too late to go after him to-night, as he lives at such a distance. You'll better come with me, my love, and I'll get you a bed for the night; and I'll direct you towards your uncle in the morning.'"

"Pray try to make your story as short as possible, and come to the charge against her as quickly as you can," said the magistrate, thinking the Caledonian was rather diffuse in his mode of telling his story.

"I'll soon be done noo. I said to her that I could not think of troubling a leddy of her respectability to get a bed to me; but she begged of me not to mention it, and assured me it would be a pleasure, and not a trouble to her. As sure as death, Sir! I thought her the kindest creatur I ever saw in my life."

"But you don't think so now, I presume?" remarked the magistrate.

Sawney held down his head, and muttered something, which

was understood to signify a concurrence in the observation of the Bench.

"You went home with her, I suppose?" continued the magistrate.

"Yes, Sir; but I would not have presumed to do such a thing, if she had not asked me. She took a-hold o' my arm, Sir; and I was almost ashamed to be seen walking with so finely-dressed a leddy." (Loud laughter.)

"Well, and what more?"

"Then I went into an elegant room, whar I saw another pretty leddy; and she also spoke in the kindest and most condescending manner to me."

"I suppose," observed the magistrate, "that you thought all the women in London were angels?"

"I just did that same, Sir, if I must tell the truth; for I never saw the leddies in our country treat strange men with so much kindness." (Renewed laughter).

"So the second was as kind to you as the first?"

"She was, Sir; indeed, if there was ony difference, she was the kindest o' the twa."

"In what way did she show her kindness?"

The poor simpleton blushed at the question, and was silent.

"Come, tell us!" said the magistrate, in half authoritative tones.

"Why, then," answered the other, in broken hesitating accents, "she cam' and sat doon on my knee." (Roars of laughter).

"Without your inviting her to do so, I presume?"

"O dear! yes, Sir. I would never have had the assurance to use such freedom with a leddy."

"Well, go on."

"Weel, after being about a quarter of an hour in the same room as the twa leddies, I said, if she would tell me whar my bed was, I would go to it, as I was very wearied; but, said I, as I'm a stranger here, might I ask of you the very great favour to keep my money to me till next morning, in case of accidents. 'Oh, with the greatest pleasure, my love!' said the one: 'Oh, certainly, my dear!' said the other. And with that I gave the one—the one noo standing there, (pointing to the bar)—a five-pound note of the British Linen Company,* and said I would be particularly obleeged to her if she would keep it quite safe to me till the morn's morning." (Loud laughter).

"And, of course, she promised she would?"

"She did, Sir: they both assured me it would be quite safe."

* The name of the leading bank in Scotland.

"And you found, next morning, I suppose, that it was so safe that you could not get a sight of it again?" (Laughter.)

"It's a' true as your honour says. I never clapped an ee (eye) on her or the money, after she got it."

"Did she leave the room as soon as you gave it her?" inquired the magistrate.

"Oh, no; she sat about a quarter of an hour longer, until I said, that if she would be kind enough to tell me whar my bed-room was, I would bid them both good night."

"And did she tell you where your bed-room was to be?"

"She said, Sir, that she would go and call the servant, who would show me where I was to sleep; and after thanking her for her kindness, and saying I was sorry to be putting her to so much trouble, she said, 'Oh! it's no trouble at all, my dear!' and then left the room."

"And was in no hurry in returning, I suppose?" observed the magistrate.

"Ots, Sir!" said the poor fellow, with great simplicity and much emphasis; "Ots, sir! she did not come back at a'." (Loud laughter.)

"And did the other remain long with you?"

"She did for some time, until I said, wondering that the other leddy was so long in returning, 'I'm afear'd that I'm gieing your frien' a great deal o' trouble?' on which, she begged me not to mention it; and said she would go and see what was detaining her."

"And she also disappeared?"

"She jost did, Sir."

"And was in no haste in returning either?"

"Faith, Sir! she did not come back again at a', mair than the ither." (Roars of laughter.)

"Well," said the magistrate, "and what did you do then?"

"To tell you the truth, Sir, I did na ken what to do."

"But what *did* you do?"

"What did I do!" repeated the raw Scotchman with great innocence.

"Yes; what *did* you do? You either remained in the house, or you quitted it."

"Oh, it's that you mean, Sir! I remained in the place until a middle-aged woman came and asked me who I wanted."

"And you told her, of course?"

"I said to her that I wanted two leddies."

"Well, and what then?" inquired the magistrate.

"'Two leddies,' says she, as if quite surprised. And I said 'Yes, mem.' On which she said, 'Pray what's their names?'"

"And you did not know, I suppose?" observed the magistrate.

"You have jost spoken the truth. I did not; and I told the woman so; adding, that I had never thought of speering at them." (Renewed laughter.)

"Well, and what happened then?"

"Why, Sir, she said I must have mistaken the house; for that no leddies lived there?"

"Well, go on," said the magistrate.

"I said I had been brought there by a leddy, who engaged to get me lodgings for the night; when she said, 'Oh, there must be some mistake! There's no lodgings here; but you'll get lodgings in the public-house over the way."

"And did you leave the place?"

"The woman made me leave it, Sir: she opened the door, and told me I could not lodge there."

"Well, and what next did you do?"

"I ga'ed o'er the way to the public-house, and told them a' that had happened; and they told me I had been regularly done for, and called a policeman for me, to whom I stated the whole circumstances; and he said he would see what he could do."

The magistrate then desired the policeman to be called. He stated that, from the description given of the prisoner, he knew her at once, and traced her to a gin shop, where she had tried to get the five-pound note changed, but without effect, as it was on a Scottish bank, and would not therefore pass current in London. He took the money from the "leddy," and conveyed her to the station-house. He then went and desired the young man to attend at the office that day.

In answer to a question from the magistrate, the prisoner declared that she did not mean to retain the five-pound note, but only went out, knowing that the young man was quite unacquainted in town, to endeavour to get it changed for him.

"Eh me!" said Sawney, holding up both his hands, and showing by his looks that, in the simplicity of his soul, he gave "the leddy" full credit for the truth of her statement; "Eh me! was not that so verra kind o' her? I'm now so sorry that I ever said a word about it." The broad accent in which this was delivered, coupled with the manner of the raw youth, threw all present into convulsions of laughter.

"If you take my advice, young man," said the magistrate, when the laughter had subsided, "you'll never again trust to the friendship or kindness of the 'ladies' who meet you in the street: but pass on, and not mind them."

"Weel, Sir," said the unsophisticated youth, with great earnestness, "if your honour thinks so, I'se tak' your advice.

I'se never open my mouth to them again, but appear as if I were both deaf and dumb." (Loud laughter.)

"As for you, madam," said the magistrate, turning to the prisoner, "it is fortunate for you that this unsuspecting lad gave you the money, instead of your having taken it. As the note has been recovered, you are discharged."

The next case I shall give is one of a different kind. It smacks of matrimonial squabbles and of poetry, in pretty equal proportions. Perhaps the most appropriate heading of it would be,

THE POETICAL COBBLER.

Sally Muggs, a little squat-looking woman, not very fair, and on the wrong side of forty, came bustling forward to the bar, and looking the sitting magistrate expressively in the face, said, "Please your vorship," and then suddenly paused.

Magistrate—Well, ma'am, and what *is* your pleasure?

Mrs. Muggs—Vy, your vorship, it is—— (Here the lady again abruptly paused, and buried her face, in quite a theatrical manner, in her handkerchief.)

Magistrate—Well, what is it? Let us hear it.

Mrs. Muggs—Please your vorship, this 'ere man at the bar is my husband.

Mrs. Muggs turned about, and emitted a disapproving glance at "the man at the bar."

Magistrate—Very well; go on.

Mrs. Muggs—And he is a mender of old shoes, your vorship.

Magistrate—Well, and what about it? Why don't you proceed?

Mrs. Muggs (with a deep sigh)—And I married him six months ago.

Magistrate—Really, my good woman, if you have any complaint to make to the bench, you must proceed to do it at once, otherwise I shall order you from the bar. You have, I understand, a charge to prefer against the prisoner; pray come to it without any further circumlocution.

Mrs. Muggs—I vill, your vorship. Vell, as I was a sayin', I married this 'ere man six months ago, and——

Magistrate—What has your marriage six months ago to do with the present case?

Mrs. Muggs—I soon diskivered, your vorship, that I had married a—Oh, Sir! I cannot utter the word.

Here Mrs. Muggs held down her head, and appeared to breathe so rapidly as to threaten instant suffocation.

Magistrate—And pray, madam, whom or *what* did you marry?

Mrs. Muggs—A—a—a—a *poet*, your vorship.

The wife of the poetical cobbler pronounced the word "poet" with a most emphatic groan, as if she had, in her own mind, associated something horrible with it.

The court was convulsed with laughter, in which the worthy magistrate heartily joined.

Magistrate— But what has the circumstance of your husband being a poet to do with the present charge?

Mrs. Muggs—I'll tell you presently, your vorship. I had some money when I married him; and so long as it lasted, he always spoke to me in pleasant poetry; but ven the money was all gone, his poetry became very disagreeable.

Magistrate—You mean, I suppose, that he scolds and quarrels with you in poetry? (Laughter.)

Mrs. Muggs—He does both of them 'ere, your vorship; but he does something more.

Magistrate—Assaults you, perhaps?

Mrs. Muggs—Yes, your vorship: he beats me, and kicks me about most cruelly, and all the while keeps talking poetry. (Renewed laughter.)

Magistrate—But pray do come to the present charge.

Mrs. Muggs—I vill, your vorship. He came home last night a little the vorse for leekur, and axed me, in poetry, for half-a-crown to spend with some fellow-snobs. I told him I had not a single penny in the house; on which he threatened, in poetry, to make gunpowder of me, if I did not give him what he wanted.

Magistrate—And was he as good as his word?

Mrs. Muggs—I'll tell you all about it. (Laughter.) I again told him I had not a farthing in the house: on which he took down my best green silk bonnet, which was hanging on a nail, and which cost me ten-and-sixpence a fortnight before, and which I bought from Mrs. ——

Magistrate—Never mind what your bonnet cost you, or who you bought it from, but tell us about the assault.

Mrs. Muggs—Yes, your vorship. Vell, as I was a sayin', he took down the bonnet, which was as handsome and fashionable a 'un as was ever a-made by any milliner in Lunnun, and which was——

Magistrate (with considerable warmth)—Pray do not expatiate any more on the good qualities of the bonnet, but come at once to the assault on yourself.

Mrs. Muggs—I beg your vorship's pardon; but I vas a-comin' to that 'ere as fast as I could. Vell, ven he took down the bonnet, he dashed it on the floor, and stamped upon it with his feet, as if he would drive the werry life out on't. "Oh, my new bonnet!" said I; and the vords wos hardly out of my mouth, when he gave another stamp on it with both his feet. "My ten-and-

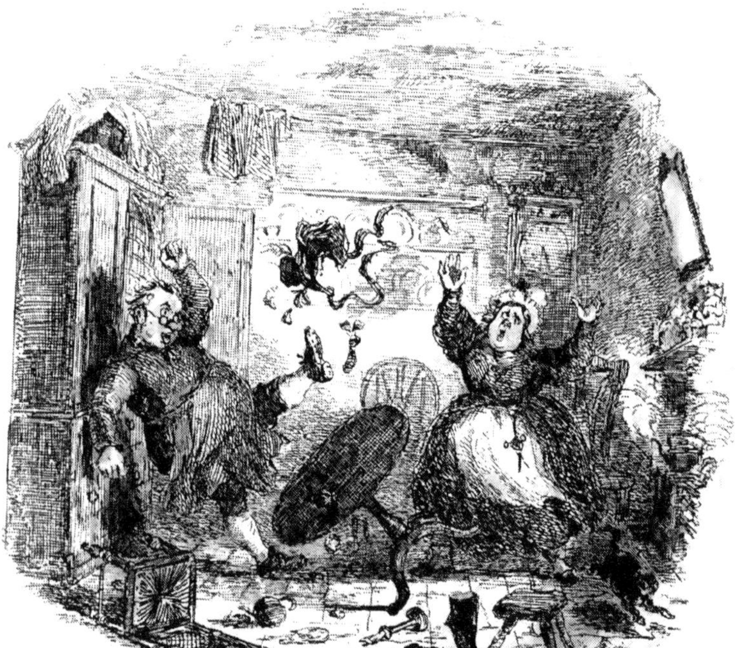

sixpence bonnet!" said I; and with that, he gave it a kick which sent it right up to the ceiling, and down again. (Loud laughter.) I then tried to snatch it up, saying, "Oh! my green silk bonnet!" on which he again put both his ugly hoofs on it, and stood with it underneath, just as if it had been a mat to wipe one's feet with. That bonnet, your vorship, wos von of the best——

Magistrate—Really, madam, if you go on in this way, I must dismiss the case at once. You are speaking only of an assault on your *bonnet*; pray come to the assault on *yourself*.

Mrs. Muggs (curtseying gracefully)—Vell, I vill, your vorship. As I was a-going to say, I tried to get the bonnet from him, and then he began to have a regular dance upon it. I stood a ghost at the sight, your vor——

"Aghast, she means, your honour; but she has no intellect—not a morsel," growled the cobbler, who had hitherto not only looked sulky, but remained silent.

Mrs. Muggs resumed—I did, indeed, your vorship; but he grinned in my face and spoke poetry. I tried to push him off the bonnet, ven he struck me so wiolently on the face, that the blood poured in rivers from my nose, and I fell down on the floor. I cried out "Murder!" and another 'ooman as lodges in the same house called a policeman, who took him into custody.

A black eye and a swollen face bore ample testimony to the forcible nature of the blows which Mrs. Muggs had received from her poetical husband.

The policeman said, that when he took the defendant into custody, he also addressed him in poetry. When he asked him,

'Why did you knock this woman down?'

he answered,

'Because she refused me half-a-crown,'

(Loud laughter.) He then added,

'I'll go to the station-house with you,
If you'll only wait a minute or two,
Till I wash my face and comb my hair—
A request which you must admit is fair.'

The defendant, who was a short, thick-set, massy-headed personage, with a most unpoetical expression of countenance, evinced, all this while, the utmost impatience to address the worthy magistrate. The latter having apostrophised the poetical cobbler with a "Now, Sir," he advanced a step or two further up the bar, and putting both his hands behind his back, looked the presiding magistrate earnestly in the face.

Magistrate—Well, Sir, what have you got to say to this charge?

'I admit that I was somewhat rude,
But not until I had reason good:

She call'd me a horrid ugly brute,
Which sure enough did put me out;
I then hit Mrs. Muggs two or three blows,
As your worship already very well knows.'
(*Loud laughter.*)

Magistrate—You seem very anxious to be considered poetical. Do you call it poetry to commit an assault of this kind?

Mr. Muggs—Do I call it poetry to beat my wife?
I do—the deed with poetry is rife.

Magistrate—You do! Will you be so obliging as to tell us (in plain prose, if you please) what kind of poetry you call it?

Mr. Muggs—Most certainly: I 'll tell you in a fraction
Of time—I call it, Sir, the poetry of *action.*

At this sally, the office was again convulsed with laughter, in which the bench heartily joined.

Magistrate (to Mrs. Muggs)—Does he always speak in this way?

Mrs. Muggs—Not always, your vorship, but he is sure to do so when he has drunk too much, and also occasionally when he is perfectly sober. He is now and then seized with fits of speaking poetry, as he calls it, and threatens at times to knock my "unpoetical soul" out of me. Mrs. Muggs, as she made the latter observation, tried to look wise, as if she had said something of surprising cleverness.

Magistrate—(to Mr. Muggs)—I understand you mend *shoes.*

Mr. Muggs—(hesitatingly)—Why—yes—I believe I *dooes.* (Loud laughter.)

Magistrate—Don't you think you would be much better occupied in attending to your business, than in making a fool of yourself by affecting to be a *poet.*

Mr. Muggs—It may be so, Sir, but I don't *know it.*

Magistrate—Well, if you persist in making an ass of yourself in this way, you must be permitted to do so; but you shall not be allowed to assault your *wife.*

Mr. Muggs—I 'll not do it again, Sir, upon my *life.* (Loud laughter.)

Magistrate—You are sentenced to ——

"Pray," interrupted Mrs. Muggs, addressing herself to the worthy magistrate, her heart having relented as she beheld her poetical husband looking touchingly towards her,—"pray, do, your honour, let him escape this time; I 'll be bound he von't beat me again, nor destroy my bonnet."

Mrs. Muggs looked as well as spoke so imploringly on behalf of Mr. Muggs, that even the magisterial nature, proof as it is generally supposed to be against entreaties of the kind, could not withstand the earnest supplications of the cobbler's lady.

Magistrate (to Mr. Muggs)—Sir, we shall allow you to get off this once at the request of your wife, but if the offence be repeated we shall deal with you in a very different *way*.

Mr. Muggs—I thank you, Sir, and wish you good *day* (Laughter.)

Mr. and Mrs. Muggs then cordially embraced each other as if their mutual affections had been wondrously improved by what had happened.

"I'm sure, Dick,"* said Mrs. Muggs, looking up touchingly in her husband's face, as he clasped his arms around her, "I'm sure, Dick, you von't do it no more."

To which tender appeal, Mr. Muggs, as Milton would have said, answered thus:—

"No, Sally, dear, I will not do't again,
Never, my angel. I will refrain,
From this time forward, and for aye,
Perish my hand, should ever the day
Arrive, in which 'twill hit thee a blow;
Oh, Sally, my love! oh, Sally, oh!
Your kindness has me quite overcome:
As I will prove whene'er we get home.
So let us hence, and leave this place;
I'm thankful we quit it with such a good grace."

The parties then retired, with their arms most affectionately entwined around each other's neck, amidst peals of laughter from all present.

A DRUNKEN FROLIC.

A young man, who afterwards proved himself to be of good *ad*dress, though his *dress* was rather awkward, and contrasted oddly with his appearance otherwise, was brought before the sitting magistrate, charged with being found drunk in the streets.

There was a general titter in the office as he advanced to the dock And no wonder; for the odd appearance he presented might well have affected the risible muscles of even Democritus himself. He carried in his hand the bonnet, and his back was graced with the coat, of a private soldier; while his small-clothes, which had once been light cassimere of a fashionable make, were so extensively plastered with patches of mud, that it was with difficulty you could ascertain what the original colour was. His waistcoat was also of a fashionable cut, and though now wofully soiled with the commodity just mentioned, had evidently been, the night before, one which Beau Brummel himself need not have been ashamed to wear. Neckerchief or

* Richard was Mr. Muggs' Christian name.

stock he had none; his neck—clearly for no other reason than the accidental absence of either stock or cloth, and not from choice—was quite exposed to the rude gaze of the policemen, and of all in the office who chose to fix their vulgar eyes on it. To add to the singularity of this part of his personal aspect, the collar of his shirt had somehow or other disappeared, as if ashamed of itself. His crest-fallen looks also added much to the oddity of his appearance.

"Well, Sir," said the magistrate, "what is your name?"

"Anthony Nonsuch," was the answer.

"And pray, what are you?"

"I am—I am—I am.—Sir, I am a *gentleman* by profession."

The first part of this answer was uttered with great hesitation, and the latter with an energy which so oddly contrasted with it, as to raise a general laugh.

"I do not know," said the magistrate, sarcastically, "what you are by profession, but you certainly are not in a very *gentlemanly situation* at present. (To the officer.) Tell us what you know of the prisoner."

"Plase your honour," said the policeman, who was an Hibernian,* "as I was on duty last *night* about one o'clock this *morning*, in Great Russel Street, Covent Garden, I saw this young man lying on his broad back in the mud while it was pouring oceans of rain. Says I to him, 'What in the name of St. Patrick was after bringing your body here?' 'Go home to Paddy's Land, you spalpeen of an Irishman,' says he. 'It wid be bether for the likes ov ye iv ye were at home in such a night as this,' says I. (Laughter.) 'Pat,' says he, 'I mane to sleep here for an hour or two.' 'By the powers, and you won't do that same,' says I; 'it's not a very comfortable bed that yourself would be after finding it,' says I. 'The sheets feel a little damp, but we must not stick at trifles,' says he. (Laughter.) 'Come, come,' says I. 'Good night, Pat,' says he; 'you be sure and call me early in the morning, my boy.' (Laughter.) Wid that, your honour, he laid hisself down again on the street, among the dubs, as if he had been slapeing on a bed of down."

"And you raised him up, of course," said the magistrate.

"I tried to do that same, plase your honour, but never an inch would he move. He felt as weighty, yer honour, as a ton of lead; so I was obliged to get the assistance of another policeman, and we put him on his feet between us."

"And they were of no use to him, I suppose, when you did so?" said the magistrate.

"Maybe yer honour's quite right there," said the Irishman,

* This occurred under the old police system, when almost all the guardians of the night were Irishmen.

with a significant shake of the head; "he could not put them beneath him at all at all."

"Did he speak when you lifted him up?"

"Did he speak, yer honour? Faith and he did that same."

"What did he say?"

"'Paddy,' says he, 'bring me a noggin of whiskey;' but I tould him, yer honour, there was none to be had. 'Why?' says he. 'Why!' says I, 'sure bekase all the public houses is shut up.' 'Is it too late,' says he, 'to get one noggin more?' 'It's meself that doesn't know,' says I, 'whether it be too late or too early; but I know that not a drop is to be had for love or money at this blessed hour of the night.'"

"Did you ask him what was his name?"

"I did, plase yer honour."

"And what did he say it was?"

"Och, and faith, yer honour, he did not speak the thruth."

"Are you quite sure of that?"

"As sure, yer honour, as it's meself is my mother's son." (Laughter.)

"And pray how did you come to know that he did not speak the truth?"

"Bekase, yer honour, it was himself that was after giving me a wrong name."

"But how did you come to know that?" repeated the magistrate with some sharpness.

"Bekase I'm sure it was not the right one." (Bursts of laughter.)

"Let us hear what it was."

"Och, I'm quite sartin, yer honour, it was not the thrue one," answered the Emeralder, showing an evident reluctance to answer the magistrate's question.

"Come, come, Sir; do tell us at once what name he gave you."

"Well, then, yer honour, if I must be after telling you, sure enough it was Daniel O'Connell." (Roars of laughter.)

"And how do you know that is not the prisoner's name?"

"Bekase, yer worship, I know Daniel O'Connell, and therefore by this same token could not be mistaken."

"The Agitator, you mean?" continued the magistrate.

"I mane Mr. O'Connell, the same fat gentleman as makes orashuns in Dublin."

"But you don't mean to say he is the only Daniel O'Connell in the world?"

"Faith, yer honour, and I never thought of that same before," answered Pat, looking quite surprised at his own stupidity.

"Well, we'll pass over his name. Did you ask him where he lived?"

"I did, yer worship."

"And what answer did he give you?"

"He said, in his own house." (Loud laughter.)

"And what did you say?"

"Must I tell your honour the very words I said?"

"Certainly."

"Then I called him a stupid spalpeen, and tould him that it was no answer at all at all that he had given meself to the civil question I asked him."

"Did he then give you his address?"

"He then said, yer honour, says he, 'Paddy, my boy, I live in Ireland,' (Renewed laughter,) and thinking that too far to remove him to that night, we brought him to the watch-house, yer honour."

"You did quite right," observed the magistrate; and turning to the prisoner, said, "Well, Sir, what have you got to say for yourself?"

"I would much rather not say anything, your worship," answered Mr. Nonsuch, in a subdued tone, and hanging his head; "the truth is, Sir, I had been dining with some friends, and took a glass too much."

"But how come you to have on this strange dress? You are not a private soldier."

"No, Sir, thank heaven, I am no soldier of any kind: I am not come to that yet. The fact is, that all I remember is this; that a young friend and myself, in coming home from the place where we had been dining, went into the tap-room of a public-house in the Strand, to have a lark; and two or three privates being drinking there, one of them proposed, for a frolic, that I should try on his red coat and bonnet, and he my black coat and hat, to see how we should severally look with this change in our apparel. I at once assented, thinking the thing was an excellent joke, and the moment he had put on my coat and hat, he bolted out of the house, crying, 'Catch me if you can.'" (Loud laughter.)

"And did you try to catch him?" inquired the magistrate.

"I did, your worship; but I lost sight of him in a few moments, and have not seen or heard of him since. I suppose the open air must have made me worse, for after losing sight of him I have no recollection of what passed."

"Well, Sir," said the magistrate, with considerable sternness, "I should think the ridiculous figure you now cut, and the situation you are now in, must be no slight punishment for your folly. You are fined five shillings for being drunk. Officer! the next charge."

"But what am I to do?" said the unfortunate wight, addressing himself to the magistrate in a tremulous tone; "what am I to do for my coat and hat? I cannot go home in this state."

"That is no affair of mine," answered the magistrate hastily. "The next charge, officer!"

"Coming, Sir," said the latter. And that moment another servant of the establishment led into the office a man, seemingly about thirty-five years of age, whose stiff gait and erect head denoted that he belonged to the military profession.

"Oh, there he is, your worship!" exclaimed Mr. Nonsuch, with some vehemence, turning about to the magistrate; "that is my coat on his back, and that is my hat in his hand," he added, pointing to the prisoner.

"Silence, Sir! order in the office!" said the magistrate, in authoritative accents.

Mr. Anthony Nonsuch remained in the place to see the upshot of the matter, his countenance irradiated with joy at the sight of two such indispensable parts of his wardrobe, and especially at the prospect of their being restored to him.

"What is this person charged with?" inquired the magistrate, addressing himself to the police constable who stood beside the prisoner.

"Please your worship," answered the guardian of the night, "as I was going my round at half-past one this morning, I saw this here man with a crowd around him, quite drunk, and hollering aloud that he had been a sodger before, but that he was a gentleman now. Seeing the trowsers, waistcoat, and stock of a private on him, with a gentleman's hat and fashionable black coat, I took him into custody, not only for being drunk and disorderly, but thinking he had stolen the coat and hat."

"What are you, Sir?" said the magistrate to the prisoner.

"A private in the 69th regiment," answered the latter.

"And what have you to say to the charge?"

The soldier admitted he had taken a drop too much, and expressed his sorrow for what had happened.

"Do that coat and hat belong to that person there?" said the magistrate, pointing to Mr. Nonsuch.

"They do, your worship," answered the soldier, after bestowing a transient glance on his companion in the previous night's frolic.

"You are fined five shillings for being drunk."

"Give me back my coat and hat, and I will pay the five shillings," said Mr. Nonsuch eagerly, addressing the son of Mars. The latter promptly complied with his wish by doffing coat and hat. The red coat and bonnet were returned to their proper owner along with the five shillings, and both parties quitted the office, Mr. Anthony Nonsuch declaring that he would take care never to get himself into such a plight again.

I shall only give one more police-office case, which may be headed—

CASE OF ALLEGED HORSE-STEALING.

Rory O'Niel, a short, thick-set, recent importation from "Ould Ireland," whose countenance was one of the most innocent-looking that ever graced the bar of a police-office, and whose black bristly head of hair had as rough an appearance as if there were not a comb in Christendom,—was charged with having stolen a horse. The charge excited more than ordinary interest, and gave rise to a variety of observations on the part of other persons in the office, touching the enormity of the crime of horse-stealing.

The complainant, a surly-looking sour-tempered personage, of middle size, and about forty years of age, stated the case with great pomposity. "The horse, your worship, with which this Irishman," pointing with an air of scorn to the prisoner, "ran away, was ——"

"He 's not spaking a word o' the blessed thruth, yer honour," interrupted poor Pat, with great earnestness of manner.

"Silence!" said the magistrate, addressing himself to the prisoner; "you must allow the complainant to state his case without interruption."

"But, yer honour, there isn't a morsel of the blessed thruth in what he 's spaking."

"Well, but you must be silent now; you 'll be heard when he 's done."

"Heaven bless yer jewel of a sowl, yer honour, for that same! If I had known that, sure it's not meself wid have throubled yer honour with a single word at present."

The complainant resumed. "The horse, Sir, with which this person ran away, was one of the finest animals in Lon——"

"Do not tell the bench anything about the qualities of your horse; that is not the matter we are called to decide," interrupted the magistrate.

"Very well, Sir," said the complainant, in a subdued tone, his vanity being clearly wounded by the observation of the magistrate. "Very well, Sir. Having, then, occasion to visit the British Museum, I desired this person, whom I saw lounging about in Great Russell Street, to hold the horse, and walk him about for an hour, saying I would, on my return, give him a shilling for his trouble."

"And he undertook to do as you requested?" observed the magistrate.

"He did, Sir: he put his hand to his hat, and said he would take particular care of the animal. On quitting the British Museum, about an hour afterwards, I found both the horse and the man were gone."

"And what did you do then?" inquired the magistrate.

"I informed the police of the circumstance, and the horse was brought back to my hotel, in Westminster, in about two hours afterwards."

The policeman, who restored the animal to the complainant, stated, that about half an hour after the time mentioned by the complainant, he saw the horse coming in the direction of Tottenham-court-road, at a furious gallop, with the prisoner on his back, but having all the appearance of one who was the reverse of comfortable in his seat. On turning the corner to go down Tottenham-court-road, in the direction of the Hampstead-road, the prisoner fell off the animal, when the latter galloped away at still greater speed. He was, however, soon seized by the bridle and stopped by a man in the street; when he ran up and took charge of him.

"Of the horse, you mean?" said the magistrate.

"Of the horse, your worship."

"So that you left the rider who had fallen off to take care of himself."

"I thought, your worship, that as the horse was very restive, if he was not taken care of, he might escape again and do greater mischief."

"Is the person here who raised the prisoner after he fell off the horse's back?"

"Yes, yer honour: it was myself that did that same act of kindness to a countryman," responded a tall, clumsy, but benevolent-looking man, in a strong Irish brogue.

"Well, I shall examine you presently," said the magistrate, addressing himself to the latter.

"Whenever your honour plases," observed the other, drily.

"You hear the charge against you, prisoner; what have you to say to it?"

"A great dale, yer honour."

"Well, make your statement as short as possible."

"I will, yer honour; but would yer honour be so condesanding as to allow me to begin first?" observed Pat, amidst shouts of laughter, caused not less by the archness with which the remark was made, than by the wit of the remark itself. The magistrate could not help joining in the general laugh.

"Well, Sir, do be so good as to let us hear your defence."

"Och! and sure that I will, yer honour, in less than a minit."

"Well, Sir, proceed."

"My defence, yer honour, is, that the gintlemin has not spoken a word of the blessed thruth, as sure as the Virgin's in heaven."

"Do you mean to say," inquired the magistrate, with some emphasis, "that the complainant did not leave his horse with you?"

"Och! sure, yer honour, and it's not meself would be after sayin' any such thing."

"What *do* you mean to say, then?"

"What do I mane to say, is it 'yer honour manes?"

"Yes. Do you mean to say that you did not run away with the horse?"

"Faith, and it's myself manes to do jist that same."

"How, then, were you seen gallopping in the direction of Tottenham-court road?"

"Och, yer honour! that's it, is it? Then I mane to say it happened in this way."

Here Pat hesitated for a moment, as if ruminating on what he would say further.

"Come, Sir: you say that you did not run away with the horse: how, then, were you seen gallopping the animal at so furious a rate?"

"Bekase, yer honour, the horse ran away with me." (Roars of laughter, in which not only the magistrate, but even the demure, sulky-looking complainant joined.)

"How do you mean?" inquired the magistrate, when the laughter had subsided.

"How do I mane? What I mane is this, that instead of meself running away with the horse on my own blessed back, the horse ran away with me on his back." (Renewed laughter.)

"You are not charged," said the magistrate, "with carrying the animal on your back."

"Am I not, yer honour?" shouted Pat, his countenance suddenly lighting up with a beam of joy. "Am I not? Then the charge is dismissed, is it?" (Laughter.)

"Not quite so fast as that," answered the magistrate, drily.

"Then what *am* I charged with, yer honour?" said Pat, with great shrewdness of manner.

"With stealing the complainant's horse."

"How, yer honour," said the prisoner, with the most imperturbable gravity of countenance, "could I stale the baste, when it ran away with me, and not me with it?"

"Come, tell us how you got on the horse's back?"

"Faith, and I will, this blessed minit, yer honour!"

"Well, let us hear. How was it?"

"Well, yer honour, as sure as I hope that my soul will be saved, I'll tell you the blessed thruth. It was in this way."

Here Pat suddenly dropped his eyes on the floor, and made a dead pause, which lasted for some seconds.

"Why don't you proceed?" inquired the magistrate, with some tartness.

"Wid yer honour be so good as to let me be after telling you what I was thinking of?" said the prisoner, with great simplicity, and slightly scratching his forehead.

"Well, what was it?" inquired the magistrate, sternly.

"Well, then, yer honour, I was thinking, in case you shouldn't belave what I say, though it's the truth of the gospel, it would be good for meself if the horse could spake, and be produced here before yer honour."

The office was again convulsed with laughter, which, indeed, it would have been impossible for the most demure to resist, owing to the air of simplicity and singularly ludicrous way in which the poor fellow made the remark.

"Well, but as we must unfortunately dispense with the presence of the horse, he being unable to give his testimony to the point, will you tell us," said the magistrate, "in a few words, how you came to get on his back?"

"I will, yer honour. As I was *standing walking* (loud laughter) with the animal, a great big spalpeen who was driving a cart, comes in over to me, and says, says he, 'That's a handsome-looking horse you have got.' 'May be, you're right there,' says I. 'Ah, Paddy!' says he, 'why don't you get on his back, and ride him about?' 'What's that to you?' says I. 'Oh,' says he, 'it's because you cannot ride, you Irish ——,' says he. 'You ——' Shall I tell yer honour the word I made use of here?"

"Do," said the magistrate, "if it's not a very bad one."

"It's partikerly bad, yer honour. Says I, 'You lie, you stupid thickskull!' On that, says he again, 'You can't put a leg on horseback. I'll bet you anything you like, you can't.' 'A noggin of gin!' says I. 'Anything you like,' says he again.' 'Well, then,' says I, 'let it be a noggin of Fearon's best.' 'Done!' says he. And with that, yer honour, to gain the wager, as sure's my name is Rory O'Niel, I leaped into the saddle, and was about to have a gintle trot, when he takes his whip and lashes the animal with all his force, and away it flew with me at full gallop, yer honour. That's the blessed thruth, as I hope to be saved!"

"We shall now hear," said the magistrate, "what the person who took the prisoner up, when he fell off the horse, has got to say. Well, Sir?" continued the magistrate, addressing himself to the witness in question.

"I'm here, yer honour."

"You say you were the first that came to the assistance of the prisoner when thrown off the horse."

"I was, yer honour."

"Tell us, then, what you know about this matter?"

"When I saw him fall," answered Rory's countryman, "I ran in over to him, not knowing at the time that he was from Ould Ireland, and said, says I, 'Are you much hurt, my darlint?' But, yer honour, the never a word did he spake in answer to my question. Says I, again, 'Are you living or dead, honey?' And sure enough, yer honour, he raised up his two big eyes, like a wild duck in a thunder storm, and said, 'Don't you see I'm dead, you spalpeen? the horse has kilt me quite?'" (Loud laughter.)

"But do you know anything as to the circumstances connected with the starting of the horse?" inquired the magistrate. "Were you near the place at the time?"

The witness stated that he was not within sight at the time the horse went off, and consequently did not know anything about that part of the matter.

The policeman, who took charge of the horse after he was caught, here came forward, and said that a highly respectable gentleman came up immediately after the accident, and when a concourse of persons were gathered around, and gave precisely the same statement as that of the prisoner, as to the circumstances under which the latter had mounted the horse.

The bench being satisfied that poor Rory had told the truth, and that, instead of deserving more punishment, he had been too much punished already, ordered him to be discharged.

"Thank yer honour, and may yer honour never be kilt by a fall from a horse, to the end of your blessed days," said Rory, amidst much laughter, on hearing the decision of the magistrate. Pat was then in the act of quitting the office, when he suddenly turned about, and addressing the bench with a remarkable peculiarity of manner, said, "But, plase yer honour, the gintleman has not given me the shilling yet, at all at all, for houlding his horse."

"You have not," observed the complainant, "entitled yourself to the shilling: you did not fulfil your engagement: you let the horse go."

"And sure, that was not my fault," answered Rory, with much dryness of manner. "The baste ran away against my will."

A loud burst of laughter followed the observation; and so pleased were the two magistrates who were present, with the readiness and wit of Rory, that they each gave him half-a-crown. The complainant, surly though he seemed to be to the last, could not resist following their example. Pat then left the office, seven-and-sixpence richer than he entered it, singing, with great seeming sincerity, "Och! long life to *all* yer honours!"

CHAPTER VII.

WORKHOUSES.

Inmates of Workhouses—The Republican character of the communities in Workhouses—Difficulty of obtaining accurate statistics regarding them—Marylebone Workhouse—Its size and statistics—Statements and calculations as to Metropolitan Workhouses generally—Farming out paupers—The horror generally entertained of the Workhouse—Description of a particular case, illustrative of the fact—The romantic incidents in the life of many inmates—The New Poor-Law Bill—Its harshness and injustice to the poor—Concluding observations.

THE workhouses of the metropolis are institutions which are rife with materials for a work whose principal object is to sketch life and society in London. In them are to be seen every variety of human character—good, bad, and indifferent. In the workhouses, also, are always to be found people of every clime: they are refuges for the destitute and the indolent of all nations. Nor ought I to omit to mention, that though the inmates of workhouses are, when once there, on precisely the same level in reference to pecuniary circumstances, yet, in the previous condition of those inmates there was as great a variety as there is in the condition of those you will meet in the public streets. Persons who once moved in the highest spheres of society are there, and so are individuals who occupied every intermediate station down to the lowest. As regards their past history, the inmates of the metropolitan workhouses are as promiscuous an assemblage as it were possible to get together. Adversity, says the adage, makes us acquainted with strange bed-fellows. Well may many of the inmates of workhouses say this. Those who were born in the splendid mansion are there reduced to the same level as those who first drew their breath in the most wretched hovel. He who rolled in wealth and luxury, is there on a footing of perfect equality with the poor wretch who had all his life long to struggle with the demon of poverty in its most repulsive aspect. I have often thought that the workhouse might, in one sense, be very fitly compared to the grim messenger whom all dread, and with whom all will sooner or later have to grapple. Like death, the workhouse is a fell destroyer: it lays the axe at the root of all the conventional differences which exist in society. It is, in this respect, the prince of destructives: it levels all distinctions. The inmates of the workhouse are a republican community on a small scale. This is of necessity the case, from the very constitution of these places. But on this topic I need not make further observations at present, as many of my remarks and statements, in the course of the chapter, will incidentally if not directly afford a further illustration of it.

The changes consequent on the introduction of the New Poor Law Bill have been so great in the metropolis, that it is not in my power to present my readers with that fullness and accuracy of statistical information respecting the workhouses, which I could have wished to give. The workhouse system, owing to the New Poor Law Bill, may, indeed, still be said to be in a state of transition; and it will be so for some years to come. New unions of parishes are constantly being formed, and other changes taking place; so that the statistics of the workhouses for one month would not be the statistics of those places in the month following. I shall, however, be able to make some statements of a statistical kind which may be regarded as, at least, approximating to the truth. I shall be enabled to do this by availing myself of the accurate and copious information which was lately furnished me when on a visit to Marylebone Workhouse. I have also visited other workhouses, but prefer singling out that of the parish of Marylebone for my statements, because it is by far the largest, and, in every respect, the most important workhouse in London. It is a building of very great size: it is not only the largest in the metropolis, but the largest in the kingdom. It is capable of containing nearly 2000 inmates. No fewer than 1600 have been in it at one time. Of course, the number of inmates varies according to circumstances. Want of trade, a bad harvest, the high price of provisions, a long continuance of inclement weather, and other causes, compel paupers to seek refuge in the workhouse, who, but for those causes, would have struggled on with the ills of poverty out of doors. The average number of inmates in Marylebone Workhouse, for some months past, has been 1200. The number of adults in the workhouse, at the close of last year, was 808: of whom 272 were men; the remaining 536 were women. The number of children was 410; of whom 242 were boys, and 168 girls. Each pauper costs the parish *3s. 6d.* per week: this applies to those who are in health. In the infirmary, each pauper costs within a fraction of *6s. 6d.* per week, including wine and other expensive medicines. The entire weekly expenses of the workhouse exceed *1000l.*; making the yearly cost to the parish about

55,000*l*. But it must be borne in mind, that the entire expenses of the establishment are not confined to within doors. The parish not being under the jurisdiction of the New Poor Law Commissioners, gives a great deal of out-door relief. On an average, the number of persons receiving out-door relief is about 2000. In times of great pressure, whether from the inclemency of the season, the want of employment, or bad harvests, the number greatly increases: some years ago it was as high as 8000. So large a number of persons are never, however, likely to be again dependent on the compulsory support of the rate-payers. At the period to which I refer, there was a gross mismanagement of parochial affairs. In proof of this, I may mention, that when an inquiry was instituted into the circumstances of the out-door pensioners on the parish bounty, a very large majority of them had no claim whatever to parochial relief, being all in the way of earning, or having it in their power to earn, a competent subsistence for themselves. One woman was found to have had four laundresses in her employ for several years, during which she had been regularly receiving a weekly allowance from the parish. In proof of the abuses that then obtained in the administration of the poor laws, I may here mention, that one of the guardians communicated to me a few weeks since, the singular fact, that out of fifty persons summoned, in one instance, to appear before the guardians to state on what grounds their claims to parochial relief rested, only one appeared in answer to the summons. The amount of out-door relief varies, according the circumstances of the parties, from one shilling and a loaf per week, to three shillings and sixpence.

As might be expected, there is a vast consumption of bread in the workhouse. The average quantity is six hundred-weight per day. The paupers are allowed three meat dinners a week. The average quantity of butchers' meat consumed per week is about 240 stone, or 3840 pounds.

The establishment is divided into two departments. The healthy department is called the workhouse: the department for the sick is called the infirmary. The lunatic paupers are not kept in the workhouse, but are farmed out. The following was the classification in the half year ending in last December:

IN THE WORKHOUSE.		IN THE INFIRMARY.	
Men	214	Men	58
Women	424	Women	112
Boys	213	Boys	29
Girls	136	Girls	32
	987		231

Total in the house - - -	1218
Casual out-door poor - - - -	1258
Permanent ditto - - - ..	604
Illegitimate ditto - - - -	51
Lunatics - - - - -	72
* Total average number relieved weekly -	3203

The number of paupers in Marylebone, including those receiving permanent out-door relief, is, to the entire population of the parish, as 1 to 50. Now, taking the population of London at 2,000,000, which is supposed to be the actual number, and assuming that the number of paupers in the metropolis bears the same proportion to the aggregate population as the paupers in Marylebone do to the entire inhabitants, that would give the number of paupers in London at 40,000. But, Marylebone is one of the wealthiest and most aristocratic parishes in the metropolis; the number of paupers there is not so great in proportion to the aggregate population as in most of the other parishes, with perhaps one or two exceptions. I am confident that, to the above number of 40,000, we may safely add at least 15,000 more, making the entire number of paupers in the metropolis, dependent on parish support, 55,000. The total amount, therefore, assuming that the average cost of paupers is the same as in the Marylebone workhouse, which is annually expended in the compulsory maintenance of the pauper population of London, would be about 550,000*l.*, or upwards of half a million.

Some of the parishes in the City, and in Southwark, "farm out" their paupers at so much per head per week. They are taken into the keeping of persons in the neighbourhood, who speculate in them just as some individuals do in providing black cattle and horses with "keep" for whatever period may be agreed on. The parties who engage to provide these paupers with food, clothing, and lodging, at the small sum—generally about four shillings per head a-week—agreed on, make, as a matter of course, the most they can of them, by causing those of them who can work, to do whatever they are most adapted for. Some of them make the workhouse clothes for the men and the boys; others make and mend shoes; others, again, prepare hair for upholstery articles; while the cooking, washing, cleaning, &c. of the workhouse, are all performed by paupers chosen for the purpose. The same principle of making all work who can, is, I believe, adopted in all the metropolitan workhouses. In Marylebone workhouse, the principle is practically carried into effect

* Shewing an increase of 113, as compared with the corresponding period of 1836.

in a manner which is pleasing to witness. In that establishment, indeed, everything appears to be conducted in a most judicious manner. And here I am constrained to say, that, of all the workhouses which I have seen, the arrangements in that of Marylebone seem to me to be better than in any other. While the strictest economy is practised, the utmost attention is paid to the comforts of the inmates. They appear to me, taken altogether, to be the happiest inmates I have ever seen in a workhouse. Under any circumstances, the workhouse is a place of misery to a sensitive and high-principled mind; but the horrors of the place can be very materially lessened by kind and humane treatment.

In Marylebone workhouse, and in most other workhouses of any note, there is a chapel in which divine service is performed, agreeably to the forms of the Church, every sabbath-day. In the former workhouse there is also an infant school, which is conducted by judicious teachers. It were highly desirable that a similar institution existed in every workhouse in the land. I regard the idea of infant schools as one of the happiest discoveries which have been made in modern times. Of nothing am I more thoroughly convinced than this, that if generally adopted, they would soon exercise a most salutary influence on the condition of mankind.

The horror with which a sensitive mind regards a workhouse, is a point which I shall afterwards have occasion to illustrate by a reference to particular cases. This sensibility is not confined to those who have been at one time in affluent or easy circumstances; though, as might be expected, it is most generally felt by them. It is gratifying to be able to state, that it obtains to a very considerable extent among the working classes; and that it causes them to submit to the greatest privations rather than submit themselves to the degradation of crossing the threshold of a workhouse. From circumstances which have come under my own personal observation, I am convinced that there are hundreds of our mechanics and working men who perish every year of absolute want, from their extreme horror of the workhouse. The feeling is one which reflects the highest honour on the artizans of the metropolis, though it is to be regretted that it should be pushed to such an extent as this.

It were impossible for a man of an observant and reflective mind, to visit the different departments of a workhouse, without indulging in a train of serious thoughts. He could not help contrasting in his own mind the present with the past circumstances of a large proportion of the inmates. He sees numbers around him who, twenty or thirty years ago, surrendered themselves to the pleasing hope that, instead of closing their lives in a workhouse, they would live and die in the possession of every earthly comfort, if not in splendour; and that, instead of being, in one sense, outcasts from society, without a single friend to console and soothe their minds with the whispers of sympathy, they would, in their declining years, be surrounded by near and dear relations. The lineaments of grief, disappointment, and self-humiliation, are visible on their faces: a solitary smile does not play on their countenances from the commencement to the close of the year. What revelations could some of the metropolitan workhouses make, of frustrated hopes, and of sudden and unlooked-for reverses! Who can tell the number of broken hearts in those places! Those only who have experienced the thing, can form any conception of the agony endured by those who formerly rolled in wealth and luxury, but who are now dependent on the compulsory contributions of a parish, when they look back on their more prosperous days. So far from wondering that the contemplation of what such persons were gives, in many cases, a shock to their minds which produces a settled melancholy, it is only a matter for surprise that it does not unhinge altogether the minds of a large proportion of them. In most other cases, the pleasing delusion of hope comes to the aid of persons suffering reverses of fortune; they flatter themselves with the hope that, amid life's varied vicissitudes, they will be one day restored to the circumstances and to the station in society, in which they formerly were; and this sustains and cheers their minds. But few indeed, and far between, are the instances in which persons of the former class enter a workhouse with the hope of ever again quitting it. Nothing but the direst necessity has compelled them to take refuge in these places: it is only when all their friends—those, I mean, who in their better days were called by the name—have deserted them, and when they see absolute starvation staring them in the face, that such individuals have been induced to submit to the alternative of seeking an asylum in a workhouse. And once in, the idea of again coming out, until they are carried out in their coffins, never for a moment enters their mind. When they cross the gate of the workhouse, they look on themselves as having entered a great prison, from which death only will release them. The sentient creations of Dante's fancy saw inscribed over the gate of a nameless place the horrific inscription,

> "All hope abandon, ye who enter here."

In like manner, the imaginations of the class of persons to whom I allude, see an admonition in the very circumstance of crossing the threshold of a workhouse, that they are never again to return to the world. By many of the inmates, the workhouse is regarded as a sort of sepulchre in which they are entombed alive. It is assuredly the grave of all their earthly hopes. It is the grave, too, if there be propriety in the expression, of their hearts. Many a broken heart, as just hinted, is there. Could one but explore the minds of the inmates, he would be appalled at the discoveries he would make.

The difference which obtains in the constitutional temperaments of different individuals, is strikingly displayed in the cases of the inmates of workhouses. There are many of those who once were Fortune's favourites, who, in being compelled to seek an asylum in one of these places, resign themselves to utter despair. They regard themselves as entirely out of the world, and as placed beyond the pale of society, as well as beyond the reach of sympathy. They see and hear their fellows in adversity, but they never bestow a thought on them. They are as much wrapt up in their own thoughts as if they were in the midst of the greatest solitude to be found on the face of the earth. They brood over their own misfortunes to the exclusion of everything else: their hard destiny preys incessantly on their minds, and you see their thoughts visibly impressed on their dark and desponding countenances. They associate with no one; they never speak, save when an unavoidable necessity is imposed upon them. Others, again, act on the principle of making a virtue of necessity; they labour to discipline their minds into submission to a fate which they cannot avert. They speak to those around them, and eagerly grasp at anything which is likely to divert their minds from unavailing regrets at their unhappy destiny. Of the latter description of inmates of workhouses, there are two classes. Besides those whose constitutional temperament is of that happy nature which leads them to extract sunshine from the darkest and gloomiest circumstances in which they can be placed, there are others whose spirits are sustained by the consolations of Christianity. They are reconciled to their condition from the pleasing conviction that it is to them a dispensation of Divine Providence, which is intended and calculated to promote their everlasting happiness in another and better world. The hopes of a happy state beyond the confines of this earth, which their religion inspires, support their minds under their accumulated adversities; and would support them, were those adversities ten times greater. I have often thought that there is not, perhaps, in the earth, a place in which the happy tendency of Christianity, even as relates to the present world, is more remarkably exhibited than in a workhouse. There, as before intimated, and as I shall afterwards have to show, all the inmates are on the same footing, as regards the present life; so that the comparative advantages of Christianity and Deism are clearly shown. The nature of this work forbids my entering on this subject in a formal manner; but I may be permitted to say, that Deism can no more be compared to Christianity, in the tendencies of the respective systems, than darkness can be to light, as regards the emotions they inspire in the mind.

The feelings are different with which different persons enter the workhouse. They are so in the case of those who have, at some previous period of their lives, been in easy or affluent circumstances. Of the lower classes—those, I mean, who have been cradled in poverty, and been all their lives steeped to the very ears in it—it can scarcely be necessary to say that, speaking of them as a body, they are altogether callous as to the degradation of becoming a workhouse inhabitant. With them, their entrance, or their remaining without, is never a matter of moral feeling: it is altogether a question of animal comforts. But with those who, as the homely phrase has it, have seen better days, there is, in this respect, a marked difference. The long series of previous privations and degradations they have endured, do in some cases so blunt the feelings, that minds which but a few years before were so excessively sensitive, that they would a thousand times sooner have suffered martyrdom, are divested of all sense of shame on their entering the workhouse. In the cases of others, again, no amount of privations or hardships can deaden their more refined susceptibilities; and they enter the place with a reluctance and abhorrence which nothing but the direst necessity could overcome. They would prefer death, did it come to them in the usual course of things. The mental struggles which they have undergone, before they could bring themselves to submit to becoming inmates of these places, are matters of which those who have not experienced those struggles can form no conception.

It were impossible to describe the feelings of a person, whose sensitiveness continued to the last, and who was once in affluent circumstances, and accustomed to the luxuries of life, on his first entrance into a workhouse. The observation applies in a special sense to a female, feminine minds being, in most cases, peculiarly sensitive in such matters. Not long since a woman, at the age of sixty, who had, about five years previously, kept her carriage, and otherwise lived in great splendour, was so reduced in circumstances as to be obliged to take refuge in a metropolitan workhouse; and gave, in a letter to a friend, a very vivid picture of what passed in her mind as she entered the place. The first reflection that overpowered her was, that she was now entirely dependent on the forced contributions of others for the means of subsistence. So long as she lived in a room by herself, miserable though the hovel was, the bounty of those who remem-

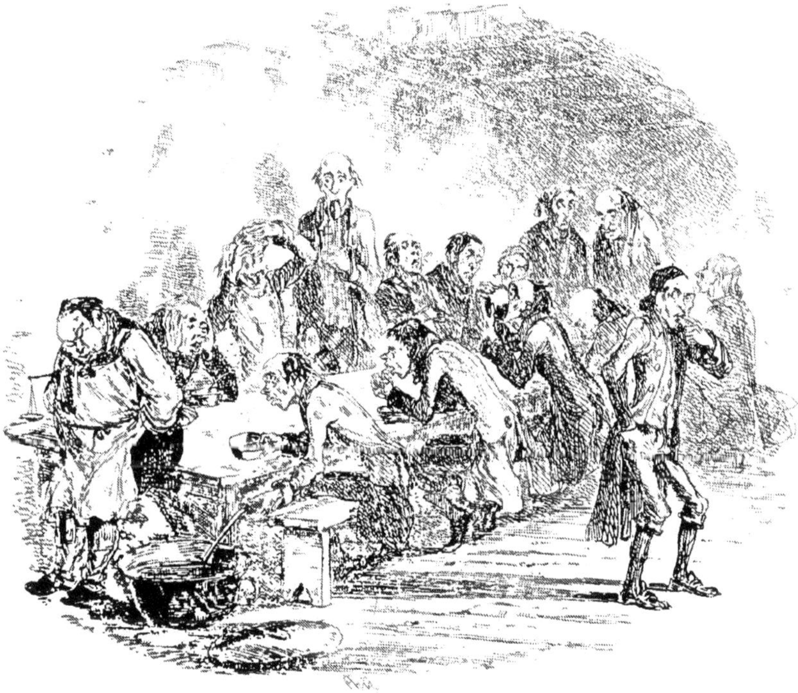

bered her in her altered circumstances was bestowed in that delicate manner which every generous mind would suggest as due to one who had but lately been so differently situated. The gifts, too, of the few friends that still stood true to her, were accompanied with expressions and proofs of sympathy with the unfortunate woman, which operated as a balm to her mind amidst all her wretchedness. But when she crossed the threshold of the workhouse-gate, she felt as if she were an outcast from the world: the heart-harrowing conviction took possession of her mind, that she must never again expect to hear the whisper of sympathy, nor see the hand of friendship extended to administer to her wants. She felt that she was now dependent on alms which were extorted by the law from the pockets of those who neither knew nor cared anything about her. To a sensitive mind, there is an infinite difference between the spontaneous benevolence of acquaintances, and the compulsory charity, if charity it may be called, of strangers. This unfortunate woman now felt degraded in her own estimation to an extent of which she had no conception before. Still she was so situated, that refuge in a workhouse was the only resource left her, if she would not literally perish from want of the necessaries of life. What also shocked her beyond expression, and made the poor creature almost literally sink under the weight of her misfortunes, was the sight of those miserable, and in many instances depraved beings, with whom she was destined to associate. The thought of the society in which she had been accustomed to move, took possession of her mind with a tenfold greater force than it had ever done before, as she beheld the poor wretches crawling about in all the abjectness and degradation of their situation. But what proved the crowning shock to her feelings, and sunk her to the lowest depths of self-degradation, was the circumstance of her being obliged to put on the workhouse-dress. On this she dwelt with a peculiar emphasis. Had she committed the most atrocious crime within the range of possibility, she could not have loathed or despised herself more thoroughly. From that moment she felt so utterly lost to the world, so ashamed of herself and her situation, that even had Fortune, in one of those caprices by which the disposal of her gifts is so often characterised, restored her, in point of pecuniary circumstances, to the condition in which she had been placed in her most affluent days, she would scarcely have been thankful for it. She felt that she could no longer, even had she been the wealthiest lady in the land, hold up her head in society; and that so far from associating with her former acquaintances, she could hardly look a stranger in the face. Milton represents his fallen angel as having sunk so deeply in the mire of depravity, that, apostrophising evil, he says, "Evil, be thou my good!" It was the same with this unfortunate lady. She now felt as if in comparative love with her degraded condition. The gifts of fortune, had they been again bestowed upon her, she would have regarded as positive evils. In the workhouse she now wished to live; in the workhouse she now wished to die.

The workhouses of London abound with the romance of real life. I have often wondered that none of our novel writers have ever thought of singling out their heroes or heroines from among their inmates. There are persons of both sexes there, whose lives would afford incidents of the most striking nature for a work of fiction, and which, if skilfully managed, could not fail to make one of the most attractive works of the kind, of modern times. Innumerable cases would be found which prove that truth is not only strange, but stranger than fiction.

Many romantic cases of this kind have been communicated to me; but in a work of this nature there is no space for relating them with any effect. All I can do is merely to relate two or three of the more prominent features of a few of them. Not long since, in the workhouse of the parish in which I live, one of the most central parishes in London, there was a female whose life had been full of romantic incidents. She was well educated, was brought up as a lady, and possessed great personal attractions. Circumstances threw her in the way of a late Turkish ambassador. He first seduced her, and afterwards took her under his protection. For some years, she lived with him in the greatest splendour, in the West-end, being treated in every respect by him as if she had been his lawful wife. And so devotedly attached was he to the young lady, that he had formed the resolution of taking her with him into Turkey. He partially executed the resolution; he took her with him, on his way home, as far as Malta; but something there occurred to cause him to abandon his intention. I have heard it said, that it was an apprehension of serious inconveniences to himself from his countrymen seeing a European female living in his house. Be this as it may, he abruptly broke off all connection with his victim at Malta, and she returned to this country. For some time afterwards, she took to the pavé; but circumstances soon compelled her to relinquish that mode of life. The next expedient to which she resorted, to obtain the means of subsistence, was betaking herself to the selling of apples and other fruit in the streets. For some time she was to be seen in the neighbourhood of Covent-garden, with a fruit-basket before her, where her beauty and appearance generally struck every one who passed her. That resource also failed her; and after several other ineffectual efforts to procure the means of subsistence, she threw herself on the parish in which she had a right of settlement, and was taken into the workhouse, where she soon afterwards died. The vicissitudes in this young woman's history were not only striking, but they followed each other with a rapidity seldom heard of, even in the pages of romance.

Some years ago, the workhouse in Shoreditch parish contained one inmate, whose history afforded a series of striking incidents in his descent from affluence to poverty. I do not now recollect his name, but the story is well known to many persons in the City-road and its neighbourhood. In addition to a moderate fortune which he inherited from his father, he had the singular luck to get two successive prizes of 30,000*l.* each, in the then government lotteries; which having been purchased at Bish's "Lucky Corner," were duly trumpeted forth by Mr. Bish in the public newspapers of the day. So long as he possessed only a competency, he conducted himself with great propriety, and carefully abstained from anything in the shape of speculation. The sudden accession of fortune, however, at once turned his head. Forthwith he started his carriage-and-four: in that, perhaps, there would not have been much harm, as the interest of his money would have enabled him to support the expense, if not addicted to extravagance in other departments of his domestic establishment. But contemporaneously with his determination to sport a splendid equipage, he was seized with the spirit of speculation. He purchased a large property in the City-road, and expended a vast sum in improving it. He entered into other foolish transactions, of a commercial nature; between which, and the general habits of extravagance he had contracted in his mode of living, he was in a few years reduced to beggary. I do not mean beggary in a figurative, but in a literal sense. And singularly enough, he chose as the scene of his mendicancy the immediate vicinity of the property in the City-road, on which he had expended so much money. There he was to be seen, day after day, for some years after, leaning against a wall, with his hat in hand, to receive the charitable contributions of the passers-by. For a time, the singularity of the circumstances which attended his appearance in the character of a beggar, procured him as much aid from the benevolent as was sufficient to support existence; but the growing infirmities of age, aggravated by a depression of spirits consequent on the sudden and extensive reverse which had taken place in his pecuniary circumstances, eventually rendered him physically incapable of appearing in the streets; and as the only resource against starvation from actual want, he was compelled to seek refuge in Shoreditch workhouse. There he brooded over the vicissitudes of the latter part of his life, for a year or two, and then died.

The annals of the workhouses in the City abound with cases of sudden descents from princely affluence to utter destitution. There, such occurrences are not so much calculated to excite our surprise, or even our sympathy; because we look on it as being in the nature of things, that men engaged in extensive transactions should sometimes ruin themselves, as well as at other times make splendid fortunes. In one of the workhouses, not far from Guildhall, there was lately an inmate whose admission occurred under circumstances of unusual interest. His mind recoiled at the bare idea of being dependent on parish relief; but the necessities of his case were so great, that there was no alternative between his throwing himself on the parish and his dying of want. But the thing which drew attention in a particular manner to his case, was his appearance before the magistrates at an adjoining office, on a charge which I forget, but which very likely was that of being found sleeping in the streets, and his then showing their worships documents which proved beyond all doubt that some years before he was worth no less a sum than 500,000*l.* He had lost his money, and been reduced to beggary, under peculiar circumstances. He had been for many years a member of the Stock Exchange, and had, by a long series of successful speculations in the funds, amassed the above sum. He had previously formed a resolution, that if he should ever be worth half a million, he would purchase an estate, and retire from the City and its business. To a certain extent he adhered to his resolution. He adhered to it thus far, that he did formally quit the Stock Exchange, and entered into a negotiation for the purchase of an estate some miles from London, which, had the purchase been completed, would have doubtless caused him to settle down as a country gentleman for the remainder of his life. I do not recollect what was the sum asked for the estate, but it exceeded 150,000*l.*, and he offered within 5000*l.* of the price put upon it. The seller would not accept the offer; probably he would have compromised the matter by taking half the difference, but the other refused to advance one shilling on the sum he had offered. The negotiation was accordingly broken off; another purchaser was soon found, who gave the price asked by the seller; and the person to whom I allude returned to the Stock Exchange with the view of doing, as he thought, a moderate and safe business, until some other eligible estate should be in the market. For a short time he did do a moderate and safe business; but an opportunity of doubling his fortune, as he supposed, having presented itself, he embarked the whole of his capital in a speculation, and before six months elapsed, he was without a shilling in the world.

The cases I have just given, relate only to individuals who had to ascribe their reverses of fortune to their extravagant modes of living, to unsuccessful speculations, or to circumstances over which they had no control. Let me now glance at a case of a truly romantic nature; one which, had the details of it appeared in a work of fiction, would be at once pronounced as an outrage on all probability. I forbear to mention names, because the principal party, so far as I am aware, is still alive. Of this I am certain, that many of her nearest relations—for I refer to a young lady—are not only still alive, but occupying a prominent place in the public eye. The lady, indeed, to whom I refer, belongs to a noble family: she is the niece of a peer of the realm. She not only received a first-rate education, but was brought up in every respect as became a member of the aristocracy. She had, however, no fortune, but was dependent on her relations—her father and mother being dead—for the station she occupied in society. She was not distinguished for her personal charms, but she possessed great accomplishments and agreeable manners. She was always remarkable, even in her more juvenile days, for a certain waywardness and caprice of disposition, which no admonition or discipline could correct. Some years ago, just as her thirtieth summer had passed over her head, accident introduced her to a gentleman possessed of the princely fortune of 150,000*l*. He had just arrived in England from abroad, and only intended to make a temporary stay in England. He was at once struck with what appeared to him the young lady's charms, and being obliged to quit the country soon, had no time to go through the formalities of a protracted courtship. He accordingly embraced the earliest opportunity which presented itself of intimating to the relation in whose house the lady resided, and who was, in point of fact, though not in law, her guardian, the favourable impression she had made on him,—accompanying the intimation with a hint which could not be misunderstood, that if the proposition were likely to meet with her own and her relations' concurrence, he should lose no time in formally proposing to her. His hopes of receiving her hand were encouraged by her relatives, and he was invited to meet her again on an early day at the house in which she resided. In the interim, what had passed between them and the opulent aspirant after her affections and her hand, was duly communicated to her. The circumstance of being united to a gentleman of so large a fortune, and thus having it in her power to make so splendid an appearance in society as the mistress of a house, was duly impressed on her. The lady appeared as if she were fully convinced of the advantages of the union, without any one pointing them out to her, or expatiating on them. She, in short, left her relatives no reason to doubt that she was as ready to accept the proposals of her lover, as he was to make them. They were delighted at the thought; not only from friendship to her, but because it would be relieving themselves of a burden. The time for the appointed meeting arrived, and the parties were left together. The gentleman proposed; the lady blushed, and was silent. Silence in such matters is proverbially consent. The gentleman viewed it in this light; but, to make assurance doubly sure, pressed for a still more unequivocal affirmative answer. The lady blushed yet more deeply. He repeated his request; and the lady, as a positive proof that she acceded to it, courteously extended to him her hand. He was happy; so, to all appearance, putting out of view the tremor of the moment, was she. The day for the celebration of their nuptials arrived; and "the match" became the subject of conversation among all the lady's acquaintances. Many an heiress of noble birth envied the good fortune of the portionless Miss ——. They wished themselves in her place. The preparations for the marriage ceremony were made on a scale of the utmost splendour. A handsome sum was placed in the lady's hands by her lover, to provide herself with the bridal robes. Everything went smoothly on: the more the lover saw of the young lady, the more was he delighted with her; and the more heartily did he congratulate himself on what he regarded as his good fortune. The marriage morn arrived; and there was not a happier man in Christendom. His love had by this time become a positive passion; and he was literally "dying," as the phrase is in fashionable life, to clasp the object of his affections to his bosom in the character of his wife. Not less delighted was she, to all appearance, at the prospect of so soon exchanging the condition of a maid for that of a wife. The hour appointed for the performance of the marriage ceremony arrived: several coaches-and-four appeared at the church door, while the white favours which floated on the horses' and the servants' heads told the passer-by of what was about to take place. The clergyman was in his place, and the bride and bridegroom stood before the altar. The reverend gentleman commenced the marriage ceremony, and everything proceeded in the usual way, until he came to that part of the service which requires the bride audibly to express her willingness to be the wife of the bridegroom. The question was put in the usual way; the lady returned no answer. Her silence was supposed to be the effect of overpowered feelings, in some measure natural to the situation in which she stood. The question was repeated: still no answer. It was put a third time, when, to the utter surprise and confusion of all present, the lady emphatically and distinctly answered, "No!" and then rushed out of the church, entered her carriage, and drove home, leaving the bridegroom and the friends of both to their own reflections on the extraordinary occurrence which had taken place. To describe their amazement were impossible. The affair so utterly confounded them, and appeared so inexplicable, that not one of them could even venture a conjecture as to the cause of so singular a proceeding. The lady's friends, when somewhat recovered from the effects of so unexpected an event, begged her to make the *amende,* by proceeding again forthwith to the hymeneal altar: the bridegroom would have been satisfied with this; but she peremptorily refused. She was then implored to see the bridegroom, in order that, if she had any valid reason for the extraordinary step she had taken, she might state it to him, for her own and her relations' sake: she was inexorable. Last of all, she was asked to state to her relatives the causes which induced her to adopt so unheard-of a course: she declined to utter a word on the subject. In a short time thereafter the bridegroom quitted the country, inexpressibly mortified as well as disappointed at what had occurred. He, if I mistake not, died within three years of the "untoward event;" and she, being disowned by her relatives, in consequence of the improper course she had pursued, was, within the same period of time, an inmate in a west-end workhouse. There she continued for upwards of twelve months, when she was, at the expense of the parish, passed, at her own request, to Dublin, of which place she was a native. She never, so far as I have heard, has, up to this moment, assigned any reason for her singular refusal at the altar to become the wife of him who led her to that altar. The thing must have been the effect of caprice; it is a caprice for which she has suffered, and most probably is still suffering, a most severe punishment. A more rapid descent from the highest to the lowest station of life, or one which has happened under more romantic circumstances, has perhaps seldom occurred.

The annals of most of the workhouses in the West-end abound with the records of equally great and nearly as sudden reverses of fortune, though not, perhaps, attended with such romantic circumstances as the case I have just given. One of the guardians of the workhouse of Marylebone lately mentioned, in my hearing, at a vestry meeting, that some time previously there were no fewer than four individuals in that workhouse, all of whom, six or seven years before their entrance, kept their carriages. Of cases of this nature, in the workhouse in question, I will only refer to one; the case, namely, of a man who a few years previous to his application for admission, was worth no less a sum than 100,000*l.* There was something peculiarly interesting in his case. He was a gentleman of the highest moral principle: his strict integrity was the admiration of all who had any transactions with him. His habits were not expensive: being unmarried, he had not to keep up a large establishment; neither had he any relations dependent on him for support. In what way, then, it will be asked, did he lose, and so speedily, so large a fortune? By the same way as many others, equally rich at one time, have eventually involved themselves in ruin. The spirit of speculation was the cause of all his reverses. His propensity that way was irresistible and uncontrollable. His mind was constantly erecting castles in the air: there was scarcely a day in which he did not devise some new scheme, or embark in schemes devised by others, by which he made sure of realising thousands. Foolish as all this may appear, it is nevertheless quite intelligible in the case of a man who is constitutionally of a sanguine mental temperament. But what appears surprising is, that after finding that he was losing money by every successive project in which he engaged, he did not desist, and thus avert his entire ruin. No: the lessons of experience were lost upon him. His failure in half a dozen speculations was no reason why he should not succeed in the seventh. The event proves that his calculations are wrong in the seventh also: he admits the fact, for his pocket told him there was no denying it: but why, nevertheless, should not the eighth speculation prove sufficiently fortunate to do more than counterbalance all his losses on the previous seven unsuccessful ones? He soon finds that, instead of retrieving the portion of his fortune which he had lost, his last speculation proved the worst of all. The ninth time he makes a still deeper plunge; he risks nearly all that remains; and that all is lost. In a word, he went on with one speculation after another, until he had speculated away the last shilling he had in the world,—just as gamblers at cards or the dice, become more venturesome and more eager for play, in proportion to the amount of their losses. Friends, for a time, felt, or affected to feel, for him; but their sympathy, if sympathy it really was, never extracted a shilling from their pockets to assist him. He made every effort to obtain such employment as he was adapted for: in that he failed. For months he struggled with all the horrors of want: at last he found himself unequal to the conflict: he felt that if he attempted to stand out much longer, he must perish in the effort. He capitulated; he submitted to a destiny which no resources of his own could controul, and sought for an asylum from a world in which he had been so unfortunate, in the workhouse of Marylebone, where he died a very short time since.

The world is full of illustrations of the remark, that as one individual falls, another rises. Two persons may be next-door neighbours, or be frequently brought into close contact together,—the one is rolling in wealth, the other has difficulty in pro-

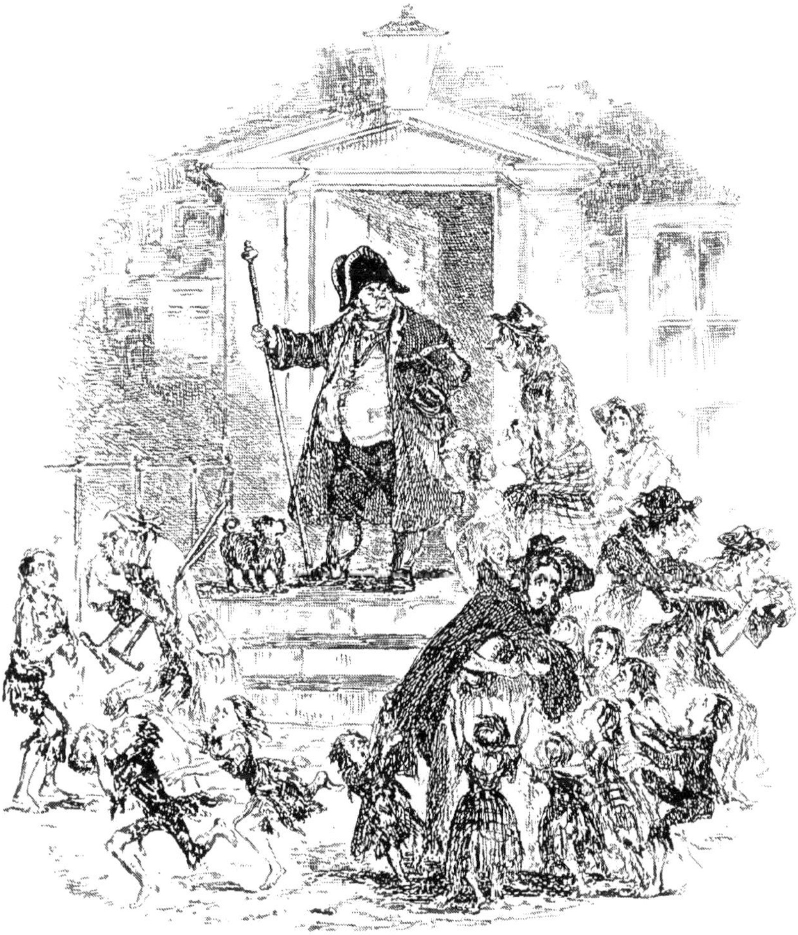

curing the necessaries of life: in twenty, fifteen, or even a dozen years, their pecuniary circumstances and position in society are completely reversed. The rich and influential individual is reduced to the very lowest depths of poverty, and of insignificance in the social scale, while the poor man is raised to affluence and importance among his fellow men. Not many months since, a remarkable illustration of what I have stated occurred in a West-end workhouse, which for particular reasons I forbear to name. A gentleman, now one of the leading men—I should say, indeed, the leading man—in a large and aristocratic parish, had, about twenty years ago, though well educated, but slender means to live on, like many other intelligent men. He was acquainted with a lady residing in the same country town as himself, who was immensely rich, and was the most distinguished of her sex among the fashionables of the place. He quitted his native town for the metropolis, where, through his talents and perseverance, he eventually raised himself to an influential position in society, and at the same time acquired a handsome independency. He was chosen one of the guardians of the poor in the parish to which I refer. He had not been in his new office for any lengthened period, when, among the names of applicants for admission to the workhouse, he found one which, as it was a very peculiar name, attracted his attention. The only person bearing that name he had ever known, was the lady to whom I have alluded. His curiosity being excited, he desired to see the particular applicant. She was brought to him, and was none other than the lady whom, but twenty years previously, he had known living in all the splendour and luxury which the world could afford. She recognised him at once: the interview, as may well be supposed, was one of an affecting nature to both parties. The gentleman felt deeply for the reverse of fortune which had befallen the lady; while her mind was overpowered at the thought of thus unexpectedly meeting with one whom she formerly knew when in circumstances so materially different. The emotions of surprise and confusion caused by the unexpected meeting, and under such peculiar circumstances, having in some degree subsided, the unfortunate lady entered into a statement of the way in which her reverses had been brought about. That statement was very brief: her tale of misfortune was soon told. Shortly after Mr. A. had left his native place, she came to town and took a large house in the West-end. Her income had been solely derived from West-India property: that property, some years since, became most seriously depreciated in value. She was obliged to borrow money on the security of her estate: the money was only lent for a limited time: the property meanwhile daily diminished in value. At length, the period for which the loan was granted, expired; and she being unable to repay the money, the estate was put up to the hammer, and brought little more than paid the loan and the expenses of the sale. In a year or two she was without a shilling in the world. Acquaintances did something for her for a time; but they, one after another, gradually deserted her. In two years more she was obliged to throw herself on the parish. She had been friendly to the gentleman in her better days, and when he was in indifferent circumstances. Now that he had been raised to an influential position in society, while she had been reduced to the lowest point in the social scale, he, equally from a sense of gratitude and a generous disposition, took advantage of the situation he held as one of the board of guardians, to render her as comfortable as possible.

Parties often meet in the workhouse under peculiar circumstances, though of a very different nature from those I have mentioned. There is no want of instances in which a high-bred and haughty lady, living at one time in the greatest luxury, has met in the workhouse, on a footing of the most perfect equality, the very mendicant of her own sex whom, in the hey-dey of her prosperity, she had desired her "pampered menial" to turn scornfully away from her door, where the poor creature had been supplicating a crust of bread for her famishing children. Little do the prosperous and affluent think in the day of their prosperity, to what complexion matters *may* come before they quit the world.

Perhaps there is no other place, speaking of assemblages of persons, in which the advantages of religion are so forcibly exhibited, as in the workhouse. I believe that every one acquainted with workhouses, be his individual opinions what they may, will bear me out when I say, that there is all the difference in the world, with regard to the manner in which they meet their reverses, between a person of genuine piety and one who has no proper sense of religion at all. The former is not insensible to the circumstances in which he is placed, and was equally reluctant with the other to be placed in those circumstances; but you see that the one bears up under his reverses with far more fortitude and tranquillity of mind than the other. How could it be otherwise? The pious inmate is sustained and cheered by a firm persuasion—no matter, in so far as his present state of mind is concerned, even were that persuasion groundless—of a happy hereafter. The irreligious person has no hope beyond the present world: possibly he does not even extend his thoughts beyond the precincts of time. In that case, all must be dark and gloomy enough; but far darker—much more gloomy still—must be the picture, if his views *do* extend to a future state, and yet he have no hope that that state will be to him one of happiness.

A singularly striking proof of the power of religion in administering to the happiness of mankind even in this world, was afforded in the case of a woman who died within the last year in the workhouse of St. Pancras. She was one of those of whom I have been speaking, who had undergone very great reverses of fortune. She had lived at one time in great splendour, keeping her carriage, taking a prominent part in the gaieties of the day, and living in utter thoughtlessness of a world to come. By a succession of reverses which followed each other with a remarkable rapidity, she was reduced to absolute destitution, and applied as a last resource for admission into the workhouse. For some time after her admission, her countenance betrayed the troubled state of her mind. It was not only that she repined at the altered situation in which she was then placed, but she felt appalled at the retrospect of the thoughtless life she had hitherto lived. A variety of circumstances conspired to turn her mind to the consideration of religious matters. The pages of inspiration were daily perused by her; and, in a very short time, she became a decidedly pious woman. From that moment her countenance assumed a wonderful serenity of expression; and so far it faithfully indexed the state of her mind. She afterwards repeatedly declared to one of the officers of the workhouse, that, possessing as she then did the peace which the gospel inspires, she felt herself an incomparably happier woman in the workhouse, than ever she had done when in the zenith of her prosperity, and when living in all the splendour and dissipation of fashionable life.

Cases of a similar kind are of quite frequent occurrence; but anything of a theological nature being foreign to the objects of "Sketches in London," I will not advert to any more of those cases in detail.

Among the class of inmates to be found in workhouses, who once moved in the more respectable spheres of society, the number of members of the learned professions is proportionably small. You meet with few decayed medical gentlemen; perhaps fewer still of decayed lawyers; and certainly fewest of all of individuals who were brought up for the pulpit. I may here also remark, that improvident as the habits of literary men proverbially are, remarkably few of them seek an asylum in the workhouse. I know of no class of men among whom a greater number of cases of hardship and privation occur, than among those who devote themselves to literary pursuits. In another work,* I have ad-

* The Second Series of "The Great Metropolis."

verted at considerable length to the deplorable circumstances of thousands in London, who make literature a profession. And yet, with very few exceptions indeed, the horror with which they regard the workhouse is so great, that nothing can overcome it. I believe innumerable instances might be adduced in which literary men have died from absolute want, rather than enter a workhouse. Their extreme sensitiveness on this point may be, in a great measure, accounted for from the refined and soul-elevating nature of their pursuits.

The best time for seeing a workhouse to advantage, is at meal-time; and of the three meals, that of dinner is to be preferred. In the larger workhouses, there is no apartment sufficiently commodious to accommodate a fourth part of the inmates, and consequently they take their meals in different places. The greatest number I have seen at dinner at once, was about 120. Nothing can exceed the avidity with which the paupers devour their meals. You would fancy that they lived for no other purpose than to eat. That certainly was the chief object they had in view in entering the workhouse; and they cling till the last to the idea, that eating is their principal business. The subject is one which would admit of some observations of a humorous nature; but I am restrained from any effort to excite a smile, by the consideration that the unfortunate inmates of a workhouse are not legitimate subjects for humour. I trust that, however much I may be disposed to relish anything of a humorous nature, I am not one of those who would indulge that taste at the expense of suffering humanity.

The guardians of the poor in most of the workhouses, have a fixed day, once a week, for the purpose of granting out-door relief. The scene on such occasions is usually one of a grotesque nature. Ragged mothers, with children in their arms, and children at their feet, are seen congregated together in vast numbers at the place of distribution; while old infirm men, and young men who are in destitute circumstances, are interspersed in very fair proportions. There is not only their ragged appearance, but their starved looks: you see, from their faces, that few and far between are their ample meals, even of the plain and homely fare to which they are accustomed. The scenes, however, of this kind which possess the greatest interest, are exhibited at those workhouses which are under the operation of the New Poor Law Act, and where, consequently, the applicants are uncertain whether they are to be successful in their supplications for bread or not. A few weeks since, I witnessed a scene of this kind, of a very touching nature. It was at the workhouse of a small parish, and the number of applicants who had besieged the office, whence the loaves are distributed, was under one hundred. A more miserable group of human beings I have never seen; a more wretched assemblage, judging from their outward appearance, I should suppose, are but seldom to be witnessed in any civilised country. When one succeeded in getting a loaf, every eye was directed to it in a moment, with an eagerness and intensity of gaze which told much more forcibly than words could, the hunger which the poor creatures were enduring. The eyes of the children looked with a specially expressive gaze at the article of food. But what was most eloquent and affecting of all, as showing the agony which the poor young creatures were suffering from want of food, was the almost ferocious-like manner in which they seized the loaf, the moment their mothers got one, and the ravenous voracity with which they began to eat it. And to add to the wretchedness of their situation, caused by destitution and hunger, the parish functionaries, dressed in their little brief authority, treated the poor unhappy applicants as if they had been no better than so many reptiles crawling on the ground. As if the poor were not made sufficiently miserable by the hard destiny of their lot, these officials must needs add to their woes by their overbearing and outrageous manner towards them. Why cannot those entrusted with the distribution of relief to paupers, treat the poor wretches who are obliged to fawn on them and lick the very dust before them, with decency at least, if not with respect? In several instances this, let me say in justice, is done; why not in all? Do such persons forget that the poor are human beings as well as themselves; and that, though doomed to grapple with the evils of pauperism, they have their feelings and susceptibilities as well as others; Are we not all, including the humblest and most dependent of human creatures, descended from the same common parent? Are we not all influenced by the same motives and feelings? Are we not all members of the great community of man? Shall we not all, whatever may be the accidental distinctions which exist in our relative circumstances at present, be soon placed on a footing of the most perfect equality? Where will be the difference between us some years hence? Shall we not all be on the same level in the grave? Is it not true, though a reflection so mortifying is carefully excluded from the minds of many of those who have it at present in their power to tyrannize over and trample on the poor, that ere many years shall have passed away, no one will be able to distinguish the bodies of these persons, from those whose feelings they have flagrantly outraged by their harsh and haughty manner, when doling out a miserable pittance to them, or when refusing to grant them a morsel of bread though famishing from want? There is one other consideration which may possibly have more weight than any of those to which I have alluded. Let me remind the man who takes advantage of the situation in which he is placed, to insult and wound the feelings of the unhappy pauper whom destiny has placed in his power, that he himself *may* before he dies stand in the same situation as the wretched person whom he now treats with so much contumely and heartlessness. Such things have been; such things will be to the end of time. The records of workhouses contain many instances of persons, whose office it once was to dole out a scanty pittance to the poor, becoming themselves the recipients of parish bounty in precisely the same way.

Many paupers spend what is called "a little life" in the workhouse. I knew a Scottish peasant, who died at the advanced age of eighty in the very cottage in which he was born, never having, during all that lengthened period, been one night absent from his home. The case of the man who had been upwards of forty years a prisoner in the Bastile, is known to most of my readers. The first was a singular length of time for an individual to live in one spot, and sleep in the same bed. Scarcely less wonderful is the circumstance of a person being upwards of forty years in prison; for one would suppose that it would be impossible to survive so lengthened an incarceration in a gloomy and unhealthy dungeon. I know of no instance of location in a workhouse for so many years; but I have heard of a pauper female who was an inmate of one of the most centrical of our metropolitan workhouses for upwards of thirty years. One cannot reflect on such a fact, without thinking of the many changes which took place in the world during her location in one spot. She first entered the place immediately previous to the commencement of the French Revolution: it was over for several years before she died. How many kings were dethroned and empires overthrown, while she remained in the same place! And how vast the changes which had occurred on the face of society while she remained there! How great, even, the changes which had taken place on the surface of a large portion of the physical world, during that lengthened period of time! Immense tracts of waste land had been brought under cultivation; marshes had been converted into dry and fruitful soil; plantations had grown into forests; the size of existing towns and villages had been vastly extended; and new villages and towns had started up in places in which were no human habitations when this pauper first threw herself on her parish. In London alone, what extensive changes had taken place! What vast additions had been made to its dimensions and population! How few, comparatively, of those who were inhabitants of the metropolis when she entered the workhouse, were among its population immediately before she died! One race had passed away and another taken its place in the interval. The appearance also of the town itself had undergone extensive changes: old streets were thrown down, and new ones built in their places. But even confining oneself to the changes which had occurred in the workhouse, under her own eye, how many and great must these have been! Not one of those who were the inmates of the place when she entered remained in it one-half of the time she did. How many entrances and exits must she have witnessed in her time!—the entrances all of one kind; the exits of two kinds: some going out in the hope of being able to earn a subsistence for themselves; others being carried out to be consigned to the grave.

Such are some of the thoughts which would naturally arise in a reflective mind, on hearing of the circumstance of a person being an inmate of a workhouse for so long a period as thirty years. The train of thought might be followed out to a great length; but this is not the proper place for moralization.

It is a fact which is worthy of mention, that the best regulated workhouses are conducive to health rather than otherwise. I ascribe this, in a great measure, to the circumstance of the rules of these establishments being of such a nature as to ensure greater regularity of habits than the inmates were previously accustomed to. They are there regular in going to bed, regular in rising, and regular in their meals; and every one knows how great an influence regularity in such matters has on the health of mankind. A guardian of one of the workhouses in the centre of the metropolis, lately mentioned to me some singular cases of paupers having entered those establishments in a very bad state of health, brought on by irregularity of living, and of their complete restoration to health after being a short time there. The case of the female to whom I have already alluded, as having for thirty years been an inmate of a workhouse, was one of those he mentioned. When she applied for admission she was labouring under illness, brought on by irregularity, to such an extent, that no one who saw her supposed she would survive a month. The medical gentleman who had attended her pronounced her case to be hopeless; and yet the regularity of habits enforced by the rules of the workhouse, restored her in a few months to perfect health; and that health continued for the long period already mentioned.

In a chapter devoted to the Workhouses of London, it will be expected that, as the great majority of those workhouses are under the operation of the New Poor Law Amendment Act, I should express some opinion of that measure. That opinion, if I must express it, is in decided opposition to it. No man can be more thoroughly impressed with the conviction than I am, that the grossest abuses prevailed under the old system; and that a reform, or amendment of that system, was most imperatively called for. The great defect of that system, or of the way in which it was administered, was the encouragement it held out to idleness and fraud. A clever rogue of indolent disposition, could always contrive to make a very comfortable living of it, under the old system. A case was mentioned to me a few weeks ago, in which a woman was in the habit of receiving four shillings per week from the parish of St. Paul, Covent Garden, while carrying on business on a rather extensive scale, and renting an excellent shop, as a bonnet maker, in the Mile-end-road. In another case, a party receiving parish relief was followed to his home, and on his table there was found awaiting his arrival, and the arrival of some "jolly paupers" he had invited to partake of it, a piece of roast beef which was equally pleasant to the eye and grateful to the olfactory nerves. In the case of a third person, that person was dexterous enough in the arts of deception to impose on no fewer than four parishes at one time, in each of which she professed to have a right of settlement, and from all of which she continued for some years to receive three or four shillings, besides a certain quantity of bread, per week. Innumerable other instances might be adduced in which parties received relief who had not the slightest claim to it; and to support whom in vice and idleness, poor industrious rate-payers were ground down to the earth. But the great objection to the New Poor Law Amendment Act is, that it has leaped from one extreme to another. The errors in the administration of the law to which I have referred, might easily have been remedied without the interposition of the legislature at all. The Poor Law guardians of the parish of Marylebone have afforded practical proof of this. They have adopted a course equally humane and judicious: one which combines the strictest justice to the rate-payers, with the greatest attention to the claims of the poor. They have appointed a certain number of men whom they call inspectors, and in whose judgment and humanity they can repose confidence, to institute a careful inquiry into the circumstances of all who apply for parochial relief. The consequence is, that persons having no claims on parish aid, are refused such aid; while those who really are proper objects for parochial assistance, at once receive it. The same enlightened caution is observed in the administration of the Poor Laws in the parish of St. Pancras; and the result has been, that in both these parishes the poor-rates have been reduced much more than one-half—nearly, I believe, two thirds—without in the slightest degree entrenching on the legitimate claims of the pauper portion of the population. And why, I should like to ask, might not a similar system have been adopted throughout the country? Nothing, surely, could be more simple in theory, and nothing could be more easy in practice.

The clause in the New Poor Law Bill which refuses relief to those who will not accept that relief except in the character of inmates of the workhouse, is as unsound in policy as it is harsh and despotic in principle. Why not give them as much out of the workhouse as it requires to support them in it? Where would be the loss to the parish in this? Why say to the poor applicants that they must either perish of want, or break through all their strong and tender attachments to home? Why thus gratuitously tear asunder all the ties which bind one to his own abode, however humble it may be? "Home is home, however homely," says the adage. Ay, and the humble hovel of the poor has its attractions and charms to them, as well as the splendid mansion has *its* attractions and charms to its wealthy possessor. To wrench the unhappy pauper from the lowly abode to which he clings with a tenacity of grasp which nothing but the horror of absolute starvation can induce him to relinquish, is a piece of cruelty at which every humane breast must revolt, and is a positive disgrace to a Christian country. Who would believe it, did not the fact stare us in the face, that in the second quarter of the nineteenth century, the legislature of Great Britain should say to a pauper, unable to earn a subsistence that he must either submit to be torn from his home and his wife and children, or die of absolute want? There is not a breast in which there is an atom of humanity, that does not rise up in revolt against such legislation.

One most objectionable regulation of the workhouse system—a regulation enjoined by the New Poor Law Bill—is, the denial of the consolations of religion to those whose conscientious scruples will not allow them to worship according to the forms of the established church. A more flagrant and uncalled-for outrage on all the higher and more hallowed feelings of one's mind, could not be committed. A regulation more at variance with the spirit of Christianity, or more repugnant to that spirit of civil and religious liberty which is the glory of this country, could not be devised. It is one worthy of the worst days of religious intolerance. That a protestant legislature, in the thirty-eighth year of the nineteenth century, should have sanctioned such a clause, is one of those facts which would be pronounced incredible, if they did not unhappily stare us in the face. Why not let those who have been all their lives connected with Dissenters, and have heard from sabbath to sabbath the truths of the gospel preached by pastors in their own communion; why not let such persons, if able, attend on the sabbath the minister of their own choice? What probability is there, that the preaching of one against whom the pauper Dissenters are prejudiced—if prejudiced must be the word—will be either pleasant or profitable? In order to a profitable hearing of the Word, it is necessary that a feeling of esteem, if not of affection, for the preacher, should be entertained. And this esteem or affection must be based on the circumstance of the preacher holding the same views on all important religious questions as the party who hears him. We all know how strong are the dislikes of many Episcopalians to the principles of Dissent. I know many members of the Church of England who would prefer absenting themselves from public worship altogether, to entering a Dissenting meeting-house. Not less strong are the antipathies of many Dissenters towards the established church. They could not worship with their Episcopalian brethren, without doing violence to all their most cherished feelings on the subject of religion. I think that there are many, both of Dissenters and Churchmen, who carry their dislike of each other's mode of worship too far. But even where I think them in error, I would treat them with tenderness. There is nothing incompatible in disapproving of this prejudice, and yet respecting it so far as to extend the utmost indulgence to those who are its subjects. Let me not be here supposed to be arguing the matter on sectarian grounds: not less decidedly would I denounce the conduct of the Dissenter who would, if he had the power, compel the Churchman either to listen to the doctrines of the gospel from the lips of a Dissenting pastor, or not hear those doctrines at all. In everything appertaining to religion, there ought to be the most unbounded liberty—the most perfect toleration. The conscience ought to be utterly unfettered. There should be an unrestrained freedom of thought—the most entire liberty of action, so long as that action does not interfere with the rights and privileges of any other member of the community. The great truth cannot be too frequently repeated—it cannot be kept too prominently before the eyes of those invested with authority—that man is not responsible to his fellow men for his religious opinions; that he is responsible only to his Maker. He, therefore, who seeks to interpose between a man's conscience and his Maker, on the most important of all questions, places himself in a position of moral peril of awful magnitude.

But, for the reasons before stated, I forbear to discuss the question in its theological bearings. Once for all, let me say, that the refusal to allow a Dissenter in the workhouse to attend, on the sabbath day, on the ministrations of a pastor of his own persuasion—one, it may be, from whose lips he had heard the living Word for a long series of years—is not only at manifest and direct variance with the spirit of Christianity, but it is an act of inhumanity, a piece of heartless cruelty—and as gratuitous as it is heartless—which may well, as Cowper says, cause us to

> "Hang our heads to think that we are men."

Then there is the separation regulation. It is difficult to speak of this regulation in measured language: it is a standing outrage on human nature; a foul stain on the national character; one of the blackest pages in England's history. Posterity will ask, could there have been one particle of humanity, to say nothing of Christianity, in the composition of those who were parties to the framing and enforcing such a regulation? To me it has always appeared as the very quintessence of cruelty. It erects a Juggernaut in every workhouse in the land within the sphere of the New Poor Law Bill: and like the Juggernaut of the East, it can already boast of its numerous victims. Who can tell the number of hearts which it has already broken? Who can compute the number of human beings who are destined to be crushed by its moral pressure, should it unhappily be permitted for any length of time to stain the pages of our history? Let not this be mistaken for mere declamation; let it not be understood as only figures of speech. When I say that the separation regulation, in the administration of the New Poor Law Act, has its victims, I speak of facts which consist with my own personal knowledge. Ay, and strange as the statement may appear, it has its victims without as well as within the walls of the workhouse. Not long since, I heard from the lips of one of the most worthy ministers in the metropolis, one very affecting proof of the operation of this regulation. The anecdote, it may be proper to mention, was related from the pulpit, not for the purpose of condemning the New Poor Law Bill, but with the view of illustrating a religious topic. As I cannot give the anecdote in the minister's words, I must give it in my own. Two persons, man and wife, of very advanced years, were at last, through the infirmities consequent on old age, rendered incapable of providing for themselves. Their friends were like themselves, poor; but so long as they could, they afforded them all the assistance in their power. The infirmities of the aged couple became greater and greater; so, as a necessary consequence, did their wants. The guardians of the poor—their parish being under the operation of the new measure—refused to afford them the slightest rel ef. What was to be done? They had no alternative but starvation or the workhouse. To have gone to the workhouse, even had they been permitted to live together, would have been painful enough to their feelings; but to go there to be separated from each other, was a thought at which their hearts sickened. They had been married for nearly half a century; and during all that time had lived in the greatest harmony together. I am speaking the language of unexaggerated truth when I say, that their affection for each other increased, instead of suffering diminution, as they advanced in years. A purer or stronger attachment than theirs has never, perhaps, existed in a world in which there is so much of mutability as in ours. Many were the joys, and many the sorrows, which they had equally shared with each other. Their joys were increased, because participated in by both: their sorrows were lessened because of the consolations they assiduously administered to each other when the dispensations of Providence assumed a lowering aspect. The reverses they had experienced in the course of their long and eventful union, had only served to attach them the more strongly to each other, just as the tempestuous blast only serves to cause the oak to strike its roots more deeply in the earth. With minds originally constituted alike, and that constitution being based on a virtuous foundation, it was, indeed, to be expected that the lapse of years would only tend to strengthen their attachment. Nothing, in a word, could have exceeded the ardour of their sympathy with each other. The only happiness which this world could afford them was derived from the circumstance of being in each other's company; and the one looked forward to the possibility of being left alone when the other was snatched away by death, with feelings of the deepest pain and apprehension. Their wish was, in subordination to the will of the Supreme Being, that as they had been so long united in life, so in death they might not be divided. Their wish was in one sense realized, though not in the sense they had desired. The pressure of want, aggravated by the increasing infirmities of the female, imposed on her the necessity of repairing to the workhouse. The husband would most willingly have followed, had they been permitted to live together when there, in the hope that they should, even in that miserable place, be able to assuage each other's griefs, as they had so often done before. That was a permission, however, which was not to be granted to them. The husband therefore determined that he would live on a morsel of bread and a draught of cold water, where he was, rather than submit to the degradation of a workhouse in which he would be separated from her who had been the partner of his joys and griefs for upwards of half a century. The hour of parting came; and a sad and sorrowful hour it was to the aged couple. Who shall describe their feelings on the occasion? Who can even enter into those feelings? No one. They could only be conceived by themselves. The process of separation was as full of anguish to their mental nature, as is the severance of a limb from the body to the physical constitution. And that separation was aggravated by the circumstance, that both felt a presentiment, so strong as to have all the force of a thorough conviction, that their separation was to be final as regarded this world. What, then, must have been the agonies of the parting hour in the case of a couple whose mental powers were still unimpaired, and who had lived in the most perfect harmony for the protracted period of fifty years? They were, I repeat, not only such as admit of no description, but no one who has not been similarly circumstanced, can even form an idea of them. The downcast look—the tender glances they emitted to each other—the swimming eye—the moist cheek—the deep-drawn sigh—the choked utterance—the affectionate embrace; all told, in the language of resistless eloquence, of the anguish caused by their separation. The scene was afflicting in the extreme, even to the mere spectator. It was one which must have softened the hardest heart, as it drew tears from every eye which witnessed it; what, then, must the actual realization of it in all its power have been to the parties themselves? The separation did take place; the poor woman was wrenched from the almost death-like grasp of her husband. She was transferred to the workhouse; and he was left alone in the miserable hovel in which they had so long remained together. And what followed? —What followed! That may be soon told: it is a short history. The former pined away, and died in three weeks after the separation; and the husband only survived three weeks more. Their parting was thus but for a short time, though final as respected this world. Ere six weeks had elapsed they again met together;

> " Met on that happy, happy shore.
> Where friends do meet to part no more."

Here, then, were two victims, under circumstances of a most affecting nature, to the separation regulation in the administration of the New Poor Law Bill. Have I overcharged the picture? I have fallen far short of the reality. Not even those who felt the agonies and anguish to which I have referred, could have portrayed it, even had they been gifted with the highest intellects. The thing was to be experienced, not described.

It it said by the advocates of the regulation, that paupers themselves have no objection to be separated from each other, because that, generally speaking, they have become old and unable to assist each other, before they throw themselves permanently on the parish. The man who makes such a representation libels the unhappy poor, and gives utterance to a calumny on human nature itself. The feelings of attachment with which the poor regard each other, are as strong and tender as those which exist among the higher classes of society. What if they be even *more* strong and tender, because less alloyed by conventional considerations and circumstances? The imputation that a pauper husband and wife care not for one another, but are glad to be separated, when they are advanced in years, is a calumny of the most cruel kind; and one more destitute of even the shadow of a foundation, was never, I will venture to say, invented. Here I do not speak from conjecture: I have had many opportunities of making myself acquainted, from personal observation, with the principles, feelings, and habits of the poor; and justice to them requires that I should vindicate them in the mass, from so heartless and unfounded a charge. Those who have once been in affluent circumstances and wallowed among the luxuries of life, are far more likely to be insensible to the pains of separation than the poorer classes. The husbands and wives of the rich and the noble have various enjoyments apart from those arising from their attachment to each other, which naturally enough enables them to submit more readily to the dispensation which disunites them. No so the ill-fated poor: the only sweet in their cup of life, apart from the hopes of a happy hereafter, is the sympathy with which they regard each other. That sympathy supports them amid all their toils and trials; and having weathered the storms and tempests of life together, is it not monstrous to suppose, that in their declining years they should lose their mutual attachment to such an extent as not only to feel no pang at the prospect of separation, but even to delight in the idea? Cold-blooded, and revolting to all the better feelings of our nature, is the philosophy, if so it must be called, which presents us with so frightful a picture of our pauper population; a picture which, happily, is as unfaithful as it is unseemly to look at.

But why thus reason on abstract principles with those who seek to justify the separation of man and wife, on the assumption that the poor have no affection for, or attachment to, each other? Has not that assumption been already proved to be groundless, by the resistless logic of facts? Has not the calumny been sufficiently exposed by the reference I have made to a poor but virtuous and noble-minded husband and wife? Their case, be it remembered, is not the exception, but the rule. They were but the faithful representatives of their unfortunate class.

It is gratifying to perceive that a feeling of indignation against this unnatural and anti-christian regulation is spreading throughout the land with a rapidity, and is acquiring a force, which is sure ere long to sweep it away for ever. Every friend of humanity ought to foster this feeling wherever he finds it, and to inspire it in those breasts in which it has not yet had an existence. Surely the miseries of the poor are sufficiently great already; surely the horrors of a workhouse are already formidable enough, without gratuitously adding to that misery, and deepening those horrors, by a regulation of this nature. It is clearly one of the purposes of the Deity, that those who in his providence have been united together in marriage, should not be separated but by himself; and, in accordance with this manifest design of the Creator, the minister of the gospel who pronounces them man and wife, solemnly says, as directed by the marriage ceremony, "Those whom God hath joined together, let no man put asunder." The administrators of the New Poor Law Bill have set this solemn injunction at defiance; they have acted in direct opposition to it. The moral responsibility they have thus incurred, is of fearful magnitude.

Of the regulation which prohibits the visits to the workhouse of the friends of the inmates, I have hitherto said nothing. It is one which is of a piece with the general harshness of the administration of the law. In what way must the mind of the man be constituted, who first conceived the idea of refusing to the wretched pauper the meagre consolation of a visit of any remaining friend he had when he flung himself, as a last resource, into a workhouse? In his nature, there must, indeed, be little of the milk of human kindness. There exists not the shadow of a pretext for this heartless severity. Are we to be told, that if permission were conceded to the friends of paupers to visit them in the workhouse, the regulation would be attended with inconvenience? That has been said; but it has not, to use the mildest language, the slightest foundation in fact. Alas! by the time a poor wretch has been compelled to seek a refuge in the workhouse, the number of his friends has been sadly reduced. Fortunate, indeed, may he consider himself, if there be a single individual among his former acquaintances, even where their name was legion, who feels for and sympathises with him to such a degree as to prompt that individual to pay him an occasional visit in the workhouse. Reverses have a wonderful effect in lessening the number of one's friends. In how many instances does adversity scatter one's friends to the four winds of heaven? In how many instances do they all vanish as suddenly as if they had, by some magical influence, been spirited up to some other planet? How many paupers are there in every workhouse, who, were the doors open at all times to the visits of friends, would never be inquired about by a single human being in the world? How miserable and groundless, then, the pretext that inconvenience would result from admitting the few persons who might feel disposed to pay an occasional visit to those in the workhouse whom they had known in other and better days? Surely so poor and cheap a consolation, as the sight of one who commiserated them in their unhappy condition, might be allowed the inmates. But no: they must needs be shut up from every manifestation of the sympathy of their fellow-creatures, as if they had committed some atrocious crime, by which they had forfeited all claim to the kindly consideration of mankind. Not even when visited with sickness, unless there be some humane individual among the leading officers who interposes on their behalf, will a friend be permitted to see them. More horrible still: there are numerous instances on record, in which near relatives have been refused permission to see a dying pauper! Will it be believed that cases have occurred—and, it is to be feared they are not few or far between—in which a dying pauper, sensible that his end was approaching, has had his last request that a beloved daughter might be sent for, to see him close his eyes in death, and that he might give her his parting blessing,—haughtily refused him? An instance occurred a few months since in a workhouse in the suburbs of the metropolis, in which intelligence was accidentally conveyed to a daughter that her father was on his death-bed: she hurried that moment to the workhouse, but was refused admission. With tears in her eyes, and a heart that was ready to break, she pleaded the urgency of the case: the functionary was deaf to her entreaties: as soon might she have addressed them to the brick wall before her. His answer was, "It is contrary to the regulations of the place: come again at a certain hour." She applied to the medical gentleman who attended the workhouse, and through his exertions obtained admission. She flew to the ward in which her father was confined: he lay cold, motionless, and unconscious before her—his spirit was gone: he had breathed his last five minutes before.

Well may we exclaim, when we hear of such things, "Do we live in a christian country? Is this a civilised land?"

CHAPTER VIII.

LUNATIC ASYLUMS.

Difficulty of obtaining accurate information on the subject of Lunatic Asylums in London—Private madhouses—Their number, and the number, &c., of their inmates—Public Lunatic Asylums—St. Luke's—Bethlem—Hanwell Asylum—Insanity on one particular point, while on all other points the party is quite rational—Sanity on one point, while on all others the parties are insane—Diversified ways in which insanity manifests itself—Partiality of particular lunatics to particular employments—Instances given—Cunning of some lunatics—Their great physical energies—Harsh Treatment they sometimes receive—General Remarks.

The subject of Lunatic Asylums in the metropolis, is one of great though painful interest. It is one with the statistics of which the public are but very imperfectly acquainted. This is easily accounted for. There is no accessible work, so far as my knowledge extends, to which persons desirous of obtaining information on the subject may refer. It is only by consulting a variety of pamphlets, the reports of committees appointed to manage the affairs of lunatic asylums, and parliamentary papers, that any approach can be made to an accurate knowledge of the statistics of insanity in London. In none of my previous chapters have I had to encounter so many obstacles in my endeavours to acquire that information on the subject which could either satisfy my own mind, or which appeared to me likely to prove satisfactory to my readers.

Before speaking of the public lunatic asylums in the metropolis, it may be proper to devote a small portion o fmy pages to private madhouses. The number of these has varied, for some years past, from 36 to 42. The latest authentic information on the subject to which I could obtain access, gives the number at 38. The number of patients in these private establishments, varied, before the Hanwell Lunatic Asylum was so generally preferred for pauper maniacs, from 2 to 560. As many as the latter number have been inmates of Hoxton House at one time. This establishment, it is proper to state, is by far the largest private madhouse in the united kingdom: it is doubtful whether it be not the largest in the world. Next to it, in point of size, and in respect to the number of patients usually in it, is the White House, Bethnal Green; and the third largest, is Bethnal

House. Of several smaller ones in the same neighbourhood, I say nothing. How it happens that that part of the metropolis has been for many years the locality of so many private lunatic asylums, especially as St. Luke's is so near to it, is a point which I cannot determine. In these three establishments there have, for a long series of years, been a greater number of insane persons than in all the other private madhouses in London taken together. Of pauper lunatics in these private houses, the number a few years since,* was 1369; of whom 596 were males, and 773 females. The number of inmates, not paupers, was 942; of whom 512 were males, and 430 were females; making the total number of inmates 2311. The number of cures performed in the course of the year to which I refer, was 121: of this number, 30 were male paupers, 37 female paupers, 36 males not paupers, and 18 females not paupers. The expenses vary, as a matter of course, with the diversity which obtains in the previous circumstances of the patients. In some cases the terms are as high as 200*l.* per annum. This class of inmates, it is unnecessary to say, receive a diet superior to that of the others, and have more attention paid to their cleanliness, and to their comfort in every other respect. Each of them has a keeper to himself. The price usually paid for the maintenance of pauper lunatics was formerly 11*s.* 6*d.* per week; but now, at the Hanwell Asylum, it is only 5*s.* 3*d.* This, it will be seen, is a reduction of more than one half. The consequence, as might be expected, has been, that the pauper lunatics in those parishes which are in Middlesex, have been all taken from the private madhouses, and sent to the Hanwell institution. Of this institution, I shall have occasion to speak by-and-by.

The public asylums in London are only two in number. They are St. Luke's and Bethlem. The first is situated in Old Street, in the parish of St. Luke; and the other is over the water, a little beyond the Obelisk. The first of these establishments is, in a great measure, supported by the bequests of benevolent individuals. With the interest of this money, and the amount received for the different patients, the usual expenses are nearly paid: whatever deficiency there is, is made up from the City funds. The average number of patients may be given at 250. There is one regulation in this institution which deserves to be noticed: the ordinary class of patients are only taken in for one year, which is called a probationary period. If not cured by the end of twelve months, their friends are written to, to come and take them away. It is true, that there is a fund

* I have not been able to obtain information as to these establishments, up to the present day.

belonging to the institution, left by a charitable person, for the permanent support of incurables; but it is only adequate to the maintenance of a limited number; and so great is the anxiety of individuals to get their insane relatives thus provided for, for life, that as many as forty candidates have, on some occasions, been put forward for a place in the incurable department, when one vacancy has occurred.

A marked change has taken place in the management of this institution, within the last quarter of a century. Previous to that time the grossest abuses prevailed in it. They were made the subject of a parliamentary inquiry, and excited great and general attention. That one human being could treat another human being in the way in which some of the inmates of this asylum were treated, at the period to which I refer, is one of those facts which may well make us blush for our species. One young lady, possessed of great accomplishments, and who had been for many years a governess in a respectable family, had been chained for some years to a wall, and was so inadequately clothed as to be almost in a state of nudity. That there was nothing in her conduct of so violent a nature as to justify this extreme rigour—to call it by the mildest name—was proved by the fact, that when liberated and clothed, she walked about among the other patients, in the most peaceable and inoffensive manner, and employed herself in needlework.

There was another case—not to mention any more—of an individual named Norris, who had been chained to his bed for nine successive years, during which period he had never been within the sight of fire. In addition to irons on his legs, of great massiveness, he had a collar round his neck, fastened in such a way to his bed as to compel him to lie almost constantly on his back. It was true, that he was very violent, and made an attempt on the life of one of the servants of the establishment; but means could have been taken to prevent any future attempt of the kind without resorting to such an extreme expedient as chaining him down to his bed in the manner I have described. For many years past, however, St. Luke's Asylum has been one of the best conducted institutions of a similar kind in the country. The inmates are treated with gentleness, and are allowed every liberty consistent with their own safety, and the safety and comfort of their fellow-patients.

Bethlem Asylum, which, as already mentioned, is situated on the other side of the water, near the Obelisk, contains, on an average, from 180 to 200 inmates. It is a well-conducted institution. The cures have been as numerous in it, considering the general character of the cases, as in any other similar institution that could be named.

Perhaps a greater number of lunatics whose names have been brought prominently before the public, have been, from first to last, in that asylum, than in any other similar institution in the country. The man who shot at George the Third has been there for a long series of years; for I believe he is still alive; and the maniac who set fire to York Minster is among its present inmates.

Hanwell Asylum does not come so properly within the scope of this work; and yet, as ten or twelve of the largest parishes of London send all their pauper lunatics to that institution, it must not be omitted. The entire average number of patients in Hanwell Asylum has been, for some time past, about 600; all of whom are paupers, and are supported at the expense of their respective parishes. This institution has been attacked, both in parliament and out of parliament, on the ground of the disparity in the number of cures effected in it, as compared with most other public institutions for the reception and treatment of insane persons. It is true, the number of cures has been, proportionally, much less in Hanwell Asylum than in most other similar institutions supported at the public expense; but those who rest their condemnation of it on this simple fact, do it a very great injustice. Mr. Gally Knight, the member for Nottingham, attacked it on this ground last session of parliament. "I hold," said he, "in my hand a calculation, resulting from an examination of twenty-six lunatic asylums. From this calculation it appears, that the proportion of recoveries in asylums under the treatment now ordinarily pursued, is 40 per cent.; and that the lowest proportion in any asylum, but that at Hanwell, has been 33 per cent.; but the recoveries at Hanwell, in an equal space of time, have not amounted to 19 per cent. Again, from a return which was made of the state of various asylums in England, it appears that, whilst out of 100 patients treated at the other fourteen asylums, 46 were discharged cured, only 18 have been discharged cured out of an equal number, at Hanwell. Here is a frightful disparity; and how is it to be accounted for? That is what I am anxious to ascertain. Has Hanwell laboured under any disadvantages, from which other asylums are free? On the contrary, Hanwell is a comparatively new asylum; and, therefore, should not be embarrassed by that *residuum* of incurables, which is the difficulty with which other asylums have to contend. Neither will it be found, that Hanwell has had an unusual number of old cases; by which I mean, patients who have been some time insane previous to admission, and whose cure is thereby rendered so much the less probable. I hold in my hand a report from the medical superintendent, which proves that, in the first year, only such were admitted as were the most likely to benefit by the institution; that is to say, only recent cases; and I am in a condition to prove, that, since that time, the same cautious selection has been observed. It is not, therefore, in this manner that the paucity of cures can be accounted for.* * * * But if the cures have been few, the deaths have been many. In 1831, out of 427 patients, there died 99; in 1833, out of 537, there died 77; in 1834, out of 580, the number who died was 71; in 1835, out of 611, there died 65. In the same time, out of 1132 patients admitted into Nottingham Asylum, there died 42; out of 1183, there died 326 at Hanwell."

These were certainly startling statements; and when I heard the honourable gentleman make them in the House of Commons —for I chanced to be present at the time,—I was anxious to hear how they were to be met and answered. From the observations of several members who spoke on the subject, it appeared that Mr. Gally Knight must have been unacquainted with several most important facts connected with the case.

With regard to the comparative number of deaths in the Hanwell institution, and at the Nottingham Asylum, Sir George Strickland showed, conclusively, that the greater proportion which existed at Hanwell could not be ascribed to any abuses, or defective administration of affairs, in the latter place; for "the same governor, the same physician, had conducted both establishments. It can, then, I think," continued Sir George "be hardly possible, that the man who has conducted the asylum at Nottingham, upon an average of 18 per cent. of deaths, should now, at Hanwell, have 32 per cent. of deaths. I must say, therefore, that the information of the honourable member appears a little strained."

In reference to the paucity of cures, Mr. C. Barclay observed, "It has been stated that the proportion of cures effected at Hanwell is much smaller than at other places. Now, I am bound, in justice, to say, from the information I have received, that by far the greatest proportion of lunatics sent to the Hanwell Asylum, are incurables, who have been in other asylums. I am informed, that out of 600 patients now at Hanwell, 500 belong to the class of incurables." In an official letter to the magistrates of the county, in 1836, respecting the diet of the patients, Sir William Ellis, the medical superintendent*, substantiates this statement of Mr. Barclay. He says—" Nearly

* While this sheet is passing through the press, Sir William Ellis has resigned his situation as medical superintendent of Hanwell Asylum; and Lady Ellis, as matron of the institution. Dr. Mullingen, the author of a late work under the title of "Curiosities of Medical Experience," has been selected out of nearly one hundred candidates, in the room of Sir William Ellis. The salary is 500*l*. a-year.

all the patients admitted into this institution are old incurable cases, who have been the probationary time of twelve months, either in Bethlem or St. Luke's, or have been confined in some private madhouse; and as they remain here until death, we have consequently a great many who, from old age or debility, require a different diet from others of the patients." This statement of Sir William's at once accounts for the paucity of cures, and the greater number of deaths, in the Hanwell Asylum, as compared with similar institutions.

It is in contemplation to enlarge Hanwell Asylum to such an extent as to provide accommodation for 900 inmates. At present it is not capable of containing more than from 610 to 620. Of late it has been quite full; and many applications for admission have been refused on account of want of room. It is believed, that when the proposed additions are made to it, there will not be any necessity for further enlargement; the number of pauper lunatics belonging to the county, rarely exceeding from 1000 to 1050.

In studying the particular forms in which insanity developes itself, I have often been struck with the utter absence of reason on particular points, while on other topics the parties could talk with the most entire coherence and rationality. A curious instance of this occurred, within the last few months, in the case of a young man with whom I had some acquaintance. He had received all the advantages of a university education, and had come to London from Scotland in the hope of being able to turn his talents and acquirements to account in this great city. His hopes, unfortunately, were not realized; and the circumstance preyed much on his spirits. The first indication I had of his mind being unhinged, was in the fact of his fancying that all the people, with but one exception, in London, had entered into a conspiracy against him. He imagined that persons whom he never saw, and whose names he only knew by report, were writing to the police authorities to have him taken up on charges of the most serious nature. For several months he came, almost daily, to me, with what he conceived some new proof of the universal conspiracy against him. I endeavoured for a long time to reason him out of his ungrounded notions, but I found I had attempted a hopeless task. On every other point but this, he was as sane as any man in London; and even when conversing on that point, he displayed a singular ingenuity in his efforts to convince me that his opinions were well grounded.

There are other lunatics, again, who are insane on every point but one, and on that one are perfectly rational. I knew a maniac who had been a distinguished lawyer before his intellect was affected, and who, though his conversation and conduct were most insane in reference to all other subjects, was rational in the highest degree whenever professional matters were talked of. His opinions on all legal difficulties were as good after his insanity, as they were when he enjoyed his reason in all its perfection; and what was more, he could go through, with the greatest method and clearness, the most intricate details of a most difficult case. So long as he confined himself to professional topics, he displayed the soundest judgment: on all other subjects he talked the greatest nonsense.

It is curious to reflect on the infinitely diversified ways in which insanity manifests itself. It is true, that with some maniacs, the disease exhibits itself in no particular form. You see their insanity in every word they speak, in every action they perform, nay, in almost every look they give to the persons or objects around them. In their cases, instead of the imagination running wild on any particular subject, they appear to have no imagination at all. Their minds seem a perfect blank. With a majority, however, the case is different. Their fancies are not only most extravagant, but are usually exercised with the same subject. One of the most common notions which lunatics entertain is, that they are persons of distinguished rank and of great consequence in the world. A very favourite delusion is, that they are kings or princesses. Two remarkable instances of this kind lately occurred, in the cases of persons who were not only not in any asylum, but were walking at large through London. The cases to which I refer will at once recur to the minds of my readers. One gentleman, it will be recollected, fancying himself to be the rightful sovereign of the country, was in the habit of using improper language towards our young Queen when she appeared in the neighbourhood of Kensington Palace. Another, it will be remembered, made several efforts to obtain an entrance into Buckingham Palace, under the impression that he was the legitimate successor of William the Fourth to the throne of these realms. In the London lunatic asylums there are at present a great many persons who entertain similar notions. One fancies himself the king of France; another imagines he is the monarch of the world; a third deludes himself with the idea that he is Napoleon Bonaparte. The number of Dukes of Wellington is very great; nor is there any want of Lords Melbourne. Others, again, identify themselves with the leading characters of past ages. Not long since, there was a lady of great literary accomplishments in one of the private madhouses—whether she be still alive or not, I am not in a condition to say—who imagined herself to be Mary Queen of Scots. In Bethlem there was lately a lunatic—and I believe he is there still—who fancied himself to be the Redeemer of the world. Several cases have occurred, in which the parties imagined that they were the Deity himself. Such lunatics are, in most cases, in the habit of assuming great things: they look down on all the other inmates, and show, by the whole of their demeanour, that they deem it an act of great condescension to speak to, or even look at, their fellow-unfortunates.

In many cases, lunatics exhibit the same predilections and partialities as they did before they were bereft of reason. Not long ago, a gentleman who was exceedingly fond of stenography previous to the derangement of his intellects, and who amused himself in his leisure hours, by filling a scrap-book which he kept with selections from English modern literature, taken in shorthand,—incessantly wrote shorthand to his own dictation, after he was placed in an asylum. Mothers who were passionately fond of their children, and whose death, it may be, was the cause of their insanity, still fancy they see those children, and address their conversation to them. Many a widow thinks and talks of her departed husband, to the exclusion of everything else: and the cases are without number, in which females whose lovers either proved inconstant or were snatched away from them by death, have their thoughts, if thoughts they can be called, occupied entirely and incessantly with the former objects of their affections.

Some years since, there was an inmate in one of the lunatic asylums, who evinced a most extraordinary taste for writing. He had been a gentleman passionately attached to literary pursuits when in possession of his reason; and the notion that he was still engaged on literary works, seemed never, for a moment, to forsake him. I was struck with his appearance as well as his occupations; for notwithstanding the unmeaning movements of his eye, and the want of a definite expression in his countenance, there was something in his largely developed forehead, and about his face generally, which must have left an impression on every one who saw him, that he must, at one time, have been one of the finest and most intellectual-looking men that ever dignified the human form. I could learn nothing of his history prior to the visitation which deprived him of his reason, farther than that he belonged to a family of great influence and respectability in the country, and that he was not only a gentleman by birth, but a perfect gentleman in his mind, his manners, and his conduct. He had been, at the time I saw him, nearly twenty years in the asylum, and during all that period, except in the hours allotted to sleep and meals, wrote on without intermission. Being of a peaceable disposition, he had full liberty to rise and walk about, either in the ward in which, along with about twenty others, he was placed, or in the ground outside the institution; but he constantly sat, from morning to night, in one particular part of the ward. In his notions of writing, there was something peculiar. If a quantity of clean paper were placed before him, nothing would induce him to take up the pen: the only thing on which he would write was the margin of a book. Whether or not he read any part of the print was a point on which I could get no information from the party who directed my attention to the unfortunate man; but it was clear that his impression was, that he was making notes or remarks on the book on the margin of which he was writing. His words were all correctly spelt, but his sentences were so incoherent that it was impossible even to conjecture what ideas had been passing through his mind. In his penmanship there was something singularly neat and beautiful: it was a remarkably small hand, and was not disfigured by the omission of words, or cancels or blots of any kind. The writing, too, was very close, so that the appearance of the page—the margin being entirely written at the top and bottom, and on both sides—was worthy of preservation as a curiosity. The book on which the unhappy man was employed, when I saw him, was one of the octavo size, with a very large margin; and he had written on about three hundred pages of it. It is worthy of remark, that he not only employed himself in constantly writing in the way I have mentioned, but that he never raised his head from the stooping position in which he wrote. This was surprising; for one would have thought the pain of perpetual stooping must have been too great for him to endure; and that, for the purpose of relieving or resting himself, he would occasionally have raised his head, and assumed an erect position. He not only never spoke to any one, but took no notice of any visitor who entered the place; neither could any noise, or other occurrence in the ward, ever for a moment withdraw his attention from his employment. So thoroughly did he appear to be absorbed with his writing, that I am convinced he would not have raised his eyes from the book had the house been falling about his ears. I never saw a man engaged in any occupation who evinced so great a pleasure in it: a smile of enjoyment constantly played on his countenance. He incessantly spoke to himself, but always in so suppressed a whisper that not even the words, far less the sentences, could be understood.

I knew another literary lunatic, if the expression be a correct one, who manifested nearly as strong a taste for reading as the one to whom I have just referred did for writing. He has been repeatedly known to read for five or six consecutive hours without pausing for a moment; and what makes the circumstance the more surprising is, that he always read aloud, and with considerable rapidity. He had been a good English scholar, and was noted for the accuracy of his pronunciation and the graces of his elocution; but all traces of anything worthy the name of elocution were now lost; and as to pronunciation, what it was may be inferred from the fact that he would pronounce the word "reflections" as "roultoulfoulchiness." In fact, he rarely pronounced a word in such a way as that any one who heard him could ascertain what term it was he was mutilating. That notwithstanding his singular partiality for reading, he attached no meaning, even of his own, to the passages he perused, was clear, from the fact that though he had never known anything of any other language than the English, yet a Latin, Greek, or Hebrew book was as acceptable to him—so would have been a work full of Egyptian hieroglyphics—as one written in his own tongue.

Since on this subject, I may mention another instance of the ruling passion for literary, or rather, in this case, scientific pursuits, being strong after the dethronement of reason. The unfortunate man had been a distinguished mathematician before he was visited with the dispensation which deranged his intellects; and his chief occupation, after the occurrence of that calamity, was, as he supposed, to solve difficult problems. On one occasion, an acquaintance of mine seeing a pile of papers, all full of figures, before him, asked him what was the problem he was endeavouring to solve. His answer was one of the most striking that ever escaped human lips. "I have been trying," he said, in a tone and manner which would have become the wisest of men; "I have been trying to calculate the duration of eternity." What an answer! What an idea to enter the mind of a maniac! I was never so forcibly struck with anything I have heard in my life: the very conception was sublime in the highest degree. The wisest of us may learn an important lesson from the employment, on this occasion, of this lunatic. If men would but sit down, and *try* to calculate the duration of eternity—in other words, overlook for the moment the impossibility of the thing, and proceed as if the problem were one which could be solved—it would awaken in the mind the most salutary as well as solemn considerations, and probably be the means of infinite good to the person so employing himself. When Simonides, in answer to an inquiry made of him as to the nature of the Supreme Being, applied himself, for several consecutive days, to the consideration of the awful topic, he found that the more he thought on the subject, the more he was lost in its unfathomable depths. So, in like manner, the man who would set himself down, like this unhappy maniac, to try to calculate the duration of eternity, would find that the more he thought on the matter, the farther he was from the solution of the question; and surely such a train of thought, and such a result, would have a beneficial effect on his mind.

There was something sublime, if there be not an inaccuracy in the expression, in all the manifestations of this individual's madness. He never occupied his thoughts, if thoughts they could be called, with things of an earthly nature: his mental aberrations were always in the direction of the spiritual world. He fancied himself to be on terms of the closest intimacy with a large community of immaterial beings, and that a constant correspondence by letter was carrying on between him and them. He replied, at great length, to written communications which he imagined himself to have received from some of their number, and replied to those imaginary letters in a most elaborate manner. One of his answers to a supposed communication from one of his correspondents in the air, fell into my hands, and was in my possession for some time. It was closely written on three sides of a folio sheet of paper, and afforded abundant proofs, that previous to the deprivation of his reason, he must have been a man of distinguished scholastic attainments, as well as great intellectual vigour. There were various classical allusions in the letter, which indicated an intimate acquaintance with the writings of the philosophers of ancient Greece and Rome. I was not able to detect a single instance of orthographical inaccuracy, or any defect in the punctuation; neither did I discover any violation of the rules of grammar. But for the incoherency of some of the expressions, coupled with the nature of the subject, any one who had seen the letter, without being apprized of who the writer was, would have supposed that it was the production of some literary character. This insane man individualized all his ideal correspondents: he ascribed to them various distinctive peculiarities of circumstances and character, and invested them with a great diversity of offices and rank. When writing to those of inferior rank, his manner was easy and familiar; when corresponding with those of a higher station in his imaginary community, he wrote with the profoundest respect. The letter to which I have already referred, as having been given to me, was regularly folded up, and addressed thus:—

(Post Paid.) *To*

His Most Noble and Serene Highness,

The Grand and Imperial Possessor

Of the Principal Palace

In the Spiritual Kingdom.

(In great haste.)

When I first knew this unhappy man, he was not in a lunatic asylum; and he was then in the constant habit of putting all his letters into the post-office with his own hand, in order, as he fancied, to insure their due transmission to their several destinations. Who can read such things without being affected with the thought, that a man of great literary attainments and of powerful intellect, should be reduced to such a state of mental imbecility!

In many cases, lunatics are exceedingly cunning, and display a remarkable readiness of resources in unexpected emergencies. I could mention many instances of this, but will content myself with one. There was lately, and I am not sure whether there be not now, in one of our asylums, a lunatic, who, on the loss of his reason in the first instance—for he was repeatedly cured, though he always relapsed again—lived in a neighbouring county. Belonging as he did to a family of wealth and respectability, he was provided with a keeper as soon as the first symptoms of the disease appeared. It was hoped that the unfortunate man's lunacy would be of but temporary duration; and that, by committing him to the care of a keeper, his friends would be spared the pain of sending him to an asylum. His insanity, however, lasted much longer than his relatives had fondly hoped it would; and it was therefore eventually determined to send him to an institution for the reception of persons labouring under mental aberration, in the hope that, through the superior treatment he would there receive, an additional chance of recovery might be afforded him. On the day previous to that appointed for his being sent to the asylum, he overheard his brother giving instructions to his keeper on the subject. He took no notice of the circumstance that night, nor next morning; but when told that he, accompanied by his companion—the name by which his keeper was always called—was to have a long drive in the gig that day, he expressed himself as quite delighted with the idea, and displayed a willingness to take an airing which strongly contrasted with the reluctance he had before shown to leave the house. After breakfast, the gig was ready, and both started for the county town—about twelve miles distant—in the suburbs of which the asylum was situated. The lunatic was unusually cheerful and docile all the way; and here I should remark, that his manner was sometimes so collected and rational, that it would have been difficult to convince a stranger that his intellects were in the slightest degree affected. On reaching the principal hotel, both parties came out of the gig with a view to get some refreshment, and to enable the keeper to make some necessary preliminary arrangements for the reception of his charge into the asylum. The former, after being some time in the house, quitted the apartment into which they were shown, for a few seconds, not deeming it necessary either to take the lunatic with him, or to turn the key of the door. The latter, watching the opportunity, agreeably to a previous determination to that effect, stole out of the house the moment the other had quitted the apartment. On the keeper missing the lunatic on his return, an alarm was given, and in less than five minutes, at least a dozen persons were engaged in an active search for the unfortunate man, the suddenness of whose disappearance was quite unaccountable to his keeper. No trace of him was to be found for two hours, and the impression began to become general among all acquainted with the circumstance, that he had by some means or other destroyed himself. Just as all hopes of ever seeing him alive again were on the eve of expiration, the lunatic appeared, to the infinite astonishment and joy of the person entrusted with his safe keeping. But where he had been during his absence, was a point which, notwithstanding all the efforts that were made with that view, could not be elicited from him. Where does the reader suppose he was, or in what way employed? That was a piece of information which his keeper learned to his cost in a few hours after the lunatic's return. The latter had been to the asylum for which his friends had destined himself, and having procured access to the proper party, gave his keeper's name as his own, and represented him as being Mr. So-and-so, the brother of Mr. ———. As it was not only well known at the asylum that the latter gentleman had a brother who was at that time labouring under insanity, but as, on the previous day, notice had been received that the lunatic was to be sent to the asylum, the remainder of his story was the more readily believed. "Now," says he, addressing himself to the manager of the institution, "the lunatic is remarkably clever and singularly cunning; and—"

"Oh, a great many of our patients are so," interrupted the superintendent of the institution. "We see instances of cunning and shrewdness every day, which the wisest of us could not exceed."

"I have no doubt of it," observed the lunatic, with the greatest apparent self-possession, and seemingly in the most rational manner possible. "I have no doubt of it; none whatever. I have seen many cases of it myself; but this unhappy man exceeds in cunning and shrewdness any one I ever heard of. Why, he would almost deceive the——"

"Oh, he won't deceive us," interrupted the other hastily; "we are too well accustomed to such things."

"I am happy to hear it," continued the lunatic. "My only reason for coming out here, before taking him with me, was, that I might acquaint you with the circumstance beforehand."

"That was unnecessary: let him try all the tricks he chooses, they will be lost here," remarked the other, with a self-consequential air, as if he were beyond the power of ingenuity to deceive.

"Very good," observed the lunatic, in a satisfied tone. "I shall bring him here in an hour or so: I have left him at the Fountain hotel, in the care of a friend."

"We shall be ready for him," said the superintendent of the place, in that careless sort of tone which is so characteristic of men in authority.

"Good morning, Sir," said the lunatic, turning on his heel as he was about to quit the apartment.

"Good morning," echoed the other, in the same half-civil, half-reserved tone as before.

"Oh, I beg your pardon!" said the lunatic, hastily turning round, and advancing a few steps towards the manager of the institution; "I beg your pardon, Sir, but I entirely forgot to mention the particular way in which his madness manifests itself."

"Ay, true; that is of some importance to us," observed the other. "In what way is it?"

"Why, he has the notion that every one else is mad but himself."

"Oh! that is quite a common impression among persons in his state."

"Yes; but singularly enough, his notion is, that I am the insane party, and that he is my keeper. You may rely upon it, that the very moment we arrive, he will affirm in the most positive terms, and with the utmost earnestness of manner, that such is the fact; and then he will desire you to take me into the asylum."

"Poor fellow!" said the other, with some slight indications of feeling. "Poor fellow!—but there is nothing too extraordinary for these unhappy beings to fancy."

"I thought it right to inform you of the fact," said the lunatic, "in order that you might not be taken by surprise."

"Oh, there was not the slightest danger of that. We are too well accustomed to such things, to be deceived either by their affirmations or representations."

"Good morning, then, for the present," said the lunatic, as he quitted the superintendent's apartment.

"Good morning," mumbled the latter.

In about two hours afterwards, a gig, with two persons in it, was seen to drive up to the gate of the institution: it was opened, and both proceeded to the door. As they entered the place,—"Here is an unfortunate individual," said the lunatic address-

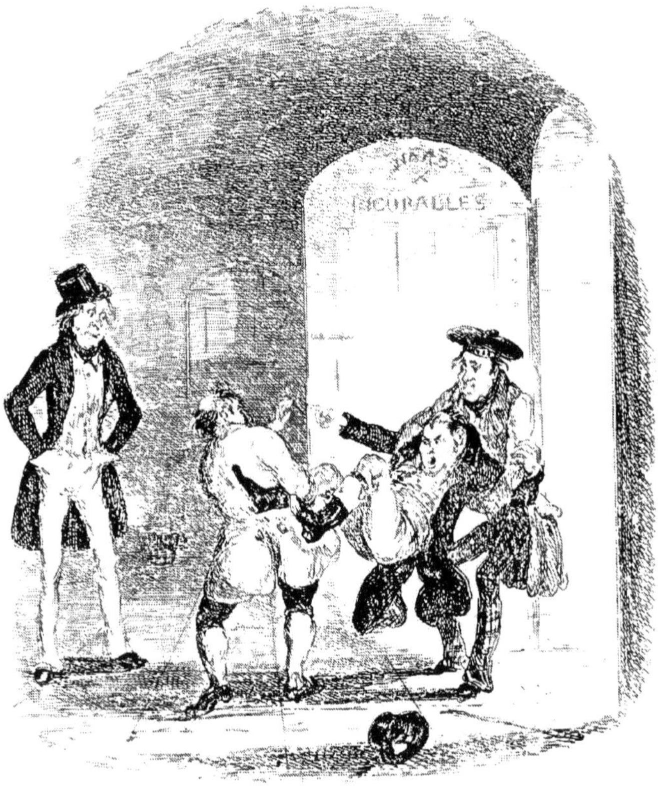

ing himself to the superintendent, "whom you will be kind enough to take every care of."

The other was so confounded by the unexpected observation, that he was unable, for some seconds, to utter a word.

"Very good," said the superintendent of the institution; "we'll take care of him," at the same time laying hold of the astonished keeper of the lunatic, by the breast of the coat.

"Sir—sir—sir!" stammered the confounded man; "you labour under a mistake: that," pointing to the lunatic, "is the person to be committed to your care. I—I—I—brought him here."

"No doubt of it," said the overseer, still dragging the hapless wight forward, assisted by another servant of the establishment, to the part of the asylum for which he was intended.

"Gracious Heavens, Sir? what is the meaning of this?" exclaimed the luckless party, half suffocated with astonishment and indignation, and struggling hard to disengage himself from the grasp of the parties.

"Come away, my good man, quietly with us," said the superintendent, soothingly.

"By all that's sacred, Sir!" shouted the other, with the utmost vehemence, "*I'm* not the lunatic; that is he," again pointing to the actual party.

"I knew it all: I told you how it would be," said the latter, in a steady voice, and with the greatest self-possession.

"This way," said the superintendent, carelessly, still dragging the unfortunate party forward.

"It's a mistake, Sir, by——"

"Oh, there's no mistake, my good man; no mistake," interrupted the guardian of the place.

"No mistake," echoed the lunatic, with the most perfect nonchalance, displaying all the while the most rational demeanour.

"Sir," shouted the unfortunate party; "Sir, are you serious? Are you aware of what you're about?"

"Perfectly serious, perfectly aware of what we're doing," replied the superintendent, drily.

"Sir, I'm not the lunatic; that is the lunatic," pointing a third time to the proper party. "Let go your hold, or you retain it at your peril," vociferated the other.

"Never mind the poor fellow: I told you how he would conduct himself, and what he would say," observed the lunatic.

A few pulls more, and the astonished and enraged party was actually dragged into his destined apartment. When both the superintendent and the inferior servant let go their hold, I leave the reader to fancy what were the feelings of the poor wight.

"Quite safe now; he's in our custody now; and you are relieved from all further responsibility," said the superintendent to the insane party, the moment he had shut the door on the supposed lunatic.

"All right," said the real lunatic, as if relieved of a heavy load of responsibility. "The family of the unfortunate man will make the necessary arrangements as to expense."

"Oh, that's all settled already; the necessary arrangements were made yesterday, when the first intimation of his coming here was sent to us."

"So I understood," said the lunatic, in a matter-of-course sort of style; and with that, he quitted the place; and springing into the gig, which had remained at the gate all this time, drove away home again, as if he had been the most sane man in his majesty's dominions.

It is impossible to describe the mingled surprise and consternation with which his relatives and friends were seized on his return home. Their first apprehension on missing his keeper, was, that he had murdered him on the way; and their fears were only partially calmed by his assuring them, in answer to their inquiries as to what had become of his companion, that when they both proceeded to the asylum, the parties having charge of the institution insisted that he was the lunatic, and took him under their care accordingly. An express was sent off to the asylum, to inquire whether the parties had been there at all, when the messenger found, to his unutterable surprise, that the facts were as the lunatic had represented; and as the messenger's statements and protestations as to the mistake which had been committed, were equally discredited with those of the unfortunate party himself, the latter was not liberated until the following day.

The great physical exertion of which many insane persons are capable, as compared with their strength when in a sound state of mind, has often been the surprise of those who have had an opportunity of witnessing the circumstance. I knew one lunatic who was constitutionally weak and infirm while possessed of his reason, but who, when deprived of it, became so vigorous or strong, in a physical sense, that it required three men to hold him. Not less surprising is the amount of fatigue which lunatics are frequently capable of enduring. Some years ago, I knew a gentleman who had been kept some weeks by his relations, after he had become insane, before being sent to a madhouse, and he was for nearly forty consecutive days, that he did not sleep above one hour out of the twenty-four, and even then without putting off his clothes; and yet he did not appear as if the least exhausted by his deprivation of sleep and rest. I should also

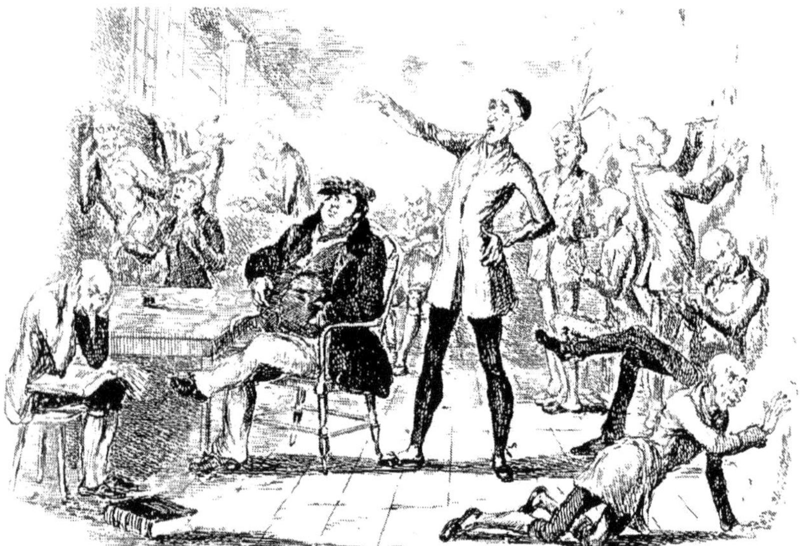

mention, that during all that time, he continued to talk to those about him with scarcely the intermission of a moment. The fluency of his conversation, and the cleverness and point of many of his observations, I should likewise state, quite astonished me. In no case did he hesitate an instant either for ideas or words; nor did he, in a single instance, stutter or use an improper term. About the same time, I chanced to see, in the house of her parents, a young female lunatic, now, I am sorry to say, in an asylum, who, I was assured, spoke without intermission for eight successive days and nights without ceasing, on being first seized with insanity. She never closed her eyes in sleep during all that time; and what made the circumstance of her being able to endure so much physical fatigue the more astonishing, was, that every sentence she uttered in the course of the eight days, was spoken with as much distinctness, and in as loud a tone, as if she had been addressing some public meeting of moderate size. She, also, like the lunatic just referred to, was of a feeble constitution, of sickly appearance, and often complained of bodily weakness as well as of general bad health.

I know of no sight more affecting in a world in which there are so many affecting sights, than that of the interior of a madhouse. What could be more melancholy than to see an assemblage of our fellow beings, all of whom were at one time equally gifted with ourselves, with the greatest and best of the Deity's gifts to men—the gift of reason—divested of all traces of rationality, and showing by their conduct that, in that respect, they are much below many of the lower animals! The spectacle is a truly pitiable one. Some time ago, I was in an asylum in which there were about thirty lunatics in one ward. It was a sight not to be looked on without feelings of the most painful nature under any circumstances; but to myself, and to those who were with me on the occasion, it was doubly touching, in consequence of the particulars communicated to us respecting several of the unhappy individuals by one of the officers of the institution. It was, therefore, not necessary in our case, that we should put our imaginations in requisition, and endeavour to form some idea of the circumstances in which the helpless beings before us were previous to the derangement of their intellects, and then contrast those circumstances with the condition in which we beheld them. The contrast could not have been more striking, had we given full reins to our fancy as to what they previously were, and how they had been circumstanced. Some of them had distinguished themselves by their scholastic attainments: of one of the parties, indeed, it might be said, that too much learning had made him mad. There were others who had earned for themselves a reputation in scientific and philosophical pursuits; while there were at least three who had been in excellent business as professional men. Two were connected by close relationship with aristocratic families; and all of them, in one word, had been accustomed to every earthly abundance. The high terms, indeed, of admission and maintenance, in the particular part of the institution in which they were placed, afforded presumptive proof that either they themselves must have possessed some property, or that their relations must have been in easy circumstances. Some of them had been the idol of their circle of acquaintances; others had been revered and beloved as husbands, parents, brothers, sons, or near relatives. They had been themselves happy in the bosom of their families; and were the source of joy and felicity to all within their domestic sphere, just as the sun is the source of light and heat to the world. One had been but a few months married; another was on the eve of union with an amiable and virtuous woman. How altered their situation now! What could be more striking than the contrast between what they once were, and what I beheld them? The joys of friendship or affection were no longer theirs. Friend! The word was to them an unmeaning sound. Wife, mother, father, brother, sister, children, were terms which might now be uttered in their hearing without calling up one idea in their minds: they were to them as unmeaning as the wildest sounds which ever escaped the lips of the savage who roams the forest. In the moral world, all was a perfect blank: in the mental world, all was either utter darkness itself, or it was peopled with the strangest and most fantastic shapes. Even the physical world could only be said to have remained to them in a qualified sense. To many of them the change in the seasons afforded no enjoyment. They seemed incapable of perceiving any difference between the inclemency of a severe winter, and the geniality of the summer season. To them it mattered not whether the sun shone or shrouded himself amidst the clouds; whether it was fair or foul; whether it was night or day. None of these changes, ever-recurring though they be, and though bearing so largely on the happiness of the human race generally, ever appeared to have come within the circle of their consciousness. They could be said, indeed, to exist in no other sense than as mere animals; and as animals, moreover, of the very lowest class. Where, I again repeat, could one go to witness a more touching scene than this? In every situation of life, and amidst the infinitely varied circumstances of this ever-changing world, the man of reflection finds something to excite his commiseration, and to call forth his sympathies; but in the wide range of human misfortune and human misery, there is no misfortune so great, no misery so deep, no spectacle so truly pitiable, as that which the interior of a lunatic asylum presents to our contemplation.

And yet there are persons—will the fact be believed?—who can treat these poor creatures with the greatest harshness and cruelty. Some years ago, the most horrible disclosures were made before a committee of the House of Commons, as to the unredeemed inhumanity with which the inmates of a private lunatic asylum were treated by those who had the charge of them; and this not occasionally, but habitually. Until those disclosures were made, and were verified beyond all possibility of doubt, I had thought that such instances of barbarity could never have occurred in a Christian or civilized land. As the asylum to which I refer still exists, I will not name it. Part of the cruelties exercised were of such a nature as to render a detail of them unfit to meet the public eye. Other instances of the barbarities systematically committed in the institution, can only be described in general terms. But, in order to preclude the possibility of being suspected, either unintentionally or otherwise, of any, even the slightest exaggeration on this subject, I will quote some portions of the evidence given. Similar cases of cruelty have occurred of a much later date; but for reasons which will occur to most persons, I go as far back as to evidence published several years since by a select committee of the House of Commons, appointed to inquire into the state of private madhouses in the metropolis. I shall only further premise, that a number of such cases of ill-usage, as those recorded in what follows, were brought to light by that committee, and by the committee which sat on the same subject, at a much later date.

Mrs. Mary H——— *called in, and examined.*

What was the motive of your coming to this committee?—I came to answer any questions that the committee might put to me respecting madhouses.

How long have you been come to England?—I arrived here on Saturday night.

Where did you come from last?—From M———.

Did your brother write you to attend this committee?—He did.

How long were you resident in the house of Mr. ———, at ———? —Three years, within six weeks.

In what capacity?—Housekeeper.

By whose recommendation did you gain that situation?—Mr. Rogers told me of the situation, and I went to Mr. ———.

Your brother was then acting as surgeon to the establishment?—He was.

It was through his recommendation to Mr. ———, that you obtained the situation?—It was.

During the time that you were resident as housekeeper at Mr. ——'s, did you observe anything in the management of that house which, knowing the objects of the inquiries of this committee, you think it necessary to state?—I know that patients were very ill-treated; a vast number of them.

How long have you left?—I left on the 6th of August, in 181—

State to the committee what those acts of ill-treatment were, to which you have alluded.—Samuel R——'s ill-treating Mr. Driver, a farmer, from the country.

Did you see that yourself?—I did.

State what you saw.—It was one morning, when I was sitting behind the table, at breakfast time, I heard a terrible noise on the gentlemen's side up stairs. I went up in consequence, and found Samuel R—— ill-treating Mr. Driver, by beating him with a pair of boots, in a most dreadful manner.

Was he in bed?—Yes, he was in bed: he had beat him out of bed, and the young man ran down the gallery, with Samuel after him.

Was he in his shirt?—Yes.

What steps did you take?—I went to Mr. ——, and told him of it.

What was Mr. ——'s answer?—He said he knew Samuel was a cruel brute.

Was nothing further done than making that observation?—Nothing more.

You did not hear Mr. —— reprimand Samuel R—— for that conduct?—No, I did not.

Is there any other case that you can state, as to the harsh treatment by this keeper of the patients under his charge?—His general conduct was extremely brutal.

In what way?—In kicking the patients, and thumping them sadly.

In striking them with his fists, and kicking them?—Yes. Captain D—— he used extremely ill, when he was under his care.

In what way?—In striking him, and using him extremely ill.

Was Mr. —— acquainted with his conduct to Captain D——?—He was.

How do you know that?—I heard the conversation.

What was that conversation?—Mr. John D——, Mr. ——, and Mr. R——, were together, in the poor women's yard; they heard a noise, and looked through the pales, and saw Sam striking Captain D—— in a dreadful manner while confined in a waistcoat. They came up to the house together, and I heard Mr. D—— say, "Sam is too great a brute to have the management of patients, and —— you ought to send him away." Mr. —— said, "I will see about it," or something to that effect

In what year did that happen?—I believe about ten or eleven months before I left the house; but I cannot exactly say.

How long was R—— a keeper after that time?—I left him a keeper when I came away.

Will you take upon yourself distinctly to state to the committee, that, to your knowledge, Mr. —— was acquainted with the cruel conduct of R—— to the patients under his charge, and yet continued him as keeper up to the period of your quitting the establishment?—Yes.

Have you any other statement to make, as to the conduct of R—— ? —He used to treat Mr. Holmes exceedingly bad.

In what way did he treat him bad ?—By striking him.

Was it the constant practice of R—— to strike the patients in the house ?—It was.

Was there anything particular in the conduct and behaviour of the three patients whom you have mentioned, that seemed to render coercion and severe treatment more necessary in their case than in that of other patients ?—No. Captain D—— was in a very high state of disorder; but after taking to his bed, it was myself that waited and attended on him, and gave him every thing, which he took without the least force.

With respect to Mr. Driver, in what state of disease was he ?—He was a little high at times, but nothing to require his being confined, or anything of that kind.

Was he manacled ?—Very seldom.

With respect to Mr. Holmes ?—He was perfectly harmless.

Were you acquainted with a person of the name of Isabella Adams ? —She was a patient in the house.

What species of patient ?—She belonged to St. G——'s parish.

Was she often in a state of great irritation ?—Not very frequently.

When she was in that state, where was she confined ?—She was confined in a place in the yard.

Describe the nature of that place.—It was originally a pig-stye : it was run up high on purpose for her. I have seen her confined there for three weeks together.

Was she ironed ?—She had been ironed there in the crib, with wrist-locks and leg-locks, and a chain two or three times across her body.

Was there an iron bar placed between her legs, in order to prevent her joining her feet together ?—There was. Mr. —— had the bar made on purpose for her.

For what purpose was that bar, as she was chained to her crib ?—It was not used when she was chained to her crib, but when she was allowed go go about.

For what purpose was it used ?—To confine her, that she should not get away ; to prevent her from escaping.

For how long together have you ever seen her using that bar ?—Indeed, I cannot say. At different times she has had it.

For a month together ?—I do not conceive she wore it so long as that.

A fortnight ?—Perhaps a week.

Describe the nature of the bar, and the way it was used.—It was confined to each ankle with a chain, coming up her body, which was attached to her handcuffs.

Do you know what was the weight of that chain ?—I cannot say, indeed.

What was the size of it ?—It was very large.

As thick as your middle finger ?—It might possibly be as thick as that.

Could she walk with it ?—Yes.

Was she a very furious patient ?—No ; a very harmless patient ; you might sit and talk to her when she was in the highest state.

Was she ever employed in domestic purposes about the house ?—Yes, she was.

In what situation ?—Scouring the rooms.

Was she ever employed in the kitchen ?—Not while I was there.

Have you ever heard she was before ?—I have; but not while I was there.

Was there a female keeper in that establishment, of the name of B—— W—— ?—Yes.

What was her character ?—She was a very turbulent woman; very harsh and cruel to the patients.

Did you ever see her ill-treat Isabella Adams ?—Yes.

Describe what you have seen her do to her.—I have seen her lock her down in her crib with wrist-locks and leg-locks, and horsewhip her; and I have seen the blood follow the strokes.

Have you seen her often horsewhip her ?—I have, sundry times: three or four times.

Did she do it of her own freewill and pleasure, or did she do it by the order of any one else?—By the order of Mr. ——.

Did you hear Mr. —— give those orders ?—He gave them to me; and I begged him to tell B—— himself.

What were those orders, to the best of your recollection ?—B——, I desire you to go and take Isabella Adams, confine her to her crib, and give her a good horsewhipping.

Do you recollect what she had been doing ?—She had been trying to make her escape.

Did you ever complain to Mr. —— of the ill-treatment that Isabella Adams received ?—Yes.

What was his answer ?—He said that he had leave from the gentlemen of the parish; that they told him, the best thing he could do was to give her a good horsewhipping.

Has she made her escape out of the house more than once ?—Several times.

What was the nature of the whip that B—— used to horsewhip Isabella Adams with ?—A whip with a whalebone handle, and a long lash: a sort of dog-whip.

Was the situation in which Isabella Adams was confined, extremely cold ?—Very cold.

What covering had she ?—A rug.

Did she appear to suffer from cold ?—She was extremely ill for some time after she came out.

Ill of what ?—She used to go double, and was very much emaciated.

Was she much straitened for room ?—No; she had the usual allowance of room.

Had she a good allowance of food ?—She had the common allowance for poor people: sometimes she did not take her food for two days together.

The above were not isolated cases: a great many, fully as bad, and several even worse, were brought to light, not only by the committee of 1816, but by that of 1827. I have selected the above cases, simply because they are more fit for publication than many others. It was proved, by the examination of witnesses of undoubted integrity, that in one house a number of patients were regularly chained, in the coldest days of winter, to the walls of their cribs, from Saturday afternoon, at four o'clock, till Monday morning, at eight; and that it was no uncommon thing to have them washed in a tub of water with a mop, when there was ice on the water. It was proved, that one poor unfortunate man had had his eye knocked out by the keeper, whom he had offended: that another had been dreadfully cut on the head by a forcible blow with a key; and that, in a number of cases, death had been the result of the cruelties which had been practised towards the poor creatures by those who were paid to protect them, and to afford them all the comfort in their power.

But this is a topic on which I will not dwell. Since then, happily, a great improvement has taken place in the treatment of insane persons in private madhouses. In some of these establishments, it is but justice to say, the unfortunate parties are as well taken care of, and are in every respect as comfortable, as if they were with their friends at home. I need hardly add, that as there is so great a difference in the treatment of the unfortunate insane in different private madhouses, even where the terms are the same, the friends of any such unhappy persons incur a fearful responsibility, when they fail to make the proper inquiries as to which of the asylums afford the best protection, and practise the kindliest treatment.

It was the detection of the gross abuses and shocking cruelties which obtained in many of the leading private madhouses in London some years ago, which led to the erection of the Hanwell Lunatic Asylum. To the pauper lunatics of the county, that asylum has, indeed, proved a boon of incalculable value.

In the course of my inquiries into the statistics of lunatic asylums in the metropolis, I ascertained that many of the inmates had been confined for fifteen or sixteen years, without having once, all that time, crossed the threshold of the institution. There were several who had been shut up in these asylums for twenty years; and, in one or two cases, there were parties who had been there upwards of a quarter of a century*. What, per-

* Mr. Bakewell, the keeper of a private madhouse at Spring Vale, near Wakefield, stated, in his evidence before a Committee of the House of Commons, appointed to inquire into the subject of insanity, that he knew a man who had been, for the singularly long period of *fifty* years, a lunatic in a private asylum; and that, during all that time, he had been confined to a small dark dungeon of an apartment, almost in a state of nudity, and never rising off the heap of straw which was all he had for a bed during all that time. I ought also to mention, that he never once saw fire, or felt its genial warmth, in the course of those fifty years. Neither was he visited, ex-

haps, is more remarkable is, that in various instances, the maniacs who were longest in the institution were amongst the most frantic and ungovernable of the inmates, and were consequently obliged to be repeatedly kept, by chains or otherwise, closely to their own apartments. What struck me as very singular, was the fact of the human frame being able to support so much mental violence, or such a high state of excitement, as the technical phrase is, for so long a period; and this, too, without one moment's lucid interval. Yet so it was. And what is more surprising still, these persons were, in most cases, among the most healthy inmates in the various institutions. This is a physiological anomaly for which I am unable to account. I can easily enough conceive how a lunatic may endure more than ordinary physical fatigue, and make more than the usual physical exertion for the first few weeks after he is visited with the malady; on the same principle as a person, stimulated by ardent spirits, or fired by some other exciting cause, often displays an amount of physical strength to which he would be unequal in ordinary circumstances: the difficulty with me, in the case of the class of lunatics to which I refer, is, how their frames can bear up under this constant violence of manner, this unintermitting high state of excitement, for a long succession of years.

It is a fact which will surprise those who were not before aware of it, that many cases have been discovered, in the recent annals of the private madhouses of London, of persons having been for a long period—in some instances, for several years—confined in these institutions, who, before they were sent thither, and all the time they were inmates, were as sane as any man in Great Britain. It will be asked, how came they, then, to be sent to these places? In a number of cases they were so from their friends mistaking certain peculiarities or eccentricities in their manner, for insanity. Not later than towards the close of the last session of parliament, I heard Mr. Wakley, the member for Finsbury, state in his place in the House of Commons, that he himself knew a gentleman, then moving in a respectable sphere of society, who a short time before had been consigned by his friends to a lunatic asylum, under the impression that he was insane. And what does the reader suppose was the ground on which those friends rested their belief in his insanity? Simply, as Mr. Wakley stated to the house, that he happened to feel very strongly in favour of a certain class of political principles—whether Tory, Whig, Radical, or Republican, Mr. Wakley did not say,—and that his zeal for the spread of his views led him to be somewhat forward in endeavouring to make proselytes to

cept a very few times, by any human being. Half a century in one spot, and without the sight of fire! To what affecting considerations is the fact calculated to give rise!

his principles. Poor fellow! he was a living martyr to his political faith, with a vengeance.

Novelists and writers of tales often construct their stories on the singularly affecting circumstances under which lovers, friends, and acquaintances, sometimes meet. I know of no meeting which could be more affecting to the relatives and friends of the parties, than that of those who were dear to each other, in a lunatic asylum. Some years since, a father and grown-up daughter, who were most affectionately attached to each other, were both inmates of St. Luke's at the same time; both having by a painful coincidence been visited with insanity within a short period of each other, though neither, so far as I have been able to learn, ever exhibited any symptoms of it before. And within the last few weeks, a case has been verbally communicated to me, by a gentleman who was personally cognizant of the fact, in which two brothers, between twenty and thirty years of age, were both visited with mental alienation within a few weeks of each other; and so decided was their insanity, that it became necessary to send both to an asylum. They were both sent to the same institution; and, touching thought! sent on the same day, and in each other's company. It was a remarkable fact in the case of these unfortunate young men, that not only was their attachment singularly strong towards each other, but their tastes, views, and habits, were so alike as to amount to a species of Siamese sympathy. And yet, when they became insane, nothing could exceed the dislike which the one entertained to the other: they seemed then to act on the principle of antipathy: what the one liked, the other hated, and *vice versa*.

In a former part of the chapter, I adverted to the fact of some lunatics talking with great rationality on all other points but one; a modification of the disease generally called monomania, or hallucination of mind. In most of the cases of this kind which have come under my observation, the parties have exhibited a marked predilection for dwelling, in their conversation with others, on the particular topic on which their minds were insane—so very strong a predilection for talking on the subject, that it was with difficulty you could divert their minds for a short time from it. There are occasional cases, however, in which the insanity of individuals not only manifests itself on a particular point, but they can, if not led to that point by accident, abstain from introducing it into conversation with others, and probably, also, from thinking of it themselves, for weeks and months at a time. The most remarkable case of this kind which has been brought before the public, for some years past, was that of Captain Good, now an inmate in Bethlem, and to which I referred, when speaking of lunatics fancying themselves to be sovereigns. It will be remembered, that about six months ago, this individual—a gentleman by birth, education, and manners—committed two or three outrages on the Queen, and was afterwards ascertained to have been as decidedly mad as a human being could well be imagined to be. Yet it was proved by the landlady, with whom he had lived for several months in Regent-street, that his conduct, so far as she saw, was perfectly rational and orderly. Nothing was seen amiss in his manner, even on the days on which he behaved so insanely in the presence of the Queen. His brother also stated, that he had heard whispers of his being insane some time before this; but that, after a lengthened interview, and a great deal of conversation on every variety of topic with him, he thought for some time that he was as sane as himself. It seems to have been the thought of the Queen, or of Kensington Palace, in which she then resided, that brought to his mind the point on which he was deranged, and made him so outrageous. It also appeared, that the moment the Queen was out of his sight, or he had quitted the neighbourhood of Kensington, his mind resumed its sanity: for it was proved that he talked and acted quite rationally, an hour or two after he had conducted himself so frantically in the presence of Her Majesty. It will be remembered that the unfortunate man was brought before Lord Chief Justice Denman, in the Court of Queen's Bench, in November last, in consequence of the outrage he had offered to her Majesty. As the whole of the proceedings afforded a curious illustration of the particular way in which insanity works on some minds, I will here quote the report without alteration which appeared in the public journals, of the examination he underwent before Lord Denman.

Saturday, November 18, 1837.

This morning, on the sitting of the Court, Captain John Good was brought in, and placed upon the floor of the court; he was very well dressed, and had a star on his left breast: he kept his hat on his head.

Usher—Take off your hat, Sir. Captain Good—I will not: I am the King of England.

Earl Spencer, Earl Glenelg, Sir John Nicol, Sir Herbert Jenner, and Sir Frederick Pollock, then entered the court, and took the oaths of allegiance. On their swearing to be true and faithful to Queen Victoria, Captain Good said, "A usurper; what a villanous oath that is!"

The privy councillors having retired, Captain Good was politely asked by the officers of the court to come forward.

Captain Good then addressed their Lordships—I beg to observe, my Lord, that this is an illegal Court; the Court of a usurper; the Court of Princess Victoria, the usurper. The throne of England is mine; I am King John the Second.

Lord Denman, with much mildness—Should you not take off your hat? Captain Good—I can't take off my hat, my Lord, without giving up my claim to the throne of England, which I do not intend to do, I assure your Lordship. My Lord, in my mother's lifetime, you once acted honourably and nobly.

The indictment was then read, which charged him as a man calling himself John the Second, and also with having used seditious language in the presence of Her Majesty.

Captain Good—This is a —— infernal ——. I will have you off the throne.

Upon being asked whether he was guilty or not guilty, he said, "I will not plead before this Court; it is the Court of a usurper."

The Attorney-General—I now, my Lord, pray an inquest, under the 29th & 30th Geo. III., to try whether this gentleman is now of sound mind, or insane.

Lord Denman—Is the Sheriff in attendance?

This being answered in the affirmative,

The Attorney-General said—My Lords, at common law, it has been determined that the second section of the act applied to misdemeanours.

Captain Good—You want to get rid of a bad prosecution. You want to get rid of it on the ground of my insanity. I am as sane as you are.

A jury was then sworn, to try whether John Good was insane or not.

Captain Good—Why am I not tried for high treason?

The Attorney-General—Gentlemen of the jury, in a few words, I may explain the nature of these proceedings. The unfortunate gentleman who stands before you, is indicted for having spoken seditious words in the presence of her Majesty, as her Majesty was returning from Brighton to the Palace, on the 4th of November; and there is every reason to believe that he is not responsible for his acts. By the humanity of the common law of England, no person, who is in an unsound state of mind, shall be put upon his trial; and it is directed, that when any person shall be called upon to plead to an indictment, and there is reason to believe him not to be of sound mind, an inquest shall be immediately taken, to ascertain that fact; and if he is found to be insane, his trial must be postponed until he shall have recovered. A most salutary act passed in the 39th & 40th years of George III., wherein it is enacted, that where any person, indicted for any offence, shall, upon his arraignment, be found to be insane, he is not to be discharged until the pleasure of the sovereign shall be known; but that the finding of the jury be recorded; and the Court shall make an order that he be placed in confinement at the pleasure of the sovereign, as her Majesty shall think fit.

Captain Good—That statute was made on purpose for me.

The Attorney-General—By another section of that act, it is enacted, that if any insane person, without actually committing an offence, shall try to commit one, that that person may have proceedings taken against him; and that that person may be put into confinement, so that he may be no longer dangerous.

Captain Good—That statute was made expressly for the purpose of meeting my case.

The Attorney-General—I will now state the history of this unfortunate gentleman. He served ten years in the army, and was a most excellent officer, having the good opinion of all men. In the year 1834, he left his regiment (10th Foot), and was promoted to half-pay. He had always conducted himself in the most proper and gentlemanly manner; but it unfortunately happened, about the month of October last, that his understanding became impaired: he was still, however, rational upon every subject but one. He had taken the strange notion into his head, that he was entitled to the throne of England: he said he was the son of George the Fourth; and insisted upon it, that he ought to reign over this kingdom. He had remained under that delusion to the present hour; and you have been witnesses of that delusion, by his conduct in this court. When the oaths of allegiance were being administered, he said her Majesty was a usurper. I shall prove to you, that in the month of October last, in the presence of his own brother, he declared he did not stand in any relationship to him; and that he was the sovereign, and had the right to command the services of all the officers in the army. Down to the present hour, he labours under that delusion. Gentlemen, I will call the surgeon who has attended him lately, and he will tell you, that whenever he talks upon this subject, he breaks out in the manner you have heard. He says her Majesty is a usurper. Under these circumstances, he is not a fit subject for punishment; he will be humanely and properly taken care of, and will not longer be dangerous, as he would, if suffered to go at large. I am sure, if he were of sane mind, he would be a most loyal subject of the sovereign, and would be the first to come forward to protect her.

W. H. Good, Esq., having been called,

Captain Good said—When a villain comes before his lawful sovereign, and shall conspire and compass the death of his liege lord, he shall be hung, drawn, and quartered; and (addressing his brother, who was then passing him in his way to the witness-box,) that is your sentence, and your death is recorded in the Court of King's Bench.

W. H. Good, Esq., was then examined by Mr. Wightman.

You are the brother of Captain Good, I believe?—I am the brother of Captain John Good.

You are in the 10th regiment of Foot?—I am.

Was your brother also in the 10th regiment?—He was also in the 10th regiment, for a period of nine or ten years.

When did he leave that regiment?—I think in the year 1834, on promotion to half-pay.

Did you remain with the regiment after he quitted?—I did, till August last.

Did you then see your brother?—I arrived in London the 1st of October; I left the Mediterranean in August.

Did you call upon your brother?—I called upon my brother on the 12th.

Where did you find him?—118, Regent-street.

Captain Good—You know, you villain, you are not my brother: how dare you claim relationship to the blood-royal of England?

Evidence continued.—Tell us what passed between you?—He received me first in a rational manner; and I had reason then to hope that the reports I had heard, as to his state of mind, were unfounded. Very shortly afterwards, he stood up, and asked me in what relationship I considered him to stand towards me? I replied, that of brother. He said, "No, Sir; you are the son of an officer in my service, and occupy your proper place in society. I am King of England. I am King John the Second." From that time, his language was incoherent. He said Queen Victoria was a usurper, and that he would have her off the throne.

Captain Good—You are trembling on the verge of the grave, Sir, remember.

Examination continued.—Did you leave him?—I left him at that time: he disclaimed me as his brother. In the afternoon of the same day, I paid him another visit; and I found he had given orders that I should not be admitted. As soon as I entered the room where he was, he told me that he was King of England, and took up his hat, and walked away, repeating again that he was lawful heir to the throne.

Have you seen him since?—I saw him once in Waterloo-place: we passed each other, but did not speak.

That was the last personal communication?—Yes; that was the last personal communication.

By Lord Denman.—Had you been on affectionate terms with your prother?—Most particularly so.

There was no cause of quarrel?—None whatever.

Alice Collins was then called; but Lord Denman asked if it was requisite to go further. His Lordship then addressed the jury.—Gentlemen, I don't know whether you want any further evidence. There might be a question, whether the unfortunate man should not be called upon; but that would be an improper mockery, and would only lead to lengthened observations, without altering the result. If you are of opinion that this unfortunate gentleman is not of sound mind, you will say so by your verdict.

Jury—Perfectly unsound.

The Attorney-General—It is now my duty to move, my Lords, that this finding be recorded; and that your Lordships will be pleased to order that John Good be kept in strict custody till her Majesty's pleasure be known.

Lord Denman—Be it so.

Captain Good—I declare, before this Court, that I will impale the royal family; that I will drag, from the sepulchre at Windsor, the bones of their ancestors, and burn them before their faces; that I will order a brig-of-war to be anchored off the Tower, in which their bones shall be placed, and cast into the deepest part of the Atlantic. I will draw out their bowels. I will draw out the bowels, and embowel the Russian and Dutch embassies, the true foes of England, and hang them on the Tower. This is my sentence, pronounced on the floor of the Court of

King's Bench; and, so help me God! I will perform it; for I will regard as an accomplice any one who dares to intercede for them.—(This was delivered with great warmth, accompanied with considerable action.)

Lord Denman—Let him now be taken back to the custody from which he was brought here.

Captain Good then turned round, and quietly walked out, having first said, in an authoritative tone, "Make way." He was guarded by a number of officers, but treated throughout by all as a gentleman.

There is every reason to believe that insanity has not yet been treated with that scientific skill of which the disease is susceptible. This, at all events, is the impression of most of our present eminent physicians. The question then suggests itself, How are the defects of the system of treatment which at present obtains, to be remedied? This is a question which it is not for me, or for any one who, like myself, is unconnected with the medical profession, to answer. I may, however, observe, that the general opinion among the most distinguished physicians of the present day—those, especially, whose attention has been particularly directed to the subject—is, that there ought, as the groundwork of any efficient system of treatment in cases of mental alienation, to be a union of moral and medical remedies. One physician of great celebrity has recorded his conviction, that "medical advice is likely to be useful in cases of insane persons." He adds, "It is most useful in the early stages of insanity; but it is useful also in the progress of the disease, particularly when it recurs in paroxysms; and it is occasionally useful in confirmed lunacy, though the good effect of it is less certain in the advanced stages of the disease. This, however, is analogous only to what is found to be the case in other distempers. I consider insanity to be connected with bodily indisposition throughout its course, though this be less apparent in some cases than in others." In connection with the medical part of the treatment of lunatics, it is necessary that the greatest attention should be paid to diet—a fact which, it is to be feared, is too generally overlooked. Sir Anthony Carlisle, in his examination before a select committee of the House of Commons, in 1827, on the subject of insanity, expresses himself on this point as follows: "I am quite convinced, from experience, that both for the moral health—that is, the remedying the derangement of the mind—and for the continuance of bodily health, diet is one of the most essential things; and that it should be specifically directed in each case, and that it requires medical direction in each case." Again: "Were I the superintendent, and answerable to the governors of an institution of that sort (a public madhouse), and were they, from a feeling of economy or saving, to coerce me in the treatment of a lunatic, or set of lunatics, with regard to diet, I would say

'You neither do the patient justice, nor do you permit me to exercise my judgment.' Their diet must be of the best kind, and not of the grossness of diet in general: it must be fresh meat, and not salt meat. In those institutions where economy is a great matter, I have seen coarse pieces of salt beef, coarse cheese, and not the best kind of bread, and unwholesome vegetables. There is no chance of restoring a man whose disordered mind depends on a disordered stomach and disordered bowels, if he is taking that food. If a man is kept in a state of dreaming while he is awake—for, in many instances, insanity consists in a man not being able to distinguish between his waking and sleeping powers; if a man's powers are asleep, he becomes a lunatic while he is awake; for most men are lunatics when they are asleep with a disturbed state of the stomach; and if a man is thrown into that state, that he is confused while he is awake, he becomes a continued lunatic, and has no chance. There is an operation of the mind, arising from the disturbance of that function, which physic can never cure, if a man is eating that which disturbs his brain, and keeps it from that quiescence and rest which the health of the mind requires."

The moral remedies to be resorted to, in the treatment of insanity, are as much dependent on the peculiar condition of the patient, as are the medical remedies. In the fifth report, written two years ago by Sir William Ellis, of the state of matters in the Hanwell Lunatic Asylum, Sir William has some judicious observations on this point. He says—"By inducing the patient to exercise and combine the mental faculties which remain to him, these become strengthened, and others are gradually developed, until the mind is eventually restored to its original powers. It must be evident, that to carry this plan into execution, a greater diversity of employment and amusement must be carefully selected, and continued with unremitting attention for years, according to the different tastes and various habits of the patients. By keeping the attention completely engrossed, so as to allow the mind no time to dwell on its prevailing delusions, these almost imperceptibly fade away; and, after a period, vanish altogether."

In conformity with these views, it is one of the leading features in the system of treatment adopted at the Hanwell institution, to employ the patients in some way or other, but always in a manner agreeable to themselves, in every case where practicable. Sir William Ellis, in the report of 1836, and from which I have already quoted, says, in reference to this—"During the year, upwards of 360 patients* have been constantly more or

* Out of 600; a very large proportion, when allowances are made for advanced years, physical infirmities, and other accidental causes.

less employed, either in the house, or in the grounds when the weather has been favourable; and it is with thankfulness recorded again, without a single accident. The delight," adds Sir William, "experienced in witnessing the benefit derived by this system, is, in some measure, a compensation for the additional duties and dangers it necessarily entails."

Religious as well as moral remedies may, in some, though in comparatively few cases, be had recourse to with success, in the treatment of insanity. Sir William Ellis makes some very important remarks on this point. "In former years," says he, "from the very incorrect notions entertained of this disease, religious and moral instruction of any kind was never thought of being afforded to the insane. Happily, a better knowledge, and a better state of feeling, now exist. And it is at this time generally admitted, that though, on some points, the mind may be insane, yet on others it may be perfectly rational. And it is no ordinary blessing to many of the sufferers, that a just sense of religion often remains when every other feeling seems obliterated. An act of parliament now provides, that the religious services, according to the established church, should be performed in all large asylums in this country. Here the patients have the instruction of the Rev. J. Stoddart, the chaplain to the institution; and a more orderly and attentive congregation cannot be assembled together. Some of the committee, and other gentlemen, have frequently been present, and have expressed their astonishment and delight at witnessing the reverence and decorum of the patients."

These are important facts in the history of insanity, and if duly improved may be of great service in the treatment of many lunatics. They have only been recently discovered; and were the subject to be more fully studied by scientific men, and the facts discovered and the observations made by them, were from time to time to be published, in the form of periodical papers or reports—there can be little question that certain principles could be laid down in the treatment of the disease, which, when taken in its earliest stages, would insure the speedy recovery of the patient, except in a few very peculiar cases.

CHAPTER IX.

BARTHOLOMEW AND GREENWICH FAIRS.

Prefatory remarks—Bartholomew Fair—The numbers which attend it—Descriptive observations—Greenwich Fair—The numbers which frequent it—The voyage downward—Throwing the stick, and other games—The park—The hill—Blackheath—The appearance of the Fair—Supply of commodities—Exhibitions—Theatres—Gamblers, and gaming—Swings—Booths—Immoral tendency of the Fair.

THE Fairs in London and its vicinity are still important *af*-fairs, though not so much so as formerly, in the estimation of the working classes of the metropolis; and any work, professing to treat of Babylonian life and habits, which did not embrace this subject, would be manifestly incomplete.

Some years ago, there were a greater number of fairs in the metropolis and its suburbs, than there are at present. The two of greatest note which now exist, are Bartholomew and Greenwich Fairs. A few years ago, there were Bow Fair, Stepney Fair, Edmonton Fair, and Brook-green Fair, besides one or two others of minor interest. These fairs have all been done away with by the civil authorities, in consequence of the injury to public morals which resulted from them. On this last point I shall make a few observations in the conclusion of the chapter.

Bartholomew Fair, or Bartlemy Fair, as the cockneys call it, is held once every year. It takes place in September, in Smithfield market, which is in the very heart of London, and is opened with great pomp and circumstance by the Lord Mayor and others of the city authorities. It always lasts three days. During each of these days, it is numerously attended; but the second day is usually the best, both with respect to the numbers who attend, and the spirit with which matters are conducted.

Among the lower classes of London, the return of Bartholomew Fair is looked forward to with great interest and anxiety. The numbers of both sexes—I am not sure whether there be not more females than of our sex—which attend this fair, must appear incredible to those who have not been made acquainted with the fact from personal observation. I am convinced I am under the mark, when I say that 100,000 persons are present each of the three days, from two to eight o'clock; and if to these be added, those who visit the Fair for an hour or two only, and then quit it, I am satisfied the number who have been at the Fair, each of the three days, is above, rather than below, 150,000. That I may not be suspected of exaggeration in this estimate, it may be proper to mention, that Smithfield-market embraces a space equal to nearly five acres. Let the reader be informed, that not only is this extensive space so densely crowded with human beings, that they have the appearance of a solid mass, but that the Fair, or, at any rate, the crowd of persons, extends itself some distance up all the streets which lead into the market-place: let him only be informed of this, and he will, in all probability, come to the conclusion that I have considerably underrated, rather than over-estimated, the numbers who patronize Bartholomew Fair.

It is here, perhaps, worthy of a passing remark, that the very spot on which Bartholomew Fair, with all its fun and frolic, is held, is the very spot on which blazed the fires of Smithfield which consumed so many distinguished Protestant martyrs, two centuries ago. Who can help being struck with the difference between the purpose to which Smithfield-market then was, and now is, applied!

To enumerate the amusements provided for the holiday cockneys at Bartholomew Fair were a hopeless task: they are legion itself. Everything that can please the palate, delight the eye, or gratify the ear, is there to be seen or heard. The "shows," or exhibitions on a larger scale, have all their bands of music; while inside, you'll see "sich vonders as no von ever saw afore." In the sweetmeat and toy departments of the Fair, the variety and abundance are so great that you are quite confounded with the scene. I have heard a young man ask his sweetheart what she would like, pointing to a stall on which were displayed, in rich abundance and most tempting condition, sweetmeats innumerable; and I have seen her so completely at a loss to make up her mind as to which she would prefer, that the fable of the ass perishing of hunger between the two bundles of hay has come across my mind with a force I have very rarely known it do on any other occasion. In fact, it is no uncommon thing, in such circumstances, for the lover to be obliged to decide, as well as to pay for the object of his affections.

I pass over the leading features of Bartholomew Fair, because the remarks and statements I shall have to make when speaking of Greenwich Fair, will equally, or in a very great measure, apply to it. The most marked difference, perhaps, between the two fairs, consists in the circumstance of Greenwich Fair being most liberally supplied with dancing booths, while Bartholomew Fair has no such attraction for the youths of the metropolis. A substitute, however, is found in the large rooms of some of the neighbouring public-houses.

For the reason just mentioned, I now quit Bartholomew Fair, and proceed to its rival at Greenwich. The latter fair is not nearly so numerously attended; a circumstance which is at once accounted for from the fact of its being four or five miles distant from the centre of London. As far as I can ascertain from the imperfect data accessible to me, I should represent the number of persons who usually attend Greenwich Fair as somewhere about 50,000; full 40,000 of which number, I should suppose, are visitors from London. Formerly, there were only two modes of conveyance to Greenwich—the steamers and the turnpike-road: now there are three, the railway having been opened upwards of a year since. Before the opening of the railway, there were always a great many pedestrians to be seen on the road to Greenwich Fair: now, there are very few. Scarcely any now go by the usual coaches. It was calculated that, at last Easter Fair, the number who went and returned by the railway, and the number that patronized the steamers, was pretty equal; giving, on my estimate, about 20,000 to each. The journey down to Greenwich is always an important affair in the estimation of the patrons of the Fair.

No one can form any idea of the sights which are to be witnessed, and the occurrences which take place, at our metropolitan fairs, who has not been present at them. Bow Fair, Stepney Fair, and several other fairs I had seen when they existed; Bartholomew Fair I had been at on two occasions; but, until last Easter Monday, I had never visited Greenwich Fair. Anxious to describe what had come under my own eye, instead of trusting to the representations of others, I that day started for Greenwich, at four o'clock in the afternoon. On passing down Cannon Street, the first thing which attracted my attention was an athletic, surly, hodman-looking personage, walking backwards and forwards, placarded before and behind with immensely large sheets of paper affixed to boards, and on which were the words, in most gigantic letters, "Greenwich Fair."—"Greenwich Fair, Sir?" "Greenwich Fair, Ma'am?" growled the bearer of these prodigious placards, as he looked into the face of every person whom he deemed likely to be on his or her way thither.

"Has the vessel yet started?" I inquired, as he accosted me with his everlasting "Greenwich Fair, Sir?"

"Not yet, Sir; but the'r a-going directly," he answered; adding, "This way, Sir; down this lane, Sir," pointing to a lane, the name of which I forget.

"Are there no vessels to be had at the usual place?" I inquired, still proceeding in the direction of London Bridge.

"This is the way to the vessels, Sir," was the reply, from one, again pointing down the lane,

"But I'll get a vessel, won't I, at the usual place?"

"I assure you, Sir, the vessels are here," was the answer. I saw at once how the matter stood, and was pleased to find, *notwithstanding* the placard-bearer's forbidding look and rude manner, he had such a perception of the moral beauty of truth, as to resist the temptation to tell a fib.

"You don't mean to say," I repeated, "that there are no vessels to Greenwich to be had at the Bridge?"

"Vy, Sir, I have already given you my vord, that the wessels are down this 'ere vay." Again his hand pointed in the old direction.

"Woy, yes, Zur," said a waggon-driver, with a short smockfrock, a dove-tailed hat, and half-boots with immensely thick soles, who was standing at the time at the door of an adjoining wine-vaults, with a pot of Whitbread and Co.'s Entire in his hand; "Woy, yes, Zur, there be lots on 'em at the bridge; but you see, Zur, as how there be two companies, vich be a-cuttin' o' one another's throats. That's how it is, Zur."

"Oh, I see," said I; "and that, I suppose, is——"

I was interrupted by the placard-bearer observing, with great earnestness, "Yes, Sir; but our wessels only charges sixpence, and the other coves charges ninepence. We be the hopposition, Sir. I'm sure you'll go on one of our 'uns."

The latter sentence was delivered in a tone and manner so very winning, and so unlike anything which one could have expected from a person whose physiognomy was so unprepossessing, that there was no resisting it.

One of the vessels was just on the eve of starting as I got on board: in other words, "the steam was up." On various occasions I have seen steam vessels, when on pleasure trips, sufficiently crowded. In July, last year, I sailed round the Isle of Wight in a steam-vessel much more crowded than I should like to see again on a similar occasion; but never did I see such a dense mass of human beings on the deck of any vessel, as I witnessed on this Greenwich steamer. It was with difficulty that those who were the last to go on board could procure standing-room. As for walking about on the deck, that was out of the question. The sailors, if the term be not a misnomer as applied to those who conduct steam-vessels down the river to Greenwich and back again, had literally, when working the vessel, to elbow their way through the crowd of passengers on deck.

And then the miscellaneous character of these passengers.

There you saw a bevy of young dandies, as prim and spruce as it were possible to imagine, puffing cigars, and ogling the girls around them. Of dress-makers' apprentices there seemed a fair sprinkling, and of male apprentices to various trades there was no lack; but the preponderance of the passengers were clearly journeymen mechanics and kitchen-maids. You would have fancied, to see the swarms of the latter who found their way to Greenwich on Easter Monday, that every kitchen in London had emptied itself of its biped contents. Some of them had their sweethearts; others had evidently gone on spec.—that is to say, trusting to meet by chance with some of their male acquaintances, either there or on their way thither or home again. You saw small colonies of Sallys in every part of the vessel. The remains of kitchen smoke which were visible about some of their caps or bonnets, and the patches of what is, I believe, technically called "black," which still graced their physiognomies, told, in language not to be mistaken, what were the avocations of a large proportion of the females on deck. But if any one could have been so slow to learn as not to have been instructed by what he saw around him, his ears must have come to his aid, and performed an office in which his eyes had so unaccountably failed; for every word they exchanged with each other smacked of the kitchen. There were the usual number of "La's!" "Well, I never—" seemed to be perpetually on their lips; while the invariable mode of resenting, or appearing to resent, the conduct of the young men, when the latter were amusing themselves at their expense, was by giving them a gentle slap on the face, and shouting out, with a shrillness of pronunciation peculiar to those who grace the kitchen—"A-done!" If one Sally asked another Sally what she thought of some male acquaintance whose name was mentioned, the sure answer was, turning up her nose as she spoke, with a view to express disdain—"Oh, shocking! I can't a-bear him." "How do you like that gown which that young ooman sitting opposite there has on?" "Oh, shocking! I can't a-bear it." Then there was an endless mention of the name of "Missis." "Missis was so cross ven I sought leave to-day;" "Missis is such a rum 'un;" "Missis is so difficult to please;" "Missis says she von't allow no follo'rs; but I contrives to see Tom Toggs for all that."

In the voyage downwards, nothing particular took place. The only occurrence worthy of mention was that of a young man's hat having fallen off his head while looking over the side of the vessel. The general laughter which followed must have been very annoying to the poor fellow, considering at the same time the loss of the hat, and the inconvenience of having his head exposed all the way to a very cold north-easterly wind. Besides, who could tell whether the unlucky wight had "the wherewith," as one of the passengers suggested, to get another? My hypothesis, judging from his appearance, was, that his coffers were by no means abundantly replenished with the circulating medium. Be this as it may, he was doomed to experience the truth of the old adage, that evils do not come alone. I have mentioned a couple of the evils which on this occasion simultaneously befel this young man: the evils, namely, of losing his hat, and then having his ears assailed with a loud and universal laugh from his fellow-voyagers to Greenwich at the occurrence of the calamity. A third evil was in store for him, which was that of the disaster being converted into a subject of wit at his expense by every person on board who could say, or imagined he could say, a clever thing on the impulse of the moment. "Why don't you take off your hat?" said one, in a gruff grunting sort of voice. A roar of laughter followed. "Wy doan't you put it on, old 'un?" said another small, shrill, squeaking voice, the proprietor of which was evidently a tailor. The laughter was renewed with additional vigour. The dying lion felt more mortified at being kicked by the donkey, than regret at the mere circumstance of dying; and surely the fact of being made the butt of a tailor's jokes must have been to this poor fellow more annoying by far than even the loss of his hat. Another passenger inquired whether the hat was "a vashing beaver von?" while a fourth inquired whether it was "a gossamer ventilator?" Loud laughter followed each of the witticisms which were levelled at the unfortunate young man through means of his lost hat. It was easy to perceive that he was inwardly wishing that some half-dozen or so of his tormentors were in the same locality as his chapeau, namely, either at the bottom of the Thames, or on their way to it.

So much for the voyage downwards. "Going down," as it is called, whether by the river, the railway, or the road, is considered by all the patrons of the fair as an essential part of the day's gratifications. On debarking—to keep up the nautical phraseology—we were furnished with abundant earnests of the amusements which awaited those who were disposed to enjoy them. The game of throwing the stick seemed to be an especial favourite with the holiday people: it was prosecuted with a vigour which I have never seen equalled. Within one hundred yards from the landing-place, there were at least forty proprietors of "the holes and the sticks," and all of them appeared to be driving a most extensive business: judging from what I saw, I should add, that they were doing a profitable one also; for out of about thirty throws, I only observed the player win once.

As the game of throwing the stick is unknown in many parts of the country, I shall describe it in as few words as possible,

The persons who attend the fair for the purpose, dig three holes, each about half a foot in diameter, in the ground; and in each of these holes place a stick, three, or three and a half feet in height. The sticks are each about one yard distant from the other, and on the top of each stick is placed a snuff-box, a pen-knife, or some other trinket, whose nominal value is from sixpence to a shilling, but which only costs the proprietor of "the stand" three or four pence. Any one who chooses to try for either of the articles on the tops of the sticks, is allowed to do so on the payment of a penny. For this "small sum of one penny" he gets three chances, or throws; three sticks, about two and a half feet in length, being put into his hand for the purpose. The particular part from which he is to throw is duly marked out for him, which is eighteen or twenty feet from the sticks themselves.

Those who have never seen the thing played before, eagerly purchase their "pennyworth of chances," fancying that they have only to hit the sticks and knock down the articles on the top of them, to entitle themselves to the articles so knocked down. I was amused with a countryman of my own, at the last Greenwich Fair, in connexion with this throwing the stick. He had evidently never seen anything of the kind before, and had all the appearance of being a recent importation from the other side the Tweed. "Try a penny'orth, Sir,"—for the poorest and most homely dressed persons are all "Sirs" to the owners of the sticks and holes;—"Try a penny'orth, Sir, o' them 'ere sticks," said one of these personages to poor Sawney, who had the appearance of a gardener, as he stood by, looking with great simplicity at the three articles on the tops of the sticks.

"Can I try at ony ane I like?" inquired the Scotchman, looking at the sticks which were proffered him, but not withdrawing his hands from his trousers' pockets, where they were most probably "gripping" what little "siller" he possessed.

"O, certainly," answered the other, who was a little thick-set, sly-looking personage.

"May I airch (throw) at the middle ane wi' the snuff-mull on the top o't?" asked the Caledonian.

"At any one you like," replied the other, not very clearly comprehending the import of the terms "airch" and "mull."

"Weel, then," said my countryman, withdrawing his hands from his pockets, and holding them out to receive the three sticks; "weel, then, here's the penny, and gie's the rungs."

"Jist ha'd oot o' the way there," said the Scotchman, with a rich Paisley brogue, addressing himself to some boys who stood rather near the sticks; "jist ha'd oot o' the way there for a minit, and I'll soon bring the snuff-mull doon."

The Scotchman threw his "rung," as he called it, and sure enough he hit the stick and down fell the snuff-box in the hole.

"Jist gie me my mull; I was sure I would knock it doon," said Sawney to the proprietor of the stand.

"It's in the hole,
Upon my soul,"

said the other, taking up the snuff-box and replacing it on the top of the stick. "You must make it fall on the ground," he continued.

"Awa wi' ye're nonsense; nae matter whar it fa's, so as it's fairly knocked doon; fetch it to me," observed the Scotchman.

"No, no," said the other; "that would never do."

The Caledonian grumbled and disputed for some time; but on being assured by the bystanders that such was the invariable practice, he at last reluctantly relinquished what he had thought his righteous claim to the snuff-box.

"Try again, Sir; per'aps you'll be more luckier next time."

Sawney did as he was bid by the proprietor of the "mulls" and the knives and the sticks, and "airched" a second time; but the "rung" missed.

"Third time's always more luckier than a first or second," suggested the other.

The Scotchman threw a third time, and hit the stick; down, of course, went the snuff-box.

The usual couplet,

"It's in the hole,
Upon my soul,"

again greeted the ears of the unfortunate speculator.

"Try another penny'orth," said the proprietor, coaxingly holding out the three sticks again to Sawney. The latter hesitated for a few moments, and then dragged out another penny from his pocket; in consideration of which he received the trio of "rungs" which had already proved such traitors to him. Again he threw them, but with no better success than before.

"Can't *always* win, Sir (though the poor fellow had not won at all); there's a lucky penny'orth this time. Sure to win the third time," said the cunning rogue, in most coaxing accents, who had fleeced him, as he again presented to him the three sticks.

"Awa wi' them! awa wi' them!" said Sawney, indignantly turning away his head from the "rungs," just as a patient does from some nauseous medicine.

"There's luck in odd numbers, Sir; the third time's sure to gain, Sir," continued the other, still pressing the penny'orth of sticks on the Caledonian.

"Get ye gone, ye cheating rascal!" shouted the Scotchman, now losing all temper with the loss of his twopence; "if ye offer me your rungs again, I'll break them o'er your back."

It is needless to say, that the sticks were not again offered to Sawney: their proprietor addressed his solicitations to try their luck, to other greenhorns, of whom there was no lack.

I was struck with the fact, that the great majority of the new-comers proceeded, as if by a kind of instinct, to the Park. One thing which might of itself have attracted a large number of persons to this classic ground, was the loud unintelligible noise which a woman was making within a few yards of the gate. The cause of the noise, as well as the words she uttered—if words they could be called, which nobody could understand until they got quite near to her—was a profound mystery when it first entered the ears of the visitors. The most natural hypothesis, had there been a disposition to speculate as to the cause of the strange sounds which this woman emitted, would have been, that some one had been either murdered or dangerously hurt, and that such unfortunate person was lying dead or damaged at her feet; for while speaking, or rather vociferating, she held her right hand in a slanting direction upwards in the air, while with her left she steadily pointed to something on the ground. The singularity of her attitude was still further increased by the stooping position in which she stood. The very moment I saw her, she brought forcibly to my mind the late Mr. Thelwall in one of the attitudes in which he always put himself when wishing, in his lectures on oratory, to convey to the minds of his audience some idea of the way in which Mark Antony delivered his funeral oration over the dead body of Cæsar. My surprise, and the surprise of others who, like myself, had been attracted to the spot by the mysterious sounds, may be imagined, when, on advancing towards the place where she stood, surrounded by a seemingly very attentive audience, I found the subject of her vehement oratory was—a sack of nuts which had been spread out on a piece of canvass on the ground! Who could refrain from a hearty laugh, when finding the reality so very different from what any one could have expected? Had I guessed till the crack of doom, before quitting the place in which I first heard the noise, what the cause of that noise was, I am perfectly certain I should never have come to the conclusion that it was the woman's vehement commendation of some two or three bushels of nuts. "Here they are fresh good full sweet a penny a half-pint from the bag this morning best sort not a bad 'un among the lot," was the favourite eulogium which this nut-vender pronounced on her commodities! And she sometimes delivered the whole encomium without drawing her breath, and therefore all the words appeared, as they came from her lips, as if incorporated with each other. In fact, her panegyric on the superior qualities of her nuts looked, in some cases, as if all the above words had been but one. The next time, again, in which she repeated her praises of her goods, she pronounced the words so slowly and distinctly, resembling a sort of chaunt, that you would have fancied no two of them had any connexion together. They were uttered thus: "Here—they—are—fresh—good—full—sweet—a—penny—a—half—pint—from—the—bag—this—morning—best—sort—not—a—bad—'un—among—the—lot." And what rendered the whole affair the more extraordinary, was, the singular manner in which, in her more energetic moments, she howled out the praises of her nuts. She reminded me of the wild sounds which the Bedouin Arabs were in the habit of uttering when performing their gymnastic and other feats at the Colosseum, a year or two ago. She had the most powerful voice I ever heard in a woman. She had all the appearance of being a great patron of malt liquor. If one were acquainted with her domestic history, I have no doubt it would be found that she is one of the most extensive consumers to be met with, of Whitbread and Co.'s Entire. She was a woman of great size, and appeared to have the strength of a Hercules. How she was able to vociferate so constantly, was to me a matter of surprise. Had a woman of ordinary lungs, and the average physical strength, bawled for one quarter of an hour, instead of a whole day, at the rate she did, such woman would have made herself hoarse, and become utterly exhausted by the effort: but all her exertions seemed to produce no impression on our heroine. Her face, which was as round and red as a full-moon when she first presents herself above the horizon, afforded no indications of weariness; nor did her voice show the least symptom of exhaustion. If sufficiently plied with porter, I have no doubt she could have held on for twenty, instead of for ten, consecutive hours. What amused me much, was the singular dexterity with which she introduced, as if by way of parenthesis, into her commendation of her nuts, any observation which circumstances rendered necessary; but never for a moment losing sight of the main object, namely, the disposing of her half-round, half-oval commodities. If a boy, for example, picked up a nut on the sly, either when falling from the half pint jug while transferring "a penny'orth" to some customer who had been overcome by the charms of her eloquence, or when one had crossed the edge of the canvass on which the stock lay, she would reprove him for his crime without for a moment losing sight of her main object. "Here they are fresh (you little rascal, return that nut, or I'll break your bones) good full sweet a penny (and you too, you vagabond, just put it back into the heap) a half-pint from the bag this (stand back there you girl with the red head and dirty face) morning best sort not a bad 'un among the lot." The only fault to be found with the matron's praises of her nuts, was a want of variety in her words: the above was the only prose eulogium she pronounced upon them. She had another, which was in poetry. When she fixed her eye on some particular person among the crowd who surrounded her commodities, she snatched up a nut, and thrusting it into the hand of the intended victim to the tune of a "penny'orth," exclaimed,

"Here, take a nut, and break 'em,
And if you find a bad 'un, don't take 'em."

And great was the amount of business which our retailer of nuts did in the course of a day. As she could not conveniently fill and empty the half-pint jug, and attend to her vociferating duties at the same time, she had a boy, very possibly her son, who acted in the capacity of assistant: he executed the orders, but all the money was paid to her. It was not the least amusing part of the affair, to hear her lisping out the praises of her articles with a sixpence or shilling in her mouth, while counting the "change" of those who tendered her silver in payment of their penny'orths. There were numerous other nut-venders in the Park; but little, comparatively, was the extent of the business which they did. I am serious, when I say, that I do believe she drew more money for her nuts than any half-dozen of persons in the same line of business. It is due to their sagacity to state, that all of them stationed themselves at a respectful distance from the locality which she chose as the scene of her merchandise. They knew that if near her they would have had no chance.

Proceeding up the hill, so great a favourite with lovers, I found it crowded in every part with young people, amusing themselves with the popular exercise of trying how fast they could run down without losing their equilibrium. Many of them—even persons of both sexes, who had got out of their teens some years ago—received some awkward tumbles. I was only surprised that the tragical termination which characterised the ascent of "Jack and Gill," of nursery celebrity, up some acclivity with whose geographical position I am unacquainted, was not literally realized. To me it was, to speak quite soberly, a matter of wonder that, like poor unfortunate Jack, no one "broke his neck" when he "fell down." Had such a disaster occurred, one could not have regretted it so much as one does its occurrence in the case of little "Jack," the nursery hero. Poor dear boy, he ascended the hill for a most praiseworthy object, namely,

"To fetch a pail of water;"

and it was while so laudably employed that the awful catastrophe of breaking his neck occurred; but the parties who "went up" Greenwich hill, did so for the purpose of foolishly running down again. If, therefore, any fatal accident had been the result of their folly, less sorrow would have been felt than in other circumstances. It happened, however, that no necks were broken on the occasion. The disaster of greatest magnitude which occurred under my observation, took place in the case of a genteel good-looking girl, seemingly a servant, about twenty years of age. She fell with tremendous force on her face, and what "the fancy" call the claret, suddenly gushed from a prominent part of her phiz. If anything could have made the disaster worse, it would have been the inexpressibly droll observation which a youth, about fourteen or fifteen years of age, made, on being asked by a person who was passing, "what was the matter with the young woman, that so many persons were standing around her, and she was holding her pocket-handkerchief to her face?" "Oh, nothing!" said the young rascal, with the most perfect *nonchalance;* "she was only having a game at running down the hill, when she lost her balance, and trode upon *her nose: that's all.*" The idea of *treading* on one's *nose* struck me as irresistibly droll.

On the top of the hill a very animated scene was exhibited, in the shape of a keenly-contested battle. The belligerents were, for the most part, young men, fifty or sixty on either side; and what does the reader suppose were the weapons of their warfare? Their fists? No.—Sticks? No.—Stones? No.—What then? Why nothing else than that description of apples called pippins! With these they pelted one another most cordially, and many were the severe hits which were received on both sides. The chief source of regret was, that those who were no parties to the fight, but were walking quite pacifically disposed along the summit of the hill, occasionally came in for their share of the "hits," as they were called, which were so liberally given and received by the opposing parties. I recollect, when a boy, reading a private letter from a relative, in which an account was given by one who took a part in it, of an important action between the English and French armies; and after detailing, in graphic terms, the numbers he saw momentarily falling around him on the field of battle, and the circumstances under which some of his comrades were killed, he added—as well as I can remember the words:—"but sad and sorrowful as I was, at seeing so many men—many of them my acquaintances, in the enjoyment of perfect health, and in the prime of life—dropping down, and expiring around me, I felt far more deeply affected at the fate of a poor rifleman who, after being wounded, had managed to craw-

from the scene of action, but was shot by a Frenchman just at the moment when, in all probability, he thought he had escaped all further danger." In like manner, numerous as were the militants whom I had seen wounded, and some of them very painfully so, in this battle on the top of Greenwich hill, I did not feel for them a fraction of the concern which I felt for a young inoffensive girl who, though she kept at a reasonable distance from the scene of action, had a large breach made in her Leghorn bonnet—to say nothing of a very unpleasant "whack" on the head—by means of an apple. Whether this was the result of design, or of accident, I cannot say: I should hope, for the credit of human nature, that the thing was purely accidental. I am willing to believe, that depraved and ignoble as many of the frequenters of metropolitan and suburban fairs are, there are few of them so utterly lost to all sense of the claims which the sex have on protection at our hands, as to be capable of perpetrating so daring an outrage as aiming a hard apple at a female's head.

Not knowing whose cranium might receive the next apple, I lost no time in quitting the scene of conflict, and advanced to the Heath. And what a scene did I witness there! There were, at least, from fifty to sixty four-footed asses on the roadside: how many asses of another kind there were present, is one of those difficult problems which it is beyond my power to solve. In point of numbers, I shrewdly suspect the biped animals, with long ears, were larger than that of the four-footed quadrupeds that were so tastefully put into classes along the side of the road. The asses on all-fours were placed there for the purpose of asses, who walk in another form, riding about the Heath on their backs. Each had a saddle, such as it was, covered over with a ragged piece of cloth, which, in most cases, had, in its better days, answered the purposes of a smock-frock, or been dignified with the name of a shirt. I pitied the poor animals, while I felt indignation and contempt towards those—and sorry am I to say, the cases were not few—who could severely lash and otherwise cruelly treat them. Persons of both sexes, and of advanced years, largely patronised the proprietors of the donkeys, by hiring the latter out to ride. Had they contented themselves with sitting on the backs of the poor beasts, I should have been silent; but, not satisfied with that, they must needs lash and strike the unoffending creatures with great severity, under the pretext of causing them to move at a more rapid pace. There were, I understand, several of the officers of the Society for the Prevention of Cruelty to Animals present; but there was either not a sufficient number, or they were remiss in the performance of their duties. Not to mention other instances of cruelty which occurred under my own eye, there was one of a most flagrant nature. Two young ruffians, about fourteen or fifteen years of age, followed one poor miserable donkey, on whose back a clumsy grown-up fellow, of great specific gravity, sate. It would, positively, have been, in the language of certain philosophers, more in accordance with "the fitness of things," had this lumbering athletic fellow carried the feeble worn-out donkey, instead of the ass carrying him. As the poor creature was unable to do more than move at a slow pace with the two-legged animal on its back, each of the young barbarians already alluded to applied a large stick to its sides with all their force, with the view of goading it on to greater speed.

But for the cruelties practised towards the helpless jack-asses, one could have heartily laughed at the odd exhibitions made by many of the equestrians. Kitchen-maids, cookeys, and various other riders, of both sexes, had never been on the back of any four-footed beast before. The females screamed and clung to the saddle as if it had been an affair of life or death, if the donkeys happened to trot for a pace or two; and not a few of them fell altogether, to the manifest gratification of the long-eared quadrupeds which had been burthened with them but a moment before.

I was much amused with a cockney youth, seemingly about twenty years of age, of very affected manners, who was ambitious of exhibiting his person on the back of a donkey. Advancing towards one of the stands, on which there stood fifteen or twenty of these animals, with their proprietors all anxious to be employed, he accosted the latter in what is called a puppyish air and manner, with "Well, old fellows, who has got the best donkey for a ride?"

"Here you are, Sir," shouted a dozen voices, each donkey proprietor drawing his animal towards the cockney.

"I can't ride on all of them; which is the best?" said the dandy, resting his hands on his sides, and strutting about with an air of great consequence.

"This von's the best, Sir," cried one.

"No, it ain't," vociferated another. "This 'ere hanimal is betterer nor any won on the stand."

"Both on 'em's told you a gallows lie, Sir; none of their hasses can lift a leg; but here's a beast of the right sort," said a third.

"Here's a capital good 'un, Sir; three years old next grass-time, Sir," was the recommendation of his donkey, which was given by a fourth.

"My von's the best as vas ever seed, Sir; ven he's once a-set a-going, he'll never stop, Sir. It's truth I say, Sir," remarked a fifth.

"Then," said the cockney, "I'll take him."

"Yes, Sir," observed another opposition proprietor of a couple of donkeys; "but there's no setting him a-going. Nobody ever saw him trot a step."

"Here's a reg'lar trump of an hanimal, Sir," said another; "you've only to touch him this way, and off he gallops at once."

As the donkey proprietor spoke, he pretended to touch the ass's side with his fingers, and, sure enough, the animal made two or three abortive attempts at a leap.

"Ay, there's some spirit in that donkey," said the cockney youth, not aware that the cunning rogue of a proprietor had achieved the two or three bungled leaps which the animal gave, by pricking it with a pin. "What is the charge?"

"It depends on how far you ride, Sir."

"From one end of the heath to the other?"

"Only a shilling, Sir."

"Then, here goes."

And so saying, the cockney was astride the ass's back in a twinkling.

"The shilling, Sir, if you please," said the proprietor of the animal, with a knowing look.

"Why, isn't it time enough when I have had my ride?" said the dandy, pulling a shilling out of his pocket, and transferring it to the other.

"Always in advance, Sir," answered the ass-proprietor, archly, pocketing the silver image of William the Fourth.

"Now then," said the cockney, applying a switch to the sides of the donkey, and looking as if he supposed he was about to start off at the rate of fifteen miles an hour. "Now then."

The animal either did not hear, or did not heed, the "Now then" of the cockney. "Why, he woan't go," said the latter, in a tone of voice, and with a look at the proprietor of the beast, indicative of surprise and disappointment.

"He will, by-and-by," said the other, coolly.

"But I want him to go now."

"Werry good, Sir; as soon as you and the hanimal pleases."

The dandy-rider was confounded at the consummate *nonchalance* of the person whose ass he was patronising. "I say, old fellow, I won't stand any nonsense, and pay for it too. Either make your ass go, or give me back my shilling," remarked the cockney youth, in half-indignant tones.

"We never gives back any shiners, Sir, arter we've got 'em," answered the other, with the same dryness of manner as before.

"Then, Sir, *make* your beast go."

"That's more than I can always do, Sir; he's a little hobstinate at times, as all hasses are; but when once he sets off, there's ne'er a better runner on the Heath."

"Yez, Zur," interposed a clownish-looking fellow, with a smock-frock and a dirty demure-looking face; "but the worst of it is, he *never sets off at all.*"

I had a shrewd suspicion that such was the fact, before the latter personage made the observation; and after two or three more equally ineffectual attempts to cause the animal to start, the dandy rider became a proselyte to the same opinion.

Finding he might as soon have expected to move Greenwich church, as to move the animal on whose back he sat, he dismounted, muttering imprecations of no very pleasant kind, both on the ass and its owner. His imprecations were equally disregarded by both.

"Try this one, Sir;" "Here's a prime 'un, Sir;" "No mistake with this 'ere hanimal, Sir;" "Here's the reg'lar racer, Sir;" were only a few of the many sounds which greeted his ears as he alighted. In short, in a few seconds, he was surrounded by a congregation, to the number of twenty or two dozen, of jack-asses and their owners; the latter of whom respectively besieged him with their applications to try their "hanimals," with a vehemence and perseverance amounting to positive persecution. At first, savage and surly at the "hobstinacy" of the beast he had but a few moments ago bestrode, he refused to listen to any of their solicitations; but one of the ass-owners was so very eloquent in his entreaties for a trial of his donkey, that the cockney at length acceded to his request; stipulating, however, beforehand, that he would not pay his shilling until satisfied of the racing capabilities and disposition of the animal. He mounted the beast, and the owner, a young knowing-looking fellow, immediately pricked it with a pin, when it set off at a smart trot. "Ah, I told you that's your sort, Sir; that's the hanimal as can run in slap-up style," said the proprietor of the beast, keeping up with it, and prompting it forward by repeated applications of the pin to its side. "Ay, this *is* something like an ass," said the cockney. "Here, take your shilling," he added, pulling up the donkey for a moment, and putting that amount of the coin of the realm into the hand of the cunning rogue. "Now then, long-ears," said the dandy, apostrophising the donkey, and applying the switch to it, with the view of setting out on a regular gallop along the road.

The animal moved not a step.

"Halloa, old donkey! what's the matter that *you* woan't go?" said the spruce rider, applying his heels to the sides of the animal.

The latter was appealed to in vain. There it stood as motionless as the bronze horse with the statue of George the Third on his back, near the Italian Opera House.

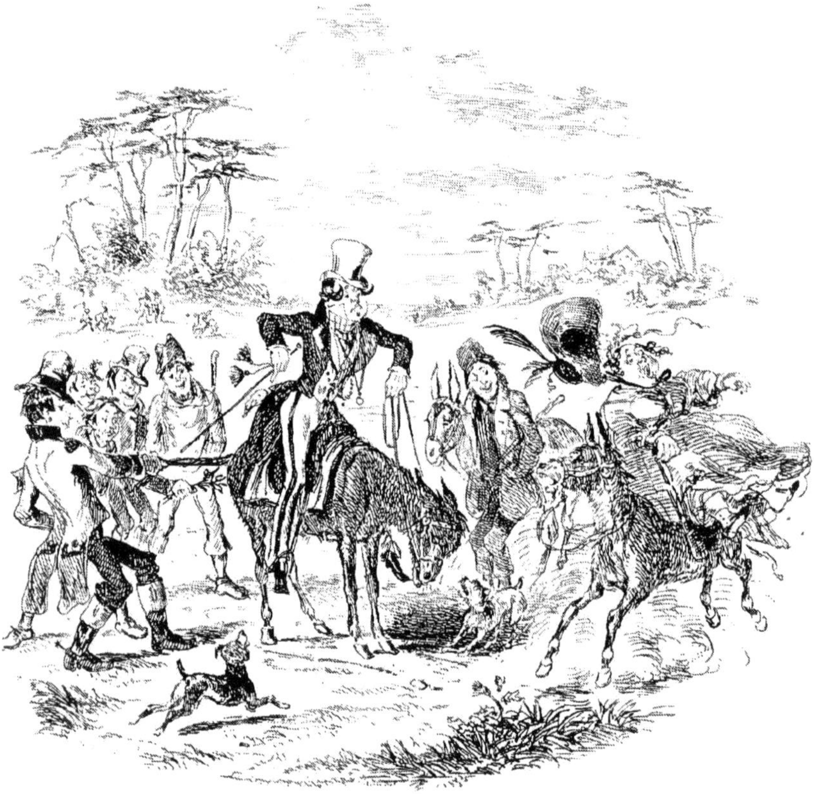

"I say, old fellow," said the cockney, now transferring his appeal from the ass to its owner; "I say, old fellow, why doan't the animal go?"

"Can't tell, Sir; he knows the reason best himself," answered the other, with inimitable coolness.

"Is there no way of *making* him go?"

"He won't be made, Sir; he never does anything by force. If you wait until he comes to himself, he'll start off agin."

"But when will that be?"

"Aye, that's more than I can tell; but not before he pleases."

The cockney looked first at the donkey, and then at its owner, as if he could have eaten both by way of revenging himself for the obstinacy and laziness of the one, and the consummate coolness of the other. He then suddenly dismounted, heaping curses both loud and deep on asses of all descriptions; not excepting himself, for being such an ass as to be thus taken in, and laughed at into the bargain, by the donkey owners of Blackheath.

A Greenwich Fair, without a greater or less number of fights, would be a modern miracle. How many took place during the fair in question, is a point with the statistics of which I am unacquainted. I witnessed one which threatened, at one time, to be productive of no inconsiderable number of broken heads, if not of personal damage of an irretrievable nature. In this fight, to which there were several parties, both soldiers and sailors, true to their proverbial character, took a *marked* part. "Drunk as usual," one soldier displayed a wonderful ingenuity, both by his words and actions, in inviting aggression; and he soon got it to his heart's content. "He met with his marrow," as the phrase is, in the person of an athletic Irishman newly arrived from the neighbourhood of Derrynane Abbey. "By the great Dan himself," said Pat, "if it's a fight he's after wanting, it's meself will give him that same." "Come on, then," mumbled the soldier, staggering slightly from the effects of drink. "May be I won't," said Paddy, advancing as he spoke, and planting some heavy blows in the face of his red-coated opponent, which made him reel yet worse than the liquor. A regular fight ensued, in which sailors and soldiers and other persons took part with a marvellous promptitude, until it became quite a general affair. The police interfered; and when they had put a stop to the combat, the soldier, who was instrumental in beginning it, was found lying on the ground, "floored," as the Fancy say, either by his Irish antagonist or by his no less formidable, because more frequent and insidious adversary, Barclay and Co.'s porter. He was carried away on the stretcher to the station-house, where he lay as straight as a pole and as silent as a bell without a tongue; though a few minutes before, he was all noise and bluster and "botheration."

I refer to the fights which are so common at all our metropolitan fairs, chiefly for the purpose of expressing my surprise and regret that so many persons, with a good coat on their backs and intelligence in their countenances, should not only stand by, without endeavouring to put an end to such brutal and barbarous exhibitions, but should encourage the parties in their disgraceful practices.

The fight or affray which I witnessed, occurred in the park; from which I proceeded to the heart of the fair. There were congregated in the narrow limits of, perhaps, one hundred and fifty yards long, by six or seven yards broad, a mass of human beings, numbering, I should think, not less than 30,000. They were so densely packed together, that it was quite a Herculean task to force one's way through them. On either side of the market-place were stalls and caravans, and other things, to which I know not what name to give, of all sizes and descriptions. I hold it impossible that any human being, be his imagination as fertile as it may, could previously have formed any idea of the vast variety of expedients which were resorted to at this fair, with the view of eliciting money from the pockets of the visitors. Of eatables, of all descriptions, there was a most abundant supply: apples, oranges, and nuts, stared you in the face in every direction; while gingerbread was presented in an inconceivable diversity of forms. Nor was there any lack of liquids: there was an ample supply of chalk-and-water, which, for the purposes of sale, was baptised milk; there were little cans of table-beer, and ginger-beer, and soda-water; but the speculators in these liquids found, before the fair was over, that they had reckoned without their host. The weather, as before stated, was intensely cold, which is always fatal to the sale of beer of all kinds, especially in the open air; and which is still more fatal to the sale of ginger-beer and soda-water. Loud were the luckless proprietors of these liquids in their praises of the quality of the article they were anxious to vend; but all the eloquence and ingenuity in the world would not have insured a demand in this case. In fact, the shivering persons who stood in the market-place, would not have drunk either soda-water or ginger-beer on this occasion, had they been paid for doing it. Ardent spirits were the order of the day, and the order of the hour and minute also, during the three days the fair lasted. "Summut to warm us," was the universal motto of the parties; and the effects of the quantity of these spirits quaffed on the occasion were visible in the scenes of drunkenness and disturbance which presented themselves wherever you turned your eye.

Of showy articles, or things which were merely intended to please the eye, there was also a most liberal supply. The assortment of dolls was varied and abundant. It struck me, indeed, as a sort of libel on the frequenters of the fair, that so many dolls should be exposed for sale; for if there be meaning in facts, as there is in language, the circumstance plainly implied that the dealers in them assumed that the young men and women who attended the fair were but so many children, though children of a larger growth. My only surprise was, that they did not resent the thing as a personal insult, when accosted, as they were at every step they took, with—"Buy a doll, Sir," "Buy a doll, Ma'am," the article which they were invited to purchase being at the same time thrust in their faces. Crackers, scratchers, little drums, sixpenny looking-glasses, watches which never went and never were meant to go, being, like the razors which Peter Pindar has immortalized as made not to shave but to sell; and innumerable other articles which, to use a favourite expression of George Robins, were too tedious to mention,—were all exposed to the eye, under the most attractive possible circumstances. "There was," as an Irish girl emphatically exclaimed in describing the scene to an acquaintance she met outside the market-place, "*such* a power of fine things!"

In the article of "sights," again, Greenwich Fair was, if that were possible, still more amply supplied. You would have fancied, from the number of caravans, booths, and other places for the exhibition of wonders of all kinds, artificial and natural, that the marvels of the whole world had been congregated within the limited space appropriated to Greenwich Fair. The seven wonders of the world, is a phrase which became familiar to us in our younger years: perhaps it is one of the first phrases we remember to have been current in the days of our childhood. Here we had, instead of seven, at least a hundred wonders of the world. And what was worthy of observation was, that every individual wonder was more wonderful—that is to say, if you took the proprietor's word for it—than any other wonder. The great difficulty with those who had but little copper in their pockets, though, peradventure, abundantly supplied with another well-known metal in their faces; the great difficulty with them was to make a selection. The figures which were daubed on the canvas which was displayed at the front of the caravans and other wooden erections, were most inviting; indeed, as is usually the case, the representations far surpassed the things represented. But in addition to the attack they made on your curiosity and your pockets, through the medium of your eyes, there were dead sets made at you through the medium of your ears. Nothing could exceed the earnestness or the eloquence with which the various proprietors of the exhibitions praised the articles exhibited. There was "the Lincolnshire Ox, the most biggest hanimal of the kind as was ever seen, and whose tail alone was not quite so thick as the mast of a man-of-war." My astonishment was, how such a "prodigiously-sized" beast could have been got into a sort of caravan of such limited dimensions, that I should have fancied a cow of the ordinary stature would not have had turning room in it. Whether the proprietor of this gigantic Lincolnshire ox was a disciple of Procrustes, and made the ox to fit the place, if the place did not fit him, is a problem which I was prevented from solving, as circumstances interposed to deny me the gratification of seeing the "wonderful hanimal." The next-door neighbour of the "most biggest ox as was ever seen," but belonging to a different owner, was "the most extraordina sheep with four legs and the half of a fifth 'un." The patrons of the fair were pressingly invited to "walk up, and see wit their own eyes this truly vonderful production of the vorks o natur." I was sorry to see that the proprietor's emphatic an repeated appeals were, in a great measure, lost on the dens crowd to whom they were addressed. They proved that they had no relish for "sheep with four legs and the half of a fifth 'un." Adjoining the last "vonderful production," there was a "vonderful pig;" not the old pig of literary reputation, nor the Learned Pig, as the swinish scholar and philosopher was usually called. No: this was a pig, whose wonderful qualities were of a physical, instead of an intellectual nature. "It was a pig as was so fat as never to rise off the place vere she lay, and as could not stand upon her legs ven she was fairly put on 'em." Judging from the portrait, if there be propriety in the expression, of this "wery extrahordinary hanimal," which appeared as large as life on the canvas that graced the front of the place of exhibition, I should certainly say that her pigship must have been among the "swinish multitude," what the celebrated Daniel Lambert was among animals of the biped class. Her belly not only trailed on the ground, but, if the representation was a correct one, her excessive corpulence had given her a globular appearance. I thought with myself, what a treat must her pigship be to the lovers of fat pork, when she falls into the hands of the butcher. A few yards from the spot in which the fat pig starred it, there was a collection of animals forming a sort of miniature menagerie. The figures on the canvas outside were newly painted, and were unusually inviting to go inside. But lest the representations outside were not of themselves sufficiently powerful motives to induce the spectators to go in, to these were superadded the motive, which could not fail to arise from the singularly winning way in which the owner of the animals implored them to inspect the beasts. "Ladies and gen'lemen, if the hanimals within here be not a treat to any one as sees 'em, then I pledge myself to eat up every beast in the caravan alive, the tiger and all. But, ladies and gen'lemen, I'm quite certain of it, that you will all be vonderfully pleased. Those who are not satisfied with this extrahordinary sight—the like of which was never seen before, and never will be agin—may have their 'tin' back again; and so they will have the splendidest sight as is in London for nothing. And, ladies and gen'lemen, I am sure you all knows that it cannot be less. Do walk up this way, if you please; walk up this way. All the hanimals to be seen for the small charge of threepence." Of the giant Rockman, and the dwarf Jarmain, each of whom had his place to himself, and to whom the payment of a penny always proved a passport; of them I say nothing. They were confessedly extraordinary enough in their respective lines; but I pass them by, for the purpose of saying, that the most wonderful live exhibition in the fair was, if the owner might be credited, that of some extraordinary unheard-of animal which walked partly on his legs and partly in an all-four's form, and which moved like an extraordinary quadruped mentioned in Captain Marryat's "Peter Simple," as having been exhibited at Bartholomew Fair, which measured fifteen feet from the tail to the head, and thirteen feet and a half from the head to the tail! But there would be no end to particularizing the live stock exhibited on this occasion. Every showman had, if you were good-natured enough to take his own word for it, something "far more better" than any of his neighbours; and he was greatly surprised, as well as indignant, at the perversion of public taste, when he saw other exhibitions patronised while his was deserted. With menageries, on a small scale, Greenwich Fair was most liberally supplied; and if the assertions of the parties who invited the curious in such matters to come and inspect them, might be believed, there were in all those menageries "lots of hanimals of a most extrahordinary kind."

In the theatrical way there was a good deal of business done. I should think the number of portable theatres, of one kind or other, could not have been much under a dozen; and so great was the taste for the drama, that theatrical speculations answered much better than any other kind of speculations. "The successor on the boards" of the late eccentric Richardson, appeared to be by far the most extensively patronised. The Clown was, as usual, the great attraction. The spectators stared and laughed, and laughed and stared again, at his ludicrous evolutions. Some of the audience, including chimney-sweeps, tap-room boys, and others, to whom the Clown's movements were perfect novelties in their way, turned up the white of their eyes in the plenitude of their amazement at the wonders he performed; and most unequivocal were the marks, in so far as a vehement clapping of hands and loud laughter were concerned, of the approbation with which they greeted his exploits. If any one wished to see the legitimate drama burlesqued with the greatest possible effect, he ought by all means to make part of the audience in one of the portable theatres at Greenwich Fair. The price of admission is reasonable enough: a fourteenth part of what it costs at Drury Lane or Covent Garden will procure him a place either in the pit or gallery. In other words, one's dramatic taste may be indulged in the theatrical establishments at Greenwich Fair, on the payment of sixpence for the pit, or threepence for the gallery. And who will say that the charge is extravagant? Boxes, there are none; and even the order of things, as regards the pit and gallery, are reversed: for the gallery—at least, in those establishments I have been in—is on the ground-floor, while the pit is six or seven feet above the gallery. However, such things will happen; or, as the proprietors themselves say, there is no use in being *too* particular. The character of the pieces performed, and the quality of acting, are precisely such as I so fully described in my chapter on "Penny Theatres;" and therefore it is not necessary to repeat the description here. Any actor is at liberty, in an emergency, to say what he pleases, or to act as he thinks fit. All that is stipulated for on the part of the proprietors, is, that something be said, and that something be done.

If Drury Lane and Covent Garden have their rivals in Greenwich Fair, so has Astley's. Not only are there equestrian performances "which has never been ekvalled in this 'ere vorld before," but there "is the truly vonderful feats on the tight rope, and various hother exhibishuns too tedious to mention, all performed in the best style." I went into one of these rivals of Astley's Amphitheatre, to witness some of these "unekvalled" and "truly vonderful" "various hother exhibishuns;" but must candidly confess, that such was the worthless quality of my taste in such matters, that I was much more gratified with the ludicrous conduct and humorous remarks of some of the audience. Some of my readers may remember to have heard of a cunning rogue of a traveller who, on going to an inn, in a small town, on an intensely cold evening, found that there was only one fire, namely, the kitchen fire, burning at the time; and it was completely concealed from his view by a number of the neighbours, who were earnestly engaged in conversation together. Not one of them moved a stool or chair to allow the stranger to partake of the genial warmth, and he had no hope of succeeding by an appeal either to their politeness or humanity. At last, he resolved on trying the effect of an ingenious expedient in his endeavours to procure a place beside the grateful hearth. "Ostler," he exclaimed.

"Coming, Sir."

"Are there any oysters to be had here?"

"As many as you please, Sir; great place this for oysters, Sir."

"Very good. Well, then, you go and give half a peck of the very best you've got to my horse in the stable."

"Your *'oss*, Sir?" said the ostler, looking unutterably amazed.

"Yes, my horse," said the stranger, quite coolly.

"Bless your soul, Sir, 'osses don't eat oysters! I never heard of such a thing. You must be mistaken, Sir," suggested the ostler, with an air of respect.

"Oh no; no mistake—no mistake; you bring the oysters directly to the horse."

The other scratched his head, and mumbled out, "Yes, Sir, presently."

"As quick as you can," said the traveller.

"This moment, Sir," said the ostler, darting out of the kitchen, to provide the horse with his supper of oysters. A general rush of those who were at the fire followed, every one being more anxious than another to see how the horse would eat shell-fish; so that the stranger had the entire kitchen, fire and all, to himself. He took the best chair he could find, and seating himself at the fire, determined on making himself quite at home. In a minute or so, the ostler, accompanied by all his followers, returned to the kitchen, saying—"It's jost as I said: the 'oss von't eat ne'er a one on 'em, Sir."

"Then bring them to me," said the stranger, "and I'll eat them myself."

I was reminded of this ingenious expedient to secure a comfortable seat at the fire, when nothing but some such expedient could have succeeded, by the device to which a person resorted, to get a good place at the rival Astley's at Greenwich Fair. He had been among the latest to enter, and all the good places were pre-occupied. Incomparably the best place, at the threepenny rate of admission, was on a sort of wooden stair, by means of which the descent to, and the ascent from, the *gallery* was to be achieved. The top of this stair was on a level with the *pit*; but it was densely peopled, or, as the play-bills say, "crowded in every part." "Is there no room here?" inquired a cunning-looking countryman, as he entered the place.

No one made him any answer.

"Do, frien's, try to make room for a poor fellow," said the clodpole-looking personage, whose accent proved to demonstration that Yorkshire claimed him as her own.

The appeal was ineffectual: the portion of the threepenny audience, who had planted themselves in that particular locality, only stood more closely together.

"Well, coom, I'm cu'st, if ye bean't an uncivil set of people," said the Yorkshireman, after a momentary pause.

Censure seemed to have as little effect on them as an appeal to their politeness; for no one moved an inch to accommodate the new-comer. He paused a few seconds again, when an idea flashed across his mind. He quietly went out of the place, and let fall a green cloth curtain, which answered the purposes of a door, behind him. In a few seconds afterwards, he put the curtain partially aside, and thrusting in his head, bawled out in stentorian tones—Halloa! clear the stair there; mind your eyes; here comes a horse." Not recognising the Yorkshireman in the abrupt and unexpected apostrophe, and supposing that one of the horses about to ride in the ring was really coming down the stair, there was an instantaneous and unusual rush into the gallery. In two or three seconds, the stair was completely cleared, and the Yorkshireman promptly took possession of the best part of it.

The humorous remarks made by the audience, while the performances were proceeding, often caused bursts of laughter. In this respect, indeed, the "Merriman" found that he had a number of formidable rivals. A young woman, of a copper complexion, who monopolized the performances on the tight-rope, said, in a very affected "fine lady" sort of air, addressing herself to the Clown—"Chalk my feet, Sir." "Vouldn't your face, too, be all the better of a little on't, Ma'am?" observed a rustic-looking young man among the audience, with a dryness of manner which told with much effect. "I say, Miss," exclaimed another voice, "Vy do you always dance the same thing? Vy don't you give us 'Jack in the Green?'" Or "Vy don't you jump 'Jim Crow,' young voman?" said a third. "You hold your tongue, Sir," rejoined the Clown, authoritatively, looking in the direction of the place whence the last voice proceeded. He had scarcely uttered the words, when a small apple abruptly alighted on the crown of his head, which was graced with a nightcap of many colours. Putting his hand to the part of his head which was hit, he looked half-piteously and half-indignantly around the audience. "Who did that?" he inquired. "Nobody," answered a voice, after a momentary pause. "It was an anonymous blow," said another, amidst bursts of laughter from all parts of the house, which so disconcerted and annoyed poor "Mr. Merriman," that he was not able either to make a passable new joke the whole evening afterwards, or to retail his old ones with the slightest spirit.

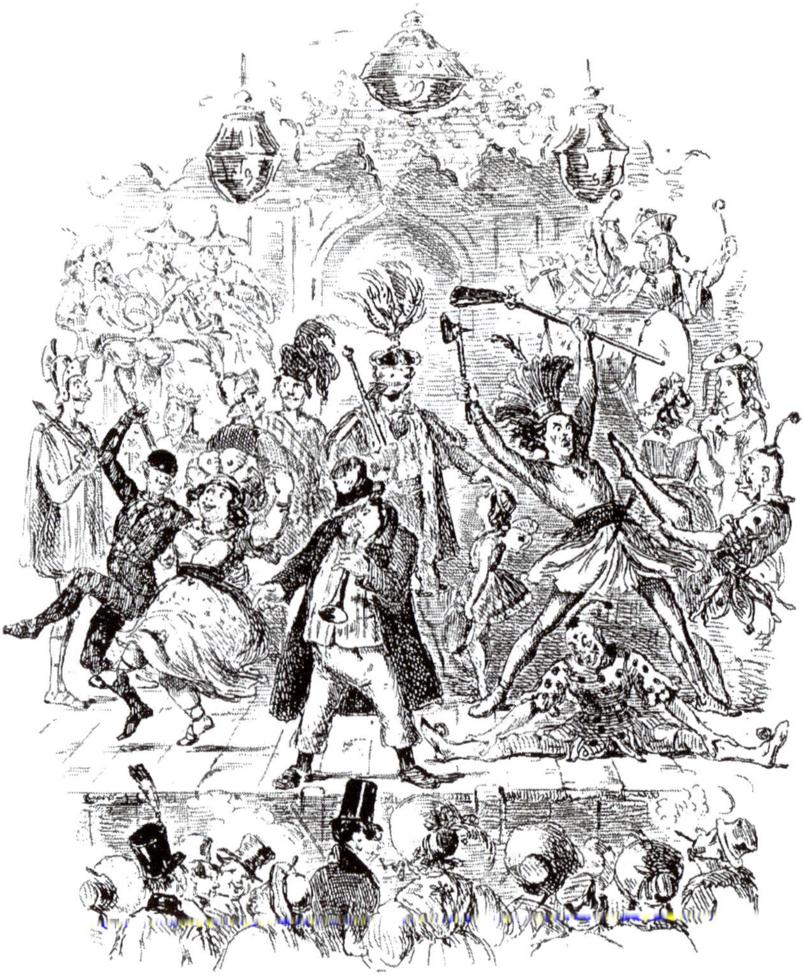

It appeared to me, that the scene on the sort of hustings outside the theatres at Greenwich Fair, was better worth seeing than the performances within. There the female actresses, if they should be dignified with the name, strutted about in a mock majesty which, in their circumstances, was truly ridiculous. They were decked out in all manner of tawdry trumpery: they had feathers in their heads; but they were such feathers as I had never seen before. Their dresses, which, I regret to say, I am incompetent to describe, were thickly studded with small fragments of some sort of metal, which, though seemingly opaque enough in ordinary circumstances, did "cast reflections" when in contiguity to the blazing lights at the front of the theatre. Nothing could be more amusing than the would-be dignified step and consequential air with which these female supporters of the drama walked about before the assembled thousands; many of whom were, no doubt, both wondering and admiring spectators. Had these actresses been so many princesses, they could not have assumed greater importance, or appeared more stiff and stately in their carriage. I thought, as I saw them, of the females who grace the train of Jack-in-the-Green, on May-day. I thought of poor Black Moll, who is doomed to dangle, dressed in white, above the doors of marine-store dealers, from one end of the year to the other. And yet, if these histrionic personages were happy in the thought of their fancied superiority to all other females, why should any one seek to undeceive them? It was edifying to witness the different objects which the parties in the front of the theatre had in view. The girls in question thought of nothing but themselves: they sought to show themselves off. The proprietor, on the other hand, had nothing in his head but how he could best induce persons to patronize his performances. His wife was wholly intent on taking money, and giving checks in return; while a poor fellow most assiduously played the Clown outside, in the character of "Spring-heeled Jack," because he saw that his own interests were bound up with those of his master.

Gambling was carried on in Greenwich Fair to a very great extent, and in every variety of form. There were roulette, hazard, and other games, at which persons might play for stakes of from one shilling upwards to a sovereign; and many were the simpletons these notable hell-keepers victimised on the occasion. This class of gamblers took care to carry on their business in places not exposed to the general gaze. There was, however, no lack of gamblers on a smaller scale, whose operations were performed in the light of day, and in the most densely crowded parts of the market. There were wheel-of-fortune men; and most promptly did these machines and their proprietors fleece the simple, soft-looking lads who ventured their pence on particular articles. In order to decoy and deceive the unsuspecting cockneys, or gullible youths belonging to Greenwich or its neighbourhood, they took care to keep the wheel in constant motion. For this purpose, they had severally one or two cunning young rascals in their employ, who, while they saw others losing their money, contented themselves with merely looking on and encouraging greenhorns to "try again," on an assurance that they were certain of gaining next time. They appeared all the while not only to have no connection with the professed gamblers, but not even to know them. The moment others ceased to turn round the wheel, they put down their halfpence; and when trying for two or three articles unsuccessfully several times, the sly rogues would, in a careless sort of tone, as if the result of the purest accident, make the observation—"Oh, never mind; can afford to lose a few browns this time; gained half-a-crown's worth of things with three hap'nies, a short time ago." This most probably has the effect of inducing some simpleton to try his luck, thinking in his own mind that there can be no good reason why he should not gain a half-crown's worth of things for his three hap'nies as well as others. He begins, and that moment the other ceases to turn round the wheel; the three hap'nies are gone, but bring no half-crown; no, not even one penny's worth of the trinkets so invitingly spread out before him. He tries other three; they follow their predecessors: three more; they are not a whit more lucky. His losses reach a shilling; he goes on, provided he has the money, until, possibly, he loses half-a-crown. Even if he does happen to gain some article which he fancied was worth eighteen-pence, he finds, on inspection, that it is not worth twopence; so that he is cheated under any circumstances.

The thimble-riggers mustered strong, and appeared to drive a profitable business. They were to be found in all the leading openings to the Fair. Much as every man of healthy moral feeling must disapprove of thimble-rigging, there was no resisting an occasional hearty laugh at the awkward circumstances under which some of the victims betrayed their simplicity. "Who lifts the thimble that kivers the pea next time?" was the everlasting question of the proprietor of the pea, the three thimbles, and the half-crown table, on which the gambling took place,—whenever there was a pause in the play; and as he spoke, he shifted about the thimbles with an almost sleight-of-hand celerity. "I knows the one it's under," whispers a greenhorn to some acquaintance.

"Are you quite sure?"

"Quite sure; could swear I knows it, and no mistake.

"Then what a fool you are, not to put down your shiners!"

Thus appealed to, down goes the crown, half-crown, or shilling, as the case may be, and the simpleton lifts the thimble. Imagine his surprise, his confusion, and mortification, when he raises it, and finds that neither pea nor anything else is there. He can scarcely credit the evidence of his eyes. He would, indeed, live and die in the belief that it had miraculously vanished, did not the proprietor lift another thimble, and exhibit the pea to the gaze of all present.

"It's all the fortune of war," says the thimble-rigger, moving about his thimbles. "Who tries his luck next? Can't always gain."

A person who is supposed, by those unacquainted with the roguery of these fellows, to have no connexion with or knowledge of them, but is one of themselves, now advances, and learning from some secret signs made by the mover of the thimbles, the one under which the pea lies, says, "I lay five shillings I know the thimble which kivers the pea."

"Here you are, Sir," says the other, putting down his five shillings.

The supposed stranger puts down his crown: he raises the thimble, and the pea is there. He is inwardly congratulated on his good luck by the spectators around, they still imagining that he is as much a stranger to the thimble-man as themselves.

"Never grumbles when I loses, though better pleased when I wins. Who tries their luck next time?" says the thimble-rigger, shifting the thimbles on the table so slowly that no one can fail to perceive under which one the pea is. "I see the one," says some greenhorn, in audible tones.

"Which one is it?" inquires the party, in a whisper, who had tried it last time, and who, though one of the rogues who are robbing simpletons, is still imagined to be a perfect stranger.

"That one," pointing to the thimble under which the pea actually is.

"Five shillings again, that I unkiver the pea," says he, with some eagerness throwing down his crown.

"Done, Sir," says the thimble-rigger, throwing his five shillings on the table also.

The supposed adventurer raises the thimble, and, behold, the pea is again there.

"You were quite right, Sir," says he, in agreeable accents, to the simpleton, at whose pockets a dead set is made.

"Oh, I knew it," says the latter, giving a consequential nod of his head, by way of showing that he was perfectly aware of his own superior imaginary discernment.

"Just speak a moment," whispers the coadjutor of the thimble-rigger to the intended victim.

"Certainly," says the latter; and both retire a few steps together. "Why don't you try for yourself, and fleece these fellows?" says the supposed stranger.

"Woy, I doan't know," says the poor simpleton.

"Suppose we run halves, when we see a good chance?" observes the other.

"Well, I doan't care, though I do," answers the greenhorn.

They return to the table: the thimble-rigger again shifts the thimbles, and invites "any one" to try his luck.

"I doan't know vich is the right 'un this time," remarks the unsuspecting simpleton.

"Ah, but I do," says the other, with a knowing nod of the head. "That's it," pointing to a particular thimble.

"Then let us put down one half-crown each."

"By all means," says the other, throwing down his half-crown.

The thimble-rigger puts down his crown, and the partner of the poor greenhorn raises the thimble; but, lo! there is no pea there. He affects to be marvellously surprised; the thing is beyond his comprehension; however, he swears that he won't be mistaken next time. Another venture is made, but with no better success. There is no limit to his amazement; the thing is altogether so unaccountable, that there must be some legerdemain in it. He gives a still greater oath that he won't be wrong next time: the victim ventures once more, on the solemn assurance that his partner in the speculation knows the right thimble this time. The latter lifts it, but still no pea is there. He stamps with his feet, strikes his forehead with his hand, makes extraordinary faces, swears so liberally both at the pea and himself, and altogether acts his part so well, that, though the victim will not trust his discernment any more, and consequently abstains from any more gambling, yet he never once questions his honesty; to say nothing of his not even suspecting that he is a partner in the robberies of the thimble-rigger. In this and various other ways simple persons, whether from London or the surrounding country, are sure to be fleeced, if they are foolish enough to play at the game of thimble-rigging.

The proprietors of swings, at the last Greenwich Fair, must have made a little fortune; for most liberally were their "machines," as they themselves call them, patronized. Not one, so long as I was there, was idle for a moment. The poor fellows who had to keep them in motion had no sinecure of it. Everybody else seemed half-perishing of cold; they were perspiring with the warmth caused by their unremitting labours. It was curious to see how differently the different persons who committed themselves to the swing felt, when they were driven about in the air. Many of the females—and I have always observed, though I cannot account for the circumstance, that the women are the greatest patrons of swings—many of the females got up a few screams in the plenitude of their affected alarm at being moved to and fro at so rapid a rate in the air; some shrieked because they did actually feel frightened, when suspended between earth and heaven, though they apprehended no such fears before entering the car; while others laughed, joked, and seemed to be as comfortable as if they had been swinging in the air all their lives. Many were made dizzy and others sick, by the motion; but there was no help for them; the swing must go for the usual time for the sake of those who were neither dizzy nor sick, but expected, and had anything to the contrary been proposed would have insisted, that, as they had paid for their pleasure, so they must have it.

The last, but assuredly not the least, of the attractions of Greenwich Fair are the dancing booths. By nine o'clock, they began to be tolerably attended: by ten they were full; that is to say, as full as was consistent with the requisite space for dancing. And yet, though thus as full as they could conveniently hold, one of the parties interested stood at the door inviting, or rather imploring, "ladies and gemmen," to go in, expressly assuring them that there was room for two or three hundred more. Most liberally was the light fantastic toe tripped: the girls seemed in perfect ecstacies: they would have danced themselves to death, if necessary; but it fortunately was not, there being at least two of them to every one of the masculine gender. Dancing, as they say in the provincial newspapers, when speaking of balls in the county town, "was kept up to a late, or rather early hour." The floor, or rather in this case the ground, was not cleared until three in the morning; and even then, the girls were loth to relinquish their occupation of it. On one side of the booths, immediately adjoining the dancing-ground, were four or five boxes constructed on the coffee-house principle, where the "partners" swigged porter or sipped brandy-and-water, as the case might be, by way of refreshing themselves after their dance. In some cases, the arms of the *beau* were to be seen affectionately entwined around the neck of the *belle*, while in others, all the indications and demonstrations of love were given by the young ladies.

Though Greenwich Fair, properly so called, is confined to the very narrow space before mentioned, it virtually extends for one or two miles along the leading roads which communicate with the town. In saying this, I do not so much mean the various stalls for the sale of sweetmeats and trinkets which are scattered so liberally about the suburbs, as to the number of idlers and holiday people who are seen lounging about in all directions, but especially at the doors of public-houses. I will venture to say, that there is scarcely a public-house within two miles of Greenwich that cannot boast, provided the weather be at all endurable, of its ten or twelve loungers about the door; some of them drinking gin, others swilling porter, a third class smoking away at a most furious rate, while many are doing all three together. Inside these public-houses, again, there is hardly standing, far less sitting room. They are crowded in every part with thirsty customers. You are quite at a loss whether most to admire the talking or quaffing capabilities of the inmates. There is nothing but noise and porter: all talk and all drink at once. To be sure, an attempt is now and then made to introduce a little harmony, in the way of a song; but the audience are anything but harmonious in hearing it. A vocalist might just as soon hope to hush into silence the roar of the ocean by the eloquence of his dulcet strains, as one might expect to restore silence in a public-house audience, on Greenwich Fair day, by the melody of his voice. Orpheus *may* have achieved the wonders ascribed to him by the power of his melody, though I have always doubted it: he *may* have tamed savage animals through means of his musical talents; but I am quite certain that all the modern Orpheuses in the world—if there be any Orpheuses extant—would not silence or secure the attention of the biped savages who, at Easter and Midsummer, patronize the public-houses in Greenwich and the neighbourhood. They are a set of inveterately noisy beings: the unrestrained exercise of their lungs seems indispensable to their enjoyment of the jovialities of the occasion.

If what I have said, as to the distance to which Greenwich Fair extends itself, in the shape of crowded public-houses, be true as regards the Woolwich and other roads, it is far more so as respects the road leading to London. The whole of that road, indeed, from Southwark to Greenwich, may be said to be only an arm of Greenwich Fair, in so far as the public-houses are concerned. Though the distance be five miles, they are all crowded with customers, and each has as much business, in the porter and gin way, as it is able to go through. I have, indeed, a strong suspicion, that many hundreds who start from town with the full intention of visiting the Fair, and sharing its fun and frolics, put a period to their journey—in other words, make a full stop—before they have gone half the way. One is cold; he goes into a public-house on the road to get a glass of spirits to warm him: a second is hot, and he must have ditto to cool him: a third is thirsty, and he must have a pint of porter to wet his throat; while a fourth, more candid than either of the others, says, according to the old story, that he must have the spirits or the porter because he likes them. But whatever be the motive or the pretext which induces the persons to whom I refer, to go into the public-house, if once they have crossed its threshold, there is no getting them out again until it is time to return home: there they enjoy, if enjoyment it may be called, their Greenwich Fair. All the public-houses on the road from London to Greenwich were, at the last Easter Fair, so much crammed with customers who had been on their way to the fair, or were on their return from it, that the windows were literally blocked up with them.

But not to attempt any further description of Greenwich Fair, let me advert for a moment, in conclusion, to the moral tendencies of that fair. I am sure the facts I have stated, and the efforts I have made to describe the scenes which are to be witnessed during the three days at Easter, and the three at Midsummer, on which the fair is held, must have satisfied every reflecting mind that nothing could be more injurious to the morals of the parties who take part in those scenes. They engender and foster habits of idleness, frivolity, intemperance, and dissipation of every kind. They deaden every delicate and amiable feeling, and inspire notions and lead to practices which are altogether unworthy of rational beings. Thousands of youths of both sexes have had to date their physical as well as moral ruin from attendance at the fairs in the metropolis and its vicinity. Every one knows how difficult it is to eradicate a taste for such scenes when once formed: it must be gratified at all hazards. It never can be satiated: the more the craving after such things is fed, the more urgent and large in its demands does it become. A love of drink and debauchery, in all their varied forms, when once inspired, is very rarely to be abated, much less annihilated, until both the mind and the constitution are irretrievably ruined by its indulgence.

I am convinced there are thousands of both sexes who are now living in the greatest destitution and wretchedness, who have to date their misery from their attendance in early life on metropolitan and suburban fairs. Some such instances have come under my own personal observation; nor could it be otherwise. It is impossible for young persons, whose judgment is immature and whose moral principles want vigour, to witness the scenes which are exhibited on such occasions, and to take part in the transactions which take place, without doing the morals of the individuals great injury. And while there is so much to condemn in these fairs, there is not a single thing to commend. I do not know of one rational amusement among all the exhibitions which are to be witnessed. I would be the last man to prohibit the youth of either sex from enjoying their amusements and recreations; but surely there could be no difficulty in pointing out the means of their rationally and innocently enjoying themselves at particular seasons of the year, instead of their patronizing the "shows" and "sights" which are to be witnessed at metropolitan and suburban fairs.

The inference from all this is plain. The civil authorities ought to put an end to such fairs. They are only the relics of a barbarous age, and were established for the sake of an ignorant and brutalized people. They are altogether unworthy the nineteenth century: they are especially unworthy a civilized and Christian land. They are a positive reflection on the intelligence and moral feeling of those in authority over us. To abolish them would be to wipe out a foul blot which now stains the character of the country, and would confer a lasting benefit on the lower classes of the metropolitan community. And that benefit would soon be visible in the improved morals and ameliorated condition of thousands of those classes. I am no advocate for the interposition of the magistrate in the amusements of the people, as a general principle; but where the obvious and admitted tendency of public amusements is of a most immoral nature, then, indeed, a case is made out for magisterial interference.

In the mean time, and until the civil authorities shall see it to be their duty to interfere, and put down the remaining fairs in the metropolis and suburbs, let me impress on parents, masters, and mistresses, that a great moral responsibility is incurred by them when they do not, in cases where they could do it with effect, interpose the shield of their authority to prevent their children or their servants from visiting such places. How parents, who have any regard for the morals or well-being of their offspring, can allow them to visit fairs, is to me altogether unaccountable. Even in the case of servants, masters and mistresses, who have any regard for the welfare of their domestics, ought to discountenance, in the most marked manner, their visits to such places.

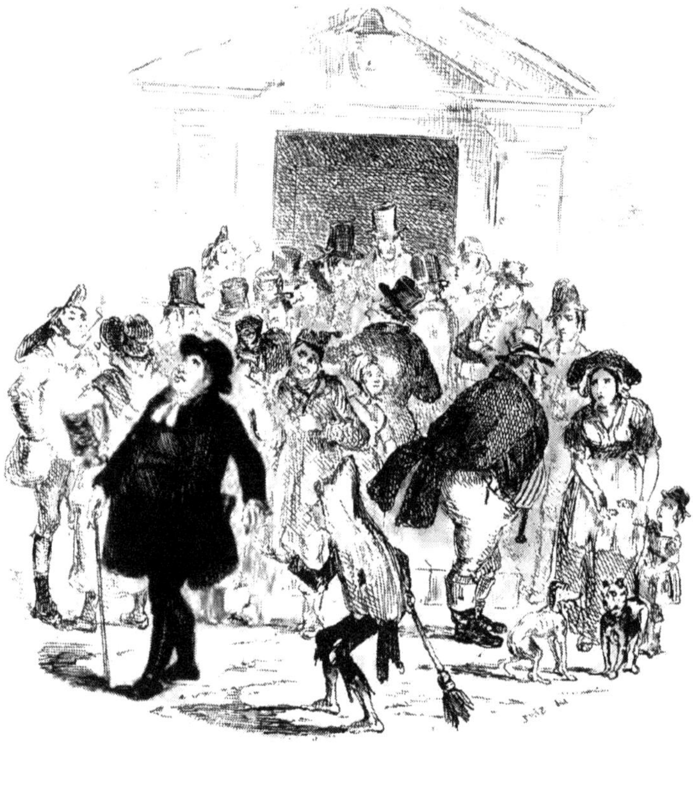

CHAPTER X.

COURTS OF REQUESTS.

Their origin and objects—Their number, and for what districts—The Westminster Court of Requests—The Court of Requests for the Borough—The Court of Requests for the City—The Court of Requests for the Tower Hamlets—The County Court of Requests—Mode of proceeding in the Courts of Requests—Number of suits instituted for various sums—Curious cases decided at these courts—Instances given—The Useless Cradle—Board, Lodging, and Love—The Ultra-Radical Patriot—The Cambric Pocket-Handkerchief—An Affecting Case—Utility of Courts of Requests.

Courts of Conscience, or Requests, as they are now generally termed, are very important institutions in the estimation of the lower classes, though known only by name to those in affluent or easy circumstances. They were first established about 300 years ago. They are Courts for the recovery of small debts by an easier, more summary, and cheaper process than exists in the ordinary courts of law. I shall, in an after part of the chapter, describe the course of proceeding adopted by the plaintiff when prosecuting his claims in one of these Courts, which are, in the hands of persons who can properly administer their affairs, exceedingly excellent institutions; and it is matter of wonder that they are not much more general throughout the country. The entire number in England and Wales does not exceed sixty-three or sixty-four. The number in London is five. They are, beginning at the west-end of the metropolis, the Court of Requests for Westminster—the Court of Requests for the borough of Southwark—the Court of Requests for the city of London—the Court of Requests for the Tower Hamlets—and the Court of Requests for the county of Middlesex. In the constitution and powers of these courts there is a very considerable dissimilarity, which I shall afterwards point out.

The Westminster Court of Requests is situated in Castle-street, Leicester-square. The administration of its affairs is intrusted to 242 individuals, called commissioners. These must be all respectable rate-payers, residing within the jurisdiction of the Court. That jurisdiction extends over the parishes of St. Margaret, St. John the Evangelist, St. Paul, Covent Garden, St. Clement Danes, St. Mary-le-Strand, St. George, Hanover-square; St. James, and St. Anne; and over that part of the

Duchy of Lancaster which adjoins the liberty of Westminster. It will thus be seen that the jurisdiction of this Court is very extensive. Formerly it was deemed advisable to have two Courts of Requests for Westminster; but two or three years since, one of them was abolished, and its business transferred to the court in Castle-street. The commissioners are chosen by the vestries of the various parishes in the district. The period for which they are elected is only one year; but they can be set aside at any time by the vestries. As the duties of the office are performed gratuitously, many of the commissioners very rarely attend. Others take great pleasure in presiding over the Court, and are very seldom absent. The average number to be seen on the bench is from five to eight. The Court has no power to adjudicate in cases above forty shillings. It is armed with the power of enforcing its decisions, by imprisoning the debtor for any period not exceeding seven days.

The WESTMINSTER COURT of REQUESTS can boast of a very fair antiquity. It was first constituted nearly a century since. There are two principal clerks, chosen by the commissioners, for assisting in conducting the affairs of the court. Their remuneration is not by fixed salary, but by certain fees on the various cases which are tried. In a parliamentary return moved for in the year 1835, the following statement on this point is given: "The emoluments of the Westminster Court of Requests consist of what remains therein, after paying the rent, taxes, and repairs of two court-houses; the salaries of the under clerks and officers, and for the printing, stationery, and other expenses incidental thereto; and are divided amongst the High Bailiff of Westminster and the two principal clerks of the said court; and were, for the five preceding years, as follows:

YEARS.	TOTAL AMOUNT OF EMOLUMENTS.			HIGH BAILIFF'S PROPORTION.			EACH CLERK'S PROPORTION.		
	£.	s.	d.	£.	s.	d.	£.	s.	d.
1830	1642	19	11	446	0	3½	598	9	9¾
1831	1221	3	9	333	13	11	443	14	11
1832	1095	18	2	315	8	1	390	5	0½
1833	1078	17	5	313	12	8½	383	2	4½
1834	996	6	7	280	10	7½	357	17	11¼

This would give an annual average amount of emoluments to each of the two principal clerks of about 400*l.*; but as one of the Courts—the one, namely, which used to sit in Vine-street, Piccadilly—has been since abolished, the reduction in the expenses must, I should suppose, be sufficiently great to make the emoluments of each of the principal clerks of the Westminster Court of Requests worth at least 450*l.* a-year.

The number of cases tried in this court in the course of a year, are, on an average, about 13,000. In 1830, the number tried was 15,439; in 1831, 13,766; in 1832, 14,429; in 1833, 13,567; and in 1834, it was 12,790. I have not access to official information respecting the number of cases tried in either of the intervening years. The average yearly expenses consequent on the hearing of the cases is, as near as may be, 2000*l.*; making the average expense of each case to be about three shillings and sixpence. An attempt has been made by the clerks to ascertain the average amount of money sued for in the course of a year; but as a great many cases are settled out of court, after the summonses have been issued, and the various amounts in such cases not being entered on the books, the clerks are afraid to hazard even a conjecture on the subject.

The Southwark Court of Requests has a more extensive jurisdiction than that of Westminster. It embraces the town and borough of Southwark, Lambeth, and the eastern half of the hundred of Brixton. It possesses the power of imprisoning the person in execution, but not for a longer period than one hundred days. It is competent to hear and decide all cases under five pounds. Five commissioners are necessary to constitute a Court when the debt is above forty shillings; and three, when the debt is under that sum. The number of commissioners is 152. They are chosen in the same way as the commissioners for the Westminster Court of Requests. When the Court was established, I have not been able to ascertain. The average number of suits instituted in this court every year, is rather above 16,000. Perhaps there is no other Court of Requests in the kingdom in which there is so slight a variation in the number of cases tried, as in the Court of Requests for Southwark. This fact will appear from the following statement of the respective numbers for the five consecutive years preceding the year 1835. In 1830, the number was 16,441; in 1831, 16,751; in 1832, 16,192; in 1833, it was 16,250; and in 1834, it was 16,450. The total average amount of debts sued for each year is about 22,000*l.*; and the annual average expenses of prosecuting this amount of debts is close on 4000*l.*, giving, as in the case of the Westminster Court of Requests, the expenses of each case at somewhere about three shillings and sixpence. The Southwark Court usually sits two days each week. It begins its sittings at ten o'clock, and rises at half-past three. It is divided into two branches; an arrangement indispensable for getting through the great quantity of business, the transaction of which devolves on the commissioners. Instead of the chief bailiff for Southwark, and the two principal clerks, as in the case of the Westminster Court of Requests, deriving their emoluments from fees on the cases which are tried before the Court, they have severally a fixed yearly salary. That of the chief bailiff is 500*l.*, while one of the two principal clerks, namely, Mr. Meymott, has 750*l.* The other chief clerk, viz., Mr. George Drew, receives the same amount of yearly salary as the chief bailiff, which I have stated to be 500*l.* The Court sits in Swan-street.

The Court of Requests for the City of London, as re-constituted under an act passed a few years since, has not the power of imprisoning for debt until after an execution has been issued against the goods, and the officer has made a return in writing under his hand that the party has no goods, or not sufficient goods. The jurisdiction of the Court is confined to the city of London. Formerly it was only competent to adjudicate on sums under five pounds; but two years since an act was passed extending its authority to all sums under ten pounds. This was understood to be only an experiment on the part of the legislature, with the view of seeing whether or not satisfactory decisions were likely to be given by courts constituted like Courts of Requests; and whether there could, if I may use the expression, be a union of "good" with cheap and expeditious justice. The experiment has been completely successful. It is doubtful, indeed, whether, on the whole, more equitable decisions could have been given in the disputed cases, had they, as formerly, been tried before the superior courts. The consequence in all probability will be, that the power of Courts of Requests generally will be extended to all sums under ten pounds; a circumstance which will be conferring a great benefit on the community. It is questionable, indeed, whether it might not be advisable to extend the authority of these courts to all sums under twenty pounds. It is certain, that originally they were competent to the adjustment of all disputed sums under the above amount; for it is to be recollected, that three hundred years ago, when Courts of Requests were instituted, two pounds were equal to at least twenty pounds of our present money. This, however, is a point which it would be inconvenient to discuss in this place.

The number of commissioners in the City Court of Requests, varies from time to time. The City being divided into twenty-five wards, commissioners from each ward sit for one calendar month in every two years; the month of October in every other year having two wards. The number of commissioners appointed by each ward varies, according to the size of the respective wards, from 25 to 50. Three commissioners constitute a court in the case of all claims under two pounds; seven are requisite when the amount in dispute exceeds that sum.

The clerks of this Court receive no fees whatever: they have fixed permanent salaries. The principal clerk has a salary of 400*l.* per annum; the first assistant clerk receives 300*l.* a-year for his services; and the second clerk has 200*l.*

The Court sits twice a-week: on Wednesdays and Saturdays. It is divided into two branches, as in the case of the Southwark Court of Requests. If the amount of business transacted in this court goes on diminishing as rapidly as it has done for several years past, it will soon become very trifling indeed. For the five years previous to 1835, the extent of the decrease in the business of the court will be ascertained from the subjoined statement:—In 1830, the number of cases decided was 9502; in 1831, it was 8825; in 1832, it fell down to 8161; in 1833, to 6951; and in 1834, it was reduced to 6560; being a diminution to the extent of nearly one-third in the short space of five years. What the cause of this rapid and regular decrease in the business of this court is, I have not the means of knowing; neither have I yet been able to ascertain whether the extension of the powers of the court to all cases under 10*l.* has as materially contributed to its regaining its former amount of business, as was expected. The total amount of debts sued for in those years is thus given: In 1830, 15,546*l.* 14*s.* 6*d.*; in 1831, 14,769*l.* 10*s.* 2*d.*; in 1832, 13,429*l.* 6*s.* 10*d.*; in 1833, 11,901*l.* 7*s.*; and in 1834, 10,702*l.* 3*s.* 4*d.* The total amount of costs incurred during the same years was 2437*l.* 1*s.* 3*d.* in 1830; 2254*l.* 17*s.* 4*d.* in 1831; 2082*l.* 4*s.* 8*d.* in 1832; 1777*l.* 10*s.* 6*d.* in 1833; and 1645*l.* 15*s.* 3*d.* in 1834. The Court sits in a street leading from Basinghall-street to the courts of Guildhall.

The COURT OF REQUESTS for the TOWER HAMLETS is of the same antiquity as the Westminster and Southwark courts. It was at first restricted to adjudication on sums under forty shillings; but five or six years since, an act was passed extending its powers to any sum not exceeding five pounds. It still does a great deal more business than any of the other courts. Some years ago, it did half as much as all the others put together. The fact of so immense a number of cases being brought before this Court is easily accounted for. Its jurisdiction not only embraces a great extent of space, and a vast amount of population, but that jurisdiction happens to include by far the poorer neighbourhoods of the metropolis. When I mention that among the districts within its jurisdiction are Whitechapel, Shoreditch, Norton Folgate, Bethnal Green, Mile-end, Bow, Shadwell, Wapping, Ratcliff, Poplar, and Stepney, I am sure the reader, who knows anything of London, can be at no loss to account for the immense number of small debt cases which are brought before the Tower Hamlets' Court of Requests. Ten years ago, the average number of cases decided at this court was nearly 30,000 every year. Since then, the number has been decreasing at a very rapid rate. In 1831 I find the number of cases disposed of was 25,890; in 1832, it was 24,194; in 1833, the latter number had undergone a reduction of nearly 7000, the returns for that year only giving 17,318 cases. In the following year, namely, 1834, the diminution seems to have been to about half the extent of the preceding year; for the number given is 13,818; while in the year 1835, the latest period to which the returns have been made to government, the number is still further reduced to 11,760. It will thus be seen that, in the short space of five years, a decrease from 25,890 cases to 11,764, has taken place in the number tried in the Court of Requests for the Tower Hamlets, which is more than one-half. To account for this very singular diminution is more than I can undertake to do. Whether the circumstance, that for some years past the commissioners have not, in point of fact, had the power of imprisoning those who cannot or will not pay, though they possess that power nominally*; whether, I say, this fact has anything to do with the decrease, I cannot tell. It may be, that the knowledge that the commissioners are not in a condition to imprison debtors, and that consequently the chances of recovering the sums sued for are diminished, has had the effect of making the smaller class of tradesmen more cautious in giving credit, and the same consideration may also have indisposed the creditors to prosecute.

The commissioners of this court are 240 in number. They are annually chosen by the parishes embraced in the jurisdiction of the Court. It is supposed that the average number that attends is twenty. The Court days are Tuesday and Friday. Its locality is Osborne-street, Whitechapel.

The Tower Hamlets' Court of Requests affords an apt illustration of the well-known adage: "Most work, least pay." The principal clerks, though they are much harder worked than the clerks of any of the other Courts of Requests in London, have the smallest pay of any. They have only 300*l.* each, without one sixpence in the shape of fees.

I come now to the MIDDLESEX COUNTY COURT of REQUESTS, which is situated in Kingsgate-street, Holborn. Its constitution is altogether different from that of any of the other courts to which I have referred. Mr. Sergeant Heath, or his deputy, Mr. Dubois, with the assistance of three individuals called jurymen, are

---

* This, perhaps, requires a word of explanation. The statute establishing the court, invests the commissioners with the power of imprisoning for forty days; but the magistrates for the city of London and the County of Middlesex having refused to permit debtors from the court to be received into the prisons under their control, the power is nominal only.

the sole dispensers of justice in it. The trio of jurymen are usually men of the humblest class of tradesmen; a fact which may be at once discovered not only by their wardrobe, but by their general demeanour. With few exceptions, they look as if they were quite unacquainted with the forms and attributes of the trial by jury. It is due, however, both to Mr. Sergeant Heath and Mr. Dubois to say, that they are generally exceedingly clear and always strictly impartial, in submitting the various cases to their consideration; so that their own innate notions of what is right must necessarily, in the majority of cases, conduct them to such a conclusion as the claims of justice require. These jurymen are chosen by the sheriff of the county. There is a new set, or, as an author would say, a new series, every court-day. It is sometimes highly amusing to see them deliberating—if deliberation it can be called, where the verdict is almost invariably returned within half a minute of the conclusion of the judge's address; it is, I say, sometimes highly amusing to see them deliberating as to the conclusion to which they ought to come. How it happens I know not; but I have always observed that the juryman who is in the middle, sits up in the miserable box allotted to them as erectly, as if it were one of his special duties to do so; and that his co-jurors on either side, just before agreeing on their verdict, stretch out their necks sufficiently far to enable them to look each other in the face, after their heads have been brought within eight or ten inches of each other. The appearance of their craniums on such occasions always reminds me of three stars—thus ***. But let that pass. Unaccustomed as men in their lowly sphere of life must necessarily be to the appellation of gentlemen, it is not to be wondered at if they should manifest extreme gratification when Mr. Sergeant Heath or Mr. Dubois, arrayed in their barrister's gown and bands, while their heads are ornamented or disfigured — whichever the reader pleases—with a wig of ample dimensions—addresses them with the most entire gravity, as "Gentlemen of the jury." It has sometimes afforded me a positive pleasure to see the happiness of the jurymen who assist in dispensing justice at the Middlesex Court of Requests, while their ears were being greeted with the appellation of "gentlemen of the jury." Whether it is merely imagination on my part, or not, I cannot tell; but I have always supposed that Mr. Sergeant Heath lays particular emphasis on the word "gentlemen."

Mr. Sergeant Heath was appointed to the presidency, or judgeship—call it which you please—of the CountyCourt of Requests in 1819; so that he has been nearly twenty years engaged in the dispensation of justice in Kingsgate-street. He has no fixed salary; but he has what is much better than any ordinary salary; for he has all the fees consequent on the administration of the affairs of the court to himself. To be sure, he has, as he himself says, to pay out of these fees the expenses of the premises in Kingsgate-street, the salaries of deputy, clerks, criers, and other officers, if other officers there be; but after he has done all this, there is a very handsome residuum behind. I cannot say—I am told nobody but himself can—what the exact amount of his annual emoluments from the court are; but I am assured they cannot be under 1500*l.*; while the probability is, they are nearer 2000*l.* One day, when I was in the court, about a month since, no fewer than four hundred summonses were issued, which, at one shilling and fourpence each, would give thirty pounds for that day alone. And as the court sits about one hundred days every year, or twice every week; and as further expenses are incurred on a large proportion of the summonses, it may easily be conceived that the learned sergeant has a very lucrative berth of it. As I have not been able to obtain access to any official accounts relative to the average number of cases now tried annually at this court, I will not hazard any conjecture on the subject: some years since, the average number was about 12,000.

The Kingsgate Court of Requests exhibits quite a scene on the morning of every Monday and Thursday. The very place, indeed, may be said to constitute a scene of itself. It is a most miserable-looking place, whether viewed from the outside or inside. It has a very dilapidated appearance outside: it is an old desolate-looking building. Mr. Heath pronounced it to be in a state of entire disrepair, on his becoming officially connected with it nineteen years ago, and he then intimated to the House of Commons the necessity of erecting a new court altogether. His views on the subject must, however, have soon after undergone a change; for the court still continues in precisely the same state as it was then. It is a very commodious place inside; capable, I should think, of easily accommodating, in a standing position, five hundred persons. I have seen as many as three hundred in it at a time, and yet there was ample unoccupied space. A more gloomy, ruinous, miserable-looking place inside is scarcely to be seen. It is in striking keeping with the condition of the great majority of those who have business to transact in it. A more ragged assemblage, or one on whose countenances, as well as exterior generally, the genius of destitution and wretchedness is more visibly impressed, it has never been my lot to witness. The spectacle is painful to behold: the appearance of most of the parties is that of squalor personified. Their counetnances are blanched, except, indeed, in those cases in which the application of water to them is of so rare occurrence that the actual complexion is concealed from the view. See what numbers of wretched mothers are there, with children in their arms, and children at their feet! The miseries of the parents are inherited by the young innocents: the latter are a mass of rags. Poor things! they know not what warmth or comfort is: the cravings of their appetites are but seldom gratified. To have a full meal—I speak, of course, of those of them that are weaned—would, indeed, be an era in their youthful existence. The smile and the laugh, which are so characteristic of their period of life when the stern hand of adversity does not press upon them, are looked for in vain in the countenances of the children who hang about their mothers in the Kingsgate-street Court of Requests. Sickliness, and want, and suffering, are so distinctly marked in their innocent faces, that no one with the slightest pretensions to humanity could look on them without feeling the deepest compassion for them. There they have sometimes to stand, as have also their mothers, for two or three hours; and this, too, in cases without number, without having tasted food that morning. If charitable individuals, on whom Providence has conferred the riches of this world, are anxious to find out, in a metropolis in which there is so much imposition and deception, real objects for their benevolence, let such persons attend the County Court of Requests on a Monday or Thursday morning, and before they are an hour there, they will meet with many miserable creatures, who are as legitimate objects of charity as any wretches on whom the sun ever shone. But this is a point to which I shall have occasion to advert again, before closing the chapter.

And yet, amidst the scenes of destitution and wretchedness which are to be witnessed in this court, you see no proofs of commiseration on the part of any one present. The miserable creatures who are summoned are too much occupied with their own wretchedness to admit of their passing a thought on the woes of others around them; while the hearts of the parties at whose instance they are summoned, are thoroughly steeled against all sympathy or pity for their victims. As regards the officers of the court, again; they are so habituated to spectacles of the deepest wretchedness, that they are scarcely conscious of seeing them at all. You hear them call out the names of the parties who are to appear before the Court, with the most entire carelessness. All is bustle and confusion as well as wretchedness in the place. The one-half, in moving from place to place, tread upon the toes of the other half. Some are constantly advancing to the inner part of the court—which I shall have to describe presently,—while others are as constantly retiring from it. In short, there is a perpetual movement in court: to this movement, the bustling officiousness of the servants often contributes in no small degree. In the middle of the place there is a wooden erection, having a good deal of the appearance of a pulpit, which one of the officers of the court ascends, and then proclaims aloud the names of the parties whose cases have reached a certain stage in their progress towards adjudication. At the farthest part of the court, and directly fronting the door, is a small apartment—not, I should think, exceeding fifteen feet square—which is specially set apart for the administration of justice. Like the body of the court, it is a miserable dingy-looking place: the windows never—not even by accident—look clean. At the farthest end, after you enter at a side-door, you see an easy antiquated chair, the covering of which is considerably the worse for the wear. Before this chair is placed a small wooden erection, which reminds one of the desks which the parish-schoolmasters in Scotland, have in one of the corners of their school-rooms. Mr. Sergeant Heath, I understand, dignifies this humble wooden affair with the name of "the bench of justice." In that arm-chair, and with his desk before him, sits the learned sergeant, his ruddy countenance beaming with good nature, yet indicating all the fancied dignity of a monarch on his throne. His wig and his bands rather awkwardly contrast with his self-complacent manner. The first article is but sparingly powdered, and the second badge of judgeship partakes of the smoky appearance of the place generally. On the learned gentleman's right hand sits an intelligent pleasant-looking clerk; while three forms, of the most homely description, seven or eight feet long, are tenanted by plaintiffs, defendants, and others, mingling together in perfect confusion. They are all impatient spectators of what is going forward, because they are anxious to know what their own fate is to be. On the left of Mr. Sergeant Heath are the jury; consisting in most cases, as before remarked, of three plain simple-like men, who, regarding the learned gentleman as oracular on all matters pertaining to the court, rarely dissent from his view of the case, as indicated in his summing-up and charge. In a range of seats, or rather forms, adjoining the jury-box, are always to be seen fifteen or twenty persons, who appear in the various capacities of witnesses, friends, or uninterested spectators. At the end of an antiquated table, directly opposite the learned sergeant or his deputy, Mr. Dubois, stand the plaintiff and defendant, and their witnesses, when the last are giving their testimony. Here the opposing parties wrangle with one another, and very often interchange, notwithstanding the repeated interpositions of the Court, some remarkably choice specimens of abuse. Innumerable are the amusing scenes which have been witnessed in this spot. Two or three specimens of these, I will give in an after part of the chapter. On the table lies a large-sized New Testament, bound in calf-skin; but the appearance of the binding is all the worse for the wear. In some places, you see the manifest effects of too much kissing. Everybody has heard the story of the Pope's toe being nearly kissed away by the frequency and energy with which it is kissed by his devotees: what wonder, then—*if* the story about the pontiff's toe be true—that the binding of the New Testament which belongs to the establishment in Kingsgate-street, should be considerably impaired by the extensive system of kissing which prevails in that court on the Monday and Thursday of every week? How many lips have been impressed on that particular copy of the New Testament! How many false oaths, alas! have been given on it! This is no uncharitable judgment. No man who has ever been in Kingsgate-street court could help being shocked, while he has witnessed the swearing to opposite facts, which is of such frequent occurrence on the part of plaintiff and defendant.

For the information of those who may be unacquainted with the subject, it may be right to describe now, in as few words as possible, the process by which a suit in the County Court of Requests may be prosecuted towards a conclusion. First of all, you go and take out your summons, which will cost you one shilling and fourpence. This is served by one of the officers of the court on the party against whom you have brought the action. Three clear days must be allowed the defendant before he is to appear in the presence of Mr. Sergeant Heath or Mr. Commissioner Dubois. If he appear in answer to the summons, the expenses of the action, which, as in other law courts, always fall on the losing party, are as moderate as the most inveterate Benthamite, or lover of cheap justice, could desire. They will only be three shillings and sixpence; two-and-twopence being charged for the hearing of the case. If the party summoned do not appear, then you get your order against him, which will cost you two shillings. If the order does not insure his appearance that day eight days, then you get it made absolute on the payment of two shillings more, when the case is decided against the party without being heard; and after some other little but necessary forms are gone through, you can attach his person. The expenses in prosecuting a case up to the last stage in this court, cannot exceed eight shillings and tenpence.

The proceedings and expenses in the other Courts of Requests are so very similar, that it is unnecessary to refer to them in detail.

The number of suits instituted for amounts under forty shillings, where the jurisdiction of the courts extends to all sums under five pounds, compared with the number above forty shillings, must have struck every one who has turned his attention to the subject. I have not access to very recent official information on this point; but in the Southwark Court of Requests, some time ago, the number of summonses issued out of the court, in one year, for debts under forty shillings, was 10,051; while for debts above that sum, the number was only 3331. The number of attachments on debts under forty shillings was 1623; and for sums above forty shillings, 683. The number of executions on debts not exceeding forty shillings was, in the same year, 2872; for sums above forty shillings, it was 1375. The number of persons sent to prison at the instance of this Court of Requests, in the year in question was 830. So that if we take this as a fair specimen of the proportion of the imprisonments to the number of summonses issued, or the suits instituted, that proportion would be as one to sixteen. In other words, out of every sixteen persons summoned to the Courts of Requests one goes to prison, either because he cannot or will not pay the debt. Of the 13,381 suits instituted in the Southwark Court of Requests, in the year referred to, only 10,389 were heard and determined by the Court; the remaining 2992 were settled by the parties out of doors. There are always a great many debtors who resist payment to the last moment; that is to say, until the executions are on the eve of being enforced. In the year alluded to, the number who did not pay until "executed," as the technical phrase is, was 1553.*

I have referred, in a former part of the chapter, to the odd and amusing illustrations of human character which are so often afforded at the London Courts of Requests. In attempting to convey some idea of a few of those cases, it is proper to remark, that no description can do justice to them, as so much depends on the looks, tones, gesture, and manner altogether, of the parties. The first case may be entitled

THE USELESS CRADLE.

A little, massy-headed, bushy-haired man, with a bluff face answered to the name of Adam Crofts, the moment the crier of

---

* Since the above was written, I have got access to the following interesting information respecting the imprisonment of parties sued in the Southwark Court of Requests. It appears that from August 1823 to 1831, a period of eight years, the number of debtors committed to the County Gaol was 6104; and the number to the Borough Compter was 1992; making a total of 8096. Of the 6104 committed to the County Gaol, there were 2047 whose debts did not exceed twenty shillings; 1798 whose debts did not exceed forty shillings; 996 whose debts did not exceed sixty shillings; and 1263 whose debts did not exceed one hundred shillings. Of the same number, 4482 were imprisoned for a period not exceeding twenty days; 828 for a period not exceeding forty days; 380 for a period not exceeding sixty days; and 414 for a period not exceeding one hundred days. In the case of those committed to the Borough Compter, the results are similar.

the court pronounced it. He appeared before the commissioners with the view of soliciting their aid to enable him to accomplish what he had failed to effect by any means within his own reach, namely, to compel or induce—he did not care which—a Mrs. Mortimer, a plain-looking woman, seemingly about two-score years of age, to pay him the sum of seven shillings and sixpence, which he alleged she owed him; but which position she totally denied.

Commissioner—What are you, Mr. Crofts?

Mr. Crofts—I *am* Mr. Crofts, Sir, please your honour.

Commissioner—I did not ask your name.

Mr. Crofts—I beg your vorship's pardon; I thought you did.

Commissioner—What I wish to know is, what are you?

Mr. Crofts (with great surprise)—What am I?

Commissioner—Yes; what are you? The question is a very plain one.

Mr. Crofts—Well, Sir; and didn't I give you a plain answer?

Commissioner—You hav'n't given me any answer at all.

Mr. Crofts (increasingly surprised)—Yóur vorship's surely mistaken. Didn't I say I was Mr. Crofts?

Commissioner—But how do you live?

Mr. Crofts (looking quite enlightened)—Oh! that's what you mean, Sir, is it?

Commissioner—That's what I mean. Pray, then, answer the question.

Mr. Crofts—Oh, certainly, please your honour. Why, then, I live by my profession.

Commissioner (looking very much surprised)—You don't mean to say you're a professional man?

Mr. Crofts (with a self-complacent smile)—I certainly do, your vorship.

Commissioner—And to which of the professions may you belong?

Mr. Crofts—To the profession of a cradle dealer. (Roars of laughter.)

Commissioner (greatly surprised)—To the what profession?

Mr. Crofts—To the profession of a dealer in cradles. (Renewed laughter.)

The several commissioners on the bench looked at each other, and heartily joined in the general laugh.

Commissioner—Well, this is the first time that I have heard dealing in cradles dignified with the name of a profession. But let that pass; pray what is your claim against this woman?

Mr. Crofts (smoothing his hair with his hand)—I'll tell you in as few words as I can, Sir.

Commissioner—Well, be as brief as possible.

Mr. Crofts—You must know, your vorships, as I makes and sells the best cradles as vas ever made or sold; and this 'ere voman, who had only been married six months, comes past my shop, where I always keeps a large assortment of cradles of every variety and at all prices, and all warranted town-made, and the best quality as—

Commissioner (interrupting him)—Mr. Crofts, have the goodness to confine yourself to the case before the Court, and don't wander into an eulogium on the merits of your cradles.

Mr. Crofts—I beg your honour's pardon for transgressing (digressing); I'll not forget your polite hint, Sir. (Loud laughter.) Well, as I vas a-sayin', she comes one day past my shop door—and I should tell your honours that her husband was with her—and says she to me, says she, "What is the price of your cradles?" Says I to her, "Do you want a cradle, Ma'am?" Says she to me, "Of course I do, or I would not ask you the price of the articles." "Well, dear, I *don't* think you do at *present*," suggested Mr. Mortimer, mildly. "I must be the best judge of that myself, I should fancy," answered Mrs. Mortimer, with a contemptuous toss of the head. "No doubt, you must, Ma'am," said I, anxious, as your vorships will readily believe, to do business. "Very well, love," said Mr. Mortimer, soothingly "if you think you want a cradle, have one by all means." "I may require it by-and-by, and it's just as well to have it in the house beforehand," remarked Mrs. Mortimer, in a subdued tone. And says, I, "You're quite right, Ma'am; by all means, you—"

Commissioner—Pray, Mr. Crofts, be so kind as to come to the debt at once, and don't waste the time of the Court with extraneous matter of this kind.

Mr. Crofts—Vell, your worship, I'll tell you the remainder of it in half a minit. Mrs. Mortimer steps into my shop, and pointing to a particular cradle, said, "Vat's the price of that 'ere?" "Nine shillings, and not a farden more nor less," says I. "It's not worth it," says she. "I tell you vat it is, Ma'am; if you get as good a cradle as that von in this 'ere town at the money I'll make a present of it to you gratis for nothing." (Loud laughter.) "I'll only give you—"

The Court—Really this is insufferable trifling with the Court. Don't tell us anything about what you asked, or what she offered, but, say at once, did the defendant buy the cradle, and what did she give you for it?

Mr. Crofts—Bless your honours' hearts, she didn't give me nothin' at all for it, and that's the reason vy I have brought her here to-day. (Renewed laughter.)

Commissioner—Tell us, then, what she engaged to give

Mr. Crofts—She engaged to give me seven-and-sixpence, and to——

Mrs. Mortimer—It's all false, your honours; and so it is; I never bought the cradle at all.

Mr. Mortimer—It's all false, your vorships; she never bought the cradle at all.

Mr. Crofts (surprised, and with much energy)—There, now; there's a couple for your vorships! She *did* buy the cradle.

Mrs. Mortimer (with great vehemence)—I did not, you lying rascal. You sent it to us without being ordered.

Here the Court suggested to the defendant that she must not allow herself to be carried away by any temporary heat, and Mrs. Mortimer nodded to the Court in token of her intention to act on the suggestion.

A Commissioner—Did you, Mr. Crofts, send the cradle to the defendant without her having concluded a bargain with you first?

Mr. Crofts—I'll tell you how it is, Sir. I said the harticle was as vell worth nine shillings as it was worth twopence-halfpenny. "Seven-and-sixpence is the outside value of it," says she. "Let me send it to you, and you can pay it at any other time," says I. "Seven-and-sixpence," again said she; "I vouldn't give a farthin' more for it." And so saying, her husband, who spoke very little, and herself quitted my premises. I sent her the cradle next day, saying I would accept her offer.

Commissioner—When was this?

Mr. Crofts—Eighteen months ago.

Mrs. Mortimer—Don't believe him, gentlemen; it was only *seventeen* months and some odd days. (A laugh.)

Commissioner—Well, Mrs. Mortimer, you appear to have got the cradle at your own price; what are the grounds on which you refuse to pay the money?

Defendant—I never made the bargain; he did not accept the offer when I made it; and therefore I was not bound to take the article next day.

Commissioner—But why then did you let the cradle into the house? Why did you not return it at once?

Mrs. Mortimer—I did not like to be uncivil, your honours; but I sent a message to him next day to come and fetch the cradle away, as I did not vant it. He may have it now.

Mr. Crofts—But I *von't* at this 'ere distance of time. She would now return it, because as how she has no prospect of ever having a little inhabitant to it. (Peals of laughter, during which Mrs. Mortimer looked quite savage at the distinguished vender of cradles.)

Mrs. Mortimer—You're nothing but an impertinent—

The Court—Mrs. Mortimer, we cannot allow any such expressions; you must restrain yourself while here.

Mrs. Mortimer, putting her handkerchief to her eyes, sobbed out—"It's werry, werry difficult to do, Sir."

It was eventually decided that as Mr. Crofts had not accepted Mrs. Mortimer's first offer, but sent the cradle next day when she had changed her mind as to the probability of requiring a cradle at all as a piece of household furniture, and as the cradle had never been used, Mr. Crofts must take back the article, and try to dispose of it to some other customer.

"To some one who will have use for it," sighed Mrs. Mortimer.

"Vich is more than you ever vill," growled Mr. Crofts, as he turned about to waddle out of the court, manifestly chop-fallen at the result of his case. As Mrs. Mortimer left the court, she was overheard to say to a female acquaintance, that she would never again bargain for any article merely because she might possibly at some future day want it; and to express her regret that she should have priced the cradle, or bought, as she had done, a quantity of baby's clothes, before she was justified in believing they should be required.

BOARD, LODGING, AND LOVE.

The next case called on for decision was, perhaps, still more ludicrous. A thin-faced vixen-looking woman, evidently approaching her fiftieth anniversary—if, indeed, she had not already celebrated it—with a visage as dark in the complexion, and as shrivelled in the appearance, as an Egyptian mummy,—summoned a rather smart-like personage, of more than the usual altitude, for the sum of 1*l*. 16*s*. 6*d*. The plaintiff gloried in the name of Sarah Cleek, while the defendant assumed, or really was baptised in, the fashionable cognomen of Augustus Standish.

Mr. Dubois (to the plaintiff)—Pray, madam, what are you?

Plaintiff—I'm Missis Cleek, my lord; as honest and wirtuous a hooman as ever lived, though I should not say it myself.

Mr. Dubois—I did not ask your name, nor question your honesty or virtue. What I want to know is, how you get your living?

Mrs. Cleek—I takes in men, your honour.

Mr. Dubois—Do what?

Mrs. Cleek—Takes in men, your wurtship.

Mr. Augustus Standish (sarcastically, and twitching a sharp prominent nasal protuberance which ornamented his face)—She's spoken the truth, Sir. She *does* take in men.

Mr. Dubois—Takes in men! For what purpose, pray?

Mrs. Cleek—For the purpose of keeping them, Sir.

Mr. Dubois looked quite amazed, as if the whole affair had been thoroughly unintelligible to him; but a juryman speedily

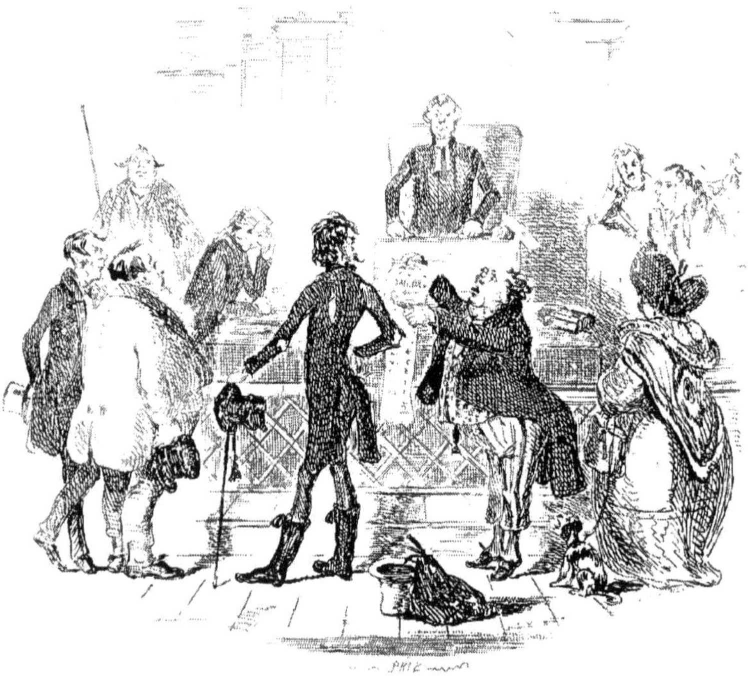
PHIZ

enlightened his ignorance, by suggesting that the woman simply meant that she kept lodgers.

"Oh! I see," said the commissioner, with some emphasis, as the light broke in on his mind. "Oh! I see the thing quite clearly. You're a lodging-house keeper?"

Mrs. Cleek—I keeps lodgings, Sir.

Mr. Dubois—And the defendant, I presume, was one of your lodgers?

Mrs. Cleek—That's just it, my lord; and he was the most worthless one I ever had.

"You were not always of that opinion, Mrs. Cleek," interposed Mr. Augustus Standish, casting an expressive glance at the plaintiff.

Mr. Dubois (addressing the defendant)—You be silent now, Sir; you shall be heard in your defence presently.

"Very good," said Mr. Augustus Standish, drily.

"He was so very bad, I presume, that you could not keep him?" suggested Mr. Dubois, addressing himself to the plaintiff.

"You've just spoken the truth, my lord," answered Mrs. Cleek, with manifest gratification.

Mr. Augustus Standish delivered himself of a tremendous groan.

Mr. Dubois—And you have summoned him for arrears of board and lodging?

Mrs. Cleek—Your lordship's right again.

Mr. Dubois—And pray what is the amount?

"Here it is, my lord," said Mrs. Cleek, handing Mr. Dubois a slip of paper, which looked as dirty as if it had just made the descent of the chimney.

Mr. Dubois (looking at the account)—One pound sixteen shillings and sixpence.

Mrs. Cleek—That's the sum.

Mr. Dubois (to the defendant)—Well, Mr. Augustus Standish, how do you propose paying this sum?

Defendant—Paying it, Sir?

Mr. Dubois—Yes, paying it!

Defendant—Don't owe the woman a farthing, Sir.

"Oh, you good-for-nothing wagabond!" vociferated Mrs. Cleek. "How *can* you say so?"

Mr. Dubois—Do you mean to say, then, that you have paid the amount?

Defendant—I never owed her a fraction in my life, Sir.

Mr. Dubois—What! do you mean to say that you never slept and boarded in her house?

Defendant—I did certainly stay in her house for fifteen or sixteen days; but that was in the capacity of a friend, not as a lodger. It was on her own invitation.

Mr. Dubois (to the plaintiff)—Is this the fact, Mrs. Cleek?

Mrs. Cleek—He's the mouth of a ——

"Stop, stop, madam, if you please," interrupted Mr. Dubois, anticipating what was coming; "there must be no improper language here. You mean," he continued, "to say it's not true?"

Mrs. Cleek—There's not a morsel of truth in it, my lord. I got acquainted with him some months ago, greatly to my sorrow (here Mrs. Cleek sighed, and attempted to cry); and having told me, about three weeks since, that he was going to quit the house in which he lodged and boarded, because, as he said, the landlady wished him to marry her, which he would not agree to, as he liked another landlady better, I said to him, "Come, and stay in my house."

Mr. Dubois—I suppose you fancied that you were yourself the *other* landlady he liked better?

Mrs. Cleek held down her head, and sighed out—"Well, if I did, he gave me abundant reason to think so."

Mr. Augustus Standish seemed all this time as miserable as if he had been on the rack.

Mr. Dubois—But though he accepted your invitation to reside in your house, he was not so affectionate to you as you had been led to expect?

"He's a brute, my lord!" replied Mrs. Cleek, with frightful emphasis; and after a momentary pause she added, bursting into a violent fit of crying, "He *is* married; he *has* a wife in the country, my lord. It was fortunate I made the discovery, my lord. We were one day sitting at breakfast together, and he said, says he, 'Mrs. Cleek, may I trouble you for another slice of toast?' Here I should state," continued Mrs. Cleek, by way of parenthesis, "that he has an awful stomach, my lord (loud laughter): he devoured the toast much faster than I could make it, and swallowed up everything as vas ever put before him. (Renewed laughter, mingled with sundry groans and inward curses from Mr. Augustus Standish.) Vell, as I vas a saying, says he, 'Mrs. Cleek, will you oblige me with another slice of that very excellent toast?' 'Certainly, my——' Before I had finished the sentence, the postman knocked at the door; and on my opening it 'Mr. Augustus Standish—sixpence-halfpenny,' says he, holding out a letter to me. I took the letter, and carried it to the brute, and——"

"Mrs. Cleek, you must be more guarded in your language," said Mr. Dubois, interrupting the voluble and violent plaintiff.

"I vill, my lord; and yet I'm so aggrawated that it's not wery easy to be calm. Vell, I carried the letter to——"

"But pray, madam, what has all this to do with the debt for which you have summoned the defendant?" interposed Mr. Dubois, again interrupting Mrs. Cleek.

"A great deal, my lord, as you shall presently see. I carried the letter to him, and immediately, on looking at its direction, the fellow exclaimed, wiolently striking his forehead with the palm of his hand—'A letter from my vife, by —— !—From my sister, I means,' he immediately hadded, correcting himself, for the purpose of deceiving me; but it vould not do. 'Oh! you wagabond! you're married, are you?' says I. 'Voll,' says he, with a terrible groan, 'I *am* married, Mrs. Cleek; there's no good in denying it.' 'You're vorse than a —— to deceive and injure a helpless female voman like me,' says I, werry hindignant; and we had a quarrel, my lord, and I turned him out of the house; and *that's* the vay in vich he howes me the money."

Mr. Dubois—I don't yet see very clearly the connexion of all this with the debt of one pound sixteen shillings and sixpence. However (to Mr. Augustus Standish), you hear the woman's statement?

Defendant—I do, Sir; but I owe her nothing. We had been acquainted for some time, and she implored me to reside in her house as her friend. She thought, Sir, that if I were once there, she would take me in, in the matrimonial way; but I am too old a bird to be caught with chaff. When she found that I had a wife, she kicked up such a rumpus, and behaved so very like a fury, that I would not have staid an hour longer in the house, though she had given me the world to do so.

Mr. Dubois—Pray, Sir, how do you live?

Defendant—In the best way I can.

Mr. Dubois—What is your profession?

Defendant—No profession at all, Sir.

Mr. Dubois—What! have you no means of living at all?

Defendant—Why, Sir, I think I must have the means of living some way or other, otherwise I could not *live;* but what the means are, is really more than I can tell. (Laughter.)

Mr. Dubois—I suppose you live by your wits?

Defendant (with much archness of manner)—Yes, Sir, when they will keep me.

Mr. Dubois—I presume you delude foolish women like the plaintiff, with the notion that you are attached to them, and then partake of their mistaken hospitality?

Defendant—Always happy, Sir, to quarter on the enemy. (Laughter.)

Mr. Dubois (looking again at the account)—I see that eight-and-sixpence of the sum is for borrowed money: that, Mr. Augustus Standish, you must pay to the plaintiff. I think the one as bad as the other. Mrs. Cleek evidently had a matrimonial design on you, when inviting you to reside in her house; while you pretended kindness to her for the purpose of living comfortably at her expense. You are both tarred with the same stick.

AN ULTRA-RADICAL PATRIOT.

The next case forcibly illustrates the folly of neglecting one's trade or calling, however humble it may be, for the promotion of political objects. The plaintiff, Mr. Robert Smith, was a most industrious journeyman brass-founder; and the defendant, Mr. John Snaggs, pursued the same calling, but was noted for the preference he gave to politics over his business. His employer, like himself, was a Radical of the first water, so that he did not lose his place in consequence of his devotion to the cause, as he always called it, of pure patriotism. The defendant had a wife and five children; but he was ready, like Hannibal of old, to "sacrifice them on the altar of his country." In so far as they were concerned, he was a patriot of the most disinterested class. If there was to be a meeting at the Crown-and-Anchor, at White Conduit House, or at Mr. Savage's in Circus-street, there Mr. John Snaggs was sure to be without fail. His wife might be sick at home, or his five children might be within a few removes of death from starvation: no matter; these were things that never moved him. He was in the habit of speaking at those meetings; and come what might at home he must needs parade his patriotism on such occasions. His wife and children were as dust in the balance compared with universal suffrage, annual parliaments, and the vote by ballot. But the character and notions of the man will best appear from what took place in court.

The plaintiff, Mr. Robert Smith, on his name being called, immediately stepped forward to state the case. He had all the appearance of a hard-working, but honest man. He was respectably attired; and while his countenance afforded every indication of a serene and happy mind, it formed quite a contrast with that presented by the defendant, Mr. John Snaggs. His apparel was a mass of rags; it was the surprise of everybody how his clothes hung together. His toes were unmannerly enough to intrude through his shoes; which last exhibited a most marked aversion to Warren's jet blacking, Hunt's matchless blacking, or any other blacking, no matter by what name it is called. His hat had once gloried in a crown; but at what period was a problem which none but himself could solve; if, indeed, even he could do it. His elbows imbibing the spirit of liberty which glowed so intensely in his own bosom, disdained to be confined within the limits of his coat-sleeves; but boldly making their way through the cloth, displayed to all around their warm attachment to freedom. In the article of apparel, indeed, he proved himself to be perfectly independent from top to toe. His face looked as if it had not been washed for a week; while any one might have sworn that his beard had not been visited by a razor for at least a fortnight. His cheeks were lank and pale, and his hands bony. He had all the appearance of a man to whom the advent of a good dinner must have proved an exceedingly rare occurrence. His wife, with a child in her arms, was equally famished-like in appearance; a circumstance which will not appear surprising when the reader is made acquainted with what follows.

The plaintiff, having been called on to state his case, proceeded to say, that the debt for which he had summoned the defendant had been contracted—if that was the proper word—under very unusual circumstances. He lived in the same house, and on the same floor as the defendant. One day, in the previous week, having expected two of his wife's friends to take pot-luck with them, his wife had determined on treating them to a little boiled beef, cooked in her own incomparable style. With this view she had purchased ten pounds of the best beef to be had in the neighbourhood, which was duly put into a pot in boiling water. The hour appointed for dinner was two o'clock. At half-past one, Mrs. Smith had occasion to go out for a quarter of an hour, to get some necessary articles for dinner. She left the key in the door, and desired the defendant or any of his family, to answer her bell if any one rung while she was absent. This was at once agreed to, and Mrs. Smith accordingly proceeded to market. "Fancy," said the plaintiff, "my wife's surprise, when she found on her return, that her friends had arrived, but that the sirloin of beef was taken out of the pot." Her first impression was, that they must have ate it themselves by way of revenge for her being out of the way when they arrived; but she soon discovered that this was an untenable hypothesis. On discovering the felony which had taken place, she held up her hands in amazement and uttered various exclamations, which the plaintiff did not think proper to repeat to the Court, and which I think it were improper to repeat here. She rushed into the room of the defendant, for the purpose of inquiring whether his wife or children had seen any one in her apartment while she was out. The Court would imagine her surprise, when she found that defendant and children were making a hearty repast, or rather *had* made a hearty repast, for it was nearly all gone, on her identical piece of meat. As soon as her astonishment and indignation would allow her to articulate, she charged the defendant with the theft, but he stoutly and unblushingly denied it. "Where, then," said she, "did you get that piece of beef on which you have been dining? It is very unusual to see *you* with a sirloin of beef." "That may be, Mrs. Smith; but usual or unusual, you see we have had as prime a piece of beef as ever——" He was interrupted by one of his own children, a boy about six years of age, who, in the simplicity of his innocent soul, exclaimed, "Oh, yes, father; now you know you did take it, for I saw you." At this critical juncture, Mrs. Snaggs, who had been out of the house for the last half hour in the hope of obtaining some provender for her famishing children, made her appearance; when the matter being stated to her, she soon extorted a reluctant admission from the defendant that he had stolen plaintiff's wife's dinner; for which offence he made a thousand apologies, and pleaded poverty, urgent necessity, and so forth. But though in the first instance he exhibited so much apparent contrition for his transgression of the laws both of good neighbourhood and moral rectitude, he afterwards chose to be insolent, and pretty plainly applied, in this particular case, his Radical notion of a universal equality of the good things of this life. It was under these circumstances that the plaintiff had summoned him to pay the price of the sirloin of beef, amounting to seven shillings and fourpence. He had preferred making the thing a matter of debt, though he had no doubt he could have proceeded criminally against the defendant.

Commissioner (to the defendant)—Well, Mr. Snaggs, you hear the plaintiff's statement; what do you say to it?

Defendant (putting himself into an oratorical attitude. as if he had meant to speak for an hour)—I have a few words to say, Sir, if you'll allow me.

Commissioner—Well, let them be as few as possible, and see that they be to the point.

Defendant—I'll take care they shall, Sir. The facts of this here case, then, are these. (Here Mr. Snaggs assumed a very consequential aspect, stretching his neck, and placing his arms a-kimbo.) The facts of this here case are these: Feeling as every man vot is born an Englishman ought to feel, that we live in wery ewentful times; and that it is every man's duty to hoppose despotism, and to stand up for liberty, I vent to Savage's Great Hall in Circus-street, to make a little bit of a speech, the night afore this here *haccident* 'appened, in support of Dr. Wade's motion for uniwersal sufferage; and I had——

"Really, my man," interrupted the Commissioner, "I don't see what earthly connexion universal suffrage or Dr. Wade's motion, or any other body's motion, has with your appropriating to yourself the dinner of the plaintiff. You must confine yourself to that."

Defendant—I was a-going your honour, to show that I had patriotism enough in my composition—for you must know, Sir, that I am an Englishman born—to sacrifice all indiwidwal considerations for the sake of the people of this 'ere country, by leaving my employment on that occasion to perform a public duty. And, Sir, I do think, that ven these wagabonds of Tories——

Commissioner (harshly)—There must be no politics here. If you do not, Sir, come to the case before the Court at once, I shall not hear a word from you.

Defendant—I'm sorry, your vorship, that I should say anythink as vould offend you. I never vishes to offend any one, but the enemies of England. I vas jist about to say, that feeling as I do, that until we have uniwersal sufferage, this country can never be prosperous or happy; and Dr. Wade and Mr. Feargus O'Connor having——

Commissioner—Really, I cannot allow this to proceed any longer. I must at once order——

Here Mrs. Snaggs, with tears in her eyes, starvation in her face, and a ragged, half-famished child in her arms, stepped forward, and begged leave to say a few words. Permission having been granted her to speak, she stated that her husband had, for more than twelve months, formed an intimate acquaintance with five or six persons calling themselves patriots (a term of which she did not know the meaning), that they talked about nothing but what they called politics; and that ever since he had formed this acquaintance, he had neglected his business to attend public meetings, leaving her and his five children whole days without a particle of food. Her own tears and entreaties, and the cries of his children, had not produced the slightest effect upon him. On the day in question, as she understood from her eldest daughter, he had been so besieged by the cries of his children while she was out, for something to eat, that, in a fit of desperation, he had gone into their neighbour's apartment, and abstracted from the pot the beef intended for their dinner. The poor woman added, that unless he gave up his patriot acquaintances and public meetings, and attended to his business, there would be no other resource for her and the children but throwing themselves on the parish.

The plaintiff here stepped forward, and said he believed that the facts of the case were such as Mrs. Snaggs had represented.

Commissioner (to the defendant)—You ought, Sir, to be ashamed of yourself. You have not only brought your wife and family to the brink of starvation, but if you persist in your "patriotism," as you call it, you will speedily ruin yourself for ever. See the difference between the circumstances of the plaintiff and your circumstances; he has every comfort which a person in his station can wish, while you and your family are in the greatest destitution; and all this because he attends to his business, while you neglect yours. You must pay the plaintiff the value of his piece of beef; and I hope you will take a lesson from what has passed. If you give another such practical illustration of your theory respecting the equality of the good things of life, you may have to answer for it in a different place.

The defendant, who up to this time took the matter quite coolly, now seemed, all of a sudden, quite impressed with a sense of the folly of his conduct, and solemnly pledged himself to abjure "patriotism" and politics in future, and to attend to his business. His poor wife heard his declaration with unspeakable joy, while the plaintiff said the circumstance afforded him so much pleasure, that he would not only not exact payment for the beef, but would cheerfully be at the loss of the expenses of the summons.

THE CAMBRIC POCKET-HANDKERCHIEF.

The next case afforded infinite amusement to all present. A slovenly-dressed but rather good-looking, portly female, seemingly about her twentieth year, and calling herself Jane Jukes, summoned Peter Straps, a stalwart, half-starved young man with carroty hair, a marked squint in his right eye, and a beard which had evidently been suffered to vegetate without interruption for at least six or seven days,—for the sum of three shillings and sixpence.

Commissioner—What is this for, Miss Jukes?

Plaintiff—Please, Sir, I'm not Miss; I'm Missis Jukes.

Commissioner—Well, no matter, Mrs. Jukes. Pray tell us what the three-and-sixpence is for?

Mrs. Jukes—It's for a cambric hankercher (a handkerchief), please your vorship.

Commissioner—What! are you a handkerchief merchant, then?

Mrs. Jukes—Oh! nothin' of the sort, your vorship. The money is for a hankercher lent, not sold.

"Sir, 'she lies like truth,' as Shakspeare says," interrupted the defendant, folding his arms on his breast, and assuming a very theatrical attitude.

Commissioner—Sir, you hold your tongue at present; you shall be heard by-and-by.

"She *gave* it me, Sir. Did I not, Mrs. Jukes (turning to the plaintiff), on receiving it from your hand, say, in one of the poems of the immortal Bard of Avon,

> 'Gifts then seem
> Most precious, when the giver we esteem?'

And did I not——"

Mr. Straps was evidently about to launch into some long exposition of the circumstances under which the handkerchief had come into his possession, when he was again interrupted by the Court, and admonished, in pretty plain terms, that if he did not wait until his turn came, the case would be decided against him.

Commissioner (to the plaintiff)—Proceed with your case.

Mrs. Jukes—If I must tell all, Sir, this 'ere man is a hactor at a small twopenny theatre in Newton-street; and he said to me, one afternoon, says he, "Jane, my love, we are a-goin' to have a werry affectin' piece of tragedy to hact to night; and as I am to have the principal character, and will have a good deal of cryin' to go through, per'aps you would oblige me by the use of your slap-up hankercher for the occasion?" "My cambric hankercher?" says I. "The best hankercher you've got," says he. And so I gave him my cambric hankercher, my lord.—(Laughter.)

Commissioner (to the defendant)—Well, Sir, what have you got to say this?

Mr. Straps (heaving a sigh, and looking very sentimental)—The truth is, your worship, there was a sprinkling of the tender passion in the matter. As Shakspeare says in his "Love's Labour Lost,"

'As love is full of unbefitting strains;
All wanton as a child, skipping, and vain;
Form'd by the eye, and therefore like the eye,
Full of strange shapes, of habits, and of forms:
Varying in subjects, as the eye doth roll
To every varied object in his glance,
So———'"

"Pray, Sir, if you please," interposed the Commissioner, before the hero of the sock and buskin had time to finish his sentence; "pray, Sir, if you please, tell us what you have got to say yourself, and not what Shakspeare says?"

Mr. Straps—Ah, Sir! as Shakspeare says, in his beautiful drama of "Troilus and Cressida,"

"Didst thou but know the inly touch of love,
Thou would'st as soon go kindle fire with snow,
As seek to———'

"Really, Sir," said the Commissioner, again interrupting Mr. Straps, "this is trifling with the Court. It must not be permitted."

Mr. Straps—Well, Sir, I should be sorry to act improperly, or to say anything disrespectful to this Court; but as I was about to state, I was at the time devotedly attached to Mrs. Jukes, and believed her to be equally so to me in return. We were, Sir, in short, pledged to each other; and under those circumstances, I thought the handkerchief was given me as a gift. But, Sir, as Shakspeare says, in his "Julius Cæsar,"

> "Ah, me! how weak a thing
> The heart of woman is!"

I soon had reason to believe that her affections were placed upon another. I remonstrated with her on the subject, which drew from her such a demonstration, as at once brought to my mind the expressive lines of the Bard of Avon, when he says, in his comedy of "Taming the Shrew,"

> "A woman mov'd, is like a fountain troubled,
> Muddy, ill-seeming, thick, bereft of beauty;
> And while it is so, none, so dry or thirsty,
> Will deign to dip or touch one drop of it."

The tragedian or comedian—for I do not know whether Mr. Straps considered tragedy or comedy his legitimate walk—delivered this latter quotation with so much rapidity, that he had got to the end of it before the Court could interrupt him. "Yes, Sir," he resumed, "she resembled a perfect fury. As Shakspeare has it,

> 'She was the very——'"

The Court—Don't give us any more of Shakspeare, but come to the point at once.

Mr. Straps—I will, your worship. I assure——

"There's not a word of truth in what he says, your honour," shouted Mrs. Jukes, interrupting Mr. Straps. "It's all false; I cut the akvantance, because he said to me, one day, that if I did not behave myself to his satisfaction after we was married, he would give me the bag, and summons my father for my board and lodging." (Roars of laughter, in which the Court joined.)

The laughter having subsided, Mr. Straps adjusted the collar of a dirty shirt, and looking the Court significantly in the face, observed with much emphasis, "As the immortal poet says, in his 'Two Gentlemen of Verona,'

> 'A fine volley of words, gentlemen, and quickly shot off.'"

The Court (with considerable sharpness)—There must be no more of this nonsense. Did you, or did you not, receive a handkerchief from the prosecutrix?

Mr. Straps—I did, Sir; I don't deny it.

The Court—Then why did you not return it?

Mr. Straps—I understood it to be a gift.

Mrs. Jukes—(with great energy)—It wasne'er a no such thing, you good-for-nothin' feller! I only lent it you.

Commissioner—Will you swear to that, madam?

Mrs. Jukes—Will I swear to it, your vorship? That I will: I'll give as many oaths to it as your vorship pleases. He only says I made him a present of it, because I married Jem Jukes in preference to him.

Mr. Straps (to the Commissioner)—There, Sir; there she goes with another thundering falsehood. But, Sir, if you will allow me, I'd rather express my sentiments in the words of the great dramatist, than in any humble phraseology of my own.

Commissioner—We've had too much of "the great dramatist" already. Madam (addressing Mrs. Jukes), you swear distinctly that the handkerchief was no gift?

Mrs. Jukes—I do, your vorship.

Commissioner (to the officer)—Hand her the book there, and administer the oath.

Officer (to Mrs. Jukes, holding out a New Testament to her)—You swear by——

"It's perjury, Sir!" shouted Mr. Straps, addressing himself to the Commissioner.

Commissioner—You hold your tongue, Sir, or the officers must turn you out.

The oath was then administered to Mrs. Jukes, Mr. Straps all the while making the most wry faces, and assuming every variety of attitude which could most forcibly express his horror of what he either conceived, or pretended to conceive, to be a false oath.

Commissioner (to Mr. Straps)—Now, Sir, she has sworn to the fact of only having lent the handkerchief to you; what has become of it?

Mr. Straps—Well, Sir, I'll tell you candidly. On the particular evening on which I got it from her, I had a very arduous part of a new piece to perform, in which,

"Albeit, unused to the melting mood,"

I had a great deal to do in the way of crying. As I was the hero of the piece, I thought it right to use the best handkerchief I could procure to dry up my imaginary tears. So far, so well, Sir; but, in the words of the mighty Shakspeare,

"A change came o'er the spirit——"

Commissioner—Never mind what came o'er your spirit; but what came o'er, or rather of, the handkerchief? (Laughter.)

Mr. Straps—I was just on the eve of telling you that, Sir. There was one scene in the piece of a peculiarly trying nature, in which no fewer than six of us were required to cry all at once. (Bursts of laughter). And as we had only this one handkerchief amongst us, we were obliged to make it serve us all. As soon as one of the weeping—that is, the persons supposed to be weeping—parties had made a pretence of drying up his tears with it, he placed it in his hands at his back, while his face was to the audience, when another actor, unperceived by the spectators, took the handkerchief, and then openly applied it to his eyes on the front of the stage. His turn done, that of another came, who also placed his hands at his back in the same way as the other, and the next in rotation laid hold of it, unknown to the audience; and so on, till the handkerchief went over the whole six, two or three times, though the spectators fancied that each of the six actors had a handkerchief to himself. (Renewed laughter.) But, Sir, I now come to the gist of my story. While thus making the tour, which it had repeatedly to do, of the half-dozen sorrowing histrionic personages, it unaccountably disappeared; in other words, some one in the crisis of the touching tragic scene, transferred the handkerchief from his eyes to his pocket; and it has not since been heard of. (Loud laughter.) This, Sir, if you will allow me, in conclusion, to quote the prince of dramatists in one of his happiest plays,

"Is the head and front of my offending,"

in regard to the handkerchief which plaintiff still calls her own; though my impression was, that being given to me, it became mine. If, however, it were in my possession, I would indignantly throw it up to her.

Mrs. Jukes (to the Court)—It's not the value of the hankercher that I cares for, or makes me summons him; it's only because he insulted me, your honour, both before and after my marriage. You (turning to Mr. Straps, and shaking her hand in his face); you know you did, you good-for-nothing, worthless baggage that you are. I have no doubt you've got the hankercher yourself.

At the latter sentence, Mr. Straps waxed mighty indignant, looked savagely at the quondam object of his affections, stamped energetically with his foot on the floor, and raising both his hands above his head, exclaimed, in stentorian tones, "Woman, the charge is false! Yes, your worship," he continued in a subdued tone, "it is, as the mighty genius I adore says in his unrivalled tragedy of 'Hamlet,'

As false as dicers' oaths;

or, as the same great authority has it in his comedy of 'As You Like It,' it is

'Falser than vows made in wine.'

Excuse my indignation, Sir; but I cannot repress my feelings when my character is attacked. I am sure, Sir, you would yourself, if placed in my unfortunate situation, feel the full force of the inimitable lines which Shakspeare puts into the mouth of Othello—

> 'Good name in man or woman
> Is the immediate jewel of their souls;
> Who steals my purse steals trash; 'tis something, nothing:
> 'Twas mine, 'tis his, and has been slave to thousands;
> But he that filches from me my good name,
> Robs me of that which not enriches him,
> But makes me poor indeed.'"

The Commissioner (smiling)—Really, Mr. Straps, I have already allowed too much of this nonsence to go on. You admit you've lost the handkerchief, and the prosecutrix has sworn she only lent it to you. There is, therefore, no alternative, but to pay the amount claimed.

"Ah, Sir!" exclaimed Mr. Straps, on hearing the decision of the Court, "this is a hard case. As the Bard of Avon says"—

"No more of the Bard of Avon, or any other bard," interrupted the Commissioner; "the case is now decided, and the money must be paid."

At this moment, a young man, having the broken-down dandy appearance of an unfortunate actor, rushed into the court, almost exhausted. He stated that he and Mr. Straps lived in the same room together, and that some time after Mr. Straps had quitted home to attend the Court, a small package containing the handkerchief had been addressed to him, with a request that it might be opened in the event of his absence. Inside, in a disguised hand, was a note to the effect that the writer had only taken a temporary loan of the handkerchief, and that hearing by accident it was to be made the subject of legal proceedings, it had been deemed right to send a special messenger with it to Mr. Straps, in order that no unpleasant results might ensue.

"Give it me," said Mr. Straps, in exulting tones, stretching out his hand to receive it. "Here, madam," turning to Mrs. Jukes, "is your handkerchief;" and gently striking his hand on his breast, exclaimed—"My character stands forth pure and unsullied as the unsunned snow."

Mrs. Jukes took her handkerchief, evidently disappointed that it had been recovered; and Mr. Straps having paid the expenses of the summons, retired from the court, ejaculating something to himself in an under-tone; most probably a quotation from Shakspeare.

The above cases are all of a laughable character, though in print they appear far less ludicrous than they are when actually before the Court. Numerous, however, as are the cases at all our Courts of Requests, but especially in the court in Kingsgate-street of a laughter-provoking nature, those of a directly opposite kind are in the proportion of six to one. Disclosures of destitution and distress are there made, at every sitting of the Court, of the most shocking nature. I myself witnessed one such case, so lately as three weeks ago, which one would have thought would have softened the hardest heart that ever formed part of humanity. A poor, emaciated, sickly-looking woman, with nothing but rags on her back, and deep-rooted care and grief in her countenance, was summoned for twenty-one shillings, being seven weeks' rent of a wretched hovel, in one of the lowest places in St. Giles's. A little, starved, pale-looking girl, seemingly ten or eleven years of age, stood by the poor woman's side. "Do you owe the debt?" inquired the Commissioner.

"I do, your worship," sighed the broken-hearted woman.

"Then why don't you pay it?"

"Because I have no means, my lord."

"Then the plaintiff (the landlord) will seize your furniture."

"Ah, Sir!" groaned the poor creature, "that's impossible; for he has taken everything that was in the house already."

"Is that true?" inquired the Commissioner, turning to the prosecutor.

"It is, Sir," answered the latter with the greatest indifference.

"And what's the meaning of bringing this action against the poor woman?"

"It's with the view of getting her out of the house, Sir; she won't leave it."

Here the poor wretched creature asked permission of the Court to say a word or two, which being granted, she stated, as articulately as the fullness of her heart and her physical exhaustion would permit her, that for a considerable time past her husband, who was a day-labourer, had been out of employment, and that one of her children had for months been confined to a sick bed; and that under these circumstances, they had no means of procuring the most necessary articles of food, or of paying their rent. When pressed for their rent she implored a little indulgence until her husband could find some employment; but the landlord (the plaintiff) had lent a deaf ear to all her entreaties, and carried away every article of furniture in the house. The poor creature added, amidst tears and sobs, that herself, her husband, and six young children, including the sick one, had not a bed left them to lie on, nor a blanket to cover them, but were obliged to lie as they best could, all huddled together on two shutters which had been got from some neighbouring windows; and that these shutters were all that was between them and a damp stone floor, during the severe weather a few months ago. They were quite willing to leave the house, but they had nowhere to go to; and no chair or stool to sit on, or bed to lie in, even if they could get some humble apartment. The unhappy woman then implored of the plaintiff to give her back one or two of the most necessary articles of her furniture, engaging if he did so, not only to quit the house—whatever should come of herself and family,—but to pay the rent she owed as soon as her husband could find work. But the man—if he should be called a man—was inexorable; he betrayed no more feeling on the occasion than the table at which he stood. How hardened can the human heart become! How unfathomable are the depths of human misery in the very midst of this wealthy and luxurious metropolis!

I will not harrow up the feelings of my readers, by a reference to any of the other cases of distress and destitution so often brought to light in our Courts of Requests. It would answer no useful purpose; it would not lessen the load of misery which the poor creatures groan under from day to day, and from year to year.

I might have largely added to the list of laughable cases which are so common in our London Courts of Requests; but the little that remains of the space devoted to each chapter, admonishes me that that cannot be done. Before concluding, I am anxious to bear my decided testimony to the great utility of these courts. Indirectly, or by implication, I have done so already. They are useful to the customer in a limited way; inasmuch as the fear of being summoned to one of them, operates in innumerable cases in which a sense of right would have no effect, and deters him from contracting debts which he does not see any probability of being able to pay. They are useful to the party of whom goods have been purchased; inasmuch as, by a short and simple process, he is enabled to compel payment when, otherwise, the party, even though possessing the means, has not the disposition to discharge his lawful obligations. Then there is the cheapness of the process of suing for the amount due or in dispute. As before remarked, it never exceeds a few shillings; so that neither party, be the result what it may, can be out of pocket to any serious extent. The extensive and populous borough of Marylebone is now applying to the legislature for the establishment of one of these local courts within its boundaries: so, also, is the borough of Finsbury. I should like to see them established in all parts of the country; they would be found exceedingly serviceable to all tradesmen and small shopkeepers. Wherever new Courts of Requests shall be instituted, they ought, as before remarked, to have jurisdiction on all sums not exceeding 10*l.*, which, as before remarked, is not above half as great as forty shillings were three hundred years ago, when these courts were established. Besides, where the powers of the existing Courts of Requests have been extended so far as to hear and decide on all sums under ten pounds—as in the case of the City Court,—the thing has been found to answer exceedingly well. Mr. Sergeant Heath has a bill now before Parliament, for the purpose of extending the jurisdiction of the County Court to all sums not exceeding ten pounds. Whether he ought to succeed in his application, constituted as his court is, is a point on which I express no opinion; but whether he ought to succeed or not, all the other Courts of Requests in London ought certainly to have jurisdiction in all cases where the amount does not exceed the sum just mentioned. My conviction is, that the powers of these courts might be even farther extended than this. I can, I repeat, see no reason why their decisions on all amounts under twenty pounds, should not be held binding on the parties. My only objection to the Courts of Requests is, that they have the power of imprisoning the debtor for certain periods. Opposed as I am to the principle of imprisonment for debt in all cases where fraud is not clearly proved, I am doubly opposed to it in the case of Courts of Requests; inasmuch as the sums over which they have jurisdiction, are so trifling. It is surely a monstrous thing, that an honest, industrious man, who may chance to owe twenty or thirty shillings to a small grocer, which, owing to sickness or the want of employment he is unable to pay at the time, should be liable to be torn from his wife and family and sent to White-cross-street, or any other prison, for seven, forty, or sixty days, according to the peculiar powers of the particular court before which his case is tried! And yet such cases not only may, but *do* occur under the existing order of things. However, there is now, happily, a feeling in the public mind, which is daily acquiring additional strength, so hostile to imprisonment for debt, that it must of necessity, before a long time has elapsed, compel the legislature to abolish such imprisonment, except in cases of gross and glaring fraud.

CHAPTER XI.

GAMING-HOUSES AND GAMBLERS.

Supposed origin of gambling—Little known of its history—Increase in the number of gaming-houses in London—Many of them kept open all day—How managed—Morals of the upper classes, in connexion with gambling—Visit to a gambling-house—Anxiety consequent upon gambling—Its pernicious effects on the mind—Suicides caused by play—The injuries it entails on relatives and families—Insidious character of gambling—Gambling in the last century—Female gamblers—Cheating at the gambling-table—Instances of the debasing tendencies of gambling—Universality of the vice—The propriety of doing something to put an end to gambling.

In my First Series of "The Great Metropolis," I devoted a chapter to the Gaming-houses of London. Since the first edition of that work was published, I have acquired a good deal of new information on the subject, which I at one time intended to have made use of in the third edition, which appeared a few months since. On second thoughts, however, I have deemed it best to resume the subject in this work; only premising that I shall not here repeat any of the facts I have stated in "The Great Metropolis," but that the matter of this chapter will be a continuation of, or supplement to, what appeared in the work in question.

The vice of gambling is of very great antiquity. It is generally believed that it was first resorted to by the Lydians, upwards of 2500 years ago, when suffering under the effects of famine. It is said that they had recourse to gambling with the view of diverting their thoughts from the privations they were enduring; and that, in the state of intense excitement into which they worked their minds, they did forget, for whole days at a time, that they had not tasted food for the previous twenty-four hours. There may be some fiction mingled with fact in this account of the origin of gambling. It is not, however, to be denied, that if the Lydians were desirous of forgetting their privations by an artificial excitement, there was no expedient to which they could have had recourse, better adapted to promote their object than the expedient of gambling. This vice prevailed to a great extent among the Greeks and Romans, as is evident from the frequent reference to it in the works of their greatest authors.

Of the history of gambling in London, little definite is known. It was very general so far back as the reign of Richard the First, and was practised to a considerable extent in the time of Queen Elizabeth. It was still more prevalent in the reign of Charles the Second; but I am not aware that any houses were then opened for the exclusive purposes of play. When they first were so, I have not been able to ascertain, the history of gambling in the metropolis being so imperfectly known. There can be no doubt that houses for the express purpose of affording knaves and fools an opportunity of indulging their propensity to play to any extent, were opened long before the public generally were aware of the circumstance. The thing was then managed with more secrecy than it is now. Then the hells were in secluded streets and lanes: now they court distinction, not only by being in the most crowded thoroughfares, but by the blaze of light which is to be seen above their doors.

About twenty years since, the number of the larger class of hells in the metropolis was supposed to be about ten or twelve. In my first series of the work already mentioned, I estimated the number, in 1836, at fifteen. Since then, there has been a considerable increase in the number. The law which came into operation in January last for closing all gambling establishments in Paris at twelve o'clock at night, has had the effect, as was to be expected, of causing a number of the Parisian speculators in hells to come over, and commence business in London. What the number of the additions which have been thus made to our gambling establishments is, I am not able to state with certainty; that being a kind of statistical information which is not very easily to be acquired, owing to the circumstance of there being certain hells which are still conducted with comparative secrecy. I should say, however, the number of gambling establishments now in London, doing business to a very considerable amount, cannot be under twenty-four or twenty-five. Indeed, I could almost myself name two dozen particular houses which are solely used for the purposes of gambling. When I wrote the work before referred to, two years since, there were only five gambling-houses in the Regent's Quadrant: now there are eight, if not nine. In Leicester-square and the neighbourhood, there have also been several recent additions to the previous number of hells.

Formerly, the gaming-houses were only open after dark: of late years, the practice of keeping them open all day has been systematically adhered to in the case of at least eight or ten of their number. In these houses, the dice are scarcely ever idle, day or night. From Sunday to Sunday, all the year round, persons are to be found in these places, losing their money, and wasting away their very bodies by the consuming anxiety consequent on their position at the hazard or roulette table.

It may be asked, how can the proprietor of one of these establishments continue to look after his own interests, if gambling goes on by day as well as night,—nature requiring, in gamblers as well as in other men, a certain amount of repose at stated intervals? In the first place, it is to be remarked, that the cases are extremely rare indeed, in which a gaming-house belongs to one proprietor. In almost every case there are three or four individuals who engage jointly in the speculation of opening such establishments, and putting down, as the phrase is, a bank against which any person who chooses may play. But even were such an establishment the property of one individual, the house, if deemed advisable, could be kept open all day as well as night, by the proprietor employing some person to act for him when not present himself. In all the gaming-houses of any note, there are unprincipled reckless persons in the pay of the hellites. They are employed in various capacities, and for various purposes. Sometimes they play for the proprietors against any person who chooses to put down his money; at other times, when there are no other individuals playing at all, they pretend to be strangers themselves, and get up sham games with the proprietors, with the view of practising a deception on any strangers who may be in the room, and by that means inducing them to put down their money. There are other occasions, again, in which they go to coffee-houses, hotels, and other places of a public nature, where they look out for simple persons possessed of property, whom they may decoy into the particular hells with which they are connected,—always, of course, taking care to appear as if they knew nothing of any of the parties belonging to these establishments. In many instances, these persons are allowed a certain per-centage on the amount of plunder got from the persons whom they trepan into these dens of iniquity. In the larger gaming establishments, there are certain individuals kept at a regular salary for the express purpose of looking out for opulent young men. To this employment they confine themselves entirely. They are dressed in the most fashionable manner, always exhibiting a profusion of jewellery and living in great splendour when they have any particular person in their eye, in the various hotels throughout town. If report speaks truth, there are men of very high rank and standing in society, who are retained for such purposes by one or two of the largest gaming establishments in the metropolis. They are called Greeks; and the parties who are their victims, are, as I explained at some length in the work more than once referred to, very appropriately called pigeons, being, as they generally are, thoroughly plucked before they are suffered to escape out of the hands of the hellites. In some cases, in the higher class of gaming establishments, the Greeks, or decoys, being men of title or considerable standing in society, do not receive a fixed salary for seducing young men of fortune into these places for the purpose of plundering them of their property; but being in every case needy men, they nominally borrow, from time to time, large sums of money from the hell-keepers; but it is perfectly understood on both sides that the amount so borrowed is never to be repaid.

Here let me pause, to ask what must be the state of morals among a certain portion of the upper classes, when persons who are quite well known to be constantly on the watch for simple unsuspecting noblemen or gentlemen of property, in order that they may decoy them into places in which their ruin is inevitable as well as designed, are received into society with as much seeming respect and cordiality as if they were the most illustrious persons for moral worth that the world ever produced? It is a melancholy state of things; but still more melancholy is the fact, that when unsuspecting young men of property are thus seduced into gambling-houses, there are noblemen and gentlemen—by courtesy so called—who, not content with the slower process of plundering their unhappy victims by means of their superior skill at the dice or the cards, acquired from long experience, resort to habitual cheating; or at least cheating as frequently as they think they can do it without being detected. Had I written this eighteen months ago, many persons would have doubted the truth of what I say. They would have come at once to the conclusion that I was speaking from erroneous information. That will not be said now. The disclosures which took place in the Court of Queen's Bench, upwards of twelve months since, on the occasion of the trial of Lord de Roos for cheating at cards, furnished the strongest demonstration that he was not the only titled person who was in the habit of cheating in certain clubs; while there are others who, if they could not be charged with directly cheating, or cheating in their own persons, did cheat indirectly and by proxy, inasmuch as they, by their own admission, were on frequent occasions partners with Lord de Roos long after they knew that he habitually or systematically cheated. The noble lord, by the confession of the titled parties to whom I allude, thus cheated for himself and them at the same time. Are such parties, then, now excluded from fashionable society? By no means: they have not forfeited the friendship, or lost the countenance—not, at least, so far as has yet transpired—of a single aristocratic acquaintance. They are as great favourites in the circles of high life as if nothing had happened. Could any fact more strongly prove the low standard of morals which prevails among the upper classes of society?

But this is a topic which I have no wish to pursue at any

length. It is deeply to be regretted that there should be so much room for animadversion, in regard to the loose notions which obtain among a large number of the aristocracy on the question of morals.

The proprietors of the gaming-houses take every precaution to guard against the admission of parties who might lodge informations against them. In most of these establishments, the practice is to have the outer or street-door half shut. This, with a large brilliant display of gas-light above the door, is well known among those who gamble, to be an indication of the fact that play is going on in the house at the time. Within a yard or two of the street-door, is another door with an eye-hole in it, which is always covered by a sliding piece of wood in the inside. The party knocks at this inner door: the knock is not responded to by the door being opened, but one of the proprietors, or some one in their confidence, draws the piece of wood aside, and looks at the party seeking admission. If it is any one unknown to him, he asks who he is inquiring for, or what is the object of his visit: if satisfied that he is some simpleton coming for the purposes of play, the door is thrown open at once, and he is shown up stairs to the place where the wheel is revolving or the dice being thrown. If the party watching the door have his suspicions that all is not right, then the person seeking admission is refused it; and it is wonderful how quick the keepers of hells, and those in their employ, are in ascertaining who may or may not be admitted with safety. The very appearance of the party soliciting admission, the tones of his voice, or his general manner, often suffice for their purpose. Anxious to witness the proceedings in these gambling establishments, in order to describe and expose them, and fearing there might be some difficulty in getting access to them, I got one night the card of a gentleman who had been in the habit of visiting such places, but who, I have reason to believe, has by this time seen both his guilt and his folly. He desired me to give his card to a Mr. B——, the proprietor, or one of the proprietors, of a largely-frequented establishment in the centre of the Regent's Quadrant. Accompanied by a friend, whose curiosity to see the interior of a gaming establishment was most intense, I went to the place in question. The fact of my having the card of the gentleman to whom I have referred, insured our admission without a moment's delay, or a single question being asked. We were shown up three pairs of stairs to a commodious room, and were there politely accommodated with seats. The only articles of furniture we saw in the place—unless the roulette-table, the table for throwing the dice, and other requisites for play, ought to be called by the name of furniture—were eighteen or twenty handsome chairs. It will at once suggest itself to the mind of the reader, that in a large gambling establishment as this was, this number of chairs would not be sufficient to accommodate all the persons who are sometimes in it at one time. Very true; but it must be remembered that several kinds of play (roulette, for example) require the parties playing to stand, or at least a standing posture is the most convenient one. Besides, the excitement which invariably accompanies gambling is so great, that in very few cases only are the parties composed enough to remain in their seats. When my friend and I were ushered into the room on the occasion in question, there were only seven or eight persons engaged at play. One of the proprietors of the place stood at one of the sides of the table at which the play was going on at the time. He was a tall, stout, dark-looking man, with a most surly, forbidding expression of countenance. Immediately opposite to him lay a small box, in which were displayed, in the most conspicuous manner in which it was possible to place them, a number of five-pound notes. This was what is called the bank. At the edge of the table, in the immediate vicinity of the bank, was a large heap of half-crowns, probably amounting to sixty or seventy. The fact of there being so many half-crowns on the table, while neither shillings nor sixpences were to be seen, is to be accounted for from the fact that no less sums than half-crowns are ever played for at the house in question. The parties playing had also each a greater or less number of half-crowns before them. The game going on at the time was roulette; and rapidly, indeed, did the half-crowns change hands. The house, as the technical phrase is, had a run of good luck while I was there. I observed that one gentleman lost three pounds, at half-crown stakes, in less than fifteen minutes. I may here observe, that there was something very peculiar in the conduct of this gentleman: whether it arose from anything constitutional, or whether from a secret conviction that he ought not to be so employed or in such a place, I cannot tell; but the fact was, that he came into the room, and remained in it for about a quarter of an hour, and then quitted it, not only without uttering a single word, but without giving even a nod to any person in the place. One of the proprietors, according to the custom in the gambling establishments, was excessively attentive to every person who entered the room, in the way of pressing him to have something to drink. Brandy-and-water, as being the most stimulating, was the first thing he invariably asked the intended victims to take. If they declined, then they were asked, in the most insinuating manner, whether they would take anything else. The hell-keeper was manifestly much disappointed when they refused to drink; and it was to be expected he would, for his whole experience had taught him that men play most recklessly when under the excitement caused by drink. I need hardly say that the drink in such places is always given gratuitously. I observed, too, that no one is ever asked to play by the hellites. They rightly judge, that were they to solicit strangers who had not before been in the practice of frequenting gaming establishments, to put down their money, and take part in the play, they would be adopting the very course which would be most likely to defeat their designs on the pockets of such persons, as the latter would, in that case, suppose that if they played, they would run a risk of being cheated. The hell-keepers always trust to the bewitching effect of seeing others at play; for experience has taught them that few men, with money in their pockets, can resist the temptation to play which is always held out by seeing others engaged in it. And here I must take the opportunity of warning those whose eye may meet these lines, from entering a gaming-house under the impression that they will come out again without playing. I do not say the thing is impossible; but it consists with my knowledge that many men have entered those places with the firm determination that they would not gamble to the extent of a farthing, and yet have come out fleeced of the last shilling they had in their possession. Nay, I have known cases in which, after they had lost all their money, and not being acquainted with any one there of whom they could borrow more, have actually pawned their watches to enable them to continue the game. The pawning of watches, waistcoats, and other articles of apparel, to enable persons to play at the gaming-table, is quite an every-day occurrence in the case of persons who have become habituated to gaming; but in the above case, I am speaking of persons who have entered a gaming-house for the first time in their lives; and entered it, too, let it be remembered, with the firm determination that under no circumstances would they risk a shilling.

The intense anxiety with which gamblers watch the result of the game is proverbial. I had ocular demonstration of this, of the most striking kind, on the evening in question. The countenances of all engaged in play, with the single exception of that of the hell-keeper entrusted with the bank, indicated a degree of anxiety as to the result, when the stakes were large, of which none but he who has experienced it can form any idea. Has the reader ever seen a wretched culprit, charged with some serious offence, standing at the bar of the Old Bailey, or in any other criminal court, while the jury were deliberating on their verdict? If so, he must, notwithstanding all the assumed indifference which sometimes characterizes the miserable being, have seen unequivocal symptoms of the consuming anxiety as to the result which was burning in his breast. Precisely similar is the case of the gambler when he has much at stake. On the night in question, the play was deep; and so wrapt up were the parties in their work, and so absorbing was their anxiety as to the issue, that they not only did not, for several minutes at a time, exchange a word with each other, but they did not even withdraw their eyes from the dice and the table; and when the game was finished, you saw the countenance of the winner brighten up as if he had made a princely fortune, while that of the loser suddenly became as pale as if he had been told, through some supernatural agency, that he was to die the next hour.

The deep and consuming anxiety of gamblers, when at table, is natural enough in any case; but there are certain cases in which it is peculiarly so. Only imagine the case—a very common case, I regret to say—not only of a man's whole property, but even his character in the estimation of mankind, being entirely dependent on the numbers which the dice may chance to turn up; and to heighten the interest which he attaches to the result, only suppose that he has a wife and family, or it may be a mother, or sister, or other near relative, dependent on him for support: their fate is bound up in his, and that fate is to be decided by the numbers which turn up. Who but himself can form any conception of the tumultuous emotions which agitate his bosom at such a moment? What these must be, may be best inferred from the alternative so often resorted to in such cases, when the numbers turned up by the dice are adverse. In how many instances is ruin at play followed by immediate suicide? We hear of only a comparatively small number of the cases of self-destruction which occur from losses at play. How often is it stated at coroners' inquests, by the relatives of the deceased, that they could assign no reason why he committed suicide. I am convinced, that in almost every instance, especially where the party moved in a respectable sphere of life, in which no reason can be assigned by friends or relatives for the "rash act," that reason was losses at play. Acquaintances often bear testimony to the fact that the deceased was in good circumstances; and that, therefore, the fact of his committing suicide was unintelligible to them. Ay, it is true, he *was* in easy circumstances a few months, or even a few weeks, before he destroyed himself; but then, in the interim, though they knew nothing of the fact, he had gambled away the last farthing he had in the world. An instance of this occurred about ten weeks ago. A gentlemanly-looking man came up from the country, and taking lodgings in the vicinity of Leicester-square, entered some of the gaming-houses with which that neighbourhood is infested. He at once fell a prey to the keepers of these Pandemoniums. In

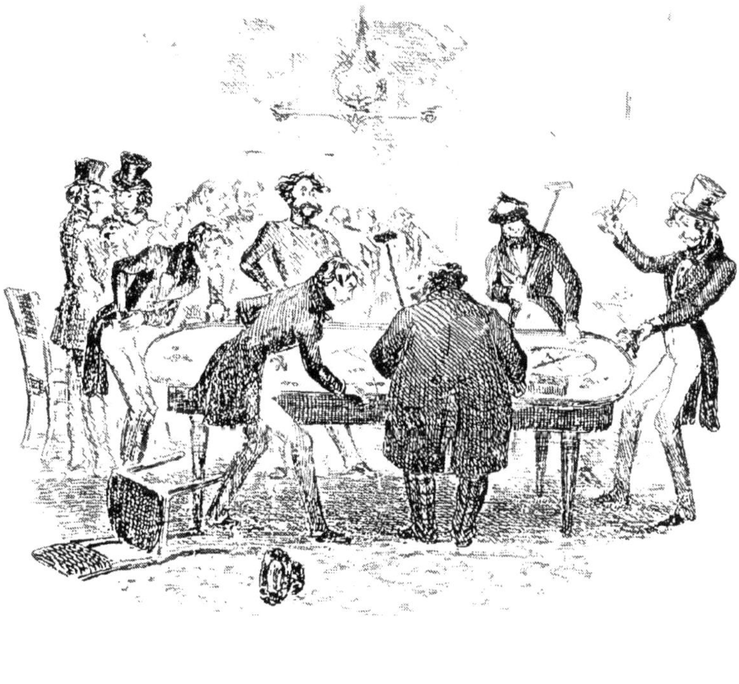

the short space of a fortnight he was plundered of from 2000*l.* to 3000*l.*, including a valuable gold watch, which he had risked when all his money was gone. He then went and blew out his brains. Of course, if any of those who knew him a month previously, and who were unacquainted with the fact of his gambling, had been asked if they knew any cause why he destroyed himself, they would have answered in the negative; adding, that he was in excellent circumstances. It is no uncommon thing for persons, who have entered one of these hells with the determination of hazarding their last shilling before they come out again, to make previous preparations for the commission of suicide, in the event of their being unfortunate. Their motto in such a case is—"Something or nothing." If the latter be the result, then out they go, and straightway carry the purpose on which they had previously resolved, into effect. In fifteen or twenty minutes afterwards their bodies are weltering in their gore*, and their spirits are before the throne of the Eternal.

The feelings of one who enters a gambling-house for the first time, are of a very peculiar and painful kind. He has a secret conviction, though too infatuated to profit by it, that in the very act of crossing the threshold of such a place for the purposes of play, he is not only sinning against Heaven, but periling his own reputation and prospects in life. He is so powerfully impressed with a sense of doing wrong, that his very head becomes dizzy, his eyes become dim, and his heart palpitates with a violence which, perhaps, he never before experienced. I have even known instances in which young men, on their first entering a gaming-house to engage in play, have almost been divested of consciousness itself. They have walked up stairs in a state of trance; reminding one, in some measure, of the mechanical motions of a somnambulist. I knew one who was so overpowered with a sense of the impropriety and perils of entering one of these hells, that he could not collect his scattered senses sufficiently to play when he had got into the room, and actually quitted it again without being able to say how many stairs he went up, or to describe the appearance of the place.

No idea can be formed by those who have not experienced it, of the intense excitement consequent on gambling. And what is worthy of mention is, that the mere circumstance of being habituated to play, does not materially abate the excitement. It is well known to those who are personally acquainted with gamblers, that they never throw the dice, deal the cards, or put down their money at roulette, when the stakes played for are

* It is worthy of remark, that very few gamblers commit suicide by hanging or drowning: they almost invariably, when they do destroy themselves, either cut their throats, or blow out their brains

large, without feeling themselves wrought up to the highest pitch of excitement. A friend of my own who went a few months since into one of these hells, says, that, among others, he saw the son of a nobleman engaged in deep play; and that though, by a run of good luck, as the phrase is, he continued to win while my acquaintance was there, his excitement was so great as to agitate his whole frame. His tongue even faltered while he attempted to speak; and he seemed so absorbed in the game, that he appeared as if insensible to everything and every one around him. Others have been known to sit for sixteen or eighteen hours at a time at the gaming-table, without feeling the slightest hunger, and without imagining that they had been so employed more than two or three hours.

I have dwelt at such length in the work to which I have already made several references, on the debasing and destructive effcts of gaming on the minds of those who give way to it, that little more is left me to say on that point. Not only does indulgence in play extinguish all the finer feelings of our nature, but it generally does it in a very short time. In the short space of two or three months, the most amiable and virtuous of men have, in innumerable cases, been transformed into a species of incarnate demons by their nightly visits to the gaming-table. Husbands that were before most devotedly attached to their wives, soon treat them with the most perfect brutality; and fathers who regarded their children with so ardent an affection, that they would have parted with everything they possessed in the world rather than that those children should be injured, would now prefer seeing them die of cold or hunger, to being themselves excluded from the gaming-house. The cases are innumerable, in which a man continues to frequent these Pandemoniums—pawning, it may be, the very clothes off his back,—while he sees his wife and children literally dying of want in some wretched hovel. In fact, the confirmed gambler is utterly lost to all virtuous feeling: he has not a trace of humanity left. An affecting instance of the suddenness with which the passion of gambling transforms a virtuous man into one of the most vicious kind, occurred within the last two or three years, under my own observation. A young man, the son of most worthy parents, who had a small competency to support them in their old age, after having spent a little fortune on his education, had, on coming from the country to London, been very successful in the profession to which he belonged. He was a handsome young man, of engaging manners, and possessed an intimate knowledge of his profession. Circumstances brought him into contact with a young lady, the daughter of a gentleman of great wealth and high standing in society. Having every reason to believe that he had only to make matrimonial advances to the young lady to insure both her own and her parents' consent to their marriage, he, after a little hesitation, did solicit the hand of the former. His proposals were accepted by her, with the most cordial concurrence of every member of the family; and in due time the marriage took place. With his bride he received a handsome sum down, and the assurance that, on the father's death, he would receive a great deal more. The first thing he did was to send 1500*l.* to his parents, in return for the expenses which his education had cost them; feeling, that but for that education, he could never have attained that position in society which he now occupied. The marriage jaunt having been performed, both parties returned to town, and he commenced business on his own account, backed by the great influence and connexions of his father-in-law. Everything went on smoothly for a time: he took a large house, at a rental of 300*l.* a-year, and furnished it in a style of great splendour: his wife and he lived on the most affectionate terms; and her friends always appeared to me to be exceedingly attached to him. In an evil hour, he met with one or more Greeks, and by them he was decoyed into a fashionable hell in the neighbourhood of St. James's-street. In a few weeks he lost every farthing of ready money he could command. His father-in-law was applied to, and advanced another sum, not aware of the purposes for which it was intended. That followed the first, in a week or two more. Another application was made to his father-in-law; but having, by this time, ascertained how the former sums had gone, he refused to advance a farthing more. This led to a quarrel, and to the young man ordering his father-in-law to quit the house, and never again to enter it. His wife took his part, and by that means forfeited the friendship of all her family. They one and all refused to have any intercourse with him or her. What was now to be done? He wrote to his father, asking him for the loan, for a few months, of the 1500*l.* he had sent him, under the pretext that he was going to appropriate it to business purposes, with a moral certainty of its producing a most handsome return. The poor unsuspecting man sent him a draft for the whole sum by next day's post. In a fortnight or three weeks, every shilling of the amount was lost in one of the dens of iniquity to which I have referred. Inventing the most plausible story his genius could suggest, he again applied to his father for the loan, for two or three months, of whatever remaining money he had, assuring him that the whole would be returned at the end of that time, with an ample consideration for the use of it. The still unsuspecting parent immediately sent him the last farthing he had, amounting to nearly 2000*l.* In a month, or rather less, that had all gone the same way as the former sum. The splendid establishment was broken up; the furniture was all sold by the creditors to whom he was indebted in his professional capacity; and he and his wife were turned into the streets without a friend or farthing in the world. He now lost all regard for his wife, as he had done already for all his friends; and in a short time afterwards, heard, with the most entire indifference, of the death of his father and the destitution of his mother. He parted from his wife without the slightest feeling of regret; and, to my certain knowledge, though brought up in the first circles of society, she was, in little more than fourteen months after her marriage, dependent for subsistence, and for a place to sleep in, on the charity of a humble tradesman; for her parents had been so offended at her conduct, in taking her husband's part when he insulted them, that it was not until they had learned that he had quitted the country altogether, that they would consent again to acknowledge her.

I give this case in illustration of the rapidity with which gambling transforms the most virtuous into the most vicious of men, because I was myself intimately acquainted with the unfortunate young man. I have modified rather than overstated the circumstances of the case, while I have purposely suppressed several facts which would have made it still more touching, lest it should be recognized by any of the friends of either the husband or the wife; and possibly, in such a case, give them a moment's uneasiness. Were I to repeat all the other instances which I have heard of a similar nature, the space that remains of this chapter would be insufficient for the purpose.

I could relate cases without number of the sudden transitions from affluence and respectability to the lowest depths of destitution and degradation, which have been brought about by a passion for the gambling-table. Not long since, a very affecting instance of this nature was brought under the personal cognizance of a number of individuals. A gentleman belonging to a good family, and who possessed a handsome freehold house and a fortune of 20,000*l*., was somehow or other trepanned into a gambling-house. He was not long there, when he thought he would play to the extent of five sovereigns. He alternately lost and gained, but quitted that evening with the same sum as he entered. He next night repeated his visit to the place, and then lost a considerable sum. A third time he crossed the portals of the Pandemonium, in the hope of regaining what he had lost on the previous occasion; but he found that he only doubled his losses. Still he clung to the hope, that by trying again he would make up for all he had lost: and with that view, and in that expectation, repeated his visits night after night. The result was, that he became a confirmed gambler. He was spell-bound to the gaming-table, and every successive loss only seemed to whet his appetite for further play. With the recklessness of a desperate man, he played still deeper and deeper with every new game, until he had gambled away the last sixpence he had in the world,—which he did in the short space of two or three months. He was a married man, with four children. The house, and the things in it, were sold. One article of wearing apparel after another, whether belonging to his wife, or himself, or his children, found its way to the pawnbrokers, as being the only means they had of procuring as much food as would sustain existence. At last the wretched family was discovered, through the merest accident, by a former friend, living in a miserable hovel in one of the lowest parts of the town; the poor wife on the eve of her confinement; the four children not only half-naked, but evidently sick and exhausted from utter want; while he himself had all the appearance of a living skeleton. I should add, that there was neither bed, table, nor chairs in the room; nothing, indeed, in the shape of furniture. The unhappy man confessed to his friend when he entered, that he had brought all the misery he then beheld, on his wife, his children, and himself, by his addiction to the gaming-table.

I have said that in many cases the last resource of the ruined gambler is suicide. Before having recourse to this expedient for ending their earthly miseries, ruined gamesters have, in numerous instances, been so utterly lost to all attachment to life, that the commission of the fatal act seems not to have cost them one moment's uneasiness. Gamblers have been known to set as coolly and deliberately about blowing out their brains as if they had only been going to light their cigars. Lord Orford, in his Correspondence with Horace Walpole, mentions two curious instances of this. Not having the work just named at hand, and not being able to refer to the particular letter in which the first of the cases is related, I cannot give it in his lordship's words. I must, therefore, give it as well as I can from memory:—One of the fashionable young men of Lord Orford's day, had been unhappily decoyed into a gambling-house, where his passion for play became so great that he spent nearly the whole of his time in throwing the dice—excepting, of course, that portion of time which was necessary for physical repose. He continued to gamble until he had not only lost a princely fortune, but had incurred a large amount of debt among his tradesmen. With the loss of his money, and the utter beggary which stared him in the face, the unfortunate victim of play lost all relish for life. He saw, or rather fancied he saw, in death the only refuge from the infamy and wretchedness which he had entailed on himself; and therefore, with the coolness and deliberation of a man in his peculiar circumstances, he determined on the commission of suicide. But though thus past all feeling for himself, he had still some lingering concern for the poor hard-working and honest tradesmen in whose debt he was so deeply; and as he was fully resolved on self-destruction, he thought he might, before carrying his fatal purpose into execution, as well do them an act of justice; though in so doing, he should do injustice to others. I suppose—though this can only be conjecture, he not having expressed any sentiment on the subject—that he thought in his own mind there could be no great harm in taking a small sum out of the pockets of a great many individuals, to make up an amount, the loss of which would be ruinous to many of his tradesmen. Be this as it may, the ruined gambler insured his life to the extent of the sum—amounting to several thousand pounds—which he owed his tradesmen, taking their claims in the aggregate. Being personally acquainted with several of the directors of the company (he called them his life-and-death brokers) in which he insured, he invited them to dinner the following day, with the ostensible view of celebrating the completion of the assurance. He also requested all his tradesmen to be present at a particular hour in the evening; an hour which would allow the party to dispatch a splendid dinner, and do ample justice to the wine. The tradesmen received strict orders to be personally present; and as the non-payment of their accounts for a long period to come was to be the penalty of not acceding to his wishes in this respect, it can scarcely be necessary to say that they were all "punctual as lovers to the moment sworn." The dinner over, and a liberal allowance of wine having been quaffed, the ruined gambler desired the servant to call up all who were in the hall below. In a few seconds the dining-room was filled with tradesmen, all eager to receive payment of their accounts. "Now, gentlemen," said the gambler, addressing his guests, and pointing to the little crowd of tradesmen,—"now, gentlemen, these are all my tradesmen; they are honest industrious men, to whom I am indebted, and as I see no other earthly means of being ever able to meet their just claims, you will be so kind as to pay them out of the sum for which I insured my life yesterday. Allow me, gentlemen, to bid you all farewell." And so saying, he pulled a pistol from his pocket, and placing it to his head, that instant blew out his brains.

The other case to which I have referred, as related by Lord Orford, I can give in his lordship's own words, having access to it in an extract in one of the periodicals of the day. Lord Orford, writing at a time when the friends of the party to whom he alludes were alive, very properly suppresses his name, contenting himself with substituting a few stars for it. "He himself," says

Lord Orford, "with all his judgment in bets, would have betted any man in England against himself for self-murder. Yet after having been supposed the sharpest genius of his time, he, by all that appears, shot himself in the distress of his circumstances. * * * The same day, he asked immediately for the government of Virginia, or the fox-hounds; and pressed for an answer with an eagerness that surprised the Duke of N———, who never had a notion of pinning down the relief of his own, or any other man's wants, to a day. Yet that seems to have been the case of * * *, who determined to *throw the die* of life or death. Tuesday se'nnight he received the answer from court, which did not prove favourable. He consulted indirectly, and at last directly, several people on the easiest mode of finishing life; and seems to have thought that he had been too explicit; for he invited company to dinner for the day of his death, and ordered a supper at White's*, where he supped, too, the night before. He played at *whist* till it was one in the morning: it was New-year's morning. Lord Bertie drank to him a happy new year. He clapped his hands strangely to his eyes. In the morning, he had a lawyer and three witnesses, and executed his will, which he made them read twice over, paragraph by paragraph; and then asking the lawyer if that would stand good, though a man were to shoot himself, and being assured that it would, he said, 'Pray stay while I step into the next room,' and shot himself. He clapped the pistol so close to his head, that they heard no report."

The above are curious illustrations of the utter indifference to life, which is so common in the case of ruined gamblers. But, perhaps, the most singular one on record occurred about fourteen or fifteen years since. A young man, having gambled away the last shilling he possessed in the world, solicited the loan of a few pounds from one of the proprietors of the hell in which he had been plundered of his money. "What security do you propose for repaying the sum?" inquired the hellite.

"My word of honour," was the answer.

"That won't do; that's poor security, indeed," rejoined the keeper of the hell, in haughty and almost insulting tones.

"Then you won't lend me a few pounds?"

"Not without security."

"Why, you surely won't refuse me a couple of sovereigns after having lost so much?"

"I won't advance you a couple of shillings without security."

The young man was, if possible, as deeply stung by this refusal as he was mortified at the loss of his money. A thought struck

* White's Club, St. James's-street.

him. "I'll give you," he said, addressing himself to the hellite, "the security of the suit of clothes on my back, which is quite new, and cost eight guineas. Will you advance me a couple of sovereigns on that security?"

"But supposing you lose, I cannot strip them off your back."

"Don't trouble yourself about that. If I lose, I shall commit suicide, which I have been meditating for some time, and you shall then have the clothes. I shall return to my lodgings before day-light, in the most worn-out and worthless dressing-gown or great cloak you can procure for me, leaving my clothes with you." The money was advanced, and in ten or twelve minutes was lost. The hellite demanded his clothes. The unfortunate youth, with the utmost coolness, stripped forthwith, and enveloping his body in a great-coat, for which no Jew old-clothesman would have given half-a-crown, quitted the Pandemonium in which he had lost his money, with the firm determination of destroying himself. Instead, however, of going home to execute his purpose, he was about to carry it into effect by suspending himself from a lamp-post, in a dark lane, near the hell in which he had lost his money; but before he had completed his preparations, he was observed by a policeman, who at once took him into custody. He was brought before the police magistrate next morning, where the whole circumstances connected with the affair transpired. It is worthy of observation, that the ruined gambler exhibited the most perfect coolness when discovered in the act of attempting to destroy himself; and that he resented the interference of the policeman, by which he was prevented from carrying his purpose into effect, as a most unwarrantable piece of impertinence. He had squandered away all his money, and now he conceived he had an undoubted right to take away his life.

In the work* to which I have two or three times alluded, I have adverted to some remarkable cases of suicide which have been committed in consequence of losses at the gaming-table. I gave those cases in detail, because, having occurred a good many years ago, they are not now likely to cause that uneasiness to the relations of the parties which they must have done at the time. I could relate many more of recent occurrence which have been made public to a certain extent; but it is better to pass them over. There are, again, many cases of suicide arising from losses at play, which are quite well known to the immediate relations of the parties, but which are carefully kept by those relations from the knowledge of the public. I myself could point to various individual cases of this kind; b

* The Great Metropolis. First Series.

that would answer no useful purpose, while it would inflict a wound in the breast of surviving relatives.

From what I have already remarked, the reader will at once infer, that an indulgence in the passion of gambling must be productive of an awful amount of individual misery to the parties themselves. Would that the misery which is the inevitable result of gambling were confined to those parties! Unhappily it is not: it extends to families, relatives, and friends; and thus indirectly spreads itself throughout the whole framework of society. Fathers are reduced to poverty by the losses at the gaming-table of their sons; wives, by the losses of their husbands; children, by the losses of their fathers; sisters, by the losses of their brothers; and so on throughout all the variety of family relationship wherever one individual is dependent on the pecuniary prosperity of another. But this is not the only way in which the baneful effects of the pernicious practice of gambling are felt by the relations of the parties. The suicides and forgeries, and other discreditable actions, which result from an indulgence in the practice of gambling, are matters which not only throw them into the deepest misery at the time of their occurrence, but which they can never look back on, at any after period of life, without the most painful feelings. There is yet another though not so manifest way in which gambling is productive of a vast amount of misery and wretchedness. I allude to the marriages which gamblers on the verge of ruin enter into with the view of retrieving their fortunes, or rather postponing their ruin for a longer or shorter period, as the case may be. In such cases, the affections are never for a moment consulted: there is no sympathy of opinion, feeling, or habit: no union of hearts. With the gambler, the transaction is one of a thoroughly sordid kind: he does not even respect the lady he is about to make his wife. It may be, he utterly detests her; but she has a fortune, and he knows of no other means of obtaining money. Of course the marriage ends in the greatest unhappiness, if not in entire separation. This, I need hardly say, chiefly applies to aristocratic marriages; and to them it applies to an extent of which I am convinced the public have no conception. Every one is aware that George the Fourth, when Prince of Wales, was, as the common phrase is, over head and ears in debt; and that it was because he would thereby be enabled to meet the claims of his creditors, that he consented to marry the Princess Caroline of Brunswick. But though this is known to every one, comparatively few people are acquainted with the circumstances under which his debts were contracted. Those debts, then, were the result of losses at the gaming-table. He was an inveterate gambler; a habit which he most probably contracted through his intimacy with Fox. It is a well-ascertained fact, that in two short years, soon after he attained his majority, he lost nearly 500,000*l.* at play. It was with the view and in the hope that marriage would cure his propensity for the gaming-table, that his father was so anxious to see him united to Caroline. And it was solely, as just remarked, on account of his marriage with that princess constituting the only condition of his debts being paid by the country, that he agreed to lead her to the hymeneal altar. The unfortunate results of their union are but too well known, not only as regarded the parties themselves, but as regarded society generally. To the gambling habits, then, of the Prince of Wales is to be ascribed all that unhappiness which he entailed on the unfortunate Caroline; and the vast amount of injury which her separation from him, and subsequent trial, produced on the morals of the nation generally.

Perhaps there is not, in the whole catalogue of vices, a single one which is more insidious than that of gambling. If a man once gives way to it—if he once yields to the temptation to play, it is a thousand to one if he ever relinquishes it until he is ruined in character and fortune. I have given, in the previous parts of this chapter, instances of a very remarkable kind, illustrative of the almost moral impossiblity of the person who has once fairly entered on play, absenting himself from the gambling-table while he has a shilling in the world. The inference from this is surely so plain, that he who runneth may read. Not only ought men to shun the gaming-houses as they would the path that leads to their own destruction, but they ought to abstain from all betting and gambling among private friends, even when only for the mere purposes of amusement. What is begun for amusement soon ends in a disposition to gamble for gain; and though the party may, in the first instance, confine his risks to trifling amounts, he will gradually venture on deeper and deeper play, until he plays sufficiently large stakes to work his own ruin. Parents ought to check and eradicate the disposition to all sorts of playing for gain among their children. The spirit of the gambler is often, I am convinced, imbibed in our boyish years, though it may not develop itself in any striking manner until we have reached the years of maturity.

The disclosures which were made on the trial of Lord de Roos, proved that not only does the practice of gaming prevail to a great extent among the upper classes of society, but that many of our nobility and gentry are in the habit of playing what is called deep game. In this respect, however, our present aristocracy have the advantage over the higher classes of the last century. With the single exception of a noble marquis, two noble earls, and three or four members of the peerage of inferior rank,

I am not aware of any of our present aristocracy whose gambling achievements can at all be compared with those of scores of the nobility and gentry of the middle and latter part of the by-gone century, whom it were easy to name. And, perhaps, among all the aristocratic gamblers of the last century, the Duke of Bedford, and Charles James Fox, the illustrious orator and statesman, were the greatest. The Duke of Bedford felt the excitement consequent on gambling to be, in one sense, necessary to existence: life was to him a positive burden when not indulging his favourite propensity. Even sickness itself, when that sickness did not prostrate his mental powers, failed to extinguish his disposition to gamble. But as I have referred to the singularly strong propensity which the late Duke of Bedford felt for play, in the work to which I made allusion in the outset, I will say nothing more relative to his Grace in this volume. I am not sure, after all, whether his friend, Mr. Fox, was not a still greater gambler. At all events, Fox was one of the most inveterate players that ever put a knee under the table. It is a well-attested fact, that one evening he lost the immense sum of 25,000*l*. No less undoubted is the circumstance of his having, on another occasion, continued at play for twenty-two consecutive hours! It is also, perhaps, worthy of mention, that, singularly enough, he lost 500*l*. every hour, without a single instance of what is technically called "a turn" in his favour; making a total loss for the twenty-two hours' sederunt, of 11,000*l*. The fact of Fox having been able, in a physical point of view, to continue twenty-two consecutive hours in one position, and at one employment, proves, in the most conclusive manner, the stimulating nature of gambling. At any other employment, nature would have been unequal to the effort; she must have sunk in the attempt. It is due to the memory of Fox to say, that he was one of the few inveterate players of his day who were never known to resort to unfair practices. There was something, indeed, of a very peculiar nature in the constitution of his mind. Unlike all other gamblers of whom I have ever heard, his losses, even when ruinous, never seemed to cause him a moment's regret or uneasiness. A contemporary and friend of his has mentioned, in his memoirs of the eminent men of that period, that at six o'clock one morning, after having the previous night lost the last farthing he had in the world at the gaming-table, he was found reading, in the original, the works of one of the most distinguished philosophers of ancient Greece. His own favourite observation, in reference to his gambling propensities, was, that next to the pleasure of gaining was the pleasure of losing at play.

In the time of Fox, and indeed during the entire latter half of the last century, gambling obtained to a very great extent among the female as well as among the male aristocracy of the country. Those unacquainted with the fact will be startled to hear, that to such an alarming height did the spirit of gambling among the female portion of the nobility and gentry rise, in the middle of the eighteenth century, that it was deemed necessary, by way of example to others, to prosecute publicly some of the most distinguished ladies in the land for allowing gambling in their houses. The Countess of Buckinghamshire was convicted of this offence, and fined 200*l.*; Lady E. Luttrel was fined 50*l.* for the same offence; and so were several other distinguished females.

How far the spirit of gambling is still cherished by the female aristocracy of England, is a point on which a diversity of opinion prevails. My own impression is—and that impression is founded on facts which have been privately communicated to me—my own impression is, that gambling is practised to a far greater extent among the female branches of the aristocracy than is generally supposed. The truth is, that people have little suspicion of a disposition to gamble on the part of the aristocratic ladies of the land, because the latter are prudent enough to take every possible precaution to conceal the fact from the public gaze. Not only are there no houses kept by their own sex solely for gambling purposes, but they do not even go to one particular house belonging to any one of themselves for many nights in succession. The understanding among them is, that, unless under peculiar circumstances, they shall not indulge their propensity for play for more than six consecutive nights in the same house. The aristocratic female gamblers are divided into various small coteries; and they take each other's houses in rotation, except when particular circumstances occur to interfere with such arrangement. They meet together on such occasions ostensibly as tea parties; and so skilfully and adroitly is the thing managed, that there are often gambling lady-parties in a husband's house without his ever dreaming of such a thing. It is due, however, to these ladies to say, that so far as I am aware, they not only refuse to have anything to do with the dice, but that they never even play deeply. The cards only are patronised by them; and the stakes are usually a sovereign each. Not long since, a countess died at an advanced age, who was one of the most inveterate gamblers of her sex in modern times. This lady did nothing else but gamble. Living apart from her husband, and having no family or any one else to interfere with her, she gave full rein to her propensities in this respect. It is a fact which is worthy of mention, that notwithstanding her passionate fondness for gambling, she almost invariably lost. It was calculated that her average losses exceeded fifty pounds per week during the eight months in the year which she regularly played. The passion for the card-table clung to her to the very last; it was only when physically unfit for play that she relinquished her gambling pursuits. I know of another lady, living by herself, but intimately related to several of the first families in the country, who never, unless confined to her bed, suffers a single night to pass without taking part at the card-table. The lady sees no company, solely because that would interfere with the indulgence of her disposition to play. She is now upwards of seventy, and yet she displays a flow of spirits and liveliness of manner, when at the card-table, which would be worthy a girl just emerging from her teens. She does nothing else but gamble; unless, indeed, I ought to except a glance at the morning newspaper, and a half-hour's "dip" into some circulating-library book. The infirmities incident to advanced age require that she should not over-exert herself at home; but the moment she sits down at the card-table she appears as if she were another person. All her ailments seem to take unto themselves wings and fly away the instant the cards are produced. I could make some curious disclosures respecting the practice of gaming among the aristocratic ladies of the land; but anything which would point in a particular direction in such a case would be in bad taste, and might be unpleasant to the relations of the parties, whose feelings ought to be consulted in the matter.

We have often heard of the long time it has taken to decide a game at chess, when the parties were both first-rate players, or were very equally matched. Instances of this kind have occurred in playing at cards, where the opposing parties were both honest. It also repeatedly occurs when it so happens that both parties are dextrous at cheating. A rather singular instance of this kind took place in London a short time since. A Frenchman had become proverbial among those with whom he was in the habit of playing, for the unerring certainty with which he gained from all who ventured to play with him. At last, as might be expected, seeing no chance of winning, every one refused to engage in the unequal trial of skill. An Englishman who had heard of the triumphs of Monsieur, expressed his readiness to enter the lists with him. The parties played for three hours without intermission, and at the end of that time were, in respect to winning or losing, much about the same as when they commenced. They then stopped to have a little refreshment. "Sare," said the Frenchmen, in a sort of whisper, to a party who accompanied the Englishman, "your friend is a very clever man at de cards; deuced clever, Sare." "He is a very clever fellow," observed the Englishman. "I shall try him again," said Monsieur. As he made the observation, he proceeded to the room in which they had been playing, and which was fixed on as the scene of their future contest. He had scarcely quitted the place, when the other made his appearance, and observed that the Frenchman was the most skilful player he had ever met with. The parties again met, and the cards were again produced. The game was renewed at eleven o'clock, and continued without intermission till six next morning. At the end of that time, to the surprise of each other, they found that they had left off just as they had begun. They were respectively the more astonished at this, as neither had ever before met with his equal. "Sare," said the Frenchman, "you are de best player I ever met with."

"And you, Monsieur," returned the other, "are the only gentleman from whom I could gain nothing."

"Indeed, Sare," said Monsieur, hesitatingly.

"It's a fact, I assure you."

"Sare, I'm quite surprised at your skill."

"I'm no less so at yours, Monsieur."

"You're the most skilfullest man at de cards in England."

"Not while you are in it, Monsieur," replied the Englishman, with a smile.

"Sare, I *cheated*, and yet could not gain from you," remarked the Frenchman, hurriedly and with great emphasis, feeling it impossible any longer to restrain his surprise at the circumstance of being unable to play a winning game with the Englishman.

"And, Monsieur, I did the same with you, and yet you are no loser," remarked the other, with a corresponding energy of tone.

The enigma was now solved: both had been cheating the whole night, though each was unconscious of the dishonest practices of the other. And so equally matched were they in their dexterity at cheating, that each rose from the table with the same amount of money as that with which he sat down. The cheats cordially shook hands, seemingly much gratified that they had at last ascertained how it was that neither could gain from the other.

Persons who have never been in a gambling-house, have very erroneous notions of how matters are conducted in those sinks of iniquity. They suppose that there is the conversation, the witty remark, the repartee, the laughter and good-humoured uproar, if I may use the expression, which are the usual characteristics of social parties. There could not be a greater misapprehension as to the real state of things. Gamblers know no friendship except in those cases in which two or more of the hellites, or professed gamblers, conspire together for the purpose of fleecing some unfortunate person who, in an evil hour, has been induced to enter one of these Pandemoniums. Not a word of conversation is to be heard: no smile is ever seen to light up the countenances of those at play. What I witnessed in this respect, in the gaming-house in the Regent Quadrant, is nightly to be seen in every hell in the metropolis. In every face you see the deepest anxiety and the most grasping avarice clearly depicted; while in the countenances of those who have been plundered of their money, and have their last farthing at stake, you see a positively horrible expression. Despair in its most frightful aspects is visibly impressed in their looks. In many instances, you witness an unearthly, I had almost said a demoniacal expression of countenance. It requires no effort to infer from their looks what awful emotions are agitating their bosoms. Every eye is fixed on the table, and on the dice, or cards, or ball, according to the nature of the play that is going on at the time. The stillness of the place is only broken by the rattling of the dice, the motions of the wheel and ball, or by the person who presides over the game announcing the result, or requesting the players to make their game anew. In the very silence of the place there is often something awful; made, of course, infinitely more so by the intense interest which the parties feel in the result of the game. The only occasions on which the voices of the parties are to be heard, is when some unhappy man, who has been robbed of his money by foul play, accuses the hellites, or the persons in their employ, of having cheated him. The charge of cheating is one at which these fellows invariably affect to be mightily indignant; and the more guilty of the crime, the louder they usually are in their blustering, and in their pretended regard for their characters. The victim who has the temerity to charge them with false play, is sure to be a sufferer in person as well as in purse. Not content with heaping every abuse on his head, and uttering the most dreadful imprecations, they usually resort, with the view of silencing the party preferring the charge, to arguments of a physical kind; that is to say, they have recourse to personal violence; and as the one invariably takes the part of the other, it is unnecessary to say that the unfortunate victim has no chance with them. In the leading gaming establishments, they have a bully, of superior pugilistic capabilities, regularly retained for the purpose of inflicting fistic punishment on any party who may become troublesome because he has been plundered of his money. The cases are innumerable—they are of nightly occurrence, though the parties are restrained from a desire not to expose themselves, from prosecuting the hellites for assault—in which poor simpletons, who have been fleeced of their last farthing, have received the most flagrant personal maltreatment* because they have ventured to charge the parties who have plundered them of their money, with unfair play. I could refer to various instances

* It may be right to say, that this applies chiefly to the transactions which take place in the minor hells.

of this kind which have been communicated to me by the parties who were the victims: that, however, is unnecessary. I will only add, that a variety of cases have occurred, in which the remonstrating party has not only been grossly assaulted, but has actually been murdered, or has afterwards died of the injuries he had received. Nor is this anything but what might be expected; for the hellites are the most thoroughly abandoned class of men under heaven. Their moral sense has been utterly deadened by the series of crimes which they had committed before they became the proprietors of gaming-houses: of humanity, there exists not the slightest vestige in their bosoms. In short, they will never hesitate at the commission of any crime, no matter what its enormity, provided they think there is a probability of their escaping the retribution which the laws of their country in all such cases inflict.

And the practice of gambling, it is right to remark, has the same effect on almost every one who gives himself up to it, whether a gaming-house proprietor or not. The instances are exceedingly rare, in which the habitual gambler is not one of the most vicious members of society. To this point I have alluded in a previous part of the chapter. An utter disregard of all virtue and friendship is a necessary consequence of gaming. The man who, when he enters a gambling den for the first time, would not be induced to do an unjust or unworthy action for the world, will, by the time he has been a few months a gambler, perpetrate the most atrocious actions without a compunctious visiting at the time, or a pang of regret at an after period. Nor is there anything too mean or ignoble for them to do, provided it will administer to their propensity for the gaming-table. A few months' attendance in one of these fearful places robs a man of all self-respect. I could give innumerable illustrations of this, by a reference to individual cases. I shall only allude to one; it came under my own observation a year or two ago, and possesses some singular features:—A young man of most respectable connexions, and who possessed great talents in the profession to which he belonged, had, in the course of two or three years, got into a business which was producing from 1000*l.* to 1200*l.* per annum. He had every prospect of his business considerably increasing. I am convinced, from what I myself knew of the circumstances, that in three or four years more he would have annually made by his professional exertions from 1500*l.* to 2000*l.* Unfortunately, however, he had not the good sense to let well alone. To make a fortune gradually, and by means of his professional talents, appeared to him a too commonplace sort of affair. His fortune must not be made by the drudgery of business: it was far more aristocratic, and much more

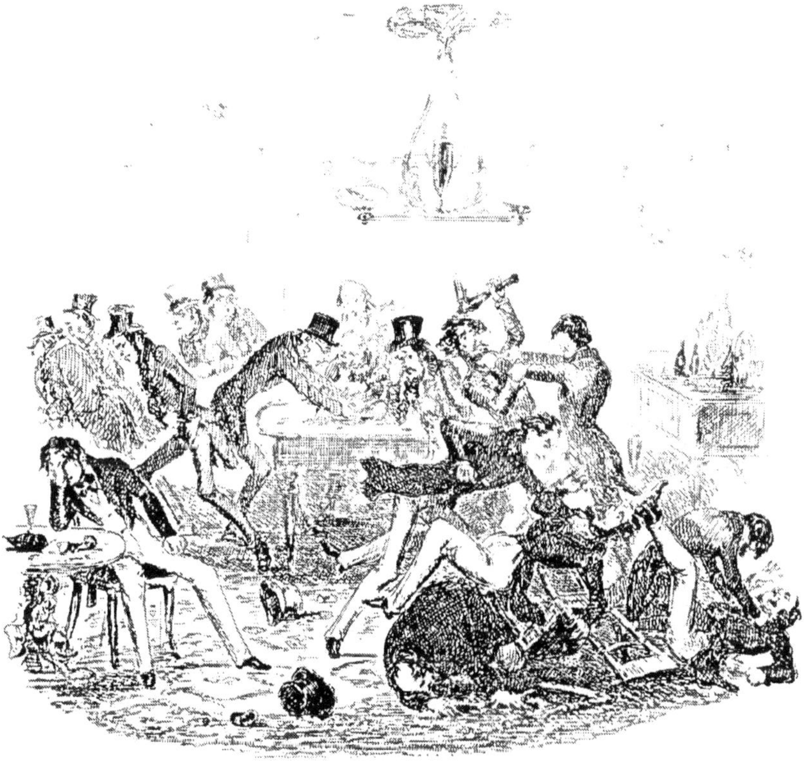

like a man of spirit, to become rich all at once. He had been told—by those of course whose interest it was to deceive him—that he might make a fortune in a few weeks, by a succession of what are called "hits" at the gaming-table. He listened to the voice which sought his ruin: he entered a Pandemonium; and in a few weeks not only was all his available money in the coffers, or, to speak with technical precision, "the bank" of the hellites, but also all the borrowed money he had been able by any effort to raise. Instead of learning wisdom from sad and painful experience, and abjuring gambling for ever, he only became the more desperately wedded to the dice-box and the cards. What might have been expected, speedily took place: he lost his business entirely, was disowned by his friends, and became a positive outcast from society. As he could not under any pretext or by any ingenuity he possessed get his acquaintances to advance him a sixpence more, he put his wits to the rack to devise methods by which he could obtain money, or that which would produce money, with the least amount of legal risk. He was in the habit of going to the houses of former friends wherever he would still be admitted, and stealing whatever portable articles of value came within his reach. He managed his felonies very adroitly. His favourite practice was to call at those early hours when the mistress of the house was not likely to be seen, owing to her being in dishabille, and when the probability consequently was, that he would be shown into the drawing-room until such time as she could put herself into a condition to see him. In such cases, his custom was to snatch up whatever he deemed most suitable for his purpose; and when walking out, to tell the servant that he would not wait for Mrs. So-and-So, but would call again in a day or two. As the lady of the house would not under these circumstances be, in many cases, in the particular room until some other person called, the article stolen would not be missed, and thus an innocent party might be blamed. In one such case, not seeing any other article sufficiently portable for theft, he actually stole a pocket bible. On another occasion, finding nothing of any value which was not too bulky for the purposes of transfer to another locality, he actually stole a Macintosh cloak which hung in the passage leading from the street-door. But of all the thefts—many of them dexterously committed—of which this young man was guilty, the most remarkable and the most ungrateful one was the following. He had gone to an old acquaintance, and laying before him the deplorable circumstances to which he had been reduced, pointed out to him a certain situation which was vacant, and besought him to use his exertions to procure it for him. His friend, though perfectly aware that the altered position in which the young man stood, was to be ascribed wholly to his own foolishness, was so convinced of his being incapable of doing a dishonest action, that he became positively indignant when any charge of dishonesty was preferred against him in his hearing. Anxious to do him a service, he took the young man with him to the office of the gentleman in whose establishment a situation was vacant. The parties were shown into a particular room by themselves; and on the other being called to speak to the gentleman who had the situation to dispose of, he said to the young man, "Now you wait here until I return, and I will let you know the result of the application. I wish to Heaven it may be successful; at all events, I will do everything in my power to get the place for you. I will be back in a few minutes." The friend of the young man then quitted the apartment, leaving his cloak in the care of the youthful ruined gambler. He had no sooner quitted the apartment, than the young man snatched up the cloak, which was quite new, and had cost six guineas, and proceeded forthwith to a pawnbroker's with it. It is unnecessary to say that he never afterwards inquired whether his friend was unsuccessful in his application in his behalf or not.

But stealing was not the only means to which this youthful victim of the gambling-table resorted in order to procure money wherewith to indulge his propensity for play. He was in the habit of making up false parcels, and delivering them at certain offices and houses, pretending they had come a distance, and demanding several shillings for their carriage. In order to practise the imposition more effectually, he dressed himself in the clothes of a porter, and so well imitated the manner and mode of speaking of that class of men, that no one ever suspected he was an impostor. In this way he contrived to raise, in small sums of two and three shillings at a time, a considerable amount of money. By-and-by, however, he overdid the thing. He went a second time to a place in which he had in this way before swindled a gentleman out of several shillings, when he was taken into custody, tried at the Old Bailey, convicted, and sentenced to twelve months' imprisonment; which sentence he is now undergoing. Thus, in the short space of three years, this young man, whose circumstances were so excellent and his prospects so bright, has been reduced not only to absolute penury, and to the loss of friends and of society, but to the degradation attaching to a convicted and imprisoned swindler.

I have before referred to the various games which are most general in the hells of the metropolis: that at which the greatest amount is lost or won in the shortest space of time, is French Hazard. This is the game which is almost invariably played in Crockford's, and all the Pandemoniums in which the nobility and gentry play. The loss of 10,000*l*., 15,000*l*, and even 20,000*l*., at this game, by one person in one night, is an event which is by no means of rare occurrence. It is well known, that a distinguished gambler ventured, a few years since, no less than 5000*l*. on the result of a single game at French hazard; which game only occupied a few minutes in playing.

Gambling is an almost universal vice. Though more prevalent in some countries than in others, it obtains to some extent in every country. The mode of gambling is infinitely diversified; but each country has its favourite game. Lewis and Clarke, in their "Travels to the Source of the Missouri," give an account of the mode in which the Indians in that part of America gamble. These travellers say—"The games are of two kinds. In the first, one of the company assumes the office of banker, and plays against the rest. He takes a small stone, about the size of a bean, which he shifts from one hand to the other with great dexterity, repeating at the same time a song adapted to the game, and which serves to divert the attention of the company, till, having agreed on the stake, he holds out his hands, and the antagonist wins or loses as he succeeds or fails at guessing in which hand the stone is. After the banker has lost his money, or whenever he is tired, the stone is transferred to another, who in turn challenges the rest of the company. The other game is something like the play of nine-pins: two pins are placed on the floor, about the distance of a foot from each other, and a small hole made behind them. The players then go about ten feet from the hole, into which they try to roll a small piece resembling the men used at draughts. If they succeed in putting it into the hole, they win the stake: if the piece rolls between the pins, but does not go into the hole, nothing is won or lost; but the wager is wholly lost if the chequer rolls outside of the pins. Entire days are wasted at these games, which are often continued through the night, round the blaze of their fires, till the last article of clothing, or even the last blue bead, is won from the desperate adventurer."

D'Israeli, in his "Curiosities of Literature," gives some curious particulars respecting the vice of gambling, as practised in the East. He says:—"Dice, and that little pugnacious animal the cock, are the chief instruments employed by the numerous nations of the East, to agitate their minds and ruin their fortunes: to which the Chinese, who are desperate gamblers, add the use of cards. When all other property is played away, the Asiatic gambler scruples not to stake his wife, or his child, on the cast of a die, or courage and strength of a martial bird. If still unsuccessful, the last venture he stakes is—himself!

"In the island of Ceylon, cock-fighting is carried to a great height. The Sumatrans are addicted to the use of dice. A strong spirit of play characterises a Malayan. After having resigned everything to the good fortune of the winner, he is reduced to a horrid state of desperation: he then loosens a certain lock of hair, which indicates war and destruction to all the raving gamester meets. He intoxicates himself with opium; and working himself up into a fit of phrenzy, he bites and kills every one who comes in his way. But as soon as ever this lock is seen flowing, it is *lawful* to fire at the person, and to destroy him as fast as possible. I think it is this which our sailors call, 'To run a muck.' Thus Dryden writes:

> 'Frontless, and satire-proof, he scours the streets,
> And runs an Indian muck at all he meets.'

Thus also Pope—

> Satire's my weapon, but I'm too discreet
> To run a muck, and tilt at all I meet.'

"Johnson could not discover the derivation of the word *muck*. I think I have heard that it refers to their employing, on these fatal occasions, a muck, or lance; but my recollection is probably imperfect.

"To discharge their gambling debts, the Siamese sell their possessions, their families, and, at length, themselves. The Chinese play night and day, till they have lost all they are worth; and then they usually go and hang themselves. Such is the propensity of the Japanese for high play, that they were compelled to make a law, that 'Whoever ventures his money at play, shall be put to death.' In the newly-discovered islands of the Pacific Ocean, they venture even their hatchets, which they hold as invaluable acquisitions, on running matches. 'We saw a man,' as Cook writes in his last voyage, 'beating his breast and tearing his hair, in the violence of rage, for having lost three hatchets at one of these races, and which he had purchased with nearly half his property.'

"The ancient nations were not less addicted to gaming. In the same volume are collected numerous instances amongst the ancient Persians, Grecians, and Romans! the Goths, the Germans, &c. To notice the modern ones were a melancholy task: there is hardly a family in Europe who cannot record, from their own domestic annals, the dreadful prevalence of this unfortunate passion. Affection has felt the keenest lacerations, and genius been irrecoverably lost, by a wanton sport, which doomed to destruction the hopes of families, and consumed the heart of the gamester with corrosive agony."

I could have given various passages from the works of travellers in every part of the world, to prove my position, that the vice of gambling is almost universal; thus proving equally the curse of civilized and barbarous society. That, however, is unnecessary. How it has thus come to be universally prevalent, is a question which I am incompetent to solve.

I believe there is one feature in the gambling of London peculiar to the English metropolis. I refer to the fact of the metropolitan gamblers making stated visits to particular towns in the provinces, for the purpose of prosecuting their "professional" pursuits. All the places at which horse-racing, or sporting amusements of any kind, take place, are regularly frequented by the hell-keepers of London. Epsom, Ascot, Southampton, and other favourite resorts of the patrons of the turf, are honoured during the racing days with a number of portable hells. The proprietors of the London Pandemoniums establish these movable branch hells in the course of a few hours. A marquee or tent suffices for the external part of the erection; and the bank, the dice, the wheel, the balls, and sundry packs of cards—not forgetting an ample supply of intoxicating liquors—are found all that is necessary, in the shape of furniture, for the interior. I went into one of these portable hells at the Southampton races of last year; and during the time I remained there, I saw a number of gentlemen plundered of very considerable sums. The hellites reaped a rich harvest on that occasion. After living for some days in Southampton in the greatest splendour, it is understood, they returned to town laden with the spoils of simple unsuspecting victims. At the Epsom races, too, of the present year, a friend of mine, who was foolish enough to play—which is almost synonymous with losing one's money,—states that gambling was carried on by London hellites to an extent of which none but those who were present, and witnessed the transactions with their own eyes, could have any idea. And yet, though thus notoriously carried on under the immediate observation of the magistrates and the police, no one interfered to prevent her Majesty's subjects from being robbed of their money.

With regard to the gaming-houses in London, I must say, in conclusion, that the existence of so great a number of them, and so openly, is a positive disgrace to a civilized, not to say a christian land. The legislature could easily put them down if it pleased; but, unfortunately for society, it does not choose to interfere. The reason is pretty obvious. A large proportion of our legislators in both Houses are themselves confirmed gamblers: nothing, therefore, is to be expected from parliament in the way of suppressing the hells which infest the metropolis.

What, then, is to be done? Must the evil, in all its awful magnitude and crying enormity, be suffered to exist unmolested and ungrappled with? Must the demon of the gambling-table in the metropolis be permitted to have his thousands of victims every year, without one effort being made to rescue a greater or less number of them from his grasp? I know of no way in which anything effective can be done to stay the wheels of this destructive Juggernaut—destructive at once of the fortunes and morals of its worshippers—unless it be by the wise and good doing all they can to expose the vice, so as that it may be seen in all its native and horrible hideousness. For this purpose, it were extremely desirable that some sort of society, consisting of virtuous and intelligent individuals, were formed, with the view of bringing to light the odious deeds practised in the hells of London; and the awful results, in the shape of suicides, trials at the Old Bailey, want, and wretchedness, which follow. I am sure that if young men were sufficiently aware of the nature of these infamous dens before entering them, they would as soon think of walking into the fire as of crossing their threshold. It appears to me, that a small cheap periodical, detailing individual cases of ruin effected in the hells of the metropolis, and exhibiting the characters of the desperate and unprincipled fellows who keep them,—would be productive of great good. Such a publication would be sure to have a large sale; for nothing could be more interesting—indeed, I may say, romantic—than the incidents with which the annals of metropolitan gambling abound.

I am sure there would be no want of materials for conducting such a periodical for at least some years to come. Many a victim of play would feel a melancholy pleasure in recording in it his own misfortunes. It would be to him some alleviation of his own regrets and mortification, to think that he had turned his crimes, or follies, if we must use the mildest term, into the means of teaching virtue or wisdom to others. There are certain weekly journals which now devote a certain portion of their space in every successive number to what they call an exposure of the Hells of the metropolis; and if, with all the drawbacks which attach to the character of the publications in question, men are found to relate, through them, the consequences of their having frequented the gambling-houses, how much more certainly might the conductors of any respectable periodical, whose object really was to expose and suppress gambling, rely on receiving an ample supply of authentic materials wherewith to work on?

Why such a society as that I have recommended should not be formed, I can see no reason whatever. We have not only societies of every form and class for the promotion of morality and religion, but we have societies for the express purpose of grappling with and putting down a variety of specific vices. We have a most excellent society for putting an end to cruelty to animals: we have sundry societies for the cure of intemperance, including societies which only have for their object to do away with the consumption of ardent spirits, and societies of a yet more radical character, namely, to prohibit the use of wine, or ale, or beer, or any other liquor whatever having in it intoxicating qualities. We have a Universal Peace Society; a society whose object is to grapple with and put down the vice of war, and to promote peace and harmony among all mankind. We have, in short, societies for the promotion of almost everything that is holy, just, and good, and the correction and extinction of everything that is evil. And why not a Society for the Suppression of Gambling? If the evils which result from this vice be as numerous and great as we have stated—and they are far more numerous, and of much greater magnitude—then surely a more wise or commendable course could not be adopted by the friends of humanity and virtue, than to form such a society at once. I am convinced it would be most liberally and most generally supported. Many an unhappy victim of the soul-and-body-destroying vice of gambling, would be glad to co-operate in rescuing others from the gulf into which he had flung his character and fortune. Many a parent would rejoice in countenancing, by every means in his power, the efforts which would be made by such a society to prevent young men and others from falling headlong into the pit prepared for them by the hellites. I do believe that the effects of such a society would speedily be to create in the country so strong an impression against the pernicious vice of gambling, that men would not only themselves feel ashamed that it should be known that they had ever crossed the portals of a gaming-house, but that people in general—I mean in England—would be ashamed to receive those persons into society who were notorious gamblers. I have a strong impression, that it is not until gambling be regarded as a vice which disqualifies a man for admission into society, that it will be compelled to hide its diminished head. At present, among the higher classes—among a certain portion of them, at least—instead of being ashamed of the practice of gambling, many persons are forward to make a boast of their having been at play, even when they have lost their money.

In the mean time, and until some great effort be made by a body of individuals to bring public opinion to bear against the destructive vice of gambling, I would warn all those into whose hands this work may fall, to guard against indulging to too great an extent in what is called "a hand at cards" among private friends. The vice is one of a most insidious kind: it imperceptibly grows on those who once give way, in however slight a degree, to it. Its rise and progress to a confirmed incurable passion can, in thousands of instances, be traced to playing at cards for purposes of pure amusement in parties of friends. They begin, as before remarked, by playing for the most trifling stakes, and not having the slightest wish to gain a sixpence; but it will invariably be found, that the longer persons play even at these games for amusement, and where the stakes are consequently trifling, the more does the disposition to proceed with the game grow upon them; and that, from an utter disregard, or rather entire thoughtlessness about gain, they become mortified and depressed when they lose, and elated when they win. It is ten to one but such parties, provided they repeat time after time playing for amusement, very soon become anxious to play solely for money, without the slightest reference to amusement. For a time they may confine their play to parties of private friends; but sooner or later, if the disposition to gamble for gain be not checked, they will undergo the natural transition from the private party to the public Pandemonium. And scarcely less certain is the relinquishment of the cards for the more speedy decision of the game by means of the dice-box. Gamblers are always impatient for the result. They cannot brook delay or protraction. So much depends on the throw, that it is no wonder they wish the point of who is to be the gainer or loser to be decided with the greatest practicable expedition. It is to the circumstance of a passion for expeditious as well as deep play having become general, I might almost say universal, among gamblers, that we are to ascribe the fact of most persons running their course, or, in other words, squandering away their fortunes, whether great or small, in so very short a period

CHAPTER XII.

THE METROPOLITAN AND CITY POLICE.

Introduction of the new system—The old police—Number, salaries, &c., of the new police—Their organization—Pensions for the aged and infirm of their number recommended—Character of the new police—Difference between them and the old police, in regard to their trustworthiness and efficiency—The city police—Its composition, and the expense of its maintenance—Number of the City police—Contemplated amalgamation of the Metropolitan and City police—Diminution of crime since the introduction of the new police—Their ingenuity in tracing out guilty parties—Reference to the French system of police.

THE sixth chapter of this work was devoted to the Police-offices. The present will be exclusively occupied with the Constabulary Force, including both the Metropolitan and City Police.

The constabulary system which now exists is only, as most of my readers are aware, of recent origin. It was introduced by Sir Robert Peel in 1829. Previous to that time, the police of the metropolis was in a most defective and inefficient state. It was the subject of loud and general complaint. For upwards of a quarter of a century the principles on which the old police force were established, had been unqualifiedly condemned by every one who had ever turned his attention to the subject. And no wonder: for the number of felonies, and other offences of every kind against property, which were weekly committed without the parties being detected, or, at all events, without being brought to justice, was almost incredible. Nor could it have been otherwise; for, in the first place, no attention was paid to the character of the persons chosen to the office of constables. They were almost, without exception, Irishmen of the very worst class in point of moral character; and, in addition to this, the smallness of their wages—from 13*s.* 6*d.* to 17*s.* per week—necessarily rendered them more liable to be bribed, than if they had been better paid. They were not only notoriously in the pay of the keepers of flash-houses, and other places for the concoction of schemes for the commission of crime, but they might, in the majority of cases, be bribed at the instance of any private gentleman who, to use their own phraseology, "did the handsome," by "tipping" them half a sovereign, however serious might be the charge on which he had been taken into custody. They were not, in fact, inspired with the spirit of their office. They had no pleasure in taking offenders into custody. They did not, as the new police do, engage in the duties of thief-catching with gusto. They preferred being suffered to crawl about as if there had been no such animal as a thief in the metropolis, or to doze away their time in a comfortable sleep, with their heads resting on their arms, in their little portable boxes. Their cowardice, too, as a body, was proverbial. Who does not remember the everlasting "rows" which the young men of the metropolis used to have with them on their return home from their convivial meetings." The "Charlies, as the old watch were usually called, were always considered legitimate subjects for a "sound drubbing." The fact was, that between the timidity of some, and the helplessness of others—for many of them were very feeble and advanced in life—they often were assaulted by half-drunken youths with impunity. With the present policemen, "young blades," as the phrase is, take special care not to interfere. One very rarely hears of any one attacking them. The reason is obvious. They are a body of men of great physical vigour and activity; and in the great majority of cases, are men of spirit and courage. A more feeble and inefficient set of men than the old police could scarcely have been got together. But, in addition to the mental and physical incompetency of the old constabulary force for the performance of the duties which were entrusted to them, the want of intercourse with each other greatly impaired their efficiency. They were chosen by the various parishes, and all the police in a particular parish were entirely under the control of the authorities of that parish. The consequence was, that there was nothing like concert among them. Responsibility did not rest anywhere. The authorities in one parish had their constant quarrels and bickerings with the authorities of other parishes, which was the direct way to prevent any general understanding among them in regard to the best means of repressing crime.

The amount of crime committed in the metropolis under this defective system of police was, as might have been expected, very great. No man's property was safe; and the difficulty which was then experienced in bringing the offender to justice, had the effect of preventing many of the parties robbed from engaging in the pursuit. Thus the inefficiency of the police establishment encouraged men, on the one hand, to commit crime, while, on the other, it deterred the parties against whom crimes were committed, from incurring the trouble and expense of bringing the offenders to justice. Crimes were committed under this system in open day, and under circumstances which would otherwise have been deemed of a most daring nature. Every one not only complained of the defective state of the police while in this condition; but various were the suggestions thrown out from time to time in the public journals, with the view of remedying the evils. But no sufficiently comprehensive scheme was thought of until, in 1829, Sir Robert Peel brought forward his plan for a more efficient system. The difference in the amount of crime now, and what it was previous to the introduction of the new police force, is a point to which I shall return in an after part of the chapter.

When the new police were formed in 1829, the total number was 3314. These consisted of 17 superintendents, 68 inspectors, 323 sergeants, and 2906 constables. Since then, the number has been gradually increasing. What it is at present, I have not been able to learn; but six months since it was, in round numbers, 3500. These 3500 are entrusted with the protection of the persons and property of about a million and a half of her Majesty's subjects; that being supposed to be the amount of the metropolitan population, exclusive of the City. If this estimate of the population ot London outside the walls of the City be correct, it would give us one police constable to every 425 persons.

The new police are under the control ot two commissioners, each having a salary of 800*l.* per year. The present commissioners are Colonel Rowan and Mr. Richard Mayne. The 17 superintendents have each an annual salary of 200*l.* The 68 inspectors severally receive a yearly salary of 100*l.*; the 323 sergeants individually receive 58*l.* per annum for their services; while the pay of the common constables is 19*s.* per week. Where the party is single, a deduction of one shilling is made in the event of lodgings being found for him. If married, and lodgings are found for the party, a special agreement must be made in each case. In addition to his weekly pay of 19*s.*, the private constable is entitled to as much clothing as is equal to two suits in the course of a year. The entire yearly expense ot the metropolitan police is 240,000*l.* Of this sum, 60,000*l.* is paid out of the consolidated fund, and the rest is made up by a rate on the parishioners.

The district embraced by the metropolitan police is formed into seventeen divisions. The number of men and officers, and the constitution of the force, is the same in each division; but "in laying out the division, attention has been paid to local and other circumstances determining the number of men required, the superficial extent varying in the several divisions, and consequently that portion of each which is committed to the care of each man." Each division is subdivided into eight sections, and each section into eight beats. "The limits of each of these," says the form ot instruction issued, "are clearly defined: each is numbered, and the number entered in a book kept for the purpose. Each division has an appropriate local name, and is also designated by a letter of the alphabet. There is in every division a station, or watch-house, placed as conveniently for the whole as may be, according to circumstances. From this point all the duty of the division is carried on." It is also stipulated in the "Instructions" given, that the men belonging to each section shall, as far as may be found practicable, lodge together near to the place of their duty, in order to render them speedily available in case the services of such as are off duty should be required for any special emergency. There is a distinct company for each division; and each company is divided into sixteen parties, each party consisting of one sergeant and nine men. Four sergeant's parties, being a fourth part of the company, form one inspector's party. The whole company is under the command of a superintendent. Every police constable is conspicuously marked with the letter of a division, and also with a number corresponding with his name in the books belonging to the body. The object of this is, to enable the public at once to identify the party in the event of there being any ground of complaint against the constables, whether by overdoing their duty, or not doing it all. The letter of the alphabet marked on the collar of each policeman's coat, denotes the particular district in which he serves. A represents Whitehall; B, Westminster; C, St. James's; D, Marylebone; E, Holborn; F, Covent Garden; G, Finsbury; H, Whitechapel; K, Stepney; L, Lambeth; M, Southwark; N, Islington; P, Camberwell; R, Greenwich; S, Hampstead; T, Kensington; and V, Wandsworth.

The course to be adopted when a person wishes to become a member of the metropolitan police force, is sufficiently easy and simple. He has only to present a petition to the commissioners, accompanied with a certificate as to good character from two respectable householders in the parish in which he resides. Inquiry is then made relative to the parties signing the certificate; and it being found that they are respectable men, whose testimony as to the applicant's character may be relied on, his name is put on the list of eligible candidates for the situation whenever a vacancy shall occur. I need scarcely say that, before appointment, the party is examined by a surgeon, to see that he suffers under no physical defect which would prevent the efficient discharge of his duties. It is also requisite that he should be under thirty-five years of age, and that he be five feet eight inches in height. The average time which an applicant has to wait, after his name has been inserted in the list of persons eligible to the office, is about eight weeks. Should, however, a party deem it an object to get appointed with the utmost practicable expedition, he may succeed in the short space of ten or twelve days, by getting some personal friend of either of the commissioners to use his influence on the applicant's behalf. The usual form of a petition and certificates from rate-payers, and so forth, are dispensed with in such cases. All that is necessary on the part of the applicant is, that he be able-bodied, the proper height, and not beyond his thirty-fifth year.

Nothing could be more complete than the organization of the metropolitan police. Each party or company is divided into fours; the first four being on duty for a given time, and the other four coming to their relief, just as in the case of soldiers, whenever their allotted period has expired. It is the duty of the sergeant to see that this arrangement is strictly attended to, and also that the parties take the night and day watches alternately. Two of the inspectors are always on duty at once. One of them examines into the state of matters throughout the division; for which purpose he is constantly going about among the men: the other inspector is stationed at the watch-house to receive charges, complaints, and all applications for assistance. The various sergeants throughout the division regularly report to the inspectors the existing state of affairs within their respective districts. When the men are relieved, they must all assemble at a particular spot, just as when about to go on duty, in order that the sergeant may see that they are all sober, and as correctly dressed as when he marched them to the scene of their duties. It is thus impossible that any dereliction of duty or improper conduct can take place in the case of any of the men, without its being immediately brought under the notice of the superintendent; and, through him, where the case may be such as to require it, under the notice of the commissioners. The latter gentlemen may dismiss any of their men at a moment's notice, and without assigning any reason for such dismissal. It is from time to time impressed on the mind of each police constable, that he must make himself perfectly acquainted with all the parts of the streets, courts, thoroughfares, outhouses, &c., of the section of the metropolis constituting his beat. He is also expected—a thing which may at first sight appear impossible—"to possess such a knowledge of the inhabitants of each house as will enable him to recognize their persons." He is further expected to see every part of his beat once in ten, or at least fifteen minutes, unless in such cases as it may be deemed necessary to remain in a particular place for a longer period, to watch the conduct of some suspected person. A printed copy of instructions as to how he shall act in almost every conceivable case, is given to the police constable on his appointment to the office; so that if he either neglect or exceed his duty, the fault—with a very few exceptions, in which there may exist doubts as to the course he should adopt—is sure to rest with himself.

The new police are a remarkably fine body of men. As only nine years have elapsed since their formation, and as no one was admitted who was not under thirty-five years of age, they are all in the prime of life. Then their constant exercise has a natural tendency to render them healthy: nor must it be forgotten, that the circumstance of being five feet eight inches in height insures their being at least the ordinary size. And their natural advantages in these respects are improved by their manner of dressing. They are not only always clean, but the form of their clothes is well adapted to exhibit their persons to the best advantage.

It is to be regretted, for their own sakes, and indirectly for the sake of the public, that no provision in the shape of pension is made for those of the new police who may be disabled from the performance of their duties while engaged in the public service, or when old age overtakes them. Many instances have occurred in which the most meritorious of their number have been so severely assaulted—sometimes by drunken "gentlemen," at others by sturdy beggars—when in the performance of their duty, as to be unable afterwards either to perform the duties of policemen, or to provide for themselves or family by engaging in any other occupation. Now it is surely manifest injustice to allow men to be incapacitated for all future work through personal injuries received in consequence of a zealous and faithful discharge of their duties, and yet deny them any provision for their support. But apart from their liability to receive personal injuries of the serious nature alluded to, there is the certainty, if their life is to be spared, of old age, with all its concomitant infirmities. What a miserable prospect for these men do advanced years present! By the time they attain a certain age, they will, in the nature of things, be unfit for the continued discharge of the duties of their office; and just at that moment they will be turned adrift without a farthing in the world, and without the physical ability to earn as much as would procure them the most scanty means of subsistence. How galling must be the reflection to them, that they have spent their best days in the public service, and are now, like the aged greyhound in the fable, unable any longer to catch the hare,—to have all their former meritorious conduct forgotten, and themselves dismissed! Were their pay such as that with prudence and economy they might contrive to make some provision for old age, the matter would be different; but it is barely sufficient, in such a place as London, to afford them the means of a homely subsistence. No man, not prepared to deny himself the most common necessaries of life, could save a sixpence out of nineteen shillings per week. The consequence of this insufficient pay, and no pension in the case of accident or being overcome by old age, must necessarily be to diminish their zeal and enterprise in the public service, and to cause them to avail themselves of any opportunity which presents itself of getting a livelihood in some other way. It is well known that many of the most meritorious of their number have quitted the service and engaged in other avocations. This would not be the case, were some provision for the future made for them by means of a pension. It would not be necessary that that pension should be large. Just as much—say six or seven shillings a-week—as would be sufficient to protect them against actual starvation, or the other horrible alternative, the workhouse, would, I am sure, be satisfactory to them. Some time ago, there was a report in the newspapers that something was in contemplation by the Home Secretary, with the view of making some permanent certain pension for the police, in case of accidents, or the approach of old age; but I am not aware that the report was founded in truth. If, however, some such provision be not made for them, not only will they be most ungenerously and ungratefully treated by the country, but the circumstance will speedily impair the efficiency and lessen the respectability of the body; and the public will consequently be the sufferers, in the diminished security of person and property.

The new police were for some time very unpopular. There was a natural tendency in the minds of the people to look with suspicion on a body with very enlarged powers, and which had been constituted in a manner different from any previous constabulary force which had been known in this country. These suspicions were converted into positive apprehensions by the clamorous opposition got up to the new police by one or two journals circulating largely among the lower orders of the community. Every movement they made was narrowly watched; and every action they performed was made the subject of severe criticism,—often of downright misrepresentation. The result was, that the public prejudice, especially as regarded the working classes in the metropolis, became so strong against the new constabulary force, that the impression began to gain ground that the experiment—for it was admitted by Sir Robert Peel and others to be in some respects nothing more than an experiment—would not succeed, but that the body must be broken up, and a recurrence to something like the old system take place. The vast diminution, however, in the amount of crime committed in town, and the great addition to the number of cases in which the offenders were detected, taken into custody, and prosecuted to conviction, soon became sufficiently apparent to remove gradually the prejudices so strongly and generally entertained against the new force, and to make it popular with the public. The experience of nine years has confirmed the predictions of good from it, made by the authors of the measure. Person and property are now incomparably safer than they were under the old system. The new police are now the objects of universal approbation, and most deservedly so. But this is a point to which I shall afterwards have occasion to make incidental allusions before I come to the end of the chapter.

I have not access to an official account of the number of persons taken into custody by the metropolitan police for any of the last four or five years. In 1831, the number of persons they took into custody was 72,824; of whom 45,907 were males, and 26,917 were females. This, on an average, would give the number of persons taken into custody every year by each policeman, as eighteen or twenty; 3300 being about the number of constables in the metropolitan police establishment at the period in question. And how, it will be asked, were all the charges brought against those 72,824 persons disposed of? In this way: —2955 of them were committed for trial; 21,843 were summarily convicted: 24,585 were discharged; and 23,787, being cases of drunkenness unaccompanied with any other crime, the parties were dismissed by the superintendents when they became sober.

The integrity and trustworthiness of the new police, considered as a body, are above all praise. It is surprising in how few instances charges of corruption have been preferred, far less proved, against any of their number. One scarcely ever hears of such a charge. There seems to be a spirit of rivalry as to who shall be the most honest—if the expression be a proper one—as well as to who shall be the most active and enterprising among the body. This is a feeling which ought to be cultivated by the commissioners and the government. Somebody, on one occasion, made the remark to me, in conversing on this point, that so great is their delight and such their honesty in the discharge of their duties, that if they found their own fathers or brothers committing a cognizable offence, they would not hesitate an instant in conveying them to the station-house. This is, no doubt, overcolouring the thing; still I am convinced that their faithfulness to the trust reposed in them is so great, that the motive must be exceedingly powerful indeed which could prevail on them to betray that trust. One such instance, and only one, consists with my own knowledge. A policeman, having undoubted evidence of a lady uttering forged five-pound notes, knowing them to be forged, determined on taking her into custody as soon as he should have such evidence as would prove conclusive in the eye of the law.

That evidence he eventually obtained; and accordingly proceeded, dressed in plain clothes*, to her house for the purpose of taking her into custody in the quietest and most delicate manner possible. On calling at her residence, which was in the West-end, and had a handsome exterior, he was shown up to the drawing-room, where he stood for a few seconds confounded with the dazzling brilliancy of everything around him. The lady promptly made her appearance, and he was about to intimate to her, in the politest way possible, the purport of his visit. He was, however, so overpowered by her surpassing beauty and dignified appearance, that he was unable to utter a word; and actually, solely from the impression the lady's beauty and manner made upon him, quitted the place without performing his duty, or even hinting to the lady what the object of his visit had been; but contented himself with getting up the most ingenious pretext he could, for having called on her. She did not even know, for some years afterwards, that he belonged to the constabulary force. Fortunately for him, he had acted in this instance without consulting any of his colleagues or superiors; and consequently he could decline performing his duty without exposing himself to any serious personal consequences. This, in my opinion—and the fact may be relied on,—is one of the most striking conquests which ever female beauty achieved. What a proof of its power! Disarming a policeman and deterring him from the discharge of his duty in the way I have described, reminds me of the resistless fascinations of poor Sheridan's manner. I forget whether it be Byron or Moore, but one of them has related an anecdote of his having, by his exceedingly winning manner and address, staved off the legal proceedings which an attorney had instituted against him to recover an amount of money which he owed to a third party. This single fact spoke more for the singularly fascinating manner of Sheridan, than a huge quarto volume could have done.

Before the establishment of the new force, charges of corruption were not only frequently preferred, but proved against the police. The Parliamentary Committee of 1828, after referring to the great number of compromises which parties robbed† had

* I should also state that he was an inspector, and had a very gentlemanly appearance.

† These parties chiefly refer to bankers. To give some idea of the extent to which bank robberies were then carried, it may be interesting to quote some extracts from the evidence of the Parliamentary Committee just mentioned. They say—"Two banks that had been severally robbed of notes to the amount of 4000*l*., recovered them on payment of 1000*l*. each. In another case, 2200*l*. was restored out of 3200*l*. stolen, for 230*l*. or 240*l*. This bank having called in their old circulation, and issued fresh notes immediately after the robbery, the difficulty thus occasioned was the cause of not much above 10*l*. per cent. being demanded. In another case, Spanish bonds,

made with the thieves, goes on to express its conviction at some length—a conviction founded on the evidence, on oath, of various witnesses—that some of the leading individuals connected with the police establishments of that period had been guilty of very serious corruption. In one case, eight hundred pounds more was received by the police officer who negotiated for the recovery of stolen property than the thieves asked or received. It is, no doubt, true, that in many instances the police, on becoming the instruments through whom compromises between the thieves and the parties whose property was stolen should be effected, were actuated by no dishonest motive; or rather did not see anything morally wrong in getting forty or fifty pounds to themselves for the part they took in the negotiation, in cases where, otherwise, no part of the property would have been recovered. Still the thing was decidedly improper, and was attended with the worst results. The committee in question, in reference to this, very justly remark, "That the frequency of these seemingly blameless transactions has led to the organization of a system which undermines the security of all valuable property; which gives police officers a direct interest that robberies to a large amount should not be prevented; and which has established a set of putters-up and fences, with means of evading, if not defying, the arm of the law, who are wealthy enough, if large rewards are offered for the detection, to double them for their impunity; and who would, in one case, have given a thousand pounds to get rid of a single witness. Some of these persons ostensibly carry on a trade: one

---

nominally worth 2000*l.*, were given back on payment of 100*l.* A sum, not quite amounting to 20,000*l.*, was, in one case, restored for 1000*l.* In another, where bills had been stolen of 16,000*l.* or 17,000*l.* value, but which were not easily negotiable by the thieves, restitution of 6000*l.* was offered for 300*l.* The bank, in this case, applied to the Home Office for a free pardon for an informer, but declined advertising a reward of 1000*l.*, and giving a bond not to compound as the conditions of such grant. In another case, 3000*l.* seems to have been restored for 19*l.* per cent. In another case, where the robbery was to the amount of 7000*l.*, and the supposed robbers had been apprehended, and remanded by the magistrates for examination, the prosecution was suddenly desisted from, and the property subsequently restored for a sum not ascertained by the Committee. In the case of another bank, the sum stolen not being less than 20,000*l.*, is stated to have been bought of the thieves by a receiver for 200*l.*; and 2800*l.* taken of the legal owners as the price of restitution. The Committee does not think it necessary to detail all the cases which have been disclosed to them; but though it is evident they have not been informed of anything like all the transactions that must have occurred under so general a system, they have proof of more than sixteen banks having sought by these means to indemnify themselves for their losses: and that property of various sorts, to the value of above 200,000*l.*, has, within the last few years, been the subject of negotiation or compromise. They have found it difficult, for many reasons, to ascertain, in several of the cases they have examined, the actual payments made to the thieves or receivers; but they have proof of nearly 12,000*l.* having been paid to them by bankers only, accompanied with a clearance from every risk and perfect impunity to their crimes." What a state of things is here disclosed! It is no wonder though the integrity of the police of that period was suspected.

who had been tried formerly for robbing a coach, afterwards carried on business as a Smithfield drover, and died worth, it is believed, 15,000*l.* Your Committee could not ascertain how many of these persons there are at present; but four of the principal have been pointed out. One was lately the farmer of one of the greatest turnpike trusts in the metropolis. He was formerly tried for receiving the contents of a stolen letter; and as a receiver of tolls, employed by him, was also tried for stealing that very letter, being then a postman, it is not too much to infer that the possession of these turnpikes is not unserviceable for the purposes of depredation. Another has, it is said, been a surgeon in the army. Two others of the four have no trade, but live like men of property; and one of these, who appears to be the chief of the whole set, is well known on the turf, and is stated, on good grounds, to be worth 30,000*l.*" Such a state of things no longer exists. There are still receivers of stolen property, but none in this wholesale and open way. The vigilance of the police has put an end to this system. Not only have the present police largely contributed to the suppression of crime in the metropolis by their own watchfulness, activity, and enterprise, but they have indirectly contributed to the improved state of things by the spirit of emulation which they have excited in the leading men belonging to the City Police, and the officers attached to the various police office establishments in London.

The city of London has a police establishment of its own, over which the Court of Aldermen and other functionaries have an entire and exclusive control. The constabulary force of the City is divided into two classes—a day and a night police. The day police consists of one superintendent, at a salary of 143*l.* per annum, exclusive of 9*l.* 18*s.* for clothes; two inspectors, with a yearly salary each of 87*l.* 2*s.*, and 7*l.* 8*s.* 9¾*d.* for clothing; one inspector, at an annual salary of 83*l.* 4*s.*, and 7*l.* 8*s.* 9¾*d.* for clothing; one sergeant (Smithfield), whose yearly salary is 66*l.* 6*s.*, with 4*l.* 16*s.* 3¾*d.* for apparel; nine sergeants, at an annual salary each of 58*l.* 10*s.*, and 4*l.* 16*s.* 3¾*d.* for clothing; seventeen constables (Smithfield), severally at yearly salaries of 57*l.* 4*s.*, and 4*l.* 16*s.* 3¾*d.* for clothing; three constables at 12*l.* 6*s.* each, with 4*l.* 16*s.* 3¾*d.* for wearing apparel; and sixty constables, each at 49*l.* 8*s.* yearly salary, with 4*l.* 16*s.* 3¾*d.* for clothing. In addition to these, there are sixteen or eighteen constables, of different grades; but all in some way or other are connected with the ordinary police establishment at the Mansion-house and Guildhall. The entire yearly expense of maintaining the day constabulary force of the City, including the salaries of a clerk and a surgeon, and the pensions allowed to eleven old and infirm police servants of a former day, was, in 1835, 7,262*l.* 12*s.* 9½*d.* It is much about the same now.

The nightly police of the City, exclusive of 65 superintending watchmen, 91 patrolling watchmen, and 47 beadles, numbers 453. Each of these is paid by the hour. Threepence per hour is the sum allowed; which, for twelve hours per day, would give one guinea per week each. The yearly salaries of the superintendants vary in different wards from 85*l.* down to 52*l.* The wages of the patrolling watchmen fluctuate between nine* shillings and twenty-five shillings per week each; while the annual pay of the beadles varies from 50*l.* to 100*l.* The entire expense of the nightly watch of the City is 34,924*l.* 18*s.* 6*d.* per annum.

The whole yearly expense of the police of the City is divided into three branches, thus:—

Marshal and Marshalmen	£1,675	6	0
Day Police	7,262	12	9¼
Nightly Watch	34,924	18	6
Making a total of	£43,862	17	3¼

It will thus be seen that, considering the proportion in regard to numbers which the City bears to the metropolitan police, the latter are considerably less expensive than the former; while any one who knows anything of the comparative efficiency of the two forces, must give the palm of superiority at once to the metropolitan body. This superiority is easily accounted for. In the choice of men for the metropolitan police, private influence, except in very rare cases, is not exercised; and were it so, would not be attended to: in the choice of men for the City police, a good deal of this influence is exercised with effect. Again, all the metropolitan policemen are young and active: in the case of the City constabulary body, many of them are considerably advanced in life, and consequently are not so full of enterprise and spirit. But that, perhaps, which chiefly gives the superiority to the metropolitan police is, the admirable manner in which they are organized. It were difficult to conceive of anything more perfect than is the organization of that body.

It is understood that the Home Secretary is anxious for a junction or amalgamation of the metropolitan and City police forces, but that the civic authorities are opposed to it. Their opposition to any such proposal was to be expected. They have always shown themselves to be exceedingly jealous of their own peculiar privileges, and determined to preserve them even in cases where the public interest would have been manifestly and more materially promoted by their relinquishment. But if they will

* Of course, it will be understood, that where the salary is as low as this, there is hardly any duty to be performed.

not listen to any proposal for placing their constabulary body under the control of the Home Secretary, as the metropolitan police are, why do they not assimilate their own force as much as possible, in regard to their organization, to the metropolitan body?

It must be admitted, that an improvement has taken place of late in the City constabulary force. They are far more effective than they were before the metropolitan body was established; but it is not to be denied, that a great deal more might yet be done, even without the City authorities relinquishing their exclusive control over their constables.

I have said that there has been a great diminution in the amount of crime committed in London, since the institution of the new police. Almost all the extensive confederations which then existed for the purpose of carrying on a regularly organized system of robbery, and other crimes against property and person, have been broken up, and scattered in all directions. We no longer hear of acts of wholesale plunder, or of thieves being leagued together, and carrying on an organized system o war against property, in bands of twenties or thirties. What is now done, in the way of housebreaking or felony, is usually done by some adventurer on his own account, or by small partnerships of two or three. Nor do we now hear of the ingenuity of former thieves, in defeating the ends of justice; an ingenuity which often gave an air of rich romance to the adventures of the parties. The thieves of the present day, owing to the vigilance of the new police, have but few and slender opportunities of displaying any ingenuity they possess; in other words, their "affairs" are not now attempted on that large and daring scale on which they were formerly done. Ingenuity itself finds it impossible to get even skilful plans of robbery laid, far less executed. The achievements of our present thieves are poor and spiritless, compared with the triumphs of their predecessors ten or twelve years since. What the state of crime in the metropolis then* was,

---

* A history of the state of crime in the metropolis, from the beginning of the last century up to the present period, would form a very curious chapter. About a hundred years ago, the number of robbers in London was so great, and such was their daring and desperate character, that persons were afraid, even in the middle of the day, to cross Moorfields, then an open sort of common, or of going alone to any of the unfrequented parts of the suburbs. The number of robberies then committed in daylight, in the suburbs of London, was very great. At night they were, as might be expected, still greater. Some curious accounts, relative to the state of crime in the metropolis, in the early part of the last century, will be found in several of the works respecting London, which appeared during the first half of that century. In the early part of the second half of last century, there seems to have been no improvement, as regards the number of robberies committed; though they appear to have been, in most cases, attended with less personal violence, and to have been committed under circumstances of greater secrecy. Henry Fielding, the celebrated novelist, and who was one

may be inferred from the statements made by authorities of undoubted veracity, and who had ample opportunities of forming an accurate opinion on the subject. The Parliamentary Committee which sat in 1828, to inquire into the state of the police in the metropolis, brought a great many facts to light, illustrative of the extent to which crime then prevailed in London. An author, who had the very best opportunities of acquiring correct information on the subject, says that the number of persons who then lived by thieving in the metropolis, could not be under 30,000; and that the amount of property annually stolen must have been close on 2,000,000*l.* Now, I will venture to say—and

---

of the magistrates of Middlesex at the time, wrote a small work, about the year 1755 on the subject of the prevalence of the crime of robbery in London at that time. It was dedicated to Lord Hardwicke, then Lord Chancellor of Great Britain, and was intitled "An Inquiry into the Causes of the Increase of Robberies, &c." Mr. Fielding commences his work in these words:—"The great increase of robberies within these few years, is an evil which, to me, appears to deserve some attention; and the rather, as it seems, though already become so flagrant, not yet to have arrived to that height of which it is capable, and which it is likely to attain; for diseases in the political as in the natural body seldom fail going on to their crisis, especially when nourished and encouraged by faults in the constitution. In fact, I make no doubt, but that the streets of this town, and the roads leading to it, will shortly be impassable, without the utmost hazard; nor are we threatened with seeing less dangerous gangs of rogues among us than those which the Italians call the banditti." Again:—"For my own part, I cannot help regarding these depredations in a most serious light; nor can I help wondering that a nation so jealous of her liberties, that from the slightest cause, and often from no cause at all, we are always murmuring at our superiors, should tamely and quietly support the invasion of her property by a few of the lowest and vilest among us. Doth not this situation in reality level us with the most enslaved countries? If I am to be assaulted, and pillaged, and plundered; if I can neither sleep in my own house, nor walk the streets, nor travel in safety, is not my condition almost equally bad, whether a licensed or unlicensed rogue, a dragoon or a robber, be the person who assaults and plunders me? The only difference which I can perceive is, that the latter evil appears to be more easy to remove. If this be, as I clearly think it is, the case, surely there are few matters of more general concern than to put an immediate end to these outrages, which are already become so notorious, and which, as I have observed, seem to threaten us with such a dangerous increase. What, indeed, may not the public apprehend, when they are informed, as an unquestionable fact, that there is at this time a great gang of rogues whose number falls little short of a hundred, who are incorporated in one body, have officers and a treasury, and have reduced theft and robbery into a regular system. There are of this society, men, who appear in all disguises, and mix in most companies. Nor are they better versed in every art of cheating, thieving, and robbing, than they are armed with every method of evading the law, if they should ever be discovered, and an attempt made to bring them to justice. Then, if they fail in rescuing the prisoner, or (which seldom happens) in bribing or deterring the prosecutor, they have, for their last resource, some rotten members of the law to forge a defence for them, and a great number of false witnesses ready to support it."

"And when Colquhoun wrote his "Treatise on the Police of the Metropolis," which was in the year 1800, the state of crime in London appears to have been of the most frightful kind. He states that persons could not "travel on the highways, or approach the capital in any direction after dark, without risk of being assaulted and robbed, and, perhaps, wounded or murdered." The same author further observes, that "we cannot lie down to rest in our habitations without the dread of a burglary being committed, our property invaded, and our lives exposed to imminent danger, before the approach of morning."

I speak from several years' personal observation of what has been going on at the Old Bailey—that the amount of property yearly stolen in London does not amount to 100,000*l.*; and that the number of regular thieves, or those who live by theft, is under 5000. With respect to crimes against the person, they are now comparatively rare. Every one, in fact, who lives in London, feels a consciousness of security, both in regard to his person and property, which was not felt before the establishment of the new police. I am aware that the great diminution in the amount of crimes in the metropolis, which has taken place within the last eight or ten years, is not to be entirely ascribed to the establishment of the new police. The progress of education, and other accidental causes, have doubtless contributed in some degree to the happy result; but the principal instrument in the accomplishment of this salutary change, must be admitted by all who have paid any attention to the subject, to be the metropolitan constabulary force.

Many of the police are singularly ingenious in tracing out guilt, and in discovering the guilty, when they have reason to suspect the one, or have the smallest clue given them to the other. Some years since, a curious instance of the dexterity with which a suspicion, resting on very slender grounds, was converted into positive proof, was given by a policeman who is either now dead, or has quitted the service. The policeman in question, having occasion one day to be in New Bond-street, was much struck with the splendid appearance of a carriage he saw standing at a jeweller's door. Several other persons having been equally struck with it, had assembled at the door of the tradesman to see the person to whom it belonged. The policemen saw that that person was a dashingly-dressed, most lady-like woman, seemingly about forty years of age. He inquired of the by-standers who the lady was, but no one present could furnish him with the desired information. While he was making his inquiries, he chanced to overhear the proprietor of the shop say to her, that the twenty-pound-note he held in his hand, and had received from her, was forged; adding, while returning it to her, that she could pay the ten shillings'-worth of articles she had purchased at any other time. This circumstance, in conjunction with something peculiar he observed in the manner of the lady, awakened his suspicions, and he determined to follow her to the next place to which she should direct the coachman to proceed. In prosecuting his resolve, he engaged a hackney-coach, and followed her to a house in Park-lane. Having remained there for some time, he ascertained that she was not likely to go out again a-shopping that day. Next day, about the time at which ladies usually set out on their shopping excursions, he took care to be in the neighbourhood of the lady's house. The carriage presently came to the door; and the lady having made her appearance, and desired the coachman to drive to a particular shop in Ludgate-hill, sprang into the vehicle and drove off. As on the previous day, the policeman hired a coach, and having leaped into it, desired Jehu to drive with the greatest possible expedition to the same place. He reached it before the lady, but did not enter the shop until he saw her in the act of descending from her carriage. He asked a sight of the lowest priced articles in the shop, satisfied that when a lady so splendidly dressed entered in the capacity of a customer, the attentions of the shopmen would be withdrawn from him to be lavished on the lady. The event turned out exactly as he expected. He was forgotten, while there seemed to be the greatest rivalry among the shopmen as to who should show the lady the most marked attention. She made purchases to the amount of one pound ten shillings, and again tendered a twenty-pound note in payment of them. The proprietor of the premises, after narrowly scrutinizing the note, observed that there were a great many forged notes in circulation at that time, and that the note in question had a very equivocal appearance. She affirmed it was good with much energy, and with an air that seemed to indicate, that she was indignant at the bare thought of having a forged note in her possession. Afraid of offending one who he thought might become a good customer, the shopkeeper, though not without some misgivings, took the note, and returned the eighteen pounds ten shillings. The lady then bade him good morning, and re-entering her carriage, desired her coachman to drive to a particular shop in Cheapside. There she was followed by the policeman; and there he saw her purchase fifteen shillings'-worth of trinkets, again tendering a twenty-pound note for payment, and receiving the nineteen pounds five shillings of change. The policeman was now satisfied beyond all doubt, that as she tendered a twenty-pound note by way of payment of the articles she had purchased, while he knew her to have eighteen pounds odd of loose money in her possession, she must not only be guilty of uttering forged notes, but that she was aware that they were forged. He followed her in the same way to a third shop, where he saw the same thing repeated, which, of course, made him yet more confident in the soundness of his opinions. Still he wanted conclusive evidence to prove the charge. He watched her movements for some time, and got access to the most conclusive evidence. He then took her into custody. It was discovered that she lived with a gang of male rogues who forged the notes, and caused her to utter them, thinking there was, in that way, less risk of being detected. Seeing the case so clear against her, she committed suicide by taking laudanum.

Another successful instance of the ingenuity displayed by the police in detecting crime, and securing the conviction of the offenders, occurred in the spring of last year. Information had been communicated to the police magistrates in London, that the town and neighbourhood of Salisbury had been inundated with counterfeit silver of every denomination, from crown pieces down to sixpences; but that all the efforts of the magisterial authorities in that place had failed to obtain a clue to the offenders. One of the cleverest of the inspectors of the London police was consulted on the subject, and he at once undertook to discover and bring the parties to justice. Having, from the success of former exploits in the same way, every confidence in the ingenuity and ability of the inspector, the magistrates signified their willingness to leave the matter wholly in the officer's hands. The plan which the latter adopted in the execution of his enterprise was one which would not have suggested itself to ordinary minds. He desired a person, in whom he could confide, to go down immediately to Salisbury, and in the disguise and character of a pedlar, to visit all the lower class of public-houses in the town and neighbourhood. He further instructed him, in the event of seeing in those houses suspicious characters, to treat them with gin, or ale, or whatever else in the way of drink they preferred, and to make himself as familiar as possible with them. He was to cultivate their acquaintance with the greatest assiduity; to give them hints that he himself was prepared for any desperate enterprise, in the way of robbery or otherwise, provided he got any other parties to assist him; and, in short, have recourse to every possible expedient to get them to make such disclosures to him as would not only satisfy himself, or might satisfy any other reasonable mind that they were the guilty parties, but as would constitute, or lead to, such evidence as the law would admit. The pioneer of the police officer had been only two days in Salisbury, when he came in contact with two or three persons whom he at once suspected to belong to the gang of coiners of false money. At first they fought shy of him; they appeared decidedly averse to his acquaintanceship; but in the course of two or three days more, their prepossessions against him wore off, and they entered into familiar conversation with him. The result was the confirmation of his suspicions as to what they were. The next point to which he directed his attention was the ascertaining what their number was; for he knew that in such cases they took care not to assemble all together in any particular place in public, as that might lead to suspicion. This secret he also soon wormed out of his newly-formed acquaintances. Having succeeded so far, he wrote, agreeably to instructions, to the officer in London by whom he was employed.

His employer immediately proceeded to Salisbury; but "lay by," as the phrase is, for ten or twelve days, until his beard should grow to such a length as, with other ingenious expedients, should enable him to disguise himself sufficiently for the execution of his plans. He at once conjectured—and in his conjecture he was right—that the gang of coiners were from London, and that, if not disguised, he would be recognized before he should be able to carry his schemes into effect. His beard having grown to a great length, and having for some days omitted to wash his face or hands, and having also put on a ragged suit of clothes, he ventured into the public-houses which they frequented, got acquainted with them through the "workman" he had sent to prepare the way before him, and in a few days was, with one and all of them, a regular "Hail fellow! well met." He soon ascertained that they were all to meet at a particular house, in a low secluded part of the town, on a particular night; and to make assurance doubly sure that this meeting was to take place for the purpose of a new coinage, he proposed treating them on the night and hour they had fixed for their meeting, in a public-house which he mentioned. They one and all said the business on which they were to meet that night was so urgent, that it must be attended to; but they should be most happy to have their glass with him any other evening he might appoint. Thus assured beyond all doubt that "an affair" was to come off on the evening in question, he got assistance from the magistrates of the place, and proceeded to the house in which they were met. His anticipations were all realized: there was the whole gang of them—nine or ten in number—busily employed in the very act of coining various descriptions of money. Every one of them was taken into custody, and all of them were convicted at the next assizes, and visited with due punishment.

With the view of illustrating how quick the police are in discovering an offender when a crime has been committed, I may mention an anecdote which has been verbally communicated to me. The anecdote will at the same time show the regular business-way in which they perform the duties of their office. Some years ago, a robbery of property to a considerable amount had taken place in the City. Circumstances caused suspicions to fall on a particular person well known for having been engaged in similar enterprises before. He was taken into custody, and brought before the magistrates on the following day. A young woman, servant in the house in which the robbery had been committed, and who had seen the thief go out of the door after committing the robbery, was called before the magistrate to speak to the question of identity. The prisoner being put to the bar, she, without a moment's hesitation, and in the most positive

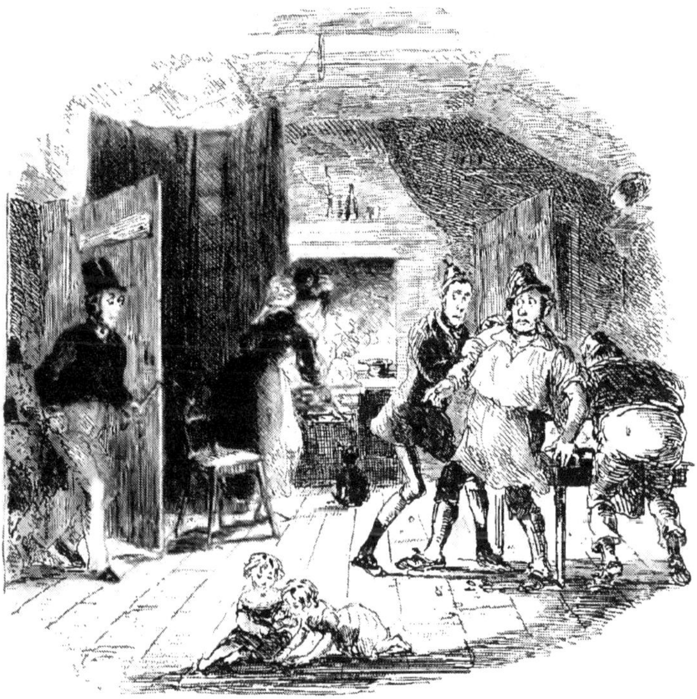

manner, swore to his being the person. The prisoner vehemently declared his innocence, and begged the magistrate to remand him for a single day, saying he would be able in that case to prove an alibi. His request was complied with, and he was remanded till the following day. In the interim, Forrester, the enterprising officer of the Mansion-House, was served with a notice to appear on behalf of the prisoner. On being placed next morning in the dock, he asked Forrester whether he did not see him at least four miles distant from the place where the crime was committed, at the very time it was perpetrated. "I cannot tell," remarked Forrester, in that cool and easy manner so characteristic of the higher class of police officers; "I cannot tell you in a moment; but I will let you know in a few seconds," putting his hand into his coat-pocket, and pulling therefrom a small memorandum-book*. He turned over a few leaves, and began reading, in an under tone, as follows:—"Met Tom Swagg, and spoke to him this evening, at half past seven precisely, at the west end of Oxford-street. Monday, February 20, 1828." Then closing his memorandum-book, and raising his head, he turned to the prisoner, and remarked that he had seen him at the particular hour on the particular evening in question, at least four miles distant from the place in which the robbery was committed. "Then, my girl," said the magistrate, turning to the young woman who had deposed to the identity of the prisoner; "then, my girl, you must have been mistaken in your man."

"No, your worship; I'm sure that's the one I seed," said the girl, manifestly with the greatest confidence.

"Just look him closely in the face again," requested the magistrate.

The girl renewed her inspection of the prisoner, but at a distance of several yards, while the light in the office was not particularly good.

"Just step a little nearer; go up close to him," said the other magistrate, who was on the bench.

The witness advanced to the place where he stood, and looked up eagerly, and with an air of sharpness, in his face. "Oh, my G——!" she suddenly exclaimed, raising both her hands, and evincing very great excitement of manner, "that's not him: I've perjured myself! He was not pock-pitted; this man is; but I never saw two men so like each other in my life."

"I'll bring the right person here in an hour," observed Forrester, addressing himself to the bench; and he quitted the room

* In their memorandum-books the police note every meeting they have with, or sight they get of, the most noted thieves, provided the place be some distance from where they reside. This is found of great service in directing them to the proper quarters whenever any robbery is committed, and the guilty parties are not taken into custody.

with the rapidity of lightning. In less than an hour, he returned with another person, who was afterwards proved, on the clearest and most conclusive evidence, to be the real delinquent, and who eventually, indeed, confessed his guilt. It was the latter observation of the girl, namely, that she never saw two men so like each other in her life as the prisoner and the thief, that furnished in this case the clue to the real culprit. The idea flashed across Forrester's mind that a particular person must be the criminal, as he bore a remarkable resemblance to the prisoner.

But ingenious as are many of our policemen in the expedients to which they resort in discovering and capturing criminals, none of them have, in this respect, approached to Vidocq, the celebrated French policeman. Perhaps, the most ingenious and best managed of his innumerable expedients, when bent on thief-catching, was that which he adopted when he visited Madame Noel. This lady, though moving in a respectable sphere in Paris, not only had a son a notorious thief, but acted as a sort of protectress to all the thieves who came in her way. Her house was at all times open to them; and to it they flew in crowds, in the hour of peril, as to a place of refuge. Vidocq having ascertained this, and feigned the name of Germain, a noted thief, of whom he was sure she must have often heard, though he chanced to know she had never seen him, disguised himself in tattered clothes, and having purposely blistered his feet by a chemical preparation that he might the more engage her attention, proceeded to her house one evening. The remainder of the adventure must be given in Vidocq's own words:—

"'Ah! my poor boy,' cried Mother Noel, 'one has no occasion to ask where you come from; I am sure you are famished?' 'Oh! yes; very hungry,' said I; 'I have not taken any thing for four-and-twenty hours.' Immediately, and without waiting for any explanation, she left the room, and returned with a plate of meat and a bottle of wine, which she set down before me. I did not eat—I devoured—I choked myself to get on faster; all disappeared, and between one mouthful and another I had not uttered a word. Madame Noel was enchanted with my appetite; when the table was cleared, she brought me a *goutte*. 'Ah, mother!' said I; throwing myself on her neck, 'you restore me to life. Noel did well to say you are good!' and I went on to tell her that I left her son twenty-eight days ago, and to give her intelligence respecting all the convicts in whom she was interested. The details into which I entered were so true and well known, that it was impossible for her to have the least idea that I was an impostor.

"'You have heard of me before now,' I continued. 'I have had many hard rubs. My name is Germain, or Captain—you must have heard my name.'

"'O yes, yes, my friend,' she said; 'I used to hear of nothing but you. O my God! my son and his friends have talked enough of your misfortunes: welcome, welcome, my dear Captain. But, good heavens! what a condition you are in; you must not remain in this state. It seems too that you are troubled with a villanous cattle that torments you. I must get you a change of linen, and manage to clothe you more decently.'

"'I expressed my gratitude to Mother Noel; and when I thought I might, without impropriety, I inquired what had become of Victor Desbois and his comrade Mongenct. 'Desbois and the *drummer!*' answerered she. 'Ah, my dear! don't speak of them; that rascal Vidocq has caused them so much trouble, since an officer called Joseph (Joseph Longueville, formerly inspector of police,) met them twice in this street, and gave information of their frequenting this quarter, that they have been obliged to leave, not to fall into his clutches.'

"'What!' said I, in a tone of disappointment, 'are they not in Paris?'

"'Oh, they are not far off,' replied Mrs. Noel; 'they have not lost sight of the Mainmast. I see them now and then, and I hope it will not be long before they pay me a visit. I think they will be delighted to find you here.'

"'I am sure they will not be more happy than I shall be; and if you would only write a line to them, I am certain they would send for me directly.'

"'If I knew where they were, I would go myself to find them for you; but I am not acquainted with their retreat, and the best thing we can do is to wait patiently till they come.'

"In my character of new-comer, I excited all the solicitude of Mother Noel. 'Does Vidocq know you: and his two bull-dogs, Levesque and Compère?'

"'Alas! yes; they have already arrested me twice.'

"'Then you must be on your guard. Vidocq assumes all kinds of disguises to entrap unfortunates like you.'

"It required all my knowledge to maintain my position; for Madame Noel had every custom and peculiarity of the *bagnes* at her fingers'-ends. She not only retained the names of all the robbers she had seen, but was also acquainted with the most trifling circumstances of the lives of most of the others; and she recounted with enthusiasm the history of the most famous, especially of her son, for whom her veneration was as great as her affection.

"'This dear son,' said I; 'you would be very glad to see him?'

"'Oh, glad! yes, indeed!' she ejaculated.

"'Well, then,' I said, 'you will enjoy that pleasure very soon. Noel has arranged everything for an escape: he only waits a favourable moment.'

"Madame Noel was delighted at the idea of embracing her son: she actually shed tears of joy. I confess that I was much moved; and at one time I deliberated within myself, whether for the time I should not pass over my duties of secret agent: but on reflecting on the crimes of these people—bearing in mind, above all, the interests of society—I remained firm and immovable in my resolution to pursue my enterprise to the end.

"In the course of conversation, Mother Noel asked me if I had *any affair in view* (any project of robbery); and after having offered to procure me one, if I had not, she put some questions, in order to learn whether I was skilful in forging keys. I answered that I was as dextrous as Fossard. 'If this be so,' said she, 'I am easy; you will soon be set up again; and as you are so adroit, I will go to a hardware-shop and buy a key, which you can fit to my safety-lock and keep, so that you may go out and come in whenever you please.'

"I expressed my gratitude for her goodness; and as it was getting late, I went to bed, ruminating on the means of extricating myself from this hornet's-nest, without running the risk of assassination, if by chance the rogues whom I was looking after should arrive before I had taken my measures.

"I did not sleep at all, and got up the moment I heard Madame Noel lighting the fire. She saw that I was an early riser, and told me she would go and get me what I wanted. Soon after, she brought me a key without web, some files, and a little vice, which I fixed at the foot of the bed, and instantly set to work in presence of my hostess, who seeing that I understood the business, complimented me on my dexterity. That which she most admired was the expedition I used. In fact, in less than four hours, I had finished a very workmanlike key. On trying it, it opened the door almost perfectly; a touch or two of the file made it a capital piece of work; and, like the others, I could introduce myself into the house at pleasure.

"I boarded with Madame Noel. After dinner I told her that I was anxious to take a turn in the dusk, in order to see if *an affair I had had in view* was still feasible. She approved my idea, but recommended me to take particular care. 'This scoundrel Vidocq,' observed she, 'is much to be feared; and if I were in your place, before trying anything, I would prefer waiting till my feet were cured.' The assurance that I would soon return quieted her fears. 'Well then, go,' said she; and I went out limping."

The expedient, after all, notwithstanding the ingenuity of its conception, and the remarkable skill displayed in its execution, it is right to say, was unsuccessful. Vidocq did not, on that occasion, capture the "customers" of whom he was in pursuit.

Before concluding, it is but right to mention, that notwithstanding the efficiency of the metropolitan police, it is far inferior in this respect to the police of France. For many years the subject of police has been reduced in Paris into what may be called a system, based on philosophic principles. Colquhoun, in his "Treatise on the Police of London," mentions an anecdote which was verbally communicated to him by one of the then English ambassadors at the court of France, relative to the singular state of efficiency to which the police force of Paris had then been brought. As the anecdote is short, and affords an interesting specimen of the romance of real life, I shall here transcribe it. It is thus related by Colquhoun:—"A merchant, of high respectability, in Bordeaux, had occasion to visit Paris upon commercial business, carrying with him bills and money to a very large amount.

"On his arrival at the gates of Paris, a genteel-looking man opened the door of his carriage, and addressed him to this effect: 'Sir, I have been waiting for you some time; according to my notes, you were to arrive at this hour; and your person, your carriage, and portmanteau, exactly answering the description I hold in my hand, you will permit me to have the honour of conducting you to Monsieur de Sartine.'

"The gentleman, astonished and alarmed at this interruption, and still more so at hearing the name of the lieutenant of the police mentioned, demanded to know what Monsieur de Sartine wanted with him; adding, at the same time, that he never had committed any offence against the laws, and that he could have no right to interrupt or detain him.

"The messenger declared himself perfectly ignorant of the cause of the detention; stating, at the same time, that when he had conducted him to Monsieur de Sartine, he should have executed his orders, which were merely ministerial.

"After some further explanations, the gentleman permitted the officer to conduct him accordingly. Monsieur de Sartine received him with great politeness; and after requesting him to be seated, to his great astonishment, he described his portmanteau, and told him the exact sum in bills and specie which he had brought with him to Paris, and where he was to lodge, his usual time of going to bed, and a number of other circumstances which the gentleman had conceived could be known only to himself. Monsieur de Sartine having thus excited attention, put this extraordinary question to him:—'Sir, are you a man of courage?' The gentleman, still more astonished at the singularity of such an interrogatory, demanded the reason why he put such a strange question; adding, at the same time, that no one had ever doubted his courage. Monsieur de Sartine replied, 'Sir, you are to be robbed and murdered this night! If you are a man of courage, you must go to your hotel, and retire to rest at the usual hour; but be careful that you do not fall asleep: neither will it be proper for you to look under the bed or into any of the closets which are in your bed-chamber (which he accurately described): you must place your portmanteau in its usual situation, near your bed, and discover no suspicion. Leave what remains to me. If, however, you do not feel your courage sufficient to bear you out, I will procure a person who shall personate you, and go to bed in your stead.'

"The gentleman being convinced, in the course of the conversation, that Monsieur de Sartine's intelligence was accurate in every particular, refused to be personated, and formed an immediate resolution literally to follow the directions he had received. He accordingly went to bed at his usual hour, which was eleven o'clock. At half-past twelve (the time mentioned by Monsieur de Sartine), the door of the bed-chamber burst open, and three men entered, with a dark-lantern, daggers, and pistols. The gentleman, who, of course, was awake, perceived one of them to be his own servant. They rifled his portmanteau undisturbed, and settled the plan of putting him to death. The gentleman hearing all this, and not knowing by what means he was to be rescued, it may naturally be supposed he was under great perturbation of mind during such an awful interval of suspense; when, at the moment the villains were prepared to commit the horrid deed, four police officers, acting under Monsieur de Sartine's orders, who were concealed under the bed and in the closet, rushed out, and seized the offenders with the property in their possession, and in the act of preparing to commit murder.

"The consequence was, that the perpetration of the atrocious deed was prevented, and sufficient evidence obtained to convict the offenders. Monsieur de Sartine's intelligence enabled him to prevent this horrid offence of robbery and murder; which, but for the accuracy of the system, would probably have been carried into execution."

This is a curious anecdote. The fact was, as stated by Colquhoun, that the French system of police was then in its best days. It had arrived at the greatest degree of perfection ever reached by any constabulary system in the world.

THE END.

J. BILLING,
PRINTER AND STEREOTYPER,
WOKING, SURREY.

Lightning Source UK Ltd.
Milton Keynes UK
UKHW020739270722
406450UK00005B/669

9 780526 827343